JOURNAL FOR THE STUDY OF THE OLD TESTAMENT
SUPPLEMENT SERIES
180

Sheffield Academic Press

The Search for Quotation

Verbal Parallels in the Prophets

Richard L. Schultz

Journal for the Study of the Old Testament
Supplement Series 180

Copyright © 1999 Sheffield Academic Press

Published by Sheffield Academic Press Ltd
Mansion House
19 Kingfield Road
Sheffield S11 9AS
England

Printed on acid-free paper in Great Britain
by Bookcraft Ltd
Midsomer Norton, Bath

British Library Cataloguing in Publication Data

A catalogue record for this book is available
from the British Library

ISBN 1-85075-496-9

CONTENTS

PREFACE

'All minds quote. Old and new make the warp and woof of every moment. There is no thread that is not a twist of these two strands. By necessity by proclivity and by delight we all quote.' What Emerson writes in his essay on 'Quotation and Originality'[1] regarding human speech and writing in general often has been claimed for the Hebrew prophets in particular. Linguistically identical or similar passages such as the familiar 'swords into plowshares' texts in Isa. 2.4 // Mic. 4.3 (cf. Joel 3.10; Heb. 4.10) occur with striking frequency both *within* and *between* individual prophetic books of the Old Testament, naturally raising the question of whether or not they result from one prophet quoting the words of another.

Not surprisingly these verbal parallels have attracted the attention of many biblical scholars. Commentaries often note the existence of verses that are similar to those which they are explaining but usually merely give the references parenthetically. Old Testament introductions discuss the literary connections between various books. Reference Bibles cite such passages in their marginal annotations. Indeed one might be able to claim without exaggeration that most of the monographs and essays which discuss the prophets at length at least mention the existence of these verbal parallels.

But precisely how should one best explain the existence of such passages? Do they unquestionably bear witness to the dependence of prophets on the utterances of their predecessors or do they suggest that they were dependent rather on formulaic language and well-known traditions? If the former is the case how does one determine who is quoting whom? What would be the implications of this practice of quotation, if confirmed, for one's understanding of the prophets? Unfortunately almost no consensus has emerged among biblical scholars with

1. R.W. Emerson, *The Complete Works of Ralph Waldo Emerson*. VIII. *Letters and Social Aims* (12 vols.; New York: W.H. Wise & Company, 1920 [1875]), p. 178.

regard to these questions even though they enthusiastically have engaged in the 'search for quotation'.

The purpose of this study is to make a thorough investigation of quotation in general, not simply within the Old Testament prophetic corpus, in order to better understand the nature and function of the phenomenon. This will involve the analysis of scholarly literature which already has addressed the subject of prophetic quotation and the examination of non-biblical literature containing quotation. A deepened awareness of both the dynamics of quotation as well as the limitations on interpretation which the textual data require should result in a more accurate assessment of the exegetical significance of verbal parallels and provide a check against their misuse in supporting a wide variety of critical theories. Above all, it is hoped that this study will help to move the discussion of prophetic quotation beyond the current methodological impasse to a new appreciation of this versatile and powerful element of prophetic rhetoric.

This monograph represents a thoroughly updated revision of a PhD dissertation which was submitted to Yale University Graduate School in May 1989 under the title 'Prophecy and Quotation: A Methodological Study'. Accordingly I would like to acknowledge my debt of gratitude to my dissertation advisor, Professor Brevard S. Childs, whose patience and encouragement were as important in this endeavor as were his helpful suggestions and sometimes painful criticisms. I similarly would like to express my appreciation to Robert R. Wilson of Yale University and to James Kugel, now of Harvard University, for their guidance during the early stages of this study. When it became necessary to investigate those literatures in which I was far from expert, I was assisted by William K. Simpson, William W. Hallo and the late Marvin H. Pope of Yale. Mr A.R. Millard and Mr C.J. Eyre of the University of Liverpool were most generous in sharing bibliographical references relating to Chapter 3. John Hollander of Yale read and offered helpful comments regarding Chapter 6 and Eckhard Schnabel and Grant R. Osborne of Trinity Evangelical Divinity School offered advice regarding Chapters 4 and 7, respectively.

I would be remiss if I did not thank Yale University for granting me a graduate fellowship, without which my doctoral study there would have been impossible. The library and faculty resources of Yale University contributed greatly to the conception and the accomplishment of this project. I am also grateful to David J.A. Clines and John Jarick of

Sheffield Academic Press for accepting this monograph for publication in the *JSOT* Supplement Series and for their patience in awaiting the long-delayed revisions of the original manuscript. Above all, I would like to thank my wife Carol for her faithful support throughout the years in which I was engaged in this project and for her careful proofreading of the manuscript. Although she has made many memorable statements during this time that are worthy of 'quotation', her contribution to this work definitely deserves far more than a footnote!

ABBREVIATIONS

AB	Anchor Bible
ABD	David Noel Freedman (ed.), *The Anchor Bible Dictionary* (New York: Doubleday, 1992)
ABL	R.F. Harper, *Assyrian and Babylonian Letters Belonging to the Kouyunjik Collections of the British Museum* (Chicago: University of Chicago Press, 1914)
ADAIK	Abhandlungen des deutschen archäologischen Instituts, Kairo
AfO	*Archiv für Orientforschung*
AJSL	*American Journal of Semitic Languages and Literatures*
AnBib	Analecta biblica
ANET	James B. Pritchard (ed.), *Ancient Near Eastern Texts Relating to the Old Testament* (Princeton, NJ: Princeton University Press, 1950)
AnSt	*Anatolian Studies*
AOAT	Alter Orient und Altes Testament
ASTI	*Annual of the Swedish Theological Institute*
ATD	Das Alte Testament Deutsch
AUSS	*Andrews University Seminary Studies*
BEvT	Beiträge zur evangelischen Theologie
BETL	Bibliotheca ephemeridum theologicarum lovaniensium
BHS	*Biblia hebraica stuttgartensia*
Bib	*Biblica*
BibB	Biblische Beiträge
BibOr	Biblica et orientalia
BSac	*Bibliotheca Sacra*
BIFAO	*Bulletin de l'Institut français d'archéologie orientale*
BJRL	*Bulletin of the John Rylands University Library of Manchester*
BKAT	Biblischer Kommentar: Altes Testament
BN	*Biblische Notizen*
BTB	*Biblical Theology Bulletin*
BWANT	Beiträge zur Wissenschaft vom Alten und Neuen Testament
BZ	*Biblische Zeitschrift*
BZAW	Beihefte zur ZAW
CBC	Cambridge Bible Commentary
CBQ	*Catholic Biblical Quarterly*

CompLit	*Comparative Literature*
ConBOT	Coniectanea biblica, Old Testament
CTA	A. Herdner (ed.), *Corpus des tablettes en cunéiformes alphabétiques découvertes à Ras Shamra–Ugarit de 1929 à 1939* (Paris: Imprimerie nationale Geuthner, 1963)
DBSup	*Dictionnaire de la Bible, Supplément*
EHAT	Exegetisches Handbuch zum Alten Testament
ETL	*Ephemerides theologicae lovanienses*
EvT	*Evangelische Theologie*
ExpTim	*Expository Times*
FRLANT	Forschungen zur Religion und Literatur des Alten und Neuen Testaments
FzB	Forschung zur Bibel
GKC	*Gesenius' Hebrew Grammar* (ed. E. Kautzsch, revised and trans. A.E. Cowley; Oxford: Clarendon Press, 1910)
GM	*Göttinger Miszellen*
GTJ	*Grace Theological Journal*
HAT	Handbuch zum Alten Testament
HDR	Harvard Dissertations in Religion
HKAT	Handkommentar zum Alten Testament
HSM	Harvard Semitic Monographs
HTR	*Harvard Theological Review*
HUCA	*Hebrew Union College Annual*
IBC	*Interpreter's Bible Commentary*
ICC	International Critical Commentary
IDBSup	*IDB*, Supplementary Volume
IEJ	*Israel Exploration Journal*
Int	*Interpretation*
ITC	International Theological Commentary
JAAR	*Journal of the American Academy of Religion*
JAOS	*Journal of the American Oriental Society*
JARCE	*Journal of the American Research Center in Egypt*
JBL	*Journal of Biblical Literature*
JCS	*Journal of Cuneiform Studies*
JEA	*Journal of Egyptian Archaeology*
JETS	*Journal of the Evangelical Theological Society*
JNES	*Journal of Near Eastern Studies*
JQR	*Jewish Quarterly Review*
JRT	*Journal of Religious Thought*
JSJ	*Journal for the Study of Judaism in the Persian, Hellenistic and Roman Period*
JSNTSup	*Journal for the Study of the New Testament*, Supplement Series
JSOT	*Journal for the Study of the Old Testament*

JSOTSup	*Journal for the Study of the Old Testament*, Supplement Series
JSPSSup	*Journal for the Study of the Pseudepigrapha*, Supplement Series
JSS	*Journal of Semitic Studies*
JTS	*Journal of Theological Studies*
KAT	Kommentar zum Alten Testament
KeHAT	Kurzgefaßtes exegetisches Handbuch zum Alten Testament
KHAT	Kurzer Hand-Kommentar zum Alten Testament
LSS	Leipziger Semitischen Studien
MDAIK	*Mitteilungen des deutschen archäologischen Instituts: Abteilung Kairo*
MVAG	Mitteilungen der vorderasiatisch-ägyptischen Gesellschaft
NCB	New Century Bible
NICOT	New International Commentary on the Old Testament
NKZ	*Neue kirkliche Zeitschrift*
NovT	*Novum Testamentum*
NTS	*New Testament Studies*
OBO	Orbis biblicus et orientalis
OLZ	*Orientalistische Literaturzeitung*
Or	*Orientalia*
OTL	Old Testament Library
OTS	*Oudtestamentische Studiën*
PBS	Publications, Babylonian section. University of Pennsylvania Museum
PTR	*Princeton Theological Review*
RA	*Revue d'assyriologie et d'archéologie orientale*
RB	*Revue biblique*
REg	*Revue d'égyptologie*
RevQ	*Revue de Qumran*
RHR	*Revue de l'histoire des religions*
RSR	*Recherche de science religieuse*
SAK	*Studien zur altägyptischen Kultur*
SBLDS	SBL Dissertation Series
SBLMS	SBL Monograph Series
SBS	Stuttgarter Bibelstudien
SBT	Studies in Biblical Theology
SEÅ	*Svensk exegetisk årsbok*
SJT	*Scottish Journal of Theology*
SPB	Studia postbiblica
ST	*Studia theologica*
STDJ	Studies on the Texts of the Desert of Judah
TBl	*Theologische Blätter*
TBü	Theologische Bücherei
TLZ	*Theologische Literaturzeitung*

TRE	*Theologische Realenzyklopädie*
TSAJ	Texte und Studien zum antiken Judentum
TSK	*Theologische Studien und Kritiken*
TTS	Trierer theologische Studien
TUGAL	Texte und Untersuchungen zur Geschichte der altchristlichen Literatur
TynBul	*Tyndale Bulletin*
TZ	*Theologische Zeitschrift*
UF	*Ugarit-Forschungen*
VT	*Vetus Testamentum*
VTSup	*Vetus Testamentum*, Supplements
WBC	Word Biblical Commentary
WMANT	Wissenschaftliche Monographien zum Alten und Neuen Testament
WO	*Die Welt des Orients*
WTJ	*Westminster Theological Journal*
WUNT	Wissenschaftliche Untersuchungen zum Neuen Testament
YOS	Yale Oriental Series
ZÄS	*Zeitschrift für ägyptische Sprache und Altertumskunde*
ZAW	*Zeitschrift für die alttestamentliche Wissenschaft*
ZDPV	*Zeitschrift des deutschen Palästina-Vereins*
ZTK	*Zeitschrift für Theologie und Kirche*

Part I

THE STUDY OF PROPHETIC QUOTATION

Chapter 1

PROPHECY AND QUOTATION IN OLD TESTAMENT RESEARCH

One cannot read extensively in the Old Testament prophetic corpus
without encountering entire verses or individual phrases, both within
and between the various books, which are strikingly similar in formulation. Such parallel passages represent an important component of
prophetic rhetoric which must be reckoned with in any attempt to
assess the nature of the prophetic task and the relationship between
distinct prophetic writings. However, despite the considerable scholarly
effort already devoted to the study of such passages, little progress has
been made. Little or no consensus has emerged regarding what distinguishes a quotation from a mere verbal coincidence or vague reminiscence or which criteria are most useful for correctly identifying,
explaining the origin of, and assessing the significance of literary
borrowing.

In order to understand why so little methodological clarity prevails in
an area of study which could shed additional light on a variety of critical issues and enrich the exegesis of numerous texts, it should prove
helpful to examine the various ways in which the problem has been
treated since the rise of the critical study of the Old Testament.
However, it is difficult to trace accurately the historical developments
in the investigation of this aspect of prophecy. Unlike many areas of
Old Testament scholarship in which each succeeding generation has
built upon the preceding generations' work, modifying, amplifying,
updating, rejecting where necessary, until recently, few students of
prophetic quotation have acknowledged or even been aware of others
who tilled the same soil. Thus much potentially valuable material has
been forgotten, and each generation has begun anew with the same
basic questions.

Furthermore, for many scholars these repeated passages have been
peripheral to their central concerns and, accordingly, have received

attention only as they impinged on or supported those scholars' theories. Even contemporaries, though sharing a common interest in such passages, have made very different use of the same data and often have come to opposite conclusions. It is not surprising, then, that little progress has been made. Before beginning my historical survey of the study of prophetic quotation, several explanations are necessary.

First of all, 'verbal parallels' is the term that will be used in this work to designate the occurrence of two or more passages of distinctive content, ranging in length from a few significant words to several sentences, which display identical or minimally divergent wording. The word 'verbal' distinguishes these passages from those which treat similar themes or topoi but whose wording does not correspond. The term 'prophetic quotation' will be reserved for those passages in which, for the sake of argument or to characterize a particular scholar's position accurately, it is suggested that the parallel results from one prophet's conscious repetition of words previously spoken or written by another prophet.[1] Secondly, in order to limit the scope of this investigation, only those verbal parallels found within the prophetic corpus will be examined, excluding parallels between prophetic passages and historical, legal, psalmic or Wisdom texts.[2] Finally, for the most part, little

---

1.   The issue of terminology will be addressed more fully in Chapter 7.

2.   Numerous parallels are quoted or listed by T.K. Cheyne, *The Prophecies of Isaiah: A New Translation with Commentary and Appendices* (2 vols.; New York: Thomas Whittaker, 5th edn, 1890); R.B. Girdlestone, *Deuterographs: Duplicate Passages in the Old Testament. Their Bearing on the Text and Compilation of the Hebrew Scriptures* (Oxford: Clarendon Press, 1894); and A. Bendavid, *Parallels in the Bible* (Jerusalem: Carta, 1972). Studies of such parallels include L.M. Eslinger, 'Hosea 12:5a and Genesis 32:29: A Study in Inner Biblical Exegesis', *JSOT* 18 (1980), pp. 91-99 (cf. W.D. Whitt, 'The Jacob Traditions in Hosea and their Relation to Genesis', *ZAW* 103 [1991], pp. 18-43); L.T. Brodie, 'Jacob's Travail (Jer 30: 1-13) and Jacob's Struggle (Gen 32:22-32): A Test Case for Measuring the Influence of the Book of Jeremiah on the Present Text of Genesis', *JSOT* 15 (1981), pp. 31-60; W. Brueggemann, ' "Vine and Fig Tree": A Case Study in Imagination and Criticism', *CBQ* 43 (1981), pp. 188-204; and A. Hurvitz, *A Linguistic Study of the Relationship between the Priestly Source and the Book of Ezekiel: A New Approach to an Old Problem* (Cahiers de la Revue Biblique, 20; Paris: J. Gabalda, 1982).

The only other extensive survey of the interpretation of verbal parallels in the prophets is by P.T. Willey, *Remember the Former Things: The Recollection of Previous Texts in Second Isaiah* (SBLDS, 161; Atlanta: Scholars Press, 1997), who devotes a chapter (Chapter 1) to the subject. In comparison with the following

attempt will be made to assess the strengths and weaknesses of the efforts of individual scholars in addition to setting out their contribution to the understanding of verbal parallels within the prophets.

Early Studies

The idea of prophetic quotation can be traced back to the very beginnings of biblical interpretation. The Talmud contains a pertinent saying of Rabbi Isaac, who cited the verbal parallel of Obadiah 3 and Jer. 49.16 as an illustration: 'The same communication is revealed to many prophets, yet no two prophets prophesy in the identical phraseology.'[3] Patristic writers attributed the consistency and harmony of prophetic speech to the fact that they all had been 'given utterance through one and the same spirit'.[4]

However, Heinrich Ewald's *Die Propheten des Alten Bundes*, published in 1840, was the first influential work to devote several introductory pages to prophetic quotation.[5] Ewald conceived of the prophets as heroic figures who periodically were overwhelmed by a higher power, becoming recipients of divine truths. As Wellhausen, Ewald's student, also would stress, the prophets were seen as the dominant force in the formulation of Israelite faith. According to Ewald, the history of Israelite prophecy could be divided into three distinct periods. During the first period, from Moses to Amos, the initial development of the institution took place. During the second period, from Amos and Hosea to the reign of Manasseh, prophecy achieved its classic form and 'reached the peak of its effectiveness, addressing an unadulterated and beneficial message to its own age and remaining unforgettable and eternally valid for all time'.[6] The final period, from the fall of Judah

---

survey, the focus of her analysis is narrower in one respect, being limited to parallels to Second Isaiah, and broader in another, including parallel themes and traditions as well as formulations.

3.   *B. Sanh.* 89a, *The Hebrew-English Edition of the Babylonian Talmud* (ed. I. Epstein; trans. M. Simon and I. Slotki; Hindhead, Surrey: Soncino, 1948).

4.   Theophilus of Antioch, *Theophilus to Antolycus* 2.35; cf. also 2.9, in A. Roberts and J. Donaldson (eds.), *The Ante-Nicene Fathers*. II. *Fathers of the Second Century* (10 vols.; trans. M. Dods; Grand Rapids: Eerdmans, 1979), pp. 94-121 (108, cf. also p. 97).

5.   H. Ewald, *Die Propheten des Alten Bundes* (3 vols.; Göttingen: Vandenhoeck & Ruprecht, 1867–68; originally published as 2 vols. in 1840–41).

6.   Ewald, *Die Propheten des Alten Bundes*, I, p. 43. This and all subsequent

onward, was marked by a visible and irreversible decay in prophetic activity, since the golden age of the revelation of divine truths was already past.

Because of the great emphasis which Ewald placed on the prophets' roles as creative innovators, literary borrowing posed a problem. Ewald viewed quotation as being more frequent in written than in oral prophecy, hence primarily a feature of the final centuries of Israelite history, when prophecy already was in decline. The words of the classical prophets formed a repository which proved to be both a help and a hindrance: 'This wealth thwarted their further activity, and many earlier items were repeated by later prophets, revised to a greater or lesser degree, as if they felt that they could produce nothing better themselves.'[7]

The fact that not only late prophets but also the classical prophets occasionally cited earlier oracles presented a further problem.[8] Ewald argued that this should not be viewed as a sign of diminished creativity, since the latter used them in a manner which clearly could be distinguished from the former. In fact, a basic criterion for recognizing different periods of prophecy was provided by the proper evaluation of prophetic repetition and re-echoing (*Wiederholungen und Wiederhalle*). Unlike the later 'imitators' who, according to Ewald, digested and wove earlier passages into their own words, due to their own linguistic poverty, the classical prophets intentionally and without pretense repeated earlier oracles solely in order to append their own considerations. Thus Ewald deemed it essential to study each verbal parallel closely in order to evaluate whether it exhibited simple repetition or complete reworking. However, despite the programmatic nature of his introductory comments, Ewald paid little attention to quotation in his discussion of the individual prophets. Nevertheless, he was among the first to incorporate the phenomenon into his larger conception of the nature of prophecy.

Although by no means as influential as Ewald, Augustus Küper, one of his contemporaries, authored one of the most frequently cited studies of prophetic quotation, *Jeremias librorum sacrorum interpres atque*

---

foreign language quotations in this study have been translated by the author.

7.   Ewald, *Die Propheten des Alten Bundes*, I, p. 46.

8.   Ewald noted that, even in the classical period, quotations were especially frequent in oracles against foreign nations. See my discussion in Chapter 8 with reference to Isa. 15–16 // Jer. 48.

vindex, in which he undertook a thorough investigation of the literary relations between Jeremiah and the rest of the Old Testament.[9] He offered a general assessment of prophetic quotation in his later work, *Das Prophetenthum des Alten Bundes*.[10] Like Ewald, his primary concern was to understand the significance of quotation within prophecy as a whole. However, unlike Ewald, who viewed the history of prophecy as one of blossom followed by decay, Küper conceived of prophecy as 'a coherent well-ordered organic whole, the individual parts of which are intimately related to one another'.[11] More specifically, he asserted that Isaiah's oracles (chs. 1–66) were foundational for all subsequent prophecy.

Accordingly, Küper suggested not only that quotations were frequently employed—indeed, quotations represented the clearest evidence for his view—but also that one could resolve easily the questions of priority simply by comparing the way in which each passage presented the parallel material. Although each author might have a characteristic manner of adapting quotations to his own purposes, certain broad features applied to all cases. In the original context the concepts are vaguer, expressed in general, summarizing objective terms; in the context where it is re-employed there is a concrete expansion and practical application of the basic ideas, expressed in terms of contemporary events and historical details. For example, earlier eschatological promises are described in far-reaching universalistic terms, while they are reused in narrower nationalistic settings. Küper sought to defend this approach by using passages drawn from his earlier work on Jeremiah, but it was clear that this criterion did not work equally well with all types of passages.

Foremost among the conservative apologists in the mid-1800s was

9.   A. Küper, *Jeremias librorum sacrorum interpres atque vindex* (Berlin: Georg Reimer, 1837). Küper's work was noted, among others, by Girdlestone, *Deuterographs*, p. 164; Cheyne, *The Prophecies of Isaiah*, II, p. 251; C.P. Caspari, 'Jesajanische Studien. I. Jeremia ein Zeuge für die Aechtheit von Jes. c. 34 und mithin auch für die Aechtheit von Jes. c. 33, c. 40-66, c. 13-14, 23 und c. 21, 1-10', *Zeitschrift für die Gesamte Lutherische Theologie und Kirche* 4 (1843), pp. 1-73 (4 n. 3); and C.W.E. Nägelsbach, *The Prophet Isaiah* (trans. S.T. Lowrie and D. Moore; A Commentary on the Holy Scriptures by J.P. Lange, 11; New York: Charles Scribner's Sons, 1878), p. 23.

10.   A. Küper, *Das Prophetenthum des Alten Bundes* (Leipzig: Dörffling & Franke, 1870), especially in an appendix to his discussion of Isaiah, pp. 274-91.

11.   Küper, *Das Prophetenthum*, p. 64.

Carl Paul Caspari, whose introductory essays on the books of Isaiah and Micah and detailed studies of individual texts were exemplary for their thoroughness and methodological rigor.[12] Caspari was concerned with defending Lutheran orthodoxy against the views of Ewald, de Wette and Hitzig. In his 73-page essay 'Jesajanische Studien. I. Jeremia ein Zeuge für die Aechtheit von Jes. c. 34', he offered a useful discussion of the proper evaluation of verbal parallels within the prophets. According to Caspari, there were seven ways to account for similar passages:[13]

1. The similarity is due to the similarity of subject which both prophets are addressing in their respective prophecies, as well as the fact that the prophet's conceptual, imagistic and linguistic world is relatively limited in scope, often resulting in the use of the same expressions.

2. The author of A, having read B's prophecies, unconsciously or intentionally employed the appropriate concepts, images and expressions of the latter which remained in his memory to present the substance of his prophecy.

3. B read A's prophecies and borrowed concepts, images and expressions from the latter.

4. An oracle of an older prophet formed the basis for the prophecies of both prophets, each drawing upon it independently.

5. The passage was introduced from an earlier oracle into a later prophecy through revision or interpolation.

6. The passage was interpolated into an earlier prophecy from a later prophecy.

7. Both passages are by the same prophet.

Caspari suggested that any of these reasons or a combination of them could apply to any given set of relationships, although he gave few suggestions as to how one decides between them. However, he felt that

12. C.P. Caspari, *Beiträge zur Einleitung in das Buch Jesaia und zur Geschichte des jesaianischen Zeit* (Berlin: L. Oehmigke's Verlag, 1848); *idem*, *Über Micha den Morasthiten und seine prophetische Schrift: Ein monographischer Beitrag zur Geschichte des alttestamentlichen Schriftthums und zur Auslegung des Buches Micha* (Christiania: P.T. Malling, 1852), pp. 440-41, 444; *idem*, 'Jesajanische Studien. I.', pp. 1-73.

13. Caspari, 'Jesajanische Studien. I.', pp. 4-8.

an exegete should not resort to method 4 unless methods 1–3 could not apply and he doubted that methods 5 and 6 occurred frequently.

To a much greater degree than Küper, Caspari's interest in quotation was based on its usefulness in defending the traditional position regarding the unity and eighth-century composition of Isaiah. As a result, he was concerned primarily with the issue of how to determine which prophet was borrowing from the other (i.e. deciding between methods 2 and 3). In the course of his study of the relationship between Jeremiah and Isaiah 34 several criteria emerged:

> For which prophet is literary borrowing more typical?
> In which types of prophetic material is literary borrowing most frequent?
> How well does each passage fit into its respective context?
> Can any plausible motivation for this borrowing be suggested?
> Which parallel is more concise and plainer in expression?
> Is the language of the passage typical of the prophet's language elsewhere?

Although not clearly dependent on Caspari's work, other scholars who have used verbal parallels to date literature have utilized similar questions to adjudicate the direction of the borrowing. However, Caspari's examination of numerous passages produced a cumulative weight of evidence greater than most have assembled.

In the late nineteenth century, Robert Girdlestone was clearly the Old Testament scholar who devoted the most attention to the study of quotation. Although best known for his *Synonyms of the Old Testament*, he addressed this topic in four of his other works.[14] The real value of his contribution is that he placed prophetic quotation within the larger context of the other repeated passages, or 'deuterographs' as he termed them, which are found throughout the Old Testament.

While his contemporaries were engaging in heated debate over critical issues, Girdlestone represented a throw-back to an earlier age when

---

14. Girdlestone, *Synonyms of the Old Testament: Their Bearing on Christian Doctrine* (Grand Rapids: Eerdmans, 2nd edn, 1956 [1897]); *Deuterographs*; *idem*, *The Foundations of the Bible: Studies in Old Testament Criticism* (London: Eyre & Spottiswoode, 2nd edn, 1891); *idem*, *The Building Up of the Old Testament* (New York: Fleming H. Revell, 1912); *idem*, *The Grammar of Prophecy: A Systematic Guide to Prophecy* (Grand Rapids: Kregel Publications, 1955).

traditional views were unassailed. For him, the major threat posed by quotation was to the orthodox doctrine of inspiration: Was prophetic quotation consonant with the prophets' claim of the divine origin of their message? Girdlestone defended the practice: 'Inspiration does not imply originality, and prophets borrowed freely from one another without mentioning the fact. When we compare their writings ... we cannot fail to detect this spiritual communism among the prophets.'[15] This view was expressed more fully in his introduction to *Deuterographs*:

> We seem driven to the conclusion that it was a literary habit with many of the sacred writers to incorporate parts of the compositions of their predecessors or contemporaries and even to repeat themselves. When a prophetic book was issued it became public property. Anyone could use it or make extracts from it ... The more widely its contents were circulated the better.[16]

Indeed, duplicate passages are so common, it is 'sometimes difficult to determine what is a quotation and what is a mere verbal coincidence'.[17] Of necessity, then,

> The study of quotations is quite a science. We have to be on our guard against mistaking resemblances for references. Some expressions may be common property to several Hebrew writers; they may have almost become idioms in the language; and we cannot say that the writers borrowed them from one another. Also, there are proverbial expressions common to two writers which cannot fairly be called quotations.[18]

Regrettably, although Robert Girdlestone clearly was interested in methodological problems, even he had little to suggest in terms of criteria for distinguishing between quotation and coincidence. Rather, he sought to demonstrate which text was original on a passage-by-passage basis. Perhaps this was due to the fact that his primary reason for collecting duplicate passages was not to answer higher critical questions but to offer evidence of the process of the 'building up of the Old Testament'.

During the last half of the nineteenth century, the primary interest in prophetic quotation continued to be due to its use in polemics over

15. Girdlestone, *The Grammar of Prophecy*, pp. 10-11.
16. Girdlestone, *Deuterographs*, p. xxi.
17. Girdlestone, *Deuterographs*, p. xxi. By 'coincidence', Girdlestone meant that 'similar persons under like circumstances naturally say the same thing, especially when inspired by the same Spirit'.
18. Girdlestone, *The Foundations of the Bible*, p. 50.

dating, and the authorship of Isaiah remained a major object of dispute.[19] For the most part, questions regarding the dating or unity of prophetic literature were decided on the basis of other considerations, quotations being used primarily to undergird the position held by a particular scholar. As it became increasingly apparent in subsequent decades how subjectively the criteria for determining priority could be applied and how easily the textual data could be used to support opposing viewpoints, parallel passages came to play a lesser role in adjudicating issues of dating.

In the meantime, however, the chronological argument from parallel passages continued to develop. One of the more extreme examples was the argument from silence which went beyond drawing conclusions from *quoted* passages to drawing conclusions from *unquoted* passages. For example, it was claimed that if Isaiah 40–66 truly preceded the oracles of Jeremiah, then one would expect the former to quote from the latter more often, especially its references to the destruction of Jerusalem and the temple. Since Jeremiah's prophecy of doom imperiled his life, he would be likely to invoke Isaiah's authority to defend his message. In his Isaiah commentary, Carl Nägelsbach addressed this issue in some detail. He agreed that it was fair to assume that, if Jeremiah mentioned the prophets who preceded him (Jer. 26.4-6), he probably also would cite some of their sayings. However, Nägelsbach argued, he was not obligated to quote any particular passage simply because it might have fit nicely into one of his oracles. The fact that a prophet did not borrow from a given prophetic book or section thereof did not prove that the book was not yet in existence or unfamiliar to the prophet.[20]

In light of the preceding comments, it is understandable that T.K.

---

19. Nägelsbach, *The Prophet Isaiah*, pp. 22-24, for example, in the introduction to his commentary on Isaiah, listed 18 verbal parallels and promised to mention and examine a much larger number of parallel passages as he proceeded through the book. However, his main concern was not to assess the exegetical or theological import of the parallels but to demonstrate that the passages in question were not quotations by the author of chs. 40–66 of passages in Jeremiah, Ezekiel, Zephaniah, Nahum or other post-eighth century prophets but quotations *of* Isa. 40–66.

20. Nägelsbach, *The Prophet Isaiah*, pp. 22-24. See also M. Delcor, 'Les sources du Deutéro-Zacharia et ses procédés d'emprunt', *RB* 59 (1952), pp. 385-411 (410 n. 41), who argued that Isa. 24–27 could not be from the Persian era because then Deutero-Zechariah 'would have to [*eût dû*]' use them.

Cheyne conceded that 'an exaggerated value is sometimes attached to the argument from parallel passages'.[21] A British contemporary of Girdlestone whose critical views were greatly influenced by Ewald and Wellhausen, Cheyne nevertheless did not simply reject earlier approaches. In 'The Critical Study of Parallel Passages', an essay appended to his Isaiah commentary, he claimed that the examination of verbal parallels offered a 'much-needed corrective of the various kinds of theoretical bias. The criticism of the Old Testament... may yet derive some light from a discriminating selection of parallel passages; and so, still more manifestly, may its exegesis.'[22] In effect, Cheyne was calling for a return, albeit with more critical discernment, to the traditional practice of interpreting Scripture by Scripture.

To facilitate the re-examination of the book of Isaiah, he listed several hundred parallel passages to both the acknowledged and the disputed prophecies of Isaiah, drawn from earlier and later books as well as from books of uncertain dating. Cheyne also cited parallels between the 'acknowledged' and the 'disputed' prophecies of Isaiah, 'less with a view of furnishing material for the higher criticism than of helping the reader to form a fuller idea of the literary and prophetic physiognomy of the book'.[23]

Cheyne viewed these 'affinities' in forms of expressions as indicative of affinities in fundamental conceptions and beliefs and as an ample demonstration of 'how instinctively the prophets formed as it were a canon of prophetic Scriptures for themselves, and also how free they were from the morbid craving for originality'.[24] Reflecting his position as a transitional figure in England between traditional and critical approaches, Cheyne ascribed the parallel passages 'to the overruling

21. Cheyne, *The Prophecies of Isaiah*, II, p. 241.
22. Cheyne, *The Prophecies of Isaiah*, II, p. 241.
23. Cheyne, *The Prophecies of Isaiah*, II, pp. 245-46. Cheyne discussed many of those individual passages in his Isaiah commentary and in his *Introduction to the Book of Isaiah* (London: A. & C. Black, 1895) but did not 'believe that the existence of such numerous links between the two portions of Isaiah is of much critical moment: There are points of contact, as striking, if not as abundant, between Old Testament books which no sober critic will ascribe to the same author' (*The Prophecies of Isaiah*, II, p. 246).
24. Cheyne, *The Prophecies of Isaiah*, II, p. 253. According to Cheyne, *The Prophecies of Isaiah*, II, p. 241, 'self-abnegation is the mark of prophetic writers quite as much as their editors'.

divine Spirit, or to the literary activity of the Soferim, or to both wor-
king in harmony'.[25]

T.K. Cheyne's work on Isaiah clearly represented a high-water mark
in the early study of prophetic quotation. No scholar who preceded or
followed him exhibited such a balanced interest in the phenomenon.
Examining its implications for an understanding of parallel passages
within all types of Old Testament literature, prophetic rhetoric as a
whole, and the book of Isaiah in particular—including its authorship,
exegesis and literary structure—he combined traditional concerns with
newly advanced critical insights from the continent. He was aware of
the work of others in the same area, such as Küper and Caspari,
acknowledged the need for restraint in drawing conclusions, since the
inquiry was 'peculiarly liable to be impeded by prejudice',[26] and was
among the first to use studies of quotation in comparative literature to
illuminate the biblical data.[27] Nevertheless, his call for a fresh evaluation of prophetic quotation went unheeded and his contributions in this
regard were soon forgotten.

A contemporary of Cheyne in Germany, Eduard König, expressed a
similar opinion regarding the abuse of parallel passages in critical
theory.[28] One of König's abiding concerns was the validity and limitations of linguistic arguments in general, especially as they were being
employed in the Pentateuchal criticism of his day. Since alleged quotations made up part of the textual data which were utilized in such lin-

25. Cheyne, *The Prophecies of Isaiah*, II, p. 246.

26. Cheyne, *The Prophecies of Isaiah*, II, p. 248.

27. Cheyne, *The Prophecies of Isaiah*, II, pp. 234 and 241. See the presentation
of the validity of this approach in Chapter 6.

28. F.E. König discussed the general validity of linguistic arguments in the following works: *De criticae sacrae argumento e lingua legibus repetito: Ratione
ducta maxime Geneseos capp. 1–11 eius historiam, naturam, vim examinavit*
(Leipzig: J.C. Hinrichs, 1879); *idem*, 'Der Sprachbeweis in der Literarkritik,
insbesondere des Alten Testaments', *TSK* 66 (1893), pp. 445-79; *idem*, *Einleitung
in das Alte Testament mit Einschluss der Apokryphen und der Pseudepigraphen
Alten Testaments* (Bonn: Eduard Weber's Verlag, 1893). The specific implications
of his views for the question of prophecy and quotation are presented in F.E.
König, *Das Buch Jesaja eingeleitet, übersetzt und erklärt* (Gütersloh: C.
Bertelsmann, 1926); *idem*, 'Die letzte Pentateuchschicht und Hesekiel', *ZAW* 28
(1908), pp. 174-79; *idem*, 'Gibt es "Zitate" im Alten Testament?', *NKZ* 15 (1904),
pp. 734-46; *idem*, *Stilistik, Rhetorik, Poetik in Bezug auf die biblische Literatur
komparativisch dargestellt* (Leipzig: Dieterich, 1900).

guistic arguments, he devoted an essay to the question 'Gibt es "Zitate" im Alten Testament?'('Are there "Quotations" in the Old Testament?') König did not deny the presence of quotations in the Old Testament but claimed that the term was being applied promiscuously to passages without any firm evidence. For example, a repeated phrase such as כשׁד משׁדי יבוא, 'it will come like destruction from the Almighty' (Isa. 13.6 and Joel 1.15), especially in view of its alliterative character, should be labeled an idiomatic expression which probably traced its origin to the 'unconscious creative soul of the language [*Sprachseele*]'.[29] Even if it once was the possession of an individual, it later simply became part of the common linguistic stock of the particular language and, therefore, was not a true quotation. The same considerations would apply to formulaic religious expressions.

In the above-mentioned article, König was not attempting a comprehensive examination of 'quotation'. Rather, he was seeking to establish a basis for critiquing those scholars who, in his opinion, were misusing the term. One such scholar was J.O. Boyd who attempted to demonstrate Ezekiel's dependence on the Pentateuch.[30] König accused Boyd (and others) of making the following 'unproven and unprovable' assumptions:

1.   That the linguistic store available to a particular author consisted solely of the previously written literary documents that have been preserved until the present.

2.   That lexical materials can be used to prove the identity of authorship of two given texts or to demonstrate that one author is quoting another.

3.   That these expressions were unique to the cited literary contexts and not common to everyday Hebrew, and thus can be used to prove literary dependence.

4.   That historical traditions were known only through narrative texts and not through oral tradition (*Volksüberlieferung*).

5.   That the primary characteristics of a quotation are the *division*, *repetition* and *variation* of the elements of the borrowed text.[31]

Regarding the last of these, König argued that it would be more

---

29. König, 'Gibt es "Zitate" ', p. 739.

30. J.O. Boyd, 'Ezekiel and the Modern Dating of the Pentateuch', *PTR* 6 (1908), pp. 29-51, especially pp. 44-47.

31. König, 'Die letzte Pentateuchschicht und Hesekiel', pp. 176-78.

likely for such features to be due 'simply to the exigencies of context and grammatical connection' and might indicate not a quotation but simply the imitation of selected expressions.[32]

The examples of Cheyne and König vividly illustrate the diversity of the background and interests of those who examined prophetic quotation around the turn of the century. Cheyne addressed the topic as a part of a commentary on Isaiah, stressing its positive exegetical benefits; König discussed it from the standpoint of Pentateuchal source analysis, stressing the negative results of its misuse. Both, however, offered useful methodological suggestions which had little or no lasting impact.

By the advent of the twentieth century, most of the traditional views regarding the literary integrity of the prophetic books had been abandoned as a result of critical investigation, although a sizable minority of scholars continued to voice its dissent. Consequently, most studies of prophetic literature during the first half of this century used quotations not primarily to establish or support dates but to examine the relationships between various books or sections thereof, the dates of which were presupposed. Of primary importance in this regard was the 1892 Isaiah commentary of Bernhard Duhm,[33] which not only separated chs. 40–66 from 1–39, but also presented a convincing case for making a further division between exilic 40–55 and postexilic 56–66. This led to a new interest in comparing Jeremiah, Ezekiel and 'Second' Isaiah as three prophets sharing a common age, a common concern about the fall of Jerusalem, and, presumably, common themes and expressions. Other resultant subjects of investigation were the date and authorship of 'Third' Isaiah and the nature of the relationship between 'Second' and 'Third' Isaiah. Duhm's earlier work followed the emphases of Ewald and Wellhausen on the personal revelatory experience of the prophets, and his commentaries reflected this resultant concern to distinguish between 'authentic' and 'inauthentic' sayings attributed to the prophet. This new literary-critical approach led to an additional refinement in the subsequent examinations of verbal parallels between prophets, for only 'genuine' sayings could be taken as evidence of quotation, while 'nongenuine' verbal parallels had to be detected and eliminated as later additions.

By the early decades of the twentieth century, prophecy no longer

32. König, 'Die letzte Pentateuchschicht und Hesekiel', p. 179.
33. B. Duhm, *Das Buch Jesaia: Übersetzt und erklärt* (HKAT, 3.1; Göttingen: Vandenhoeck & Ruprecht, 4th edn, 1922 [1892]).

was viewed as a monolithic, organic whole which could be described in broad generalizations, as in the writings of Ewald and Küper. Gunkel's form-critical work effected a basic shift away from a focus on the prophets as creative geniuses who were privy to mysterious divine disclosures to the investigation of the forms of prophetic speech. This resulted in a greater appreciation of the varied origins and usage of prophetic forms and genres and of the diversity within the prophetic corpus. The prophets soon came to be seen not primarily as innovators but as spokesmen who were dependent on both earlier institutions for their forms and earlier traditions for their content.

This shift in emphasis gave new impetus to the study of prophetic quotation, as scholars began to examine how several prophets made use of the same traditions or how one prophet took up and reissued, with modifications, elements of the messages of his predecessors. Thus literary criticism as practiced by Duhm and form and tradition criticism as pioneered by Gunkel had a major impact on changing the way in which verbal parallels were studied.

Affinities between Prophetic Books

Among those twentieth-century scholars whose primary interest in prophetic quotation continued to be due to its relevance to questions of literary chronology was Millar Burrows. Burrows's 1925 Yale dissertation[34] served to undergird the late pre-Maccabean dating of Ezekiel that his mentor, C.C. Torrey, had proposed. The express purpose of his thesis was to determine what bearing Ezekiel's relation to other writings had on the problem of the date and composition of Ezekiel. Accordingly, he immediately acknowledged the need for 'definite criteria of priority and dependence so that snap judgments and momentary impressions may not be confused with reasoned and well-founded conclusions'.[35]

In order to provide a check on these criteria as they apply to Ezekiel, Burrows studied the various ways in which Ezekiel used materials borrowed from pre-exilic literature, identifying eight different categories: (1) direct quotation, (2) repetition of borrowed expressions, (3)

---

34. M. Burrows, *The Literary Relations of Ezekiel* (Philadelphia: Jewish Publication Society of America, 1925).

35. Burrows, *The Literary Relations of Ezekiel*, p. ix.

adoption of characteristic expressions, (4) variation, (5) division, (6) combination, (7) elaboration, and (8) allusion. In short, Ezekiel exhibited 'every conceivable form of literary dependence',[36] though seldom reproduced more than a few words without at least some modification in form. Burrows conceived of Ezekiel as one who 'inwardly digested' earlier literature, so that his style is a 'veritable tissue of reminiscences'[37] that extends beyond diction to the thoughts expressed previously. He suggested three guidelines which he then applied to his study of Ezekiel's literary relations with exilic and postexilic literature:

1.   No one criterion can be made into a hard and fast rule to test Ezekiel's priority or dependence.
2.   No form of dependence, no mode of using material furnished by another writer, can be considered incongruous or unlikely in Ezekiel's, excepting only the exact verbal reproduction of extended passages.
3.   If Ezekiel is clearly connected with any book of marked originality in style and conception or of marked independence of other writers, it will be fair to assume, *ceteris paribus*, that Ezekiel is dependent.[38]

Ironically, although Burrows's caution in claiming literary influence has been repeatedly lauded by others,[39] few have adopted his conclusions regarding the date of Ezekiel. Indeed, the inherent subjectivity of his adopted methodology was made apparent by Georg Fohrer's 1952

36.   Burrows, *The Literary Relations of Ezekiel*, pp. 13-14.
37.   Burrows, *The Literary Relations of Ezekiel*, p. 14.
38.   Burrows, *The Literary Relations of Ezekiel*, p. 15.
39.   See the remarks by Curt Kuhl in his review of Burrows, *The Literary Relations of Ezekiel*, *TLZ* 53 (1928), pp. 121-22; also C.C. Torrey, *Pseudo-Ezekiel and the Original Prophecy* (YOS, 18; New Haven: Yale University Press, 1930), p. 92; S. Spiegel, 'Ezekiel or Pseudo-Ezekiel?', *HTR* 24 (1931), pp. 245-321 (310). Burrows's introductory remarks on methodology have been the basis for the approach taken in two dissertations at Southern Baptist Theological Seminary: J.K. Eakins, 'Ezekiel's Influence on the Exilic Isaiah' (ThD dissertation, Southern Baptist Theological Seminary, 1971), and V.J. Eldridge, 'The Influence of Jeremiah on Isaiah 40–55' (ThD dissertation, Southern Baptist Theological Seminary, 1978). More recently Hurvitz, *A Linguistic Study*, p. 16 n. 10, drew on Burrows's arguments. This dependence suggests that Burrows's study either is the best or the only well-known twentieth-century discussion of the methodological issues involved in determining literary influence—and that over half a century ago!

study, *Die Hauptprobleme des Buches Ezechiel*,[40] which used the same data to support an early exilic date for the origin of the prophecy. Whereas Burrows conceived of Ezekiel using Jeremiah as a long-published book, Fohrer believed that the former even may have been among the original audience which heard the latter's oracles.[41]

A more thorough study of the relationship between these two prophets was undertaken by J.W. Miller.[42] Miller sought to submit Rudolf Smend's list of 62 'borrowings' (*Entlehnungen*) from Jeremiah[43] to a methodologically more rigorous investigation. He began by eliminating 41 of them 'due to their inauthenticity, on the basis of language or content considerations, due to poor textual transmission, due to insufficient evidence of "borrowing" '.[44] Even the 21 passages which remained were by no means certain borrowings. Miller complained that it was inadequate to examine each alleged parallel individually, devising ad hoc explanations to account for similarities.[45] For

40. G. Fohrer, *Die Hauptprobleme des Buches Ezechiel* (BZAW, 72; Berlin: Alfred Töpelmann, 1952).

41. Fohrer sought to demonstrate this by examining 30 passages in which a dependence of Ezekiel upon Jeremiah had been alleged. Although Fohrer concluded that only six of them were so clearly influenced by Jeremiah that literary dependence seemed certain, these were sufficient to convince him that Ezekiel had read at least an earlier version of Jeremiah's book. Fohrer did not state explicitly whose list of alleged parallels he was re-examining. Beginning with 47 passages, he eliminated 17 of them as later additions to either Jeremiah or Ezekiel before categorizing the remaining 30. Fohrer also studied Ezekiel's relationship with postexilic literature, primarily prophetic books, cf. *Die Hauptprobleme*, pp. 154-64.

Eakins, 'Ezekiel's Influence on the Exilic Isaiah', p. 200, concluded that there was 'no evidence to suggest that Exilic Isaiah was influenced significantly by Ezekiel in the realm of expression'.

42. J.W. Miller, *Das Verhältnis Jeremias und Hesekiels sprachlich und theologisch untersucht mit besonderer Berücksichtigung der Prosareden Jeremias* (Assen: Van Gorcum, 1955).

43. R. Smend, *Der Prophet Ezechiel* (KeHAT; Leipzig: S. Hirzel, 2nd edn, 1880), pp. xxiv-xxv.

44. Miller, *Das Verhältnis Jeremias und Hesekiels*, p. 1.

45. One of the studies Miller criticized in this respect was that of Karl Gross, *Die literarische Verwandschaft Jeremias mit Hosea* (Leipzig: Universitätsverlag von Robert Noske, 1930). Gross described his approach as a literary-critical textual comparison in which he examined each parallel passage for positive indications of literary borrowing, such as uniqueness of comparison, rarity of usage, exactness of repetition or clear reversal of concept. Gross identified 55 passages in Jeremiah in which a quotation of Hosea was certain or likely, 36 from the first period of

example, the familiar 'Peace, and there is no peace' of Jer. 6.14 and Ezek. 13.1 (שלום ואין שלום) may be used by Ezekiel (1) as an ironic saying current in his day; (2) as a saying originated by Jeremiah and personally heard from his mouth; (3) as a saying adopted by Jeremiah's audience as a fitting saying and transmitted to Ezekiel in this form; or (4) as a statement which Ezekiel read in the book of Jeremiah.

This example served to demonstrate that Rudolf Smend's approach of merely listing parallels led nowhere. If any meaningful comparison between Ezekiel and Jeremiah was to be made, a dependable method first had to be developed. Miller's approach was to isolate a datable portion of Jeremiah's writings that may have been completed by the time of Ezekiel's prophetic call—the 'Baruch scroll', consisting primarily of prose speeches from chs. 1–25. As a result of his study, Miller concluded that Ezekiel had carefully studied a copy of the 'Baruch scroll' as well as the salvation speech of chs. 30–31, and perhaps 29.1-23. However Ezekiel's acquaintance with other oracles of Jeremiah was minimal, so that verbal parallels to them in his prophecies reflect, at most, only an oral acquaintance, the majority simply displaying the coincidentally similar linguistic features of a common age and task. Miller's re-examination of alleged literary borrowings by Ezekiel in the first part of his monograph formed the basis for his theological comparison of the two prophets in which the direct influence of Jeremiah on Ezekiel's message could be more accurately assessed.

The literary relations of 'Second' Isaiah also have received considerable attention. Umberto Cassuto offered a lengthy essay, 'On the Formal and Stylistic Relationship between Deutero-Isaiah and Other Biblical Writers',[46] as a sample study of how 'to ascertain which authors, and to what degree, contributed to the formation of the style and phraseology of this prophet, and conversely, which writers, and in what measure, drew upon his work and imitated him'.[47] Cassuto listed, without much comment, numerous parallel passages between 'Second'

Jeremiah's ministry (up to 621 BCE), 14 in the time between 609 and 597, and 5 after 597. According to Gross's analysis, a total of 41 passages from Hosea had been borrowed.

46. U. Cassuto, 'On the Formal and Stylistic Relationship between Deutero-Isaiah and other Biblical Writers', in *idem*, *Biblical and Oriental Studies*. I. *Bible* (trans. I. Abrahams; repr.; Jerusalem: Magnes Press, 1973), pp. 141-77, originally published in *Rivista Israelitica* 8–10 (1911–13).

47. Cassuto, 'On the Formal and Stylistic Relationship', p. 142.

Isaiah (chs. 40–66) and Jeremiah, Ezekiel, Nahum and Zephaniah. Cassuto observed that passages in Jeremiah and 'Second' Isaiah which shared identical phraseology often dealt with the same subjects or themes, such as the anti-idolatry polemics, the redemption and future prosperity of Israel, and oracles against Babylon.

Proceeding to consider Ezekiel, Cassuto presented a dozen passages from 'Second' Isaiah which have formal parallels in both Ezekiel and Jeremiah, due to the fact that both exilic prophets were inspired by the same model. However, he also admitted that some expressions which are common to two or more prophets may still be insignificant, since they are found throughout biblical literature and even have approximate echoes in ancient Near Eastern literature outside the Bible. Cassuto concluded, therefore, that some of the expressions found only in the two exilic prophets also may have been drawn independently from a common source which has long since perished. Thus there is no evidence to show that 'Second' Isaiah was directly indebted to Ezekiel.

The next study of the relationship between Jeremiah and 'Second' Isaiah was done in 1958 by Werner Tannert,[48] whose approach was similar to that of J.W. Miller. Tannert complained that previous studies of parallel passages between the two prophets had concentrated on the exegesis of individual texts, often making overly hasty generalizations which ignored the question of the tradition-historical connections between their messages. Tannert sought to gather and evaluate all the relevant material in which a literary connection was possible and to classify it according to major prophetic themes, such as election, salvation for the exiled, judgment as purification, and the transformation of the preaching of doom into a message of salvation. Tannert found a great variety in the manner and degree of dependence, especially in individual expressions, images and concepts, although some of the connections were due to the independent use of the same traditions. Although Jeremiah's message was influential on 'Second' Isaiah throughout his life, his dependence was greatest during the early part of his ministry.

In 1969, a further comparison was undertaken by Shalom Paul.[49] His

48. W. Tannert, 'Jeremia und Deuterojesaja: Eine Untersuchung zur Frage ihres literarischen und theologischen Zusammenhanges' (PhD dissertation, University of Leipzig, 1956), known to me only through the summary in *TLZ* 83 (1958), pp. 725-26.

49. S.M. Paul, 'Literary and Ideological Echoes of Jeremiah in Deutero-Isaiah',

purpose was not only to include 'expressions and verses which were adopted verbatim, but also ... Deutero-Isaiah's more subtle and artistic adapting and refashioning of material from Jeremiah, in order to create a total [*sic*] new pattern of imagery'.[50]

Paul found previous comparative studies to be inadequate because:

1. They have noted sporadic surface parallels between the two without subjecting the corresponding contextual relationship and linguistic overtones to further analysis.
2. Their remarks usually are scattered throughout their commentaries rather than being presented in a systematic fashion, which would enable one to appreciate the full extent of the influence.
3. Many points of contact, to the best of my knowledge, have been overlooked so far.[51]

However, their methodological weaknesses could not be remedied simply by presenting more passages in a systematic fashion and examining their contexts, and Paul did not advance the problem much beyond the work of others. In fact, by including among his examples formulaic expressions which were found not only throughout the Old Testament but also in cuneiform inscriptions, he blurred the line between intentional and coincidental correspondences, a distinction which Cassuto had maintained carefully. In spite of this, he continually used the Jeremiah parallel and its context to explicate and even emend enigmatic passages in 'Second' Isaiah, assuming that the latter was dependent upon the former on the basis of similarity in wording and the repetition of rarely used terms.

Attracted by the unresolved question of the influence of Jeremiah upon 'Second' Isaiah, Victor Eldridge undertook a comprehensive re-examination of the passages listed by Cassuto and Paul.[52] In order to diminish methodological hindrances to an accurate assessment of the relationship between these two prophets, Eldridge suggested the following steps:

in P. Peli (ed.), *Proceedings of the Fifth World Congress of Jewish Studies (1969)* (5 vols.; Jerusalem: World Union of Jewish Studies, 1972), I, pp. 102-20.

50. Paul, 'Literary and Ideological Echoes', p. 102.

51. Paul, 'Literary and Ideological Echoes', p. 103. Paul was referring to the commentaries of A. Dillmann, B. Duhm, E.J. Kissane, J.L. McKenzie, K. Marti, J. Mulenburg (*sic*), C.R. North, C.C. Torrey and P. Volz on ('Second') Isaiah, and of W. Rudolph and J. Bright on Jeremiah. He seemed unaware of the more systematic work of either Cassuto or Tannert.

52. Eldridge, 'The Influence of Jeremiah on Isaiah 40–55', *passim*.

1.   To identify the points of similarity between texts such as words, phrases or ideas common to both passages.
2.   To determine the degree to which these words or phrases are characteristic of Jeremiah and Deutero-Isaiah, compared with their usage elsewhere.
3.   To examine the significance of the contexts for understanding the meaning of the passages being compared.
4.   To determine the genres being used and the degree to which the parallels may be explained in terms of that genre.
5.   To attempt to discover the theological significance of the passage in the overall message of each prophet.[53]

Eldridge's study concentrated on two issues: (1) whether it is legitimate to claim the direct dependence of 'Second' Isaiah on Mowinckel's source A; and (2) what bearing the parallels have on the question of the authorship or date of Jer. 10.1-16, 30-31, and 50-51 (Source D).[54]

As a result of his numerous textual comparisons, Eldridge concluded that 'Second' Isaiah made 'selective use of his [Jeremianic] heritage—only that which was particularly apposite to his purposes was utilized'. This explains why his borrowing concentrated on certain passages while other large sections were deemed irrelevant and thus ignored. Furthermore, differences in wording were due to the fact that 'Second' Isaiah 'constantly refashioned his borrowed material to make it pertinent to the new situation'.[55]

---

53. Eldridge, 'The Influence of Jeremiah on Isaiah 40–55', p. 63.

54. S. Mowinckel, *Zur Komposition des Buches Jeremia* (Oslo: Jacob Dybwad, 1914). According to Eldridge, 'The Influence of Jeremiah on Isaiah 40–55', p. 64, of Cassuto's 129 verses in Jeremiah having affinities with 'Second' Isaiah, 39 were from Mowinckel's A, 1 from B, 6 from C, and the rest from D; of Paul's 66, 28 were from A, 0 from B, 1 from C, and the rest from D.

55. Eldridge, 'The Influence of Jeremiah on Isaiah 40–55', p. 252. The most recent contribution to the question of the relationship between prophetic books is J. Untermann, *From Repentance to Redemption: Jeremiah's Thought in Transition* (JSOTSup, 54; Sheffield: JSOT Press, 1987), who in excursuses briefly discusses the relationship between Hosea and Jeremiah (pp. 165-66), Jeremiah and Ezekiel (pp. 167-70), and Jeremiah and Isaiah (34–35) 40–66 (pp. 171-75). See also U. Wendel, *Jesaja und Jeremia: Worte, Motive und Einsichten in der Verkündigung Jeremias* (Biblisch-theologische Studien, 25; Neukirchen–Vluyn: Neukirchener Verlag, 1955), who examines the influence of the oracles (not the writings) of 'First' Isaiah on Jeremiah, offering a helpful list of 'correspondences' (*Entsprechungen*) between the two on pp. 227-33.

Two recent monographs on 'Second' Isaiah's use of earlier prophetic and non-prophetic traditions offer contrasting approaches and conclusions regarding verbal parallels in the book of Isaiah. According to Patricia Willey,

> Second Isaiah displays such a significant density of linguistic correspondence to certain other biblical texts—and only certain texts—that the similarities between them could not easily have happened by coincidence, similar traditioning, or the work of secondary redactors.[56]

By analyzing 'Second' Isaiah's utilization of previous texts, she sought to understand the prophet's rhetorical context and strategy in invoking them. Because of the impossibility of using verbal parallels to date texts, she limited her comparison of specific verbal similarities to texts which arguably pre-date 'Second' Isaiah, including the Pentateuch, Psalms, 'First' Isaiah and Lamentations.[57] Willey viewed 'Second' Isaiah

> not as a learned scholar writing in response to other learned scholars, but as a prophet negotiating through the maze of other words that may claim authority, in order to assert a new understanding of the divine will in the exilic situation.

In doing so, however, the prophet must demonstrate this stood in continuity with past intepretations.[58]

Willey analyzed verbal parallels as 'intertextual allusion', drawing on the theoretical and methodological reflections of Mikhail Bakhtin, Michael Fishbane and Richard Hays. Central to her approach are Hays's seven 'tests' for allusion in the Pauline epistles:

56. Willey, *Remember the Former Things*, p. 3.

57. According to Willey, *Remember the Former Things*, p. 57, some previous studies 'have expected precise repetitions, others have allowed too much imprecision. Some have let uncertainty about dating keep them from making intertextual claims, while others have ignored the problematic nature of dating, or even allowed perceived intertextual relationships to determine it'. She sought to focus on the significance and interpretation of verbal parallels, but the validity of her analysis remains dependent upon her identification of parallels despite minimal verbal correspondence (according to Willey, 'Second' Isaiah usually refers to other texts only 'by short phrases and brief images' [*Remember the Former Things*, p. 116]), her assumption of the literary integrity of 'Second' Isaiah (i.e. chs. 40–55), and the correctness of her reconstructed literary chronology.

58. Willey, *Remember the Former Things*, pp. 67, 70.

1. Availability: Did the author have access to the claimed source?
2. Volume: How extensive is the explicit repetition?
3. Recurrence: Are there other parallels between the two texts?
4. Thematic Coherence: Do the words have similar meanings in the two texts?
5. Historical Plausibility: Is it likely that the later text would be understood as echoing an earlier text?
6. History of Interpretation: Has this allusion been recognized previously?
7. Satisfaction: Does the proposed interpretation of the alluding text illuminate the surrounding discourse?[59]

Willey concluded that 'Second' Isaiah made varied use of previous texts, sometimes closely preserving their original forms, sometimes recasting or even reversing them. Each reuse exhibited aspects of continuity as well as discontinuity. According to her analysis, Isaiah 49–54 is the most densely and continuously allusive part of the book, exhibiting more continuity with Nahum and the Psalms than with Jeremiah and Lamentations and showing little influence by 'First' Isaiah or the other seventh-century prophets.

In a 1994 University of Chicago thesis, revised as *A Prophet Reads Scripture: Allusion in Isaiah 40–66*,[60] Benjamin Sommer independently examined a set of allusive texts similar to those selected by Willey, though attributing chs. 35 and 56–66 to 'Second' Isaiah, as well, basing this in part on his analysis of their 'poetics of allusion'. Similar to Willey, he concluded that 'Second' Isaiah is one of the most allusive

59. M.M. Bakhtin, *The Dialogic Imagination: Four Essays by M.M. Bakhtin* (ed. M. Holquist; trans. C. Emerson and M. Holquist; Austin: University of Texas Press, 1981); M.A. Fishbane, *Biblical Interpretation in Ancient Israel* (Oxford: Clarendon Press, 1985); R.B. Hays, *Echoes of Scripture in the Letters of Paul* (New Haven: Yale University Press, 1989), pp. 29-32. See my discussion of inner-biblical exegesis and intertextuality in Chapter 2.

60. B.D. Sommer, '*Leshon Limmudim*: The Poetics of Allusion in Isaiah 40–66' (PhD thesis; University of Chicago, 1994); *idem, A Prophet Reads Scripture: Allusion in Isaiah 40–66* (The Contraversions Series; Stanford: Stanford University Press, 1998); cf. also *idem*, 'Allusions and Illusions: The Unity of the Book of Isaiah in Light of Deutero-Isaiah's Use of Prophetic Tradition', in R.F. Melugin and M.A. Sweeney (eds.), *New Visions of Isaiah* (JSOTSup, 214; Sheffield: Sheffield Academic Press, 1996), pp. 156-86.

ancient Israelite authors, who should be viewed as a prophet in his own right, not as a disciple or epigone. According to Sommer, 'Second' Isaiah's oracles have no original connection with or close affinity to 'First' Isaiah, for his use of the oracles of 'First' Isaiah cannot be distinguished from his use of Jeremiah. Unlike Willey, his methodology concentrated on inner-biblical exegesis (or allusion), as analyzed by Fishbane, rather than on broader intertextual relationships.

Sommer's major contribution was in developing and applying a more rigorous method for interpreting allusion. In distinguishing allusion from several related terms, namely intertextuality, influence, echo and exegesis, he characterized allusion as a marked reuse of an earlier text in which the verbal repetition's diachronic dimension and rhetorical or strategic but non-interpretive purpose are discernible. He noted the wide range of often contrasting reasons for allusion: to acknowledge and to assert influence, to affirm one's closeness to or to distance oneself from earlier texts, to utilize a knowledge base shared with one's audience, and to display the author's and reader's erudition. Sommer added an eighth 'test' to Hays's list of seven noted above: 'the critic must be reasonably sure that a similarity does not result from common use of an Israelite or ancient Near Eastern literary topos'.[61]

In his analysis of allusion in 'Second' Isaiah, Sommer identified and illustrated five types of reuse of earlier texts: reversal, reprediction (historical recontextualization of positive or negative oracles), fulfillment of earlier prophecies, typological linkages, echo. Sommer criticized Steck for drawing conclusions from

> alleged allusions or redactional connections [which] consist of concordance-like listings of parallels whose compositional significance is unclear given the commonplace nature of the vocabulary and the absence of a studied re-use of older passages.[62]

However, his own extensive reliance on the 'occurrence' of four stylistic features—(1) the 'split up pattern' (breaking up a borrowed phrase into two parts which are separated by several words or even verses); (2) sound-play (similar sounding but not identical words); (3) word-play (homonyms) and (4) parallel word pairs (substituting a related word in the alluding text for the word commonly paired with it

---

61. Sommer, *A Prophet Reads Scripture*, pp. 219-20 n. 12. Sommer also criticizes some of Hays's tests as 'very loose', especially tests 4, 5 and 7.

62. Sommer, *A Prophet Reads Scripture*, pp. 296-97 n. 50.

that occurs in the source text)—in identifying allusion introduced a major subjective element into the analysis. Accordingly, there is little warrant for viewing most of his 'allusions' as 'prophetic quotation', even though he began with the same lists of verbal parallels suggested by Cassuto and Paul discussed above. Using such a flexible set of stylistic devices as indicators of allusions he could claim that almost every phrase in the fourth 'Servant Song' hints back to at least one earlier prophetic passage![63]

According to Sommer, allusions are found in every chapter of 'Second' Isaiah, most passages drawing upon several sources, primarily, however, upon earlier prophecies. The prophet thereby declares: 'I am a reader, a traditionalist, a recycler.'[64] In his opinion, 'Second' Isaiah alluded most frequently to ('First') Isaiah and Jeremiah frequently because, as well-known prophets, they were the most useful sources of authority, and so he drew liberally upon their rebukes, encouragements, laments and eschatological oracles, though seldom revised or exegeted them.

The work of scholars such as Burrows, Fohrer, Miller, Cassuto, Tannert, Paul and Eldridge, both in listing parallel passages and utilizing various criteria for eliminating the more dubious examples, though motivated primarily by concerns over the origin and growth of the prophetic literature and marred by their often contradictory conclusions, laid the foundation for more constructive comparisons between the rhetoric and messages of various prophets, a task which Miller, Tannert and Eldridge undertook with varying degrees of thoroughness and success. The gradual shift from chronological to theological concerns was accompanied by an increasing use of literary-critical (Miller), tradition-critical (Tannert) and form-critical (Eldridge) tools in determining literary relationships. However, although Miller and Eldridge utilized lists of verbal parallels supplied by others, there was little evi-

---

63. Sommer, *A Prophet Reads Scripture*, pp. 64-66 and 93-96. These features are first defined by Sommer in Chapter 2 but employed throughout the monograph in identifying allusions. According to Sommer, *A Prophet Reads Scripture*, pp. 75-76, Isa. 40.1-10 alludes to Isa. 28.1-5 because these passages share six words or phrases: the topos of the fading flower (ציץ נבל, twice in each), valley (גיא), such common words as 'people' (with pronominal suffix, עמו/עמי) and 'hand' (with preposition, מיד/ביד), the 'phrase' הנה+חזק+אדני, and the word-play צבאה/צבי ('magnificence'/ 'term of service').

64. Sommer, *A Prophet Reads Scripture*, p. 166.

dence that any of those who studied the relationships between prophetic collections gained much insight from the methodologies of their prede- cessors. The recent dissertations of Willey and Sommer show more awareness both of previous studies of verbal parallels in the prophets and of the need for a rigorous methodology in identifying and interpret- ing them. They also reflect the growing influence of literary approaches in biblical studies as well as the increased emphasis on assessing the specific use made of earlier texts rather than simply compiling lists of verbal parallels between two books.

Affinities between Sections of the Book of Isaiah

While some scholars were examining the linguistic links between two or more prophetic books, others were studying the affinities between what they considered to be two prophetic voices within a single book. One focus of attention in the early 1930s was 'Second' Isaiah and its posited reuse by 'Third' Isaiah, as exemplified by the debate between Odeberg, Volz and Elliger.

In some respects, the study of quotations between sections of one prophetic book is similar to the study of quotations between prophetic books, since critical scholars have viewed both types of parallels as resulting from one prophet borrowing from another. However, whereas parallels between different books usually have been understood as resulting from the latter prophet addressing the same concerns and subjects as the former, verbal parallels between 'Second' and 'Third' Isaiah have been seen paradoxically not only as providing further evi- dence for distinguishing two prophetic 'voices' but also as helping to explain the inclusion of both within the canonical book of Isaiah.[65]

Hugo Odeberg[66] examined the use that 'Third' Isaiah made of earlier biblical literature, including 'Second' Isaiah, noting examples of 'dependence', 'quotations' and 'reminiscences'. Tallying the results of his detailed verse-by-verse study, he observed that 'Third' Isaiah's

---

65. Few still hold to the 'accidental' theory, that suggests that chs. 40–66 were added to 1–39 simply to fill up a partially empty scroll. See the discussion by P.R. Ackroyd, 'Isaiah I–XII: Presentation of a Prophet', in W. Zimmerli *et al.* (eds.), *Congress Volume: Göttingen 1977* (VTSup, 29; Leiden: E.J. Brill, 1978), pp. 16-48 (18-19).

66. H. Odeberg, *Trito-Isaiah (Isaiah 56–66): A Literary and Linguistic Analysis* (Uppsala: Lundeqvist, 1931).

dependence on terminology and phraseology was divided fairly equally between 'First' Isaiah, 'Second' Isaiah, Amos, Hosea and Micah. He therefore drew two conclusions: (1) 'Third' Isaiah cannot be identified with the main author of 'Second' Isaiah or the author of any part of chs. 40–55. (2) Furthermore, since 'Third' Isaiah's use of 'Second' Isaiah was the same as his use of other earlier literature, there was no inherent connection between the two. Thus the suggestion that 'Third' Isaiah was a student or disciple who carried on the work of his predecessor was unsubstantiated and incorrect. 'Third' Isaiah's apparent attraction to 'Second' Isaiah was merely due to the fact that both of them had the publication of promise oracles as one of their functions:

> There is no other intrinsic relation between Deutero-Isaiah and Trito-Isaiah than that necessitated by their belonging to the same historical continuity in the development of Jewish religion. Trito-Isaiah's dependence is a dependence, mainly on a book, on recorded words, on traditions, not on a person.[67]

This becomes obvious when one realizes that nearly every term of 'Second' Isaiah which 'Third' Isaiah reused had, according to Odeberg, a 'different shade of meaning'[68] in its new context, sometimes even reflecting a failure to understand its original meaning.

Paul Volz's views concerning 'Third' Isaiah were somewhat similar.[69] In his commentary on Isaiah 40–66, he argued that the frequent quotation of 'Second' Isaiah by 'Third' Isaiah, often 'accompanied by a shift in meaning' (*Umbiegung*),[70] is decisive for the separation of chs. 56–66 from 40–55. According to Volz, 'Second' Isaiah certainly would not have done this to his own words. In some passages, such as chs. 60–62, the relationship to 'Second' Isaiah is much closer. This supported Volz's conception of Isaiah 56–66 as consisting of many individual pieces, originating between the seventh and third centuries BCE. Accordingly, 'Third' Isaiah's special attraction to 'Second' Isaiah was

67. Odeberg, *Trito-Isaiah*, p. 28.
68. Odeberg, *Trito-Isaiah*, p. 27.
69. P. Volz, *Jesaia II* (KAT, 9; Leipzig: Deichert, 1932). However, Volz and Odeberg differed in their response to K. Elliger's monograph *Die Einheit Tritojesajas* (BWANT, 45; Stuttgart: W. Kohlhammer, 1928). Odeberg agreed with Elliger's view of the authorial unity of 'Third' Isaiah but felt that he dated the collection too early. Volz completely rejected the unity of 'Third' Isaiah for reasons set forth in his commentary.
70. Volz, *Jesaia II*, p. 198.

due to the impact of the reading of the latter's oracles in the synagogue!

Karl Elliger's comprehensive study of the relationship between 'Second' and 'Third' Isaiah,[71] which appeared the next year, disputed many of Volz's contentions. Elliger agreed with Volz that there were *quantitative* differences within 'Third' Isaiah in its use of 'Second' Isaiah. However, in his opinion, they were to be accounted for by the fact that certain literary genres within 'Second' Isaiah were more appropriate to 'Third' Isaiah's message than others and by the fact that some of 'Third' Isaiah's oracles were produced immediately after reflection on the words of his master, 'Second' Isaiah, while others were not. However, Elliger emphatically denied that there was any *qualitative* difference in 'Third' Isaiah's use of 'Second' Isaiah. It is true that some of the contents of 'Second' Isaiah were more consonant with 'Third' Isaiah's perspective than others, but a proper interpretation of any of his quotations will demonstrate that indeed no 'shift in meaning' occurred in the process of adapting them to his purposes. In any case, there is no evidence of multiple authorship within 'Third' Isaiah.

Elliger's argumentation regarding 'Third' Isaiah's use of quotation was based on his detailed study of 'Second' Isaiah. For Elliger, 'Second' Isaiah and 'Third' Isaiah were not simply convenient labels for chs. 40–55 and 56–66. Rather, they represented the literature produced by master and disciple. Elliger viewed 'Third' Isaiah as the collector and first editor of Isaiah 40–55 (similar to Williamson's recent claim that 'Second' Isaiah was the primary editor of 'First' Isaiah; see discussion below, pp. 48-49). According to Elliger, many of the passages within 40–55 with close parallels in 56–66, which Volz interpreted as quotations of 'Second' Isaiah by 'Third' Isaiah, actually were 'Third' Isaianic additions to 40–55 and therefore quotations by 'Third' Isaiah of himself! Each prophet/author represented within chs. 40–66 had his own distinct manner of quotation and thus provided a criterion by which to determine the origin of any given passage. When 'Second' Isaiah quoted himself, he only repeated brief phrases, always with variation of the original wording. 'Third' Isaiah not only repeated his own previous statements with word-for-word exactness but also quoted

---

71. K. Elliger, *Deuterojesaja in seinem Verhältnis zu Tritojesaja* (BWANT, 63; Stuttgart: W. Kohlhammer, 1933), cf. especially 'Exkurs Nr. 2 zur Einheit von Jesaja 56-66. Eine Auseinandersetzung mit P. Volz, *Jesaja II* s. 197ff.', pp. 278-303.

his master for lines at a time. Later additions were characterized by a skillful reworking of a variety of quoted materials into a new literary composition. Utilizing this strictly defined method of analysis, it was possible for Elliger to draw very different conclusions from Volz or Odeberg about the relationship between 'Third' Isaiah and 'Second' Isaiah, even though basing his study on an examination of the same passages.

With Walther Zimmerli's highly regarded essay, 'Zur Sprache Tritojesajas', published in 1950,[72] this discussion was elevated beyond the intramural debate regarding the inter-relationship to a theological appreciation of it. Rather than addressing the issue of the unity and authorial distinctness of 'Third' Isaiah, Zimmerli examined the use which 'Third' Isaiah made of 'Second' Isaiah, seeking to determine the influence of older religious language on the formulations of a later period. First, Zimmerli divided the verbal parallels between them into 'quotations' (*Zitate*), 'freer imitations' (*freiere Nachahmungen*) and 'brief accidental similarities' (*kleinere gelegentlichen Berührungen*), although not explaining his criteria for assigning a particular passage to one of these categories. When he then studied the passages within each of these groups, he discovered that each group reflected a similar approach to reapplying 'Second' Isaiah's language. In general, the language of 'Second' Isaiah suffered in the process of being actualized by 'Third' Isaiah, becoming 'religiously sanctified vocabulary'.[73] Literal terms were reused in a diminished figurative sense, concrete speech was spiritualized, vividness of expression was muffled, images were awkwardly or inappropriately reapplied, specific statements became conventional formulations, key concepts of 'Second' Isaiah were subordinated to 'Third' Isaiah's new concerns. Although Zimmerli admitted that some passages reflected no apparent conceptual shift when reused by 'Third' Isaiah, this failed to modify his assessment of the prophet's significant freedom in adapting borrowed language to his own purpose.

He concluded:

72. W. Zimmerli, 'Zur Sprache Tritojesajas', in *Gottes Offenbarung: Gesammelte Aufsätze zum Alten Testament* (TBü, 19; Munich: Chr. Kaiser Verlag, 1963), pp. 217-33, reprinted from *Schweizerische theologische Umschau* 20 (1950), pp. 110-22.
73. Zimmerli, 'Zur Sprache Tritojesajas', p. 220.

No fixed system for using Deutero-Isaiah's sayings could be observed. In addition to the word-for-word quotation of entire phrases, we found roughly equivalent free reminiscences within individual sayings. In addition to the faithful adoption and analogous reuse of images, whether developed more fully or broken up for dramatic effect, we also found completely new associations or merely formulaic-figurative uses.[74]

Although methodologically not above reproach,[75] Zimmerli's treatment of prophetic quotation pointed the way to a more fruitful assessment of the phenomenon.

In 1969, the relationship between 'Second' Isaiah and 'Third' Isaiah received an important new examination by Paul Hanson, as a part of his Harvard dissertation tracing the development of prophecy to apocalyptic.[76] Building on the work of both Elliger and Zimmerli, Hanson's study of 'Third' Isaiah moved the discussion toward identifying historical and sociological factors influencing the borrowing.

Hanson was critical of Elliger, declaring that an argument based on linguistic, stylistic and lexicographic data is incapable of settling questions of authorship and pointing out the inherent circularity in Elliger's reasoning.[77] However, he similarly attributed the relationship between Isaiah 40–55 and 56–66 to a prophetic group who 'quote from or allude to words of the master, applying his thoughts to their new situation'.[78] Like his predecessors, Hanson noted that chs. 60–62 evidence a closer dependence on 'Second' Isaiah than the rest of 'Third' Isaiah. In his opinion, this was due to the fact that they represented the earliest oracles of Isaiah 56–66, produced by a group that optimistically viewed Israel's judgment as past history and looked forward to its imminent salvation, drawing on 'Second' Isaiah to formulate their program for

74. Zimmerli, 'Zur Sprache Tritojesajas', p. 233.

75. See the critique by F. Maass, 'Tritojesaja?', in *idem* (ed.), *Das ferne und nahe Wort: Festschrift Leonhard Rost* (BZAW, 105; Berlin: Alfred Töpelmann, 1967), pp. 153-63.

76. P.D. Hanson, *The Dawn of Apocalyptic* (Philadelphia: Fortress Press, 1979).

77. Hanson, *The Dawn of Apocalyptic*, p. 38, accused Elliger of circular reasoning in that he explained passages within Isa. 40–55 with verbal parallels in 56–66 as either (1) Trito-Isaianic passages included within 40–55, (2) Deutero-Isaianic passages which Trito-Isaiah had imitated or (3) later interpolations, depending on which best fit into his theory. However, Hanson's statement in which he discussed this is worded in such a way as to suggest something very different, i.e. that there are Deutero-Isaianic passages included in 56–66, a claim that Elliger never made.

78. Hanson, *The Dawn of Apocalyptic*, p. 45.

restoration. Later historical realities led to disillusionment and a rejection of this vision. Subsequent 'programs' had less in common with 'Second' Isaiah's expectation and, accordingly, displayed less literary dependence on him.

Hanson considered it more important to study *how* the reiteration of 'Second' Isaiah's language and themes functions in a new setting than to try to determine *who* is responsible. Like Zimmerli, Hanson saw this reuse as indicating a reverence for earlier prophetic utterances, although a considerable draining of language occurred. Original contexts were ignored, metaphors became obtuse, poetic beauty was lost. However, the theological significance of this reapplication of older prophecies far outweighed the linguistic devaluation which resulted in a 'poor imitation, the product of a committee approach paraphrasing an older classic'.[79] Although Paul Hanson with his contextual-typological approach may not have spoken the final word on the relationship between these two sections of the book of Isaiah, he, like Zimmerli, moved beyond the polemics over dating to examine the *function* of quoted material in the prophets.

In recent decades, a new approach to verbal parallels within the book of Isaiah has been developed, especially by German scholars, primarily utilizing a redaction-critical methodology and often giving special attention to the relationship between 'First' Isaiah and the rest of the canonical book. In this regard, one can refer especially to the work of Rendtorff, Hermisson, Steck and the Dutch scholar Beuken.[80] Rendtorff,

---

79. Hanson, *The Dawn of Apocalyptic*, p. 71.

80. R. Rendtorff, 'Zur Komposition des Buches Jesaja', *VT* 34 (1984), pp. 295-320; H.-J. Hermisson, 'Deuterojesaja-Probleme: Ein kritischer Literaturbericht', *VF* 31 (1986), pp. 53-84; *idem*, 'Einheit und Komplexität Deuterojesajas: Probleme der Redaktionsgeschichte von Jes 40–55', in J. Vermeylen (ed.), *The Book of Isaiah: Le livre d'Isaïe. Les oracles et leurs relectures unité et complexité de l'ouvrage* (BETL, 81; Leuven: Leuven University Press, 1989), pp. 287-312; O.H. Steck, *Bereitete Heimkehr: Jesaja 35 als redaktionelle Brücke zwischen dem Ersten und dem Zweiten Jesaja* (SBS, 121; Stuttgart: Katholisches Bibelwerk, 1985); *idem*, *Studien zu Tritojesaja* (BZAW, 203; Berlin: W. de Gruyter, 1991); W.A.M. Beuken, especially *Jesaja* (De Prediking van het Oude Testament; Vols. 3A, 3B; Nijkerk: G.F. Callenbach, 1989); also 'Does Trito-Isaiah Reject the Temple? An Intertextual Inquiry into Isa. 66.1-6', in S. Draisma (ed.), *Intertextuality in Biblical Writings: Essays in Honor of Bas van Iersel* (Kampen: Kok, 1989), pp. 53-66; *idem*, 'Isaiah lxv–lxvi: Trito-Isaiah and the Closure of the Book of Isaiah', in J.A. Emerton (ed.), *Congress Volume: Leuven 1989* (VTSup, 43; Leiden: E.J. Brill, 1991), pp. 204-21;

for example, noted how various key words, such as נחם (comfort) and
און (evil), occur in structurally strategic locations throughout the
canonical book of Isaiah, sometimes with very different associations
(cf. צדק/צדקה, 'righteous'/'righteousness'), indicating a close redactional linkage of the three main sections of the book. Steck attributed
various thematic and verbal parallels, such as the image of the 'highway of the return' to a redactor, such parallels serving as editorial
sutures which sewed various parts of the book together. Hermisson uses
'quotation' as a criterion for identifying editorial comments: these must
be viewed as later additions since a prophet is unlikely to quote himself
or interpret his own oracles. Beuken has offered detailed studies of the
extensive use that 'Third' Isaiah makes of his Isaianic 'predecessors',
'First' and 'Second' Isaiah.

The most detailed redactional analysis of 'Second' Isaiah's contribution is offered in Hugh Williamson's 1994 monograph *The Book Called
Isaiah*.[81] The purpose of Williamson's study is to demonstrate (contrary
to the position taken by Willey and Sommer):

1. That Deutero-Isaiah was especially influenced by the literary
    deposit of Isaiah of Jerusalem. 'Second' Isaiah's primary
    dependence is upon 'First' Isaiah.
2. That he regarded the earlier work as in some sense a book that
    had been sealed up until the time when judgment should be
    passed and the day of salvation had arrived, which day he
    believed himself to be heralding.
3. That in order to locate his message in relation to the earlier
    and continuing ways of God with Israel he included a version
    of the earlier prophecies with his own and edited them in such
    a way as to bind the two parts of the work together.[82]

As primary evidence in support of this thesis, Williamson analyzed

---

idem, 'Isa. 56.9-57.13: An Example of the Isaianic Legacy of Trito-Isaiah', in
J.W. Henten *et al.* (eds.), *Tradition and Re-Interpretation in Jewish and Early
Christian Literature: Essays in Honour of Jürgen C.H. Lebram* (Leiden: E.J. Brill,
1986), pp. 48-64.

81. H.G.M. Williamson, *The Book Called Isaiah: Deutero-Isaiah's Role in
Composition and Redaction* (Oxford: Clarendon Press, 1994).

82. Williamson, *The Book Called Isaiah*, pp. 240-41. Williamson thus disputed
the view set forth by Hermisson, 'Deuterojesaja-Probleme', especially p. 67, that
'Second' Isaiah evidenced little connection with 'First' Isaiah.

verbal parallels within Isaiah 1–55, some of which he views as evidence of the influence of 'First' Isaiah on 'Second' Isaiah, others of which he explains as editorial insertions by 'Second' Isaiah into 'First' Isaiah of the former's key words and themes. Thus, in his analysis, despite the fact that an identical phrase occurs in both Isa. 5.26 and 11.12 (ונשא־נס לגוים, 'We will raise a banner for the nations'), the former has influenced Isa. 49.22 which reverses the image and, in turn, has influenced the use of נס (banner) in 11.12.[83] Williamson's methodological thoroughness and caution are exemplary, as is his critique of numerous other approaches to verbal parallels and the growth of the book of Isaiah. Allusions are identified primarily on the basis of rare but significant repeated words which often use the terms in a different manner or for a different purpose. However, the potential for circular reasoning in determining whether verbal parallels in 1–39 to 40–55 have *influenced* and been *inserted by* 'Second' Isaiah is apparent, though Williamson consistently argued that the influence always proceeds from the prophet for whom a given expression or emphasis is more typical or appropriate.[84]

The examination of the relationship between 'Second' Isaiah and 'Third' Isaiah and between 'First' and 'Second' Isaiah, like the investigation of the relationship between Jeremiah, Ezekiel and 'Second' Isaiah, reflects three tendencies: (1) There has been a continuing interest in the significance of verbal parallels as a primary indicator of those affinities. (2) The treatment of these 'quotations' has changed with the development of new critical approaches to the prophets, encompassing concerns regarding chronology, tradition history, prophetic schools, actualization, and sociology, redaction criticism, inner-biblical exegesis and intertextuality. (3) No agreement has been reached regarding the proper method for identifying, explaining the origin of, and assessing the significance of quotations between these two sections of the book of Isaiah. Although the criteria for identifying allusions have become increasingly sophisticated, a troubling degree of subjectivity remains in employing them.

---

83. Williamson, *The Book Called Isaiah*, pp. 63-67, 125-43.

84. Williamson's analysis of the influence of Isa. 28 on the formulation Isa. 40 is remarkably similar to that of Sommer, noted above, p. 41 n. 63 (*The Book Called Isaiah*, pp. 77-79).

Tradition-Historical Approaches

Although Gunkel's influence on the evaluation of verbal parallels within the prophets was indirect and gradual,[85] Sigmund Mowinckel, one of his students, developed several of his emphases in such a way that a radical reassessment of prophetic quotations ensued. Gunkel's stress on the oral origin and growth of the prophetic literature and his suggestion of the linkage between prophecy and cult formed the basis for Mowinckel's thesis of oral tradition as the primary medium for the transmission of prophecy and his positing of certain prophetic books as the literary deposit of cultic prophets.[86]

Mowinckel's work was instrumental in shaping a 'Scandinavian school', which began surveying the prophetic corpus as a whole, gathering textual evidence that supported their theory of oral tradition. At the time, most scholars viewed verbal parallels as examples of *literary* borrowing. However, the members of the Scandinavian school re-examined this issue and concluded that the data suggested instead that these doublets arose during the period of *oral* transmission, long before any literary fixation occurred.[87] Hence it was incorrect to speak of literary dependence of one prophet on another; in fact, even the concept of 'quotation' was inappropriate.

85. The influence of Gunkel's form-critical approach on the study of prophetic quotation has been minimal. However, one might cite G. von Rad's form-critical study of 'The Levitical Sermon in I and II Chronicles', in *The Problem of the Hexateuch and Other Essays* (trans. E.W.T. Dicken; New York: McGraw–Hill, 1966), pp. 267-80, which is seen to be built around quotations, some of them from the latter prophets; and Joachim Begrich's *Studien zu Deuterojesaja* (TBü, 20; Munich: Chr. Kaiser Verlag, 1963), pp. 169-70, originally published as BWANT, 77; Stuttgart: W. Kohlhammer, 1938, in which he used a form-critical argument, for example, to determine whether Isa. 35.10 or its parallel in Isa. 51.11 is the original location of the saying.

86. Mowinckel's brief monograph, *Prophecy and Tradition: The Prophetic Books in the Light of the Study of the Growth and History of the Tradition* (Oslo: Jacob Dybwad, 1946), offers a convenient summary of his views in this regard.

87. The following discussion is dependent on the work of D.A. Knight, *Rediscovering the Traditions of Israel: The Development of the Traditio-Historical Research of the Old Testament, with Special Consideration of Scandinavian Contributions* (SBLDS, 9; Missoula, MT: SBL, 1973), especially his summary of Norwegian or Swedish literature that is unavailable in translation. Summarizing their contributions as a whole necessarily involves some over-generalizations, but space does not permit a more detailed examination of their individual differences.

This general assessment of their work is not to suggest that unanimity prevailed among them. Ivan Engnell's views were representative of the strict position:

> If one finds a formula, expression, or tradition unit which appears in more than one context, one should refrain from immediately thinking of a 'borrowing' or a 'citation', discussing priority, and asking whether Amos borrowed from Joel or Joel from Amos. Rather, in most cases we would do best to consider that the prophets and the circles of the pious men who stand behind them carry and transmit further a living, religious, often cultically rooted tradition and thought-pattern that expressed itself in traditional forms, drawn from a common fund of stylistic-formal terminological material.[88]

Engnell interpreted such doublets in the text as offering positive proof of the oral transmission of materials. Geo Widengren, however, disputed this conclusion: 'The doublets *per se* have nothing at all to do with the solution of the question of oral transmission or not.'[89] Widengren believed that writing was the usual mode of transmitting traditions; oral transmission was employed primarily by semi-nomadic societies.

Helmer Ringgren attempted to derive an objective test by which to adjudicate the conflicting claims.[90] By comparing a series of Old Testament passages which are recorded twice, he found evidence of errors deriving from both oral and written transmission and concluded that 'there existed an oral tradition along with the written one regarding the correct reading of the consonantal text which survived up to the time of the Massoretes'.[91] Unfortunately, the value of Ringgren's study was seriously undermined by the fact that, although he felt able to distinguish between errors due to written transmission and errors due to oral transmission, which were far more numerous, he was unable to distinguish between oral errors and intentional changes.

The Scandinavian scholars accounted for repeated passages in a

---

88. I. Engnell, 'Profetia och tradition: Några synpunkter på ett gammaltestamentligt central-problem', *SEÅ* 12 (1947), pp. 94-123 (106-107). Holding similar positions were also H.S. Nyberg and H. Birkeland.

89. G. Widengren, *Literary and Psychological Aspects of the Hebrew Prophets* (Uppsala: Lundeqvist, 1948), p. 80.

90. H. Ringgren, 'Oral and Written Transmission in the Old Testament: Some Observations', *ST* 3 (1949), pp. 34-59.

91. Ringgren, 'Oral and Written Transmission', p. 59.

number of ways. In their opinion, although some glosses in the prophets may have consisted of quotations or reminiscences of other scriptural passages,[92] most true doublets arose during the oral stage. Unattached oracles were always in circulation. 'Tradition circles' gathered around the individual prophets and were constantly growing. Since there was not always a clear demarcation between the circles which surrounded other prophets,

> it was possible for traditional material [*Traditionsgut*] to migrate from one circle to others and thereby be placed in different contexts. This led to the break-up of traditional material, resulting in parallel series of sayings in which some but not all were identical. In the series A+B+C, B could be separated and continue to develop in the context D+B+E.[93]

Thus one finds originally anonymous oracles which are now transmitted under the authority of two different prophets.

Doublets within a single prophetic book had a different origin. Widengren asserted that, as in the Koran, these passages simply bear witness to the fact that the same words were spoken by the prophet more than one time under different circumstances.[94] Harris Birkeland offered a more complex explanation: these internal parallels usually are not as close in wording as external parallels and therefore probably had independent origins. In the course of transmission, they were drawn to material in other tradition complexes because of their inherent similarity ('like attracts like') and thus were incorporated into new complexes. Later redactors who reordered material according to dating schema often ignored the presence of these internal doublets and once again separated them. In each of these cases, therefore, it is incorrect to speak of literary dependence or intentional borrowing.[95]

From a historical perspective, it is significant that most biblical scholars have rejected or ignored the basic premise of the Scandinavian school regarding prophetic materials; otherwise their distinctive contribution effectively could have terminated the quest for prophetic quotation. However, several of their emphases have continued to find qualified acceptance in modern treatments of the prophets, such as their

92. J. Lindblom, *Prophecy in Ancient Israel* (Philadelphia: Fortress Press, 1962), p. 290.

93. H. Birkeland, *Zum hebräischen Traditionswesen. Die Komposition der prophetischen Bücher des Alten Testaments* (Oslo: Jacob Dybwad, 1939), p. 19.

94. Widengren, *Literary and Psychological Aspects*, p. 80.

95. Birkeland, *Zum hebräischen Traditionswesen*, p. 19.

assertion that, since the prophetic literature represented the culmination of a long process of transmission that involved the revision, supplementation and reapplication of original sayings by prophetic 'schools', it was futile and even counterproductive to concentrate on identifying and interpreting the *ipsissima verba* (the very words) of the prophets. This same attitude was expressed also in a variety of more recent studies that examined the redactional shaping of prophetic books, concentrating on the significance of that material which Duhm and his literary-critical successors previously had dismissed as secondary glosses and additions.

Exemplary in this regard was Ina Willi-Plein's *Vorformen der Schriftexegese innerhalb des Alten Testaments*,[96] which traced the 'further history' (*Nachgeschichte*) of prophetic words as a means of illuminating the tradition- and redaction-history of prophetic books. According to Willi-Plein, 'a substantial portion, perhaps the bulk of Old Testament literature, in terms of its literary character, consists of secondary references to older material'.[97] Some of the passages which she studied involved prophetic quotation and thus her approach is useful to summarize, even though her primary interest lay elsewhere.

Flatly rejecting the Scandinavian view, Willi-Plein held that most traditional material was already fixed in written form at an early stage in the formation of the prophetic corpus. In a manner reminiscent of Ewald, she viewed the early prophets as foundational, since later prophets modified, explained, expanded and even reversed their words, using prophecy to interpret prophecy. As a result, the prophets of the seventh century were less independent than their predecessors; they were 'classicistic' rather than 'classical'. Willi-Plein found textual evidence of this process in Jer. 26.18's quotation of Mic. 3.12, and Zech. 1.12's reference to Jer. 25.11 or 29.10. Accordingly, when attempting to identify quoted material, Willi-Plein always sought an exegetical purpose which might account for this literary borrowing.

Another continuing influence of the Scandinavian school was in its distinction between cultic and non-cultic prophecy, especially Engnell's division of the resultant literature into *diwan* (books primarily shaped by oral transmission, including Hosea, Amos, Micah and Proto-Isaiah, focusing on the words and actions of the prophets) and 'liturgy'

96. I. Willi-Plein, *Vorformen der Schriftexegese innerhalb des Alten Testaments* (BZAW, 123; Berlin: W. de Gruyter, 1971).

97. Willi-Plein, *Vorformen der Schriftexegese*, p. 2.

(prophetic literature whose artistic shape suggests that it was set down in written form from the beginning, including Nahum, Habakkuk, Joel and Deutero-Isaiah).[98] This led to the treatment of prophets such as Nahum, Habakkuk and Joel as representatives of an 'alternative prophetic tradition' which stood apart from the 'mainstream'. Richard Coggins challenged this approach in a 1982 essay,[99] in which he repeatedly cited verbal parallels as exhibiting an interdependence and close connection between these and 'mainstream' prophets.

Coggins distinguished two types of dependence: the literary dependence of one prophetic collection on another, and the dependence of several prophets on the language of the Jerusalem cult. With regard to the striking parallel between Isa. 52.7a and Nah. 1.15a ('[Look/how beautiful] on the mountains, the feet of one who brings good news, announcing peace...'), Coggins suggested that it derives from the fact that both prophets had Jerusalemite backgrounds and concerns. Similarly, verbal links between Habakkuk 2 and Isaiah 14 point to the dependence of both upon the characteristic language used in the Jerusalem cult.

According to Coggins, this hypothesis of 'borrowing' language from the Jerusalem cult might also have a bearing on other tradition-critical problems. With regard to the prominent 'day of the Lord' language, he asserted:

> It does not seem necessary to postulate any complicated theory of literary dependence. It may be that each of these passages is ultimately dependent upon the usage of the cult, taking up a theme that could be applied either positively against the enemies of the community or negatively against the community itself.[100]

Similarly, the oracles against the foreign nations which share many expressions may have arisen from the prayer for victory over foreign enemies, which was a function of the Jerusalem cult. Although Coggins did not rule out the possibility of prophetic quotation, his proposal

---

98. I. Engnell, 'Prophets and Prophetism in the Old Testament', Chapter 6 in *A Rigid Scrutiny: Critical Essays on the Old Testament by Ivan Engnell* (trans. and ed. J.T. Willis; Nashville: Vanderbilt University Press, 1969).

99. R. Coggins, 'An Alternative Prophetic Tradition?', in R. Coggins, A. Phillips and M. Knibb (eds.), *Israel's Prophetic Tradition: Essays in Honour of Peter R. Ackroyd* (Cambridge: Cambridge University Press, 1982), pp. 77-94.

100. Coggins, 'An Alternative Prophetic Tradition?', p. 90.

claimed for the cult some of the choicest examples that have been cited in the scholarly literature.

It is appropriate to conclude this historical survey with the work of Peter Ackroyd. From his first scholarly essay to his most recent publications, he combined a rigorous methodology[101] with an interest in the significance of quotation within the prophets as a whole[102] and its implications for a proper interpretation of individual texts.[103] His fascinating essay, 'The Vitality of the Word of God', noted the repetition of prophetic utterances as an aspect of 'the shaping of the Old Testament material ... by the living application of the recognized word of God ... to the ever new needs of a community sensitive to the vitality of that word'.[104] Published more than two decades ago, it succinctly summarizes the methodological problem of prophetic quotation which has plagued scholars for a century and a half:

> When almost identical oracles occur in two different prophets, the solution sometimes proposed is that one quoted from the other, or that both utilized a common source ... for example ... in Isaiah 2, 1-4 (5) and Micah 4, 1-4(5). Few Old Testament scholars would wish to maintain a strictly literary view of such quotation, as if prophets had available to them books of earlier material to which they had recourse when inspiration failed or when they wished to illustrate a point, as when a preacher quotes the poets ... Yet the attempt to establish quotation, whether from literary source or fixed oral tradition, is still much in vogue, and is still frequently employed as a criterion for the relative dating of Old Testament passages, in spite of the fact that actual quotation is often difficult to prove and the direction of quotation even more difficult.[105]

Despite the rather pessimistic tone of Ackroyd's comments, his more recent work demonstrates that even he has not abandoned the quest for a proper approach to verbal parallels within the prophets.[106]

101. P.R. Ackroyd, 'Criteria for the Maccabean Dating of Old Testament Literature', *VT* 3 (1953), pp. 113-32, a summary of some of the conclusions of his PhD dissertation, 'The Problem of Maccabean Psalms' (Cambridge University, 1945).

102. P.R. Ackroyd, *Continuity: A Contribution to the Study of the Old Testament Religious Tradition* (Oxford: Basil Blackwell, 1962).

103. Ackroyd, 'Isaiah I–XII', pp. 16-48.

104. P.R. Ackroyd, 'The Vitality of the Word of God in the Old Testament: A Contribution to the Study of the Transmission of Old Testament Material', *ASTI* 1 (1962), pp. 7-23, especially p. 7.

105. Ackroyd, 'The Vitality of the Word of God', pp. 8-9.

106. See his comments in 'Isaiah I–XII', pp. 21-25.

The Current State of the Discussion

As should be clear from the preceding survey, although the phenomenon of verbal parallels within the prophetic corpus has provoked much discussion, its very nature has substantially impeded progress in its evaluation. This overview, of necessity, has been selective, focusing on those scholars whose work, though not always the most influential, reflected an honest attempt to wrestle with the methodological issues which accompany the claim of prophetic quotation. I will conclude by summarizing the approaches taken in the past, noting the problems which remain to be solved, and suggesting several corrective measures which need to be taken if progress is to be made in the future.

Characteristics of Past Studies

The interest in verbal parallels has continued unabated during the past century and a half, with numerous scholars addressing the topic. However, the phenomenon of prophetic quotation has been more like a mine in which each generation has searched independently for gems than a torch which was passed on from one generation to the next. The verbal parallels often were treated like clues awaiting discovery and interpretation by the scholar-detectives who sought to unravel the mysteries of the origin of the prophetic corpus. Although fraught with methodological difficulties, the study of prophetic quotation is certain to continue, even if some consider those difficulties to be insoluble.

The study of prophetic quotation consistently has been treated as a means to an end. The primary concern of scholars never has been the phenomenon of verbal parallels but the bearing it might have on a particular theory of dating, authorship or interrelationship. As a result, subjectivity tended to play a significant role: methodological problems were downplayed, superficial comparisons were made, the relevant data were investigated only in as much detail as was necessary to serve a particular scholar's purpose. Lengthy systematic studies were rare; commonly, only several pages in a monograph or a few paragraphs in an essay were devoted to a discussion of quotation. Few scholars offered more than one study in which verbal parallels were a significant focus of attention.

As might be expected, the way in which verbal parallels were evaluated was affected greatly by general historical developments in the critical study of the Old Testament. The same passage which was viewed in the late nineteenth century as a divinely inspired quotation might be viewed in the course of the twentieth century as an inauthentic gloss, a felicitous result of the process of oral transmission, or an ingenious redactional reinterpretation. On the positive side of the ledger, new perspectives sometimes helped to shed light on enigmatic verbal parallels; on the negative side, verbal parallels became the clay which a scholar could mold according to the latest scholarly fashion.

Scholars, for the most part, worked independently on the problem. Although occasionally one might use the list of verbal parallels prepared by another as a starting point, there was seldom evidence that the students of prophetic quotation consciously built on the work of their predecessors. Interaction with others usually was limited to a disagreement with, if not a complete rejection of, their views. Even then one suspects that criticism of the methodology of another scholar was the second step: motivated by a basic disagreement with the conclusions of other scholars, one then proceeded to attack their use of the data. For example, it seems that Volz's and Elliger's primary object of dispute was their position regarding the unity and dating of 'Third' Isaiah; their debate over the evaluation of verbal parallels was ancillary.

The same methodological questions were asked repeatedly throughout the history of the study of verbal parallels, with a variety of answers being given:[107]

1. How can one best account for this verbal parallel?
2. Is this really a quotation?
3. Why was this passage quoted?
4. How can one determine in which direction the literary borrowing took place?

Which question was most prominent in a particular discussion and how thoroughly it was treated depended on the scholar's primary concern. For example, Caspari focused on the direction of the borrowing; whether or not borrowing had occurred did not receive much discussion. Miller was interested in weeding out passages incorrectly identi-

107. The first two questions are related, for even though a verbal parallel may be capable of another explanation, it still may be a quotation. Alternatively, although a convincing case can be presented for considering a text a quotation, it still may have another origin. The third question was seldom explicitly asked or answered, although clearly an underlying motivation for studying quotation was to explain why certain passages were repeated, while others were not. The fourth question was most frequently, though not always convincingly, answered.

fied as quotations but also in explaining the origin of the verbal parallels. Paul simply assumed that all of the parallels he identified were examples of 'Second' Isaiah borrowing from Jeremiah.

Each scholar utilized some type of criterion, whether explicit or implicit, to determine the answer to these questions. Even those who were accused of offering ad hoc arguments on a passage-by-passage basis had some criteria in mind. Some considered a passage to be a quotation simply because it was included in another scholar's list. The direction of borrowing usually was determined on the a priori basis of the prevailing scholarly consensus regarding literary chronology rather than as a result of a passage-by-passage comparison. To summarize, scholars who studied verbal parallels in the prophets had little in common in terms of motivation, presuppositions or approach. However, they did share a common methodological problem which they often sought to address in some way before proceeding to evaluate the phenomenon.

Persistent Problems

The methodological problem confronting scholars has three major components:

Identifying quotations. It is by no means the case that every striking verbal parallel was automatically labeled a 'quotation'. Rather than attributing all similarities in wording to one prophet consciously citing another, scholars have proposed numerous alternative explanations—coincidence, unconscious imitation, divine inspiration, formulaic, proverbial or cultic language, oral transmission, mutual dependence on unpreserved material, similarity of background and circumstances, redactional glosses. Although some of these alternative explanations no longer may be considered viable options and not all of them would apply equally well to a given passage, nevertheless, progress has been made in determining what influences might have produced a verbal parallel if it is *not* a quotation. However, completely reliable criteria for identifying what *is* (or even *may be*) genuine quotation have yet to be discovered. Part of the problem is terminological: Is 'quotation' clearly synonymous with 'literary borrowing' or 'conscious imitation'? The other part is syntactical: given the absence of clear indicators, such as introductory formulae or quotation marks, determining dependence remains little more than an educated guess.

Assessing the nature of the borrowing. Several centuries ago, a verbal parallel between the books of Ezekiel and Isaiah might be assessed simply as a case of Ezekiel quoting Isaiah. However, today the situation is understood as being considerably more complex. In the light of subsequent developments in the critical study of the prophetic books, one might consider all of the following alternatives: Ezekiel is quoting (1) the words of Isaiah the eighth-century prophet; (2) an edited collection of Isaiah's oracles; (3) a later prophet of the 'Isaiah school'; or (4) a saying originated by Isaiah which by Ezekiel's day had become formulaic or proverbial. Alternatively, the parallel in Ezekiel could be (5) a post-Ezekiel redactional addition; or (6) even stem from a later prophet or editor within the Isaiah 'tradition' who is quoting Ezekiel.

Determining the direction of borrowing. Before the rise of critical studies, it was a simple matter to determine who was borrowing from whom, except in the cases of contemporaries such as Isaiah and Micah and prophets such as Habakkuk, Nahum and Joel whose historical background is difficult to determine. A new critical consensus regarding the dating of some of the prophetic literature has emerged, once again encouraging a priori determinations of the direction of dependence. However, with regard to contemporaries and prophetic literature whose date is still being debated and as a means of testing again critically determined chronologies, criteria are still essential for ascertaining who the borrower is. As the polemics of the late nineteenth century illustrate, most criteria are extremely flexible, able to be used persuasively by either side: did the quoter expand or abbreviate borrowed material? Did he gather together multiple fragments from his predecessor and build them into a new composite oracle or did he break up the longer saying of a predecessor into seed-thoughts to be scattered wherever appropriate throughout his oracles? Did he carefully adapt a borrowed saying so that it fitted more perfectly into its new setting than in its original location or is an awkward contextual fit evidence that he sought to preserve the saying exactly as he found it? Although such criteria are essential, their application is almost unavoidably subjective.

Implications for Future Studies of Prophetic Quotation
Given the foregoing discussion, one might be tempted to abandon the entire enterprise as beyond remedy. However, as already indicated, interest in the phenomenon has continued and will continue, despite the

present methodological impasse. Therefore, it is preferable to suggest some corrective measures and alternative approaches which may serve to curb the promiscuous attribution and evaluation of quotation and redirect some of the scholarly energy devoted to the problem in a more fruitful direction. The purpose of this work is to propose some new possibilities for the study of verbal parallels within the prophets.

1. Given the multiplicity of possible origins of verbal parallels and the difficulty of determining whether and in which direction borrowing occurred, greater caution must be exercised in the evaluation and appropriation of verbal parallels in the construction of a variety of hypotheses. Chapter 2 will summarize and critique the range of uses which scholars have made of the phenomenon in critical theory despite offering little or no methodological demonstration that the passages under consideration are actually quotations. It also will be necessary to set out some of the presuppositions about the prophetic literature that have been foundational to the work of these scholars.

2. In light of the methodological impasse, it is appropriate to ask again some fundamental questions: Did prophets actually quote their predecessors? If so, why did they not indicate this fact more clearly? Did they expect their audience (and later readers) to recognize their quotations as such? An even more basic question is: What does one mean by 'quotation'? (Chapter 7 will discuss the lack of clarity in terminology and definitions.)

3. Given the history of a century and a half during which the biblical data have been examined repeatedly with no substantial methodological progress being made, there clearly is a need for some new sources of insight into the phenomenon. Chapters 3–6 will suggest some of the ways in which the study of quotation in ancient Near Eastern literature (from Egypt, Mesopotamia, Ugarit), the writings of early Judaism (Ben Sira and the Qumran Hodayoth), Old Testament proverbial and narrative literature, and modern literature may contribute to the understanding of prophetic quotation.

4. There is a need to give more attention to the significance of verbal parallels within the prophets. Too often in the past, interest in a verbal parallel ceased as soon as it was labeled as 'not a true quotation'. However, given the difficulty of determining what is a 'true quotation', it may prove enlightening to consider alleged examples of quotation alongside all other types of verbal parallels, regardless of origin, in order to determine what kinds of material were repeated most fre-

quently and to assess the impact of repeated passages on the reading of the prophetic corpus.

5. If 'quotation' is to continue to be a meaningful term, its use will have to be controlled by a much stricter definition than has been implied by its past employment. Rather than attempting to compile a hypothetically 'complete list' of all quotations between two given prophetic collections, as exemplified by the work of scholars such as Miller, Gross and Paul, one should seek to assess more objectively a small number of the best examples. Attention should be given also to determining how such passages function within their new contexts rather than solely how they can be used to support larger theoretical constructs. The remaining chapters of this study will be devoted to the re-examination of verbal parallels and quotations within the book of Isaiah and between Isaiah and other prophetic books.

Although these issues can be dealt with only in a preliminary manner here, my goal is to point the way beyond the current methodological impasse toward a more promising approach to this intriguing though elusive component of prophetic rhetoric.

Chapter 2

THE ASSESSMENT OF PROPHETIC QUOTATION

When one immerses oneself in the voluminous secondary literature that discusses prophetic quotation, whether as a central concern or only peripherally, it is both fascinating and deeply disturbing to discover how certain some scholars can be regarding the significance and implications of the phenomenon without offering any substantive evidence that the texts which they are considering actually incorporate identifiable quotations. Although, as has been seen in the previous chapter, many have acknowledged how problematic it is to adopt such an attitude, the following approach is far too common: having listed a number of verbal parallels, perhaps also giving their texts in translation, the scholar declares that they involve prophetic quotation and immediately proceeds to treat those passages as offering a body of objective data whose contribution to his area of interest can be assessed readily.

Why have so few scholars felt the need to begin their study of verbal parallels with any discussion of the methodological issues? One can only speculate, since reasons seldom are given. On the one hand, it seems that most consider the data to be self-vindicating, that the existence of the verbal parallels is so immediately evident to all who examine them that one safely can take their identification to be a certainty. Indeed, there is some force to this position, since many of the verbal parallels are cited repeatedly in the literature. However, even a superficial comparison of any lists of parallels between two particular prophetic books or any sections thereof will reveal a significant divergence in the passages chosen.[1] What one considers a 'striking parallel' another will deem to be an insignificant similarity. Therefore, one

---

1. This may be due partly to the fact that such scholars are intending to offer only an illustrative, not an exhaustive, list of passages. However there is also significant disagreement over which passages clearly exhibit dependence. See the discussion of Ezekiel on pp. 31-34 above.

simply cannot assume an adequate scholarly consensus when claiming 'A is a verbal parallel to B'. Furthermore, even when one has shown that passage A is *verbally parallel to* B, only the first step has been taken toward demonstrating that A is *dependent on* B.

On the other hand, examining each of the individual passages for evidence of literary dependence would require more effort, time and pages than most scholars are willing to invest. In addition, a more detailed (and, consequently, accurate) assessment of the data might radically reduce the number of relevant passages and might even negate the hypothesis which they are cited to support. It is not surprising, therefore, that most choose, for one reason or another, simply to concentrate their attention on the *interpretation* rather than the *identification* of parallel passages.

In order to demonstrate the methodological weaknesses of this approach, it is necessary to be aware of the wide variety of ways in which verbal parallels within the prophets have been employed in developing numerous scholarly hypotheses as well as the underlying presuppositions which make such theorizing possible. The purpose of the following survey is to examine and illustrate the most significant ways in which the import of the phenomenon of prophetic quotation has been interpreted and appropriated.

The Dating of the Literature

The possibilities are legion. As was suggested in Chapter 1, the most extensive use of verbal parallels has been in the chronological ordering of the literature. When parallels are identified between two prophetic books, it generally is assumed that one is dependent on the other and, accordingly, the date of the latter forms the *terminus ante quem* (fixed date before which) for the former's composition.

Although some indication has already been given in Chapter 1 of the use of verbal parallels in the determination of the date of Ezekiel (Burrows), Isaiah 40–55 relative to Jeremiah (Caspari) and Isaiah 56–66 relative to 40–55 (Odeberg, Volz, Elliger), the most vivid illustration is the dating of Joel. Georg Fohrer saw the interdependence of the prophets as a primary means of dating Joel's activity, citing Joel's dependence on Isaiah, Jeremiah, Ezekiel, Obadiah, Zephaniah and Malachi in suggesting an early-fourth-century date.[2] However, the fact

2.   G. Fohrer, *Introduction to the Old Testament* (trans. D.E. Green; Nashville:

that estimates of Joel's date of composition range from the ninth to the second century[3] suggests that this criterion can be used with considerable flexibility.

Other scholars were more cautious than Fohrer: S.R. Driver listed ten reasons for holding to a late date for Joel before invoking literary parallels as offering corroborating evidence. Even then he admitted that

> from several of these parallels, it is true, no conclusion of any value can be drawn: the fact of there being a reminiscence, on one side or the other, is sufficiently patent; but unless it is known independently that one of the two writers was earlier than the other, there is nothing to shew [*sic*] which is the original.[4]

Interestingly, the dating of Joel is one issue regarding which the methodological or theological a prioris have little significance. The staunchly conservative E.J. Young shared the view of Eichhorn, Ewald and de Wette that Joel was the elder contemporary of Amos, while British evangelical L.C. Allen held to an early postexilic date (520–500 BCE) in agreement with Jacob Myers and Gösta Ahlström.[5] This may imply that the ambiguous nature of the textual data forbids dogmatism. However, the decision which one makes in this regard has a major impact on how one incorporates the numerous verbal parallels between Joel and other prophetic books into one's conception of Joel's prophetic work and, consequently, on how one exegetes the book. On one end of the spectrum is Delitzsch:

Abingdon Press, 1968), p. 429. Fohrer used this dependence as his first criterion in dating Joel, although he gave no indication that he was discussing the evidence in the order of its importance.

3.   See the brief summary in M. Bič, *Das Buch Joel* (Berlin: Evangelische Verlagsanstalt, 1960), p. 9.

4.   S.R. Driver, *The Books of Joel and Amos* (Cambridge: Cambridge University Press, 1915), p. 22.

5.   E.J. Young, *An Introduction to the Old Testament* (Grand Rapids: Eerdmans, 1960), p. 256; J.G. Eichhorn, *Einleitung in das Alte Testament* (5 vols.; Göttingen: Carl Eduard Rosenbusch, 4th edn, 1823–25), IV, p. 300; Ewald, *Die Propheten des Alten Bundes*, I, p. 69; W.M.L. de Wette, *A Critical and Historical Introduction to the Canonical Scriptures of the Old Testament* (trans. T. Parker; 2 vols.; Boston: Little, Brown & Company, 2nd edn, 1858 [1817]), II, pp. 442-43; L.C. Allen, *The Books of Joel, Obadiah, Jonah and Micah* (NICOT; Grand Rapids: Eerdmans, 1976), p. 24; J.M. Myers, 'Some Considerations Bearing on the Date of Joel', *ZAW* NS 33 (1962), pp. 177-95; G.W. Ahlström, *Joel and the Temple Cult of Jerusalem* (VTSup, 21; Leiden: E.J. Brill, 1971), p. 119.

> It is undisputed that Joel stands in the relative position of a model which is copied by the entire prophetic ministry of the age of Uzziah and Jeroboam, and from Amos onward there is scarcely a prophet...in whom we fail to meet with reminiscences of Joel.[6]

On the other end of the spectrum is Wolff:

> In its details, the language of Joel is determined by the earlier prophetic movement (*von den älteren Propheten bestimmt*)... As a learned prophet he is occupied directly... but, above all, indirectly with the systematic treatment of transmitted prophetic words. He interprets even contemporary events on the basis of earlier prophecy.[7]

Wolff's perspective is not a new one; already in 1881 Joel's complete dependence on his prophetic predecessors was so often stressed that Reuss complained: 'But is it fair to ask whether the whole is suited to give the impression that the author was unable to write a single line without repeatedly stealing a phrase from here or there in the earlier literature?'[8]

Why is it that the textual data can be used to support opposite conclusions? It is not the case that scholars have made totally arbitrary decisions regarding the direction of the dependence. Although each scholar who has studied the problem has used some criteria in making his or her determination, the major difficulty lies in the very nature of the criteria chosen. An examination of J.A. Thompson's reasons for considering Joel to be the quoter whenever a literary relationship can be determined may reveal the inherent weaknesses in this approach.

Thompson offers five arguments for Joel's dependence:

1. In 2.32 (= Heb. 3.5) Joel himself indicates that he is quoting Obadiah 17 by the phrase 'As the LORD has said'.

---

6. F. Delitzsch, 'Zwei sichere Ergebnisse in Betreff der Weissungsschrift Joels', *Zeitschrift für die Gesamte Lutherische Theologie und Kirche* 12 (1851), p. 307, cited by K.F. Keil, *Manual of Historico-Critical Introduction to the Canonical Scriptures of the Old Testament* (trans. G.C.M. Douglas; 2 vols.; Edinburgh: T. & T. Clark, 1869–70), II, p. 377. Similarly, Eichhorn, *Einleitung in das Alte Testament*, IV, p. 304: 'Because of his originality, Joel deserved to be imitated, and that also occurred to a considerable extent.'

7. H.W. Wolff, *A Commentary on the Books of the Prophets Joel and Amos* (trans. W. Janzen, S.D. McBride, Jr and C.A. Muenchow; Hermeneia, 29–30; Philadelphia: Fortress Press, 1977), pp. 10, 14.

8. E. Reuss, *Die Geschichte der Heiligen Schriften: Alten Testaments* (Braunschweig: C.A. Schwetschke & Son, 1881), p. 244.

2. In several cases the similar phrases are integral parts of larger contexts in the other prophets, but only parenthetical theological interpretations in Joel.
3. In some verses Joel combines phrases from different prophetic passages.
4. Some of the parallels consist of phrases of other prophets and are therefore probably quoted.
5. In two cases Joel gives the reverse of ideas, each of which is found elsewhere twice and therefore probably in the original form.[9]

At first reading, these arguments, especially taken together, seem conclusive. Nevertheless, there is good reason to question their reliability. First, the use of כאשר אמר יהוה ('as the LORD has said') as indicating a quotation is suggestive, especially given the resultant identity between the phrase in Joel and Obadiah בהר־ציון (ובירושלם) תהיה פליטה ('on Mt Zion [and in Jerusalem] there will be deliverance') if one follows the *BHS* editor in transferring the reference to Jerusalem to the following clause. The use of כאשר (as) in such a connection is uncommon, and in passages such as Jer. 27.13; 40.3 (both with דבר, 'has spoken'), 48.8 (without כ, 'as'), and Amos 5.14 (of human speech), it may refer to previous statements.

However, even then, כאשר אמר יהוה could be viewed as simply one of many formulaic introductions to direct or indirect speech and, as such, not inherently indicative of a quotation any more than the more frequently occurring כה אמר יהוה (thus says the LORD). In fact, the examples cited in the previous paragraph have no clear Old Testament passage in mind. The use of the introductory formula (כ) אשר אמר/דבר יהוה does not necessarily signal the quotation of another biblical writer, nor does Joel (granting Thompson's position) syntactically indicate the remainder of his alleged literary borrowings. Therefore, one could as easily conclude that Joel is citing a previous statement of Yahweh not

9. J.A. Thompson, *The Book of Joel* (IBC, 6; Nashville: Abingdon Press, 1956), pp. 731-32. Thompson offers a fuller discussion of the issue in 'The Date of Joel', in H.N. Bream, R.D. Heim and C.A. Moore (eds.), *A Light unto my Path: Old Testament Studies in Honor of J.M. Myers* (Philadelphia: Temple University Press, 1974), pp. 453-64.

recorded in Scripture (similar to Isa. 28.12) upon which Obadiah may
be dependent.[10]

Secondly, again, the verbal identity of Joel 1.15 and Isa. 13.6
(כי קרוב יום יהוה [ו]כשד משדי יבוא, 'for the day of the LORD is near; it
will come like destruction from the Almighty') or Joel 2.2 and Zeph.
1.15 (יום חשך ואפלה יום ענן וערפל), 'a day of darkness, a day of clouds
and blackness') is undeniable. However, to claim that the latter passage
in each parallel is clearly more integral to the context, while the former
is only parenthetical is a highly subjective judgment. First of all, one
might also argue that, if one views the prophetic corpus from a literary
perspective, it would be understandable for a passage which is
'peripheral' to its original context to be placed, when quoted, into a
context that is specifically structured to integrally accommodate it.
Furthermore, given the complexity of the tradition-historical development of the concept of the 'day of the LORD', it is precarious to
attempt to trace direct dependence too closely. Even Amos, whose early
date is undisputed, in 5.18-20 builds on an already formulated day of
the LORD expectation.[11] Joel's brief reference to the day of LORD
may suggest its early position within the growth of the tradition, while
Zephaniah's fuller description is indicative of a later stage. Finally, Joel
1.15's 'parenthetical' reference to the day of the LORD may be due to
the fact that it adumbrates his fuller description in 2.1-11.

Thirdly, to argue that Joel combines phrases from different prophetic
passages suggests, if not presupposes, a rather denigrating view of
Joel's prophetic activity as lacking any fresh message or creativity and
therefore rather mechanically piecing together scraps of earlier oracles
into a patchwork composition. Rudolph emphatically rejected this

10. See Wolff's lengthy discussion of introductory formulae in 'Das Zitat im
Prophetenspruch: Eine Studie zur prophetischen Verkündigungsweise', in *idem*,
Gesammelte Studien zum Alten Testament (TBü, 22; Munich: Chr. Kaiser Verlag,
1964 [1937]), pp. 36-129. Wolff, *Joel and Amos*, p. 68 n. 96, also notes the use of
the phrase with reference to the Nathan oracle of 1 Chron. 22.10 in 2 Chron. 6.10
and 23.3. Wolff is more hesitant than Thompson to consider this Joel's explicit
quotation of Obadiah: 'The inclusion of "as Yahweh has said" at this point shows
that we have a conscious proclamation of transmitted material, and not perchance a
new oracle of Yahweh.' 'He does so exactly in that form which is attested for us in
Ob 17', *Joel and Amos*, p. 68.

11. See Wolff, *Joel and Amos*, pp. 33-34, 255-56, and the discussion of
R. Coggins above, p. 54. Thompson's most important examples of parallels between
Joel and other prophetic books involve 'day of the LORD' passages.

view: 'Joel is not one who pours over older prophetic writings and patiently pieces them together into mosaics; instead he freely fashions [his sayings] out of a living tradition, which he himself thereby contin- ues.'[12] Unless one presupposes that Joel is late, it is just as possible to suppose that several other books contain phrases which independently and perhaps even coincidentally correspond to phrases in Joel.

To take one of Thompson's examples, to state that 'Joel 3.16 = Amos 1.2; Isa. 13.13; Ps. 61.3', as if to suggest that 3.16 is composed of three borrowed beads artificially strung together to form a new necklace, is quite misleading. The identity of Amos 1.2 and Joel 3.16, יהוה מציון ישאג ומירושלם יתן קולו ('The LORD roars from Zion and Thunders from Jerusalem'), is well known and arguments for priority are indecisive. However, it is not clear that ורעשו שמים וארץ, 'the sky and the earth will tremble' (3.16) is derived from על־ כן שמים ארגיז ותרעש הארץ ממקומה, 'Therefore I will make the heavens tremble; and the earth will shake from its place', or that ויהוה מחסה לעמו ומעוז לבני ישראל, 'But the LORD will be a refuge for his people, a stronghold for the people of Israel' (3.16) derives from כי־היית מחסה לי מגדל־עז מפני אויב, 'For you have been my refuge, a strong tower against thy foe' (Ps. 41.3 [4]). The former also could be an eschatologizing reuse of the theophanic language of Judg. 5.4 and Ps. 68.8 (Heb. 9). In the case of the latter, Ps. 46.1(2) is as close in wording to Joel as Ps. 61.3, while Isa. 25.4 at least employs the same nouns as Joel (מחסה...מעוז, 'refuge...stronghold'), while Psalm 61 does not. It is reasonable to expect 'day of the LORD' passages to share common motifs and themes and to expect a cultic prophet to use cultic language without claiming literary borrowing to account for all similarities.

Fourthly that 'I, the LORD, am your God and there is none else' (Joel 2.27) sounds like 'Second' Isaiah, and 'and you shall know that I am the LORD your God' (Joel 3.17) sounds like Ezekiel is clear; but such similarity does not require the dependence of the former on the latter. Frequency of use does not imply exclusive possession of a for- mulation such as ואין עוד, 'and there is no other'. One can hardly expect Joel, within the scope of 70 verses, to contain as many repeated phrases as a longer prophetic collection. One could as reasonably argue that 'Second' Isaiah 'found' the phrase in Joel and liked it so well that

---

12. W. Rudolph, 'Wann wirkte Joel?', in Maass (ed.), *Das ferne und nahe Wort*, pp. 193-98 (196).

he used it repeatedly in a variety of contexts. With respect to the second phrase, Zimmerli[13] has demonstrated that the use of the 'recognition formula' (*Erkenntnisformel*), though prominent in Ezekiel, also is scattered throughout the Old Testament. Accordingly, Joel could have derived his usage from Pentateuchal traditions which predated Ezekiel.

Finally, if any of the criteria for priority or dependence are subjective, then Thompson's final one is supremely so. If it were not for the fact that Isa. 2.4 parallels Mic. 4.3, which Thompson claims Joel to be reversing, the evidence would be completely ambiguous as to who was reversing whom. Even the existence of these parallels is not clearly supportive of his viewpoint. On the one hand, if Isaiah is a reversal of Joel, one might hold that Micah saw the reversal of Joel as so striking that it bore repeating or that both independently reversed Joel. On the other hand, Micah might have quoted Isaiah without any knowledge of Joel or Joel might have reversed Isaiah without any knowledge of Micah. Therefore, the repetition of one of the passages has no decisive bearing on the question of priority. Given the fact that the most frequently offered explanation of the identity of Isa. 2.2-4 and Mic. 4.1-3 is that both drew independently on an unpreserved third source,[14] a real possibility is that Micah, Isaiah *and* Joel all based their oracle on that shared tradition. Hence, the parallel to Joel in Isaiah and Micah might be completely irrelevant to the question of a relative chronology of the three prophets.

The foregoing critique of Thompson's criteria is not intended to suggest that all criteria for determining who depended on whom are useless. Nor is it being claimed that Joel's date is early. Rather, my purpose is simply to illustrate my contention that most criteria are satisfying only to those who already are convinced of the correctness of a particular date for a given prophet and the resultant chronological relationship between that prophet and other biblical books.

Most scholars acknowledge the potential for subjectivity in applying these criteria and seek to remedy the situation by invoking the value of multiplied examples. Typical of this approach is G.B. Gray, author of a lengthy study of the parallel passages in Joel and their use in determining the date of the book, who states that the whole argument from the

---

13. W. Zimmerli, 'Erkenntnis Gottes nach dem Buch Ezechiel', in *Gottes Offenbarung: Gesammelte Aufsätze zum Alten Testament* (TBü, 19; Munich: Chr. Kaiser Verlag, 1963), pp. 41-119.

14. See the discussion of Isa. 2.2-4 and Mic. 4.1-3 in Chapter 8.

parallels is 'cumulative'.[15] It is true that ten verses in which Joel's dependence is 'demonstrated' are weightier than one as evidence for its late date.

However, this argument, as well, is fraught with questionable pre-suppositions. First of all, given the subjective nature of the criteria of priority discussed in the previous section, ten examples may not be stronger than one which is argued more convincingly. Secondly, the claim is made sometimes that there are only two alternatives: either Joel is very early or very late (i.e. he is in every case the quoted or the quoter).[16] Accordingly, every example points unambiguously to the same conclusion. Of course, if Joel were the earliest writing prophet, by definition he could not quote any extant prophetic predecessor,[17] and, if he were the latest, he would always have to be the quoter. However, the position expressed above involves more than that. On the one hand, it assumes that Joel contains nothing which makes it worthy of signifi-cantly influencing other writers.[18] On the other hand, it sees quotation as primarily a characteristic of only a few late lesser prophetic figures. Jacob Myers assails that view: 'One cannot say definitely that because a given writer quotes earlier materials therefore he is always the borrower and that others coming after him never quoted from him.'[19] Since Rudolph makes a strong case for a late preexilic date,[20] Joel could also be viewed as having an intermediate position, both quoting and being quoted. Indeed, the available data at least suggest that each prophet, in turn, was influenced in some way by his predecessors.

Thirdly, this approach assumes a simplistic conception of the unity of prophetic collections, as if every parallel between Joel and another prophetic book involves the prophet Joel quoting another canonical prophet or vice versa. The literary unity of Joel,[21] as well as of other

15. G.B. Gray, 'The Parallel Passages in "Joel" in their Bearing on the Question of Date', *The Expositor* 4.8 (1893), pp. 208-25 (222).

16. See Reuss, *Die Geschichte der Heiligen Schriften*, p. 259; and Gray, 'The Parallel Passages in "Joel" ', p. 213.

17. However, Ewald, *Die Propheten des Alten Bundes*, I, pp. 69-70, argued that even the earliest canonical prophets (Joel, Hosea, Amos, Isaiah) drew upon still earlier prophetic oracles which are no longer preserved.

18. Gray, 'The Parallel Passages in "Joel" ', p. 213.

19. Myers, 'Some Considerations Bearing on the Date of Joel', p. 183.

20. Rudolph, 'Wann wirkte Joel?', pp. 193-98.

21. See Wolff, *Joel and Amos*, pp. 6-8; and Allen, *The Books of Joel, Obadiah, Jonah and Micah*, pp. 133-36. Here the redactional complexity of the book of Joel

members of the prophetic corpus, is much debated. If a parallel involved a late addition to the book of Joel, it would have no bearing on the chronological relationship between the prophet Joel and the prophet containing the parallel. If the historical notations in prophetic super-scriptions or narratives are no longer to be taken at face value as providing valuable historical data, as they were in the pre-critical era, then every passage must be shown to be either original or a datable late addition—indeed, if Willi-Plein is correct, quotations by nature may be suspect of being secondary.[22]

Similarly, the cumulative argument assumes that the only (or most) correct way of explaining verbal parallels is to determine who is quoting whom. Rudolph, however, notes that another viable alternative exists: 'It is not a case of literary dependence but of being rooted in a common tradition.'[23] If Rudolph is correct, *both* prophets containing a given parallel may be dependent on a common tradition but *not* on each other. Thus, all that the careful comparisons between parallel passages reveal is simply how a given tradition has been adapted and integrated into each prophet's message.

Although one could proceed to consider other examples of the use of prophetic quotation in determining literary chronology, the example of Joel suffices. As inviting as the phenomenon of verbal parallels is to the scholar seeking to date the prophetic literature, one must conclude with S.R. Driver: 'Nothing is more difficult... than from a *mere* comparison of parallel passages to determine on which side the priority lies... In other words, the parallels cannot be used for *determining* the date of Joel.'[24]

The Process of Textual Transmission

Although the most common use of verbal parallels in critical theory has been in the dating of literature, the earliest use of these passages was in

is being acknowledged as possible but not necessarily asserted.

22. Willi-Plein, *Vorformen der Schriftexegese*. See the discussion above, p. 53.

23. Rudolph, 'Wann wirkte Joel?', p. 196; similarly Coggins, above p. 54.

24. S.R. Driver, *An Introduction to the Literature of the Old Testament* (New York: Charles Scribner's Sons, 6th edn, 1897), pp. 312-13. In this respect he also criticized the work of Küper and C.P. Caspari. For a thorough study of Joel's use of earlier texts, see S. Bergler, *Joel als Schriftinterpret* (Beiträge zur Erforschung des Alten Testaments und des antiken Judentums, 16; Main: Peter Lang, 1988).

the discipline of text criticism. In 1774, Henry Owen suggested that, in the attempt

> to discover, remove, and rectify corruption ... the [approach] most obvious and determinate, yet somehow strangely overlooked or at least applied in a very imperfect manner [is] to compare together ... the several correspondent passages of Scripture ... [which are] far more numerous, ample and various, than most Readers could, at first, conceive.[25]

Owen distinguished five classes of passages:

1. genealogical registers, master-rolls, and so on, doubly inserted;
2. historical narrations repeated;
3. sentiments, messages, and so on, twice recited;
4. quotations made by one prophet from another;
5. quotations or repetitions borrowed by the same prophet from himself.[26]

Owen listed 11 parallels in the fourth category and 23 in the fifth but drew few conclusions, recommending the actual textual collation to those 'who are happily endowed with more leisure, and disposed to try their skill this way'.[27]

Although he may not have fit Owen's description exactly, J.G. Eichhorn was the first major scholar to take up the challenge:

> Parallel passages are not simply sources of variants but also an excellent means for evaluating them and for discovering and correcting errors which have arisen, as long as one does not believe that related passages must have been identical down to the smallest detail.[28]

After noting Owen's five classes, Eichhorn reorganized his examples under three headings which eliminated Owen's special focus on prophetic quotations:

---

25. H. Owen, *Critica Sacra; or, a Short Introduction to Hebrew Criticism* (London: W. Bowyer & J. Nichols, 1774), pp. 5-7. This essay was also, probably mistakenly, attributed to Benjamin Kennicott.

26. Owen, *Critica Sacra*, p. 8. Owen's category of self-quotation, i.e. the prophet repeating himself, will be discussed in Chapter 7.

27. Owen, *Critica Sacra*, p. 10.

28. Eichhorn, *Einleitung in das Alte Testament*, I, p. 390. In the fourth edition, Eichhorn's discussion of parallel passages is considerably longer than that which is in the second edition. Eichhorn may have not been the first to respond to Owen, since a bibliographical note to his *Critica Sacra* indicates that a supplement in answer to some remarks by Raphael Baruh appeared in the following year.

1. Repeated historical passages
    a. Genealogies
    b. Narratives
2. Repeated laws, songs and oracles.
3. Repeated concepts, sayings, proverbs, and so on.

Eichhorn acknowledged the value of these repeated passages for both higher and lower criticism, especially as evidence that many striking errors in the text could be traced back to earliest times. Whereas Owen was interested in formulating specific rules for the text-critical use of verbal parallels, Eichhorn was too cautious: 'Each parallel passage demands its own approach (*Specialkritik*), according to the fortuitous circumstances which produced it... The specific rules employed in their evaluation must emerge from each individual passage.'[29] Nevertheless, he felt that a discriminating examination of parallel texts might determine whether the same or a different author was responsible for the repetition and whether changes in readings were intentional or accidental.

In this regard, it is clear why the most extensive use of verbal parallels has been in the chronological ordering of the literature. To a greater or lesser extent, nearly every critical application of the phenomenon is dependent on the relative dating of the literature. In order to use parallels text-critically, one usually seeks first to determine which passage is the original. This is not an easy task for, as Eichhorn pointed out, in one parallel the more forceful, more natural, superior reading may be the original, in another it may be the correction.[30] Thus the text critic must be satisfied with probabilities or even possibilities rather than certainties.

Helmer Ringgren's text-critical examination of parallel passages already has been noted.[31] In comparing the well-known pairs, Isa. 2.2-4 and Mic. 4.1-3, he concluded that nearly all the variants between them are explained best as resulting from mistakes in oral transmission. In the parallel between Jer. 48.29-36 and Isa. 16.6-12 he also found

29. Eichhorn, *Einleitung in das Alte Testament*, I, pp. 296-97.

30. Eichhorn, *Einleitung in das Alte Testament*, I, p. 398. J.W. Miller similarly cautioned textual critics not to use the data offered by verbal parallels too schematically, *Das Verhältnis Jeremias und Hesekiels*, p. 119.

31. See above p. 51; also H. Ringgren, 'Oral and Written Transmission in the Old Testament: Some Observations', *ST* 3 (1949), pp. 34-59.

evidence of graphic (copying), hearing and memory errors. However, what seemed like a valuable approach, when launched by Owen and Eichhorn, foundered on Ringgren's obvious inability to distinguish, in many cases, between errors and intentional alterations.

The literature devoted to prophetic quotation is, nevertheless, filled with numerous emendations on the basis of verbal parallels. A single passage may illustrate the problem. A variety of positions have been taken on the basis of the verbal parallel between Isa. 48.6bß וּנְצֻרוֹת וְלֹא יְדַעְתָּם, 'of hidden things unknown to you', and Jer. 33.36b וּבְצֻרוֹת לֹא יְדַעְתָּם, 'and unsearchable things you do not know'. Cheyne emended the text in Isaiah to וּבְצֻרוֹת to agree with Jeremiah, while Ewald and Duhm emended Jeremiah to וּנְצֻרוֹת on the basis of Isaiah. Cassuto also agreed that Jeremiah should be read וּנְצֻרוֹת, but on the basis of manuscript evidence (6 Kennicott Orientales manuscripts, the Targum and Rashi). Ehrlich read נְצֻרוֹת in both passages, parsing the verb as a niphal participle of יצר (form). Paul suggested that גְדֹלוֹת וּבְצֻרוֹת, 'great and unsearchable things', in Jeremiah might have been influenced by the similarly expressed description of the walled cities in Deut. 1.28; 9.1 and Josh. 14.12.[32] Jeremiah's expression certainly is the rarer, and the variant may reflect an effort to simplify the reading, perhaps influenced by Isa. 48.6. Despite Paul's claim that Jer. 33.3 has 'clear Deutero-Isaianic overtones',[33] the most likely solution is to deny any influence in either direction. The parallel simply is too brief and inconsequential to support any emendation. In any case, the complexity of the text-critical use of verbal parallels is very apparent.

The view that variant readings, such as וּנְצֻרוֹת in Jer. 33.3, resulted from the influence of verbal parallels has been given greater credence due to the textual study of the Dead Sea Scrolls. Although William Brownlee also was alert to this phenomenon,[34] Shemaryahu Talmon has devoted the most attention to the influence of parallel passages on the

---

32. Cassuto, 'On the Formal and Stylistic Relationship', p. 156 n. 52; Paul, 'Literary and Ideological Echoes', p. 112 n. 43.

33. Paul, 'Literary and Ideological Echoes', p. 112 n. 43.

34. See W.H. Brownlee, *The Meaning of the Qumrân Scrolls for the Bible* (New York: Oxford University Press, 1964), especially Chapter 8, 'The Interpretative Character of the Isaiah Text', section 6, 'Assimilation to Parallel Passages', pp. 182-88, in which he discusses the *enrichment* of the text from parallel passages in Isaiah and other books and *harmonization* by alteration.

growth of the text, each study delving more deeply and creatively into the subject.[35]

By comparing readings found in Qumran biblical manuscripts with those of the MT and LXX and in biblical quotations employed in Qumranic compositions, Talmon observed a similar type of variant in each source, which was distinguished from the usually identified variants by four characteristics:

1. They result from the substitution of words and phrases by others which are used interchangeably and synonymously with them in the literature of the Old Testament.

2. They do not affect adversely the structure of the verse, nor do they disturb either its meaning or its rhythm. Hence they cannot be described as scribal errors.

3. No sign of systematic or tendentious emendation can be discovered in them ... They are characterized by the absence of any difference between them in content or meaning.

4. They are not the product of different chronologically or geographically distinct linguistic strata.[36]

Talmon called these variants 'synonymous readings'. A synonymous reading often occurred in the Qumran manuscript in place of an alternative reading in the MT or was paired with it within the same verse to form a 'double reading'. Talmon also identified similar synonymous readings which were used interchangeably in parallel passages within or between biblical books in the masoretic tradition. Rather than imposing linguistic uniformity on these repeated verses, the biblical editors and redactors preserved both readings, since neither was decidedly superior.

This 'discovery' by Talmon helped him to account for some of the divergences between numerous parallel passages. For example, this explained why Isa. 2.2-4 had the order גוים...עמים, 'nations ... peoples', while Mic. 4.1-3 had עמים...גוים, 'peoples ... nations' 'The stylistic inversion of synonymous words is now shown to constitute the

---

35. S. Talmon, 'Double Readings in the Massoretic Text', *Textus* 1 (1960), pp. 144-84; *idem*, 'Synonymous Readings in the Textual Traditions of the Old Testament', *Scripta Hierosolymitana* 8 (1961), pp. 335-83; *idem*, 'Aspects of the Textual Transmission of the Bible in the Light of the Qumran Manuscripts', *Textus* 4 (1964), pp. 95-132; *idem*, 'The Textual Study of the Bible: A New Outlook', in F.M. Cross and S. Talmon (eds.), *Qumran and the History of the Biblical Text* (Cambridge, MA: Harvard University Press, 1975), pp. 321-400.

36. Talmon, 'Synonymous Readings', p. 336.

differentiating factor between two textual variants of the same verse'.[37]
In addition to the inversion of synonyms, there were many examples of
substitution of one word for the other, as in Isa. 2.20 // 31.7 where אִישׁ
(each) replaces הָאָדָם (the man) and יִמְאָסוּן (reject) replaces יַשְׁלִיךְ (throw
away):

ואת אלילי זהבו	אלילי כספו	האדם את	ישליך	ביום ההוא	2.20
ואלילי זהבו	אלילי כספו	איש	ימאסון	ביום ההוא	31.7

In Talmon's opinion, this phenomenon often served a distinct
function in structuring smaller and larger textual units. The double
reading מפני רעתם אשר עשו להכעסני ללכת לקטר לעבד לאלהים אחרים
in Jer. 44.3, 'because of the evil they have done, they have provoked me
to anger by burning incense and by worshipping other gods', was seen
as a 'transitional doublet' between לעבד אחרים לאלהים, 'to serve other
gods', used exclusively in the first part of the book (8.2; 11.10; 13.10;
16.11, 13; 22.9; 25.6; 35.15), and לקטר לאלהים אחרים, 'to burn incense
to other gods', used in 44.5, 8, 16, 17, 18, 19, 21, 23, 25 (as well as
1.16 and 19.4).[38] Furthermore, the inversion of synonymous elements
(chiasm) may be used (1) to indicate that a statement is being repeated
but reversed, for example, Isa. 40.21 הלוא תדעו הלוא תשמעו, 'Do you
not know? Have you not heard?' // Isa. 48.8 גם לא־שמעת גם לא ידעת,
'you have neither heard nor known'; (2) to mark the presence of an
inner-biblical quotation, for example, Jer. 51.58, which inverts 'for
nothing' and 'fuel for the fire',

ויגעו עמים בדי־ריק ולאמים בדי־אש ויעפו	Jer. 51.58
וייגעו עמים בדי־אש ולאמים בדי־ריק יעפו	Hab. 2.13

and (3) to form by inclusio a self-contained sub-unit.[39]

והייתם לי לעם ואנכי אהיה לכם לאלהים	Jer. 30.22
אהיה לאלהים לכל משפחות ישראל והמה יהיו־לי לעם	Jer. 31.1

So you will be my people, and I will be your God	Jer. 30.22
I will be the God of all the clans of Israel, and they	Jer. 31.1
will be my people.	

Although Talmon offered his essays as programmatic and illustrative
rather than conclusive and comprehensive studies, his work has several

37. Talmon, 'Synonymous Readings', p. 340.
38. Talmon, 'The Textual Study of the Bible', p. 353.
39. Talmon, 'The Textual Study of the Bible', pp. 358-78. See also P.C.
Beentjes, 'Inverted Quotations in the Bible: A Neglected Stylistic Pattern', *Bib* 63
(1982), pp. 506-23.

important implications. First of all, the common practice of comparing and harmonizing parallels by emendation or conflation in order to restore the 'original text' may be incorrect in many cases. If synonymous readings were produced intentionally and preserved, the effort to decide which is 'superior' is futile and misdirected. Secondly, Talmon's uncovering of this type of intentional variation should alert one to the likelihood of many other kinds of intentional, purposeful alterations. Accordingly, the exactness of linguistic correspondence may be a faulty criterion for determining what is or is not a quotation. Thirdly, the fact that Talmon was able to make a fruitful textual study of the nature and function of verbal repetition and variation without first explaining the origin of the verbal parallel suggests that an overemphasis on identifying quotations and determining the direction of borrowing may have diverted our attention from other valuable approaches to the data. Finally, the many examples of conflation within the Qumran manuscripts, deduced by Talmon on the basis of parallel passages within the masoretic tradition, imply that readers of the biblical writings may have been aware of the phenomenon of prophetic quotation at a very early stage in the history of the study of the text. Thus Talmon's work argues both for more restraint and more innovation in the text-critical comparison of verbal parallels.

The Influence of Prophetic 'Schools'

Reference has already been made to several aspects of Mowinckel's continuing influence on the study of the prophets in general and on the evaluation of verbal parallels in particular. Mowinckel's emphasis on the primacy of oral tradition in the transmission of prophetic oracles, which, for the most part, took place at cultic centers, led naturally to the suggestion that disciples were responsible both for passing on and ultimately for writing down the prophetic legacy.

Mowinckel was particularly interested in the influence of the disciples of Isaiah, devoting an entire monograph to *Jesaja-Disiplene*.[40] According to Mowinckel, the 'circle', 'school' or 'group' of disciples which Isaiah gathered around himself was responsible not only for the preservation, collection, growth and editing of Isaiah (1–39), but also for the books of Micah, Zephaniah, Nahum, Habakkuk, as well as the

---

40. S. Mowinckel, *Jesaja-Disiplene: Profetien fra Jesaja til Jeremia* (Oslo: H. Aschehoug & Co., 1926).

Song of Moses, and the Deuteronomic law book.[41] Thus these disciples produced the continuity between the prophets which can be observed in the writings stemming from the period marked by the 'transformation of the pre-exilic prophecy of judgment to a nationalistic prophecy of happiness'.[42] Mowinckel found a textual basis for positing disciples in Isa. 8.16, an analogy for their activities in the accounts of the 'sons of the prophets' associated with Elijah and Elisha, and evidence of their work in the verbal, stylistic and thematic similarities between the above-mentioned prophetic books.[43] Although he did not refer specifically to prophetic quotation, it is clear from his examples that verbal parallels were important to the development of his argument.

Mowinckel's *Prophecy and Tradition* offered a further application of his view of disciples. Not only were the words of the 'master' repeated by his disciples, but also the words of the latter, who were prophets in their own right, sometimes were taken to be sayings of the former. The familiar parallel between Isaiah 2 and Micah 4 was offered as proof of this, the oracle being explained as created by an unknown Isaiah disciple, passed on to Micah who also belonged to the Isaianic circle, and incorporated along with genuine Isaianic sayings into the Isaiah collection.[44]

Mowinckel found another confirmation of his theory in the ongoing expansion of the book of Isaiah. Mowinckel viewed 'Second' Isaiah as a single individual who sprang from the prophetic milieu provided by the continuation of the pre-exilic Isaianic disciple circle. 'Third' Isaiah, in turn, was produced by a new 'school' created by 'Second' Isaiah. That all three 'Isaianic' collections were historically part of a continuum was proven decisively, according to Mowinckel, by the placement of chs. 34–35 which are 'strongly "Deutero-Isaian" sounding' and in

41. Mowinckel, *Jesaja-Disiplene*, p. 13.

42. E. Nielsen, *Oral Tradition: A Modern Problem in Old Testament Introduction* (SBT, 11; Naperville, IL: Allenson, 1955), p. 14.

43. Mowinckel, *Jesaja-Disiplene*, pp. 14-15. The similarities he noted include: between Isaiah and Micah—'remnant': Isa. 4.2; 10.20-22—Mic. 2.12; 4.7; 5.6-7; 'Messianic prophecy': Isa. 7.14—Mic. 5.2; 'naked and barefoot': Isa. 20.3—Mic. 1.8; 'woes': Isa. 5.8ff.—Mic. 2.1f.; 'drunken prophets': Isa. 28.7ff.—Mic. 2.11; 'Hear, O earth!': Isa. 1.2—Mic. 1.2; between Isaiah and Zephaniah—'Day of the LORD': Isa. 2.15—Zeph. 1.16; between Isaiah and Habakkuk—'tablet': Isa. 8.1; 30.8—Hab. 2.2; between Isaiah and Nahum—'eating of the first ripe fig': Isa. 28.4—Nah. 3.12 (incorrectly listed as Hab. 3.12 by Mowinckel).

44. Mowinckel, *Prophecy and Tradition*, p. 67.

'spirit, style and tone "Trito-Isaian" ' but are used to cap off the 'book' of Proto-Isaiah.[45]

Although Mowinckel's larger thesis regarding the role of the Isaiah circle in producing a variety of prophetic and non-prophetic works has not been accepted widely, his theory of disciples carrying on the work of prophetic 'masters' has been enormously influential on subsequent research into the formation of prophetic books. Within the Scandinavian group, Harris Birkeland was a staunch supporter. Inspired also by Nyberg, Birkeland sought to set out in greater detail the stages in the building up of prophetic collections and to survey the prophetic books for indications of the process.[46] By the time Johannes Lindblom completed his great work on the prophets, an entire 'curriculum' for the disciple schools had been hypothesized by this group of scholars who concluded that 'for most of the prophetic literature which has been transmitted to us we are above all indebted to the disciples of the prophets'.[47]

Outside of Scandinavia, Mowinckel's impact also was felt. As already noted, Elliger, Zimmerli and Hanson each made reference to the verbal parallels between 'Second' and 'Third' Isaiah in developing Mowinckel's proposal that the latter was the work of an individual disciple (Elliger, Zimmerli) or a group of disciples (Hanson) of the former.[48] Suddenly, groups of disciples were 'discovered' around nearly every prophetic figure. Zimmerli spoke of a 'school of the prophet which edited the prophecies of Ezekiel, commented upon them, and gave them a fuller theological explanation'.[49] Wolff posited both a disciple who expanded Hosea's own writings and composed the third-person *memorabile* (a factual account and interpretation of a prophet's call and actions) and 'the old school of Amos' which promulgated his oracles as well as incorporating 'new formulations and supplementations'.[50] Almost any phenomenon noted within the prophets could be

---

45. Mowinckel, *Prophecy and Tradition*, pp. 67-70.

46. Birkeland, *Zum hebräischen Traditionswesen*, esp. pp. 19-22.

47. Lindblom, *Prophecy in Ancient Israel*, p. 163.

48. See the discussion above, pp. 42-49.

49. W. Zimmerli, *A Commentary on the Book of the Prophet Ezekiel Chapters 1–24* (trans. R.E. Clements; Hermeneia, 26; Philadelphia: Fortress Press, 1979), p. 70.

50. H.W. Wolff, *A Commentary on the Book of the Prophet Hosea* (trans. G. Stansell; Hermeneia, 28; Philadelphia: Fortress Press, 1974), p. xxix; *Joel and Amos*, pp. 108-11.

attributed to some group of disciples that bore particular traditions. To give an example, Victor Eldridge, in explaining the similarities between Jeremiah 50–51 and Isaiah 13–14; 34; and 40–55, suggested that 'Second' Isaiah may have emerged from a mid-sixth-century group of prophets which included disciples from both the Isaiah and Jeremiah traditions.[51]

Although it is clear that many of the contemporary proponents of schools or circles of disciples are not as concerned with verbal parallels within the prophets as was Mowinckel, a critique of his approach nevertheless may have implications for recent appropriations of his views. Mowinckel based his theory on four types of evidence, none of which is overly convincing. First, the enigmatic 'prooftext' of Isa. 8.16 has, of necessity, borne a heavy load, yet the adjective למוד is not translated as 'disciple(s)' in its other five occurrences,[52] and Clements may be correct in rendering the word 'those I have instructed' in Isa. 8.16 and identifying them with the witnesses Uriah and Zechariah who are mentioned in 8.2.[53] The specific role of Baruch with reference to the book of Jeremiah is still being debated, but it is not obvious that 'disciple' is a more appropriate designation for him than 'scribe'.[54]

Secondly, whether or not the group called 'the sons of the prophets' is an appropriate analogy is also questionable. Although several of their activities in the time of Elijah and Elisha are detailed, there is no suggestion that theirs was the task of preserving, interpreting or augmenting the sayings of their master.[55]

Thirdly, although a disciple might be expected to quote his master, the vast majority of striking verbal parallels within the prophets occur between books for which no master–disciple relationship has been suggested. Although the idea of disciples is based in part upon the existence of verbal parallels, it by no means adequately accounts for them. In fact, a careful examination of the thematic, stylistic and linguistic

51. Eldridge, 'The Influence of Jeremiah on Isaiah 40–55', pp. 186-87.

52. Isa. 50.4 (twice); 54.13; Jer. 2.24; 13.23.

53. R.E. Clements, *Isaiah 1–39* (NCB; Grand Rapids: Eerdmans, 1980), p. 100.

54. For a recent discussion of Baruch, see P.-M. Bogaert, 'Le personnage de Baruch et l'histoire du livre de Jérémie', in E.A. Livingstone (ed.), *Studia Evangelica. VII. Papers Presented to the Fifth International Congress on Biblical Studies Held at Oxford, 1973* (TUGAL, 126; Berlin: Akademie Verlag, 1982), pp. 73-81.

55. See the discussion of the 'sons of the prophets' by R.R. Wilson, *Prophecy and Society in Ancient Israel* (Philadelphia: Fortress Press, 1980), pp. 140-41.

links between the works of Mowinckel's 'Isaianic school' reveals that no close dependence upon Isaiah is necessary to speak of doom, a remnant, nakedness, figs, and other matters. Although a connection is possible, common historical circumstances, a common message, and a common rhetorical heritage may explain satisfactorily most of these similarities in wording. Simply being a prophet was sufficient cause for quoting one's predecessors.

Fourthly, perhaps the strongest argument for Mowinckel's view is the existence of prophetic collections which were expanded greatly beyond the original oracles attributed by scholars to the prophet under whose name the collection circulated. Since the traditional view of Isaianic authorship largely has been rejected, the idea of a school of Isaiah offers a plausible reason for the canonical linking of chs. 40–55 and 56–66 to 1–39. Surprisingly, there actually are relatively few verbal links between 'First' Isaiah and 'Second' Isaiah, other than the use of 'the Holy One of Israel',[56] which is an unexpected situation if a disciple was the author of the latter. Furthermore, if Zimmerli's and Hanson's denigrations of 'Third' Isaiah's draining and misconstrual of the language of his master, 'Second' Isaiah, are appropriate,[57] the latter made a poor choice in selecting disciples to carry on his message. The idea of disciples may be an intriguing thesis, but it is not proven correct simply because it offers a possible explanation for verbal parallels and other phenomena of the text.[58]

56. For a rather comprehensive list of stylistic resemblances between Isa. 1–39 and 40–66 see J.H. Raven, *Old Testament Introduction: General and Special* (New York: Fleming H. Revell, 1906), pp. 190-91. However, the clearer parallels in 1–39 to phrases in 40–55 would be considered by most contemporary scholars to be later additions to 1–39 influenced by 40–55, see Clements, *Isaiah 1–39*, p. 21.

57. See above, pp. 45-47.

58. Zimmerli, for example, has argued that some verbal parallels within a book are due to a prophet reinterpreting his own oracles, 'Das Phänomen der "Fortschreibung" im Buch Ezechiel', in J.A. Emerton (ed.), *Prophecy: Essays Presented to Georg Fohrer on his Sixty-Fifth Birthday, 6 September 1980* (BZAW, 150; Berlin: W. de Gruyter, 1980), pp. 174-91. Furthermore, Duhm's arguments for his divisions between 'First', 'Second' and 'Third' Isaiah have not found universal acceptance. Regarding 'Third' Isaiah, see Maass, 'Tritojesaja?', pp. 153-63, and Chapter 8 n. 103 below. According to A.R. Millard, 'The Old Testament in its Ancient World: Aspects of Prophetic Writings', *The Scottish Bulletin of Evangelical Theology* 7 (1989), pp. 88-99; *idem*, 'La prophète et l'écriture Israël, Aram, Assyrie', *RHR* 202 (1985), pp. 125-45, evidence from the ancient Near East

It is interesting to observe, as noted at the beginning of this section, that a major motivation in Mowinckel's developing a thesis about disciples was to answer the question of who was responsible for the oral transmission of prophetic sayings. However, this aspect of the Scandinavian approach has not been sustained by further research, and many scholars would claim rather that oracles may have been written down soon after their initial pronouncement. Despite this and other weaknesses of Mowinckel's views, the concept of a school of disciples has not been modified significantly from what was set forth in *Jesaja-Disiplene*, as is apparent from Klaus Koch's concluding remarks on the prophets of the Assyrian period:

> Perhaps it was Isaiah's disciples (8.16) who made a beginning here, forming a school in Jerusalem in which material deriving from Amos and Hosea was passed down, too. We may perhaps assume that for generations there was a kind of school of Isaiah followers. This seems likely because at the close of the Assyrian period Isaiah's, in particular, is the proclamation from whom a number of other prophets (Joel, Nahum, Zephaniah) pick up the threads.[59]

The Beginnings of Exegesis

It already has been noted how the students of prophetic quotation have used the phenomenon in their efforts to date the literature and restore the original text of the parallels. Schools of prophetic disciples were suggested as being responsible for the occurrence of numerous verbal parallels within the prophets. Scholars also sought to explain *why* earlier sayings were reused in later prophetic writings. Although some attributed the repetition to the accidents of oral transmission, others saw a purposefulness in their employment. Two of the long-standing views that have achieved greater prominence in recent decades are (1) that quotation is for the purpose of reinterpretation; and (2) that quotation is for the purpose of enhancing one's authority.

It commonly is acknowledged that the history of biblical interpretation commenced within the biblical period itself.[60] The nature of this

suggests by analogy that biblical prophecies would have been recorded immediately and, once recorded, not altered.

59. K. Koch, *The Prophets*. I. *The Assyrian Period* (trans. M. Kohl; Philadelphia: Fortress Press, 1983), p. 168.

60. See, in addition to those mentioned in the following note, F.F. Bruce, 'The Earliest Old Testament Interpretation', *OTS* 17 (1972), pp. 37-52; and G. Vermes,

reworking of earlier materials has been described in various ways. Stade (1881) spoke of 'Wiederaufnahme und Umdeutung' (resumption and reinterpretation), Müller (1907) of 'Entlehnung und Glossierung' (borrowing and glossing), Robert (1934) of a 'procédé anthologique' (anthological procedure), Hertzberg (1936) of 'die Nachgeschichte alttestamentlicher Texte' (the further history of Old Testament texts), Auerbach (1953) of 'die grosse Überarbeitung' (the great revision), Seeligmann (1953) and Bloch (1954) of 'midrash', Gelin (1959) of 'relectures' (rereadings), Michel (1966) of 'die schriftgelehrte Auslegung' (scribal interpretation), Grech (1969) of 'interprophetic reinterpretation', Willi-Plein (1971) of 'Vorformen der Schriftexegese' (early forms of scriptural exegesis), Schreiner (1973) of 'Nachinterpretation' (later interpretation), Mason (1973) of 'inner biblical exegesis', Day (1980) of 'inner scriptural interpretation', and Fishbane (1985) of 'biblical interpretation'.[61]

'Bible and Midrash: Early Old Testament Exegesis', in P.R. Ackroyd and C.F. Evans (eds.), *The Cambridge History of the Bible. I. From the Beginnings to Jerome* (Cambridge: Cambridge University Press, 1970), pp. 199-231.

61. B. Stade, 'Deuterosacharja: Eine kritische Studie', *ZAW* 1 (1881), pp. 1-96; 2 (1882), pp. 151-72; D.H. Müller, 'Ezechiel entlehnt eine Stelle aus Zephanja und glossiert sie', in *Biblische Studien*. III. *Komposition und Strophenbau* (Vienna: Alfred Hölder, 1907), pp. 30-36; A. Robert, 'Les attaches littéraires bibliques de Prov. i-ix', *RB* 43 (1934), pp. 42-68, 172-204, 374-84; 44 (1935), pp. 344-65, 502-25; H.W. Hertzberg, 'Die Nachgeschichte alttestamentlicher Texte innerhalb des Alten Testaments', in P. Volz, F. Stummer and J. Hempel (eds.), *Wesen und Werden des Alten Testaments* (BZAW, 66; Berlin: Alfred Töpelmann, 1936), pp. 110-21; E. Auerbach, 'Die grosse Überarbeitung der biblischen Bücher', in G.W. Anderson *et al.* (eds.), *Congress Volume: Copenhagen 1953* (VTSup, 1; Leiden: E.J. Brill, 1953), pp. 1-10; I.L. Seeligmann, 'Voraussetzungen der Midraschexegese', in G.W. Anderson *et al.* (eds.), *Congress Volume: Copenhagen 1953* (VTSup, 1; Leiden: E.J. Brill, 1953), pp. 150-81; R. Bloch, 'Ecriture et tradition dans le judaïsme: Aperçus sur l'origine du midrash', *Cahiers Sioniens* 8 (1954), pp. 9-34; A. Gelin, 'La question des "relecture" bibliques à l'intérieur d'une tradition vivante', in J. Coppens, A. Descamps and E. Massaux (eds.), *Sacra Pagina* (2 vols.; Gembloux: Duculot, 1959), I, pp. 303-15; D. Michel, 'Zur Eigenart Tritojesajas', *Theologia Viatorum* 10 (1965–66), pp. 213-30; P. Grech, 'Interprophetic Reinterpretation and Old Testament Eschatology', *Augustinianum* 9 (1969), pp. 235-30; Willi-Plein, *Vorformen der Schriftexegese*; J. Schreiner, 'Interpretation innerhalb der schriftlichen Überlieferung', in J. Maier and J. Schreiner (eds.), *Literatur und Religion des Frühjudentums: Eine Einführung* (Würzburg: Echter Verlag, 1973), pp. 19-30, R.A. Mason, 'Some Examples of Inner Biblical Exegesis in Zech IX-XIV', in E.A. Livingstone (ed.), *Studia Evangelica. VII. Papers*

Spanning a century, the development of this approach reflects on a smaller scale the general characteristics of the examination of verbal parallels sketched in the first chapter. The phenomenon of verbal parallels was not always the central concern, some (such as Auerbach and Hertzberg) making no mention of it, and little effort was made to demonstrate that 'quotation' actually had occurred, various terms being used without any explanation. The scope of the literature on this aspect of prophecy is broad enough to warrant a complete study; the purpose here simply is to illustrate some of the ways in which scholars have understood verbal parallels as serving an interpretive purpose and to suggest some of the weaknesses in the methods they employed in developing this perspective. We will divide these studies into three groups in order to facilitate their comparison, although there clearly is some overlap and mutual influence: anthological style, proto-midrash, and reinterpretation.

Anthological Style

Anthological style is associated with André Robert and his French followers and was expounded most fully in his comprehensive study of the literary connections of Proverbs 1–9.[62] The 'anthological procedure', as Robert termed it, consisted of 'the reemployment of the words or formulae of earlier Scriptures, either verbatim or with equivalent expressions'.[63]

Robert viewed anthological style as particularly dominant in the Wisdom literature but also found it in Chronicles and many of the latter prophets, as in Isaiah 60–62's use of 40–55, Jeremiah's use of Hosea and Isaiah, Ezekiel's dependence on the Holiness Code, Amos, Hosea, Isaiah, and especially Jeremiah, and the influence of Isaiah 40–55, Jeremiah, and the Pentateuch on the Servant Songs. Because his approach was primarily philological, he could trace literary dependence on a word-for-word basis, as several of his often repeated examples

---

Presented for the Fifth International Congress on Biblical Studies Held at Oxford, 1973 (TUGAL, 126; Berlin: Akademie Verlag, 1982), pp. 343-54; J. Day, 'A Case of Inner Scriptural Interpretation: The Dependence of Isaiah XXVI.13–XXVII.11 on Hosea XIII.4–XIV.10 (Eng. 9) and its Relevance to Some Theories of the Redaction of the "Isaiah Apocalypse" ', *JTS* NS 31 (1980), pp. 309-19; Fishbane, *Biblical Interpretation in Ancient Israel*.

    62. Robert, 'Les attaches littéraires bibliques de Prov. i-ix'.

    63. Robert, 'Littéraires (Genres)', *DBSup*, V, pp. 405-21 (411).

demonstrate: Prov. 8.14 borrows the description of divine wisdom from Isa. 9.5 and 11.2, and the נקם יום, 'day of vengeance', of Prov. 6.34 must be viewed in the light of the impending judgment announced in Isa. 34.8; 35.4; 61.2; and 63.4.[64]

In many cases, the later author simply took up the language and thoughts of his predecessors with no appreciable change; in others he gave them a new meaning in adapting them to his purposes. According to Robert, tracing these literary connections helps to establish not only the genres of literary works but also their historical and theological roots: 'The anthological procedure...attests at the same time to the continuity of the theological tradition as well as to its astonishing advancement'.[65]

In one respect, Robert simply was putting a different label on the phenomenon of verbal parallels which many others had already observed. However, his effort to make a comprehensive study of all the apparent literary relationships between a text and its predecessors provided a tool which some of his followers would abuse and others would profitably employ. Paul Humbert in 1944 published a monograph on Habakkuk listing, almost in concordance fashion, all of the Old Testament references where the words of this minor prophet recurred.[66] Dhorme correctly questioned the validity of Humbert's purely verbal approach when even the similarity of the subject treated might be expected to give rise to analogous styles, expressions and words.[67]

A different approach was taken by Delcor in his study of Deutero-Zechariah.[68] Delcor sought to determine Deutero-Zechariah's manner of borrowing by observing its links with other books, but unlike Robert and Humbert he traced dependence primarily in terms of common themes. For example, he viewed Zech. 9.16 as 'clearly dependent on'[69] Isa. 62.3 since both speak of Israel as a crown, even though different terms are used. He saw a connection between Zech. 9.11 and Isa. 40.2;

---

64. Robert, 'Les attaches littéraires bibliques de Prov. i-ix', pp. 60, 187-89.

65. Robert, 'Littéraires (Genres)', p. 417.

66. P. Humbert, *Problèmes du livre d'Habacuc* (Neuchâtel: Secrétariat de l'Université, 1944).

67. E. Dhorme, review of *Problèmes du livre d'Habacuc* (Neuchâtel: Secrétariat de l'Université, 1944) by P. Humbert, in *RHR* 131 (1946), pp. 176-82 (179).

68. Delcor, 'Les sources du Deutéro-Zacharia', pp. 385-411.

69. Delcor, 'Les sources du Deutéro-Zacharia', pp. 388, 408.

42.22, simply because both promise release from captivity; and between Zech. 10.8 and Isa. 5.26; 7.16, since all three speak of the LORD whistling (שרק). Delcor's observations were almost identical to Robert's, concluding with regard to Deutero-Zechariah: 'A concept or image borrowed from a given context preserves the meaning of that context. But, we must add immediately, our author by no means loses his freedom of movement. He is not the slave of the text.'[70]

B. Renaud, another student of 'les attaches littéraires' (literary connections), was especially interested in the relationship between Micah 4–5 and Isaiah 1–12.[71] Focusing primarily on repeated phrases of two or more words in length, Renaud noted how the meaning was sometimes identical and sometimes reversed. This led him to posit a very complex relationship between the two collections: Micah 4–5 was dependent on Isaiah but not original to the book of Micah. According to Renaud, Isaiah 1–12 contained not only original oracles, but also later interpolations, some of them placed in the book by the editors of Micah. In other words, none of the verbal links between Isaiah 1–12 and Micah 4–5 resulted from one of the contemporary eighth-century prophets quoting the other. Although Robert conceived of the underlying motivation of the 'anthological procedure' as interpretive and theological, for Renaud its value was primarily in tracing the redactional development of prophetic collections. From the very beginning, however, there was a tendency to hang weighty conclusions from slender threads of evidence. In most examples which were cited, common employment of selected words and themes could as easily occur by coincidence as by conscious reuse, and divergences in their usage might as easily argue for no inherent link as for purposeful reinterpretation.[72]

---

70. Delcor, 'Les sources du Deutéro-Zacharia', p. 408. Delcor included among Deutero-Zechariah's common procedures in reusing a passage 'schematization', 'recapitulation' and 'telescoping', p. 411. A more recent and methodologically more rigorous examination of 'anthologic' allusion in Zechariah has been offered by K.R. Schaefer, 'Zechariah 14: A Study in Allusion', *CBQ* 57 (1995), pp. 66-91.

71. B. Renaud, *Structure et attaches littéraires de Michée IV–V* (Cahiers de la Revue Biblique, 2; Paris: J. Gabalda, 1964).

72. For example, Renaud assumes a relationship of dependence on the basis of the following parallels between Isa. 55–66 and Micah, all of which, according to him, concern the pilgrimage of the peoples to Zion: Isa. 66.12 // Mic. 4.2 (probably 4.1 was intended)—use of root נהר ('flow'); Isa. 58.14 // 4.1 (probably 4.4 was intended)—'for the mouth of the LORD has spoken' (Micah adds 'of Hosts'); Isa.

Proto-midrash

If the 'anthological procedure' approach was flawed by its reliance on insufficient textual data, the 'midrashic' approach to 'prophetic quotation' was flawed by an inconsistent understanding of what was meant by 'midrash'. Since the early application of the term to biblical materials often was pejorative,[73] Seeligmann's 1953 essay, in which he argued 'that the earliest midrashic exegesis developed organically out of the peculiar nature of the biblical literature',[74] was important for its more positive assessment of midrash.

Seeligmann saw 'flexibility, playfulness, and actualization' as characteristic features of midrash and found similar hermeneutical principles operative in Old Testament passages which quote or allude to earlier passages. 'Many such quotations and allusions contain a modification or reinterpretation, that is, in a sense, an exegesis of the original passage',[75] noting particularly Jeremiah's use of Hosea, Ezekiel's use of Zephaniah and Jeremiah, and 'Third' Isaiah's use of 'Second' Isaiah. According to Seeligmann, in many cases the ambiguity of the repeated phrase lends itself to being given another meaning in its new context. As an example, Seeligmann cited Jer. 49.3's כִּי מַלְכָּם בַּגּוֹלָה יֵלֵךְ כֹּהֲנָיו וְשָׂרָיו יַחְדָּיו, 'for Moloch will go into exile, together with his priests and officials', reuse of Amos 1.15 (וְהָלַךְ מַלְכָּם בַּגּוֹלָה הוּא וְשָׂרָיו יַחְדָּו, 'Their king will go into exile, he and his officials together') in which Jeremiah plays on the double meaning of מַלְכָּם (their king or Moloch).[76]

Even more responsible than Seeligmann for the recent revival of

---

59.6 // Mic. 4.7 (59.21 intended)—מֵעַתָּה וְעַד־עוֹלָם (from this time on and forever); Isa. 60.1 // Mic. 4.13—קוּמִי (Rise!); Isa. 62.10 // Mic. 2.13 'passing through the gate(s)'; Isa. 60.22 // Mic. 5.1—use of צָעִיר (small) and word-play on אֶלֶף (clan); Isa. 60.22 // Mic. 4.7—לְגוֹי עָצוּם (strong nation) (*Structure et attaches*, pp. 68-70).

73. As in J. Wellhausen, *Prolegomena to the History of Ancient Israel* (trans. J.S. Black and A. Menzies; New York: Meridian Books, 1957), p. 227, regarding 1–2 Chronicles: 'Midrash is the consequence of the conservation of all the relics of antiquity, a wholly peculiar artificial reawakening of dry bones, especially by literary means.'

74. Seeligmann, 'Voraussetzungen der Midraschexegese', p. 151. Actually, R. Gordis had written even earlier about midrash in the Old Testament, 'Midrash in the Prophets', *JBL* 49 (1930), pp. 417-22, but his essay had little influence.

75. Seeligmann, 'Voraussetzungen der Midraschexegese', pp. 151, 181.

76. Seeligmann, 'Voraussetzungen der Midraschexegese', p. 161. Seeligmann, 'Voraussetzungen der Midraschexgese', p. 171, and others also saw striking examples of 'midrashic' exegesis in Daniel which will not be discussed here.

interest in midrash was Renée Bloch.[77] Although aware of Seeligmann's essay, she was influenced more by Robert. What Robert cited as examples of the 'anthological procedure'—Chronicles, Proverbs 1–9, Isaiah 60–62 and the Servant Songs—Bloch labeled midrashic.[78] Bloch made this identification of biblical midrash on the basis of her list of the key features of rabbinic midrash: (1) it has its point of departure in Scripture; (2) it is homiletical in character; (3) it involves a careful study of the text; (4) it involves adaptation to the present.[79] Bloch found the roots of midrash in the general tendency of the biblical authors to ground themselves in their predecessors, a practice which increased in the postexilic period as writers addressed the problems of the present in the light of past Scripture.

Inspired in part by Bloch, a number of scholars offered more detailed studies of Old Testament midrash. Sandmel examined Pentateuchal narratives, Weingreen the legal material, Sarna Psalm 89, Childs and Slomovic the Psalm titles, Willi the Chronicles, Sanders the development of the text, and Vermes a variety of examples of 'pure' and 'applied' exegesis. One also could include Willi-Plein's study of interpretation within the redactional additions to the minor prophets, since she sought to explain each in terms of rabbinical hermeneutical rules.[80]

77. Bloch, 'Ecriture et tradition dans le judaïsme'; *idem*, 'Ezéchiel XVI: Exemple parfait du procédé midrashique dans la Bible', *Cahiers Sioniens* 9 (1955), pp. 193-223; *idem*, 'Midrash', in *DBSup*, V, cols. 1263-81; *idem*, 'Note methodologique pour l'étude de la littérature rabbinique', *RSR* 43 (1955), pp. 194-227.

78. Actually, Robert noted that both 1–2 Chronicles and apocalyptic literature share many features with rabbinic midrash, *Initiations Bibliques: Introduction à l'étude des saintes écritures* (ed. A. Robert and A. Tricot; Paris: Desclée de Brouwer, 1948), pp. 279-80, but did not, as far as I have been able to ascertain, label the 'procédé anthologique' as a whole 'midrashic'.

79. Bloch, 'Midrash', col. 1265. Bloch's fifth feature, omitted because it is less relevant to the discussion here, concerned the difference between halakhah and haggadah.

80. S. Sandmel, 'The Haggada within Scripture', *JBL* 80 (1961), pp. 105-22; J. Weingreen, *From Bible to Mishna: The Continuity of Tradition* (Manchester: Manchester University Press, 1976); N.M. Sarna, 'Psalm 89: A Study in Inner Biblical Exegesis', in A. Altmann (ed.), *Biblical and Other Studies* (Cambridge, MA: Harvard University Press, 1963), pp. 29-46; B.S. Childs, 'Psalm Titles and Midrashic Exegesis', *JSS* 16 (1971), pp. 137-50; E. Slomovic, 'Toward an Understanding of the Formation of Historical Titles in the Book of Psalms', *ZAW* NS 91 (1979), pp. 350-80; T. Willi, *Die Chronik als Auslegung: Untersuchungen zur literarischen Gestaltung der historischen Überlieferung Israels* (FRLANT,

However, despite the enthusiastic response to the thesis of Seeligmann and Bloch, methodological confusion was everywhere evident. Since each scholar offered his or her own definition of midrash, it was easy to locate and explain biblical examples which fit the definition. Midrash was defined on the basis of its content, process, function, attitude, purpose or literary features.[81] Wright, on the one hand, sought to limit midrash to a literary genre, thus rejecting nearly all of Bloch's examples. Childs and LeDéaut, on the other hand, strongly objected to Wright's attempt to separate the forms of rabbinic midrash from its technique and method.[82] More recently, Gary Porten sought to avoid the difficulties posed by either too broad or too narrow a definition:

> I would define *midrash* as a type of literature, oral or written, which stands in direct relationship to a fixed, canonical text, considered to be the authoritative and the revealed word of God by the midrashist and his audience, and in which this canonical text is explicitly cited or clearly alluded to.[83]

Whether or not Porten's proposal will win any more supporters than previous efforts remains to be seen. It is clear, in any case, that for Porten the phenomenon of quotation is still central to the concept of midrash. Furthermore, Porten's definition has an advantage over many others which put a primary stress on midrash's effort to make an ancient text relevant and meaningful to a contemporary audience.[84] In terms of this examination of prophetic quotation, this would suggest that quotation occurred primarily for the sake of the previous author's words rather than to enrich the later writer's message. This may account

---

106; Göttingen, Vandenhoeck & Ruprecht, 1972); J.A. Sanders, 'Text and Canon: Concepts and Method', *JBL* 98 (1979), pp. 5-29; Vermes, 'Bible and Midrash'; Willi-Plein, *Vorformen der Schriftexegese*. See also A. Shinan and Y. Zakovitch, 'Midrash on Scripture and Midrash within Scripture', *Scripta Hierosolymitana* 31 (1986), pp. 257-77.

81. G.G. Porten, 'Defining Midrash', in J. Neusner (ed.), *The Study of Ancient Judaism*. I. *Mishnah, Midrash, Siddur* (New York: Ktav, 1981), pp. 55-92 (60-61).

82. A.G. Wright, 'The Literary Genre Midrash', *CBQ* 28 (1966), pp. 105-38, 417-57; B.S. Childs, 'Midrash and the Old Testament', in J. Reumann (ed.), *Understanding the Sacred Text: Essays in Honor of Morton S. Enslin* (Valley Forge, PA: Judson Press, 1972), pp. 47-59; R. LeDéaut, 'A propos d'une définition du midrash', *Bib* 50 (1969), pp. 395-413.

83. Porten, 'Defining Midrash', p. 62.

84. See the definitions cited in Porten, 'Defining Midrash', pp. 59-60.

for some of the verbal parallels within the prophets but it is an inadequate explanation for the majority of them. Until a fuller understanding of the nature and purposes of rabbinic midrash has been achieved, the continued search for midrash in the Bible may be popular but not very conclusive.[85] In the meantime, it may be more profitable to examine alleged prophetic quotations for clear evidence of exegetical reworking, rather than risking a misconstrual of the data by looking at the phenomenon solely from the perspective of later rabbinic approaches.

Reinterpretation
Those who see interprophetic interpretation as a primary motive for quotation differ from the previous two groups in several ways. On the one hand, the reuse of biblical words and phrases is all that is essential to the 'anthological procedure'. A theological intent may or may not be present. On the other hand, despite the disagreement over what constitutes midrash, those who have identified examples of proto-midrash in the Old Testament have done so on the basis of a specific set of rabbinical expository features which they have found exemplified by biblical texts. The third group simply insists that some type of reinterpretive use of a previous text is being made, without specifying any particular exegetical rules. Furthermore, whereas some, such as Delcor, who have studied the 'anthological procedure' have concluded that the meaning of the phrase in its original context usually is preserved, proponents of proto-midrash—given the fact that midrash treats the Old Testament as a timeless, contextless totality[86]—often claim the opposite. For the third group, the question of the preservation of the original meaning and context can be answered on a case-by-case basis. Finally, whereas the felicitous formulations of a former age may be incorporated into the *anthological procedure whether or not* it is hermeneutically relevant in its new context, and many advocates of biblical midrash suggest that its purpose is to *make* an earlier text relevant, the third group holds that the

85. Fortunately, the study of Old Testament midrash has not yet gone to the extremes of the study of New Testament midrash. For an introductory survey, see M.P. Miller, 'Targum, Midrash, and the Use of the Old Testament in the New Testament', *JSJ* 2 (1971), pp. 29-82; and R.T. France and D. Wenham (eds.), *Studies in Midrash and Historiography* (Gospel Perspectives, 3; Sheffield: JSOT Press, 1983)

86. See J. Kugel, 'Two Introductions to Midrash', *Prooftexts* 3 (1983), pp. 131-55.

later interpreter cites an earlier statement precisely because it *is* relevant.[87]

Before examining the work of several individuals in the third group, another clarification is necessary. As already noted above, not all of the exponents of inner-biblical exegesis were concerned with quotation. This is because there are two ways to reinterpret a text. One is to cite and then expound it, the other is to build immediately onto the text, in which case citation is unnecessary, whether the interpreter is the prophet himself, as Zimmerli has argued in many passages in Ezekiel,[88] a disciple or a later editor. Willi-Plein explained this process:

> If it is Yahweh's word which has been communicated to the prophet, then, at any time, it can be modified by a new word of Yahweh or its actual meaning clarified. As long as prophecy is a living phenomenon, a prophetic word which already has been promulgated can be supplemented by a new prophecy ... [89]

Since the latter approach does not involve verbal parallels and since it is often difficult to determine whether the further exposition of a given verse is original or a later interpretive addition, the present survey will concentrate exclusively on the former.

Surprisingly, although many scholars have been interested in inner-biblical exegesis and its implications, most of their discussions have been quite general, few of them offering a detailed examination of any of the examples they cited. One early exception was David Henry Müller who studied Ezekiel's borrowing and glossing of a passage from Zephaniah.[90] Müller saw the reworking of Zeph. 3.1ff. in Ezek. 22.24ff. as so thorough that 'none of the later great commentators such as Rashi or Ibn Ezra could have offered such a precise and careful commentary'.[91] As in most verbal parallels, one of his goals was to demonstrate that Ezekiel and not Zephaniah was the borrower.

The primary parallel consists in the list of officials given in Zeph. 3.3-4 (שׂר, שׁפט, נביא, כהן [prince, judge, prophet, priest]) which Ezekiel repeats, reorders, revises and expands. However, one suspects that it

---

87. See Ackroyd, 'The Vitality of the Word of God', p. 18; and Mason, 'Some Examples of Inner Biblical Exegesis in Zech IX–XIV', p. 354.

88. Zimmerli, 'Das Phänomen der "Fortschreibung" im Buch Ezechiel'; *idem, Ezekiel 1–24.*

89. Willi-Plein, *Vorformen der Schriftexegese*, p. 10.

90. Müller, 'Ezechiel entlehnt eine Stelle'.

91. Müller, 'Ezechiel entlehnt eine Stelle', p. 34.

might be more accurate to state that it is Müller who did the most reordering and revising. The actual parallel and Müller's emendations are as follows:[92]

Zephaniah	Ezekiel (MT)	Ezekiel (Müller)
1. her princes (שׂר) like lions (v. 3)	her prophets— like a lion (v. 25)	her *princes* (נשׂיא)
2. her judges— like wolves (v. 3)	her priests (v. 25)	her priests
3. her prophets (v. 4)	her princes (שׂר)— like wolves (v. 27)	her *judges*
4. her priests (v. 4)	her prophets (v. 28)	her prophets
5.	the people of the land (v. 29)	

The clearest example of citation, revision and expansion is with respect to the priests. According to Müller, Ezekiel promoted the priests from fourth (in Zephaniah) to second position. The accusations begin almost identically:

Zephaniah:	חללו־קדש חמסו תורה	כהניה
Ezekiel:	חמסו תורתי ויחללו קדשׁי	כהניה

Zephaniah: Her priests profane the sanctuary and do violence to the law

Ezekiel: Her priests do violence to my law and profane my holy things

(Talmon might see this as an example of inversion to mark a quotation), but then Ezekiel adds:

> ...they have made no distinction between the holy and the common, neither have they taught the difference between the unclean and the clean, and they have disregarded my sabbaths, so that I am profaned among them (Ezek. 22.26).

Müller was convinced that Ezekiel is not only dependent on Zeph. 3.3-4 but in the larger context, viewed the 'superscription' in Ezek. 22.24 ('You are a land that is not cleansed, or rained upon in the day of indignation.') as a paraphrase of Zeph. 3.2 ('Woe to her that is rebellious and defiled, the oppressing city')! Although it appears likely that Ezekiel indeed had Zephaniah in mind when formulating this section, the precise reason for and rhetorical effect of this interpretive borrowing was not stated by Müller. While some of his suggestions were

---

92. Müller's emendations are אשׁר נשׂיאיה from קשׁר נביאיה (v. 25), which has LXX support (ης οι αφηγουμενοι), and שׁפטיה from שׂריה (v. 27).

accepted by Zimmerli,[93] one wonders whether Müller was more interested in laying bare Ezekiel's exegetical technique or in deriving a
plausible explanation for his own reconstruction of the text. Nevertheless, in its basic approach, Müller's article was remarkable for 1905.

More recently, another case of inner-scriptural interpretation was
examined by John Day who sought to demonstrate the dependence of
Isa. 26.13–27.11 on Hos. 13.4–14.10.[94] Day used a cumulative argument, noting that, of eight parallels, all but one occur in the same order
in both sources. He also considered it significant that both passages
came at the end of their respective compositions. Of the eight parallels,
only one consists of verbal similarities, the others exhibiting thematic
similarities, such as identical images (birth pangs, east wind, dew,
vineyard), or motifs (deliverance from Sheol, idolatry, need for discernment). Day made a strong case for some type of dependence
involving Hosea and Isaiah, though he simply assumed that Isaiah is
the borrower. Although one might question the evidential value of
some of his thematic parallels, one must agree with him that verbal
parallels are not essential in order to claim literary borrowing.[95]

---

93. Zimmerli, *Ezekiel 1–24*, pp. 465-69. Zimmerli, like Müller, also noted the
parallel between Zeph. 3.8c-d and Ezek. 22.31.

94. Day, 'A Case of Inner Scriptural Interpretation', pp. 309-10, cited the following parallels:

    1. Israel knows no lords/gods but Yahweh
            Hos. 13.4; cf. Isa. 26.13 (LXX)
    2. Imagery of birthpangs but child refuses to be born
            Hos. 13.13; cf. Isa. 26.17-18
    3. Deliverance from Sheol
            Hos. 13.14 (LXX, etc.); cf. Isa. 26.19
    4. Imagery of destructive east wind symbolic of exile
            Hos. 13.15; cf. Isa. 27.8
    5. Imagery of life-giving dew
            Hos. 14.6 (Eng. 5); cf. Isa 26.19
    6. Israel blossoming and like a vineyard
            Hos. 14.6-8 (Eng. 5-7); cf. Isa. 27.2-6
    7. Condemnation of idolatry, including the Asherim
            Hos. 14.9 (Eng. 8); cf. Isa. 27.9
    8. The importance of discernment; judgment for the wicked
            Hos. 14.10 (Eng. 9); cf. Isa. 27.11

95. D. Baltzer, *Ezechiel und Deuterojesaja: Berührungen in der Heilserwartung der beiden grossen Exilspropheten* (BZAW, 121; Berlin: W. de Gruyter,

What is more important, however, is to examine the use that he made
of the parallels. Day drew two kinds of conclusions from his study.
First, with respect to some of the eight parallels, he used the Hosea
passage to help clarify the Isaiah passage (he emended Isa. 26.13 to
conform more closely to Hos. 13.4 and suggested that 'Israel' in Isa.
27.6 and 'Jacob' in 27.9 may refer to the Northern Kingdom, since their
parallels in Hosea are directed to the Northern Kingdom) and vice versa
(he argued for a positive rendering of Hos. 13.14 partly due to Isa.
26.19 and claimed that the idolatry condemned in Hos. 14.9 is Asherim
worship since that is what is condemned in the parallel in Isa. 26.9).
Secondly, on the basis of the eight parallels, he concluded that Isa.
26.13–27.11, if not also all of Isaiah 24–27, is the work of one author
but presumably not a member of a 'distinctive Isaianic school'.[96]

Rather than critique Day's conclusions, it is sufficient to ask some
questions which he apparently was content not to try to answer. First,
why did the author of the 'Isaiah' passage choose precisely Hosea 13–
14 as the basis for his concluding poetic passage? Day's explanation
that 'the author, probably writing in the early postexilic period, found

1971); and R. Fey, *Amos und Jesaja: Abhängigkeit und Eigenständigkeit des Jesaja*
(WMANT, 12; Neukirchen–Vluyn: Neukirchener Verlag, 1963), offered full-length
discussions of the relationship between two prophetic books on the basis of
thematic rather than verbal parallels. E.W. Davies criticized Fey's claim of
dependence in *Prophecy and Ethics: Isaiah and the Ethical Traditions of Israel*
(JSOTSup, 16; Sheffield: JSOT Press, 1981), pp. 36-38. Similarly, most of Day's
parallel themes and motifs occur so commonly in biblical and other ancient Near
Eastern literature (despite his disclaimer, 'A Case of Inner Scriptural Interpretation', p. 316) and are employed so differently in the two prophets that it is
unnecessary to claim dependence in order to account for them. See also Day's general survey of 'inner-biblical interpretation' in 'Prophecy', in D.A. Carson and
H.G.M. Williamson (eds.), *It Is Written: Scripture Citing Scripture. Essays in
Honour of Barnabas Lindars* (Cambridge: Cambridge University Press, 1988), pp.
39-55.

    96. Day, 'A Case of Inner Scriptural Interpretation', p. 319. For a thorough
demonstration that Isa. 24–27 is deeply rooted in the 'Isaianic tradition', see M.A.
Sweeney, *Isaiah 1–4 and the Post-Exilic Understanding of the Isaianic Tradition*
(BZAW, 171; Berlin: W. de Gruyter, 1988); and especially his essays, 'New
Gleanings from an Old Vineyard: Isaiah 27 Reconsidered', in C.A. Evans and W.F.
Stinespring (eds.), *Early Jewish and Christian Exegesis: Studies in Memory of
William Hugh Brownlee* (Atlanta: Scholars Press, 1987), pp. 51-66; also *idem*,
'Textual Citations in Isaiah 24–27: Toward an Understanding of the Redactional
Function of Chapters 24–27 in the Book of Isaiah', *JBL* 107 (1988), pp. 39-52.

the prophecy of Hosea, with its message of a glorious future for Israel following the judgment of exile, a source of hope and inspiration',[97] is inadequate to account for either his choice of this oracle over others promising an equally glorious future or his selection of precisely these eight 'themes' to reuse. Secondly, is there really any evidence in Isaiah 26–27 of an *interpretation* of Hosea? Does the Isaiah passage actually offer a reinterpretation of Hosea's birth pangs, east wind, dew or vineyard imagery? Borrowing or literary dependence and exegetical reworking are clearly distinct procedures and Day offered little or no evidence of the latter.

Thirdly, although it is possible that Day's exegetical remarks regarding Isaiah mentioned in the previous paragraph are correct (Day based his emendation in Isa. 26.13 as much on the LXX reading as on the Hosea parallel and admitted that 'Israel' and 'Jacob' in Isa. 27.6, 9 probably do *not* refer to the Northern Kingdom), does an awareness of the Hosea parallels substantially aid one in understanding Isaiah 26–27 as a whole? Fourthly, what is the significance of the verses in each passage which Day did not mention? Hosea 13.4–14.10 consists of 22 verses of which Isaiah 26–27 'borrows' from only 9. Were the other 13 less useful for the author's purposes? Isaiah 26.13–27.11 consists of 20 verses, only 12 of which contain 'borrowings' from Hosea. What is the relationship of the other material in the passage to the Hoseanic themes? Accordingly, in light of all the intervening verses, is Day justified in claiming that the dew image of Hos. 14.6 // Isa. 26.19 'serves to counteract the effect of the destructive east wind' of Hos. 13.15 and Isa. 27.8?[98] Day may have proven a case of *dependence* but not of 'inner scriptural *interpretation*' as his title implied.

The most thorough application of this approach to Isaiah was Wolfgang Lau's study of 'scribal prophecy' in Isaiah 56–66.[99] On the basis of their interpretive approaches to earlier prophetic material, Lau distinguishes various 'hands' in Isaiah 56–66: 'Third' Isaiah (responsible only for chs. 60–62), three separate 'tradition circles', and individual traditions. As soon as the oracles of 'Second Isaiah' were written down, their scribal 'continuation' (*Fortschreibung*) commenced, as they were actualized and (re-)interpreted, the *same* message being reapplied to changing circumstances. Unlike Steck who, influenced by Zimmerli,

---

97. Day, 'A Case of Inner Scriptural Interpretation', p. 317.
98. Day, 'A Case of Inner Scriptural Interpretation', p. 313.
99. Ackroyd, 'The Vitality of the Word of God', p. 9.

blurred the line between 'Fortschreibung' and 'Redaktion', Lau viewed these 'continuers' as *authors* (or 'desk' prophets) rather than *editors*.[100] In Lau's opinion, scribal prophets normally signaled their intended references to other texts through the use of word-for-word quotation (not through countless cross-references, as Steck suggested), also demanding, accordingly, a learned readership. As authoritative writings, various texts could be juxtaposed or recombined without contradiction, though often taking on different meanings in their new context.

Four dominant themes account for the majority of the scribal utilizations of earlier Isaianic texts, according to Lau: Zion, the servant of God, the Holy One of Israel, and the Exodus. On the basis of his interpretive procedure, Lau traced a trajectory in the development of the 'highway of the return' image in Isaiah, more specifically, of the phrase פנו דרך, 'prepare the way', which occurs in Isa. 40.3; 57.14, and 62.10 (and סלו סלו, 'Build up, build up', which occurs in the 57.14 and 62.10). Because the author of 57.14 no longer expects a real exodus to take place, this author must be distinguished from (and later) than both 'Second' and 'Third' Isaiah,[101] which are quoted in this verse. Much of Lau's analysis apparently is undergirded by two questionable premises: (1) when an expression occurs only twice within the Old Testament, one of the texts likely stems from a later dependent author; (2) when an author makes repeated use of the same images or concepts, he cannot use them in significantly different ways.

Lau's view of verbal parallels virtually rules out self-quotation, downplays the effect of literary context on meaning and conceives of authors as drawing constantly (and consciously) upon a limited number of prior texts in addressing any subject. Such a rigid understanding is bound to lead Lau to an inflated assessment of the amount of 'scribal prophecy' to be found in 'Third' Isaiah.

This criticism of the work of Müller, Day and Lau does not imply a rejection of the claim that prophetic quotation often may result from inner-biblical exegesis. As Peter Ackroyd once claimed, 'Quotation

---

100. W. Lau, *Schriftgelehrte Prophetie in Jes 56–66: Eine Untersuchung zu den literarischen Bezügen in den letzten elf Kapiteln des Jesajabuches* (BZAW, 225; Berlin: W. de Gruyter, 1994).

101. Lau, *Schriftgelehrte Prophetie*, pp. 8-9; cf. also his detailed critique of Steck's approach, pp. 14-18. See O.H. Steck, *Old Testament Exegesis: A Guide to the Methodology* (trans. J.D. Nogalski; SBL Resources for Biblical Study, 33; Atlanta: Scholars Press, 1995), pp. 81-82.

may indeed only be claimed with certainty where reinterpretation is evident, indicating dependence upon an earlier form of the same material and its re-handling with a distinctively new point of view in mind'.[102] Where such reinterpretation plausibly can be demonstrated, the likelihood of coincidental verbal parallels or unconscious borrowing is much diminished, and the identification of verbal parallels can be used more confidently to enrich the exegesis of the respective passages. However, this seldom has been undertaken in any thorough-going manner. Many scholars have been interested in the general implications of the phenomenon of verbal parallels within the prophetic corpus; but in terms of a specific application of prophetic quotation to the interpretation of individual passages, these verbal parallels remain a largely untapped resource.

An important exception to the preceding remarks is Michael Fishbane, whose magisterial work *Biblical Interpretation in Ancient Israel*, expanding on two previous essays on the subject, was published in 1985. Fishbane's volume is exemplary in displaying a rigorous, though not unflawed, methodology and an extensive bibliography throughout. Although there is some overlap between his and this study, the scope of *Biblical Interpretation in Ancient Israel* is both broader and narrower. It is broader in that it deals with scribal, legal and haggadic exegesis, as well as exegesis of oracles which he labels 'mantological'; it is narrower in that it focuses primarily on those passages in which 'the Hebrew Bible cites itself before a new interpretation of the older text, whether the citation is complete or fragmentary', or to use Fishbane's preferred terminology, in which 'a nexus between a given *traditum* and its exegetical *traditio* can be analytically recovered and demonstrated', since 'similar phenomena need not be exegetically related'.[103]

102. Lau, *Schriftgelehrte Prophetie*, pp. 118-21.

103. Fishbane, *Biblical Interpretation in Ancient Israel*, pp. 11-12; *idem*, 'Torah and Tradition', in D.A. Knight (ed.), *Tradition and Theology in the Old Testament* (Philadelphia: Fortress Press, 1977), pp. 275-300; *idem*, 'Revelation and Tradition: Aspects of Inner-Biblical Exegesis', *JBL* 99 (1980), pp. 343-61. Fishbane summarizes his work on inner-biblical exegesis in *The Garments of Torah: Essays in Biblical Hermeneutics* (Bloomington: Indiana University Press, 1989), Chapter 1: 'Inner-Biblical Exegesis: Types and Strategies of Interpretation in Ancient Israel', pp. 3-18. Fishbane deals with 'inner-prophetic' interpretation in Isaiah on pp. 289, 495-99 of *Biblical Interpretation in Ancient Israel*. Fishbane derives his terms 'traditio' and 'traditum', which he applies to written traditions, from D.A. Knight's

Therefore, on the one hand, Fishbane is not interested in even exten-sive verbal parallels within the prophets if reinterpretation is not evident; on the other hand, many of his examples involve the atomistic reuse of individual terms from one passage by another, such as the 'interweaving' of Isaianic oracles (Isa. 2.1-4 and 2.5-22) in the postex-ilic proclamation of Isaiah 60 (specifically, in vv. 3, 5, 14, 17). Although he summarizes Müller's essay (see pp. 91-93 above), surpris-ingly few of Fishbane's examples are 'inner-prophetic', in which one prophet cites and interprets another prophetic text. Nevertheless, the methodological foundation which he has laid can facilitate the fruitful analysis of numerous prophetic texts.

Recently, however, Lyle Eslinger has recommended eliminating the designation 'inner-biblical exegesis' and replacing it by 'inner-biblical allusion'.[104] Eslinger's suggestion essentially involves replacing the category 'inner-biblical exegesis' by 'intertexuality'. According to Peter Miscall, 'intertextuality' is to be understood as a covering term for all the possible relations that can be established between texts. The relations can be based on anything from quotes and direct references to indirect allusions to common words and even letters to dependence on language itself. According to T.K. Beal, Fishbane, in his treatment of inner-biblical exegesis, is examining 'biblical intertextuality', though limiting himself to more determinate intertexual relations.[105] Thus

analysis of oral tradition (see Chapter 1 n. 87). For a critique of Fishbane's termi-nology and methodology, see J.L. Kugel, 'The Bible's Earliest Interpreters', *Prooftexts* 7 (1987), pp. 269-83; and W. Roth, 'Interpretation as Scriptural Matrix: A Panel on Fishbane's Thesis', *BR* 35 (1990), pp. 36-57 (with contributions by L.J. Hoppe, R.D. Haak and P.A. Viviano).

104. L.M. Eslinger, 'Inner-biblical Exegesis and Inner-biblical Allusion: The Question of Category', *VT* 42 (1992), pp. 47-58.

105. P.D. Miscall, 'Isaiah: New Heavens, New Earth, New Book', in D.N. Fewell (ed.), *Reading between Texts: Intertextuality and the Hebrew Bible* (Louisville, KY: Westminster/John Knox Press, 1992), pp. 41-56 (44); T.K. Beal, 'Glossary', in Fewell (ed.), *Reading between Texts*, pp. 21-24 (22). See also Fishbane's brief dis-cussion of intertextuality, *The Garments of Torah*, pp. 127-28. Gail O'Day, 'Jeremiah 9:22-23 and 1 Corinthians 1:26-31: A Study in Intertextuality', *JBL* 109 (1990), pp. 259-67 (259-60), similarly views Fishbane's work as the 'single most important contribution to the study of intertextuality in scripture'.

According to T.K. Beal, 'Ideology and Intertexuality: Surplus of Meaning and Controlling the Means of Production', in Fewell (ed.), *Reading between Texts*, pp. 27-39 (29), the term 'intertextuality' was coined by Julia Kristeva in a 1969 publi-cation. For helpful theoretical discussions and examples of 'biblical intertextuality',

'intertextuality' could be viewed as the larger category of literary relationships which includes those 'verbal parallels' which result from quotations. However, as van Wolde correctly has noted, true intertextual
exegesis replaces the 'chronological or diachronic approach of comparative exegesis' with the synchronic approach. (Otherwise, intertextuality is being used, according to van Wolde, merely 'as a modern literary
theoretical coat of veneer over the old comparative approach'.)[106] Thus
'quotation', in a sense, becomes an inappropriate term for intertextual
analysis. Eslinger's goal in abandoning inner-biblical exegesis is to cir-
cumvent problems caused by trying to determine literary chronology.
However, most recent 'intertextual' analyses of verbal parallels in the
Old Testament are based upon some predetermined diachronic relationship between texts; nor is it clear that Eslinger's suggested reliance on
what he terms 'the Bible's own plot line' completely avoids these
difficulties.[107]

The Struggle for Authority

Students of prophetic quotation have often asked the question: Why
would one prophet cite the sayings of another? One of the answers

see S. Draisma (ed.), *Intertextuality in Biblical Writings: Essays in Honor of Bas
van Iersel* (Kampen: Kok, 1989). Miscall recently has published a commentary
which expands on his essay in Fewell's volume, focusing on intertextual relations
throughout the book of Isaiah, *Isaiah* (Readings; Sheffield: JSOT Press, 1993).
Miscall refers to these as 'parallel passages', though admitting that 'one reader's
parallels may not exist for another', p. 20. For a thorough discussion and critique of
intertextuality as a method of biblical interpretation, see H.K. Berg, *Ein Wort wie
Feuer: Wege lebendiger Bibelauslegung* (Munich: Kösel; Stuttgart: Calwer Verlag,
1991), Chapter 10. Unfortunately, as D. Polaski has noted, 'Reflections on a
Mosaic Covenant: The Eternal Covenant (Isaiah 24.5) and Intertextuality', *JSOT* 77
(1998), pp. 55-73 (58), the term 'intertextuality' already 'has accumulated a bewildering variety of definitions and uses'.
    106. E. van Wolde, 'Trendy Intertextuality?', in Draisma (ed.), *Intertextuality in
Biblical Writings*, pp. 43-49 (43, 46).
    107. Eslinger, 'Inner-biblical Exegesis and Inner-biblical Allusion', p. 56. Note
the cautious wording used by A.E. Hill, *Malachi* (AB, 25D; New York: Doubleday,
1998), who in explaining his 'Appendix C: Intertextuality in the Book of Malachi',
pp. 401-12, speaks of 'interdependence' rather than 'dependence', p. 401.
However, the choice of the former term may represent simply a strategy for avoiding addressing difficult questions rather than a different way of conceiving of the
text and its interpretation.

frequently given concerned the inherent authority of previous prophetic proclamations. Nothing is more typical of the prophetic literature than the repeated formulaic claim that what the prophet declares is the very word of the Lord. Hence it is not surprising to find the words of earlier prophets repeated in the prophetic literature of a later generation.

Although scholars have long suggested that earlier oracles were reissued because they were authoritative, only recently have a number of sociologically oriented studies proposed that the authority thus borrowed by quotation was essential to the prophet's societal status. The most thorough work utilizing this approach was Robert Wilson's *Prophecy and Society in Ancient Israel*.[108] On the basis of anthropological case studies of intermediary figures in modern societies, he concluded that the existence of a support group is essential to the functioning of a prophet. Therefore, sociological factors also may play a significant role in influencing a prophet's rhetoric.

Wilson noted several ways in which the necessity of a support group might result in 'verbal parallels' within the prophets. First of all, two prophets may speak and act in a similar way and may express similar points of view because they are both members of the same support group. For example, some of the linguistic affinities between Hosea and Jeremiah may be due not to the latter's actual conscious quotation of the former but to the fact that his 'possession behavior included the use of the stereotypical language of his support group, the Ephraimite priests of Anathoth'.[109] Building on his identification of two major traditions within Israelite prophecy, Ephraimite and Judean, Wilson suggested further that prophets might be expected both to use the stereotypical speech patterns of their tradition and to echo the oracles of their predecessors within the tradition. This would account for the verbal links between Amos, Isaiah, Micah and Zephaniah.

According to Wilson, conformity with the stereotypical patterns and expectations of the support group would serve to enhance the individual prophet's authority, especially within that group. Authority became a major concern in the postexilic period, leading to a number of changes in Israelite prophecy. Some late prophets, in order to enhance their prophetic authority, chose to 'make extensive use of quotations and in

---

108. See also the brief discussion in D.L. Petersen, *Late Israelite Prophecy: Studies in Deutero-Prophetic Literature and in Chronicles* (SBLMS, 23; Missoula, MT: Scholars Press, 1977), pp. 14-16.

109. Wilson, *Prophecy and Society*, pp. 226, 236.

this way claim the authority of the quotations' original prophetic sources', drawing on 'language and concepts from traditions that had been distinct in the pre-exilic period'.[110]

Wilson's monograph clearly made a significant contribution to the assessment of verbal parallels within the prophets. By focusing on the sociological factors influencing prophetic speech, he warned against devoting exclusive attention to the individual prophet's role in receiving, interpreting and communicating the divine word. In his opinion, reuse of earlier traditions was not determined solely by their authority and exegetical value for the prophet but also by the potential response of his audience in general and his support group in particular to his quotations and stereotypical speech forms. Furthermore, by suggesting that the inherent or attributed authority of an earlier prophet might be 'borrowed' by a later prophet/author by repeating his words, Wilson offered a powerful motivation for quoting one's predecessors.

However, although Wilson made no attempt to account for all the verbal parallels, an unqualified acceptance of his basic thesis might lead to an inadequate assessment of the phenomenon. First of all, there is the danger that the Ephraimite and Judean traditions would be viewed as holding exclusive 'rights' to the use of particular language and concepts and, accordingly, one must account for any exceptional use of its 'property' by a prophet from outside the camp. Wilson acknowledged that already with Ezekiel the distinction had broken down, but he attributed the mixture of features from both traditions within his oracles to Ezekiel's own idiosyncratic synthesis.[111] Wilson's parade example of postexilic mixing is Joel whose date is still much disputed. Secondly, given the frequency of alleged quotations within and between all periods and representatives of Israelite prophecy, it is unlikely that the enhancement of authority was always the motive lying behind quotation. One may affirm that earlier oracles were reused because they were authoritative for the audience without necessarily assuming that the borrower himself lacked sufficient authority to function properly within society.

In light of the preceding discussion, it can be seen that prophetic authority may be fundamentally a *social* rather than a *theological* reality. Accordingly, Burke Long argued that it is prejudicial to speak of *true* or *false* prophecy. It would be more accurate, in his opinion, to

110. Wilson, *Prophecy and Society*, pp. 291-92.
111. Wilson, *Prophecy and Society*, p. 284.

see prophetic conflict as a question of 'contested authority'.[112] As might be expected, the phenomenon of prophetic quotation also has played a significant role in the scholarly discussion of the issue of true and false prophecy.

A further suggestion is that false prophets might be guilty of faulty or ill-timed quotation of true prophets, especially in the case of Hananiah. According to Buber, Hananiah was 'a parrot of Isaiah'[113] who failed to realize that the prophetic promise of an earlier age might not apply to a different historical moment. By severing the integral connection between promise and condition, he falsified the true proclamation of Isaiah. Osswald expressed this idea similarly: 'The genuine prophet must be able to determine, whether a particular historical hour is under God's wrath or his love.'[114] To quote a past promise in a time of wrath is to utter false prophecy. Recently, James Sanders described the problem as primarily hermeneutical in nature: 'To adapt any "text" or tradition to any "context" without employing the fundamental hermeneutic of monotheizing within the dynamics of that situation is in canonical terms falsehood.'[115] God's sovereign freedom to act forbids the static repetition and rigid reapplication of old oracles to new settings.

Although the term 'quotation' may be inaccurate here, since one cannot document from the Old Testament that any of the false prophets cited the actual words of their canonical predecessors, such as Isaiah,[116] further support for this view has been found in Jer. 23.30: '... I am

112. B.O. Long, 'Prophetic Authority as Social Reality', in G.W. Coats and B.O. Long (eds.), *Canon and Authority: Essays in Old Testament Religion and Theology* (Philadelphia: Fortress Press, 1977), pp. 3-20 (6).

113. M. Buber, 'Falsche Propheten', *Die Wandlung* 2 (1947), pp. 277-81 (278); similarly E. Jacob, 'Quelques remarques sur les faux prophètes', *TZ* 13 (1957), pp. 478-86 (484).

114. E. Osswald, *Falsche Prophetie im Alten Testament* (Sammlung gemeinverständlicher Vorträge und Schriften aus dem Gebiet der Theologie und Religionsgeschichte, 237; Tübingen: J.C.B. Mohr [Paul Siebeck], 1962), p. 22.

115. J.A. Sanders, 'Hermeneutics in True and False Prophecy', in G.W. Coats and B.O. Long (eds.), *Canon and Authority: Essays in Old Testament Religion and Theology* (Philadelphia: Fortress Press, 1977), pp. 21-41 (40; cf. also 21).

116. More accurate would be Wilson's description of them as 'Jerusalemite prophets, who continue to advocate the royal theology of the inviolability of Zion', *Prophecy and Society*, p. 239. An effort to synthesize the message of the false prophets in Jeremiah was made by R.E. Manahan, 'A Theology of Pseudoprophets: A Study in Jeremiah', *GTJ* 1 (1980), pp. 77-96.

against the prophets, says the LORD, who steal my words from one another.' Similarly to Buber, Kraus understood this usurpation as 'their unsanctioned employment and application of the prophetic tradition's salvific oracles'.[117] Given the frequency of prophetic quotation within the canonical literature, this verse raises serious questions about the validity or meaning of the accusation. One approach is to see it as a futile attempt by Jeremiah to discredit his opponents by character assassination, since he lacked any valid criterion for proving their falsity. Typical of this view was Robert Carroll's explanation:

> This curious charge could be made against many of the prophets represented in the biblical traditions because so much of the material there consists of reworked oracles and elements common to different prophets... Furthermore the influence of earlier prophets on Jeremiah should be contrasted with this attack on the other prophets so as to indicate the pejorative nature of his [Jeremiah's] description of their activity as stealing [...] a certain hysterical note of desperation.[118]

Another approach was taken by Hossfeld and Meyer who felt that Kraus's interpretation was not supported by the text. According to them, the phrase 'my words' should not be understood as the equivalent of 'the words which I revealed through your predecessors' but as an imprecise expression for 'words allegedly originating from me'.[119] Devoid of any divine source of revelation, these false prophets either must invent their own message (v. 16: 'they speak visions of their own minds') or imitate each other. As an example of the latter, Jeremias cited 1 Kings 22 in which the false prophets proclaim 'the same word of Yahweh as a unified group'.[120]

---

117. H.-J. Kraus, *Prophetie in der Krisis: Studien zu Texten aus dem Buch Jeremia* (Biblische Studien, 43; Neukirchen–Vluyn: Neukirchener Verlag, 1964), p. 55. According to Kraus, this interpretation goes back to Rashi and Kimchi who built on *b. Sanh.* 89a.

118. R.P. Carroll, *When Prophecy Failed: Cognitive Dissonance in the Prophetic Traditions of the Old Testament* (New York: Seabury, 1979), p. 192. See also Ackroyd, *Continuity*, p. 9; and J.L. Crenshaw, *Prophetic Conflict: Its Effect upon Israelite Religion* (BZAW, 124; Berlin: W. de Gruyter, 1971), p. 59.

119. F.L. Hossfeld and I. Meyer, *Prophet gegen Prophet: Eine Analyse der alttestamentlichen Texte zum Thema. Wahre und falsche Propheten* (BibB, 9; Fribourg: Schweizerisches Katholisches Bibelwerk, 1973), pp. 84, 176 n. 128. I. Meyer, *Jeremia und die falschen Propheten* (OBO, 13; Göttingen: Vandenhoeck & Ruprecht, 1977), p. 139 n. 3, called this expression a 'Breviloquenz'.

120. J. Jeremias, *Kultprophetie und Gerichtsverkündigung in der späten*

Although it is clearly beyond the scope of this survey to rehearse the complex issues associated with true and false prophecy,[121] it is necessary at least to respond to the possible implications of Jer. 23.30 for my larger study. First of all, even if 'Jeremiah's' accusation (which is presented as the first person message of Yahweh) is a desperation tactic, it is unlikely that he is denying, overlooking or being deceptive about his own dependence on his predecessors. Rather, in light of the larger context, Jeremiah's perspective must be seen as follows: Denying their divine commission and access to the divine council (vv. 21-22), he must also deny both the validity of their message and the legitimacy of its sources.

Although Werblowsky has noted that the phrase מגנבי דברי איש מאת רעהו, 'who steal my words from one another' (lit. 'a man from his neighbor'), is inappropriate for describing the relationship of false to (earlier) true prophets,[122] the possibility still remains that a false prophet conceivably could quote earlier prophetic words. Indeed, if one motivation behind this borrowing was authority enhancement, the false prophet might even be expected to do so. In this case, true and false is not a question of the hermeneutics employed but of the person doing the borrowing, unless one denies that any divine initiative lay behind the institution of Israelite prophecy.[123] Just as authorized students may borrow any of the books of their university library and every use they make of them in research, whether 'good' or 'bad', is legitimate, while

---

Königszeit Israel (WMANT, 35; Neukirchen–Vluyn: Neukirchener Verlag, 1970), p. 187.

121. Crenshaw, *Prophetic Conflict*, offers a good survey of the issues and positions taken concerning true and false prophecy as well as a lengthy bibliography.

122. R.J.Z. Werblowsky, 'Stealing the Word', *VT* 6 (1956), pp. 105-106, understood the root גנב (usually: steal) as involving a word-play with the meaning 'nocturnal vision', as attested by its Arabic cognate *ganaba*. איש מאת רעהו would be an appropriate designation for two contemporary true prophets but, in this context, not for a false prophet quoting a contemporary true prophet, since the radical opposition between their messages is the point at issue.

123. W. Zimmerli, 'Prophetic Proclamation and Reinterpretation', in D.A. Knight (ed.), *Tradition and Theology in the Old Testament* (Philadelphia: Fortress Press, 1977), pp. 69-100, has demonstrated the freedom with which prophets affirmed some traditions while reversing others, apparently without worrying about being accused of false prophecy. Wilson, *Prophecy and Society*, pp. 157-66, noted that, at least for the 'Deuteronomists', the criteria for distinguishing between true and false prophecy were person-centered.

unauthorized borrowers are guilty of stealing, no matter what use they make of these books, so Jeremiah's total rejection of his prophetic opponents in ch. 23 reflects not hysteria but his personal confidence that there is a qualitative difference between his and their prophetic activity.

The Growth of the Canon

The suggestions that quotation occurred in order to reinterpret or to borrow the authority of a previous oracle raises the question of why there was a need for or interest in reinterpretation or what kind of authority the sayings possessed. Ultimately, this is the question of canon: Does the phenomenon of prophetic quotation indicate that the literature already was achieving a fixity of form and commanding the obedience of the community that are the twin hallmarks of canonical Scripture?

Some answered the question in the negative. Sid Leiman stated it bluntly: literary affinities 'reveal nothing about the canonical status of the earlier book'.[124] Leiman felt that unless an earlier book was cited verbatim and by title, one could not assert with certainty the canonical status of that book. Conversely, if any prophetic book had achieved that status during the pre-exilic period, it could not have escaped mention. Similarly, von Rad argued that the free use of passages from the prophets in the levitical sermons of Chronicles can only mean that the preacher 'does not regard those traditional works as being in the strict sense canonical'.[125]

However, whether they stated it explicitly or not, many who assessed verbal parallels saw them as implying the incipient canonicity of the repeated text. Among nineteenth-century scholars, Cheyne felt that parallel passages 'show how instinctively the prophets formed as it

---

124. S.Z. Leiman, *The Canonization of Hebrew Scripture: The Talmudic and Midrashic Evidence* (Hamden, CT: Archon Books, 1976), pp. 17, 25-26.

125. Von Rad, 'The Levitical Sermon', p. 280. Similarly, Y. Hoffman, 'The Technique of Quotation and Citation as an Interpretive Device', in B. Uffenheimer and H.G. Reventlow (eds.), *Christian and Jewish Hermeneutics through the Centuries* (JSOTSup, 59; Sheffield: JSOT Press, 1988), pp. 71-79 (78), states: 'Sometimes biblical sources are referred to only implicitly since they were not yet recognized as holy, let alone canonical', although he cites no evidence to support this claim.

were a canon of prophetic Scriptures for themselves'.[126] Others saw
interdependence between the prophets as indicating the development of
the canon as a whole. Küper noted that the prophets' 'mutual utilization
[of one another's] produced the cohesion and gradual development
within our canonical writings',[127] while Girdlestone viewed the
prophets as making a conscious 'selection from among many possible
materials ... for a wider circle of readers in the far future'.[128] Although
few contemporary scholars would hold such a simple view of the
'building up of the Old Testament', many would see in the reuse of
earlier oracles for interpretive purposes at least 'the rise of a canonical
consciousness' (*Kanonbewusstsein*),[129] as Seeligmann described it.
Willi-Plein, for example, identified a clear historical development
within the exegetically motivated redactional additions to the minor
prophets that occurred 'with growing canonization, i.e. the equal value
of and regard for the biblical books' and which led one 'to draw upon
similar passages, beyond the boundaries of the book in question, for the
purpose of clarifying or correcting a text'.[130]

Recently, a number of scholars have explored a new aspect of the
canonical significance of prophetic quotation. Brevard Childs has been
a prime mover in this enterprise, noting how quotation not only *indicated* the proto-canonical authority of earlier passages but also consciously *contributed* to the growth of canon. Childs saw signs of
original passages in Ezekiel 'being expanded in the light of the larger
canon, the borrowed material functioning as an interpretive commentary', and of Joel's editor 'reaffirming Israel's tradition of divine revelation' by incorporating numerous citations into his message. In the
case of Micah, original thematic links with Isaiah have been increased
considerably by a common redactional tradition that resulted in numerous verbal parallels, effectively causing these two prophetic books to
serve as a commentary on each other and 'to be heard together for

126. Cheyne, *The Prophecies of Isaiah*, II, p. 253.

127. Küper, *Das Prophetenthum*, pp. 63-64.

128. Girdlestone, *The Building Up of the Old Testament*, p. 31.

129. Seeligmann, 'Voraussetzungen der Midraschexegese', p. 152, see also
pp. 176-81. Following him, Childs, 'Midrash and the Old Testament', p. 53; and
Fishbane, 'Torah and Tradition', p. 289; and *idem*, 'Revelation and Tradition',
p. 359, also spoke of a 'canonical consciousness'.

130. Willi-Plein, *Vorformen der Schriftexegese*, p. 264; also p. 2: 'the quasi
canonical status of the attested word'.

mutual enrichment'. In Zephaniah, 'the original layer of prophetic preaching has been largely obscured' by being 'blended with other prophetic voices ("First" and "Second" Isaiah, Amos) which have been used in fashioning a prophetic compendium'. Finally, with respect to Zechariah, 'the same blocks of authoritative scripture ... were exercising an effect on the composition of both sections', canonically linking them together.[131]

Dale Schneider devoted a Yale dissertation to an assessment of the significance of verbal parallels within the prophetic corpus for an understanding of 'The Unity of the Book of the Twelve'.[132] Disputing Wolfe's earlier study in which he denied that the prophets' message ever made reference to anything spoken or written previously, hence all parallels stemmed from scribal editors in the third century BCE,[133] Schneider sought to demonstrate that many of the citations were original. As an example, he proposed that Joel consciously made his book 'fit' between Hosea and Amos, in the process of drawing on their authority to endorse his message (cf. Joel 2.19 // Hos. 2.23-24 and Joel 2.27 // Hos. 13.4; Joel 4.16 // Amos 1.2 and Joel 4.18 // Amos 9.13), 'presenting it as the continuation (or application) of prophecies which had already been confirmed by events'.[134]

A much more thorough-going analysis of the significance of verbal parallels in tracing the redactional growth of the Book of the Twelve was presented in James Nogalski's dissertation, subsequently published as two BZAW volumes.[135] In the first volume he discussed 33 'allusions and citations', in the second 77 (though there is some overlap), 80 per cent of which are internal to the corpus of the minor prophets. Some of these consist merely of 'catchwords', which others have noted but not interpreted as offering 'a springboard into the editorial work of the Book of the Twelve', each minor prophet thereby being

131. B.S. Childs, *Introduction to the Old Testament as Scripture* (Philadelphia: Fortress Press, 1979), pp. 368, 293-94, 435-36, 438, 462, 482.

132. D.A. Schneider, 'The Unity of the Book of the Twelve' (PhD dissertation, Yale University, 1979).

133. R.E. Wolfe, 'The Editing of the Book of the Twelve', *ZAW* 53 (1935), pp. 90-129.

134. Schneider, 'The Unity of the Book of the Twelve', pp. 79-87.

135. J. Nogalski, *Literary Precursors to the Book of the Twelve* (BZAW, 217; Berlin: W. de Gruyter, 1993); *idem, Redactional Processes in the Book of the Twelve* (BZAW, 218; Berlin: W. de Gruyter, 1993).

linked to its successor within the sequence.[136]

Gerald Sheppard, also influenced by Childs's work on canon, under-stood canonization as 'hearing the voice of the same God through his-torically dissimilar traditions'. In his opinion, the anthological midrash presented by Robert and Bloch (see the discussion above, pp. 84-88) 'reflects an effort to exploit the full recurrences of a theme throughout a given canonical book or within a collection of canonical books' and 'assumes the same word of God lies behind all parts of a book or all books in a collection'. Furthermore, he saw the verbal links between Joel and Amos, which Childs and Schneider also had mentioned, as giving evidence of 'canon conscious redaction', an editorial attempt to relate one canonical book to another book or collection.[137]

In one respect, whether one views prophetic quotation as reflecting a growing 'canonical consciousness' or merely an earlier oracle's inher-ent authority may be simply a semantic distinction or may depend entirely upon whether one focuses on the message as literature or on the messenger as inspired prophet. Nevertheless, Childs has correctly noted that the phenomenon of prophetic quotation not only indicates the quasi-canonical status of earlier oracles when they were appropriated by later writers or editors but also represents one aspect of the very process of canonization, that the reuse of earlier sayings not only supplies a clue as to how those texts were read in Old Testament times but also how the completed canonical books are to be read today. However, Childs and other scholars have only sketched in briefest fashion the direction such canonical readings of prophetic quotation might take.[138] A more detailed examination may reveal further some of

136. Nogalski, *Literary Precursors to the Book of the Twelve*, pp. 16-17. R.H. O'Connell, *Concentricity and Continuity: The Literary Structure of Isaiah* (JSOTSup, 188; Sheffield: Sheffield Academic Press, 1994), pp. 22, 29, somewhat similarly seeks to demonstrate that 'corresponding devices', i.e. recurrent literary patterns that are discernible in the arrangement of vocabulary and thematic materi-als, 'govern the book as a whole and thereby give it unity' as the creation of a sixth-century author/compiler. His argument is less convincing due to the complexity of the concentric structures that he suggests. See also the essay by E. Bosshard, 'Beobachtungen zum Zwölfprophetenbuch', *BN* 40 (1987), pp. 30-62, who notes a correlation (in order of occurrence) between verbal parallels involving the individ-ual prophets in the Book of the Twelve and the major sections of Isaiah (pp. 30-36).

137. G.T. Sheppard, 'Canonization: Hearing the Voice of the Same God through Historically Dissimilar Traditions', *Int* 36 (1982), pp. 21-33 (23-24).

138. Here one might mention J. Blenkinsopp, *Prophecy and Canon: A*

the manifold ways in which the prophetic corpus was shaped to continue to speak authoritatively to future generations.

Problematic Assumptions

The preceding survey has highlighted the fascinating variety of applications and interpretations which scholars have made of alleged quotations within the prophetic corpus. Verbal parallels have been viewed as pointing to deficient creativity, textual fluidity, prophetic schools, waning authority, proto-midrashic exegesis, redactional shaping and incipient canonicity. An effort has been made to indicate that these approaches, though illuminating, often are built upon an insufficiently supported methodological foundation. Underlying these studies are several presuppositions which are possibly correct but unproven and perhaps unprovable.

The Accessibility of Previous Oracles
Other than the Jerusalem elders' citation of Micah in Jeremiah's day (Jer. 26.17-19), Daniel's reference to Jeremiah's prophecy of the 70 years (Dan. 9.2), and some oblique references to the words of earlier prophets in Ezekiel (Ezek. 38.17) and Zechariah (Zech. 1.4), verbal parallels offer the only evidence that oracles were known to contemporary or later prophets, or to the general populace—which is also essential, since most scholars seem to imply that the employment of quotation must be apparent to the audience in order for it to function as intended. The possible explanations for verbal parallels are rather limited. One might invoke divine inspiration, as some late-nineteenth-century conservatives did, although this would not ensure audience recognition, or, in the case of verbal parallels among contemporaries,

Contribution to the Study of Jewish Origins (Notre Dame: University of Notre Dame Press, 1977); R.E. Clements, 'Patterns in the Prophetic Canon', in G.W. Coats and B.O. Long (eds.), *Canon and Authority: Essays in Old Testament Religion and Theology* (Philadelphia: Fortress Press, 1977), pp. 42-55; and J.A. Sanders, *Torah and Canon* (Philadelphia: Fortress Press, 1972); *idem*, 'Adaptable for Life: The Nature and Function of Canon', in F.M. Cross, W.E. Lemke and P.D. Miller, Jr (eds.), *Magnalia Dei: The Mighty Acts of God. Essays on the Bible and Archaeology in Memory of G. Ernest Wright* (Garden City, NY: Doubleday, 1976), pp. 531-60, who, in the interest of brevity, have not been discussed, since prophetic quotation played a minor role in their work.

they might have actually heard the message proclaimed. Oral tradition has been much invoked, but did this form of transmission spread prophetic messages to all of Israelite society or only to those fortunate enough to frequent a particular cult site or to belong to that prophet's school of disciples?

Even if oracles were recorded in writing soon after their proclamation, multiple copies may not have been available. Therefore, is the common portrayal of the later quoter as a scholar who minutely examined earlier documents (as Michel viewed 'Third' Isaiah) appropriate? In order to ensure the fixation of oracles in written form, must one assume that quotation is almost exclusively a late postexilic feature, the work of scribes and redactors rather than classical prophets? Unlike the members of Scandinavian school, the proponents of inner-biblical 'canonizing' exegesis must assume that the careful adaptation of a few select passages rather than the accidental duplication of orally carried oracles was the rule. Given the fact that many if not most verbal parallels *could* have resulted from coincidental correspondence due to similarity of subject and the constraints of Hebrew (and Semitic) idiom, to assume accessibility on the *basis* of verbal parallels is a questionable procedure.

The Stability of the Text

Both those who are interested in textual criticism and in inner-biblical exegesis must assume that prophetic oracles not only were accessible but also fixed in formulation. In order to use verbal parallels to correct the text or identify changes which the later user made in adapting the passage to his purpose, one must hold that the form of the text which is presently preserved is identical to the form that the quoter knew and be confident that one can infallibly distinguish between accidental and intentional alterations. This requires the scholar to assert either that quotation was a late activity of redactors using written texts or that oracles underwent little or no modification between their initial proclamation and their canonical fixation. Talmon's work has demonstrated that the textual and the literary process often overlapped and that the period of textual fluidity continued for centuries, making it more difficult to maintain that an early stabilization of the text occurred.

The Authority of Earlier Sayings

At first glance, it seems to be a safe assumption that the oracles of Israel's prophets were authoritative. However, if one moves backward from the point in time in which a given prophet's sayings achieved their final canonical status, one might well ask when and for whom his words became authoritative. Even the most superficial reading of the narrative accounts of the prophets' relationship to society in general and especially the power structure reveals that, at least initially, their authority claim often was rejected and their message went unheeded. Robert Wilson's entire analysis of intermediaries as functioning either centrally or peripherally within society assumes that the prophet's authority frequently was recognized only by his support group, as the numerous disputes with the 'false' prophets aptly illustrate. Despite the prophet's repeated invocation of divine authority to back up his words, apparently the words often were heeded only after the threatened judgment fell. Most students of prophetic quotation are more concerned with the status of the prophet's words at the time they were quoted than with their initial authority, yet it cannot be unequivocally established from the text that every quoted prophet's oracles possessed a generally acknowledged authority for the quoter's audience.

The Identifiability of Quotation

The final presupposition was also the point of departure for this chapter. Nevertheless, it must be reiterated here as well that few who seek to evaluate the phenomenon of verbal parallels make any effort to demonstrate that the texts that they are examining actually contain intentional interprophetic quotations. Peter Ackroyd's comments in this regard are to the point:

> The whole matter of quotations is one which is often too lightly treated and dependence is often deduced on evidence which is much too slender. Account needs to be taken of the probability or otherwise of dependence, and the possibility that quotation may be in either direction. Frequently the resemblances are better to be explained as due either to dependence upon a common tradition or to the use of set phrases found in religious compositions of almost any period of Old Testament history.[139]

Although it is by no means being suggested here that true quotations are non-existent or even infrequent or that, given the difficulty of

---

139. Ackroyd, 'Criteria', p. 118.

identification, all efforts at assessing the phenomenon should be abandoned, it ought to be clear from the preceding discussion that many who have constructed elaborate theories utilizing verbal parallels have built upon a sandy foundation indeed.

The Need for a New Approach

It has been noted above that verbal parallels within the prophetic books, though an oft-noted and much-discussed phenomenon, only rarely have been subjected to a rigorous examination. This is due in part to the fact that no consensus has yet been achieved concerning the proper methodology for such a study. To be sure, as the historical survey in Chapter 1 revealed, many scholars have touched briefly on methodological issues, but their work has had little lasting impact.

In concluding Part One of this study, it is appropriate to point out the major obstacles which have led to this impasse in the interpretation of prophetic quotation, in order to begin moving toward possible solutions. Two major difficulties have already been mentioned. First of all, in Chapter 1, it was pointed out that verbal parallels may result from a number of factors other than conscious literary quotation, and it is often very difficult, if not impossible, to determine which of these factors were responsible.[140] Secondly, in Chapter 2, it has been demonstrated that no criteria are adequate to prove infallibly that borrowing has occurred in one direction rather than the other, thus it is not always easy to proceed beyond the mere identification of a verbal parallel.[141] (Further difficulties related to those two will be discussed in Chapters 7 and 8 below.) Thirdly, since similar phrases within the prophets may have a great variety of origins, it is difficult to know which term it is most appropriate to employ in describing them. As a result, several widely divergent labels may be applied by various scholars to the same passage. However, since terms seldom are defined or differentiated, this lack of terminological clarity makes it impossible to know what type of dependence or degree of correspondence is implied thereby.

Finally, there is the methodological obstacle presented by the critical understanding of the nature of the prophetic literature. Ever since traditional views regarding authorship were abandoned and the historical

---

140. See above, p. 58.

141. See above, pp. 63-71. The best recent discussion of this subject is Hurvitz, *A Linguistic Study*, pp. 13-18.

information offered by superscriptions and narrative accounts was deemed unreliable or relevant only to a limited passage, an unending debate has ensued regarding the growth of and chronological relationships between the various prophetic books, and it appears to be highly unlikely that a new consensus soon will emerge. Rather than a book being viewed as the literary record of one prophet's ministry, the material now is commonly seen as remaining in flux for centuries, individual oracles being expanded, revised, updated and reapplied as they were read and used by generations of the faithful. Accordingly, a given verbal parallel may have been incorporated at any stage in the process.

Though the study of the prophetic corpus has been enriched by an awareness of its complexity, its exegesis has suffered proportionally due to the resultant confusion over how a multi-layered text, including its verbal parallels, is to be interpreted. As soon as the multi-layered nature of a text is posited, any number of plausible explanations for a particular verbal parallel can be given and absolute certainty in the matter becomes impossible. In itself, this development is not all that distressing, but, as a by-product, when the effort to determine dependence is abandoned, the verbal parallel often ceases to be of further interest to the exegete. Rather than understanding verbal parallels as a significant component of prophetic rhetoric which demands careful analysis, most commentators simply list them, then ignore them. Although some have raised their voice in protest against this hermeneutical slight,[142] the exegetical potential of this phenomenon still remains largely untapped.

In the preceding chapters an attempt has been made to demonstrate that complex methodological problems beset anyone who seeks to assess the import of verbal parallels within the prophets. Although such passages frequently have been discussed, little real progress has been achieved: one either capitulates before the difficulties posed by questions of terminology, dating and text form and simply acknowledges

---

142. Jeremias, *Kultprophetie und Gerichtsverkündigung*, p. 14 n. 2, in discussing Nah. 1.15, says, 'It is incomprehensible how recent commentators on Nahum are satisfied merely to remark "vgl. Jes. 52:7" '! Coggins, 'An Alternative Prophetic Tradition?', p. 82, complains similarly, 'to a remarkable extent commentators [on Isaiah] seem able to wax lyrical about the passage in Isaiah 52 without any reference to Nahum'.

verbal parallels without incorporating them in any way into one's interpretation or one simply ignores the difficulties, resulting in a multitude of mutually contradictory interpretations of the data. If the identification of verbal parallels is going to enrich the exegesis of the prophets in any way, a new approach to the phenomenon must be suggested.

In the ensuing chapters, several potential sources for shedding additional light on prophetic quotation will be examined: quotations in four types of non-prophetic literature. Although methodological issues have been addressed with respect to each of these literatures, their relevance to the biblical phenomenon has never been assessed in any thorough manner.

First, quotations within ancient Near Eastern literature will be examined in order to determine how Israel's neighbors drew upon their traditional literature in formulating new compositions. This may give some indication of how literary borrowing occurred in the world of the Old Testament, using documents whose analysis is not as affected by religious concerns as the biblical texts. Next, the use of the prophetic books in early Judaism will be investigated, concentrating on the Hebrew texts of Sirach and the Qumran Hodayoth, proceeding from the premise that if any patterns of quotation prevailed during the formation of the Old Testament, they also might be identifiable in the books composed in the centuries concluding and immediately following the Old Testament period. Finally, following a brief overview of the treatment of the quotation of proverbial sayings and other speakers in the Old Testament literature, a survey will be made of studies of quotation in modern literature, where interest now focuses not simply on how to identify quotations but rather on how quotations should be 'read'. It is hoped that the analysis of quotations in each of these types of literature along with the examination of the respective methodologies which have been employed will result in both a fresh approach as well as methodological refinement in the study of verbal parallels within the biblical prophets.[143]

143. In the final section of this study the insights gained through these surveys will be applied to selected verbal parallels within Isa. and between Isa. and other prophetic books.

Part II

QUOTATION IN NON-PROPHETIC LITERATURES

Chapter 3

QUOTATION IN ANCIENT NEAR EASTERN LITERATURE

To turn to the literature of ancient Egypt, Mesopotamia and Ugarit in order to understand the Old Testament prophets better is hardly a new enterprise. For at least a century extra-biblical parallels to the literary forms, themes, formulations and social roles of the prophets have been suggested in the scholarly literature.[1] Although some of these similarities may be coincidental, the Assyrian royal inscriptions in particular are deemed to have profoundly influenced 'Second' Isaiah.[2] However, the concern here is not with inter-cultural but rather with intra-cultural literary borrowing. Specifically, the primary question is: Did ancient Near Eastern scribes and authors quote their literary predecessors? If so, how did they indicate this, and what was their purpose and procedure in such citations? Although it is not the goal to achieve a comprehensive study of such internal parallels—if such were even possible[3]—

1. For helpful studies see especially Wilson, 'Prophecy in the Ancient Near East', Chapter 3 in *Prophecy and Society in Ancient Israel* (Philadelphia: Fortress Press, 1980), pp. 89-134, and the bibliography which he cites; also M. Weinfeld, 'Ancient Near Eastern Patterns in Prophetic Literature', *VT* 27 (1977), pp. 178-95; S.A. Kaufman, 'Prediction, Prophecy, and Apocalypse in the Light of New Akkadian Texts', in A. Shinen (ed.), *Proceedings of the Sixth World Congress of Jewish Studies* (3 vols.; Jerusalem: Jerusalem Academic Press, 1977), I, pp. 221-28; and Millard, 'La prophète et l'écriture Israël', pp. 125-45; *idem*, 'The Old Testament in its Ancient World', pp. 88-99.

2. See J.W. Behr, *The Writings of Deutero-Isaiah and the Neo-Babylonian Royal Inscriptions: A Comparison of the Language and Style* (Pretoria: University of Pretoria, 1937); S.M. Paul, 'Deutero-Isaiah and Cuneiform Royal Inscriptions', *JAOS* 88 (1968), pp. 180-86; S.L. Peterson, 'Babylonian Literary Influence in Deutero-Isaiah: A Bibliographic and Critical Study' (PhD dissertation, Vanderbilt University, 1975); and H.M. Barstad, 'On the So-Called Babylonian Influence in Second Isaiah', *Scandinavian Journal of Theology* 2 (1987), pp. 90-110.

3. W.W. Hallo, 'New Viewpoints on Cuneiform Literature', *IEJ* 12 (1962),

even a selective investigation[4] may prove to be of great interest and relevance to the biblical phenomenon.

Quotation in Egyptian Literature

Quotations in Egyptian literature have received more scholarly attention than those in Mesopotamian literature,[5] and, not surprisingly, most of the citations discussed are found in Wisdom literature, although the reuse of numerous phrases from the classic Middle Egyptian tales and various ritual texts has also been studied.[6] This immediately presents a methodological problem. First of all, one might well expect traditional wisdom sayings to be transmitted for generations and to be included in more than one collection. This hardly would serve to demonstrate that one wisdom composition which contains a particular saying is quoting another such composition. For example, several of the parallels which

pp. 13-26 (20 n. 34): 'The whole problem of such "internal parallels" in the various separate ancient Near Eastern literatures is worthy of investigation.' Another related subject is the question of inter-cultural literary borrowing. See, for example, the recent essay by J.H. Tigay, 'On Evaluating Claims of Literary Borrowing', in M.E. Cohen, D.L. Snell and D.B. Weisberg (eds.), *The Tablet and the Scrolls: Near Eastern Studies in Honor of W.W. Hallo* (Bethesda, MD: CDL Press, 1993), pp. 250-55, which discusses methodological issues involved in analyzing the alleged verbal parallel between the *Gilgamesh Epic* and Eccl. 9.7-9.

4.   For many of the bibliographical references in this Chapter I am indebted to Professor W.K. Simpson and Professor W.W. Hallo of Yale University as well as Mr A.R. Millard and Mr C.J. Eyre of the University of Liverpool.

5.   The most thorough studies are those of H. Brunner, 'Zitate aus Lebenslehren', in E. Hornung and O. Keel (eds.), *Studien zu altägyptischen Lebenslehren* (Göttingen: Vandenhoeck & Ruprecht, 1979), pp. 105-71, and 'Zitate', in W. Helck and W. Westendorf (eds.), *Lexikon der Ägyptologie* (7 vols.; Wiesbaden: Otto Harrasowitz, 1986), VI, cols. 1415-20; and W. Guglielmi, 'Zur Adaption und Funktion von Zitaten', in H. Altenmüller and D. Wildung (eds.), *Festschrift für Wolfgang Helck zu seinem 70. Geburtstag* (SAK, 11; Hamburg: Helmut Buske Verlag, 1984), pp. 347-64; cf. also C.J. Eyre, 'The Semna Stelae: Quotation, Genre, and Functions of Literature', in S. Israelit-Groll (ed.), *Studies in Egyptology Presented to Miriam Lichtheim* (Jerusalem: Magnes Press, 1990), pp. 134-65 (153-60).

6.   Brunner, 'Zitate', col. 1417. As in Old Testament studies, there is not total agreement among Egyptologists regarding what constitutes Wisdom literature and, accordingly, which works should be included. See M.V. Fox, 'Two Decades of Research in Egyptian Wisdom Literature', *ZÄS* 107 (1980), pp. 120-35.

Hellmut Brunner considers to be quotations, Battiscombe Gunn thinks are more likely to be proverbs used independently.[7] Furthermore, it cannot be assumed necessarily that any saying found within a given piece of literature, such as *The Teaching for Merikare*, is an original creation of its author.

In order to overcome these difficulties, this survey will focus on parallels occurring in non-Wisdom texts where a repeated usage is less expected. Of course, the subjective element cannot thus be completely eliminated, for the possibility always remains that both writers may be making independent use of an unpreserved or perhaps yet-to-be-discovered source, or that the saying is merely a proverbial, idiomatic or formulaic expression for which the label 'quotation' is inappropriate. However, an excessive skepticism or agnosticism regarding the identifiability of quotations also seems unwarranted; the evidence deserves to be evaluated as objectively as possible.

Indeed, there is good reason to claim that earlier classics were frequently and extensively quoted. *The Instruction of the Vizier Ptahhotep* claims as a purpose 'to speak to him the words of them that listen and the ideas of the ancestors, of them that hearkened to the gods', and *Merikare* advises, 'copy your forefathers, for [work] is carried out through knowledge; see, their words endure in writing'. *In Praise of Learned Scribes* asks, 'Is there anyone here like Hor-dedef? Is there another like Ii-em-hotep?', and goes on to name other 'learned men who foretold what was to come'.[8] On the one hand, given the Egyptians' high regard for their ancestors, especially their learning, it is hardly unexpected to find numerous statements repeated from earlier texts. On the other hand, as early as the 'Complaints of Khakheperre-Sonb', which Lichtheim dates to the Twelfth Dynasty (c. 1900 BCE), a strong desire for originality (and, conversely, an 'anxiety of influence') is expressed:

7.   Brunner, 'Zitate aus Lebenslehren', pp. 133-38; and B. Gunn, 'Some Middle-Egyptian Proverbs', *JEA* 12 (1926), pp. 282-84. For the specific examples, see nn. 41-43 below.

8.   *ANET*, p. 412; W.K. Simpson (ed.), *The Literature of Ancient Egypt: An Anthology of Stories, Instructions, and Poetry* (trans. R.O. Faulkner, E.F. Wente, Jr and W.K. Simpson; New Haven: Yale University Press, 1973), p. 182; *ANET*, p. 432.

Had I unknown phrases, / Sayings that are strange,
Novel, untried words, / Free of repetition;
Not transmitted sayings, / Spoken by the ancestors!
I wring out my body of what it holds,
        / In releasing all my words;
For what was said is repetition, / When what was said is said.
Ancestor's words are nothing to boast of,
        / They are found (useful) by those who come after. [9]

Sometimes such quotations were clearly indicated by some type of introductory formula. Proverbial sayings in *The Eloquent Peasant* are preceded by such phrases as 'the proverb that people say' (*pꜣ ḥn ni mdt ḏdw rmṯ*), 'such is the precept' (*wḏ*), 'according to the saying' (*ḏd*), and 'your maxim' (*ts*) [10] More significant, however, are those instances in which the saying is not an undocumented proverb but an identifiable statement from another extant text. In *Ostracon O.I.C. 12074*, a scribe says to his son, 'You are in the situation of him who said' (*pꜣ nty ḥr ḏd*) and goes on to quote, somewhat inaccurately, a first person statement of *The Eloquent Peasant*.[11] *The Installation of the Vizier* cites a saying from *Ptahhotep*, marking it as a quotation by the words 'for men say' (*mk tw ḏd tw*).[12] Most remarkable is the case of Dua-khety's *Satire on the Trades* in which he directly names his source: 'Read then at the end of the Book of Kemyet this statement in it saying: as for the scribe …' (*gmi.k ts pn im.s m ḏdt*).[13]

Clearly, at least some of those who quoted earlier sayings were aware of what they were doing and were not averse to admitting their literary borrowing and even indicating its source. However, the fact remains that most citations went unmarked other than by the implicit signs of

---

9.   M. Lichtheim, *Ancient Egyptian Literature: A Book of Readings* (3 vols.; Berkeley: University of California Press, 1973–78), I, p. 146. See G.E. Kadish, 'British Museum Writing Board 5645: The Complaint of Kha-Kheper-Re-Senebu', *JEA* 59 (1973), pp. 77-90; and B.G. Ockinga, 'The Burden of Kha kheperre sonbu', *JEA* 69 (1983), pp. 88-95, for a discussion of this text.

10.   Gunn, 'Some Middle-Egyptian Proverbs', pp. 282-84.

11.   W.K. Simpson, 'Allusions to "The Shipwrecked Sailor" and "The Eloquent Peasant" in a Ramesside Text', *JAOS* 78 (1958), pp. 50-51; and A.H. Gardiner, 'The Eloquent Peasant', *JEA* 9 (1923), pp. 5-25 (25).

12.   Brunner, 'Zitate aus Lebenslehren', p. 127; and R.O. Faulkner, 'The Installation of the Vizier', *JEA* 41 (1955), pp. 18-29 (22).

13.   W. Barta, 'Das Schulbuch Kemit', *ZÄS* 105 (1978), pp. 6-14; Simpson (ed.), *Literature of Ancient Egypt*, p. 330.

archaic language, awkward grammar or contextual abruptness. Can it be assumed that all other quoters were either ignorant or unconscious of their borrowings or deceptive plagiarists?

In order to answer this question adequately one must first settle the question of terminology and definition. Brunner proposes a series of terms, 'quotation' (*Zitat*), 'allusion' (*Anspielung*), and 'dependence/ influence' (*Anlehnung*), each, in turn, indicating a lesser degree of verbal identity, but actually prefers the more general term 'borrowing', literally 'adoption' (*Übernahme*). Earlier, Brunner refused to define his terms, claiming that 'we destroy more than we discover when we apply strict definitions to ancient Egyptian literature'. More recently, however, in his *Lexikon der Ägyptologie* article on 'Zitate', he at least offers a definition of 'quotation': 'Quotation is the taking over of a sentence or part of a sentence from a specific text, the knowledge of which the quoting author can presuppose among the linguistic community or the educated class.'[14] More helpful is the distinction made by C.J. Eyre, who suggests the following definitions: 'a quotation may be defined as a phrase used with the deliberate intent and expectation that the audience will recall a specific passage in a specific text'; 'a formula is a phrase that carries a ring of familiarity, and may be used time and again in different texts, in identical or slightly varied form, but is not intended to recall a specific text'. Eyre concedes that, in practice, the two may be impossible to distinguish due to the difficulty of determining 'compositional intent'. (It is not simply a matter of using written sources in the former and oral in the latter.) Eyre ultimately categorizes much formulaic language as 'model phraseology learnt at school'.[15] It may well be that the ancient Egyptians lacked any such distinction between degrees of verbal dependence, but that hardly permits one to avoid one's responsibility to state clearly what it is that one is investigating.

Brunner, to a much greater extent than other scholars who discuss quotations, is straightforward in discussing his methodology. He is

14. Brunner, 'Zitate aus Lebenslehren', p. 167, 'Zitate', col. 1415; Guglielmi, 'Zur Adaption und Funktion von Zitaten', p. 348.

15. Eyre, 'The Semna Stelae', pp. 155-59. Eyre notes several possibilities quite similar to those discussed in Chapter 1 with regard to prophetic quotation: 'whether the Semna stela "quotes" Ptahhotep, or whether a later redactor of Ptahhotep "quotes" the work that was inscribed on the Seman stela, or whether they both "quote" an unknown third source' (p. 160).

interested in determining, through the examination of numerous examples, what texts were frequently quoted (according to Brunner, *Ptahhotep*) and what kinds of texts did the quoting, and, more importantly, what happened to the form and meaning of the original text in the process of quotation. Because verbal and not thematic parallels are his primary concern, he sets down some minimum standards for the passages to be considered: the texts must share at least two key words (though one may suffice if it is particularly striking and central to the phrase) and 'there must be some relationship between the development of thought in the two texts'.[16]

Surprisingly, Brunner says relatively little about why quotation occurred, about what a quoter sought to achieve through his literary borrowing. For the most part, he seems content to see quotation simply as a type of 'party game of the well-educated', the quoter displaying his or her thorough knowledge of the Egyptian 'classics' by quoting them and the reader displaying his or her erudition by detecting the citation and correctly identifying its source.[17] Hence quotations are of interest primarily as illustrations of an accepted ancient rhetorical device for enriching one's style by adopting and adapting the skillful formulations of literary predecessors. For example, the Ethiopian kings quoted frequently, thereby demonstrating their linkage to Egyptian tradition. In addition, quotations serve as indicators of which texts continued to be read and known for centuries, even millennia—*The Shipwrecked Sailor* was quoted by Pianchi 1200 years after its composition! Van de Walle expresses this value most vividly when he concludes on the basis of several citations and reminiscences: 'the classics of the Middle Kingdom appear ... to have maintained an undisputed prestige'.[18]

However, an examination of the more than 70 verbal parallels cited by Brunner and others reveals that more may be involved in quotation than merely the enhancement of one's style and reputation. It appears that Egyptian scribes were not only aware of the practice of quotation but had a clear concept of what was the right and wrong way to go about it. In the *Letter of Hori* the author criticizes a scribe: 'Thou art

16. Brunner, 'Zitate aus Lebenslehren', p. 167. In his article 'Zitate', col. 1415, he has changed the criterion from one or two key words to two or three.

17. Brunner, 'Zitate aus Lebenslehren', p. 110. He also describes quotations as intended 'for intellectual connoisseurs'.

18. B. van de Walle, *La transmission des textes littéraires égyptiens* (Brussels: Fondation Egyptologique Reine Elisabeth, 1948), p. 29.

come provided with great mysteries, and thou tellest me a saying of Hor-dedef (although) thou knowest not [whether it is] good or bad. What chapter is before it? What after it?' Although it is possible that this statement means something other than that the scribe has misinterpreted or misquoted Hor-dedef,[19] several examples have been cited in which this seems to be precisely what happens.

In *The Teaching of King Ammenenes I*, the king claims, 'It was I who made barley and loved grain' (literally 'loved the grain god Nepri', *mri npri*). In the Second Intermediate Period a man named Bebi claimed similarly to have 'created barley and loved *nfr*.' According to Brunner, Bebi no longer knew of the god Nepri and therefore used the near homonym *nfr*, meaning 'beauty', which destroyed the parallelism and import of the original.[20]

Another quotation of *Ammenemes I* reflects a similar error. Helck identifies two borrowings of *Ammenemes'* statement: 'Indeed, many children are in the street' (*iw ms msw.t 'šꜣ.t m mrwt*). The first parallel, which is commonly acknowledged, is in *The Admonitions of an Egyptian Sage*: 'Indeed the children of magnates are ejected into the streets' (*iw ms msw(t) srw ḫꜣ' m mrt*).[21] According to Helck, the author of the *Admonitions* helped to clarify *Ammenemes* by substituting *srw*, 'magistrates', for '*šꜣ*', 'many'—here being understood as 'rich', and adding a verb. Faulkner, on the other hand, considers the *Ammenemes* passage to be 'a garbled quotation from *Admonitions* 6, 12–14, without the help of which the interpretation of this passage would be impossible. Even now, its bearing on the context is not clear'.[22] Helck concurs

19. Brunner, 'Zitate aus Lebenslehren', p. 108. See the translation of A. Erman, *The Ancient Egyptians: A Sourcebook of their Writings* (trans. A.M. Blackman; New York: Harper & Row, 1966), p. 221, which suggests that the problem was an inadequate mastery rather than a misuse of the text.

20. Brunner, 'Zitate aus Lebenslehren', pp. 144-45, 149; Simpson (ed.), *The Literature of Ancient Egypt*, p. 195. Lichtheim, *Ancient Egyptian Literature*, I, p. 137, translates, 'I was grain-maker, beloved of Nepri'. To compare the orthography of the near homonyms see R.O. Faulkner, *A Concise Dictionary of Middle Egyptian* (Oxford: Oxford University Press, 1962), pp. 130 and 132.

21. W. Helck, 'Eine kleine Textverbesserung', *Jaarbericht van het voorazia-tisch-egyptisch genootschap Ex oriente lux* (*Annuaire de la Société orientale 'Ex oriente lux'* 19 [1965–66]), pp. 464-67; Simpson (ed.), *The Literature of Ancient Egypt*, pp. 196, 218. The following two sentences are also quite similar in both texts.

22. Faulkner in Simpson (ed.), *The Literature of Ancient Egypt*, p. 196 n. 15.

with the latter statement and suggests that the confusion is due to a textual corruption, citing a second 'quotation' in *The Instruction of a Man for his Son*: 'Those who are hated become as those who are loved' (*msdw ḫpr mrw.t*).[23] Helck postulates that the original statement read 'Indeed, much hatred is in the street' (*iw ms msd.t 'š₃ m mrt*). Thus, the corruption of *msd.t* (hatred) into *msw.t* (children) produced the text which *Admonitions* quoted and revised. The substitution of a more common determinative with *mr* (Gardiner A 2 'man with hand to mouth'), giving the meaning 'love', for the determinative with *mr* giving the meaning 'street' (Gardiner O 5 and 1 'winding wall' and 'house'), produced the basis for the *Man for his Son* citation.[24] Whether one accepts Helck's or Faulkner's explanation of the divergent texts, it is clear that quotations may both result *from* and result *in* confused readings. The relationship between the passages in the *Admonitions* and *Ammenemes* has been acknowledged in most of the published translations of those texts, probably due to the fact that they both consist of three consecutive sentences which are strikingly similar in wording.

What is more important, however, and much more difficult to determine, is how close and extensive the verbal correspondence had to be for ancient readers to recognize a quotation. Remarkably, the exact quotation is virtually non-existent in Egyptian literature. Orthographic changes, syntactical simplification, substitution of near synonyms, variations in word order, grammatical updating, necessary adjustments in person, number and verbal form, as well as extensive paraphrasing and expansions frequently occur. Helck may be correct when he suggests that certain elements of a sentence (Brunner's 'catchwords'?) must remain basically intact in a quotation, but if this requirement is met, a rather extensive revision of the remaining elements can be tolerated.[25]

A most instructive illustration of this principle is offered by the

---

Wilson, *ANET*, p. 442 n. 22, agrees with Faulkner's view concerning the direction of the borrowing, calling it an 'inapt quotation', also p. 419 n. 17; as does Erman, *The Ancient Egyptians*, p. 100 n. 5, calling it a corrupt version which has been interpolated, also p. 74 n. 8. Both Wilson and Erman understand the phrase as meaning 'idle talk'.

23. Helck, 'Eine kleine Textverbesserang', p. 465; Simpson (ed.), *The Literature of Ancient Egypt*, p. 338.

24. Lichtheim, *Ancient Egyptian Literature*, I, pp. 155 and 139 n. 12, follows Helck, translating both passages, 'There is much hatred in the streets'.

25. Helck, 'Eine kleine Textverbesserung', p. 466.

repeated adaptation of *Hor-dedef*'s counsel: 'Beautify your house at the necropolis and make excellent your place of the west' (*smnḫ pr.k nt ḫrt-nṯr/ siḫr st.k nt imnt*).[26] There are at least a half-dozen alleged quotations of this charge. A son in an eleventh dynasty autobiography claims to have carried out the advice not for himself but for his father, according to Brunner, thereby exceeding *Hor-dedef*'s demands, simplifying the expression from a parallelistic statement to: 'beautified his place of the necropolis' (*smnḫ.n.i st.i m ḫrt-nṯr*). The grave of Senmes, eighteenth dynasty, also offers an autobiographical statement: 'I have made secret my place in the west, my tomb in the inner part of the temple' (*sitn.n.i st.i m imnt/ is.i m ḫnw n ḥwt*). Here a radical revision makes questionable whether this is even dependent on *Hor-dedef*'s formulation: one verb is changed, another eliminated, the grammar is simplified from *nt* to *m*, and the funerary buildings in the second line are described in totally different terms.[27] *The Instruction of Ani* gives another revision: 'Beautify your place which is in the valley' (*smnḫ.t st.tw.k nty m.ʒt int*). This version reflects late Egyptian grammatical features as well as a possible accommodation to local topography in the use of *int* (= valley).[28] The latest quotation of the saying which has been discovered is found in an embalming ritual of the first or second century CE, nearly 26 centuries after *Hor-dedef* first offered his advice!—'Your tomb of the west is made beautiful, so that it makes excellent your plans of the necropolis' (*smnḫ.t.w 'ḥ' t.k nty imnt/ siḫr.f sḫrw.k ḫrt-nṯr*).[29] In this case, the verb *siḫr* now refers to successful plans rather than splendid monuments.

In the preceding examples, it has been observed how the original text of *Hor-dedef*'s words was revised through the centuries in a variety of ways in order to adapt it to new contexts. It is even more illuminating, however, to note the differing attitudes of the writers toward the statement which they are quoting. In the *Harper Song of Khai-Inheret* of the twentieth dynasty, the harper's words, which paraphrase *Hor-dedef*'s advice, offer comfort to the deceased and his family that he had done all that he could to assure his continued existence beyond death: 'Reckoned up are your works of the necropolis, beautiful is your place

26. Simpson (ed.), *The Literature of Ancient Egypt*, p. 340; G. Posener, 'Le début de l'enseignement de Hardjedef', *REg* 9 (1952), pp. 109-17.

27. Brunner, 'Zitate aus Lebenslehren', pp. 114-15.

28. Brunner, 'Zitate aus Lebenslehren', pp. 115-16; Wilson, *ANET*, p. 420.

29. Brunner, 'Zitate aus Lebenslehren', p. 116.

3. *Quotation in Ancient Near East Literature*   125

of the west' (*ipt kꜣwt.k nt ẖrt-nṯr/ mnḫ.t st.k nt imnt.t*).[30]

Less positive toward the ancient sage's counsel is another Song of the Harper, the so-called *Antef* song which comments, 'Now I have heard the sayings of Iyemhotep and Hor-dedef, which are quoted in the proverbs so much', and then skeptically queries, 'What are their cult places? Their walls are dismantled and their cult places exist no more, as if they had never been.' Although this is not another citation of the much-quoted saying of *Hor-dedef* which is being examined here, it may be a direct allusion, that is, *Hor-dedef*'s counsel proved to be fallible even in his own situation, for his own monument has crumbled into nothingness.[31] Discontentment with *Hor-dedef*'s counsel is also expressed in *Merikare* in which an ethical dimension is added: 'Make excellent your place of the west, beautify your tomb of the necropolis with equity and with the doing of truth' (*sikr st/ḥwt.k nt imnt/ smnḫ ḥwt/st.k nt ẖrt-nṯr m 'kꜣm irt mꜣ't*). In addition to reversing the order of the clauses and substituting *ḥwt* for *pr*, Merikare transforms the meaning by suggesting that moral behavior rather than tomb construction will perpetuate one's existence.[32]

A final step in the assessment of *Hor-dedef*'s ideology may be reflected in the Chester Beatty text *The Immortality of Writers*: 'Better is a book than a well-built house, than tomb-chapels in the west' (*ꜣḫ šfd r pr ḳd/ r ḥwt ḥr imn.t.t*). Buildings may crumble but books remain![33]

30. Brunner, 'Zitate aus Lebenslehren', p. 116; and M. Lichtheim, 'The Songs of the Harpers', *JNES* 4 (1945), pp. 178-212 (201-202).

31. Simpson (ed.), *The Literature of Ancient Egypt*, pp. 306-307. Lichtheim, 'The Songs of the Harpers', p. 193 n. e, suggests the allusion being made. For a recent study of this text, see M.V. Fox, 'A Study of Antef', *Or* 46 (1977), pp. 393-423.

32. Brunner, 'Zitate aus Lebenslehren', pp. 113-14. The transposition of elements or clauses within the parallel lines has been seen by some as typical of quotation. See above, pp. 74-77, and Beentjes, 'Inverted Quotations in the Bible'. G. Fecht, *Der Habgierige und die Maat in der Lehre des Ptahhotep (5. und 19. Maxime)* (ADAIK, 1; Glückstadt: Verlag J.J. Augustin, 1958), p. 42, suggests that *Merikare*'s ethical addition is a 'free quotation' from *Ptahhotep* l. 312, which reads 'The man who is exact in right-doing and who walks according to its procedure will long endure' (*wꜣ ḥ z 'qꜣ.f mꜣ't*) (Simpson [ed.], *The Literature of Ancient Egypt*, p. 167). The likelihood of such dependence is increased by the fact that this is the only section of *Ptahhotep* that mentions the tomb (l. 315). See also Posener, 'Le debút de l'enseignement de Hardjedef', pp. 115-16.

33. Posener, 'Le début de l'enseignement de Hardjedef', p. 116; and Lichtheim, *Ancient Egyptian Literature*, II, p. 177. The following lines continue this theme.

To be sure, one could argue that the ancient Egyptian's common concern with making preparation for the afterlife might lead one to utter something similar without consciously 'quoting' *Hor-dedef*. However, the fact that the statement has an identifiable literary source and parallelistic formulation suggests that is is legitimate to trace the modifications of the utterance even if it had attained quasi-proverbial status.

Although few statements are reused as often and in as many different contexts as these words of *Hor-dedef*, it is not uncommon for the language of a given saying to re-emerge as much as two millennia later than its initial formulation. Alfred Grimm discusses a striking case in which an Old Kingdom pyramid text is 'quoted' by a Ptolemaic ritual text. Here Grimm claims that a grave cult ritual was taken up in a temple ritual, the former reading 'The incense is laid upon the flame, the incense glows' (*dii sntr ḥr sdt/ wbn sntr*), while the latter's revision reads 'The fragrance of the god (is) upon the flame, its smoke glows' (*sty-ntr ḥr sdt/ wbn ḥty.f*). It is Grimm's opinion that *both* texts may be derived from a common, unpreserved papyrus *Vorlage*, but in either respect, a quotation has occurred.[34]

In a parallel like this, Brunner's two criteria for dependence both apply: the two passages share three out of five words. However, is it not just as likely that this is merely a similar ritual practice rather than a literary quotation? The 'two keyword' criterion seems unable to distinguish clearly between true quotation and formulaic, metaphorical and common gesture expressions such as the allegedly hedonistic 'follow the heart' (*šms ib*),[35] or 'follow the happy day' (*šms ḥrw nfr*),[36] 'the breath of the mouth' (*ṯ3w n r3*),[37] 'cause them to do the dogwalk' (*irt*

---

34. A. Grimm, 'Ein Zitat aus den Pyramidentexten in einem ptolemäischen Ritualtext des Horus-Tempels von Edfu: Edfou III, 130.14-15 = Pyr. 376b (Spr. 269). Zur Tradition altägyptischer Texte: Voruntersuchungen zu einer Theorie der Gattungen', *GM* 31 (1979), pp. 35-46. For other ritual 'quotations' see D.P. Silverman, 'Coffin Text Spell 902 and its Later Usages in the New Kingdom', in J. Leclant (ed.), *L'égyptologie en 1979: Axes prioritaires de recherches* (2 vols.; Colloques internationeaux du Centre National de la Recherche Scientifique, 595; Paris: Centre National de la Recherche Scientifique, 1982), I, pp. 67-70; and M. Gilula, '*Hirtengeschichte* 17-22 = *CT* VII 36 m-r', *GM* 29 (1978), pp. 21-22; along with J.R. Ogdon, 'CT VII, 36 i-r = Spell 836', *GM* 58 (1982), pp. 59-64.

35. D. Lorton, 'The Expression *Šms-ib*', *JARCE* 7 (1968), pp. 41-54.

36. D. Lorton, 'The Expression *'Iri Ḥrw Nfr*', *JARCE* 21 (1975), pp. 23-31.

37. P. Vernus, 'La Formula "Le souffle de la bouche" au moyen empire', *REg* 28 (1976), pp. 139-45, notes 16 examples.

šmt tsmw),[38] 'each embraced his companion' (*s(t) nb(t) ḥpt snw.f/s*),[39] 'from foreign land to foreign land' (*m ḫȝs.t r ḫȝs.t*).[40]

Also uncertain are proverbial-sounding sayings such as 'one does not know what may be in the heart' (*n rḫ.n.tw wnnt m ib*),[41] 'it is what God commands that happens' (*wḏt nṯr pw ḫprt/ḫpr<ti>.si*),[42] 'no one knows his lot when he plans the morrow' (*nn wn rḫ šḥrw.f/ kȝ.f dwȝw*), [43] and 'It is better for the one who does it than for the one to whom it is done' (*ȝḫ n irr r irrw n.f*).[44] Of course, it is possible that a particular author achieved a formulation so striking that it attained proverbial status (*geflügeltes Wort*), but the mere occurrence of such a saying in two texts, even if one seems intentionally adapted to its context, is no certain proof that one is dependent on the other.

A further questionable procedure is to assume a quotation even when the verbal overlap is quite minimal. Kaplony cites a line from *The Instruction of Mtty*: 'There is no bread for the rebel against him in the necropolis' (*[nis wn]t iw tȝ n rmt sb.f ḥr-f m ḫrt-nṯr*), as 'reminding one' of *The Instruction of Sehetibrê*: 'There is no grave for the one who rebels against his majesty' (*nn is n sbi ḥr ḥm.f*),[45] the texts sharing only *sbi-ḥr*. Griffith notes a parallel between *Ptahhotep*: 'Being profitable to the one who shall listen and woe for the one who shall transgress it' (*m ȝḫ.t n sḏm.tfy / m wggt n nty r th.t st*), and *Amenemope*: 'It is profitable to put them in your heart, but misery to him that neglects them' (*ȝḫ pȝ rd.t st m ib.k / wg iw n pȝ wnw st*). Here only the antithetical word pair *ȝḫ/wgg* is in common. The two possible responses to instruction—to accept or to reject—are too universal to claim dependence.[46] Finally,

38. Brunner, 'Zitate aus Lebenslehren', pp. 145-47; and A.H. Gardiner, 'The Earliest Manuscripts of the Instruction of Amenemmes I', in *Mélanges Maspero*. I. *Orient Ancien* (3 vols.; Cairo: Imprimerie de l'institut français d'archéologie orientale, 1935–38), pp. 478-96 (494-95).

39. Simpson, 'Allusions', p. 51 n. 11.

40. A. Alt, 'Zwei Vermutungen zur Geschichte des Sinuhe', *ZÄS* 58 (1923), pp. 48-50.

41. Gunn, 'Some Middle-Egyptian Proverbs', pp. 283-84.

42. Gunn, 'Some Middle-Egyptian Proverbs', p. 284.

43. Gunn, 'Some Middle-Egyptian Proverbs', p. 283.

44. Brunner, 'Zitate aus Lebenslehren', pp. 160-61; and Vernus, 'La formula "Le souffle de la bouche" au Moyen empire', p. 140.

45. P. Kaplony, 'Eine neue Weisheitslehre aus dem alten Reich (Die Lehre des Mttj) in der altägyptischen Weisheitsliteratur', *Or* NS 37 (1968), pp. 1-62 (45).

46. F.L. Griffith, 'The Teaching of Amenophis the Son of Kanakht: Papyrus

Brunner suggests an allusion to *Ptahhotep*: 'According as you reach me [i.e. my position], your body will be uninjured' (*mi pḥ.k wi/ ḥ'w.k wdȝ*), in *Merikare*: 'Then you will reach me with no one your accuser' (*iḥ pḥ.k wi nn srḥy.k*). Here only *pḥ.k wi* is in both expressions, although Brunner seeks to account for the latter's divergences.[47]

Such a cautionary note, however, should not be taken as casting doubt on all alleged quotations. Indeed, the evidence is often quite convincing. Many quotations involve texts of the same or similar genres, with parallels found within instructions, ritual texts, hymns or historical inscriptions. For example Žabkar has discussed the use of *Pyramid Text Utterance* (600 §§1652-3) to accompany a relief in Room X of the Temple of Philadelphus, editing it to fit the spatial limitations of the inscription and adapting it, applying the ritual benefits (Atum's embrace) not to the king, as in the original text, but to *Ḥaṭhor-Isis*.[48] Just as often, however, the quotations are incorporated from one genre into another. *Sinuhe*'s praise of Sesostris I's military might: 'None can stand in his presence' (*n 'ḥ'.n.tw m ḥ'w.f*) is re-employed in King Piye's victory stela description of the capture of Memphis (*n 'ḥ'.tw m hȝ.f*), conspicuous by the fact that both the preceding and following lines of the latter are framed in the second person plural.[49] A scribe tells his lazy son, 'You are in the situation of him who said, "I am killed, my asses are seized, and the complaint is taken from my mouth"' (*ḫdb.k (wi) iṯ 'wȝ <t>.i/ nḥm imw m rȝ.i*) an obvious allusion to *The Eloquent Peasant*: 'You beat me, you steal my chattels, you even take the complaint from my mouth' (*ḥw.k wi 'wȝ.k ḥnw.i nḥm k rf nḥwt m rȝ.i*).[50] In

B.M. 10474', *JEA* 12 (1926), pp. 191-231 (199); and Brunner, 'Zitate aus Lebenslehren', pp. 129-31.

47. Brunner, 'Zitate', pp. 138-39. Fecht, *Der Habgierige und die Maat in der Lehre des Ptahhotep*, pp. 27 and 51, sees a very complex quotation of *Ptahhotep* here. *Merikare* develops both meanings of the former's key words, *'ḥ'w* = lifetime, pile/treasure, *zp(j)* = deed/matter, remain, a rhetorical feature called 'amphibole': 'The disentanglement of the two-fold meaning and the mention of the key words probably is the only possible means here of pointing to the literary expressions of the intellectual tradition.'

48. L.W. Žabkar, 'Adaptation of Ancient Egyptian Texts to the Temple Ritual at Philae', *JEA* 66 (1980), pp. 127-36.

49. N.-C. Grimal, *La stèle triomphale de Pi('ankh)y au musée du Caire: Je 48862 et 47086–47089* (Cairo: Institut français d'archéologie orientale, 1981), pp. 123-24, 288, 293. Lichtheim, *Ancient Egyptian Literature*, III, p. 76.

50. See n. 11 above.

these quotations from narrative classics, a similar circumstance justified the appropriation of the same language.

In other citations, advice from instructions is used in autobiographies and legal texts to express the fact that it has, in fact, been carried out and the associated benefits are expected to accrue. *Ptahhotep* advises, when you are at the table of a superior, 'do not pierce him with many stares, … let thy face be downcast *until* he addresses you' (*m stiw sw m gmh ʿ$ȝ$ / hr.k m hrw r wšd.f tw*) and Amenemhet, high priest of Amon, reports that, with respect to his own father, he did not 'pierce him with many glances, my face was downcast *when* he spoke with me' (*n st sw m gmh ʿ$ȝ$ / hr.i m hr-i mdw.f hr.i*). In other words, Amenemhet excceded *Ptahhotep*'s demands.[51] In these and many other examples, it appears that the quotation is made not simply because of a felicitous expression of which the author was aware but rather because of the continuing relevance or authority of its contents.

Finally, there are passages in which the language of a well-known text is reused, even though the situations are not that similar, the words being quoted precisely in order to gain the reader's attention by repeating a familiar saying and to create an aura of authority and similarity of context. For example, the solemn introductory words of the *Loyalist Instruction*: 'I speak a great thing, I cause you to hear. I cause you to know: the conduct of eternity, the course of true life' (*dd.i wrt/ di.i sdm.tn/ di.i rh.tn/ shr n nhh / sšr ʿnh n mȝ'w*) are later used to introduce the concern of Neferhotep to restore the Osiris cult and, in an abbreviated form, in a Middle Kingdom stele reporting on a king's expedition as well as in an inscription of Hatshepsut telling of her Punt expedition.[52]

Guglielmi has offered a helpful summary of the formal and rhetorical functions of quotation. Formally, it can serve a structural purpose, as an introduction (*Ostracon O.I.C. 12074* begins with a quotation from *The Shipwrecked Sailor*); as a caesura and commentary, often making up the second stich of a parallelistic line; as a conclusion to a composition or section thereof (the *Harper Song of Onuris-Cha* concludes with a *Sinuhe* quotation); and as a strophic component. (*The Admonitions of an Egyptian Sage* consists of three sections dominated by self-quotation

51. Brunner, 'Zitate aus Lebenslehren', pp. 123-24; A.H. Gardiner, 'The Tomb of Amenemhet, High-Priest of Amon', *ZÄS* 47 (1910), pp. 87-99. The first half of the quotation follows the text of Papyrus Prisse, the second half London 2.

52. Brunner, 'Zitate aus Lebenslehren', pp. 156-60.

and 'foreign' quotation, with two intervening sections of equal length which are devoid of quotation, i.e. 8 vv. / 40 vv. / 25 vv. / 40 vv. / 7 vv.)

Rhetorically, quotation can be used to clarify, demonstrate and confirm, illustrate, compare, contrast and criticize, even to the extent of irony, parody and satire. Sometimes the quotation is intentionally ambiguous or hidden ('cryptic quotation'). It can serve to instruct, admonish, warn or threaten. Through its power of association it can cause another context or setting to impinge on the quoting text's context. A vivid example of this is when *Ptahhotep* ('He whom god loves is a hearkener, [but] he whom god hates cannot hear') is quoted in the *Admonitions* 13.1. Guglielmi translates: 'It was answered: "The one is, to be sure, beloved, but the other is hated, and that means, that it is everywhere the case, that they have become miserable characters!"' Here the quotation is used to contrast *Ptahhotep*'s ordered, intact world with the sage's miserable reality.[53]

It is apparent that quotation was a recognized component of ancient Egyptian rhetoric. Whatever revisions were deemed necessary to adapt a previously formulated saying or phrase to a new context were tolerated, as long as the original text was not thereby effaced beyond recognition. The rediscovery of these sometimes brilliant, sometimes pedantic or even misconstrued borrowings is useful not simply for textual criticism and the reconstruction of intellectual history, but also as a means of gaining fascinating insights into the way in which a living literary tradition was preserved and continued to function authoritatively for over two millennia.

Quotation in Mesopotamian Literature

In examining the literature of Mesopotamia several similarities can be discovered. As in the Egyptian examples just studied, quotations in Sumerian and Akkadian are especially prominent in Wisdom literature but are also incorporated from one genre into another, often appearing

---

53. Guglielmi, 'Zur Adaption und Funktion von Zitaten', pp. 352, 358-64. For Ostracon Oriental Institute 12074, see W. Guglielmi, 'Eine "Lehre" für einen reiselustigen Sohn', *WO* 14 (1983), pp. 147-68 (153). For the *Admonitions of an Egyptian Sage*, see G. Fecht, 'Ägyptische Zweifel am Sinn des Opfers: Admonitions 5, 7-9', *ZÄS* 100 (1973), pp. 6-16 (8). For *Ptahhotep* 545/546 (Déraud's numbering), see Wilson, *ANET*, p. 414.

centuries later. A special problem is posed by Sumerian, for many of the repeated phrases of Akkadian may have their origin in a Sumerian text, so that the extent of verbal correspondence to earlier formulations is more difficult to determine. In terms of its scholarly treatment, most quotations have been cited on an individual basis rather than as a part of a more comprehensive synthetic study such as Brunner's. Nevertheless, what can be learned from an examination of these citations will serve as a helpful complement to the survey of Egyptian examples.

Even a superficial overview of the verbal parallels cited by Assyriologists reveals two clear contrasts with the work of their Egyptological colleagues. First of all, in terms of content, the parallels are generally more extensive than those cited in Egyptian. Secondly, in terms of approach, these scholars are more cautious, most of them hesiating to use the term 'quotation'. This is, indeed, just the reverse of what one might expect and merits further consideration.

One perspective is that of Bendt Alster who views most repeated language in *The Instructions of Suruppak* and other Sumerian literary works as formulaic in nature. Dependent on the studies of Milman Parry in the Homeric epics, Alster sees the 'repeated use of the same phrases to express the same ideas' as characteristic of 'a traditional poetic language', rather than being the result of the author's conscious reuse, whether the repetition is within or between compositions.[54] In Alster's opinion, this rhetorical feature is primarily due to the fact that the Sumerian language is highly idiomatic in nature and its poetic diction is completely unified. Standardization has produced identity of idiom, grammatical form and meaning.

However, this is not to suggest that Alster claims that Sumerian literature is exclusively formulaic; he also acknowledges the presence of many proverbs within *Suruppak*, some of them being freely revised to fit their new setting, and even admits that the same phrases may occasionally express different ideas in different contexts. Because of his perspective, verbal parallels are never attributed to intentional quotation—one almost feels that even the possibility has been excluded by definition. Nevertheless, this does not lessen the task of the interpreter, for each parallel phrase must be analyzed both in terms of its formulation and its contextual function. Alster's approach, if embraced in its entirety might bring the 'quest for quotation' to a jolting halt, but,

---

54. B. Alster, *The Instructions of Suruppak: A Sumerian Proverb Collection* (Copenhagen: Akademisk Forlag, 1974–75), p. 20.

used with caution, clearly offers many helpful insights into the source and proper assessment of many of the repeated phrases found within Sumerian literature.

A related, but not identical, label given to verbal parallels is the Greek derivative 'topos', which is used, in preference to 'quotation', by Hallo, Hallo and van Dijk, Wiseman, Landsberger and Oppenheim, although Wiseman uses it in addition to and almost synonymously with 'quotation'.[55] 'Topos' is rather loosely defined by these scholars as a group of related stereotypical or proverbial expressions which deal with a given characteristic, action or subject, 'a stock of phrases, lines, and even whole stanzas at the disposal of a school of poets who created from them ever-new combinations'.[56] Although these topoi—such as the 'fleeing like a fluttering bird', 'the quiet city', 'the open gate of heaven', 'height of heaven', 'the blessings of inundation', 'woman as net, trap, or pit'[57]—were often 'strung up ... without much inner logic

55. Hallo, 'New Viewpoints on Cuneiform Literature', pp. 19-20; W.W. Hallo and J.J.A. van Dijk, *The Exaltation of Inanna* (New Haven: Yale University Press, 1968), p. 6; D.J. Wiseman, 'A Lipšur Litany from Nimrud', *Iraq* 31 (1969), pp. 175-83 (176); B. Landsberger, 'Jahreszeiten in Sumerisch-Akkadischen', *JNES* 8 (1949), pp. 248-97 (281); A.L. Oppenheim, 'A New Prayer to the "Gods of the Night" ', in *Studia biblica et orientalia. III. Oriens antiquus* (AnBib,12; Pontifical Biblical Institute, 1959), pp. 282-301.

56. Hallo, 'New Viewpoints on Cuneiform Literature', p. 20. Hallo also notes the discussion of D.G. Bradley, 'The Topos as a Form in the Pauline Paraenesis', *JBL* 72 (1953), pp. 238-46. See also T.Y. Mullins, 'Topos as a New Testament Form', *JBL* 99 (1980), pp. 541-47.

57. 'fluttering bird'—Hallo and van Dijk; 'quiet city' and 'open gate of heaven'—Oppenheim; 'blessings of inundation'—Landsberger; 'woman as net, trap, pit'—E. Ebeling, 'Quellen zur Kenntnis der babylonischen Religion II', *Mitteilungen der vorderasiatischen Gesellschaft* 23.2 (1919), pp. 1-82 (67); 'height of heaven'—The full formulation of this topos is proverbial in nature: 'Who is so tall as to ascend to the heavens? Who is so broad as to compass the underworld?' (*ajjû arku ša ana šamê elû ajjû rapšu ša erṣetim ugammeru*), found in the *Dialogue of Pessimism*, lines 83-89, W.G. Lambert, *Babylonian Wisdom Literature* (Oxford: Clarendon Press, 1960), p. 327. A similar proverb is found in the Sumerian *Gilgamesh*, S.N. Kramer, 'Gilgamesh and the Land of the Living', *JCS* 1 (1944), pp. 1-46 (35). Elsewhere, the topos of the high heaven and broad earth is used repeatedly; see the examples listed by Lambert, *Babylonian Wisdom Literature*, p. 327; Hallo and van Dijk, *The Exaltation of Inanna*, pp. 30-31, 60; and A. Sjöberg, *Der Mondgott Nanna-Suen in der sumerischen Überlieferung* (Stockholm: Almqvist & Wiksell, 1960), pp. 80-84.

or structural connection in longwinded conglomerations of pious phraseology' by 'dull scribes',[58] occasionally they were employed with remarkable freedom, creativity and beauty.

The concept of 'topoi' has two advantages. First of all, since they are viewed as traditional, there is no need to determine dependence or trace the topos back to its origin. At most, one can seek the earliest attestation of a particular topos. Secondly, since the topic presented is more important than the actual wording, little or no attention needs to be paid to verbal correspondence. Hence, Oppenheim is able to discuss adequately four instances of his topoi in English translation alone.[59] Once again, one must admit that the concept of topoi conforms well to what seems to have been common scribal practice and eliminates the compulsion to always seek the elusive 'author' or origin of a striking formulation. Nevertheless, in cases where verbal correspondence is extensive, the idea of quotation is still a more attractive alternative. It hardly is convincing that 'topoi' can produce even identical stanzas of poetic language.

A number of Assyriologists do not hesitate to use the term 'quotation' or to speak of 'direct dependence'. Speiser employs it in the most traditional manner, assuming literary borrowing whenever parallels appear. His two examples, however, are far from persuasive. In one study he notes a similarity between *The Poor Man of Nippur*, line 73, '[before him?] he kissed the ground before him' (*maḫaršu iššiq qaqqaru maḫaršu*) and *Enuma Eliš* 3.69, which, on the basis of variant readings, had a posited text in some copies of 'he bowed down and kissed the ground before them' (*uškēnma iššiq qaqqaru maḫaršum*).[60] In seeking to determine the direction of dependence, Speiser reasons that *Enuma Eliš* is not likely to have borrowed from 'a secular work of a rather frivolous nature';[61] rather *The Poor Man of Nippur* lifted the whole line from the 'canonical'[62] composition, the apprentice scribe, according to

---

58. Oppenheim, 'A New Prayer to the "Gods of the Night" ', p. 294.

59. Oppenheim, 'A New Prayer to the "Gods of the Night" ', pp. 282-301.

60. E.A. Speiser, 'Sultantepe Tablet 38.73 and Enuma Eliš III 69', *JCS* 11 (1957), pp. 43-44. This appears to be simply a stereotypical description of a common gesture. See M.I. Gruber, *Aspects of Nonverbal Communication in the Ancient Near East* (Studia Pohl, 12; 2 vols.; Rome: Biblical Institute Press, 1980).

61. Speiser, 'Sultantepe Tablet 38.73 and Enuma Eliš III 69', p. 44.

62. With regard to the question of the 'canonization' of Mesopotamian literature, see Hallo, 'New Viewpoints on Cuneiform Literature', pp. 22-26; and

the colophon, misreading the first word on the basis of the final word in the line. However, it seems more likely that this phrase simply describes a common gesture, as another parallel, which Speiser also cites, helps to confirm: *The Myth of Nergal and Ereshkigal*, 1.28 and 3.49, 'kneeling down, he kissed the ground before her' (*kmis(i) iššiq qaqqaru maḫriša*).

Another parallel which Speiser cites is line 76 of *The Dialogue of Pessimism*: 'Go up on to the ancient ruin heaps and walk about' (*ilīma ina muḫḫi tillāni labīrūti itallak*). In Speiser's opinion, this is 'an all too obvious borrowing from the Gilgamesh Epic': 'climb up on top of the wall of Uruk and walk about' (*elīma ana muḫḫi dūri ša Uruk imtallak*).[63] Lambert, however, counters that one is in no position to know if the author was citing *Gilgamesh*. Rather, in his opinion, Speiser once again 'underestimates the extent and exaggerates the importance of clichés'.[64]

In clear contrast to the two parallels just discussed is the impressive example noted by Borger in which a treaty between *Marduk-zākir-šumi I* of Babylon and *Šamši-Adad V* of Assyria concludes with a series of curses which is drawn almost totally from *The Code of Hammurabi*, composed an entire millennium earlier.[65] Even though curse formulae tend to be stereotypical, the degree of correspondence here is convincing. If Borger's reconstruction of the text is correct, out of 14 consecutive lines of the treaty, less than half a dozen words are not found in *Hammurabi* and nearly 100 are shared. Even more remarkable is the fact that their sequence within the code is left entirely undisturbed. No clear editing principle emerges, other than the expected elimination of first person comments of *Hammurabi*, and the possible climactic patterning of the curses so that the first curses are to afflict just the

---

W.G. Lambert, 'Ancestors, Authors, and Canonicity', *JCS* 11 (1957), pp. 1-14.

63. E.A. Speiser, 'The Case of the Obliging Servant', *JCS* 8 (1954), pp. 98-105 (104). The line is found in the *Gilgamesh Epic* 1.1.16 and 11.363. Speiser, *ANET*, p. 73 n. 6 emends im-ta-lak 'take counsel' to it-ta-lak on the basis of the reading in Tablet XI.

64. Lambert, *Babylonian Wisdom Literature*, pp. 140-41.

65. R. Borger, 'Marduk-zākir-šumi I und der Kodex Ḫammurapi', *Or* NS 34 (1965), pp. 168-69. Since Hammurabi's Laws were copied as scribal exercises for a thousand years after his time, it is not surprising to find the curses reappearing in this ninth-century treaty, A.R. Millard, private communication. See D.R. Hillers, *Treaty Curses and the Old Testament Prophets* (BibOr, 16; Rome: Pontifical Biblical Institute, 1964).

monarch while the final curses call for the destruction of his entire land as well.

Equally extensive are the numerous parallels between the *Gilgamesh Epic* and other mythological texts which Tigay studied. He notes that seven lines describing the nether world (*Gilgamesh Epic* 7.4.33-39) are identical to a passage which appears in *The Descent of Ishtar to the Netherworld* (Nineveh recension 4–10) and *Nergal and Ereshkigal* (2 [end]–3.5). Because there are further parallels between *Gilgamesh* and *Ishtar*, Tigay acknowledges the possibility of 'reciprocal influence', although the use of a common source as well as conventional material is also an option. After examining several further examples in which the parallels do not occur in all recensions, he concludes:

> This implies that not all of the parallels were put into the texts by their authors, but that some were added by later copyists. Perhaps on one occasion a copyist of *Gilgamesh* added a line from *Ishtar*. A copyist of *Ishtar*, perhaps many years later, borrowed another line from *Gilgamesh*. The process may have been repeated a few times, and in this way the number of parallels grew.[66]

The most remarkable parallel is the account of the flood in *Gilgamesh* 11.15-196 which is taken from *The Atrahasis Epic*. Tigay argues that this is the nature and direction of the borrowing because of the virtually identical lines, the fact that the flood story is integral to the plot of *Atrahasis* but incidental to *Gilgamesh*, the list of gods with which the former commences is inappropriate in the latter, and Atrahasis's name is used once in *Gilgamesh* instead of Utnapishtim. Tigay notes various differences between the two texts: grammatical forms, synonyms, additions, reformulations with or without changing meaning, assimilations, and expansions and abridgments. Most striking is the elimination in *Gilgamesh* of any reference to divine hunger and thirst. Tigay's discussion of these divergences, as well of the harmonizations and non-harmonizations of the borrowed material with the rest of *Gilgamesh*, gives some indication of how fruitful the study of verbal parallels can be when the direction of dependence is virtually certain.[67]

Lambert has also noted a number of intriguing verbal parallels

---

66. J.H. Tigay, *The Evolution of the Gilgamesh Epic* (Philadelphia: University of Pennsylvania Press, 1982), p. 174. Tigay lists these parallels on pp. 125, 126 n. 52.

67. Tigay, *The Evolution of the Gilgamesh Epic*, pp. 214-40.

involving Wisdom literature in which literary dependence is likely. He notes that three lines of K 2765, perhaps a prayer, are almost identical to *Ludlul Bel Nemiqi* 1.52-54,[68] and that *Ludlul* 2.77-78 corresponds to PBS I/I 14 obv. 10-11,[69] a '*Dingir.šà.dib.ba*' incantation for appeasing a god's wrath. *The Counsels of Wisdom*, lines 143-44 and 147, are close to *ABL* 614 rev. 8-9, a late Assyrian letter of obscure content,[70] while its lines 62-66 appear at the end of a bilingual incantation, in Lambert's words, 'certainly a direct borrowing of the text in its present form'.[71] So close is the relationship in the last example cited that he offers it as text source 'F' in the critical apparatus of the *Counsels*. The parallel was already noted by Ugnad who felt that it had 'nothing at all to do' with the incantation.[72] This may be overstating the case, for earlier in the incantation these questions are asked: 'With whom should I have eaten...drunk...made merry...clothed myself on a day?'. The *Counsels* encourages one to do good even to an enemy; then, after some damaged lines, advises 'Give food to eat, beer to drink' before the above cited parallel passage commences.[73] It may be that this text was chosen to conclude the exorcism not only because it answers the question posed earlier, but also because it promises the one who performs it *Šamaš's* favor, a comfort to the one confronting an alu demon![74]

---

68. Lambert, *Babylonian Wisdom Literature*, p. 288.

69. Lambert, *Babylonian Wisdom Literature*, p. 293. See W.G. Lambert, '*Dingir.Šà.dib.ba* Incantations', *JNES* 33 (1974), pp. 267-322.

70. Lambert, *Babylonian Wisdom Literature*, pp. 315, 397; and E. Behrens, *Assyrisch-Babylonische Briefe kultischen Inhalts aus der Sargonidenzeit* (LSS, 2.1; Leipzig: J.C. Hinrichs, 1906), p. 7.

71. Lambert, *Babylonian Wisdom Literature*, p. 97. See also G. Meier, review of *A Dictionary of Assyrian Chemistry and Geology* (Oxford: Oxford University Press, 1936), by R. Campbell Thompson, in *AfO* 13 (1939–41), pp. 71-74.

72. A. Ugnad, 'Zur akkadischen Weisheitsliteratur', *OLZ* 23 (1920) pp. 249-50. This may be the case, since the text has been identified as a 'school text' with quotations extracted from several genres, the choice of which may have been arbitrary; A. Falkenstein, *Die Haupttypen der sumerischen Beschwörung literarisch untersucht* (LSS, NS 1; Leipzig: J.C. Hinrichs, 1931), p. 4.

73. H.F. Lutz, *Selected Sumerian and Babylonian Texts* (PBS, 1.2; Philadelphia: The University Museum, 1919), pp. 66-67; R.D. Biggs, *ANET*, p. 595.

74. Lambert is helpful in pointing out these striking parallels, but disappointing in making no comment regarding why the text might have been quoted. He is one of those guilty of Alster's charge, *The Instructions of Suruppak*, p. 23: 'Entire lines which are repeated verbatim in other texts are sometimes quoted at great length, but

Another possible quotation involves the *Advice to a Prince* that begins, 'If a king does not heed justice' (*šarru ana dīni la iqūl*, 'if' is consistently left unexpressed). This is 'borrowed directly' from the first protasis of Tablet 53 of the omen series *Šumma ālu*, which uses the positive formulation, 'if a king heeds justice' (*šumma šarru ana dīnim iqūl*),[75] although the expression may be too frequently used to be significant.

A final example, and one of the most interesting, is discussed fully by Lambert and Millard in their treatment of *Atrahasis*. One of the reports compiled by Bel-lesi, an incantation priest of a late Assyrian king, cites the following lines from Tablet 2.2.11-13, 16, 19, as advice for dealing with drought:

> Seek the door of Adad, bring meal,
> In front of it. The offering of sesame meal may be pleasing to him.
> He may rain down a mist in the morning,
> So that the field will furtively bear water.

and adds, 'When rain has become scarce in the land of Akkad, do this'.[76] This direct quotation omits *Atrahasis* 14-15, 'then he [Adad] will be put to shame by the gift and will lift his hand', perhaps because it refers to the specific events of *Atrahasis*, and 17-18, 'and may furtively rain down a dew in the night', perhaps as an unnecessary parallelism. Only three changes are made in the epic's text, two of them involving the substitution of more common words for less, and one consisting of the use of 'water' (*māmū*) for 'grain' (*šu u*) in line 19. According to Lambert and Millard, this substitution could be accidental but, if deliberate, would emphasize the quotation's purpose through its use of the word 'water'. This appropriation makes a powerful statement: 'what was done on divine instigation in the beginning can be

one will rarely find any reflections as to how they came into being, and the ideas attached to these phrases are practically never analyzed.' In the preceding example from the *Counsels of Wisdom* (n. 70), Lambert cites the parallel without even noting that the phrase introducing the repeated passage may mark it as a quotation of earlier material: 'Since you are learned, read in the tablet ... ', Biggs, *ANET*, p. 595, although Lambert translates line 142, paralleled by 154, *ina iḫ zikama amur ina tuppi*, as 'In your wisdom, study the tablet', *Babylonian Wisdom Literature*, p. 105.

75. Lambert, *Babylonian Wisdom Literature*, p. 110.

76. W.G. Lambert and A.R. Millard, *Atra-hasis: The Babylonian Story of the Flood* (Oxford: Clarendon Press, 1969), pp. 27-28.

repeated at intervals throughout history'.[77]

The most recent survey of the phenomenon of literary borrowing in Mesopotamian literature is by B.R. Foster in the general introduction to his anthology of Akkadian literature, *Before the Muses*. Foster addresses the subject under the rubric 'intertextuality', noting several types of 'intertextual relationships'.[78] Some of these involve intra-generic borrowing (magical spells occurring in several versions and narrative sections being incorporated into later epics), while others are inter-generic (monumental inscriptions and hymns alluding to narrative epics, belles lettres drawing on omens series). The *Creation Epic*, probably stemming from the 'Mature Period' (1500–1000 BCE), both utilizes a variety of earlier traditions and, in turn, is often alluded to or quoted in late devotional compositions.

Foster uses a variety of terms to describe these verbal parallels: 'literary allusions', 'quotations' and 'borrowings', without defining them as distinct categories. He illustrates how the borrowing texts often transfer the accomplishments of central figures in the borrowed texts to

77. Lambert and Millard, *Atra-hasis*, pp. 27-28. For other examples of verbal parallels, see W.W. Hallo, 'Notes from the Babylonian Collection. I. Nungal in the Egal: An Introduction to Colloquial Sumerian?', *JCS* 31 (1979), pp. 161-65 ('an extract tablet combining quotations from numerous compositions, apparently in a fixed ... order', p. 161); E. Reiner, 'The Babylonian Fürstenspiegel in Practice', in J.N. Postgate (ed.), *Societies and Languages of the Ancient Near East: Studies in Honour of I.M. Diakonoff* (Warminster: Aris & Phillips, 1982), pp. 320-23 (a Neo-Babylonian letter to Esarhaddon quotes the *Advice to a Prince*); K. Watanabe, 'Rekonstruktion von Vte 438 aus Grund von Erra III a 17', *Assur* 3 (1983), pp. 164-66 (a vassal treaty of Esarhaddon quotes the *Erra Epic*).

78. B.R. Foster, *Before the Muses: An Anthology of Akkadian Literature* (2 vols.; Bethesda, MD: CDL Press, 1993), pp. 22-25. It is interesting to note that Foster utilizes the term 'intertextuality', the favored designation for verbal parallels in most contemporary studies. See also P. Derchain, 'Allusion, citation, intertextualité', in M. Minas and J. Zeidler (eds.), *Aspekte spätägyptischer Kultur: Festschrift für Erich Winter zum 65. Geburtstag* (Mainz: Philipp von Zabern, 1994), pp. 69-76, who discusses verbal parallels in ancient Egyptian texts.

Foster (*Before the Muses*) refers to a number of examples in his introduction, citing discussions in secondary literature, and lists numerous verbal parallels in his annotations to the various texts, cf. pp. 100, 159, 263, 492, 499, 594, 602, 603, 618, 626, 698, 720, 760. Unfortunately, he does not treat any of them in detail. In the second edition (1996), pp. 25-26, he notes several additional examples, including two lengthier parallels between *The Descent of Ishtar* 3.18 lines 19-20 and 106-108 in *Gilgamesh Epic* Tablet 6 lines 97-100 and Tablet 7.3 lines 19-22, respectively.

central figures in the next text, thus changing the 'intentions' of the borrowed material. He admits the difficulty of determining the direction of literary borrowing and remains cautious even when citing 'circumstantial reasons', such as when multiple allusions are 'concentrated in a single passage'.[79] One problem is that 'stock expressions' may point to 'common use of well-known material rather than borrowing'. This may apply especially to a considerable number of the noted parallels which consist merely of divine epithets and descriptions, precisely the type of formulations which one might expect to be repeated. Foster says little regarding the purposes which such borrowing served, though he claims that such material is sometimes misquoted or misapplied.[80]

The examples of quotation in Mesopotamian literature cited here indicate that, even though many of the brief verbal parallels may involve formulaic language or topoi, authors sometimes incorporated extensive passages or numerous phrases from earlier works into their new compositions. Unfortunately, since many of the texts containing these parallels presently are fragmentary, poorly understood, or without scholarly editions, it is often difficult to determine the underlying principles which motivate and guide such literary borrowing. As more texts are published and analyzed, no doubt more 'quotations' will emerge, shedding further light on the ancient writers' method. In the meantime, the parallels already noted deserve the careful interpretation which Alster recommends.

Quotation in Ugaritic Literature

Given the chronological, geographical and linguistic proximity of the Ras Shamra texts to the Old Testament, one would be remiss not to discuss the nature of verbal parallels within its literature. However, it appears, at this point in time, that quotation is rare or non-existent in the Ugaritic corpus. That is not to suggest that repeated passages are infrequent. Several types of repetition immediately come to mind. First, there are internal parallels, successive lines which are repeated within a given composition. Numerous actions are recorded not simply when they are carried out but also when they are commanded and/or reported

79. Foster, *Before the Muses*, p. 602: 'This hymn may allude to the Creation Epic', see also p. 603.
80. Foster, *Before the Muses*, pp. 25 and 618 n. 5.

to another. This type of parallel passage was first examined thoroughly by Franz Rosenthal, although he was interested primarily in their text-critical rather than their literary value.[81]

Secondly, there are lengthy passages which appear in more than one text. The most striking of these is the threefold repetition of the response to 'bad news', used to describe Anat, Athirat and Danel:

(No sooner espies she the gods,)	(*hlm 'nt tph ilm*)
Than Anat's feet do stumble.	*bh. p'hm ttt*
Behind her loins do break;	*b'dn.ksl.ttbr*
Above her face doth sweat:	*'ln.pnh td'.*
Bent are the joints of her loins,	*tġs. pnt.kslh*
Weakened those of her back.	*ảnš.dt zrh*
She lifts up her voice and cries.	*tšủ gh .wtṣh*[82]

Other than the switch from the feminine to masculine gender in the third example, the only other variation is the transposition of the second and third lines in Danel's response. Despite the length and exactness of the parallels, it seems impossible to claim that one text is quoting another. Rather this seems to be a stereotypical response to one kind of situation, with no inherent association with any specific event. However, the fact that the first two occur in one text 'cycle', will set up a particular dynamic between the two events that occasion the response and between the two who responded in this manner.

Thirdly, there are numerous formulae, which are used repeatedly. Richard Whitaker has done the most comprehensive study of these phrases, although many other scholars have noted them.[83] Whitaker, whose approach is similar to that of Alster, defines a formula as a series of units which form a full colon or full line which normally introduce or describe common actions in the narrative with or without including

---

81. F. Rosenthal, 'Die Parallelstellen in den Texten von Ugarit', *Or* NS 8 (1939), pp. 213-37. Such internal repetitions are common in ancient Near Eastern literature. See *Enuma Eliš* 1.129-61 // 2.15-48 // 3.19-52, 77-110; and J. Cooper, 'Symmetry and Repetition in Akkadian Narrative', *JAOS* 97 (1977), pp. 508-12.

82. CTA 3.D.29-33, 4.2.16-21, 19.2.93-97. H.L. Ginsberg (trans.), *ANET*, pp. 136-37; also J.C.L. Gibson (ed.), *Canaanite Myths and Legends* (Edinburgh: T. & T. Clark, 2nd edn, 1978), pp. 50, 57, 117. See also D.R. Hillers, 'A Convention in Hebrew Literature: The Reaction to Bad News', *ZAW* 77 (1965), pp. 86-90.

83. R.E. Whitaker, 'A Formulaic Analysis of Ugaritic Poetry' (PhD dissertation, Harvard University, 1970). His work is summarized in 'Ugarit Formulae', Chapter 2 in S. Rummel (ed.), *Ras Shamra Parallels: The Texts from Ugarit and the Hebrew Bible* (3 vols.; Rome: Pontifical Biblical Institute, 1981), III, pp. 209-19.

the name of the actor. In his estimation, 50 per cent of Ugaritic poetry is composed entirely of formulae while another 30 per cent is formulaic in nature.[84] As examples one might mention, 'he parts his jaws and laughs' (*yprq lṣb wyṣḥq*, CTA 6.3.16, 4.4.28, 17.2.10) and 'at the foot of El she bows and falls down / she prostrates herself and honors him' (*lp'n il thbr wtql/ tšṯḥwy wtkbd(n)h*, CTA 6.1.36-38, 4.4.25-26, cf. 3. F.18-20).

There are two problems with this approach. First, given the fact that most of the formulae which he cites represent common bodily gestures or physical movements, one may well ask whether they are used repeatedly because they are formulaic or because there is no other way in which they could be briefly and appropriately described in the language.

Secondly, in a line like 'a lip to the earth, a lip to the heavens' (*špt larṣ .špt.lšmm*, CTA 5.2.2, 23.61-62), it seems that more is involved than a mere formula. This is by no means a common gesture or action, and it reminds one of the Sumerian and Akkadian proverb or topos of the high heaven and wide earth.[85] The line that follows the phrase in the first text describing Mot's gaping jaws ' ... a tongue(?) to the stars' ([---l] *šn.lkbkbm*) is lacking in the second, which portrays the voracious appetite of the newly born 'gracious gods', perhaps because the stars are mentioned in line 54 as the recipients of offerings. While this is not a direct quotation, the descriptive language may be associated with Mot in such a way that its mere application to Shachar and Shalish may involve an allusion to and imply a comparison between their insatiable appetite and that of Mot (= death). The verbal parallels of Ugaritic thus have much in common with the formulaic repetitions of Egyptian and Mesopotamian literature but little in common with the quotations in the Old Testament prophets. However, the presence of so much repeated language within the Ugaritic corpus necessarily sets up a pattern of associations that will not escape the attention of the careful reader.

84. Whitaker, 'Ugarit Formulae', p. 209.

85. Gibson, *Canaanite Myths and Legends*, pp. 69, 126, and n. 57 above. On the phrase and its parallel in Ps. 73.9, see M.H. Pope, 'Mid Rock and Scrub, a Ugaritic Parallel to Exodus 7:19', in G.A. Tuttle (ed.), *Biblical and Near Eastern Studies: Essays in Honor of William Sanford LaSor* (Grand Rapids: Eerdmans, 1978), pp. 146-50.

Assessment

In the preceding survey of quotation in ancient Near Eastern literature an effort has been made to examine as much linguistic data as possible, as well as to note how various scholars have interpreted it. Furthermore, it occasionally has been necessary to evaluate and criticize their methodologies, since it is also a concern here to determine which approaches to the phenomenon of verbal parallels are appropriate and effective. The investigation of these repeated passages is a fascinating enterprise which merits further effort.

However, the primary goal is to ascertain whether this survey can illuminate the problem of prophetic quotation. Since the Old Testament is an integral part of ancient Near Eastern literature, one may expect that quotations will function in similar ways within the literary works of each culture, despite the manifold differences between them. If this is, in fact, the case the following observations will be helpful.

First, not every verbal parallel is a quotation or involves some type of literary dependence. Formulae and stereotypical phrases often appear to be similar to quotations, but simply reflect standardized expressions for describing characteristics, gestures, common actions, as well as repeated natural phenomena. Proverbs also are problematic since they combine striking formulation with a complete, though often generally applicable, thought. Proverbs may be considered to be a type of quotation, since similar introductory formulae are sometimes used. Yet the ideas of origin or authorship and of context, which are inherent elements of true quotation, are lacking. These other aspects of repeated language are important to note, however, since they share some of the rhetorical functions of quotation, such as style enhancement and emphasis.

Secondly, quotation is an extremely complex phenomenon. Sometimes it is clearly marked by an introductory formula but more often it is left unmarked and its presence can be detected only by contextual features, such as archaic vocabulary, grammatical awkwardness, abrupt style change, or simply the recognition that the same passage appears elsewhere. The assessment is as difficult as the detection, for the quoter can be embracing, questioning, modifying, or even rejecting the original meaning of the passage.

Thirdly, the analysis of verbal divergence is an important element in the assessment of quotation. Some changes are linguistically necessary but semantically relatively insignificant. Several changes may minimally modify the meaning while a verbatim repetition may be radically reinterpreted by being placed in a new context. A large degree of verbal divergence can be tolerated as long as the quotation is still recognizable. One technique noted in Egyptian literature is to repeat the first line of a quotation almost verbatim and then radically modify the second line. In any case, the degree of verbal correspondence does not appear to make one citation 'better' or more effective than another.

Fourthly, quoted material often is drawn from passages which deal with central religious and interpersonal concerns of life. Especially frequent in Egyptian quotations are counsel and descriptions of preparations for the afterlife and means of gaining the favor of the gods. In other words, not only is the quoted formulation especially striking, but the subject is also of inherent interest.

Finally, if most of the passages examined above constitute genuine quotations, then literary borrowing was an acknowledged and relatively widespread rhetorical device in the ancient Near East. It indicates both a continued knowledge of literature for as long as one to two millennia and its continued authority. (It also reflects the existence of multiple textual recensions of a given work.) Tigay's study of the *Gilgamesh Epic* suggests that quotation can occur and be incorporated on a variety of compositional or redactional levels, an initial quotation possibly leading to the mutual enrichment of *both* texts through further verbal parallels. Even though the purpose of some quotations remains unclear, especially for the longer Akkadian examples, the idea of the contemporary relevance or applicability rather than simply the stylistic value of the expression apparently underlies most conscious literary borrowing. Wisdom counsel is reported as carried out, mythical or fictional circumstances are experienced in real life, old rituals and curses are incorporated into new. Quotation is not simply a means of reusing words from earlier literature but also of preserving and modifying the ideas and values of a civilization. This is its power and appeal.

Chapter 4

QUOTATION IN EARLY JUDAISM

The discovery of the Dead Sea Scrolls in the mid-1940s gave new impetus to the study and comparison of the documents of early Judaism. The resultant addition of a considerable corpus of Hebrew-language texts has raised anew the question of the relationship between canonical and non-canonical Jewish literature. While some scholars have stressed the growing impact of external influences, such as Hellenism, on postbiblical Jewish thought, most assert that its primary roots are to be found in the Old Testament.

Accordingly, one of the features of the Qumran documents, which has received considerable attention is the extensive use they make of Old Testament concepts and language. This is particularly true of the Hodayoth,[1] which have been characterized as 'virtually like a mosaic of Biblical phrases and quotations'.[2] Not surprisingly, the use of the Old Testament at Qumran often has been compared with its use in the apocryphal books, especially Sirach which has been described as 'being more or less a tissue of old classical phrases',[3] and with the use of the

---

1. Hodayoth, the name commonly used for the scroll containing these psalm-like compositions, will be used in this study. Other designations include Hymns, Thanksgiving Psalms and Songs of Praise (Loblieder), cf. J. Carmignac and P. Guilbert (eds.), *Les textes de Qumran: Traduits et annotés* (Paris: Letouzey et Ané, 1961), p. 130.

2. M. Mansoor, *The Thanksgiving Hymns* (STDJ, 3; Leiden: E.J. Brill, 1961), p. 23.

3. S. Schechter and C. Taylor, *The Wisdom of Ben Sira* (Cambridge: Cambridge University Press, 1899), p. vii. See the helpful survey of biblical interpretation in early Judaism by A. Chester, 'Citing the Old Testament', in D.A. Carson and H.G.M. Williamson (eds.), *It Is Written: Scripture Citing Scripture. Essays in Honour of Barnabas Lindars* (Cambridge: Cambridge University Press, 1988), pp. 141-69.

Old Testament in the New.[4] However, quotation within the non-canonical books has not been compared in any thorough manner with the phenomenon within the Old Testament itself.[5] Even though, quantitatively,

4. See especially J.A. Fitzmyer, 'The Use of Explicit Old Testament Quotations in Qumran Literature and in the New Testament', *NTS* 7 (1961), pp. 297-333; also D.M. Smith, Jr, 'The Use of the Old Testament in the New', in J.M. Efird (ed.), *The Use of the Old Testament in the New and Other Essays: Studies in Honor of W.F. Stinespring* (Durham, NC: Duke University Press, 1972), pp. 3-65; D.J. Moo, *The Old Testament in the Gospel Passion Narratives* (Sheffield: Almond Press, 1983); E.E. Ellis, *The Old Testament in Early Christianity: Canon and Interpretation in the Light of Modern Research* (WUNT, 54; Tübingen: J.C.B. Mohr [Paul Siebeck], 1991); D.I. Brewer, *Techniques and Assumptions in Jewish Exegesis before 70 CE* (TSAJ, 30; Tübingen: Mohr Siebeck, 1992); M. Hengel and H. Löhr (eds.), *Schriftauslegung im antiken Judentum und im Urchristentum* (WUNT, 73; Tübingen: Mohr Siebeck, 1994); T.H. Lim, *Holy Scripture in Qumran Commentaries and Pauline Letters* (Oxford: Oxford University Press, 1997).

The use of the Old Testament in the New also could have been included in this chapter, but because of the linguistic problem presented by the Greek translation of the Old Testament texts and the large number of methodologically responsible studies already devoted to this subject, it was decided not to do so. It is hoped, however, that this work will prove helpful to New Testament scholars as well. Moody Smith's essay offers a useful survey of the topic, and, despite its date and apologetic purpose, Franklin Johnson's monograph, *The Quotations of the New Testament from the Old Considered in the Light of General Literature* (Philadelphia: American Baptist Publication Society, 1846) is also insightful. A more comprehensive treatment of the subject is now to be found in Chapters 11–19 in Carson and Williamson (eds.), *It Is Written*. Two recent works which break new methodological ground are Hays, *Echoes of Scripture in the Letters of Paul* and C.D. Stanley, *Paul and the Language of Scripture: Citation Technique in the Pauline Epistles and Contemporary Literature* (Cambridge: Cambridge University Press, 1992). Hays draws on work of some of the same literary theorists as Chapter 6 below in developing an intertextual and 'reader-response'-oriented approach to verbal parallels. Stanley limits the application of the term 'citation' to those verses which are (1) introduced by an explicit quotation formula, (2) accompanied by a clear interpretive gloss, or (3) stand in demonstrable syntatical tension with their present Pauline surroundings (p. 37), in comparing the Pauline citation technique to that found in Greco-Roman and early Jewish literature (Qumran, the Apocrypha and Pseudepigrapha, and Philo).

5. I am not aware of any such comparison, other than the efforts to find rabbinic-type exegesis in the Old Testament, which may involve quotation. See n. 6 and pp. 87-99, above. One should note, however, that that several scholars have applied methodologies developed for analyzing New Testament verbal parallels to Old Testament texts; cf. especially Willey, *Remember the Former Things*, who

verbal parallels may appear with greater frequency in Sirach or the Qumran Hodayoth than within the Old Testament prophetic corpus, it is not clear that there is any qualitative difference.

Geze Vermes has claimed that 'post-biblical midrash is to be distinguished from the biblical only by an external factor, canonization'.[6] Although the use of the term 'midrash' to describe such inner-biblical exegesis is disputed,[7] Vermes has shown that similar interpretive principles are employed both in Old Testament texts as well as in later midrash. This at least raises the possibility that the related feature of 'quotation' within non-canonical Jewish literature simply continues a practice which manifests itself already in the biblical texts.

The purpose of this chapter is to investigate quotation in two representative texts from early Judaism: Sirach from the traditional apocrypha and the Hodayoth from Qumran Cave 1. As in the previous chapter, general discussions of the methodological issues will be surveyed and specific characteristics of quotations in these two texts and in this type of literature will be noted. However, in this chapter I will focus on the manner in which later authors drew upon the canonical prophets, and Isaiah in particular, in order to determine whether any clear patterns of usage developed. Following separate considerations of these apocryphal and Qumran texts, the nature of quotation within the two will be compared and the implications of this survey for the phenomenon of 'prophetic quotation' will be assessed.

Quotation in the Traditional Apocrypha: Sirach

Though recent studies of early Jewish texts have abandoned the distinction between apocryphal and pseudepigraphical literature, it is nevertheless surprising that, to my knowledge, no monograph-length examination of quotation in the traditional Apocryphal has been published.[8] However, this subject was a central concern of two older

draws on the work of Hays, *Echoes of Scripture in the Letters of Paul* and Schaefer, 'Zechariah 14', pp. 66-91, who draws on J. Paulien, 'Elusive Allusions: The Problematic Use of the Old Testament in Revelation', *BR* 33 (1988), pp. 37-53.

6. Vermes, 'Bible and Midrash', p. 199. This was also essentially the view of A. Robert and R. Bloch. See also B. Vermes, *Scripture and Tradition in Judaism: Haggadic Studies* (SPB, 4; Leiden: E.J. Brill, 1961).

7. See especially Porten, 'Defining Midrash', pp. 55-92.

8. There have, of course, been numerous studies which have touched on the subject, especially with respect to the use of the Old Testament in specific books

American dissertations.[9] Leroy Hammill, in studying biblical interpretation in the Apocrypha and the Pseudepigrapha, notes that these
books contain almost no exegesis per se (i.e. formal biblical commentary) but that the *results* of such exegesis can be inferred from their use
of the Old Testament, especially in direct quotations. Such quotations
are not always easy to detect, since they are 'nearly always filled right
in with the author's own words without any mention that Scripture was
being quoted'.[10] In Hammill's observation, the use of introductory
formulae is a historical development, becoming common only in the
late first century BCE,[11] accompanied by a closer conformity to the
biblical text. He surmises that the growth of the science of biblical
interpretation, especially as practiced by Hillel, may have served to
promote a greater appreciation of the importance of the exact wording
of Scripture. It is equally plausible, however, to attribute greater
conformity to the *Masoretic* Text to the increasing stability and ascen-
dancy of that textual tradition. In any case, most biblical quotations
contain numerous divergences from either the MT or the LXX, resulting
from genuine textual variants, quotation from memory, or authorial
adaptation.

Hammill never actually defines the term 'quotation', but he seems to

and passages. See, for example, P.W. Skehan, 'Isaiah and the Teaching of the Book
of Wisdom', *CBQ* 2 (1940), pp. 289-99; and M.J. Suggs, 'Wisdom of Solomon
2:10-15: A Homily Based on the Fourth Servant Song', *JBL* 76 (1957), pp. 26-33;
S. Cheon, *Exodus in the Wisdom of Solomon: A Study in Biblical Interpretation*
(JSPSSup, 23; Sheffield: Sheffield Academic Press, 1997).

9. L.R. Hammill, 'Biblical Interpretation in the Apocrypha and Pseudepigrapha' (PhD dissertation, University of Chicago, 1950); and J.K. Zink, 'The Use of
the Old Testament in the Apocrypha' (PhD dissertation, Duke University, 1963).
Zink is apparently unaware of Hammill's work.

10. Hammill, 'Biblical Interpretation', p. 15.

11. Hammill, 'Biblical Interpretation', p. 15 n. 1, lists the following examples
of introductory formulae from the Apocrypha: Tob. 2.6; 8.6; 14.4, Sir. 48.10; Jdt.
9.2; 1 Macc. 7.16, *3 Macc.* 6.15, *4 Macc.* 2.5, 19; 17.19; 18.14, 15, 16, 17, 18, 19,
Sus. 5.53. Hoffman, 'The Technique of Quotation and Citation as an Interpretive
Device', views this rather as a *generic exigency*: Explicit quotations are rare in
pseudepigraphs (which Hoffman includes in the term 'Apocrypha') since the use of
introductory formulae served to emphasize the distinction between canonical and
non-canonical texts; they are rare in the poetic apocryphal books, since that
conformed to the biblical convention of Wisdom and psalmic literature (pp. 74-76).
(Conversely, *T. Levi* 10.5 explicitly quotes from *Enoch* in order to enhance the
latter's status.)

apply it to nearly any verbal correspondence between the Old Testament and an apocryphal book. He does draw an important distinction, however, between those quotations which are 'only convenient literary phrases which the author has taken over, or had become idioms or clichés in common use among the people',[12] and those which actually involve interpretation. Hammill claims that the former are far more numerous, especially in the poetic books, although conceding that it is often difficult to draw the line between them.

In analyzing the second category of quotations, Hammill uses rabbinic models entirely, speaking of literal haggadic, unacceptable haggadic, and halakic interpretation in the non-canonical literature. 'Legitimate' interpretation consists of (1) 'natural' interpretation, in which 'the context in which an author placed the quotation gave it the same meaning it had in the Bible',[13] although its reuse in a new context already constitutes an 'interpretation'; and (2) 'free paraphrases', which explain Old Testament texts by combining, glossing, reversing, reframing and reapplying them. In these latter restatements of a passage's thought, the original context is often completely ignored but the meaning is preserved intact.[14]

More interesting is Hammill's claim that the Apocrypha also display 'unacceptable' interpretation. After admitting that no well-formulated hermeneutical rules are employed and that the meaning of the biblical text as well as its citation is often ambiguous, he proceeds to discuss twelve illegitimate uses of the Old Testament:[15]

1. incorrect interpretation of biblical metaphors;
2. misconstruing poetic parallelism;
3. application of Scripture passages to entirely different persons or subjects;
4. etymologies and word-plays;
5. allegory;
6. deliberate misconstruction or mistranslation;
7. omissions or limitations of the thought of Scripture statements, quoting only part of a verse;

12. Hammill, 'Biblical Interpretation', p. 16 n. 1.
13. Hammill, 'Biblical Interpretation', p. 17.
14. Hammill, 'Biblical Interpretation', pp. 214-17, finds no examples of Sirach 'quoting' Isaiah but lists the following 'biblical paraphrases' of Isaiah: Sir. 17.28—Isa. 38.18, 19; Sir. 17.30—Isa. 55.8, 9; Sir. 31.25—Isa. 5.22; Sir. 35.19—Isa. 25.9.
15. Hammill, 'Biblical Interpretation', pp. 52-131.

8. unfounded inferences and assertions;
9. attempt to explain contradictions and difficult passages;
10. interpretive changes to avoid statements that might appear unbecoming to God;
11. circumlocutions for the Name of God;
12. midrashic elaboration of Scriptural phrases.

Although it is beyond the scope of this survey to discuss Hammill's examples in any detail, a brief critique is necessary. In the first place, Hammill does not clarify which criteria should be used for evaluating interpretation: acceptable to the rabbis, acceptable to the Apocrypha's original readers, or acceptable to contemporary readers? On what basis is allegory deemed illegitimate? Secondly, since there are a number of techniques which he lists under both acceptable 'free paraphrasing' as well as unacceptable interpretation, it is apparent that he is concerned more with specific applications of a principle than with the principle itself, increasing the subjectivity of his claim. Finally, since Hammill already has noted that quotations frequently involve merely the convenient reuse of biblical phrases, it is incumbent upon him to demonstrate that an *interpretation* was really intended. For example, Sir. 46.9 is cited by Hammill as misconstruing the metaphor of Isa. 58.14 (במתי-Q על-במותי ארץ, 'on the heights of the land'), taking it literally as referring to the hill country of Judah rather than figuratively as Isaiah does.[16] Since the phrase appears five times in the Old Testament and the figurative expression probably arose from a literal usage, it is not certain that Sirach 46 is even *dependent* on Isaiah 58, much less interpreting it.[17]

Whereas Hammill's primary concern is how the Apocrypha interprets the Old Testament, James Zink is more interested in matters of form and function.[18] Like Hammill, he suggests that many Old Testament phrases which appear in the Apocrypha are not purposeful citations but are simply an indication that the writer has saturated his mind with biblical terminology and has sought to imitate its style. Thus

16. Hammill, 'Biblical Interpretation', pp. 53-54.

17. It is interesting to note, however, that נהלה (inheritance) is used in the next line of both passages.

18. Zink, 'The Use of the Old Testament in the Apocrypha'. This is my observation, despite Zink's stated goal: 'To investigate the manner of usage of the Old Testament in the Apocrypha ... to determine its place in the history of the interpretation of the Old Testament', p. 15.

Zink distinguishes between mere verbal coincidence and 'explicit citation', which he defines as the apparent, *purposeful* use of an Old
Testament passage, with or without a formulary introduction, often
paraphrastic rather than exhibiting an exact verbal correspondence.
Equally purposeful but less obvious are the more numerous 'implicit
citations' which involve indirect references to, recollections of, or allusions to biblical events, statements or theological themes. Zink reserves
the use of the term 'quotation' for those explicit citations which reproduce the Old Testament wording exactly.[19]

From his study, Zink concludes that the writers of the Apocrypha
made no great effort to reproduce the text accurately or to conform their
usage to that of the original context. This, however, does not indicate a
lesser reverence for the Scriptures (or sloppy exegesis, as Hammill
claims). Rather, in Zink's opinion, 'words alone held the meaning of a
passage and, if it seemed to be relevant to their situation, that was
ground enough to take it as a support for the statements being made'.[20]

Although the actual usage of the Old Testament by different books of
the Apocrypha varies, the following example is fairly typical. In *4 Ezra*
6.56 (2 Esdras), διξιστι is used to introduce God's words from Isa.
40.15 and 17: 'As for the other nations which have descended from
Adam, thou hast said that they are nothing, and that they are like spittle,
and thou hast compared their abundance to a drop from a bucket.' Zink
presents this passage as an example of the Apocrypha's departure from
the original context, since Isaiah focuses on the contrast between the
creation and the Creator, while *4 Ezra* uses it to describe the 'utter
worthlessness of non-Jews'.[21] Upon a closer examination, this assessment does not seem very accurate. Like Isaiah 40, *4 Ezra* focuses on
the Creator and creation: this citation is in the middle of a prayer (6.38-
59) which reviews the six days of creation and then concludes that
everything was created for the sake of God's people. Furthermore,
Isaiah 40 also sets up an implicit contrast between 'my people' (Jacob/
Israel) and God and the nations with their idols. Thus the description of
the nations and the rulers of the earth (vv. 17 and 23) functions not

---

19. Zink, 'The Use of the Old Testament in the Apocrypha', pp. 13-14. Zink
appears to use the term 'quotation' in this manner on pp. 67 and 81.

20. Zink, 'The Use of the Old Testament in the Apocrypha', p. 161.

21. Zink, 'The Use of the Old Testament in the Apocrypha', pp. 158 and 34-35.
2 Esdras follows the LXX which apparently reads רֹק (spittle) instead of MT, *Tg*,
Vulg, *Syr* רֹק (dust).

simply to exalt the Creator but to comfort Israel as a people in exile. The use of this passage in *4 Ezra* is more fitting than Zink admits.

Of all the traditional apocryphal books, Sirach is probably that which makes the most extensive use of the Old Testament and, as such, vividly illustrates the methodological problems which complicate the study of quotation in early Judaism. In Sir. 33.17-18, the author describes his own procedure and purpose:

> I was the last on watch, I was like one who gleans after the grape-gatherers; by the blessing of the Lord I excelled, and like a grape-gatherer I filled my wine press. Consider that I have not labored for my self alone, but for all who seek instruction.[22]

Commentators have filled their footnotes with biblical references in an effort to identify all of these 'gleanings', a 'bewildering array', according to John Snaith, because they 'seldom indicate how close in wording or how significant in meaning the similarities may be'.[23] There is a considerable difference of opinion regarding the extent of Sirach's dependence. Schechter and Taylor list nearly 400 'phrases, idioms, typical expressions, and even whole verses about which there can be no reasonable doubt that they were either suggested to him by or directly copied from the Scriptures',[24] drawn from all but a half dozen Old Testament books. On the other end of the spectrum, Zink identifies only ten passages in which Sirach 'explicitly cites' the Old Testament.[25]

The implications of these data are similarly disputed. Schechter and Taylor disparage Sirach's work as marked by 'a mere Paitanic arti-

22. See also his grandson's preface, as well as 39.1-5 and 51.13-22.

23. J.G. Snaith, 'Biblical Quotations in the Hebrew of Ecclesiasticus', *JTS* NS 18 (1967), pp. 1-12 (1).

24. Schechter and Taylor, *The Wisdom of Ben Sira*, pp. 13-25. A. Eberharter, *Der Kanon des Alten Testaments zur Zeit des Ben Sira: Auf Grund der Beziehungen des Sirachbuches zu den Schriften des Alten Testaments dargestellt* (Münster: Aschendorff, 1911), pp. 4-6, however, suggests that these parallels be divided into three categories: allusions (*Anspielungen*), dependence/imitation (*Anlehnungen*) (= quotations), and retrospective references (*Rückbeziehungen*). Ackroyd, 'Criteria', pp. 114-18, adopts Eberharter's categories but concludes that, out of 160 supposed quotations (as listed by Schechter and Taylor, Eberharter, and others) from Psalms in Sirach, only about 15–20 passages are likely.

25. Zink, 'The Use of the Old Testament in the Apocrypha', p. 192, Sir. 1.14; 2.18; 15.19; 17.17, 27; 20.29; 27.26; 34.16; 36.24; 49.7. Zink finds less than 100 in the entire Apocrypha. Hammill, 'Biblical Interpretation', p. 212, finds 17 'quotations' in Sirach.

ficiality', a failed attempt to imitate perfectly the biblical style, while Stadelmann emphasizes the noteworthy 'interpretive work'.[26] All admit that a considerable amount of adaptation has occurred. Any assessment of these verbal parallels is entangled by four difficulties which Snaith discusses in some detail:

1. Dealing with the wide divergence between the Hebrew fragments, the Greek and Syriac translations, the rabbinic quotations and the mysterious 'Alphabet of Ben Sira', with much scholarly debate over which version is prior to the others.
2. Distinguishing the author's original quotations from the canon from glosses of editors or copyists.
3. Distinguishing deliberate reference and quotation from common literary or popular usage.
4. Determining to what extent the books of the Palestinian Canon were canonical to Sirach.[27]

Despite these problems, Snaith is convinced that one indeed can identify deliberate quotations, his primary criterion being the convergence of similar wording in both passages with similar context or subject matter.[28] Snaith's methodological rigor is commendable. However, his conclusion regarding the purposes of Sirach's borrowing—'to heighten the colour of his descriptions', and 'to create a link in the reader's mind with the biblical passage, and thus increase his appreciation of the heritage of Israel'[29]—is as unsatisfying as that of Schechter and Taylor. A brief re-examination of Sirach's use of one book, Isaiah, may help to enrich one's understanding of his literary intents.

26. Schechter and Taylor, *The Wisdom of Ben Sira*, pp. 32-33; H. Stadelmann, *Ben Sira als Schriftgelehrter: Eine Untersuchung zum Berufsbild des vormakkabäischen Sofer unter Berücksichtigung seines Verhältnisses zu Priester-, Propheten- und Weisheitslehrertum* (WUNT, 2.6; Tübingen: J.C.B. Mohr [Paul Siebeck], 1980), p. 253.

27. Snaith, 'Biblical Quotations', pp. 1-5. With regard to textual problems, see H.P. Rüger, *Text und Textform im hebräischen Sirach* (BZAW, 112; Berlin: W. de Gruyter, 1970); with regard to canonicity, see Eberharter, n. 24 above, and J.L. Koole, 'Die Bibel des Ben-Sira', *OTS* 14 (1965), pp. 374-96.

28. Snaith, 'Biblical Quotations', p. 7. Other indications of quotation which Snaith suggests include the use of 'poetic periphrasis', the rarity of words, the exact similarity of whole hemistichs, minimal adaptation, the use of introductory כי, the use of key words and phrases, the infrequency of the grammatical form, and odd word usage (pp. 6-8).

29. Snaith, 'Biblical Quotations', p. 11.

According to Middendorp, although Sirach was familiar with the entire book, his process of selection is remarkable for its omissions: no emphasis on the 'servant' or 'the day of the Lord', little attention to social and theocratic concerns, minimal actualization of promises and futuristic visions for his own day. 'The actual prophetic concern, that God speaks, shapes the history of his people, and supports justice in their corporate life, is not taken up.'[30]

Just how does Sirach use Isaiah? A definitive answer is impossible; instead a case-by-case response is necessary. As Snaith has pointed out, most lists of suggested quotations need considerable 'trimming'.[31] Of Middendorp's two dozen 'Scriptural quotations' of Isaiah, most represent merely allusions, similar themes, or coincidental repetition of common idioms or phrases.[32] Some verbal parallels, however, possibly

30. T. Middendorp, *Die Stellung Jesu Ben Siras zwischen Judentum und Hellenismus* (Leiden: E. J. Brill, 1973), p. 69. See also pp. 66, 71.

31. Snaith, 'Biblical Quotations', p. 11.

32. Middendorp, *Die Stellung Jesu Ben Siras*, pp. 66-69, lists the following passages:

Isaiah		Sirach
4.5	–	40.27
10.6	–	16.6
11.10 (14.22)	–	47.22
22.9-11	–	48.17
25.9	–	35.19d
25.10	–	16.9
34.8	–	5.7
40.14	–	42.21
40.29	–	41.2
40.31	–	43.30
42.9	–	48.25
49.6	–	48.10
56.5	–	15.6
45.7	–	11.14
52.2	–	11.12d
52.10	–	36.17
52.13-14	–	11.13
56.3	–	6.2
56.5	–	41.11
56.11	–	6.3 (19.2b; 40.3a)
59.17	–	43.20
61.2	–	48.24

have greater significance. First, a distinction must be drawn between those passages in which Sirach is merely dependent on Isaiah for a phrase and those in which he also uses it in such a way that would clearly link the two texts. As an example of the former, in Sir. 15.6 two phrases from Isaiah are combined: שָׂשׂוֹן וְשִׂמְחָה יִמָּצֵא, 'joy and gladness will be found' (51.3) and וְשֵׁם עוֹלָם, 'and an everlasting name' (56.5). In Sirach, these are presented as favors bestowed on the one who fears the LORD. Isaiah 51.3 speaks of the restoration of Zion when the desert will blossom and the promise in 56.5 is given to sabbath-keeping eunuchs who by virtue of their status would normally have their names terminated. In neither case does there seem to be an interpretation of the Isaianic text. In other words, the author of Sirach is not suggesting through this reuse that the corporate promise of Isa. 51.3 was intended to be individualized and transferred from a future eschatological to a timeless gnomic setting, or that the specific recipient of 56.5 was well suited to be generalized. Rather, in describing the benefits of divine wisdom, the author simply chose two familiar phrases for describing future blessings.

Similarly, Sirach repeatedly draws on Isaiah for phrases of indictment and judgment, transferring them from the national to the individual sphere if necessary. It is likely that Isa. 5.25 provides the rhetorical model for Sir. 48.15 (בכל־זאת לא שב העם, 'For all this the people did not repent'), that Isa. 10.6's description of Israel as a גוי חנף, a 'godless nation', is the source of Sir. 16.6's description of the wilderness generation, and that Isa. 5.22's 'woe' saying forms the basis of Sir. 31.25's negative imperative על היין אל התגבר, 'Do not aim to be valiant over wine'.[33]

In each of the preceding passages there is a clear use of Isaianic language but no obvious connection to a larger context. The following examples may involve a close linkage to the prophetic source in meaning as well as in language. In Sir. 43.30, the promise of Isa. 40.31 (וקוי יחוה יחליפו כח, 'But those who hope in the LORD will renew their strength') is reformulated as a command (מרומים תחליפו כח, 'When you exalt him, put forth all your strength'). Although Isaiah 40 relates

---

33. However, the phrases נין ונכד (offspring and descendants, Isa. 14.22–Sir. 47.22) and שד ושבר (ruin and destruction, Isa. 51.19–Sir. 40.9) are probably idiomatic and not a result of Sirach's dependence on Isaiah. All English translations of Sirach are taken from the Revised Standard Version (Oxford: Oxford University Press, 1977), unless noted.

this strength to running and walking (return from exile?), the use of the same phrase in 41.1 suggests a broader application. In that both Sir. 43.30 and Isa. 40.31 form the climax of a section on God's creative power and incomparability (Sir. 42.15–43.33, Isa. 40.12-31), it appears that the use of the phrase from Isaiah is intended to remind the reader of its Isaianic context and suggest that the proper use of divinely bestowed strength is in the praising of the Bestower.

In Sir. 11.13 several terms from Isa. 52.13-14 are incorporated (נשא בראשו וירממהו ויתמהו עליו רבים, 'and raises up his head; so that many are amazed of him', cf. שממו עליך, 'he will be raised and lifted up', רבים ירום ונשא, 'many were appalled at him'), a correspondence which is unlikely to be coincidental. Although it may be simply a reuse of appropriate exaltation language, it might suggest that Sirach understood the portrayal of the servant figure in Isaiah 52–53 as paradigmatic of the divine reversal of the lowly and lofty rather than as historically specific. A clearer case of implicit interpretation is in Sir. 48.24 where the first person addressee of Isa. 61.2, who is to 'comfort all the mourners', is identified as being Isaiah (וינחם אבלי ציון, 'and comforted those who mourned in Zion').

The final chapter of Sirach contains two striking quotations from Isaiah. In the first section, Sir. 51.1-12, a hymn of thanksgiving, the language of Isa. 63.5 is invoked (ואביט ואין ציר ואשתומם ואין סומך, 'I looked, but there was no one to help', cf. Sir. 51.7 ואפנה סביב ואין עוזר לי ואצפה סומך ואין, 'I turned every way, but there was no one to help me, I looked for one to sustain me, but could find no one' [NAB]). In Isaiah 63, the divine speaker accomplishes the eschatological redemption himself, since there is no one to help. In Sirach 51, the human speaker realizes the same and therefore cries out for the divine deliverer's aid. The final section of the chapter, 51.23-30, borrows the commercial imagery of Isaiah 55. Isaiah 55.1 is rather vague regarding what is represented by 'wine and milk' which the thirsty are to purchase without money. Sirach 51.24-25, however, is clearer: the thirsty (צמאה) are told to acquire *wisdom* (קנו לכם חכמה בלא כסף). In both passages, the metaphor stresses the great value, gracious provision and abundant availability of the possession to be acquired and thus serves to bring Sirach's treatise on divine wisdom to a stirring climax.[34]

---

34. Another intriguing verbal parallel is between Sir. 40.27 and Isa. 4.5. The Masada text which reads ועל כל כ(בוד) חפתה, 'and over all the glory its canopy' (my trans.) instead of the Geniza text's וכן כל כבוד חפתה, 'and covers a man better

On the one hand, the verbal parallels just considered do not involve elaborate rabbinic-type exegesis; few hermeneutical rules can be generated from their analysis. On the other hand, the dependence on Isaiah seeks to do more than merely enhance the style and increase the reader's appreciation of his Jewish heritage. In some parallels, a knowledge of the quotation's source enriches one's understanding of Sirach's purpose in his literary borrowing and of the meaning of individual passages. Isaiah and the other Old Testament books are more than just a linguistic 'storehouse' (*Fundgrube*);[35] interpretation is also taking place in the process of reapplying the language. The preceding analysis of Sirach's dependence on Isaiah is to be seen as illustrative and tentative. Authorial intent in cases of apparent verbal dependence is exceedingly difficult to determine, and absolute statements about what an author did or could do in his use of the Old Testament are therefore inadvisable.

However, before any further conclusions about Sirach's approach to Scripture are drawn, Sir. 36.1-17 must also be examined. Until recently, it was generally assumed that this passage was composed by Sirach, although some suggested that he used a liturgical source.[36] However, Middendorp has asserted that the passage is a hasidic addition from the Maccabean period.[37] Middendorp offers several arguments in support of his claim, including the sectional markers (ס) before and after the passage, its close connections with 1Q Milhamah (and Daniel), its use of vocabulary which does not appear elsewhere in Sirach, its eschatological–nationalistic character, and the relatively simple explanation, which Middendorp posits, for its later insertion.

Middendorp's proposal has not been widely received; the lengthiest rebuttal is that of Marböck, who offers a thorough survey of Sirach, especially chs. 44–50, in an effort to demonstrate that the 'historical perspective' of 36.1-17, the expectation of God's renewed intervention on his people's behalf and their regathering, the emphasis on Zion and

---

than any glory', is closer to Isaiah's כִּי עַל־כָּל־כָּבוֹד חֻפָּה, 'over all the glory will be a canopy', but the phrase is not discussed here because of the lack of agreement over exactly what it means.

35. Middendorp, *Die Stellung Jesu Ben Siras*, p. 69.

36. W.O.E. Oesterley, *The Wisdom of Jesus the Son of Sirach or Ecclesiasticus* (Cambridge: Cambridge University Press, 1912); and J.G. Snaith, *Ecclesiasticus, or the Wisdom of Jesus Son of Sirach* (Cambridge: Cambridge University Press, 1914), p. 174.

37. Middendorp, *Die Stellung Jesu Ben Siras*, pp. 125-32.

the fulfillment of prophecy, the passion and the polemic, far from being alien to a wise man's writings, correspond to that which is found throughout the book as a whole.[38]

One of Middendorp's arguments in support of the independence of Sir. 36.1-17, which has received less attention from his reviewers, concerns the disputed passage's use of Scripture. First, Middendorp considers it unlikely that a sage suddenly would be concerned with the actualization of the prophets. However, Middendorp's assessment of Sirach is rather one-sided: he views Sirach as a broad-minded scribe, comparing wisdom at home and abroad and emphasizing a universalistic 'fear of God'. But Sirach also stresses such common prophetic themes as the unique position of Israel (17.17; 24.8-12), God's mercy and deliverance of his own people (48.20; 50.22-24; 51.8), and his judgment of the nations (10.14-17; 35.18; 39.23; 46.1). Thus it is the scribe's duty to pay attention to prophecy about Israel (39.1; 44.3), as well as to international wisdom. In fact, much of Sirach's work has closer affinities to the Old Testament prophets than to the Wisdom books.

Secondly, Middendorp objects to the greater concentration of verbal parallels in this section: 'This abundance of borrowed biblical material in this brief passage earns its author the reputation of an epigone. Sirach hardly would have worked in this manner.'[39] However, it is not the case that verbal parallels are evenly distributed throughout the book with the single exception of 36.1-17. Nearly two-thirds of the verbal parallels with the Old Testament occur in chs. 30–51, and the prophetic parallels are more frequent in the compositions which are hymnic or lyrical rather than didactic in character. A concentration of verbal parallels similar to that of 36.1-17 can be found also in the thanksgiving psalm of 51.1-12.[40] Therefore, the mere increase in the number of

---

38. J. Marböck, 'Das Gebet um die Rettung Zions Sir 36, 1-22 (G: 33, 1-13a; 36, 16b-22) im Zusammenhang der Geschichtsschau Ben Siras', in J.B. Bauer and J. Marböck (eds.), *Memoria Jerusalem: Freundesgabe Franz Sauer zum 70. Geburtstag* (Graz: Akademischer Druck- und Verlagsanstalt, 1977), pp. 93-115. See also the critical reviews of M. Hengel, *JSJ* 5 (1974), pp. 83-87 and P. Höffken, *ZAW* 87 (1975), pp. 195-98.

39. Middendorp, *Die Stellung Jesu Ben Siras*, p. 131. Middendorp lists these borrowings on pp. 130-31 n. 2. He also speaks of 'the remarkable verbatim use of Scripture, which is not found elsewhere in Sirach in such abundance and so lacking in originality', p. 132.

40. Only 95 of the 250 verbal parallels which Schechter and Taylor list, *The*

'quotations' in 36.1-12 is not necessarily a problem. The genre simply lends itself to such extensive dependence.

Sirach 36.15—'fulfill the prophecies spoken in thy name'—leads us to expect that prophetic themes and promises will be emphasized in the prayer'[41] and that borrowing is more than stylistic. Rather, what Yahweh has proclaimed himself to be and pledged to do on Israel's behalf is invoked in a time of crisis:

v. 3	הניף על עם נכר = Isa. 19.16	מניף עליו
v. 5	אין אלהים זולתך = Isa. 45.21	ואין־עוד אלהים ... זולתי
v. 8	החיש קץ = Isa. 60.22	בעתה אחישנה
v. 8	כי מי יאמר לך מה תעשה = Isa. 45.9	היאמר חמר ליצרו מה־תעשה
v. 10	האומר אין זולתי = Isa. 47.8, 10	האמרה בלבבה אני ואפסי עוד
v. 12	נקרא בשמך ... כיניתה = Isa. 45.4	ואקרא לך בשמך אכנך
v. 16	תן את פעלת = Isa. 61.8	ונתתי פעלתם
v. 17	וידעו כל אפסי ארץ = Isa. 52.10	וראו כל־אפסי־ארץ

v. 3	Lift up (your hand) against foreign nations	= Isa. 19.16	raises (the hand) against them
v. 5	There is no God apart from you	= Isa. 45.21	and there is no God apart from me
v. 8	Hasten the end	= Isa. 60.22	in its time I will do it swiftly
v. 8	For who says to you, What are you doing?	= Isa. 45.9	Does the clay say to the potter, What are you making?
v. 10	Who say, There is no one but me!	= Isa. 47.8, 10	saying to yourself, I am, and there is none besides me
v. 12	Called by your name you bestowed the title of	= Isa. 45.4	I summon you by name and bestow on you a title of honour
v. 16	Reward those	= Isa. 61.8	I will reward them

Wisdom of Ben Sira, pp. 13-26, are from Sir. 1–29. W. Baumgartner, 'Die literarischen Gattungen in der Weisheit des Jesus Sirach', *ZAW* 34 (1914), pp. 161-98 (186), sees in Sirach 'a strange mixture of wisdom and prophecy'. Snaith, 'Biblical Quotations', p. 5, observes further that 'the words used in the prophets are prominent in "non-wisdom" parts of the book'. Middendorp, *Die Stellung Jesu Ben Siras*, pp. 113, 115-17, also notes the similarity between 51.1-12 and 36.1-17, and considers the former to be a 'later addition' for the same reasons as the latter.

41. The author in v. 17 calls it a תפלה (prayer). More specifically, Baumgartner, 'Die literarischen Gattungen in der Weisheit des Jesus Sirach', p. 183, calls it 'a public lamentation', and Marböck, 'Das Gebet um die Rettung Zions', p. 102, a 'community lament'. M.R. Lehmann, 'Ben Sira and the Qumran Literature', *RevQ* 3 (1961–62), pp. 103-16 (105), labels it a 'battle prayer/liturgy'.

v. 17	And all the ends of the earth will know	= Isa. 52.10	And all the ends of the earth will see

These are only the close verbal parallels between the prayer and Isaiah.[42] The use of borrowed language does not serve simply to remind the reader of his prophetic heritage; it becomes the very basis of the petition. It is true that this type of 'actualization' is not prominent in the rest of Sirach. The only other prayer, in 22.27–23.6, is individualistic and ethical rather than national and *heilsgeschichtlich* in orientation. However, as noted above, God's mercy, wrath and power to deliver are frequently *affirmed* throughout the book, even though they seldom are *invoked*. And, as in the examples examined above, Sirach often reapplies scriptural promises, declarations and threats but does so usually in terms of the individual rather than Israel as a whole. There is no justification for the claim that the use of Scripture displayed in Sir. 36.1-17 cannot be that of the author of the rest of the book. This prayer is the composition of one for whom the prophetic message still rings true, not of the unimaginative imitator. The examination of quotation within Sirach leads one to expect great variety in the usage of Scripture, even within an individual book.

Quotation in the Qumran Scrolls: The Hodayoth

As is evident from the above survey of verbal parallels in Sirach, the analysis of quotation is an integral part of the study of scriptural interpretation in early Judaism. However, the two are often separated in the examination of Qumran texts. Some scholars seek to identify hermeneutical principles underlying certain appropriations, comparing them to those of rabbinic Judaism or the New Testament, but pay minimal attention to how closely the original text is followed, while others

42. Other alleged parallels include:

v. 6	–	Isa.	51.9; 63.12
v. 7	–		42.13
v. 8	–		5.19
v. 11	–		11.11, 12; 23.7; 27.13; 49.6
v. 13	–		64.5
v. 14	–		2.2-4
v. 15	–		45.4
v. 17	–		40.28

compile long lists of biblical parallels but fail to discuss the specific purposes which such borrowing served. Not surprisingly, the same issues and problems encountered in relation to the Apocrypha also encumber the study of the Dead Sea Scrolls.

One rather obvious but important finding of those who have studied the Qumran documents is that the use of Scripture differs greatly according to the genre or type of literature involved, whether commentary, community code, or hymn, although a similar conviction of existing as an elect eschatological community is prominent throughout.[43] Fitzmyer concludes that no systematic or uniform pattern of exegesis can be discerned, although there is throughout the 'implicit desire to enhance some recent event in their histories or some idea or person with an Old Testament association, as a result of a certain analogy which they saw'.[44] This association was achieved through a variety of devices: actualization of the text, atomistic interpretation, use of textual variants, play on words, deliberate manipulation of the text to fit into the new context better. Some of them might seem illegitimate today, but in their case the religious purpose justified the means.

Fitzmyer distinguishes four classes of quotations:

1. Literal or Historical—Old Testament is actually quoted in the same sense in which it was intended by the original writers.
2. Modernization—Old Testament text, which originally had a reference to some event in the contemporary scene at the time it was written, nevertheless was vague enough to be applied to some new event in the history of the Qumran sect.
3. Accommodation—Old Testament text was obviously wrested from its original context, modified or deliberately changed by the new writer in order to adapt it to a new situation or purpose.

---

43. See especially D. Patte, *Early Jewish Hermeneutic in Palestine* (SBLDS, 22; Missoula, MT: Scholars Press, 1975); F.F. Bruce, *Biblical Exegesis in the Qumran Texts* (Grand Rapids: Eerdmans, 1954); and O. Betz, *Offenbarung und Schriftforschung in der Qumrantexte* (WUNT, 6; Tübingen: J.C.B. Mohr [Paul Siebeck], 1960); G. Brin, 'Concerning Some of the Uses of the Bible in the Temple Scroll', *RevQ* 12 (1987), pp. 519-28; B. Mitzan, *Qumran Prayer and Religious Poetry* (STDJ, 12; Leiden: E.J. Brill, 1994).

44. Fitzmyer, 'The Use of Explicit Old Testament Quotations', p. 331.

4.   Eschatological—Old Testament quotation expressed a promise
or threat about something to be accomplished in the *eschaton*
and which the Qumran writer cited as something still to be
accomplished in the *eschaton* of which he wrote.[45]

Fitzmyer uses the term 'quotation' cautiously, focusing on those passages which 'are introduced by special formulae and are cited to bolster
up or illustrate an argument, to serve as a *point de départ* in a discussion or to act as a sort of proof-text', although noting that some explicit
quotations lack such a formula.[46] Unfortunately, this type of caution has
not characterized most of the studies of the Hodayoth, where the tendency has been to list indiscriminately all the verbal parallels between a
given hymn and the Old Testament Scholars are not entirely to blame
in this regard, for the nature of these compositions makes it difficult to
determine whether quotation is actually involved. Unlike other Qumran
documents, the Hodayoth lack any introductory formula, the clearest
marker of quotation.[47] Furthermore, this type of liturgical poetry often
incorporates formulaic language which may also appear in similar biblical literature without necessarily involving literary dependence.

This practice of compiling a maximal list of verbal parallels has led
to the disparagement of the Hodayoth. According to Gaster, 'they are,
in the main, mosaics of Biblical quotations and ... often exhibit all the
learned and tortured exploitation of Scripture that we find later in the

45. Fitzmyer, 'The Use of Explicit Old Testament Quotations', pp. 305-306.
Fitzmyer concedes that classes 2 and 3 are often difficult to distinguish.
46. Fitzmyer, 'The Use of Explicit Old Testament Quotations', p. 299. He calls
these 'virtual citations', p. 304. This is also the approach taken by Stanley, *Paul
and the Language of Scripture*.
47. But S. Holm-Nielsen, *Hodayot: Psalms from Qumran* (Acta Theological
Danica, 2; Aarhus, Denmark: Universitetsforlaget, 1960), p. 245, notes Hod. 17.12
in which Exod. 34.6-7 is quoted as מושה ביד (being 'by the hand of Moses'). On
the subject of quotation formulae in Qumran literature, see Fitzmyer, 'The Use of
Explicit Old Testament Quotations', pp. 297-333, and F.L. Horton, Jr, 'Formulas of
Introduction in the Qumran Literature', *RevQ* 7 (1969–71), pp. 505-14. Hoffman,
'The Technique of Quotation and Citation as an Interpretive Device', pp. 76-77,
suggests several reasons why the Dead Sea Scrolls texts rarely use explicit
quotations: (1) The difficulty of finding an appropriate quotation for every new,
original idea; (2) The resultant disturbance of the fluency of the composition; (3)
The desire to blend the quoted sacred text with its suggested exegesis. The second
and third reasons may be applicable to the analysis of the inner-biblical
phenomenon.

medieval poetasters (*payyetanim*) of the synagogue'.[48] Holm-Nielsen, who has undertaken the most thorough study of the Hodayoth's use of the Old Testament, considers a description such as Gaster's to be exaggerated (though the Hodayoth do make a greater use of Scripture than most other Qumran writings) since the description suggests a uniform and random borrowing of Old Testament passages.[49]

This is clearly not the case, according to Holm-Nielsen's analysis, for the verbal parallels are predominantly taken from the psalmic and the prophetic literature, especially Isaiah, with a marked preference for Isaiah 40–66. In examining the individual psalms, Holm-Nielsen discovered that the use of the Old Testament is most extensive in the *individual* psalms which contain a mixture of complaint and thanksgiving, while in the *community* hymns the use is 'more sporadic and haphazard'. Within each group there are certain favorite Old Testament passages to cite, but these texts are seldom shared between the two groups. Therefore, greater selectivity is involved than many have noted previously.[50]

Holm-Nielsen is cautious, though somewhat confusing, in setting up his criteria for identifying quotations. He prefers to speak of 'use' of the Old Testament rather than 'quotation', since the Hodayoth's borrowing is so different from that of the New Testament, although he employs the latter term as well. Since a verbal parallel 'may simply be a matter of the use of certain permanent phrases, stereotyped expressions, customary terminology, which may well have originated somewhere or other in the Old Testament, but which existed in the everyday language of the time',[51] it is necessary to examine both contexts for an indication that this 'use' of Scripture furnishes 'information about the particular understanding of the Old Testament which was peculiar to

---

48. T.H. Gaster, *The Dead Sea Scriptures in English Translation* (Garden City, NY: Doubleday, 1964), p. 124.

49. Holm-Nielsen, *Hodayot*, p. 301. Holm-Nielsen concedes that he probably is also guilty of listing too many passages from the Old Testament but defends this tendency: 'my viewpoint is that it is better to include too many than too few, since it is so evident that these psalms are so full of the Old Testament' (p. 303 n. 7). However, in his lists of verbal parallels, Holm-Nielsen does indicate those in which the use of the Old Testament is 'uncertain' (p. 304).

50. Holm-Nielsen, *Hodayot*, pp. 312-14. This is also Patte's conclusion, *Early Jewish Hermeneutic in Palestine*, pp. 247-69.

51. Holm-Nielsen, *Hodayot*, p. 302.

these authors' or contributes 'to the elucidation of the context in the Hodayoth'.[52]

Thus Holm-Nielsen believes that genuine quotation in these texts involves 'theological content' and not simply useful language, a contextual as well as a linguistic correspondence. Interpretation is involved, but not so much in the sense of establishing a particular meaning for a given text as of reading all of Scripture in the light of the interpreters' own self-understanding.

Bonnie Kittel criticized Holm-Nielsen for his carelessness in using the term 'quotation' and his 'low view of the creativity and originality of the poet'.[53] It must be pointed out, however, that her comments are directed primarily toward his treatment of specific passages and fail to acknowledge the caution and appreciation which he displays in his general discussion of the topic.[54] Kittel suggests four categories of Old Testament borrowing to replace the two categories 'quotation' and 'original material' which, in her opinion, are currently being used:

52. Holm-Nielsen, *Hodayot*, p. 304. Although he notes that 'in most cases ... it soon becomes apparent that there is either no attention at all, or else only very little, paid to the context in the Old Testament' (p. 302).

53. B.P. Kittel, *The Hymns of Qumran: Translation and Commentary* (SBLDS, 50; Chico, CA: Scholars Press, 1981), p. 48. Kittel (*The Hymns of Qumran*, p. 49) addresses the following criticisms to both Holm-Nielsen, and Carmignac and Guilbert (eds.), *Les textes de Qumran*, and Carmignac, 'Les citations de l'Ancien Testament, et spécialement des poèmes du serviteur, dans les hymnes de Qumrân', *RevQ* 2 (1959–60), pp. 357-94: 'They include among their examples many 'quotations' ... (1) which consist of only 1 or 2 words, often not even consecutive within the O.T. verse, (2) in which the O.T. context and meaning are changed considerably, (3) which involve recurring idioms, (4) which employ different morphological forms and syntactical relationships.' The fourth of these criticisms is the most questionable, since, if strictly observed, it would eliminate precisely those quotations in which intentional adaptation has taken place, a key characteristic of quotation.

54. See Holm-Nielsen, *Hodayot*, 'The Use of the Old Testament in the Hodayot', pp. 301-15, and the discussion of his views above. As was pointed out, Holm-Nielsen does employ the term 'quotation' more freely than Kittel and often interchangeably with other phrases for rhetorical variation, since he prefers 'use' as his more restrictive term. Once this is understood, his discussion sounds much like Kittel's, especially pp. 302-305. It is true, nevertheless, that many scholars have not shown either Kittel's or Holm-Nielsen's caution in treating the verbal parallels found in the Hodayoth.

1. Quotation or allusion is used to recall a specific passage to the reader/listener's mind.
2. Biblical literary forms are imitated by the use of standardized phrases in appropriate places.
3. Biblical imagery and metaphor characteristic of certain types of literature or certain theological ideas can be identified.
4. Many thoughts are expressed simply in a manner consistent with biblical langauge [*sic*] and terminology.[55]

Kittel defines 'quotation' in terms of verbal correspondence rather than purpose—'several words ... with only the slightest variations from the original'—and, in 'allusion', looks for a convergence of 'the context, meaning, and the idiom itself'[56] in one text, much as Holm-Nielsen demanded to indicate a 'use' of Scripture. Although Kittel's categories are helpful and her emphasis on the author's creativity is needed, one must concede that, in theory, she is very much in agreement with Holm-Nielsen regarding the proper criteria for distinguishing quotation in the Hodayoth, even though she disputes his application of them.

Given the special affinity which the Hodayoth seem to have for the book of Isaiah, an examination of several of the verbal parallels which have been identified between them may help to illustrate the issues just discussed and indicate the extent to which *interpretation* of the Old Testament is taking place. That many phrases from the prophets appear in the Hodayoth has long been noted. Many of them involve imagery such as that of a woman in labor, springs of water, floods, a lion breaking bones, or descriptions of God, the wicked, and the righteous.

---

55. Kittel, *The Hymns of Qumran*, p. 50. She labels categories 2 and 3 'deliberate use of biblical expressions', while category 4 represents 'free use of biblical idiom and vocabulary'. In order for an expression to be considered deliberate rather than free, it must meet one of the following qualifications: (1) its context is the same as in the Old Testament but it is not a recurring idiom; (2) its meaning is the same as in the Old Testament, but it is not frequently employed; (3) it marks a literary form; (4) it is an Old Testament metaphor or simile characteristic of a certain type of imagery (pp. 50-51). Kittel offers helpful illustrations of her categories in her analysis of 'Alleged Quotations in Hodayot 2:20-30' (pp. 53-55). See also the comments by Chester, 'Citing the Old Testament', p. 146.

56. Kittel, *The Hymns of Qumran*, p. 51. See Holm-Nielsen, *Hodayot*, p. 303. All that Kittel says about quotation's purpose is that it is used 'to recall a *specific* passage to the reader/listener's mind ... for special effect', pp. 50, 52. Holm-Nielsen, on the other hand, offers a lengthy discussion of the purpose of the 'use' of the Old Testament, pp. 306-308.

Often these phrases are employed in very different contexts.[57]

Other parallels manifest a closer relationship between the two passages. Isaiah 9.5's description of the coming ruler פלא יועץ אל גבור, 'wonderful counselor, mighty God', is used in 3.10 as פלא יועץ עם גבורתו ('a splendid counsellor with his strength'). Here the author is restating the hope centering on the birth of a remarkable child, not merely reusing the imagery.[58] When the author of 6.7 abbreviates the description of enemies gathering for battle from Isa. 13.4 and Ezek. 32.3, על המון עם ועל שאון מ[מל]כות בהאספם ('above the noise of the people and the roar of kingdoms, when they join together [against me]...' —קול המון בהרים דמות עם־רב קול שאון ממלכות גוים נאספים, 'Listen, a noise on the mountains like that of a great multitude! Listen, an uproar among the kingdoms, like nations massing together!'), he, like Isaiah, has in mind not simply the general opposition of the foes of the righteous but an eschatological conflict which is marked by the raising up of a purified remnant (l. 8) and the burning up of the wicked (ll. 18-19). The Hodayoth author also links Isaiah 34 with the destruction of the world that will accompany that final conflict by using the reference in v. 9 to 'streams being turned into pitch' (ונהפכו נחליה לזפת) in such a setting in 3.31 (לנחלי זפת, streams of lava, cf. ll. 35-36).

Isaiah 28–33, which scholars frequently have grouped together, is drawn upon numerous times by the Hodayoth. Isaiah 28.11 (כי בלעגי שפה ובלשון אחרת ידבר אל־העם הזה) is given an interesting interpretation in 4.16, which begins almost identically (והם [ב]ל[וע]ג שפה ולשון ... אחרת ידברו לעמך), 'They speak to your people with stuttering lip and weird tongue', but then adds, 'to convert to folly all their deeds with tricks', the statement referring to the false prophets (נביאי כזב).

---

57. Such usage should not be considered 'quotation' and therefore these verbal parallels will not be discussed. Patte, *Early Jewish Hermeneutic in Palestine*, pp. 251-67, treats such phrases as part of the author's 'anthological' style.

58. This analysis of the Hodayoth will employ the Hebrew text as edited by E. Lohse, *Die Texte aus Qumran: Hebräisch und Deutsch* (Munich: Kösel-Verlag, 1986); and the English translation of F.G. Martinez, *The Dead Sea Scrolls Translated: The Qumran Texts in English* (Leiden: E.J. Brill, 1994). Regarding 3.10, see Holm-Nielsen's discussion, *Hodayot*, pp. 56-57 n. 19, of the various interpretations. Patte, *Early Jewish Hermeneutic in Palestine*, pp. 264-66, simply notes that phrases from numerous Old Testament passages, including Isa. 9.5, have contributed to the central imagery of the 'distress of a woman giving birth', but see also the discussions cited by Patte, *Early Jewish Hermeneutic in Palestine*, p. 265 n. 168. The language of Isa. 9.5 is too elevated to describe a normal birth.

The same position is also taken in its use in 2.18-19 where it is reinforced by a quotation from Isa. 30.10 (לא תחזו־לנו נכחות) in 2.15 (לכול חוזי נכחות), 'to all true observers, Give us no more visions of what is right!', an Isaianic context which clearly speaks of the people's rejection of true prophecy.[59]

A striking example of the Hodayoth's careful attention to the quoted text's context is in column 6 in which Isa. 28.15 and vv. 16-17 are quoted.

vv. 16-17: הנני יסד בציון אבן אבן בחן
פנת יקרת מוסד מוסד המאמין לא יחיש
ושמתי משפט לקו וצדקה למשקלת

See I lay a stone in Zion, a tested stone, a precious cornerstone for a sure foundation; the one who trusts will never be dismayed.

are cited in lines 26-27: תשים סוד על סלע וכפיס על קו משפט
ומשקלה א [מת] ל [נס]ות אבני בחן לבנ[נ]ו[ת חומת]
עוז ללוא תתזעזע וכול באיה בל ימוטו

For you place the foundation upon rock and the beams to the correct size, and the plumb line [...] tested stone for a strong [building] which will not be shaken. All those who enter there will not stagger.[60]

Although the New Testament interprets the stone messianically, Isaiah speaks of confidence in God rather than human covenants. The author of the Hodayoth adheres to this latter view but applies what is primarily political in intent, directed to the rulers of Jerusalem, personally (ll. 24-25—ואהיה כבא בעיר מצור), 'am I like someone entering a fortified city', although he may be speaking as a representative of the community. Here again, the author places the quotation in the context of the final conflict. Thus he appropriately also cites the preceding verse, Isa. 28.15 (שוט שוטף כי־יעבר לא יבואנו), 'When an overwhelming scourge sweeps by, it cannot touch us') in line 35, near the conclusion of the column (and poem),[61] as expressing his confidence in God's refuge

59. 2.18 also draws on Exod. 6.12, 30 in its phrase בערול שפה, 'by uncircumcised lip'.

60. The Hodayoth author plays with the twofold meaning of Isa. 28.17's משפט לקו, taking it in a literal, architectural sense here, facilitated by his adaptation על קו משפט, but using it in its theological sense, speaking of coming judgment, in 3.17.

61. Gaster, *The Dead Sea Scriptures*, p. 155, sees the poetic unit as 5.20–6.35 (36), as does A. Dupont-Sommer, *Le livre des hymnes découvert près de la mer Morte (1QH)* (Semitica, 7; Paris: Librairie d'Amérique et d'Orient Adrien

(וּמֵעֲבִיר שׁוֹט שׁוֹטֵף בַּל יָבוֹא בְמָצוֹר), 'He will make an overwhelming whiplash pass, but it will not invade the fortress'. Although adhering closely to Isaiah's context and meaning, the Hodayoth author clearly adapts the text and its meaning to fit his purpose.

One of the most interesting interpretations of Isaiah is the quotation of Isa. 33.15 in 7.2-3. Isaiah's statement (אֹזֵן אֹטֵם מִשְּׁמֹעַ דָּמִים וְעֹצֵם עֵינָיו) מֵרְאוֹת בְּרָע, 'who stops his ears against plots of murder and shuts his eyes against contemplating evil') describing the characteristics of the righteous person uses a separative מִן (19.2b; 40.3a). The Hodayoth takes the statement with a causal מִן, speaking in the first person of what the righteous one has suffered *because of* the wickedness of others, combining Isa. 33.15 with expressions from 6.10 or 32.3, and following the frequently observed practice of reversing the order of the quoted parallel clauses: 'My eyes are blind from having seen evil, my ears, through hearing the shedding of blood'[62] (שׂוּ עֵינַי מֵרְאוֹתַץ רַע אוֹזְנִי מִשְׁמוֹעַ דָמִים).

These are only a few examples of quotations in the Hodayoth. However, they are sufficient to demonstrate that, although the Hodayoth share numerous verbal parallels with the Old Testament in general, and the prophets in particular, this does not warrant the conclusion that this is due to the poverty of Jewish poetic skill, that the poems are little more than strings upon which randomly selected biblical beads were strung in a vain effort to imitate the brilliance of Old Testament literary genius. Since scholars may never be able to determine to what extent the language of the Hodayoth simply reflects the current usage of the Qumran community, it may be impossible to ascertain just how

Maisonneuve, 1957), p. 56, but Holm-Nielsen, *Hodayot*, p. 103, interprets the unit as extending through 7.5.

62. Regarding the stylistic inversion of parallel clauses in a quotation, see Talmon, 'Synonymous Readings', p. 340, and, more recently, Beentjes, 'Inverted Quotations in the Bible'. He credits M. Seidel with a similar observation (p. 508 n. 4). In Isa. 33.15, the phrase is preceded by a reference to the hands (נֹעֵר כַּפָּיו מִתְּמֹךְ בַּשֹּׁחַד, 'keeps his hand from accepting bribes'), while 7.3 continues with a reference to the heart (הֵשַׁם לִבְבִי מִמַּחֲשֶׁבֶת רוֹעַ, 'my heart is horrified at wicked schemes'), probably derived from Isa. 6.10 where 1QIsa reads הֵשַׁם rather than הַשְׁמֵן (make fat). The Hodayoth's substitution of שַׁע (be smeared) for Isa. 33.15's עַצַם (shut) is therefore probably also based on Isa. 6.10, though it could be influenced by Isa. 32.3. Dupont-Sommer, *Le livre des hymnes*, p. 57, is inconsistent in translating the מִן in the first and second clauses as 'in order not to' (*pour ne pas*) but the מִן in the parallel third clause as 'because of' (*à cause du*).

dependent it is on Old Testament Hebrew. In any case, the use of the Old Testament at Qumran involves much more than an effort to create a link with the community's historical heritage. Rather, the phrases of the Old Testament are cited repeatedly as expressing the living faith of the author, as the most fitting means of describing God, the wicked and the community of the righteous, and their interrelationship as he understood it. Beyond this, there is clear evidence that, at least in some passages, an obvious interpretation and reapplication of a cited text is being made, not simply a contextless appropriation of words.

Assessment

It would be presumptuous to claim that this brief survey offers a thorough assessment of quotation in early Judaism. Other apocryphal books and Qumran documents could have been examined in greater detail, in addition to targums, midrashic texts, pseudepigrapha and the New Testament.[63] This chapter has focused on the verbal parallels of Sirach and the Hodayoth with the Old Testament because of the amount of scholarly literature devotred to the phenomenon of quotation in these texts and because of the extensive use which these texts make of the prophets. Furthermore, they contain passages which, in style and tone, are similar in many ways to the oracles of the Old Testament prophets. Therefore, these writings serve to illustrate as well as any the problems

63. See nn. 4, 8, 9, 43 above for bibliography as well as J. Bonsirven, *Exégèse rabbinique et exégèse paulinienne* (Bibliothèque de Théologie historique; Paris: Beauchesne, 1938); J. Carmignac, 'Les citations de l'Ancien Testament dans "La Guerre des Fils de Lumière contre les Fils de Ténèbres" ', *RB* 63 (1956), pp. 234-60, 375-90; N.N. Glatzer, 'A Study of the Talmudic-Midrashic Interpretation of Prophecy', in *idem* (ed.), *Essays in Jewish Thought* (Birmingham, AL: University of Alabama Press, 1978), pp. 16-35; L. Hartman, *Prophecy Interpreted: The Formation of Some Jewish Apocalyptic Texts and of the Eschatological Discourse of Mark* (Lund: C.W.K. Gleerup, 1966); B.M. Metzger, 'The Formulas Introducing Quotations of Scripture in the New Testament and the Mishnah', *JBL* 70 (1951), pp. 297-307; Miller, 'Targum, Midrash and the Use of the Old Testament in the New Testament', pp. 79-82; J. de Waard, *A Comparative Study of the Old Testament Text in the Dead Sea Scrolls and in the New Testament* (STDJ, 4; Leiden: E.J. Brill, 1965); P. Wernberg-Moller, 'The Contribution of the Hodayot to Biblical Textual Criticism', *Textus* 4 (1964), pp. 133-75, C.A. Evans and J.A. Sanders (eds.), *The Function of Scripture in Early Jewish and Christian Tradition* (JSNTSSup, 154; Sheffield: Sheffield Academic Press, 1998); M. Albani *et al.* (eds.), *Studies in the Book of Jubilees* (TSAJ, 65; Tübingen: Mohr Siebeck, 1997).

and prospects of the study of quotation in early Judaism.

Since the above analysis necessarily has been quite selective, no attempt will be made to draw any conclusions about the differences between the use of the Old Testament in Sirach and at Qumran. A number of biblical phrases have been noted which are found in both Sirach and the Qumran Hodayoth, but they do not therefore indicate, for example, that the former is dependent upon the latter. Furthermore, the diversity in usage within the individual texts is so great that no great significance can be drawn from differences in the way that each employs a particular phrase. Carmignac's claim that the use of the same citations suggests a similar tendency toward an 'anthological style' and perhaps the use of common 'florilegia' (= anthology) goes beyond the evidence.[64] Zink, who concludes that there is great similarity between biblical interpretation in the Apocrypha and at Qumran, sees the major difference in the Apocrypha's lack of a developed eschatology and of an idea of a special person who would usher in the new age.[65] A more detailed analysis might reveal many interesting similarities and differences in the ways in which the two select, adapt, interpret and apply Old Testament texts in keeping with their own theologies and purposes, but that, unfortunately, lies beyond the scope of this work.

What are the implications of this survey for the assessment of prophetic quotation? It is necessary to begin by summarizing what has been observed concerning quotation in the non-canonical Jewish literature. First, questions of terminology and definition remain a major issue. In the past, the tendency has been to consider every verbal parallel a quotation, with the goal of achieving as extensive a list of Old Testament parallels as possible. Recently, the need for a passage-by-passage analysis of text and context has been stressed. Kittel has shown how helpful the use of more precise categories can be in reducing exaggerated claims of dependence.

Secondly, many of the verbal parallels may reflect current usage, stereotypical phrases, generally recognized figures of speech, and idiomatic expressions, as well as thorough acquaintance with Scripture, in which dependence on the Old Testament is nonexistent, indirect or unconscious.

Thirdly, the use of introductory formulae is apparently a historical

64. J. Carmignac, 'Les rapports entre l'Ecclésiastique et Qumrân', *RevQ* 3 (1961–62), pp. 209-18 (217).
65. Zink, 'The Use of the Old Testament in the Apocrypha', pp. 180-89.

development, since they appear only in the latest apocryphal books and with increasing frequency at Qumran. Since they are not employed every time a passage from the Old Testament is repeated almost verbatim by a later writer, even at Qumran, it is wrong to demand such a formula for 'true quotation' to be present. It is not clear what their use indicates about an author's attitude toward the Old Testament. Since formulae never accompany the Hodayoth citations, it may be that their use is governed by the author's purpose within a given text or passage. The infrequency of explicit quotations also may be due in part to stylistic or generic requirements.[66]

In the fourth place, the selection of Old Testament citations is influenced primarily by the author's themes and theology. The failure to quote a given book or section thereof does not necessarily suggest that it was unavailable, unfamiliar or unimportant to the author. Affinity in form and/or style with the new composition also may lead to its more frequent usage.

Fifthly, a given composition may exhibit great variety in the frequency, sources and uses made of biblical citations. A marked divergence in any of these does not inherently suggest the presence of more than one author. Certain genres and subjects more readily accommodate literary borrowing than do others.

Finally, the use of the Old Testament often involves an adaptation and interpretation which serve to apply a biblical description, promise, warning or teaching to a contemporary writer's or reader's personal or corporate experience. In such a case, a proper understanding of the quotation's original context and meaning is crucial to a proper understanding of the passage which incorporates it. This practice is to be sharply distinguished from the use of biblical language merely for its rhetorical effect. Stanley noted that there is no observable correlation between the degree of 'freedom' with which the biblical text is quoted and either the genre of the quoting text or its proclivity for citation.[67]

---

66. See also Hoffman, 'The Technique of Quotation and Citation as an Interpretive Device', pp. 71-79, who traces the development of the use of explicit quotation from the Hebrew into rabbinic Judaism, attributing it, in part, to the growing concept of canonization.

67. Stanley, *Paul and the Language of Scripture*, pp. 305-307. According to Stanley, the basic types of adaptation include omitting irrelevant words, phrases, or clauses, adjusting the grammar of the source text to suit the new context, replacing a word or phrase by a more appropriate one, adding interpretive words or phrases,

It is not surprising that early Jewish writers drew heavily upon the Old Testament which constituted a major source of their national, linguistic and religious heritage. Whether or not they already considered these books to be 'Scripture' is difficult to determine.[68] It is obvious, however, that the numerous verbal parallels which permeate their writings indicate an appreciation of and reverence for the Old Testament which transcend simple literary indebtedness. It is not an implausible step, then, to move back several centuries to the biblical prophets and explain the numerous verbal parallels within them as arising from similar beliefs: From the conviction that God's Word is reliable, that his promises may be trusted, that judgment and deliverance will come, that ancient documents speak to contemporary crises and concerns. If this is the case, then one might expect quotation to be employed within the prophets in a manner similar to its use within the non-canonical writings which followed, for the attitude toward the Old Testament which is reflected in the quotations of Sirach and the Hodayoth most likely had its origins among the producers of the Old Testament writings themselves.[69]

---

changing the word order, and extracting a useful passage from a more problematic original context, such adaptations serving (1) 'to conform the grammar of the citation to its new linguistic environment', (2) 'to improve the rhetorical impact', and (3) 'to insure that it communicates the precise point that the later author wanted to make in adducing the text' (pp. 343-47).

68. See n. 27, above, on 'canonicity', and Patte, *Early Jewish Hermeneutic in Palestine*, Chapter 2, pp. 19-30, although he does not discuss the Apocrypha.

69. Chapter 8 will seek to demonstrate that this is, indeed, the case.

Chapter 5

QUOTATIONS OF PROVERBIAL SAYINGS AND
OTHER SPEAKERS IN THE OLD TESTAMENT

When one speaks of 'quotations' within the prophets, the term is
potentially ambiguous in meaning. This was noted already by Eduard
König, who in his 1904 essay 'Gibt es "Zitate" im Alten Testament?'[1]
discussed a variety of ways in which the term may be used, such as
indicating any saying whose implied author is an unspecified impersonal speaker. This suggests that prophetic quotation can be viewed not
only as part of the larger phenomenon of literary borrowing within the
Old Testament as a whole, but also as just one of many types of
'foreign material' incorporated into a new context to serve some purpose of the author or speaker, all of which a modern writer might
correctly enclose within quotation marks to indicate the borrowing.

This wider meaning of 'quotation' has been the subject of several
lengthy studies in recent decades. Robert Gordis focused on quotation
within Wisdom literature while Hans Walter Wolff devoted his attention to quotation in prophetic speech and George Savran examined
quotation in biblical narrative. This broader understanding of quotation
has been employed by a number of scholars in addressing a variety of
textual problems. Although not specifically addressing the same problem, their insights also may offer some assistance in untangling the
methodological knot of prophetic quotation.

Gordis's interest in quotations, which spanned four decades of scholarly writings, arose in the course of his study of Wisdom literature,
particularly Ecclesiastes. Noting clauses which were grammatically,
syntactically and thematically at variance with their surrounding context, he suggested that, rather than emending them or excising them as
glosses or interpolations, they should be viewed as proverbial sayings

---

1. König, 'Gibt es "Zitate" ', pp. 734-46.

which were quoted by the writer. Expanding his approach to include non-proverbial sayings, he developed the following definition of quotation:

> Words which do not reflect the present sentiments or situation of the speaker, but have been introduced by the author to convey the standpoint either of another person or of another situation ... [including] citations from previously existing literature, whether written or oral ... [as well as] passages that cite the speaker's words or thoughts whether actual or hypothetical, past or present, which are distinct from the present context.[2]

Many of Gordis's examples were introduced by verbs of speaking or thinking; however, others lacked any such indication. Thus, Gordis spoke also of '"virtual quotations", i.e. a passage in a literary document that becomes intelligible only if the reader mentally supplies an introductory *verbum dicendi* or *cogitandi* which is not expressed in the text'.[3] Further investigation[4] demonstrated that this usage is found throughout the Old Testament, as well as in extra-biblical, oriental and rabbinic sources. While admitting that the identification of virtual quotations was rather subjective, depending on the reader's skill and insight, he cited Archer Taylor's criterion—'a passage, when it varies grammatically or syntactically from ordinary usage or from the usage of the context, can be safely declared to be proverbial'[5]—as offering a sufficiently objective basis for proceeding. One is also helped, according to Gordis, by 'a sympathetic understanding of the writer's personality'.[6] The ultimate test, however, is the degree to

2.   R. Gordis, *The Book of God and Man: A Study of Job* (Chicago: University of Chicago Press, 1965), p. 174.

3.   R. Gordis, 'Virtual Quotations in Job, Sumer, and Qumran', *VT* 31 (1981), pp. 410-27 (410-11).

4.   A chronological list of Gordis's publications on this subject includes: 'Quotations in Wisdom Literature', *JQR* NS 30 (1939–40), pp. 123-47; *idem*, 'Quotations in Biblical, Oriental, and Rabbinic Literature', *HUCA* 22 (1949), pp. 157-219; *idem, Koheleth: The Man and his World. A Study of Ecclesiastes* (New York: Schocken Books, 3rd edn, 1973 [1951]); *idem, The Book of God and Man*; *idem, The Book of Job: Commentary, New Translation, and Special Studies* (New York: Jewish Theological Seminary of America, 1978); *idem*, 'Virtual Quotations in Job, Sumer, and Qumran'.

5.   A. Taylor, *The Proverb* (Cambridge, MA: Harvard University Press, 1931), pp. 6-7.

6.   Gordis, 'Quotations in Wisdom Literature', p. 129.

which such an interpretation makes greater sense of the text. Most interesting to Gordis was the variety of functions performed by these direct or indirect quotations in verbalizing the unexpressed ideas or sentiments of the writer or speaker, conveying the sentiment of a subject other than the writer or speaker, or setting forth opposing views in argument and debate.[7]

In a 1980 essay,[8] R.N. Whybray utilized a similar approach in determining the relationship of Qoheleth to earlier Old Testament wisdom, especially Proverbs 10–29. Whybray sought to isolate sayings which (1) are self-contained, (2) correspond closely in form to those of Proverbs, (3) have themes which are characteristic of Proverbs yet are in partial or total disagreement either with their immediate contexts or with Qoheleth's characteristic ideas, and (4) have language which is free from late features.[9] His examination of those passages which fit at least two of these criteria led him to conclude that Qoheleth gave unqualified approval to some of these sayings, but only after completely reinterpreting the basic wise–foolish contrast, while giving

---

7.   In *The Book of God and Man*, pp. 174-75, Gordis listed the principal categories of quotations to be found in the Bible:

1.   Citations from the current folk wisdom (apothegm or rhetorical question).
2.   The speaker's direct quotation of the words of others (his foes, friends, God, or the people).
3.   The development of an elaborate dialogue where the identity of the particular speaker must be inferred by the reader.
4.   Presentations of the unspoken thought of the speaker.
5.   The citation of prayers offered on earlier occasions or promised for the future when deliverance comes.
6.   The presentation of ideas previously held by the speaker or writer.
7.   A hypothetical idea that might or should have occurred to the subject.
8.   The citation of a proverb, either without comment or expanded by an additional observation by the author.
9.   The use of contrasting proverbs to negate one view and affirm another.
10.   The citation of the arguments of one's opponents in debate (generally contains exaggeration and distortion).
11.   Indirect quotations with or without a *verbum dicendi*.

8.   R.N. Whybray, 'The Identification and Use of Quotations in Ecclesiastes', in J.A. Emerton (ed.), *Congress Volume: Vienna 1980* (VTSup, 32; Leiden: E.J. Brill, 1981), pp. 435-51.

9.   Whybray, 'The Identification and Use of Quotations', p. 437.

qualified approval to others. Whybray saw this reuse of earlier Wisdom sayings as indicating that, although Qoheleth regarded himself as standing within Israel's Wisdom tradition, he could use relatively little of the earlier wisdom (only 'secular' proverbs) to express or support his views.

While Gordis and Whybray identified 'quotations' within Wisdom literature, Hans Walter Wolff studied a similar phenomenon in the prophetic literature.[10] Wolff identified more than 250 passages in which 'foreign voices' are introduced into prophetic speech. These 'voices' may speak as witnesses on the prophet's behalf, express the views of his opponents, represent non-contemporary, non-present or non-human speakers, or offer future words. Although most of them are preceded by a verb of speaking or indicated in some other way, Wolff also recognized that these are sometimes omitted. In such cases, the effect of the quotation is considerably intensified: 'Its relationship to that of explicitly introduced quotations is that of the living word to the written one.'[11]

Wolff assessed these quotations as being employed by the prophets for several reasons: to enliven the speech, to clarify the message, and to serve as the vehicle of hyperbole, harshness or irony. Accordingly, the majority are fictitious, fabricated by the prophet to serve his rhetorical purposes. Many others, however, are authentic statements, including some whose origins can be located within earlier biblical material, such as the use of 1 Sam. 8.6 in Hos. 13.10. Wolff noted how these quotations often involved some modification of the original wording, exhibiting the prophet's freedom in handling traditional material ('human words'). As a result, some quotations fit nicely within the rhythm of their new contexts while others, retaining prose features, sit uncomfortably in the text. The quotations gain a new meaning or new application in their reuse and their appropriation indicates that the prophet viewed his contemporary situation as analogous in some respects to that of the original setting. In contrast, Wolff noted that the elders in Jeremiah's day cited Micah's earlier prophecy of doom (Jer. 26.18, cf. Mic. 3.12), without any variation, since it represented an earlier 'word of Yahweh' and therefore could not be handled as freely.

Wolff made the following observations regarding authentic quotations: (1) For a quotation to be considered authentic, it must exhibit a

10. Wolff, 'Das Zitat im Prophetenspruch'.
11. Wolff, 'Das Zitat im Prophetenspruch', p. 47.

complete agreement in content, although not necessarily in form, with the statement being cited. (2) The quotation contemporizes the other passage, declaring that the past word holds true for the present. (3) The prophet quoted earlier passages in order to address the question of guilt, indicating the continuity in the history of the people's sins.[12]

Wolff also identified a number of freely composed quotations in later prophetic literature. Portions of those composite quotations can be substantiated as being derived from earlier biblical material, including priestly Torah, prophetic and cultic-liturgical traditions. Among the borrowings from the prophetic tradition, he included Isa. 35.4 which uses a 'voice' from Isa. 40.9-10; Jer. 46.6 which cites an old familiar word from Amos 2.14,[13] in which a similar atmosphere of insane panic and futile flight prevails; and a section of one Moab oracle (Jer. 48.32-33) which takes up the motifs of the lament of the people from an earlier Moab oracle (Isa. 16.8-10). These composite quotations employ resonances of older prophetic passages in order to 'intuitively guide the understanding of those listening'.[14]

Wolff admitted that many authentic quotations (25-30 of them) may not be verifiable among the canonical writings. Several characteristics which they possess, however, suggest that they were not first composed by the prophet in whose oracles they appear. Among these are the use of technical terms such as מָשָׁל (proverb) or שִׁירָה (song), the prophet's recalling his own earlier words, distinctive rhythmical or rhyming patterns, the absence of any catchword connection with its context, and content indicators such as reflections of the history and thought-world of its origins, peculiar style, and incomprehensibility. The real value of Wolff's work for our purposes is his concentration on the form and function of quotation as an important component of prophetic rhetoric.

Michael Fox, in a 1980 essay, sought to introduce more methodological objectivity into 'The Identification of Quotations in Biblical

---

12. Wolff, 'Das Zitat im Prophetenspruch', p. 60.

13. In 'Das Zitat im Prophetenspruch', p. 62 n. 40, Wolff noted regarding Jer. 46: 'See in addition other sections of the chapter. Verse 10 assumes Isa. 34.6; Verse 11 can only be understood on the basis of Jer. 8.22, an example of how the quotation unfolds his own life and thereby seems not to fit (*befremdet*) in the context, cf. Volz on this passage'. Wolff denied that Jeremiah was the author of these foreign oracles because their manner of quotation was not in keeping with the prophet's 'manner' (German: Art).

14. Wolff, 'Das Zitat im Prophetenspruch', p. 62.

Literature'.[15] Although lauding Gordis's hypothesis as a heuristic principle to avoid excessive excising, emendation and transposition of
passages, Fox was critical of its overly subjective application, such as
in Gordis's translation of ‏ראיתי אני ש‎ in Eccl. 2.13 as 'I have heard it
said' (lit. 'I have seen that'), implying that a quotation was being introduced, when a normal rendering of the phrase would be insufficient to
mark a quotation.[16]

According to Fox,

> quotations are words that either 1) are taken from another source but
> used as the speaker's words or 2) are meant to be understood as belong-
> ing to a person other than the primary speaker, regardless of their actual
> source, and only repeated by him.[17]

Passages in the first category are called quotations according to their
origin while those in the second are called quotations according to the
way they are used in discourse. With regard to the latter, it is essential
to identify the citation in order to understand the passage properly. As a
result, there is a significant difference between marked and unmarked
quotations, for in 'marking' the statement, the speaker is 'deliberately
setting a distance between himself and the quoted words, possibly to
give them greater authority, possibly because he disagrees with them,
possibly some other reason'.[18] On the other hand, if quotations are left
unmarked, this may indicate that the speaker intends them to be taken
as expressing his own thoughts. 'In other words, the more important for
the meaning of a passage it is for the reader to understand that certain
words are quoted, the more clearly the writer must show him that they
are.'[19]

Accordingly, in the case of 'proverbial coinage' or 'literary borrowing', Fox's first category, formal indicators of quotation are unnecessary, for although the recognition of this type of quotation may deepen
one's understanding of the text, it will not fundamentally change it.[20]
Furthermore, although 'knowledge of the source enriches our awareness of the allusions the quotation bears ... these allusions are con-

---

15. M.V. Fox, 'The Identification of Quotations in Biblical Literature', *ZAW* 92
(1980), pp. 416-31.
16. Gordis, *Koheleth: The Man and his World*, p. 140.
17. Fox, 'The Identification of Quotations', p. 417.
18. Fox, 'The Identification of Quotations', p. 418.
19. Fox, 'The Identification of Quotations', p. 421.
20. Fox, 'The Identification of Quotations', p. 420.

trolled and restricted by their new context'.[21] For interpretive purposes, therefore, the statement, though quoted, may be treated as the speaker's own words. Indeed, unless one can identify the original context from which it is quoted, it is of little value, despite Gordis's assertions, even to recognize that quotation is taking place.

In the case of 'attributed' quotations, on the other hand, the meaning of the passage depends on the reader's recognition that a switch in voices has occurred. Unless this is obvious from the content of the passage, formal indicators are essential, such as marking by an explicit verb of speaking or thinking or virtual marking by a verb or noun that implies speech, the presence of another subject besides the primary speaker in the immediate vicinity of the quotation, or a shift in perspective indicated by a change in grammatical person or number.[22]

Fox admitted that it is often difficult to identify with any certainty whether a quotation is indeed present, as well as to determine where that quotation begins and ends. In dealing with this phenomenon, one must ask oneself why the author chose not to mark quotations more clearly, and what 'literary function ambiguity and uncertainty fulfill'.[23] However, Fox felt that it is likely that less 'signalling' of an attributed quotation would be necessary if the author was drawing on a canonical Scripture with which his readers were thoroughly acquainted and which was commonly quoted for prooftexts. In his opinion, however, this was not the case during biblical times.

In 1988, George Savran published a fascinating study of quotation in biblical narrative,[24] in which he examined the form and function of quoted direct speech, that is, those narrative passages in which one character explicitly repeats words which she or he or another character expressed earlier. Unlike Gordis and Wolff, Savran was concerned only with those statements which are attributed to a specific prior speaker.

Savran observed that verbatim repetition is relatively infrequent, only

21. Fox, 'The Identification of Quotations', p. 421.

22. Fox, 'The Identification of Quotations', p. 421-23.

23. Fox, 'The Identification of Quotations', p. 427.

24. G.W. Savran, *Telling and Retelling: Quotation in Biblical Narrative* (Indiana Studies in Biblical Literature; Bloomington: Indiana University Press, 1988). Savran refers to the studies of Gordis, Wolff, Fox, van der Woude (see Chapter 8 n. 146) and Crenshaw. See also M. Sternberg, *The Poetics of Biblical Narrative: Ideological Literature and the Drama of Reading* (Bloomington: Indiana University Press, 1985).

ten examples being identified (two to seven words in length). Changes involve shortening, lengthening and paraphrasing the previous utterance, apparently with conciseness and variation in language being high priorities, though sometimes the wording is altered in a significant and revealing manner. In his opinion, such quotation is more than a mere 'rhetorical flourish or gratuitous repetition', serving within the story as a reminder, a means of deception or an accusation. Within the narrative in general, quotation can assist in the organization of the plot, in characterization and in the expression of the author's point of view.[25]

As speech within speech, such quotation 'brings one set of words into contact and/or conflict with another' as the speaker of the quotation 'engages in a temporal dialogue between the past and present', using quotation to evoke a response. Because such quotation is identifiable and verifiable, it affords the reader a unique opportunity to compare the 'initial and subsequent formulations'. Thereby one discovers the 'power of context to transform the meaning of quotation regardless of its fidelity to the original words', as well as the significant semantic effect of even minor variations and omissions. Savran concluded that the meaning of a quotation is to be found 'somewhere between the original context and its quoted setting, drawing upon elements of both contexts, yet never fully aligned with either'.[26] Thus the proper analysis of quoted direct speech demands that the interpreter give careful attention to a number of textual features.

The studies of Gordis, Whybray, Wolff, Fox, and Savran,[27] although not primarily concerned with the type of quotation which is being discussed in this work—in fact, Wolff denied that his consideration

25. Savran, *Telling and Retelling*, p. 74.

26. Savran, *Telling and Retelling*, pp. 108, 110, 111. Savran comments regarding the effect of recontextualization: 'although the quoted words take on the meaning ascribed to them by their new context, they still retain some autonomy as identifiable prior direct speech, which carries within it some of the sense of its orignal context' (p. 110).

27. Other studies following a similar approach include: S.H. Blank, 'Irony by Way of Attribution', *Semitics* 1 (1970), pp. 1-6; N.C. Habel, 'Appeal to Ancient Tradition as a Literary Form', *ZAW* 88 (1976), pp. 253-72; T.W. Overholt, 'Jeremiah 2 and the Problem of "Audience Reaction" ', *CBQ* 41 (1979), pp. 262-73; G.V. Smith, 'The Use of Quotations in Jeremiah XV 11-14', *VT* 29 (1979), pp. 229-31; N.A. van Uchelen, 'Isaiah I 9: Text and Context', *OTS* 21 (1981), pp. 155-63.

included literary quotations such as these[28]—nevertheless offer some provocative suggestions regarding the proper methodology for studying prophetic quotation:

1. Literary quotation can be viewed as a part of the larger phenomenon of 'foreign voices' that are incorporated within the biblical text.
2. A number of formal or content markers help to indicate the presence of quotations within a passage.
3. Quotations serve a variety of functions within a literary composition.
4. The absence of any introductory formula or strict verbal agreement with the original source may be due to the speaker's or author's purpose in citing the earlier words.
5. It may not always be necessary or intended that the hearer or reader recognize the quotation in order for the passage to be understood.
6. Verbatim repetition in quotation is rare, and any divergence may have a profound effect on the meaning of the whole.
7. The recontextualization of a quoted statement results in a complex layering of meaning.

Since some of these points will be discussed more fully in Chapters 6 and 7, it will suffice, at this point, simply to note that, although an impasse seems to have been reached in the contemporary study of prophetic quotation, new approaches can be derived from the analysis of other genres and rhetorical features of biblical literature which may be applicable to this phenomenon and yield further insights into the meaning of the prophetic literature.

---

28. Wolff, 'Das Zitat im Prophetenspruch', p. 47 n. 71: 'It is to be viewed entirely differently when prophetic speech takes up the words of earlier prophets as building blocks, without stating that it involves borrowed words. This occurs in postexilic prophecy, either consciously or unconsciously. The "Apocalyptist Joel" (4.17) quotes the "prophet Joel" (2.27), and the latter builds on Deutero-Isaiah (45.5f.), who, in turn, has taken up earlier traditions (Ezek. 20.2; Deut. 4.35)'; and p. 35 n. 31: 'Naturally, I have excluded from the discussion those words which are to be classified as glosses. Entire sentences from earlier prophets are "quoted" on the margins of later prophetic writings, e.g Jer. 48.29; cf. in this regard P. Volz, *Der Prophet Jeremia*, 2 1928, p. 407.' It is for this reason that Wolff is included in this section, even though he, unlike the others, examined prophetic literature.

Chapter 6

QUOTATION IN WESTERN LITERATURE

To turn to comparative literature studies in order to seek assistance in disentangling the methodological knots of prophetic quotation may, at first glance, appear to be an acquiescence to the pressures of methodological faddism. To be sure, the discipline of biblical studies currently is being inundated by a wide variety of applications of the literary approach to the Bible. The authors of structuralist, narratological and reader-response analyses promise fresh insights into the text, and others offer New Criticism as a replacement for the antiquated historical-critical approach. Admittedly, there is a potential benefit in a 'close reading' of the text, but excesses are also prevalent. James Kugel has correctly complained that 'what is nowadays called literary criticism of the Bible often consists of the imposition onto biblical texts of ideas about genre, form, and literary convention wholly foreign to the world of the Bible's creation', often 'fundamentally distorting the object of... analysis'.[1]

The goal of this chapter, however, is not to apply the tools of literary analysis to the Bible. Rather, as in the two preceding chapters, the intent is to examine how quotation in another 'corpus'—Western literature—has been approached by the scholars of comparative literature, in order to determine whether some of their questions, cautions, methods and conclusions might shed some helpful light on the issues and problems involving prophetic quotation. The potential application of these approaches to the biblical phenomenon will be explored in the final chapters of this study.

---

1. J. Kugel, ' "James Kugel Responds." Response to "On the Bible as Literature", by A. Berlin', *Prooftexts* 2 (1982), pp. 328-32 (328). See also T. Longman III, 'An Appraisal of the Literary Approach', chapter 2 in *Literary Approaches to Biblical Interpretation* (Foundations of Contemporary Interpretation, 3; Grand Rapids: Zondervan, 1987), pp. 47-62.

Consulting studies of quotation in the documents of the ancient Near East as well as early Judaism can easily be defended on the basis of geographical, chronological, theological or linguistic proximity, but how can one justify the comparison between canonical Scripture and modern secular literature? What does Isaiah have in common with James Joyce? Much in every way.[2] Both the Old Testament prophetic books and Western literature contain verbal parallels between contemporary works as well as works separated by centuries, indicating that authors were influenced continually by their predecessors. These verbal parallels are usually unmarked, often making their identification and interpretations difficult. Some correspond completely in their formulation while other parallels share little more than a word or a distinctive grammatical form. Both frequently employ an elevated poetic style. These similarities at least suggest the aptness of a comparison, without ignoring the uniqueness of the Bible's oral origins, complex literary history and sacred purpose.

T.K. Cheyne, nearly a century ago, led the way in applying several ideas from his knowledge of world literature to the issue of parallel passages in the prophets,[3] and it is likely that some of the criteria of priority used in dating biblical materials have been derived from similar studies of the literature of antiquity.[4] However, there is a more

---

2.   Rom. 3.2 (RSV). The purpose of this biblical citation will be discussed below in n. 70.

3.   Cheyne, *The Prophecies of Isaiah*, II, pp. 234, 250. See also the more thorough approach of Johnson, *The Quotations of the New Testament*. A more sophisticated recent application of contemporary literary theory to the analysis of Old Testament quotations and allusions in the New Testament, under the rubric 'intertextual echo' is Hays's monograph, *Echoes of Scripture in the Letters of Paul*. Hays draws primarily on the work of John Hollander, *The Figure of Echo: A Mode of Allusion in Milton and After* (Berkeley: University of California Press, 1981), although he also refers to the literary studies of Thomas Greene, Harold Bloom, and Reuben Brower. (See the discussion of their contributions below.) The original version of this study was completed before the publication of Hays's study.

4.   See R.M. Meyer, 'Kriterien der Aneignung', *Neue Jahrbücher für das klassische Altertum, Geschichte und deutsche Literatur und für Pädagogik* 17 (1906), pp. 349-89; E. Löfstedt, 'Reminiscence and Imitation: Some Problems in Latin Literature', *Eranos* 47 (1949), pp. 148-64; B. Axelson, 'Lygdamus und Ovid: Zur Methodik der literarischen Prioritätsbestimmung', *Eranos* 58 (1960), pp. 92-111; A.G. Lee, *Allusion, Parody, and Imitation: The St John's College Cambridge Lecture 1970–71 Delivered at the University of Hull 11th March, 1971* (Hull: University of Hull, 1971).

compelling reason for turning again to comparative literature. Unlike the scholars who have discussed prophetic quotation, the students of comparative literature have frequently and thoroughly discussed the question of methodology. If there is any validity to the proposed approach, there are abundant resources in the 'literature about literature' from which methodological insights may be gleaned.

Indeed, it is the very embarrassment of riches that complicates the task. The materials consulted range from classical Latin epic poetry to contemporary American campaign speeches, from the study of an individual work or author to an essay on the whole English tradition beginning with Milton, from the simple aesthetic enjoyment of quotation to the terminological intricacies of its semiotics. Throughout, the effort will be to focus on the methodological prefaces rather than the detailed textual analyses. The approach here is that of the curious explorer who simply strives to climb high enough to attain new vistas and perspectives rather than that of the detective who leaves no stone unturned in the search for all available clues.

Terminology and Definitions

Before proceeding to examine the models, motives, uses and functions of quotation in literature, it is essential to achieve clarity in terminology and definitions. Here, as with prophetic quotation, a wide variety of labels have been applied to the phenomenon of verbal parallels (quotation, citation, borrowing, echo, influence, imitation, allusion) which are not completely interchangeable but often not clearly distinguished by their users. The nature of the confusion can be illustrated by noting three attempts at categorization. Wheeler, on the one hand, suggests *allusion* as the cover term for formulations (including quotation) which involve verbal repetition (and *reference* for interrelated texts which do not).[5] Hollander, on the other hand, notes three forms of *citation*: quotation, allusion and echo, each in turn exemplifying a lesser degree of verbal reduplication.[6] Anstensen reverses Hollander's classification, suggesting *quotation* as the generic term which embraces citation as well as proverbial sayings/expressions, which he further

5.   M. Wheeler, *The Art of Allusion in Victorian Fiction* (London: Macmillan, 1979), p. 3.
6.   Hollander, *The Figure of Echo*, pp. 64, 72.

divides into proverbs, proverbial phrases and proverbial allusions.[7]

More common is categorization by contrast in which quotation or allusion is set over against borrowing or repetition. Here, however, the distinction no longer concerns the degree or extent of verbal repetition but rather the authorial intent. According to Hermann Meyer,

> Borrowing differs from quotation in that it has no referential character. It is not intended to be related to its source, and this is fitting, for having recourse to its origin may result in philological clarification, but it cannot enrich the meaning or increase the aesthetic value.[8]

Hence it really is not necessary for the reader to detect a 'borrowing' in order for the passage to be correctly understood, while it is essential in the case of 'quotation', since more is involved than mere repetition.

Unfortunately, this important distinction is not always expressed in the proposed definitions of quotation. Typical is that of Wheeler: 'An identifiable word, phrase, or passage taken from an adopted text.'[9] Even broader is Morawski's suggestion:

> Quotation is the literal reproduction of a verbal text of a certain length or of a set of images, notes, sounds, movements, or a combination of all or some of these elements or some of them with a verbal text, wherein what is reproduced forms an integral part of some work and can easily be detached from the new whole in which it is incorporated.[10]

---

7.   A. Anstensen, *The Proverb in Ibsen: Proverbial Sayings and Citations as Elements in his Style* (New York: Columbia University Press, 1936), p. 27.

8.   H. Meyer, *Das Zitat in der Erzählkunst: Zur Geschichte und Poetik des europäischen Romans* (Stuttgart: J.B. Metzlersche Verlagsbuchhandlung, 1961), pp. 14-15. See also E. Miner, 'Allusion', in A. Preminger (ed.), *Princeton Encyclopedia of Poetry and Poetics* (Princeton, NJ: Princeton University Press, enlarged edn, 1974), p. 18; and T.M. Greene, *The Light in Troy: Imitation and Discovery in Renaissance Poetry* (New Haven: Yale University Press, 1982), p. 49. In this regard, Rabinowitz's criticism that Meyer's polarities distinguish 'techniques according to how accurate or explicit the copying is, but they don't discriminate among the ways the models are used' is misdirected, P.J. Rabinowitz, ' "What's Hecuba to Us?" The Audience's Experience of Literary Borrowing', in S.R. Suleiman and I. Crosman (eds.), *The Reader in the Text: Essays on Audience and Interpretation* (Princeton, NJ: Princeton University Press, 1980), pp. 241-63 (241-42).

9.   Wheeler, *The Art of Allusion in Victorian Fiction*, p. 6.

10.   S. Morawski, 'The Basic Functions of Quotation', in C.H. van Schooneveld (ed.), *Janua Linguarum: Studia Memoriae Nicolai van Wijk Dedicata. Sign, Language, Culture* (Series Maior, 1; The Hague: Mouton, 1970), pp. 690-705

More in keeping with the above categorization is Gerhard Kaiser's definition of quotation:

> The citation of foreign formulations with the goal of embellishing one's own speech (one's own text), conferring authority on it, or critically distancing oneself from such an authority, by means of a more or less explicit reference.[11]

Although one might question whether Kaiser's three functions of quotation are comprehensive enough to embrace all examples, his approach is commendable in that it moves beyond mere linguistic similarity to the question of intent.

Accordingly, it is the use of the term '(verbal) parallel' which is both most neutral and most problematic, since it often offers too little evidence for one to declare with any assurance that a given passage is derived from another. Altick and Fenstermaker speak of the seductive power of such 'sequences of lines whose resemblances are such as to suggest that the author of one sequence knew, perhaps deliberately imitated, the other', so that one jumps quickly to this desired conclusion rather than giving due consideration to other options.[12]

Models of Imitation

Precisely in regard to the authorial purpose of quotation, the study of comparative literature offers rich resources, for one is not simply limited to the analysis of examples of verbal repetition, since the very authors themselves were often far from reticent to discuss their own imitative procedures. Although one could cite statements from nearly every period of Western literature, the writers of the Renaissance were particularly given to such discussions of the theory and practice of imitation and were especially fond of using images and metaphors to characterize their approach. The best study in this regard is that of G.W. Pigman who divides these metaphors into three groups: (1) transformative, including apian, digestive; and filial metaphors; (2) dissimulative, which involve concealing or disguising the relationship between

(691). See also U. Schneider, *Die Funktion der Zitate im 'Ulysses' von James Joyce* (Studien zur englischen Literatur, 3; Bonn: Bouvier, 1970), p. 9.

11. G.R. Kaiser, *Proust—Musil—Joyce. Zum Verhältnis von Literatur und Gesellschaft am Paradigma des Zitats* (Frankfurt: Athenäum Verlag, 1972), p. 7.

12. R.D. Altick and J.J. Fenstermaker, *The Art of Literary Research* (New York: W.W. Norton, 4th edn, 1993), pp. 110-13.

a text and its model; and (3) eristic, involving an open struggle with the model for pre-eminence.[13]

Pigman's classification offers a convenient outline for considering the variety of ways in which scholars of comparative literature have approached quotation. Although some continue to label all unacknowledged appropriation as 'literary kleptomania' or 'plagiarism',[14] most consider the practice more honorable. In one respect, all writing involves imitation and repetition, since each author is heir not only to a language but also to a literature with a long and complex history and is inevitably influenced by that inheritance, whether consciously or unconsciously, whether willingly or against her or his will. The author's use of forms, genres, imagery, themes and even plots necessarily represents a selection from the vast resources offered by their cultural heritage. In this regard, originality consists not in a *creatio ex nihilo* but in the author's new use of old matter.[15]

Accordingly, the key issue in quotation is not necessarily which sources are being drawn on but rather how they are being used. Exact reproduction is not a goal to strive toward, much less the essential characteristic of quotation; instead, it may be taken as indicative of a pedantry or an intellectual poverty to be avoided at all cost. Furthermore, as Weisgerber has pointed out, 'literalness does not mean faithfulness',[16] since the new context into which the borrowed statement is placed may serve to seriously skew or even reverse its original semantic intent, even though its verbal formulation is left intact. Perhaps this is why the apian metaphor, in Pigman's reckoning, has been the most widely used description of imitation. Just as the bee who gathers pollen from a variety of blossoms transforms it into honey, so the would-be author who has gathered a multitude of felicitous and

13. G.W. Pigman, III, 'Versions of Imitation in the Renaissance', *Renaissance Quarterly* 33 (1980), pp. 1-32 (3-4). In his essay, Pigman cites numerous statements which employ these analogies. See also Greene, *The Light in Troy*, especially Chapter 4, 'Themes of Ancient Theory', pp. 54-86, which discusses Greek and Latin theory.

14. J. Rickman, 'On Quotations', *International Journal of Psycho-Analysis* 10 (1929), pp. 242-48 (247).

15. A.J. Smith, 'Theory and Practice in Renaissance Poetry: Two Kinds of Imitation', *BJRL* 47 (1964–65), pp. 212-43 (216). See also E.E. Kellett, *Literary Quotation and Allusion* (Cambridge: W. Heffer & Sons, 1933), p. 14.

16. J. Weisgerber, 'The Use of Quotations in Recent Literature', *CompLit* 22 (1970), pp. 36-45 (38).

memorable phrases from earlier literature transforms them in the process of reproduction.

If comparison with a quoted statement's source can be undertaken, a variety of divergences may be uncovered. Meir Sternberg distinguishes three modes of 'interference' with the original version: paradigmatic (e.g. lexical substitution), syntagmatic (e.g. addition, omission, reordering) and contextual (changes in time, place, genre, stylistic register), but warns that further analysis is necessary, since different forms of divergence may have the same effect, while the same form may produce different effects.[17] To analyze one such borrowing adequately, says Sternberg, one must take full account of what has been preserved and what has been modified (or omitted) in transmission. Even then one has not yet explained whether the divergences are due to a lack of access to the original, faulty memory, carelessness, contentment with a paraphrastic rendering, or conscious literary intent.

If transformation is such a frequent if not constant characteristic of quotation, correct identification and interpretation is indeed a difficult task which is further complicated by the consideration of Pigman's second category: dissimulation. In Erasmus's words: 'If we wish to imitate Cicero successfully, we must above all disguise our imitation of Cicero.'[18] The effort to conceal one's literary borrowings has been evaluated in a number of ways. Some have seen this as further proof that 'plagiarism' is the only appropriate label for this activity. Kellett views quotation as a kind of intellectuals' version of 'hide-and-seek', in which the author carefully selects apropos snippets of earlier classics and cleverly embeds them in his or her own composition in an attempt to display erudition to the readers who, in turn, upon recognizing this disguised pilferage, find titillation in their own skill as a literary detective: 'He says, "Here is a theft from Homer—track it down, and none will rejoice more than I when it is found".'[19]

---

17. M. Sternberg, 'Proteus in Quotation-Land. Mimesis and the Forms of Reported Discourse', *Poetics Today* 3 (1982), pp. 107-56 (129): 'Substitution, addition, and recontextualization, for instance, may all result in comparable shifts of meaning ... [while] the consequences of lexical substitution, say, range from the semantic to the stylistic.'

18. Cited in Pigman, 'Versions of Imitation in the Renaissance', p. 10.

19. Kellett, *Literary Quotation and Allusion*, p. 3. See Wheeler's criticism of Kellett, *The Art of Allusion in Victorian Fiction*, p. 1. H. Thun, *Probleme der Phraseologie* (Beihefte zur Zeitschrift für Romanische Philologie, 168; Tübingen:

Kellett's hypothetical quotation of the author makes it clear that, at least in his opinion, the dissimulative model of imitation is not completely sincere in its efforts to conceal. To the extent that pleasure and ornamentation, which Kellett views as the primary purposes of quotation, are dependent on reader recognition to have their desired effect, the author who is overly successful in the covert operation of citation or allusion is his or her own worst enemy. Here again the above distinction between quotation and borrowing is important. In the case of borrowing, where reader recognition is unnecessary for the reused phrase to have its desired effect, dissimulation may be essential to keep the original context from interfering with the new composition, while a surreptitious stroking is still reserved for the curious cultured reader who is able to ferret out its source. In the case of quotation or allusion, however, where its intended effect is dependent upon recognition, the author must be more cautious. To be sure, some of the reader's difficulty in identifying quotation may be due to an inadequate education or to the great distance between the reader's and the author's cultural storehouses or result from the divergence in the 'copy' from the 'original' which occurs in the process of transformation even when no dissimulation is intended. Nevertheless, in the end, the author must be blamed if the quotation falls on deaf ears. In this respect, the difference between 'good' and 'bad' quotation, from an aesthetic rather than an ethical perspective, is not a question of the exactness or appropriateness of the repetition but of its success in achieving its desired effect on the reader.[20]

If recognition is a necessary feature of quotation, it is not surprising that some authors, such as Eliot, annotated their own compositions. However, even then, the footnotes are an appended rather than integral

Max Niemeyer, 1978), p. 42, claims, with regard to quotation, 'The real (*materielle*) product is thereby ... the same. The evaluation tends to depend on the norms and ideals of the given cultural communities.'

20. See the discussion of the ethics of quotation by Sternberg, 'Proteus in Quotation-Land', p. 133; and especially by P.F. Boller, Jr, *Quotemanship: The Use and Abuse of Quotations for Polemical and Other Purposes* (Dallas: Southern Methodist University Press, 1967).

In this regard, C.D. Stanley's distinction between author-centered approaches to citation (including 'any verse that exhibits substantial verbal agreement with a known passage of Scripture') and reader-centered approaches (excluding any passages which fail to 'give the reader at least some indication that a quotation is indeed present') is helpful. Stanley, *Paul and the Language of Scripture*, p. 34.

component of the text.[21] It seems to be almost an unwritten rule of world literature that quotation, for the most part, is to be left unmarked and unacknowledged, as if to do so would be to violate some basic law of aesthetics. Thus both the author and the reader are forced to walk the tight-rope between revelation and concealment. As Hermann Meyer has aptly described the situation:

> If a quotation is so completely fused with the new literary whole that it is no longer recognizable, it loses its specific character and specific effect... The attraction of quotation lies in the peculiar tension between assimilation and dissimilation...: It is closely bound up with its new environment, but at the same time stands in contrast to it.[22]

Rabinowitz distinguishes seven categories of literary recycling on the basis of what the audience or reader of a new work knows about the work from which it borrows: plagiarism (if the discovery of the source will diminish the effect), adaptation (if the discovery is irrelevant), and retellings, parody, criticism, revisions or expansions (if the discovery is essential).[23] It must be pointed out, however, that Rabinowitz is projecting an ideal reader who will apprehend and interpret each case of borrowing precisely as the author intended. Although this may never occur in the actual process of reading, by making judicious use of dissimulation, the author may do much to guarantee a sufficient degree of success in this undertaking.

The fact that dissimulation is one of the author's imitative strategies should raise a number of questions for the interpreter. First of all, when there is considerable divergence between a passage and its alleged

---

21. However, it should be noted that, in T.S. Eliot, the annotations may represent pretensions to learnedness. See T.S. Eliot, 'Notes on "The Waste Land" ', in *The Complete Poems and Plays* (New York: Harcourt, Brace & Company, 1934), pp. 50-55; G. Williamson, *A Reader's Guide to T.S. Eliot: A Poem-by-Poem Analysis* (New York: Noonday Press, 1955), p. 120: 'Given the qualified reader, the poem must produce its effect without the notes.' Also H. Kenner, 'Notes to "The Waste Land" ', in J. Martin (ed.), *A Collection of Critical Essays on 'The Waste Land'* (Englewood Cliffs, NJ: Prentice–Hall, 1968), pp. 36-38.

22. Meyer, *Das Zitat in der Erzählkunst*, p. 12.

23. Rabinowitz, ' "What's Hecuba to Us?" ', pp. 246-99. Although Rabinowitz's study examines the way in which a new work uses an audience's knowledge of the original, it focuses on the reader's quandary over which role to assume in assessing quotation—whether to read as the reader's real self, as a part of the authorial (hypothetical) audience, or as a part of the narrative (imaginary) audience.

original, one must ask: Are the *differences* intentional or are the *similarities* coincidental? When so many of the distinctive features of the alleged original have been removed and little more than a basic image or key word remains, one must ask: can the source even be identified, since many authors employed the same metaphors and themes? Is this clearly a conscious quotation, or is this simply an ornamental borrowing which is so effortlessly interwoven with the author's own language that it must involve only an unconscious drawing upon the treasures of the memory? Can a quotation which is so disguised entail any serious communicative intent which requires the identification and assessment of its veiled source?[24]

If the dissimulative analogy raises doubts regarding the necessity or even the possibility of identifying an author's model, the eristic analogy assumes not only that the reader will recognize the literary predecessor with whom the author is competing but also that the reader will acknowledge that the author has achieved mastery over her or his 'opponent'. The eristic metaphor goes back at least as far as Longinus:

> Plato would never have reared so many of these flowers to bloom among his philosophic tenets, never have wandered so often with Homer into the regions and phrases of poetry, had he not striven, yea with heart and soul, to contest the prize with Homer like a young antagonist with one who had already won his spurs, perhaps in too keen emulation, longing as it were to break a spear, and yet always to good purpose.[25]

Pigman points out that, although emulation was considered one of the three basic types of repetition (*sequi, imitari, aemulari*), it did not emerge in the Renaissance as the technical term for the freer, transformative type of imitation partly because of its 'ambiguous moral significance'.[26] Somehow it was deemed legitimate, even noble, to imitate one's literary ancestors, but to seek to surpass them reflected an unworthy hubris.

Perhaps the peculiar historical circumstances of the Renaissance produced the prevalent attitude that the classics were simply unsurpassable. In any case, during this period, the individual author's stance toward his heritage determined whether her or his work would be the mere

---

24. See Pigman, 'Versions of Imitation in the Renaissance', pp. 12-15.

25. W.H. Fyfe (trans.), 'Longinus: On the Sublime', in G.P. Goold (ed.), *Aristotle: The Poetics, XXIII* (LCL, 199; Cambridge, MA: Harvard University Press, 1973), p. 169.

26. Pigman, 'Versions of Imitation in the Renaissance', p. 23.

display of fossils from the past or their actual revivification. As Thomas Greene expresses it:

> The characteristic risk of Renaissance imitation lay in the potential paralysis of its pieties, in a rhetoric so respectful of its subjects that no vital emergence from the tradition could occur ... The discovery of the ancient world imposed an enormous anxiety upon the humanist Renaissance, but its living poetry represents a series of victories over anxiety, based upon a courage that confronts the model without neurotic paralysis and uses the anxiety to discover selfhood.[27]

However, it should not be inferred from the preceding discussion that struggle with the past was merely a feature of the Renaissance age. According to Harold Bloom, every author is unavoidably influenced by her or his literary predecessors, whose poems are continually 'finding' her or him, hence poetic history is identical with the history of poetic influence. 'All influence is dialectical, in that it involves both gain and loss for both giver and recipient. And so all influence induces anxiety.'[28] Bloom has made an extensive study of the effects of what he terms 'the anxiety of influence', especially on post-Miltonic English poets. A person's success or failure as a poet depends on whether she or he is 'weak', merely idealizing her or his predecessors, or 'strong', appropriating her or his predecessors.

From Bloom's perspective, in order for a latecomer poet to clear imaginative space for her or his own writing, she or he must utilize a series of six 'revisionary ratios', analogous to Freudian defense mechanisms, each of which involves not so much a *re*interpretation as a *mis*interpretation of the model:

1. Clinamen, which is poetic misreading or misprision proper ...
2. Tesera, which is completion and antithesis ...
3. Kenosis, which is a breaking-device ...
4. Daemonization, or a movement toward a personalized Counter-Sublime ...
5. Askesis, or a movement of self-purgation ...
6. Apophrades, or the return of the dead ...[29]

---

27. Greene, *The Light in Troy*, pp. 30-31.

28. H. Bloom, *Figures of Capable Imagination* (New York: Seabury, 1976), pp. xi-xii; *idem*, *The Anxiety of Influence: A Theory of Poetry* (New York: Oxford University Press, 1973), p. 5; and *idem*, *A Map of Misreading* (New York: Oxford University Press, 1975), pp. 83-105.

29. Bloom, *The Anxiety of Influence*, pp. 14-16. In *Figures of Capable*

In subjecting the predecessor's work to these revisions, the author is asserting that the earlier poet was accurate up to a certain point but now needs to be both corrected and completed by the new poet. Bloom sees these revisions not as a set of hermeneutical crowbars among which to select one for dismantling the influential strong poem but as succeeding stages in the life of the strong poet, as she or he progressively overcomes her or his anxiety of influence. The ultimate victory is in the later poet's *holding* her or his poem open to its precursor where once it simply was open to its influence.[30] When one understands the dynamics of strong poetry, one realizes that poetic influence may result in greater rather than diminished originality and therefore is to be welcomed, despite the anxiety which it evokes.

Indeed, to associate the eristic model primarily with anxiety may be quite inappropriate. According to Emerson, 'a great man quotes bravely, and will not draw on his invention when his memory serves him a word as good... genius borrows nobly', for 'only an inventor knows how to borrow'.[31] Rather than over-emphasizing a general model of literary borrowing, it is essential to examine *how* and *why* such borrowing occurs.

The Motives, Types and Functions of Quotation

The use of transformative, dissimulative and eristic metaphors to describe quotation suggests that its proper analysis involves far more than what Bloom calls 'the wearisome industry of source-hunting, of allusion-counting'.[32] Although a classification of an author's quotations, allusions and references according to their sources may provide helpful insights not only into his or her reading habits but also into the 'cultural treasury' of his or her intended audience,[33] this effort is only

Imagination, pp. 1-17, Bloom traces the six steps in the life and work of Coleridge.

30. Bloom, *The Anxiety of Influence*, p. 16. The emphasis is Bloom's.

31. Emerson, *Letters and Social Aims*, VIII, pp. 183, 191, 204, cf. also 194. See the critique of Bloom's 'anxiety of influence' by Altick and Fenstermaker, *The Art of Literary Research*, pp. 130-32; and L. Jenny, 'The Strategy of Form', in T. Todorov (ed.), *French Literary Theory Today: A Reader* (trans. R. Carter; Cambridge: Cambridge University Press, 1982), pp. 34-63 (36-38).

32. Bloom, *The Anxiety of Influence*, p. 31. Bloom adds that this 'industry ... will soon touch apocalypse anyway when it passes from scholars to computers'.

33. Kaiser's study, *Proust—Musil—Joyce*, investigates the latter, especially the

infrequently followed by an investigation into the underlying motives, types and functions of the quotations thus neatly categorized. Hermann Meyer has posed the essential question in a most vivid manner: 'Can quotations be more significant than the raisins in a cake? Can their aesthetic effect transcend the momentary delight, which raisins have for the palate?'[34]

In order to probe more deeply into the significance of quotation, scholars recently have gone beyond the classification of its sources to the classification of its uses within a given work, author, period or type of literature. Although, as the following survey will reveal, there is some overlap among the various approaches for analyzing quotation, their authors' views are set forth as schematically as possible.

The popular attitude toward quotation is that it is motivated by laziness, lack of originality or courage to express one's own views, or genuine, even inordinate, affection for a predecessor's words.[35] From a psychoanalytical viewpoint, Rickman understands 'motivation' as the purposed effect of the use of quotation: to win over, to overwhelm, to conceal.[36] However, a more perceptive approach is that of G.B. Conte in his study of allusion in poetry.[37] Conte begins by listing 'forms' of allusion but makes it clear that the choice of a particular form is controlled by the author's underlying motive or purpose:

1. Metaphoric/integrative—A parallelistic relation is discovered between the poet's word and another (admired) word. As in a

society's attitude toward its literary tradition. See also Meyer, *Das Zitat in der Erzählkunst*, p. 23.

34. Meyer, *Das Zitat in der Erzählkunst*, p. 10.

35. Kellett, *Literary Quotation and Allusion*, p. 5, somewhat euphemistically, hypothesizes that quotation may have arisen from 'the prudent and economical use of materials provided by others'.

36. Rickman, 'On Quotations', p. 243. He continues, '... in terms of the pleasure-pain theory of mental action the pleasure derived is due to the fact that the sense of helplessness is averted; we have risen to the occasion, albeit with the help of another'. Kellett, *Literary Quotation and Allusion*, pp. 44-55, offers an expanded but similar list of motivations, including subterfuge, buttressing or gaining attention for one's opinion, expressing indignation, scorn, or malice, as well as obscure motives, such as a desire for rhetorical variety and ornamentation. For a thorough discussion of motivations underlying quotation in the media and public speech, see Boller, *Quotemanship*.

37. A.L. Johnson, 'Allusion in Poetry', *PTL: A Journal of Descriptive Poetics and Theory of Literature* 1 (1976), pp. 579-87.

palimpsest, scrutiny of the text reveals a second message hidden behind or within the first. In order to assure her or his own work's permanence, the poet absorbs a literary substrate already considered permanent.

2.   Reflexive—As in simile, two formal segments are reflected in each other without combining, inviting comparison but setting up a strong metaliterary tension.

3.   Ironic—A special case of reflexive allusion, it attempts to undercut the original text by arranging a context which implies a negation of the original system of values.

4.   Complimento—Its intention is to acknowledge the worth of the original model.

5.   Aemulatio—It implies a *complimento* of rivalry, wishing to outdo the predecessor.[38]

Conte's final two categories remind one of Pigman's frequent reference to 'sequi', 'imitari' and 'aemulari'. In the final analysis, Pigman views these three versions of imitation not as in opposition to one another but as a progression, lacking clear boundaries, as the author moves from non-transformative to transformative repetition, from simple reproduction to critical reflection on or correction of the model. This progression, in turn, sets up three possibilities of evaluation: The imitation is deemed worse, equal, or better than its model.[39]

A more sophisticated study of the implicit attitude of the author toward his or her literary sources has been undertaken by Thomas Greene. Although, like Pigman, he is concerned primarily with Renaissance imitation, his analysis is applicable to other literature as well. Greene describes four types of relationships between the quoting text and its model:

1.   Reproductive or sacramental—reverently rewrites a hallowed text which is a fixed object, beyond alteration or criticism.

2.   Eclectic or exploitative—treats all traditions as stockpiles to be drawn upon ostensibly at random, assuming they can be disarranged endlessly without suffering damage.

3.   Heuristic—advertises its derivation from its underlying subtexts and underscores the historicity of its sources, but then

---

38.   Johnson, ' "Allusion in Poetry" ', pp. 581-82. See also Rabinowitz's seven categories listed above.
39.   Pigman, 'Versions of Imitation in the Renaissance', pp. 25, 32.

proceeds to distance itself from them, thus drawing attention to the linguistic, cultural, historical and perspectival gulf between them.

4. Dialectical—proves its historical courage and artistic good faith by leaving room for a two-way current of mutual criticism between authors and between eras.[40]

For Greene, as well, these four types represent a progression rather than an opposition. Similar to Bloom's six revisionary ratios, an author or an age can move from the paralysis of uncritical reverence to the freedom of mutual respect and criticism, from an uncontrolled flood of influence to a carefully channeled flow which nourishes rather than drowns one's literary productivity.

Another way to categorize quotation is according to its function in its new context. Among the scholars who list basic functions there is considerable agreement concerning some of the items included,[41] as well as concerning the fact that a quotation can function in more than one way in a given context. The most common use of quotation is aesthetic or ornamental, employing borrowed language as an embellishment which adds vividness to an author's rhetoric. There is some debate regarding whether this is true quotation. However, given the multi-functional nature of repeated language, there is little doubt that quotation can have an ornamental effect even if that is not its primary purpose. Decisive in this regard is whether its aesthetic effect is enhanced or diminished by the recognition of its source. The decorative function of quotation is often linked to the author's desire to be considered erudite on the basis of his or her learned allusions, although some decorative repetitions may have been unconsciously absorbed into his or her own language through personal reading.

A second function of quotation is as an appeal to authorities, in which the author of the words is recognized clearly both as the originator of the statement and as well qualified to address the subject which is being discussed. The quoted authority then, by implication, endorses the writer's viewpoint. A third function is as an expression of a general or universal idea, usually a key theme of the quoting text. Whereas the

40. Greene, *The Light in Troy*, pp. 38-46.
41. Morawski, 'The Basic Functions of Quotation', pp. 692-96; Schneider, *Die Funktion der Zitate im 'Ulysses' von James Joyce*, p. 153; Wheeler, *The Art of Allusion in Victorian Fiction*, pp. 20-22. See also Anstensen, *The Proverb in Ibsen*, p. 4.

first function relates to *how* something is said and the second relates to *who* said it, the third focuses on *what* is said.

Since such a 'universalizing' statement is often pointed and concise in its formulation, almost gnomic in nature, one must exercise caution before declaring it to be a true quotation. More often than not, it may be a proverbial expression instead. In several respects the distinction is unimportant. For one thing, a quotation and a proverb may share the same form and usage. In fact, a quotation may, through repeated usage, gradually attain the currency of a popular proverb, whose historical or literary origin becomes forgotten and even irrelevant to its proper understanding. The transitional stage is that of the proverbial allusion, or a 'popular saying' (*geflügeltes Wort*), whose literary origin remains well known, even though it has achieved widespread currency. It is precisely at this point that the distinction between quotation and proverb is essential, for only the quotation is able to evoke a second context whenever it is invoked.[42] A similar problem concerns the distinction between the quotation and the motif, topos, and archetype. Whereas the former represents a 'foreign body' which introduces another historical context by authorial design, the latter, though operating 'within the limits of certain cultural sequences', are largely ahistorical and impose 'compositional or conceptual patterns' by their very nature.[43]

The first three functions of quotation are relatively simple to assess in comparison with the next three. The fourth function, which already has received considerable discussion, is, in Morawski's terminology, the stimulative–amplificatory quotation. This type of citation forms a building-block in the author's argument as it awakens in the memory of the reader another text and context, adding a second substrate layer of meaning to the statement. The author, in addition to citing the text, may amplify it in a variety of ways in reinterpreting it, ranging from a minor expansion to a radical reapplication to a complete negation. Unlike the third function in which the repeated idea is central, in the fourth the larger context, indeed the entire text, from which the quotation is drawn, may resonate in the new setting. Although the basic thrust of

42. See Taylor, *The Proverb*, pp. 34-38; Anstensen, *The Proverb in Ibsen*, pp. 20-27; Schneider, *Die Funktion der Zitate in 'Ulysses' von James Joyce*, p. 10; also G. Büchmann, *Geflügelte Worte: Der Citatenschatz des deutschen Volkes* (Berlin: Hande & Spenersche [Max Pasche], 1925).

43. Morawski, 'The Basic Functions of Quotation', pp. 696-98; Greene, *The Light in Troy*, p. 50.

such a quotation may be clear, its full appreciation may require a detailed examination of the two texts. Related to the fourth function and especially prominent in novels is a fifth—the use of quotation as a kind of 'short-hand notation', as typifying or characterizing a particular group, individual, time or place. Here, too, the basic idea expressed by the quotation may have determined its selection, but an understanding of the literary context from which it is drawn may be essential for it to have its intended characterizing function.

A sixth function of quotation is also an offshoot of the fourth: the structuring quotation. There are several ways in which quotation can give structure to a literary work. Hermann Meyer answers his own question—'Can quotation, despite its fragmentary nature, play a significant role in the total structure of a narrative work, which encompasses its individual parts?'[44]—with an emphatic 'yes'. Gerhard Kaiser, whose study was inspired by Meyer, concurs that the investigation of the smaller elements, such as quotations, 'must always be carried with the entire work in view', since they determine its 'microstructure'.[45] Ulrich Schneider, also following Meyer, illustrates how quotations supply the scaffolding for Joyce's *Ulysses*. By citing a passage from Homer's *Odyssey* at the beginning of each chapter, a parallel is set up between the two works, the former actually helping to structure the latter. In addition, quotations are used to establish motifs or to reintroduce central themes and keywords, to conclude episodes, thus recapitulating chapter motifs, obliquely prognosticating future events, and linking one chapter to the next, and to serve as *leitmotifs*, with quotations from one source recurring with a different meaning in each context.[46]

The use of quotation as a type of *leitmotif* has been noted also by John Hollander, especially in Milton's *Paradise Lost*. This internal reference, or self-echo, which may operate in conjunction with external allusion, is, in the final analysis, the result of an author's self-quotation. Self-quotation can result in an 'allusive resounding' not only 'across a gap' of many lines of text but between texts as well, often producing a 'kind of dramatic and typological irony'. Hollander concludes his discussion of 'Echo Schematic': 'The echo device and its variant schemes

---

44. Meyer, *Das Zitat in der Erzählkunst*, p. 10.
45. Kaiser, *Proust—Musil—Joyce*, pp. 1, 7.
46. Schneider, *Die Funktion der Zitate im 'Ulysses' von James Joyce*, especially p. 154.

of refrain and patterned repetition can have, as we have seen, a force of figuration much deeper than that of mere decorative patterning.'[47] Michael Wheeler has effectively summed up the 'structural' effect of both external and internal quotation from the same and differing sources, speaking of

> the necessarily sequential way in which we respond to allusions as we read ... even widely separated quotations from and references to the same adopted text can have an accumulative effect, later allusions 'reactivating' earlier allusions ... [resulting in] the establishment of a symbolic pattern or structure within an adoptive text through the development of some kind of a relationship with an adopted ... text. Sets of allusions to a single adopted text can provide the analogical matrix which shapes part of a novel, either overtly ... or semi-covertly ... On the other hand, allusions to a wide range of adopted texts can contribute to the adoptive text's central symbolism.[48]

Although every quotation may not contribute greatly to the overall shaping of a text, its potential structuring function may not as yet have received the attention it deserves.

A final function of quotation is the most complex, the most difficult to assess adequately, and the least thoroughly discussed. Related to what Greene calls the 'dialectical' type of imitation, the act of quotation sets in motion a hermeneutical dynamic by which the quoted and the quoting text mutually interpret each other. This dynamic has been variously described. According to Wheeler, 'When allusion ... triggers associations in our minds as we read ... both the text which we are reading and our store of accumulated associations are reshaped'. Bloom claims, in a statement previously quoted, 'All influence is dialectical, in that it involves both gain and loss for both giver and recipient', and J. Hillis Miller asks similarly: 'Is the citation an alien parasite within the body of the main text, or is the interpretive text the parasite which surrounds and strangles the citation which is its host?'

Quotation also relativizes the chronological gap between the quoter and the quotee. According to Weisgerber: 'In a way, the poetics of quotation allows us to make a journey in time. The past provides a vantage-ground from which the present can be viewed in a new

---

47. Hollander, *The Figure of Echo*, p. 60. For a further discussion of self-quotation, see Johnson, ' "Allusion in Poetry" ', p. 585; Kellett, *Literary Quotation and Allusion*, p. 6; and Weisgerber, 'Quotations in Recent Literature', p. 41.

48. Wheeler, *The Art of Allusion in Victorian Fiction*, p. 161.

perspective; ... conversely, the present also illuminates the past.' Bloom speaks of this almost magical chronological reversal as 'the uncanny effect ... that the new poem's achievement makes it seem to us, not as though the precursor were writing it, but as though the later poet himself had written the precursor's characteristic work', that later writers 'are being *imitated by their ancestors*!' In a similar manner, Hollander observes that instances of echo may be 'so scattered in the later texts that they seem to be regathered, in a reversal of direction, in the earlier one'. Indeed, 'this bidirectional quality of echo is frequently at work in major poetry, where in the structure of the poem's rhetoric, the anterior voice is made to seem the echo of the present one'.[49] No matter how differently they may express the matter, all of these scholars are agreed on the fact that quotation has a permanent interpretive effect on both the text from which it is taken and the text into which it is incorporated.

The Poetics of Quotation: The Contribution of Semiotics

As already has been noted, there are many ways to analyze quotation. One of the more recent approaches is that of semiotics and the related field of structuralism. Some practitioners of comparative literary study may consider the technical jargon and complicated diagrams of semiotics to be too far afield from the classic methods of their discipline to be useful here.[50] However, it is precisely with regard to an issue as complex as that of the mechanics of quotation that a new perspective should always be welcomed.

From a semiotic point of view, literary quotation and allusion represent unique features within a language system, in that, rather than having a simple relationship between a signifier and a signified, the signified (the quotation) is itself a signifier, or, to put it another way,

---

49. Wheeler, *The Art of Allusion in Victorian Fiction*, p. 162; Bloom, *Figures of Capable Imagination*, p. xi; J.H. Miller, 'The Critic as Host', in H. Bloom *et al.* (eds.), *Deconstruction and Criticism* (New York: Seabury, 1979), pp. 217-53 (217); Weisgerber, 'Quotations in Recent Literature', p. 42; Bloom, *The Anxiety of Influence*, pp. 15-16, 141; Hollander, *The Figure of Echo*, pp. 101-102.

50. For a general introduction to semiotics and structuralism in their application to interpretation, see R. Scholes, *Structuralism in Literature: An Introduction* (New Haven: Yale University Press, 1974); and *idem, Semiotics and Interpretation* (New Haven: Yale University Press, 1982); as well as J. Culler, *Structuralist Poetics* (Ithaca, NY: Cornell University Press, 1975).

the object of quotation is itself a subject.[51] The result is not simply 'meaning' juxtaposed with 'meaning', but rather 'meaning' within 'meaning'. In G.B. Conte's analysis:

> Allusion allows one literary text to work its way physically into another. One text may build physically on another, reutilizing and remolding the various physically memorable levels—phonic, graphic, lexemic, syntactic, rhythmic, semic—present in one small segment of the original construct.[52]

This 'literary substrate' produces 'an area of unexpected semantic overlap', since 'two significations are condensed into a single verbal segment'. This type of quotation, which Conte calls 'integrative' is relatively passive in comparison with the 'reflexive' quotation. The latter often involves dissimilar registers so that the 'tension of cohabitation' is compounded by a 'strong metaliterary tension' produced by two 'quarreling' voices, 'a willed rivalry' between the two texts, which may result in 'an expanding—or even a *repeatedly rebounding*—referential function; this comes to involve the whole literary output of the two authors, and, by extension, their paradigmatic and semiotic models for the two different worlds'. Once quotation has related two texts, they cannot again be 'disentangled'. It is 'irreparably "smeared" by the verbal segment which, as in imitative magic, resuscitates it… The reciprocal reaction between the two forms destroys the self-sufficiency of each', or, to use a different metaphor, allusion 'solders one system to another, and sets up a current of sense between them'.[53]

One of the most helpful attempts to expound the semiotic workings of quotation is the work of Ziva Ben-Porat.[54] Ben-Porat defines a liter-

---

51. Sternberg, 'Proteus in Quotation-Land', p. 108. See the discussion of Sternberg below. For an application of some of these principles to the analysis of biblical narratives, see Sternberg, *The Poetics of Biblical Narrative*, especially Chapter 11: 'The Structure of Repetition: Strategies of Informational Redundancy'.

52. Johnson, ' "Allusion in Poetry" ', p. 580.

53. Johnson, ' "Allusion in Poetry" ', pp. 581, 582, 585-86. It is not always clear when Johnson is simply summarizing Conte and when he is expressing his own views on the subject.

54. Z. Ben-Porat, 'The Poetics of Literary Allusion', *PTL: A Journal for Descriptive Poetics and Theory of Literature* 1 (1976), pp. 105-28. His discussion is considerably briefer and accordingly more lucid than the monograph of Antoine Compagnon, *La seconde main: Ou le travail de la citation* (Paris: Editions du Seuil, 1979), reviewed by P.-L. Rey, *La Nouvelle Revue Française* 318 (1979), pp. 116-18.

ary allusion as 'a device for the simultaneous activation of two texts... achieved through the manipulation of a special signal: a sign (simple or complex) in a given text characterized by a larger "referent" ' (an independent text), which 'results in the formation of intertextual patterns whose nature cannot be predetermined'. The essential element in quotation is a 'marker', consisting of some element(s) of the evoked text, which leads to the identification of the source text and simultaneously activates other independent elements of the text which remain to be identified. The interpretation of the marker in its present form and context, followed by the comparison with and interpretation of its original form (the marked) and context, makes an initial pattern between the two texts. This pattern, in turn, activates 'the evoked text as a whole, in an attempt to form maximum intertextual patterns', ultimately leading to a richer interpretation of the alluding text, as well as enriching the evoked text. Depending on the degree and extent of formal identity between the marker and the marked and the general familiarity of the marked, the marker will be either strong or weak, which may affect how quickly internal patterns are formed between the texts, especially if they are not initially related in any way.[55]

In recent decades, 'intertextuality' has become a become a prominent term in literary theory, though it is employed in a bewildering variety of ways. Though Julia Kristeva usually is credited with laying the theoretical foundation for intertextual approaches, she traces the concept back to M.M. Bakhtin who spoke of 'the dialogic orientation' of all discourse. According to Kristeva, 'any text is constructed as a mosaic of quotations; any text is the absorption and transformation of another', though she prefers the term 'transposition' because of the promiscuous usages of the term 'intertextuality'.[56] Jenny distinguishes between 'idealistic criticism' which utilizes aquatic, fluid metaphors, such as 'influences' and 'sources', from intertextual metaphors, such as texture and weave. Each source text has been so assimilated that it 'is there, potentially present, bearing all of its meaning without there being any need to utter it', thus conferring on the intertext 'an exceptional richness and density'.[57] Altick and Fenstermaker, however, use the term

55. Ben-Porat, 'The Poetics of Literary Allusion', pp. 107-12. See his diagram, p. 112.
56. Bakhtin, *The Dialogic Imagination*, p. 279; J. Kristeva, *The Kristeva Reader* (ed. T. Moi; New York: Columbia University Press, 1986), pp. 37, 111.
57. Jenny, 'The Strategy of Form', pp. 38, 45.

'intertextuality' in a more generalized manner to refer to

> the significant relationship between specific and in some way similar
> passages in two or more authors' work, the significance residing in the
> way the original meaning changed as it resonated in the work of a later
> one, where it appeared in a new context and with some—perhaps
> major—difference in purpose and effect.[58]

Literary Quotation as a Form of Reported Discourse

Another way to approach literary quotation is to view it as one of many forms of 'reported discourse'. Although sources and usages may differ, literary quotation shares much in common with other types of repeated language. A thorough study of this aspect of quotation has been made by Meir Sternberg. Sternberg analyzes quotation as consisting of four universals: (1) a representational bond, which links the quoting discourse and the original discourse, of which it is an imperfect mimesis; (2) structural framing, which surrounds and incorporates the quoted portion (the inset) into its new context; (3) communicative subordination (of the quoted portion to the quoting discourse), which is the automatic result of recontextualizing; and (4) perspectival montage or ambiguity, which is the blending and blurring of the voices and viewpoints of the original subject, with its own verbal, moral, sociocultural, thematic, aesthetic, informational, and persuasive expressive features, and the quoting subject who cites and manipulates it.[59]

Exactly how the quotation will function within a given context depends on the 'affective potential' of the original, the 'desired effect' of the frame, and the 'linguistic form' of the incorporated inset. The variables involved in the process of quotation are incredibly complex. On the one hand, the original context of the quotation 'with its own participants, spatiotemporal anchorage, sociocultural matrix, generic and linguistic conventions, and expressive goals' is never replaced or subsumed; on the other hand, since 'to quote is to recontextualize' and it is actually 'the contextual coordinates that give that sequence its meaning and function as an expressive structure', even a verbatim

---

58. Altick and Fenstermaker, *The Art of Literary Research*, p. 1. Somewhat similarly, A.H. Pasco, *Allusion: A Literary Graft* (Toronto: University of Toronto Press, 1994), p. 5, defines intertextuality as 'any textual exploitation of another text' and distinguishes three categories: imitation, opposition and allusion.

59. Sternberg, 'Proteus in Quotation-Land', pp. 107-109.

quotation 'must, to a certain degree, modify, if not misrepresent, its role and import within the original whole', not to mention the effect of deliberate manipulation.[60] Stylistic, situational and generic pressures all combine to reduce the correspondence between the original and the quote, and since the effect of a particular divergence can be determined only on a case-by-case basis, overt alteration may be more deceptive than covert changes.

The effect of quotation's recontextualization is determined by a number of factors, not the least of which is the addressee's informational access—whether or not the reader has independent access to the original. If the reader is unable to reconstruct the original, the bicontexuality of the inset is lost to her or him. Furthermore, if the reader fails even to recognize the quotation, as is often the risk when it is unmarked, the impact of this rhetorical device is effectively blunted. However, despite the anti-reproductive factors, the quoter can do much to 'moderate ... the overall effect of divergence and montage' so that the inset will be reproductive in communicative effect even though not in an absolute sense. Rather than drawing any hard and fast conclusions regarding the effect of any particular quoting strategy, Sternberg suggests 'the "Proteus Principle": in different contexts ... the same form may fulfill different functions *and* different forms the same function'.[61] What all this means is that reproduction, either in its stricter linguistic sense or its looser (and more appropriate) rhetorical sense, may be only a 'variable' and not a 'defining quality' in the description of quotation. More important is the recognition that

> each act of quotation serves two masters. One is the original speech or thought that it represents, pulling in the direction of maximal accuracy. The other is the frame that encloses and regulates it, pulling in the direction of maximal efficacy ... [and] each piece of quotation ... [is] the product of a tug-of-war, with two eternal rivals but changing factors and fortunes.[62]

Assessment

Despite Morawski's almost unbelievable conclusion that 'in literature ... the significance of the quotation does not appear to be great',

60. Sternberg, 'Proteus in Quotation-Land', pp. 121, 130-32.
61. Sternberg, 'Proteus in Quotation-Land', pp. 144, 148.
62. Sternberg, 'Proteus in Quotation-Land', p. 152.

and Schneider's warning against the danger of over-interpreting quotation,[63] most contemporary literary critics agree that quotation contains
vast treasures of meaning for those who are diligent enough to dig for
them, while most interpreters have only begun to scratch the surface.[64]
This new investigation into the functional strategies underlying quotation marks a radical change from earlier approaches:

> In the past century, allusiveness has been studied in various ways: as
> *Quellenforschungen*, as if the sources of the poetic Nile were not them-
> selves eloquent and derivative rivers; or as props to the infirmities of
> unoriginality; or as one of a set of credentials, like watermarks on paper,
> of the creative presence of an informed will.[65]

Weisgerber has offered a more positive assessment of quotation which
sets the agenda for its future analysis:

> Quotations constitute the epitome of a perennial and inexhaustible her-
> itage ... an exhortation to learn and to create, and the irrefutable evidence
> of our concern with a tradition, which we try not so much to imitate as to
> reshape and reinterpret.[66]

Before seeking to suggest some of the potential applications of the
comparative literary theory which have just been surveyed, some con-
cessions are necessary. First of all, one might criticize the approach
taken here as being too inclusive, ranging from ancient to modern
literature, from poetry to prose, and from English to a variety of foreign
languages. However, since the concern was not to examine the workings of individual quotations, which might differ according to the
language, period and genre of the literature, but to gather insights from
literary scholars' comments on the problems of methodology in studying quotation, casting the net as far out as possible seemed warranted, if
not highly desirable.

Secondly, one might criticize the survey as too undiscriminating, in
that it treated essays on allusion, echo, imitation and influence as being

63. Morawski, 'The Basic Functions of Quotation', p. 703; Schneider, *Die
Funktion der Zitate im 'Ulysses' von James Joyce*, p. 13.
64. See the comments by Ben-Porat, 'The Poetics of Literary Allusion', pp.
105-106; Greene, *The Light in Troy*, p. 1; Rabinowitz, ' "What's Hecuba to Us?" ',
p. 263; and B.A. Schlack, *Continuing Presences: Virginia Woolf's Use of Literary
Allusion* (University Park: Pennsylvania State University Press, 1979), p. x.
65. Hollander, *The Figure of Echo*, p. 72.
66. Weisgerber, 'Quotations in Recent Literature', p. 48.

as equally relevant to the subject as those concerned only with quotation. This procedure seems defensible for several reasons. Given the disagreement over terminology, it turns out that some scholars are actually discussing the identical phenomenon under different terms. Furthermore, since all such studies are concerned with some type of 'verbal parallel' to a greater or lesser extent, what they have to say about the reuse of language from earlier literature is directly relevant to the assessment of quotation. Similarly, a number of scholars have made it clear that distinctions such as quotation/allusion/echo relate to quantitative rather than qualitative differences.

Finally, one might object that the presentation of divergent viewpoints and even contradictory methodologies has been too uncritical. We might respond facilely that such intramural debate is better left to the literary experts than to dilettantes.[67] However, it must be admitted that a deliberate attempt has been made to straddle the methodological fences between formalism and deconstruction, between classical but often no longer accepted approaches and avant-garde semiotic approaches. The desire has been to listen politely to and then cautiously apply the varied insights of comparative literature to the problem of prophetic quotation.

The following insights gleaned from the preceding survey are deemed relevant to the study of the biblical phenomenon:[68]

1. The proper assessment of quotation is inherently problematic. The confusion in comparative literary theory regarding terminology and methodology demonstrates that the difficulty surrounding prophetic quotation is not due solely to the nature of biblical literature but is rather due largely to the nature of quotation itself.

2. There is no such thing as a simple quotation, though some quotations may produce less complex intertextual patterns. So much may be involved in the selection, modification and

---

67. One might cite, for example, David Hoy's qualified appreciation of Harold Bloom's work on the 'anxiety of influence', in *The Critical Circle: Literature, History, and Philosophical Hermeneutics* (Berkeley: University of California Press, 1978), pp. 159-66. See also R. de Beaugrande, 'Harold Bloom', ch. 14 in *Critical Discourse: A Survey of Literary Theorists* (Norwood, NJ: Ablex, 1988), pp. 281-307.

68. The task remains in the following chapters to test the validity of this assertion.

recontextualization of a quotation that its analysis is always a complex procedure.

3. Identification of a quotation's source is only the first step in its assessment. However, even this step is not always easy, since the verbal parallel may be the result of unconscious processes or may be derived from a 'second-hand' source, including the possibility that the phrase has already achieved a proverbial or motif/topos currency in which an awareness of its origin may long since have vanished.

4. The degree and extent of linguistic identity between the quotation and the original statement may determine whether one chooses the term 'quotation', 'allusion' or 'echo' to describe it, but is not in itself the sole indicator of faithfulness in reproduction.

5. A knowledge of both the original form and context of a quotation is essential to its adequate understanding, and 'context' may expand to include an entire work or author. In fact, the context may be even more important than the quoted statement, which may serve primarily as its marker.

6. Rare is the author, if not non-existent, who uses every quotation, even from a given source, in the same manner. The multifunctionality of quotation always must be taken into consideration. It is important to ask with regard to each quotation whether it is peripheral in the composition, serving a relatively simple purpose, or determinative, its related subtext playing a 'constitutive role' in the new text's meaning.[69]

7. The exact form which a quotation takes in a given context is the result of the interplay of numerous factors, only some of which are subject to the quoter's controlling influence, and some of which may be beyond the interpreter's comprehension. The double-layeredness of the quotation's 'meaning' lends itself to intentional ambiguities. Over-interpretation is, accordingly, as much a danger as under-interpretation.

8. From the perspective of communication theory, one must evaluate a quotation not only on the basis of authorial intent but also in terms of reader competency. One must seek to ascertain how much of an author's allusive language might

---

69. See Greene, *The Light in Troy*, p. 50.

fall on deaf ears and how much might be lost as a result. This may assist the interpreter in appreciating the writer's communicative strategies more fully.

9. Given the power of quotation to inseparably link two texts, one must acknowledge that the recognition of a quotation and its source will affect not only how the quoting text is read but also how the quoted text is read.

10. Given quotation's evocative power, self-quotation or internal repetition within a composition must be expected to occur frequently and be distinguished from external quotation because of its effective structural and recapitulative function. It need not be viewed as a merely stylistic, much less a secondary, feature.

Certainly, many more principles could be drawn from the preceding survey. If this assessment of the material is, for the most part, correct, one may ask again, this time with less trepidation, the earlier question: What does comparative literary theory have in common with the study of prophetic quotation? Much in every way![70]

70. Here the Pauline phrase has been quoted again to illustrate some of the functions of quotation. The statement is meaningful by itself as a response to the preceding question. However, a knowledge of the context of Romans adds to this the awareness that the quotation in its original context was also preceded by a question anticipating a negative answer from the audience. The positive answer which the author himself gave is then buttressed by supporting arguments and remains an important theme throughout the epistle, culminating in Rom. 11.26-36. Here the quotation is used as a structural device, marking the commencement and conclusion of this chapter's argument against an anticipated negative response. Rather than using the Pauline double question, I posed one half of the question at the beginning, the other half at the end. The second question imitates the first, yet reveals progress in its reformulation. In effect I have quoted both Paul and myself, effectively giving the final statement in this chapter a double source and triple context.

Part III

A New Approach to Prophetic Quotation

Chapter 7

PROPHETIC QUOTATION:
METHODOLOGICAL REFLECTIONS TOWARD A NEW APPROACH

One of the continuing interests of biblical scholarship is the manner in
which prophetic oracles, once uttered, were repeated and reapplied by
succeeding prophetic spokespersons to later generations of the faithful
within Israel. The history of the search for an adequate methodology
which would facilitate the detection and the evaluation of such quoted
material already has been rehearsed. Primarily, the effort was directed
at the difficult task of dating the literature, for, without relative dates,
determining the direction of the borrowing was virtually impossible. As
new ways of viewing the literary complexity of the text emerged, so did
new models for approaching the phenomenon of quotation, yet unanimity could not be achieved regarding reliable criteria for identifying
quotation or even regarding a definition of what actually constitutes
quotation. Seldom was the hermeneutical question of the purpose and
exegetical import of quotation handled, though manifold theories were
developed on the basis of generally acknowledged verbal parallels. The
lack of a methodology that would accommodate the historical and literary complexity of quotation often restricted progress in evaluating the
phenomenon.

The Basis for a New Approach

In the preceding chapters new perspectives for approaching the biblical
data have been sought. In part, the goal has been to place the biblical
phenomenon within its larger context as a part of Jewish, ancient Near
Eastern and world literature.[1] Furthermore, actual patterns of quotation

---

1.   One could conceive of the literature examined in Chapters 3, 4 and 6 as
concentric categories. In practice, however, the primary and secondary literature
consulted for each of the surveys proved to be without any significant overlap.

in other literatures were studied and the various methodologies which have been employed in evaluating them were noted. Although a comprehensive study of each literature was not attempted, it was hoped, that even a preliminary survey and analysis would yield some new suggestions for assessing the biblical data.

Quotation in the Comparative Material
To attempt to summarize the findings is problematic for several reasons. First of all, it may be ill-advised to seek to draw general conclusions when one has examined only a limited number of examples. Furthermore, the types of literature which were studied differ so greatly in context, scope, date, purpose and style as to warn against characterizing all of them in any statement.[2] Finally, since there is no unanimity regarding the proper approach to quotation in each of these literatures, absolute claims about methodology must be avoided. However, given the fact that the goal here is descriptive, that is, to note the various forms and functions of quotation, rather than prescriptive, that is, to suggest how it must function, such problems are not insurmountable if due caution is taken.

The following conclusions can serve as a starting point for examining the biblical data in the light of the comparative material:

1. *Introductory formulae* occur in all types of literature. Within Jewish literature they may be a later innovation, but the absence of formulae in the Hodayoth and their use within ancient Near Eastern literature suggest that the genre of the quoting text and the purpose for which something is being quoted are determinative. Ignorance of the source is a possible but less likely explanation. The use of introductory formulae may be accompanied by closer verbal correspondence, but this greater accuracy also may be due to the purpose of the quotation.[3]

2. A quotation, nevertheless, will be *marked* in some way, either overtly by a deictic particle or shift in person or number, or simply by a sufficient number of repeated key words and syntactical relationships so that the quoted text is recognizable. Due to a deficient knowledge of

---

2. As will be pointed out below, the methods employed in the four chapters could, in effect, cancel out each other. The data derived from each chapter will be applied selectively in formulating a composite method.

3. To facilitate the comparison, it will be noted where the point has been discussed previously: Chapter 3, p. 119; Chapter 4, pp. 147, 161, 169-70; Chapter 5, pp. 177-78.

the original audience's or reader's literary competence, it is impossible to know how much of each 'marker' is essential for recognition and how much simply served the purpose of the quotation. Obviously, if recognition was necessary for the quotation to function properly, the quoter would endeavor to make the use of quotation clear enough for the reader to identify it.[4]

3. *Divergences* between the quoted text and the quoting text may have a variety of explanations. Beside frequently cited reasons such as lack of access to the same text, quotation by memory, and lack of concern for accuracy, two primary sources of changes should be noted: (1) those necessary to adapt the text to a new context—grammatical, syntactical, stylistic, cultural; and (2) those which serve the author's purpose for the quotation—emphasis, irony, reinterpretation, application. One should attempt to account for as many changes as possible yet be wary of over-interpretation.[5]

4. The *frequency* with which quotation is employed may be a function of an individual author's style. However, the generic restraints of the quoting text may play a significant role: wisdom texts are catchalls for striking formulations. Holm-Nielsen has noted that the Hodayoth individual psalms contain more quotations than the community psalms, and Egyptian letters are filled with learned citations. (Guglielmi noted one such 'letter' which within 27 text lines contained, according to her categorization, two 'quotations' [*Zitate*], one 'reminiscence' [*Anklang*], one 'proverbial saying' [*geflügeltes Wort*], one (or two) 'allusions' [*Anspielung*], and one 'topos'. Certain historical periods may be marked by a *Zeitgeist* which promotes quotation, such as the Renaissance's return to the classics. In addition, the purpose of a composition or section thereof may be furthered by quotation, such as Sirach's prologue indicates, though a sober evaluation of the textual data reveals that the book is anything but 'a veritable tissue of biblical reminiscences'. The concentration of prophetic quotations within the prayer in Sirach 36 is clearly related to its purpose and not a proof (contra Middendorp) of distinct authorship.[6]

---

4. Chapter 5, pp. 177-78; Chapter 6, p. 201. See also Fishbane, *Biblical Interpretation in Ancient Israel*, p. 460.

5. Chapter 3, pp. 123-26; Chapter 4, pp. 147, 151-52; Chapter 6, pp. 186-87.

6. Chapter 3, pp. 117-19, 129; Chapter 4, pp. 151, 156-59, 161-62; Chapter 6, pp. 190-91. Guglielmi, 'Eine "Lehre" für einen reiselustigen Sohn', pp. 147-66, especially 151, 154.

5. The *sources* of quotation also may be a matter of the author's taste. Statistically, the Hodayoth authors had a preference for Isaiah and Psalms, though this choice may be due to the lyrical qualities of the authors and the variety of subjects treated in these lengthy books rather than to any 'theological' leaning. If the reuse is primarily for stylistic purposes, any striking formulation may be appropriate, perhaps the less familiar the better. However, in many cases, the very act of borrowing indicates not only an aesthetic appreciation of the quoted material but also a recognition of its inherent *authority*, continuing validity or contemporary appropriateness. Therefore, what is important in quotation is not the felicitous formulation alone, though this may influence its particular choice, but also the subject and content of the passage. This respect is indicated in the explicit statements in the Egyptian texts regarding the words of the ancients and manifested in the general stance of the Qumran community and Sirach toward the Old Testament. Specifically, however, quotations often deal with matters of religious duties, ritual procedures and exemplary behavior in the ancient Near Eastern materials and with vivid portrayals of judgment or promise or characterizations of the deity in his relationship to his people in early Jewish literature. However, there can be as much variety in the materials selected as there is of contexts which incorporate quotations. Beyond these few comments, statistics can indicate as little regarding why certain texts are included as regarding why others are excluded.[7]

6. In one respect, all quotation involves *interpretation*, since recontextualization inherently changes the meaning of the words quoted. Precisely what form this interpretation takes is determined by the exigencies of the quoted text and the quoting text. Holm-Nielsen sees in the Hodayoth a general reinterpretation of Old Testament texts in the light of the Qumran community's self-understanding. *Merikare* spiritualizes *Hor-Dedef*'s words, suggesting that practicing truth and justice are as good a preparation for the afterlife as pyramid building. A lesser shift occurs when later authors describe their actions or situation as similar to that of earlier literary or historical figures in Egypt regardless of differences in their circumstances. A variety of grammatical and syntactical modifications facilitate these reinterpretations, individualizing the corporate or nationalizing the individual statement, transforming a command into a statement or a statement into a command, invoking a

7. Chapter 3, pp. 119, 129, 143; Chapter 4, pp. 153-56, 157-59, 161-62, 166-67; Chapter 6, pp. 193-95.

promise in a prayer or portraying an eschatological promise as being fulfilled imminently. All of these are ways of actualizing an ancient word. Interpretation in the expected sense, that is, explaining what a previous saying means, is rare, though one might cite Sirach's identification of Isaiah as the speaker in Isa. 61.2. Perhaps the chronological or literary distance is too great to make such a use of quotation, leaving that for immediately appended explanatory glosses. Given the diverse types of reinterpretation which quotation may involve, one must be careful not to conceive of its purpose and function too narrowly or overlook its versatility in also structuring a text, directing attention and adding emphasis and rhetorical flair.[8]

7. Quotation must be carefully distinguished from *non-quotation* not simply in terms of its function but even more so in terms of its form. Because of the derivative nature of all literature, repeated language is to be found in abundance in all genres. In quotation one is looking for a phrase with distinctive formulation and content that lacks the gnomic features of proverbial sayings and does not involve gestures or other common actions, formulaic expressions which may reflect the limited resources of a language's linguistic store, or simple images that bear a general character. Obviously, the dividing line between these categories and quotation is not always clear. The lengthier the repeated phrase, the greater the likelihood of quotation. Interestingly, most of the passages examined, other than the extended Mesopotamian parallels and several Qumran examples, are quite brief. This raises the question of how long a quoted snippet must be in order to evoke a second context. On the one hand, most lists of alleged quotations should be greatly reduced, eliminating proverbs, clichés, idioms, refrains, figures of speech and topoi. On the other hand, the exclusion of such phrases from the category of 'quotation' should not eliminate them from further consideration, since, as other forms of repeated language, they may share a number of significant functions with true quotation.[9]

8. The lack of *methodological* clarity in dealing with the comparative materials reveals several facts. First of all, the desire to evaluate the data has tended to overrule the necessity of laying a firm procedural foundation. Secondly, each of the literatures surveyed deserves a more

8.   Chapter 3, pp. 128-29, 137-38; Chapter 4, pp. 147-49, 153-56, 157-59, 161-62, 165-66; Chapter 6, pp. 196-97.

9.   Chapter 3, pp. 120-21, 126-28, 131-33; Chapter 4, pp. 153-54, 161-64, 169-70; Chapter 6, pp. 183-84, 196, 202-203.

thorough, methodologically sophisticated study than this investigation allows. Ancient Near Eastern literature, in particular, is in need of further examination. Finally, the disagreement over methodology in the comparative materials reflects not so much the subjectivity of scholarly approaches as the complexity of the phenomenon of quotation. Any hopes of a simplistic solution to the problem of prophetic quotation should be dispelled immediately.[10]

The Problem of Applicability

On the basis of the study of the comparative material, a new approach to inner-biblical quotation may be formulated. Despite the necessarily selective survey of methodological treatments and the brief examinations of individual passages, the study has been highly suggestive. However, several aspects of the problem warn against a hasty or comprehensive application of these newly gained insights to the biblical data. First of all, no uniform portrait of 'the quotation' emerged in the preceding chapters so as to facilitate a definitive characterization of the phenomenon for comparative purposes. Indeed, quotation in each of the literatures studied manifests its own distinctives. Secondly, one cannot assume that any individual example of quotation noted in the preceding chapters is completely analogous to a given biblical passage. Finally, the uniqueness of the Old Testament in its complex literary development and its religious use easily could be violated by an overly zealous imposition of foreign standards on its text.

However, my purpose is to apply the principles observed in the preceding chapters selectively and cautiously to the biblical problem as a possibility for moving beyond the methodological impasse. Chapters 3 and 4 will be used primarily for deriving hermeneutical warrants of a historical nature, Chapters 5 and 6 for literary warrants. Individual examples will be used suggestively rather than prescriptively.

The Old Testament, despite its unique origin and use, shares many features with the comparative materials. Linguistically and theologically, it is the major source of the Jewish writings of the Apocrypha and the Qumran community; their use of the canonical prophets is especially prominent. If the continuity between the Old Testament and rabbinic Judaism is as clear as some have proposed, one may actually discover within inner-biblical quotation the origin of the post-biblical

10. Chapter 3, pp. 119, 133-34; Chapter 4, pp. 151, 155-56, 162-64, 169; Chapter 6, pp. 183-85, 204-205.

phenomenon and, therefore, such a comparison is an essential historical study.[11] To the extent that the Old Testament partakes of the literary conventions of other ancient Near Eastern literature—many of which served religious purposes, had a complex literary history, and achieved a quasi-canonical status like the Old Testament—prophetic quotation is likely to exemplify at least some of the features of quotations in Egyptian or Mesopotamian literature.[12] Finally, quotation as a recognized literary convention and rhetorical feature will be characterized by certain universals which transcend language, culture and time.[13] Hence the comparison of prophetic quotation with quotation in other literatures, if done with due caution, may be viewed as an appropriate undertaking.

The Problem of Terminology

It already has been noted that, since similar phrases within the prophets may have a variety of origins, it often is difficult to decide which term should be used to describe such verbal repetition. In the course of a century of study, scholars have attached numerous labels to the phenomenon, and, although many have listed the same passages as examples, it is uncertain whether their understanding of the passsages has been the same, given the terms they selected. A similar multiplicity of terms and lack of uniformity in usage was observed in the study of the comparative material. Accordingly, before proposing a new model for the analysis of such passages, it is necessary to achieve some clarity in the choice and definition of terms.

As a point of departure, it is helpful to note the various types of labels that already have been employed before suggesting an alternative. Some prefer completely neutral terms, such as Girdlestone's 'deuterographs', Cheyne's 'parallel passages' (Humbert, S.R. Driver, and König also speak of 'parallels'), Leiman's 'literary affinities', Fey's 'correspondence' (*Entsprechung*) and C.P. Caspari's 'relationship to' (*Verwandschaft mit*) and 'repetition' (*Wiederholung*). These terms are useful in that they allow one to discuss two passages without

---

11. See Chapter 2, pp. 86-90, also Fishbane, *Biblical Interpretation in Ancient Israel*.

12. See Hallo, 'New Viewpoints on Cuneiform Literature', and Tigay, *The Evolution of the Gilgamesh Epic*.

13. See Chapter 6, pp. 181-82, and Sternberg, 'Proteus in Quotation-Land'.

deciding which of the two is the original source, indeed, without even claiming that there *is* an original source. All that these terms actually designate is that these two or more passages are similar in some way.

In practice, these terms are rather deficient even in fulfilling this limited purpose. First of all, a term like 'parallel passages' implies lengthier selections, as when it is used to designate synoptic Gospel pericopes or the Chronicler's history, rather than brief phrases. Secondly, an examination of Cheyne's parallels reveals that many of them involve *thematic* rather than *linguistic* similarities.[14] In fact, most of these terms are too unspecific to imply that the repetition or relationship is in the actual wording of the parallels. Therefore, the term 'verbal parallels' will be used in this and the following chapters to designate any verbal correspondence between two texts in which actual dependence is either impossible or unnecessary (for the sake of argument) to demonstrate.

A second group of terms implies some type of dependence but is rather vague regarding its purpose: 'echoes' (van der Merwe), 'direct borrowing' (Torrey), 'imitation' (*Nachahmung*—de Wette, Ewald), 'borrowing' (*Entlehnung*—Elliger, Stade), and the very frequent but ambiguous 'reminiscence' (Delcor, Burrows, Küper). Complicating the situation is the fact that some, such as Otto Kaiser,[15] use as many as five different terms in the course of a single page in such an interchangeable manner that it seems futile to try to define any of them more narrowly. The term 'verbal dependence' will be used in this study for any 'verbal parallel' in which, for the sake of argument, or, as a result of a careful examination of the data, it is concluded that one prophet is dependent on the words of another, without stating anything about the nature or form of the 'source' or suggesting any reason for the prophet's drawing upon it.

Not surprisingly, the term used most frequently is 'quotation' (also 'citation' or *Zitat*), which appears in the writings of, among others, Girdlestone, König, Gray, Lindblom, Westermann, Zimmerli, Ackroyd, Talmon and Robert Wilson. Precisely because 'quotation' is the most specific term applied to 'verbal parallels' there is considerable debate

14. Cheyne, *The Prophecies of Isaiah*, II, pp. 241-54.

15. O. Kaiser, *Introduction to the Old Testament: A Presentation of its Results and Problems* (trans. J. Sturdy; Minneapolis: Augsburg, 1975), p. 270: 'alteration of sayings', 'phrases taken over', 'quotations', 'distinctive recasting', 'echoes'. Although some of these descriptions simply may represent rhetorical variations, it is not clear that they are synonymous and used interchangeably.

over exactly what the term entails and whether it is even appropriate to use it. Von Rad refuses to speak of quotations 'in the strictest sense' in the Old Testament unless an introductory formula is used or there is some other indication that the borrowed phrases are 'of outstanding significance'.[16] Although von Rad is concerned primarily with the use of earlier texts in the Levitical Sermons of Chronicles, Fohrer also has noted the interesting fact that no prophet ever mentions another prophet or his writings by name.[17] Leiman sees this as definitive proof that no prophetic book had achieved canonical status by this time, although other explanations also are possible.[18]

The only passage in which a prophet and his message are cited explicitly in the latter prophets is Jer. 26.18 in which the elders quote the words of Micah (3.12). One might also note Zech. 1.4, 'the former prophets proclaimed, saying, "Thus says the LORD of hosts, 'Return now from your evil ways and from your evil deeds' " ', perhaps an approximate citation of Jer. 18.11; 25.5; 35.15; or Ezek. 33.11.[19] Introductory formulae are equally rare. Driver claims that Joel 3.5 indicates that it has 'expressly cited' Obadiah 17 by appending 'as the LORD has said' (כאשר אמר יהוה) to the quotation.[20] Similarly, Ewald interprets Isa. 16.13 as pointing to a previous, unpreserved prophecy with the phrase, 'This is the word which the LORD spoke earlier con-

---

16. Von Rad, 'The Levitical Sermon', p. 279.

17. Fohrer, *Die Hauptprobleme des Buches Ezechiel*, p. 139.

18. Leiman, *The Canonization of Hebrew Scripture*, p. 25. König, 'Gibt es "Zitate"?', pp. 734-35, suggests that no introductory formula is needed if it is recognized 'that the involved words represent an earlier statement of another, and that they are being employed as a so-called popular saying (*geflügeltes Wort*), without making reference to that person'. Schneider, 'The Unity of the Book of the Twelve', pp. 196-97, argues similarly that citation formulae were *unnecessary* because the hearers already would recognize the speaker's words as those of his pre-eminent prophetic predecessors and were *undesired* because elaborate citation made for poor rhetoric, so that the emphasis was on the divine authority rather than the human agency. Fox, 'The Identification of Quotations', p. 423 n. 18, agrees in part, ('The possibility of less signalling in an attributed quotation is greater when there is a canonical scripture with which the audience is thoroughly acquainted and which is commonly quoted for proof texts.') but denies that this type of canonization occurred during biblical times.

19. See also Ezek. 38.17. The reinterpretation of Jer. in Dan. 9 is not discussed here because Daniel is not included in the second division of the Hebrew canon. See Bruce, 'The Earliest Old Testament Interpretation', pp. 43-44.

20. Driver, *An Introduction to the Literature of the Old Testament*, p. 313.

cerning Moab'.[21] Although it is common in the New Testament to use some type of introductory formula to indicate a quotation,[22] it does not seem to be an essential feature in the Old Testament, as long as the repeated phrase is familiar enough to the reader or listener to be recognized as the 'individual property' of another.[23]

In the final analysis, the crucial issue is how one defines 'quotation', a task which only a few have undertaken. König suggests the following basic description: 'all identical sayings in the Old Testament, which are repeated without referring to any individual or general subject as being the author of the original',[24] while Michael Fox explains 'literary borrowing' as 'words that ... are taken from another source but used as the speaker's words'.[25]

Neither definition says much about the purpose of the repeated words. Rather, though they do not state it explicitly, most scholars use the term merely to indicate that close (or exact) verbal correspondence prevails in a given parallel. In other words, a quotation consists of two or more passages involving no, or only minimal, divergence between their texts. Whenever any significant 'adaptation' occurs in fitting the passage to its new context, the label 'quotation' must be forfeited.[26] This is indicated by the series of terms which some scholars use. Bloch speaks of 'textual citations', 'free citations' and 'simple allusions'.[27] More familiar is the analysis of 'Third' Isaiah's use of his prophetic predecessor by Walther Zimmerli in which he divides the examples

21. Ewald, *Die Propheten des Alten Bundes*, I, p. 68.

22. Even the presence of an introductory formula does not eliminate all difficulties, since one is led to query further why Matthew prefers the general 'so it is written by the prophet' (Mic. 5.2) in Mt. 2.5-6, while specifying in 2.17-18: 'what was spoken by the prophet Jeremiah', why Mark introduces a double quotation from Mal. 3.1 and Isa. 40.3 with 'as it is written in Isaiah the prophet' (Mk 1.2-3); and Heb. 2.6 simply notes 'but one solemnly testified somewhere saying'!

23. König, 'Gibt es "Zitate"?', p. 739, 'personal property'.

24. König, 'Gibt es "Zitate"?', p. 738. König obviously disagrees with von Rad's criterion.

25. Fox, 'The Identification of Quotations in Biblical Literature', p. 417. Fox also suggests the term 'proverbial coinage' instead of 'literary borrowing' for this (p. 420), which has a very different connotation.

26. Owen, *Critica Sacra*, p. 21, even notes that 'some of these passages, as they are often applied to different Subjects, critics may perhaps look upon rather in the light of Adaptations, than in that of real and formal Quotations'.

27. Bloch, 'Midrash', *IDBSup* V, col. 1270.

into three categories: 'verbatim or near-verbatim quotation', 'free imitation and recombination' (emulation of forms and themes) and 'brief
reminiscences'.[28] Though neither Bloch nor Zimmerli explains what
marks the boundary between one category and the next or even why
making such a distinction is necessary or helpful, their sequence of
terms is logical given the above understanding of 'quotation' and is
more satisfying than some of the alternative categories which others
propose, such as Whallon's 'accidental recopyings' and 'deliberate
plagiarisms'.[29]

However, the limitation of the term 'quotation' to expressing linguistic fidelity is inadequate. Robert Girdlestone envisioned a broader
usage for the term, offering four categories of quotation:

1. The substance is used, but the words themselves are not
    actually given.
2. Passages are made use of without any attempt being made to
    quote them fully or accurately.
3. Sentences are introduced without acknowledgment, and with
    no departure from the original text, except such as may be due
    to copyists' errors, to changes in idiom, or to the fact that the
    second writer trusts his or her memory and has not the original
    document before him or her.
4. Passages are formally cited, with a reference to the name of
    the writer quoted or to the document or class of documents
    from which the extract is made.[30]

---

28. Zimmerli, 'Zur Sprache Tritojesajas', p. 219.

29. W. Whallon, *Formula, Character, and Context: Studies in Homeric, Old
English, and Old Testament Poetry* (Cambridge, MA: Harvard University Press,
1969), p. 164. Whallon basically sees all biblical diction as stereotyped in general
and neither borrowed nor lent, but also conceives of an earlier time 'when there
were no records to show who was original and who was not, when poets borrowed
freely from each other until their songs were a good deal alike, and when a man
aimed less at individuality than at making the finest poetry possible from all available resources' (p. 171). Seeligmann, 'Voraussetzungen der Midraschexegese', p.
157, lists 'dependence/imitation, modification, and paraphrase' (*Anlehnungen,
Umbildungen, und Paraphrasen*), although it is not clear that he conceives of these
as a progression. König, 'Gibt es "Zitate"?', pp. 739-46, declares that a number of
alleged examples do not merit the term 'quotation' (*Zitat*) and are more appropriately labelled 'allusion', 'variation', 'resumé' or 'backward reference' (*Zurückver-
weisung*).

30. Girdlestone, *Deuterographs*, pp. xxiii-xxiv.

In Girdlestone's opinion, quotation occurred frequently, especially the third type, because earlier biblical writings already had achieved an authoritative status and thus it was quite natural for a later writer to invoke their words. Girdlestone also realized that the meaningful reuse of material does not require, and often can be hindered by, recopying it exactly as it first appeared.

Obviously, given the fluidity in usage, nearly any definition of 'quotation' could be defended. Thus far, explanations based primarily on formal features have been considered, especially the degree and extent of verbal correspondence. However, if 'quotation' is to be distinguished clearly from its numerous near synonyms, a more functional description is necessary. Ackroyd suggested the following qualification:

> Quotation may indeed only be claimed with certainty where re-interpretation is evident. Such re-interpretation indicates dependence upon an earlier form of the same material, and its re-handling with a distinctively new point in mind.[31]

This is essentially the understanding of 'quotation' which is employed in this study. Granting the possibility that 'verbal dependence' may take a variety of forms and serve a variety of purposes, the term 'quotation' will be reserved for those examples in which an exegetical purpose in reusing earlier material can be demonstrated or where an understanding of the earlier text and context is helpful, if not essential, for a proper interpretation of the new text.

Although the selection of just three out of a plethora of terms— 'verbal parallels', 'verbal dependence' and 'quotations'—may seem arbitrary,[32] the intention is to eliminate the prevailing terminological confusion and be able to assess separately the significance of the passages in each of these categories. Selecting and defining terms is an essential first step toward the often neglected exegetical evaluation of this significant component of prophetic speech.

---

31. Ackroyd, 'The Vitality of the Word of God', p. 9. Mason, 'Some Examples of Inner Biblical Exegesis in Zech. IX-XIV', p. 353, similarly sees quotation as 'allusive' and generally faithful to the larger context from which earlier prophetic material is drawn.

32. The terms 'verbal parallel', 'verbal dependence' and 'quotation' are conceived of as concentric categories. It is not being suggested here that it is an easy task to prove that a given passage involves a 'quotation' but simply that the primary distinction to be made between 'quotation' and 'verbal dependence' is not material but functional.

A New Model

Many scholarly treatments of prophetic quotation proceed from the assumption that quotation simply involves verbal repetition, hence the closer and more extensive the correspondence the better, though such slavish dependence often is viewed as a sign of deficient creativity. The comparative data examined above suggest that this approach is inadequate. The model which is being proposed here instead involves (1) the use of two complementary criteria (verbal and syntactical correspondence and contextual awareness, the latter sometimes indicated by interpretive re-use; (2) a twofold analysis (diachronic and synchronic); and (3) an acknowledgment of the multi-functionality of quotation. After this model for 'quotation criticism' has been set out, it will be tested and illustrated in the following chapter using a variety of prophetic texts.

Criteria for Identifying Quotation

In the scholarly literature previously examined,[33] repeated efforts to devise dependable criteria which would help to determine the direction of verbal borrowing were noted. However, since criteria for *detecting* quotation were discussed far less frequently, lists of passages so identified displayed considerable divergence in length and content.

1. *Verbal and syntactical correspondence.* In the light of the promiscuous use of various terms, the three *labels* 'verbal parallel', 'verbal dependence', and 'quotation' have been suggested, conceiving of them as concentric, functional categories. The first simply implies *verbal correspondence*, the second implies *a determined direction of borrowing*, and the third *a conscious, purposeful reuse*. Each thus posits a further degree of linguistic evidence and literary intent. This categorization allows one, for example, to discuss the form and use of verbal parallels in a given text without noting their source and purpose.

However, in the treatment of quotation, contiguous categories are also helpful. One can measure the extent of the correspondence from one key term to several verses, as in the familiar parallel Isa. 2.2-4 // Mic. 4.1-3. Interestingly, within the prophetic corpus, verbal parallels seldom extend beyond a single sentence, often consisting of half of a parallelistic line. On the other end of the scale, one reaches the limits

---

33. See Chapter 1, pp. 22, 24; and Chapter 2, pp. 63-71.

of recognizability, or at least the realm of possibility rather than probability. Rather than setting an arbitrary minimum number of words, it is more useful to seek both verbal *and* syntactical correspondence, that is, phrases and not just words. Otherwise one may be dealing with motifs, themes, images and key concepts, rather than quotation. For example, Fishbane notes that the following words appear in both Isa. 2.1-22 and Isa. 60.3, 5, 14, 17: גוים, נהר, הלך, אור, זהב...כסף, and שחה ('nations', 'to stream', 'to come', 'light', 'silver...gold', 'be brought low'). The relationship may be more than coincidental, but one cannot claim, despite the number of repeated terms, that Isaiah 60 involves a 'quotation' of Isaiah 2.[34] In such cases, terms such as 'allusion' or 'thematic links' are more appropriate. This is not to say that allusion cannot share some of the rhetorical functions of quotation. However, quotation has semantic possibilities that other referential devices lack.

One can also measure the degree of correspondence on a scale from complete to very loose agreement. One might expect an inverse relationship between the extent and degree of correspondence, that is, the longer the repetition the looser it may be, the shorter the closer, if it is to remain recognizable, although here the unknown factor of familiarity also might play a significant role. Actually, the opposite is the case. In the lengthiest parallel, Isa. 2.2-4(5) // Mic. 4.1-3(5) the correspondence is remarkably close, with only a few synonymous substitutions and minor changes in word order. To cite another example, in Jer. 26.18, the most clearly marked quotation (cf. Mic. 3.12), the only deviation is one dialectal ending. On the other end of the spectrum, brief parallels often display a greater proportion of verbal and syntactic deviation. Indeed, it is this feature which makes the identification of quotation so problematic. One must conclude that the extent and degree of correspondence are related primarily to the function and purpose of a quotation, even though they also serve to increase or decrease the identifiability of a parallel.

---

34. Fishbane, *Biblical Interpretation in Ancient Israel*, p. 498. It must be noted that Fishbane does not use the term 'quotation' but rather a 'skillful interweaving of a cluster of old Isaianic oracles into a new, post-exilic proclamation'. However, given the frequency of some of these terms elsewhere in Isaiah and the nature of their use in these two passages, Fishbane's understanding of these 'parallels' as a whole also is unwarranted. The only rare term is נהר and may represent an entirely different root in Isa. 60 than Isa. 2. For a critique of a similar approach, see Chapter 2, pp. 92-96.

Here a further complication must be mentioned. The comparative material makes it abundantly clear that it is precisely those parallels that display close correspondence which often are *not* quotations but are rather formulaic, idiomatic or proverbial in origin and whose wording is so well established that it resists modification. For example, the 'sour grapes' proverb of Jer. 31.29 and Ezek. 18.2 contains only two minor divergences.[35] Refrains also display close correspondence, such as in Isa. 5.25; 9.12, 17, 21, as does the numerical saying in Amos 1.3, 6, 9, 11, 13; 2.1, 4, 6. Clearly, criteria other than correspondence are decisive in identifying quotation.

2. *Contextual awareness, including interpretive use.* If terminology is to be used meaningfully, some distinction must be made both between quotation and formulaic, idiomatic or proverbial language on the one hand and between quotation and unconscious borrowing or the solely stylistic use of borrowed language (i.e. mere verbal dependence) on the other. From the survey of the comparative material, two helpful suggestions may be cited. Hermann Meyer maintains that a quotation, unlike 'borrowing' or 'proverbial usage', has a referential character; it 'intends to be related to its source'.[36] Bonnie Kittel similarly distinguishes between (1) biblical language and terminology; (2) biblical imagery and metaphor; and (3) biblical literary forms imitated by standardized phrases; and (4) quotation (and allusion) which is 'used to recall a *specific* passage to the reader/listener's mind'.[37] Simply put, a quotation is not intended to be self-contained or self-explanatory; rather a knowledge of the quoted context also is assumed by the speaker or author.[38]

---

35. The divergences between Isa. 2 and Mic. 4 will be discussed in Chapter 8. The only divergence between Jer. 26.18 and Mic. 3.12 is that the former has עיים while the latter has עיין (both: heap of rubble). For a discussion, see Fishbane, *Biblical Interpretation in Ancient Israel*, p. 459. The only differences between Jeremiah's and Ezekiel's forms of the proverbs are that the latter has יאכלו (eat) for אכלו (have eaten) and has the definite article with בנים (children).

36. Meyer, *Das Zitat in der Erzählkunst*, pp. 14-15: 'referential character' (*Verweisungscharakter*), 'intended ... to be related to its point of origin'.

37. Kittel, *The Hymns of Qumran*, p. 50.

38. M. Silva, *Biblical Words and their Meaning: An Introduction to Lexical Semantics* (Grand Rapids: Zondervan, 1983), p. 145 n. 18, disputes the contention of B. Malinowski, 'The Problem of Meaning in Primitive Languages', in C.K. Ogden and I.A. Richards, *The Meaning of Meaning* (New York: Harcourt, Brace &

Here one must differentiate between *purpose* and *result*. The literary sleuth may be able to ferret out the source of a borrowed phrase despite a plagiarist's deceptive efforts, but this discovery will not necessarily affect the passage's meaning. However, if a quotation's source is not recognized, there is an unfortunate semantic loss, even if the passage in itself is comprehensible. This raises the difficult question of intentionality. When speaking of 'intent' no attempt is being made to psychologize the text or presume to determine all that a speaker/author/editor sought to or was able to accomplish by means of a quotation. Nor is intention being contrasted with lack of purpose. Even the speaker who surreptitiously borrows a felicitous formulation 'intends' to thereby embellish her or his language, but this has no semantic reflex. 'Intent' is being used here simply to designate one's purpose that a verbal parallel be recognized by a reader or audience. Despite the hermeneutical controversy surrounding intentionality,[39] it appears impossible to discuss quotation meaningfully without referring to intention in at least this limited sense.

An awareness of a quoted text's context can be marked explicitly in several ways. A transitional phrase, including an introductory formula, or an appended explanatory comment, can indicate that the point of the quotation does not reside in the quoted words alone but that an awareness of their source is also important.[40] Furthermore, in comparing the wording of two parallel passages, one can note changes that transform the quoted phrase's meaning, suggesting that the original wording may not have served the quoter's purpose well. Sometimes other key words or images from the quoted context are introduced into the larger context of the quotation, such as when the parallel כלה ונחרצה in Isa. 10.23 and 28.22 (destruction decreed) is reinforced by the use of שטף (overwhelming) in 10.22 and 28.15, 17-18.[41] More often, however, the

Company, 1945), pp. 296-336, especially p. 306: 'Written statements are set down with the purpose of being self-contained and self-explanatory.'

39. See W.K. Wimsatt and M.C. Beardsley, 'The Intentional Fallacy', in W.K. Wimsatt (ed.), *The Verbal Icon* (Lexington: University Press of Kentucky, 1954), pp. 3-18. For an opposing view, see E.D. Hirsch, *Validity in Interpretation* (New Haven: Yale University Press, 1967).

40. Such explanatory comments are frequent in the New Testament; see, for example, Jn 10.34-35.

41. See the discussion in Fishbane, *Biblical Interpretation in Ancient Israel*, pp. 489-91, and the treatment of Isa. 8.15 and 28.13 in Chapter 8.

relationship between the quoted and the quoting context is left implicit for readers to respond to as they become aware of either their coherence or the contrast between them.

Here Ackroyd's criterion must be considered again:

> Quotation may indeed only be claimed with certainty where re-interpretation is evident. Such re-interpretation indicates dependence upon an earlier form of the same material, and its re-handling with a distinctively new point in mind.[42]

It already has been pointed out that reinterpretation through quotation can take many forms. Ackroyd's formulation, 're-handling with a distinctively new point in mind', is, for the purposes of this study, happily vague. Whether a person quotes a statement in order to point out a perceived analogy, to ironically reverse or reject it (a possible explanation for Joel 4.10), or to refocus the statement by draining it of its contextual meaning,[43] the quoted text will be distinctively rehandled.

Because Ackroyd's qualification lacks specific examples,[44] it is unclear just what he understands by reinterpretation. Less ambiguous is Michael Fishbane, who seeks 'textual transformations, reapplications, and reinterpretations' which display a 'literary exegetical interdependence'.[45] According to Fishbane,

> the identification of ... exegesis where external objective criteria are lacking [i.e. introductory citation formulae] is proportionally increased to the extent that multiple and sustained lexical linkages between two texts can be recognized, and where the second text ... uses a segment of the first ... in a lexically recognized and topically rethematized way.[46]

Fishbane's criterion is helpful and his methodological caution well taken. However, his exclusively 'exegetical' understanding of reinter-

---

42. Ackroyd, 'Criteria', p. 118.

43. It is not clear, however, that the verbal borrowing can be described as 'mere language'. See Moo, *The Old Testament in the Gospel Passion Narratives*, p. 18. For example, one could take the phrase 'one if by land, two if by sea' from Longfellow's 'Paul Revere's Ride' and use it in such a way that it no longer refers to lanterns and a horseback journey, yet if the effect of the reused quotation were dependent upon a knowledge of the original context, it would no longer be used as 'mere language'.

44. Ackroyd is more concerned with pointing out that many 'biblical' phrases in Sir. and the Hodayoth are *not* quotations.

45. Fishbane, *Biblical Interpretation in Ancient Israel*, pp. 282, 288.

46. Fishbane, *Biblical Interpretation in Ancient Israel*, p. 285.

pretation appears, in the light of the comparative study of quotation, to be too narrow.[47]

In sum, in addition to verbal and syntactical correspondence, one should seek in quotation such a use of the borrowed phrase that a knowledge of the *quoted* context is essential in order to properly understand the *quoting* context. In some verbal parallels no such intent may be apparent or the appropriation may seem merely stylistic; in others, interpretive strategies will be quite obvious. In between, there will be passages with hints of contextual allusiveness suggesting possible motivations for the borrowing. A balance between openness to the data and methodological caution is essential.

Twofold analysis: Diachronic and synchronic. In the study of quotation in extra-biblical literature, two basic methodologies for treating quotation were observed. In chapters three and four quotation was viewed primarily as a historical phenomenon, in chapters five and six as a literary phenomenon. In the following section, an approach will be set forth and defended which combines both of these emphases.

a. *Diachronic Analysis.* Quotation is pre-eminently a historical phenomenon. Unlike a proverb which expresses a universal truth, formulaic language which is employed in predictable contexts, and those standardized phrases which describe particular activities, quotation establishes a relationship to a specific, previously expressed statement. Whether operating orally or in written materials, quotation recalls either explicitly or implicitly not only the quoted words but also the context of their original use, whether in real or fictive history. This imparts to quotation a unique chronological dimension,[48] a 'laterness' or even a

47. It must be noted that Fishbane, in the preceding passages, is describing 'aggadic exegesis' and looking for evidence of exegetical techniques similar to rabbinic procedures. He also discusses 'mantological' exegesis of prophetic oracles (Chapter 18) following a similar procedure. He is not specifically interested in the question of quotation as defined in this study. In some of his examples, in which there are only individual words and no phrases in common, the label 'exegesis' is questionable. See especially, Fishbane, *Biblical Interpretation in Ancient Israel*, pp. 497-98. For example, to describe Isa. 60.1-2, 17-18 as a 'realization of [the] promise' of 9.1, 3 ignores the content of 60.3-16, the context of 9.1-3, and the repeated use of the terminology of light and darkness throughout Isaiah

48. For a discussion of the term 'diachronic' see below, pp. 232-33.

'belatedness'[49] which is an important aspect to consider in analyzing it. If this contextual recall is lacking, one merely has borrowed language with no referential value.

The reasons for this dependence on utterances of the past vary. It simply may be that the quoter recognizes the continuing validity of the earlier statement, a validity of the statement which may be due to the speaker's status as a sage or divine spokesperson. This status may endow the words with an authority which the quoter hopes to transfer to his or her work, as in the extensive quotation of the Old Testament in the Qumran *Manual of Discipline* and *Zadokite Document*.[50] Whether or not this implies that the speaker perceives him- or herself as lacking such authority or as living in an age where such authority is diminished is not always clear, though one sees this attitude in Egyptian literature: 'Is there anyone here like Hor-dedef? Is there another Ii-em-hotep?'[51] A historical dimension is also reflected in quotations which suggest an analogy between a situation previously described and the speaker's or writer's circumstances. This analogy can be identified in fictive history, as in the Egyptian 'letter' which introduces a quote from *The Eloquent Peasant* with 'you are in the situation of him who said'.[52] A similar historical analogy is the basis of Hosea 12's recollection of the Jacob tradition expressed in much the same form as the Genesis narrative.[53]

Related to this is the claim through quotation that the speaker's

---

49. See Chapter 6, pp. 190-92; and Fishbane, *Biblical Interpretation in Ancient Israel*, p. 408.

50. For a list of the explicit quotations in these documents, see Fitzmyer, 'The Use of Explicit Old Testament Quotations', pp. 297-333, and Moo, *The Old Testament in the Gospel Passion Narratives*, pp. 18-19.

51. Wilson (trans.), *ANET*, p. 432.

52. Guglielmi, 'Eine "Lehre" für einen reiselustigen Sohn', p. 159, and Chapter 3 n. 11.

53. See P.R. Ackroyd, 'Hosea and Jacob', *VT* 13 (1963), pp. 245-59; F. Diedrich, *Die Anspielungen auf die Jakob-Tradition in Hosea 12, 1-13: Ein literaturwissenschaftlicher Beitrag zur Exegese früher Prophetentexte* (FzB, 27; Würzburg: Echter Verlag, 1977); M. Gertner, 'The Masorah and the Levites: An Essay in the History of a Concept', *VT* 10 (1960), pp. 241-84, esp. the Appendix, 'An Attempt at an Interpretation of Hosea XII', pp. 272-84; E.M. Good, 'Hosea and the Jacob Tradition', *VT* 16 (1966), pp. 137-51; L. Ruppert, 'Herkunft und Bedeutung der Jakob-Tradition bei Hosea', *Bib* 52 (1971), pp. 488-504; T.C. Vriezen, 'La tradition de Jacob dans Osee 12', *OTS* 1 (1942), pp. 64-78; Whitt, 'The Jacob Traditions in Hosea', pp. 18-43.

community is the fulfillment, as in the Qumran commentary on Habakkuk[54] or is expecting the fulfillment, as in Daniel's treatment of Jeremiah's 70 years,[55] of an earlier 'predictive' prophecy, even if this 'fulfillment' is established by reinterpreting the earlier words. In this case, the quoted and the quoting text stand at opposite ends of a historical spectrum. Another historical relationship is found in the claim that particular speakers (with their messages) stand in continuity with earlier spokespersons whom they quote, as in Ezek. 38.17-18 and Zech. 1.1-6.[56]

In his treatment of inner-biblical exegesis, Michael Fishbane suggests several reasons for the reuse of a previous text, in his terms, a 'traditum' which is reinterpreted to form a 'traditio'. In evaluating such 'traditios' one not only must recognize the 'temporal belatedness' of the latter but also seek to determine the 'historical exigencies' which produced it.[57] According to Fishbane, the interpretation and reinterpretation of oracles was caused primarily by the concern for their fulfillment. Through their rehandling, older predictions were presented as temporarily delayed in their fulfillment, were revised when expectations were not met, or were presented as intended for the contemporary era. Because such predictions projected a 'rational order on to the apparent disorder of events', their non-fulfillment posed a threat to the 'entire framework within which a believer lived', and thus reinterpretation served to reduce the resultant cognitive dissonance.[58]

One aspect, then, of the diachronic analysis of quotation, is an examination of historical factors which may have produced or influenced the use of quotation. One should examine the original setting of the passage to seek to determine whether the *setting* and not simply the *wording* led to its selection, and examine the new setting to seek to determine which historical exigencies may have led to quotation. In

---

54. See K. Elliger, *Studien zum Habakuk-Kommentar vom Toten Meer* (Tübingen: J.C.B. Mohr [Paul Siebeck], 1953).

55. Fishbane, *Biblical Interpretation in Ancient Israel*, pp. 479-89.

56. Fishbane, *Biblical Interpretation in Ancient Israel*, p. 477, associates Ezekiel's reference with Jeremiah's prophecies regarding the 'enemy from the north'. See also B.S. Childs, 'The Enemy from the North and the Chaos Tradition', *JBL* 78 (1959), pp. 187-98. The prophetic quotation in Zech. 1.4 is closest to Jer. 25.5 but also similar to Jer. 18.11; 35.15, and Ezek. 33.11.

57. Fishbane, *Biblical Interpretation in Ancient Israel*, pp. 408-409.

58. Fishbane, *Biblical Interpretation in Ancient Israel*, pp. 509-11, see also 518-19.

addition, one must analyze the wording of the quotation to see if the quoter's awareness of her or his belatedness is reflected in the text. Of course, it should not be expected that this dimension of quotation always or even frequently will be indicated clearly. There is therefore a danger that an interpreter who is seeking a historical explanation will 'discover' one which has no support in the text. However, it is essential for the interpreter to realize that the decontextualization and recontextualization which quotation involves have not only a literary but also a historical dimension.

A further aspect of diachronic analysis, and even more complex, is the analysis of the literature in which the quotation is embedded. It has been noted that it is this dimension that has received the most scholarly attention in the past and continues to be the focus or at least the basis of the study of prophetic quotation. This emphasis is understandable, since the question which arises naturally when identifying quotation is: Who is quoting whom? However, with the gradual abandonment of traditional views regarding the authorial integrity of the prophetic books, this question has become increasingly difficult to answer. Not only the relative chronology of the various books but also the dating of sections within the individual books are disputed. More difficult to resolve is the question of the redactional reshaping of individual oracles, whether alleged expansions reflect the work of the prophet, a prophetic group, an editor, or a series of later hands.[59] In Chapter 2 an attempt was made to demonstrate that the various criteria suggested for identifying the direction of borrowing are inadequate, even if combined. Nevertheless cumulative arguments continue to be constructed often using indiscriminate lists including all types of verbal parallels.

As a result, little consensus has been achieved or will be achieved with regard to the dating of many alleged prophetic quotations. The literature simply is too complex and the textual data too meager. How should one proceed, then, with the diachronic analysis of quotation? First of all, we cannot advocate the abandoning of the historical aspect of quotation. On the one hand, the positive benefits of determining the direction of borrowing are too great. Once one has identified a quotation, unless one at least suggests a direction of borrowing, little can be said with regard to its purpose. Indeed, responsible exegesis demands taking a position on the question of quotation. Too often, interpreters

---

59. See the treatment of Isa. 2 // Mic. 4 in Chapter 8.

are content merely to cite parallel verses parenthetically, as if there were no need to comment on them further. Yet if quotation truly is present, its evaluation may be crucial to understanding the text which contains it.[60]

On the other hand, the type of evaluation of quotation recommended here is not without an objective basis. By evaluating criteria other than quotation for the relative dating of prophetic oracles and by making a discriminating use of word statistics and examining evidence of interpretive reworking, one can suggest, at least in terms of degrees of probability, the direction and nature of the quotation. Here, however, caution and restraint are necessary. The tentative nature of such conclusions concerning chronology warn against using quotation as the basis for any larger theory regarding the prophetic materials. An awareness of the subjective nature of this 'dating game', in which the rules which one chooses to play by largely determine the results, will also forbid dogmatism.

The diachronic analysis of quotation, so conceived, must deal with all the complexity of the prophetic literature. One must ask whether a given quotation first functioned orally in the public ministry of a prophet and simply was preserved later in writing or whether it functions primarily or exclusively on a literary level, since certain types of verbal revisions would have been too subtle for a listening audience to note. Here, too, one must ask whether the audience or reader reasonably could be expected to be aware of the quotation, especially of brief phrases, even though this is a historical question which may be unanswerable.[61] In analyzing an example of verbal dependence within a single book, or between prophetic books, one must recognize that it may result from a prophet repeating earlier words simply because of their striking formulation and thematic appropriateness, and thus without any contextual reference, or it may be the work of a literary editor rather than of a prophet, and textual evidence must be evaluated accordingly. It is also likely that the function of a quotation has changed or at least expanded between the oral and written stage(s).[62]

---

60. See the complaints of Jeremias and Coggins in this regard noted in Chapter 2 n. 142.

61. See the discussion below, pp. 236-37.

62. See W. Zimmerli, 'Vom Prophetenwort zum Prophetenbuch', *TLZ* 104 (1979), pp. 481-96; also C. Hardmeier, 'Gesichtspunkte pragmatischer Erzähltextanalyse. "Glaubt ihr nicht, so bleibt ihr nicht": Ein Glaubensappell an schwankende

An observation from the comparative material is relevant here. In the various types of literature examined, no pattern of more or less extensive or exact verbal correspondence or the reuse of any particular content could be identified as having a temporal dimension. Thus the diachronic analysis of quotation must proceed on a case-by-case basis.[63] The extensive literature on the use of Old Testament quotations in the Qumran documents or the New Testament where the historical relationship is undisputed[64] encourages one to pursue the diachronic analysis of prophetic quotation despite the difficulties. Yet one is also cautioned to realize the limits of such analysis and not focus on the diachronic aspect of quotation alone.

b. *Synchronic analysis.* Although diachronic analysis of quotation has dominated past study of the phenomenon, the study of comparative literary theory demonstrated that synchronic analysis, though often neglected, is also essential. Here the terms 'diachronic' and 'synchronic', generally associated with the foundational linguistic theory of Ferdinand de Saussure, are being used as they have been applied to literary interpretation.[65] The former focuses on a text's function and meaning at the various stages which precede its final form as incorporated within a larger work as well as the external historico-sociological influences, sometimes inferred or reconstructed, which helped shape its development; the latter looks at a text as a part of a literary work, as a 'functional whole'.[66] To analyze prophetic quotation synchronically is to shift the attention from the question of who quoted whom, when, and for what reason (author-centered) to the question of how such repeated language functions within texts, to examine its literary workings

Anhänger Jesajas', *Wort und Dienst* 15 (1979), pp. 33-54.

63. This is not to dispute the claim that quotation as a phenomenon may be more frequent in late prophetic texts. See, for example, Wilson, *Prophecy and Society*, pp. 291-92. What is called into question here, however, is whether one can determine the date of a text (or an individual passage) on the basis of the frequency and type of quotations which it contains.

64. For a partial bibliography, see Chapter 4, especially n. 4.

65. F. de Saussure, *Course in General Linguistics* (New York: McGraw-Hill, 1966). See Culler, *Structuralist Poetics*; R.M. Polzin, *Biblical Structuralism: Method and Subjectivity in the Study of Ancient Texts* (Semeia Supplements; Missoula, MT: Scholars Press, 1977); Scholes, *Structuralism in Literature*. See also Chapter 6 n. 50.

66. Culler, *Structuralist Poetics*, p. 12.

(reader-centered). Two distinct but complementary aspects of the synchronic analysis of prophetic quotation will be discussed: (1) the function and meaning of quotation within the canonical prophetic books; and (2) the nature of quotation as a rhetorical device and its resultant effect on the reading process.

To analyze quotation synchronically involves interpreting it within the context of the entire book or books in which it is located. This places the interpreter's focus on the final canonical form of the book rather than on antecedent oral or written stages or posited historical influences. Just as the New Testament, when quoting from the Old Testament prophets, merely refers to such passages in terms of the book (or author) from which they are drawn, without any distinction being made between 'original oracles' and 'later additions', so a synchronic analysis will trust the author's or editor's implicit injunction to accept the text's final form as an original entity with its own integrity, despite the remaining literary tensions which it encompasses.

This approach has a number of implications for the analysis of prophetic quotation. First of all, from a synchronic perspective one must distinguish clearly between *internal* and *external* verbal parallels, that is, parallels *within* a canonical book and *between* canonical books. In the diachronic analysis of quotation within the book of Isaiah, verbal parallels within chs. 40–66 to passages in 1–39 usually are viewed as stemming from later prophetic voices, perhaps roughly contemporary with Jeremiah or Zechariah, rather than from Isaiah of Jerusalem's self-quotation. Although a synchronic analysis of verbal parallels *within* Isaiah need not speak of 'self-quotation' since that, in part, is also a diachronic judgment, it will, nevertheless, acknowledge that such passages are hermeneutically of a different order from verbal parallels *between*, for example, the books of Isaiah and Jeremiah and must be analyzed accordingly.[67]

Secondly, synchronic analysis focuses on quotation's effect rather than on its origin. One should examine quotation for evidence of editorial intention, since quotation's ability to evoke another context makes it useful as a structuring device, as may be the case with Isa. 48.22 and 57.21 and Isa. 5.30 and 8.22,[68] or for pointing out a perceived

---

67. For a discussion of 'internal parallels' and 'self-quotation', see Chapter 6, pp. 197-98.

68. In Isa. 48.22 and 57.21, according to Delitzsch, the phrase 'there is no peace, says the LORD, for the wicked' is used to divide Isa. 40–66 into three equal

analogy or relationship between two passages. Since the only historical dimension which synchronic analysis acknowledges is the chronological data offered by the text itself in its superscriptions and narratives,[69] quotation can serve as one means of linking two oracles even when there is no temporal framework which explicitly links them. Here, too, one must be wary of imposing diachronic categories. For example, even though Isa. 35.10 may be later than and dependent on Isa. 51.11, from a synchronic perspective it anticipates or adumbrates the latter within the book of Isaiah.[70] Thus, one should study the *effect* which a quotation has within the present canonical book as potentially indicative of an editorial *purpose*. Whether this editorial purpose is at odds with the original historical purpose or even produced the quotation in the first place is not at issue here.

Thirdly, quotation will share some of the features of other types of repeated language, such as refrains, formulae and topoi. Even though quotation is more highly evocative than the others, they can have overlapping roles within the rhetoric of a book in giving it structure and developing its themes. Given the limited data supplied by the text, the distinction between these categories necessarily may be blurred. In the absence of clear signs of reinterpretation, one may hesitate to label a particular passage as a 'quotation' of another, yet verbal parallels as such can be subjected to a comparative textual and contextual analysis which is not dependent on the correctness of diachronic decisions in

parts (9 addresses each), the variation 'my God' in 57.21 indicating 'a more excited and fuller tone', and the close of the third part (66.24) dropping this form of refrain to declare the miserable end of the wicked more vividly, similar to the substitution of an entire psalm (150) for the blessing which closes each of the first four books of the Psalter: 'The three parts, which are thus marked off by the prophet himself, are only variations of the one theme common to them all.' Duhm insists that 48.22 has no conceptual or material relationship to the preceding context: 'That it has been placed precisely here, is to be explained by the fact that the three small volumes are to have approximately the same length'. F. Delitzsch, *The Prophecies of Isaiah* (trans. J. Martin; 2 vols.; repr.; Grand Rapids: Eerdmans, 3rd edn, 1976 [1877]; II, pp. 128-29; Duhm, *Das Buch Jesaia*, p. 330. Regarding 5.30 // 8.22, see Williamson, *The Book Called Isaiah*, pp. 125-43.

69. See T. Polk, *The Prophetic Persona: Jeremiah and the Language of the Self* (JSOTSup, 32; Sheffield, JSOT Press, 1984), p. 15. Polk also speaks of the 'temporal dimension' of the reading process.

70. See Steck, *Bereitete Heimkehr*. Clements, *Isaiah 1–39*, views Isa. 34–35 rather as a summary conclusion to Isa. 1–33.

order to be valid and useful. Viewing quotation as one of several types of verbal repetition is preparatory to its assessment as a significant component of prophetic rhetoric.

Finally, in analyzing quotation, whether within or between prophetic books, one must make a detailed comparison between the parallel texts and their respective contexts. One must note the extent of the parallel and both the agreements and divergences between them. Though over-interpretation is a danger, one should seek to distinguish between those changes which appear to be primarily grammatical, necessary to adapt the text to its new setting, and those which are reinterpretive, clearly changing the scope and direction of the text. However, one must be aware that even minor variations can be highly significant semantically and that verbal agreement may be as important to note as divergence.

Furthermore, one must carefully examine both the immediate and larger contexts of the verbal parallels, since, from a synchronic perspective, the ultimate context of quotation is the entire prophetic book. The larger context may contain clues that will explain the editorial intentionality of the quotation as well as other verbal or thematic links between the two passages. Both differences and similarities between the contexts should be noted, as they will help to assess the impact of the decontextualizing and recontextualizing of the text. Even if verbal agreement is maintained, the change in context can affect its meaning radically.[71]

Here is an appropriate place to expand the discussion to the literary workings of prophetic quotation. On the synchronic level, the analysis of quotation will be similar in some respects whether the quotation being studied is found in Isaiah or in Milton. There are several aspects of literary analysis which need to be mentioned in relation to the analysis of prophetic quotation. The first concerns quotation and prophetic

71. See Chapter 6, pp. 186-87, 202-204. According to Fishbane, *Biblical Interpretation in Ancient Israel*, p. 415, 'The two steps of literary dislocation and relocation are equally transformative. But it deserves emphasis that the first phase transforms a *traditum* into a *traditio*, whereas in the second the new aggadic *traditio* becomes a *traditum* in its own right.' For purposes of analysis, M. Sternberg's three categories are helpful, 'Proteus in Quotation-Land', p. 129: paradigmatic (e.g. lexical substitution), syntagmatic (e.g. addition, omission, reordering), and contextual (changes in time, place, genre, stylistic register). According to Sternberg, 'substitution, addition, and recontextualization ... may all result in comparable shifts of meaning'.

style. A number of studies have stressed style as basically a matter of lexical choice.[72] Despite the fact that many scholars have suggested that prophetic quotation largely results from deficient creativity and an inordinate influence by one's predecessors, or the sociological necessity of meeting listener expectation or rescuing earlier oracles from failure,[73] the relative infrequency and freedom of employment of quotation suggest rather that it is a matter of conscious stylistic choice.[74] Given the constraints imposed on prophetic speech by the message to be proclaimed, the common forms used to convey it, and the lexical stock of the Hebrew language, the prophets display a remarkable rhetorical variety. The significance of choosing between a simple statement and a quotation, with its virtually polysemous ability to 'call up meaning', should not be overlooked.

Secondly, quotation raises the question of 'reader competence'. Despite a confusing terminology which speaks, for example, of 'intended', 'implied', 'hypothetical', 'ideal', 'optimal', 'informed' and 'competent' readers,[75] the relevance of the discussion to this study is clear: What does the author of quotation assume about a reader's or audience's ability to discern the author's verbal dependence and purpose? Without seeking to give a definitive answer, several aspects must be probed. From one's own personal experience with quotation, it is clear that the absence of introductory formulae in prophetic quotation cannot mean that its detection is not intended. Our comparative study indicates that quotation is much more than a game for the intellectual

---

72. See M. Silva, 'The Pauline Style as Lexical Choice: Γινωσκειν and Related Terms', in D.A. Hagner and M.J. Harris (eds.), *Pauline Studies: Essays Presented to Professor F.F. Bruce* (Grand Rapids: Eerdmans, 1980), pp. 184-207, and the literature he cites.

73. See the discussion above, especially Chapter 3, pp. 118-19 and Chapter 2, pp. 99-104. For the question of the 'failure' of prophecy, see Carroll, *When Prophecy Failed*, and Fishbane, *Biblical Interpretation in Ancient Israel*, pp. 476-77.

74. This is not to imply that some verbal parallels within the prophets may not also, as in early Jewish literature, result from the *unconscious* influence of one's prophetic predecessors.

75. See R.A. Culpepper, *Anatomy of the Fourth Gospel: A Study in Literary Design* (Philadelphia: Fortress Press, 1983); R.M. Fowler, 'Who Is "the Reader" of Mark's Gospel?', in K.H. Richards (ed.), *SBL Seminar Papers: 1983* (Chico, CA: Scholars Press, 1983), pp. 31-53; *idem*, 'Who Is "the Reader" in Reader Response Criticism?', *Semeia* 31 (1985), pp. 5-23.

elite to play. If quotation is not detected, there is a significant semantic loss, yet such failure usually does not render a text incomprehensible. Synchronic analysis does not mean taking a text as a self-contained, self-explanatory entity without requiring the reader to bring any knowledge of, for example, prophetic oracles that are quoted to a reading of the text, but rather that the author included within the text all essential explanatory material that the reader is not assumed to bring to the text. The issue of reader competency also raises the question of how much subtlety is to be sought in an author's reformulation and recontextualization of borrowed statements. Certainly, some word-plays could function only in a studied text and would escape the casual listener.[76]

Finally, synchronic analysis, in contemporary theory, has emphasized not only the literary text as a 'functional whole' but also the dynamics of the reading process itself. Reading is viewed as an active temporal experience. The encounter with quotation with its 'backwards' reference to that which has preceded in the same or a previous text is part of this temporal process. Many theorists see here a resultant semantic reverberation, that the linking of two texts and contexts through quotation causes each passage to be read in the light of the other. Sometimes this results in a reversal of actual textual chronology, as in the story about the naive reader who complained that Shakespeare was full of quotations![77] The extent to which this and other aspects of synchronic analysis can be applied convincingly to biblical examples must be explored with caution. However, comparative study suggests that this type of analysis is essential if the nature and purpose of quotation is to be assessed accurately.

The dangers of an exclusive approach. A twofold analysis is being proposed here because an exclusive emphasis on either the diachronic or the synchronic aspect involves an inadequate understanding of quotation. In the past, students of prophetic quotation have focused on its historical aspect. Efforts have concentrated on determining the direction of borrowing and what this indicates about the growth of a prophetic book and the relationship between various prophets or

---

76. This is certainly an assumption which underlies much of Fishbane's work. See especially his *Biblical Interpretation in Ancient Israel*, pp. 520-21; also Michel, 'Zur Eigenart Tritojesajas', pp. 213-30.

77. See Chapter 6, pp. 199-202.

prophetic groups. Beyond general statements about a prophet's use of his predecessors, often little effort has been made to move beyond the identification of verbal parallels to their analysis.[78] However, to note historical factors which produce quotation without studying their effect is a task left incomplete. The only evidence one has of quotation in ancient Israel is preserved in the canonical texts and they, ultimately, must be the object of analysis.

In linguistics, de Saussure held that synchronic analysis held priority over diachronic.[79] The resultant emphasis on the former often occurred at the expense of the latter, despite repeated claims that the former does not deny the latter.[80] When de Saussure's approach was applied to the Bible, as one of the roots of the 'Bible as literature' movement, the resultant studies often did injustice to the actual nature of biblical literature, especially its complex history of development.[81] Especially with a phenomenon such as quotation which is inherently 'historical' in nature, an approach which neglects diachronic analysis is equally deficient.

A twofold analysis will help to provide a check against the dangers of both over-interpretation and under-interpretation. It will warn against an interpretation of prophetic quotation which is totally dependent on a reconstructed historical setting as well as against an overly subtle reading following modern literary conventions and attributing omnisignificance to each element of textual and contextual modification. Here no clear-cut 'method' is being set out, which spells out exactly how the diachronic dimension relates to the synchronic.[82] Rather a new attitude is being proposed which recognizes the necessity as well as the limita-

---

78. This is the basic thrust of the historical survey in Chapter 1. Exceptions include R.N. Whybray in his commentary *Isaiah 40–66* (NCB; London: Marshall, Morgan & Scott, 1975), as well as earlier commentators such as Cheyne and Nägelsbach.

79. De Saussure, *Course in General Linguistics*, p. 90.

80. See Polzin, *Biblical Structuralism*, pp. 17-18; Scholes, *Structuralism in Literature*, p. 17; R. Jakobsen, 'pure synchronism now proves to be an illusion', cited in E.V. McKnight, *Meaning in Texts: The Historical Shaping of a Narrative Hermeneutics* (Philadelphia: Fortress Press, 1978), p. 247.

81. For a critique, See J.L. Kugel, 'On the Bible and Literary Criticism', *Prooftexts* 1 (1981), pp. 217-36.

82. Polzin, *Biblical Structuralism*, p. 48, notes that even Paul Ricouer 'admits that he has no answer on how to meaningfully relate diachronic or genetic biblical interpretations to synchronic ones'. In some quotations, the diachronic features will be more prominent, in other the synchronic features.

tions of both diachronic and synchronic analysis of prophetic quotation and which probes the possibilities on a case-by-case basis before drawing any overarching conclusions about its nature and function.

Multi-functionality. A final aspect of the analysis of quotation is the question of function. Some of the purposes which prophetic quotation may serve have been mentioned already: to actualize an earlier oracle, to reinterpret a text, to give structure to a text or link several passages, to acknowledge the validity of a previous statement and appropriate its authority, to utilize a felicitous or familiar formulation for its aesthetic or emotional impact. As a rhetorical device, quotation is multi-functional. Its function on an oral level may well differ from its function within the present canonical text. The quoted words in their recontextualized form bear a meaning which is independent, in part, from the meaning called up from the underlying quoted text, a palimpsest-like layering of meaning. In analysis, the reader may tend to focus on only one of these functions, yet he or she must be cognizant of the other ways in which the same quotation may function simultaneously. It is also important to note that some of these functions may be the exclusive property of quotation while others are shared by a number of rhetorical devices.[83]

Some of these functions, such as exegesis as Fishbane describes it, clearly assume an intentionality on the part of the author or editor. Yet the obstacles posed by the 'intentional fallacy'[84] warn against setting demonstrable intentionality as a primary criteria for the identification of quotation. This is the advantage of a synchronic approach, which can assess the effect of certain rhetorical devices within a text without necessarily proving that they were consciously designed by their originator. The absence of an unambiguous marking of prophetic quotation by means of an introductory formula already suggests that it operates differently than the Old Testament quotations in the New Testament. In Chapter 8 the approach proposed here will be applied to a variety of verbal parallels, probing the limits as well as the possibilities of diachronic and synchronic analysis, while seeking to learn more about the nature and function of prophetic quotation.

83. See Chapter 6, pp. 195-99, 202-203.
84. See n. 39 above and the discussion of the 'intention of the text' in Polk, *The Prophetic Persona*, pp. 16-18, 177-79.

Chapter 8

THE ANALYSIS OF PROPHETIC QUOTATION

In Chapter 7 some methodological suggestions for the assessment of prophetic quotation have been offered. In this chapter these suggestions will be utilized in the analysis of a number of verbal parallels, both within the book of Isaiah and between the book of Isaiah and other prophetic books, probing the limits on interpretation which the various texts impose. The goal is not so much to offer an alternative exegesis of these, for the most part, much-discussed texts, as to explore the nature and function of the quotations which they contain and determine the significance of quotation for the proper understanding of such passages.

Isaiah 11.6-9 and 65.25

The most extensive verbal parallel within the book of Isaiah involves the portrayal of the 'peaceable kingdom' in 11.6-9 and 65.25. Before examining the larger contexts and reviewing the previous discussion of these passages, a detailed comparison of the verbal correspondence will be made.[1]

Text

וגר זאב עם־כבש ונמר עם־גדי ירבץ	6	65.25 זאב וטלה ירעו כאחד
ועגל וכפיר ומריא יחדו ונער קטן נהג בם:		
ופרה ודב תרעינה יחדו ירבצו ילדיהן	7	
ואריה כבקר יאכל־תבן:		ואריה כבקר יאכל־תבן
ושעשע יונק על־חר פתן	8	ונחש עפר לחמו
ועל מאורת צפעוני גמול ידו הדה:		
לא־ירעו ולא־ישחיתו	9	לא־ירעו ולא־ישחיתו
בכל־הר קדשי		בכל־הר קדשי

---

1. Textual citations are from the Masoretic Text as printed in *BHS*. Significant text-critical variants will be discussed.

כי־מלאה הארץ דעה
את־יהוה כמים לים מכסים:

אמר יהוה:

The wolf will live with the lamb,	6	The wolf and the lamb 65.25
The leopard will lie down with the goat,		will feed together,

the calf and the lion and the yearling
together; and a little child will lead
them

The cow will feed with the bear,   7
their young will lie down together
and the lion will eat straw like the ox

and the lion will eat
straw like the ox

The infant will play near the hole of the   8
cobra,
and the young child put his hand into the
viper's nest.

but dust will be the
serpent's food

They will neither harm nor destroy   9

on all my holy mountain,
for the earth will be full of the
knowledge of the LORD as the waters
cover the sea.

They will neither harm
nor destroy
on all my holy mountain,
says the LORD.

Criteria for Indentifying Quotation

What is remarkable here is that each verse in Isa. 11.6-9 is reflected in
Isa. 65.25, but each incompletely and each to a different degree. 11.6-7
describes how both wild and domesticated animals and their young will
live and eat together peacefully, mentioning five pairs of animals.[2] In
the first, second and fifth pair, the wild animal is mentioned first; in the
remaining two the domesticated animal is first. 65.25aα contains only
the first and the fifth pair, in the same order as in 11.6-7. 25aα begins
with the wolf (זאב), as does 6aα, but uses the rarer טלה for lamb rather
than כבש found in 6aα.[3] The first verb in 25aα, ירעו (feed), is found in

2.   If the MT is followed, a third animal, the yearling (מריא) is mentioned in v.
6bα. Most commentators, following the lead of LXX, posit a verbal form, such as
ימראו. C. Schedl retains the MT on the basis of 'logotechnisch' considerations,
*Rufer des Heils in heilloser Zeit: Der Prophet Jesajah Kapitel I-XII logotechnisch
und bibeltheologisch erklärt* (Paderborn: Ferdinand Schöningh, 1973), pp. 329,
332. Since 11.6b has no parallel in 65.25, the matter has little bearing on this discussion.

3.   טלה (sing.) is used elsewhere only in 1 Sam. 7.9, the pl. only in Isa. 40.11.

v. 7a, not v. 6, which does not speak of eating, unless one emends מְרִיא
(yearling) to יִמְרָאוּ (graze). כְּאֶחָד (as one) of v. 25 corresponds to יחדו
(together) in v. 6bα and 7bα, the former occurring elsewhere only in
Ezra 2.64; 3.9; 6.20, Neh. 7.66, Eccl. 11.6 and 2 Chron. 5.13.[4] 6aα links
the animals with עִם־ (with), while 25aα uses a simple waw. The second
half of 25aα is identical to 7b, and 25b is identical to 9a, but adds the
concluding formula אָמַר יהוה (says the LORD). In contrast, 25aß does
not share a single word with v. 8, even though both portray the future
harmlessness of the serpent, albeit using different figures. Summarizing, then, 6-7 // 25α, 8 // 25aß, 9a // 25b. Of the 44 words[5] in 11.6-9a,
12 are found in identical form in 65.25, 1 in a different form (תרעינה/
ירעו), and in 3 cases approximate synonyms are used instead (טלה/כבש
[lamb], כְּאֶחָד/יחדו [together], צפוני ... נחש/פתן [serpent]). Conversely, of
65.25's 18 words,[6] 13 appear in 11.6-9a(!) in identical or similar form.

The most significant divergence between 11.6-9 and 65.25 is that
11.9b, which explains the restored harmony as resulting from 'the
knowledge of Yahweh' which then will fill the land, is lacking in 65.25.
There are two more noteworthy differences, beyond those previously
mentioned. In 11.6-9, harmony between human and animal as well as
between animals is portrayed, while in 65.25 only the latter is in view.
Furthermore, 11.6-9 offers a more colorful description, using verbs
such as גּור, רבץ, נהג (מרא), שׁעע and הדה ('live', 'lie down', 'graze',

---

כבש is used 107 times, including Isa. 1.11 and 5.17, כבשה is used 8 times. Beuken,
Jesaja, IIIB, p. 92, sees the choice of טלה in 65.25 as an allusion to 40.11, also
arguing that the verb רעה is selected over other verbs in 11.6-7 due to its thematic
significance within 'Second' and 'Third' Isaiah. See similarly O.H. Steck, ' "ein
kleiner Knabe kann sie leiten": Beobachtungen zum Tierfrieden in Jesaja 11, 6-8
und 65, 25', in J. Hausmann and H.-J. Zobel (eds.), *Alttestamentlicher Glaube und
biblische Theologie* (Stuttgart: W. Kohlhammer, 1992), pp. 104-13 (109).

According to J.T.A.G.M. van Ruiten, 'The Intertextual Relationship between
Isaiah 65, 25 and Isaiah 11, 6-9', in F. García Martínez, A. Hilhurst and C.J.
Labuschagne (eds.), *The Scriptures and the Scrolls: Studies in Honour of A.S. van
der Woude's 65th Birthday* (Leiden: E.J. Brill, 1992), pp. 31-42 (37), the author of
65.25 uses the wolf and the lion to represent, respectively, all predatory and non-
predatory animals.

4.   Excluding כְּאֶחָד + מִן which reflects a different idiom. See also כְּאִישׁ אֶחָד
Judg. 20.8, 1 Sam. 11.7. יחדו is used elsewhere in Isaiah in 60.13; 65.7; and 66.17,
also Ezra 4.2; Neh. 4.2; 6.2, 7; 1 Chron. 10.6; 12.17.

5.   Not counting the conjunction *waw* and inseparable prepositions directly
attached to other words.

6.   Omitting אָמַר יהוה.

'lead', 'play', 'put'), whereas 65.25 unifies all of the imagery around the topos of eating (לחם, אכל, רעה, 'feed', 'eat', 'food'), although the basic idea is the same (9a // 25b—this cannot be due to the emphasis on eating in 65.2-5, as has been suggested).

These observations lead to the second criterion, that of contextual awareness. Should the speakers/authors of Isa. 11.6-9 and 65.25 be viewed as making independent use of a familiar topos of peace in the animal kingdom or is one of the texts clearly dependent on the other? It has been noted that similar scenarios can be found in several ancient texts, the closest parallels being the Sumerian myth of Enki and Ninhursag and Virgil's Fourth Eclogue.[7] Although it is possible that the Hebrew prophets were aware of this mythical motif which may have been disseminated widely throughout the ancient Near East, the correspondence between the two texts within the book of Isaiah is closer than that between them and any of the extra-biblical parallels cited: not only the identical phrases but also the identical order of the elements in both passages suggest verbal dependence.

Neither passage is explicitly marked in its context. In Isaiah 11 the transition is made by the use of the waw-consecutive perfect וְגָר, 'and he will live', and the unit is clearly demarcated by the formula והיה ביום ההוא, 'in that day' in vv. 10 and 11.[8] In 65.25 the commencement of the passage is more abrupt, with asyndetic זאב (wolf). An abrupt transition is a possible but by no means certain indicator that 'foreign material' is being inserted into the context at this point. No effort has been made to integrate the verse syntactically into the larger context, although the use of the first person 'my' continues the divine speech. The word order of the first clause places emphasis on the animal pair while distinguishing the scenario from that which precedes. The closing formula אמר יהוה has been viewed elsewhere as marking quotation.[9] However, its use in the closing chapters of the book of Isaiah is too frequent to posit a

---

7.　See H. Wildberger, *Jesaja 1–39* (BKAT, 10; 3 vols.; Neukirchen–Vluyn: Neukirchener Verlag, 1965–82), I, p. 456. For a discussion of the prophets' possible use of this motif, see B.S. Childs, *Myth and Reality in Ancient Israel* (London: SCM Press, 1960), pp. 65-69.

8.　The oracle also begins with a *waw*-consecutive perfect ויצא in Isa. 11.1. See also vv. 2, 3, 4; 5.3. For a discussion of the implications of the formula, as marking a secondary addition and/or an eschatological passage, see Wildberger, *Jesaja 1–39*, I, pp. 111-12.

9.　See Joel 2.32 (= Heb. 3.5) and Isa. 16.13.

similar use here (65.7, 8, 13, 25; 66.1, 9, 12, 20, 21, 23).[10]

A superficial comparison of the two passages might lead one to consider either 65.25 to be simply a resumé of 11.6-9 or 11.6-9 to be an expansion of 65.25. This would account for the repetitions as well as the omissions or additions. However, this still would not explain the various substitutions and changes already observed, some of which, especially the treatment of the snake motif, seem to indicate more than merely stylistic variation. Rather, despite the similarities, the imagery of the two passages is shifted in different directions. Whether this shift indicates a reinterpretation will be investigated below.

Summarizing our initial investigation, the extensive correspondence between Isa. 11.6-9 and 65.25 suggests that the relationship between them extends beyond that of a common topos to verbal dependence. Verbal correspondence is limited to these verses; the larger contexts lack further lexical linkages. Neither text makes a clear reference to the other, nor does a knowledge of one appear essential for understanding the other, though such knowledge helps to clarify some of the differences between them. In sum, the data suggest that the author of one of the passages probably is quoting the other, although the nature and purpose of this reuse remain to be explored.

Diachronic Analysis
In order to determine the historical exigencies which may have produced this quotation, the larger contexts which contain these two passages will be examined first. In the absence of any explicit indication of why the portrayal of animal harmony was repeated or even any observable divergences between the parallels which clearly have a historical dimension, a close analysis of the larger units is essential.[11]

First, diachronic elements contained in the immediate and larger contexts of the parallel passages will be noted: Isa. 11.6-9 completes what often is described as the climactic promise oracle of the first section of the book of Isaiah.[12] It complements 11.1-3a, which describes

10. There is no obvious significance to the variations in its formulation or its placement within the clause.

11. Except for the use of כאחד (as one) in 65.25 which could be viewed as indicating a later usage replacing יחדו (together).

12. Isa. 1–12 generally is viewed as the first section of Isaiah. Whether or not this passage is 'messianic' is disputed. According to R. Kilian, 'the messianic character of this passage is generally (*fast allgemein*) acknowledged', *Jesaja 1–39*

the origin and charismatic endowment of the future ruler, and 11.3b-5, which describes his righteous rule by portraying the peaceful conditions which then will prevail. In its present literary context, the promise of a future ideal Davidic king responds to the twin threat to the monarchy posed in Isaiah's day by Judah's corrupt leadership (7.13; 10.1) and the mighty Assyrian Empire (8.4, 7; 10.5). Precisely when this ruler will reign is unclear, but the position of 11.1-9 directly following 10.5-34 (to which it also is loosely linked by the use of the tree imagery in 10.33-34; 11.1)[13] suggests that it will follow God's coming judgment upon Assyria (10.12, 24-25).

Isaiah 65.25 similarly concludes a promise oracle.[14] By juxtaposition, ch. 65 offers the divine response to the lament and petition (63.7–64.12) of the survivors of the destruction of Judah's cities and Jerusalem's temple (64.10-11).[15] The following oracle addresses those who would rebuild the temple (66.1). Thus, in its present literary setting, ch. 65 addresses a situation nearly two centuries later than that of ch. 11. This is also underlined by the reference to the 'former troubles' and 'former things' in 65.16-17 as an oblique reference to the past judgment on Israel and Judah.[16] 65.13-15 contrasts the future fate of

(Erträge der Forschung, 200; Darmstadt: Wissenschaftliche Buchgesellschaft, 1983), p. 10. Whether or not 11.1-9 should be associated with 9.1-6 is discussed by W. Werner, *Eschatologische Texte in Jesaja 1-39: Messias, Heiliger Rest, Völker* (FzB, 46; Würzburg: Echter Verlag, 1982), pp. 75-81.

13. See also 10.17, 18-19; 11.10 and compare the linking use of darkness/light imagery in Isa. 8.20, 22, 23; 9.1.

14. Hanson views the entire chapter as one salvation-judgment oracle, *The Dawn of Apocalyptic*, pp. 134-35, 145. The focus of this study is primarily on vv. (16) 17-25 which contain only promise. Elliger, Westermann and Whybray view these verses as forming a separate unit; Oswalt links 65.17-25. to ch. 66 as constituting the final section of the book.

15. See Hanson, *The Dawn of Apocalyptic*, p. 81; and K. Pauritsch, *Die neue Gemeinde: Gott sammelt Ausgestossene und Arme (Jesaia 55-66): Die Botschaft des Tritojesaia-Buches literatur-, form-, gattungskritisch und redaktionsgeschichtlich untersucht* (AnBib, 47; Rome: Biblical Institute Press, 1971), pp. 16-17 n. 47. Most commentators, however, deny that this connection between the two passages is original. See Whybray, *Isaiah 40–66*, p. 266.

16. See Childs, *Introduction to the Old Testament as Scripture*, pp. 225-28; and R.E. Clements, 'The Unity of the Book of Isaiah', *Int* 36 (1982), pp. 117-29. C.R. North, 'The "Former Things" and the "New Things" in Deutero-Isaiah', in H.H. Rowley (ed.), *Studies in Old Testament Prophecy* (New York: Charles Scribner's Sons, 1950), pp. 111-26. Whybray, *Isaiah 40–66*, p. 276, sees a shift in the mean-

God's servants with that of the apostates; v. 16 forms a transition to vv. 17-19 which announce God's new creative work in which Jerusalem again will be a delight. Verses 20-23 portray the satisfying life which then will prevail. Verses 24-25 bring the description of future bliss to a climax, v. 24 speaking of God's immediacy by using the קרה/ענה (call/answer) word pair,[17] and v. 25 promising peace within the animal realm.

Precisely what motivated the reuse of this description of animal harmony is difficult to ascertain. As a particularly striking image of a world very different from that known to humanity, it simply may have offered an attractive formulation to express the degree of transformation which the future would bring. In comparing both contexts, several observations can be made. First of all, other than the verbal parallel, no effort is made to link the two oracles explicitly. It is not obvious that the quoter is seeking to evoke the entire context of the quoted passage. Furthermore, one oracle is not presented as the fulfillment of the other nor is the verbal parallel so central to the meaning of either oracle as to suggest that a later prophet is appropriating the authority of an earlier prophetic spokesperson by quoting them. One can suggest, however, that a prophet, in quoting the portrayal of 'animal harmony', is affirming the continuing validity of this promise which was delivered in response to an earlier historical situation.

Here one is confronted by the basic question which dogs the analysis of every such parallel: Who is quoting whom? Fohrer and Torrey, among others, hold that Isaiah 11 contains a quotation from Isaiah 65, while the majority of scholars, more recently Wildberger and Westermann see the reverse to be the case.[18] Duhm claims that borrowing occurred in both directions, 65.25a being derived from 11.6-8, while 65.25b is the source of 11.9a.[19] Non-committal is Soggin, who

ing of the 'former things': in 'Second' Isaiah it refers to Yahweh's past great deeds, in 65.16 to the 'troubles of God's people from 587 B.C. onwards', in 66.17 to the 'whole created order'.

17. Isa. 55.6; 58.9; 65.1; 66.4.

18. C.C. Torrey, *The Second Isaiah: A New Interpretation* (New York: Charles Scribner's Sons, 1928), p. 107; G. Fohrer and E. Sellin, *Introduction to the Old Testament* (trans. D.E. Green; Nashville: Abingdon Press, 1968), p. 371; Cheyne, *Introduction to the Book of Isaiah*, pp. 66, 372; C. Westermann, *Isaiah 40-66* (trans. D.M.G. Stalker; OTL; Philadelphia: Westminster Press, 1969), p. 410. Wildberger, *Jesaja 1–39*, I, pp. 444, 326: 'It is generally assumed'.

19. Duhm, *Das Buch Jesaia*, pp. 108, 481: 'In v. 25a Trito-Isaiah unabashedly exploits 11.6-8'. Also G.B. Gray, *A Critical and Exegetical Commentary on the*

prefers 'to speak in terms of identical literary genres, avoiding the word "dependence" '.[20]

Some attempt to use traditional criteria for determining dependence. Feldmann considers 65.25 to be 'a summarizing repetition' of 11.6-9, while Torrey claims that 11.6-9 is 'very plainly an expansion of 65:25'.[21] For them, the same data lead to mutually contradictory conclusions. Others offer more specific reasons for their decision. Interestingly, those who view 11.6-9 as the source of 65.25 argue primarily on the basis of their relative dating of the larger oracles containing the image, giving little attention to the form and contextual appropriateness of the verbal parallel itself.

However, those who view 65.25 as the source of 11.6-9 note the following: (1) Since 11.9b is found in Hab. 2.14 and 11.9a is found in Isa. 65.25b, it is likely that 11.9 is the quoting text in both cases. (2) The phrase 'my holy mountain' appears elsewhere in Isaiah 56–66 (56.7; 57.13; 65.11; 66.20) but nowhere else in Isaiah 1–39. (3) The pronoun 'my' fits well in Isaiah 65 which contains first person divine speech but is out of place in 11.9 where the surrounding context, including v. 9b refers to Yahweh in the third person. (4) In the context of 11.6-9, v. 9b (which is lacking in 65.25) describes the animals as 'full of the knowledge of the LORD', an unlikely concept.[22] If one attempted to determine the direction of the borrowing on the basis of these criteria alone, one might conclude that 65.25 is the *source* of the quotation. However, the weight of each of these reasons can be reduced by other considera-

Book of Isaiah I-XXVII (ICC; New York: Charles Scribner's Sons, 1912), pp. 219, 223.

20. J.A. Soggin, *Introduction to the Old Testament from its Origins to the Closing of the Alexandrian Canon* (trans. J. Bowden; OTL; Philadelphia: Westminster Press, 1976), p. 261. Similarly, Pauritsch, *Die neue Gemeinde*, pp. 185-86, says regarding 65.25: 'The verse derives its analogous motif (*Entsprechungsmotiv*) from the portrayals of Paradise.' H. Barth, *Die Jesaja-Worte in der Josiazeit* (WMANT, 48; Neukirchen–Vluyn: Neukirchener Verlag, 1977), p. 60 n. 256, also views 65.25a and 11.6-8 as 'parallel in subject matter' (*sachlich parallel*), 'without any demonstrable literary dependence'.

21. F. Feldmann, *Das Buch Isaias übersetzt und erklärt* (HAT, 14; 2 vols., Münster: Aschendorff, 1925–26) as cited by E. Sehmsdorf, 'Studien zur Redaktionsgeschichte von Jesaja 56-66', *ZAW* 84 (1972), pp. 517-62 (522); Torrey, *The Second Isaiah*, p. 107.

22. See Gray, *Isaiah I-XXVII*, pp. 222-23. A. Schoors, *Jesaja* (De Boeken van het Oude Testament, 9A; Roermond: J.J. Romen & Sons, 1972), p. 94.

tions. For example, there is no inherent reason not to conclude that Isa.
11.9 is the *source* rather than the *result* of two verbal borrowings (as
claimed in the first argument).[23]

For the most part, decisions about the direction of dependence are
determined by the scholars' tradition- and literary-critical analyses of
the respective texts. The dominant question is whether the parallel portraying animal harmony, along with the related explanation (11.9a;
65.25b), is integral, that is, original to the oracle containing it. The
status of 11.6-9 is dependent on one's understanding of the *Sitz im
Leben* of the so-called messianic passages in the book of Isaiah. Was
the 'messianic hope' awakened by Isaiah's own confrontation and dis-
appointment with the current Davidide Ahaz or was it a late eschatological hope? Did it center on a historical figure, an idealized king
described in oriental hyperbolic language, or a superhuman leader?[24] If
one seeks a concrete historical setting, does the text point to an Isaianic
date, as Alt has posited for 9.1-6, a later pre-exilic situation as posited
by Crook and more recently by Vermeylen, or a time after the dynasty
had been deposed (so Clements)?[25]

Although Wildberger has offered a thorough defense of the traditional attribution of Isa. 11.1-9,[26] most scholars question the Isaianic

23. See the discussion in Chapter 2, pp. 63-71 with regard to Joel. Wildberger,
Jesaja 1–39, I, p. 458: 'The suffix קׇדְשִׁי makes the listener ... aware that here it is
not a case of a poet breaking forth into non-binding visions of the future but of a
prophet speaking by divine commission.' The most thorough defense of 65.25's
dependence on 11.6-9 is by Steck, ' "ein kleiner Knabe kann sie leiten" ', pp. 104-
13.

24. A vast amount of literature has been devoted to this question. For a sum-
mary account, see the discussion in recent commentaries such as Wildberger,
Jesaja 1–39, and Clements, *Isaiah 1–39*, and the literature they cite; also Werner,
Eschatologische Texte in Jesaja 1-39, pp. 17-88.

25. A. Alt, 'Jesaja 8, 23–9, 6: Befreiungsnacht und Krönungstag', in *idem*,
Kleine Schriften zur Geschichte des Volkes Israel (3 vols.; Munich: Beck, 1953), II,
pp. 206-25. M.B. Crook, 'A Suggested Occasion for Isaiah 9, 2-7 and 11, 1-9', *JBL*
68 (1949), pp. 213-24; J. Vermeylen, *Du prophète Isaïe à l'apocalyptique: Isaïe, I-
XXXV, miroir d'un demimillénaire d'expérience religieuse en Israël* (Etudes
Bibliques; 2 vols.; Paris: J. Gabalda, 1977–78), I, pp. 271-75; Clements, *Isaiah 1–
39*, p. 123.

26. Wildberger, *Jesaia 1–39*, I, pp. 442-46. Wildberger's linguistic arguments
are criticized by Werner, *Eschatologische Texte in Jesaja 1-39*, p. 71, but Werner's
defense of an exilic or postexilic date on the basis of 'word choice', pp. 73-74, has
been criticized, in turn, by C. Hardmeier, 'Jesajaforschung im Umbruch', *VF* 31

authorship, the unity of the oracle, or both. On the one hand, Barth attributes 11.1-5 to Isaiah but argues that vv. 6-8 represents a secondary addition (nowhere else in the Old Testament or ancient Near Eastern literature are the 'royal ideology' and 'animal harmony' linked), and that v. 9 is a redactional modification which transfers to the people the qualifications ascribed to the Messiah in vv. 1-5 (its use of two quotations giving it a gloss-like character).[27] On the other hand, Clements dates the entire oracle, 11.1-9, to the late-sixth or early-fifth century and argues that the pictures it contains are intended to complement each other, since 'the fact that ... (v. 9) has connections with other parts of the Old Testament does not in itself prove that it is a secondary insertion'.[28]

Similarly debated is the status of 65.25. Chapter 65 usually is attributed to 'Third' Isaiah, although the identification and even the existence of this person or group still is disputed.[29] Elliger dates the passage to shortly after 515 BCE, while Volz, on the basis of v. 11, suggests a second-century date.[30] Hanson defends the original integrity of the entire chapter, except for several minor glosses, while Sehmsdorf distinguishes within 65.16b-25 an original core (vv. 16-19a), a deuteronomistic redactional layer (vv. 19b-24), and an even later addition (v. 25). A paradox of the modern study of the prophets is that Isa. 11.6-9 can be defended as Isaianic while its verbal parallel, 65.25, is viewed as a late apocalyptic addition.[31]

(1986), pp. 3-31 (13-19). See also J. Vollmer, 'Jesajanische Begrifflichkeit?', *ZAW* 83 (1971), pp. 389-91.

27. Barth, *Die Jesaja-Worte*, pp. 60-63. C.R. Seitz, *Isaiah 1–39* (Interpretation; Louisville, KY: Westminster/John Knox Press, 1993), pp. 106-107, while acknowledging that 'it does not sound as though this holy mountain [vv. 6-9] is in need of royal government [vv. 1-5]', argues that the images of v. 4 and v. 9 must be held in tension and not 'played off against each other'.

28. Clements, *Isaiah 1–39*, p. 124.

29. For a summary of views, see Vermeylen, *Du prophète Isaïe*, II, pp. 451-54; Hanson, *The Dawn of Apocalyptic*, pp. 32-46; and especially C.R. Seitz, 'Third Isaiah', *ABD*, III, pp. 501-507.

30. Elliger, *Die Einheit Tritojesajas*, p. 103; Volz, *Jesaia II*, pp. 284-85.

31. Hanson, *The Dawn of Apocalyptic*, pp. 135, 141-42. Sehmsdorf, 'Studien zur Redaktionsgeschichte von Jesaja 56-66', pp. 518-30. Differing slightly, Vermeylen, *Du prophète Isaïe*, II, p. 493 n. 1, claims that 65.19b-24 reflects a knowledge of Deut. rather than a deuteronomistic redactional layer. Westermann, *Isaiah 40–66*, pp. 410-11, similarly considers 65.25 (and 65.17) to be a secondary apocalyptic addition. However, van Ruiten, 'The Intertextual Relationship between

The extensive disagreement over the dating and integrity of Isaiah 11 and 65 has enormous implications for the interpretation of the verbal parallel which they contain. First of all, given the degree to which the evaluation of quotation is dependent upon historical reconstruction, virtually no diachronic analysis can expect to receive widespread acceptance. The purpose will differ in accordance with the direction and dating of the borrowing.[32] Secondly, if the verbal parallel originated as a secondary redactional addition, then the quotation probably never had any oral life but functioned exclusively on the literary level. There is no need to ask whether the hearers of a later prophet could be expected to be sufficiently familiar with the content of the oracle now recorded in Isa. 11.1-9 (which certainly is conceivable, given its vivid portrayal of hope for the monarchy) to recognize its quotation as now contained in Isaiah 65. Thus the quotation may never have been known outside the context of the present book of Isaiah. To be sure, some of the divergences between these verbal parallels are too subtle to be recognized without study, but this does not necessarily imply that the quotation could not have functioned orally as well. Furthermore, the later the quotation was incorporated into the Isaianic corpus, the less its meaning changed in accordance with its changing contexts.

Before summarizing the diachronic analysis of Isa. 11.6-9 and its parallel in 65.25, several observations can be made. First of all, on the

Isaiah 65, 25 and Isaiah 11, 6-9', pp. 31-32, correctly notes that v. 25 is integrally imbedded in its literary context, the harmonious state of the animal world reflecting the harmony between Yahweh and his servants, as portrayed in v. 24. He points also to several striking parallels between vv. 24-25 and v. 12. For a thorough discussion of the integral structure of Isa. 65 and its similarity to 66, see O.H. Steck, 'Beobachtungen zur Anlage von Jes 65-66', *BN* 38/39 (1987), pp. 103-16. According to Steck, 65.16b is expounded in vv. 17-25 and 17-18a in 18b-25, while 25 points back to 18b-19 (p. 104). Accordingly, Steck defends the literary- and tradition-critical integrity of chs. 65–66.

32. According to Barth, *Die Jesaja-Worte*, p. 60 n. 256, Isa. 65.25b is quoted in 11.9 because 65.25a and 11.6-8 are already parallel in content without demonstrating any literary dependence. Similarly Vermeylen, *Du prophète Isaïe*, II, p. 497, explains 11.6-9 as incorporated into 65.25 in order to extend the optimistic scene of vv. 16-24 and interpret it in terms of 65.11-15: the Jewish traitors, here symbolized by the serpent, will have no part in the coming salvation. Volz, *Jesaja II*, p. 287, on the other hand, explains the quotation in 65.25 as resulting from the author's habit of harmonizing his promise oracles and the congregation's earlier writings, thus expressing the return to paradisaical conditions in Jahwe's new creation in terms of the portrait in Isa. 11.

basis of the study of the widespread use of quotation within ancient Near Eastern literature, it is incorrect to suspect that a verse is secondary simply because it contains a quotation. Nor is it necessary to view this either as 'epigonic allusions ... the result of the serious scrutiny of the words of Isaiah of Jerusalem by late prophets', or as a 'chance, occasional, or casual phenomenon'.[33] Similarly, prophecy containing quotation is not to be understood a priori as second-rate, as evidence of diminished creativity or inspiration. Rather it can be a highly nuanced rhetorical device which, accordingly, was used sparingly. The fact that studies have noted 'Third' Isaiah's frequent dependence on 'Second' Isaiah and his tendency to repeat his own words gives this rare parallel in 'First' Isaiah greater significance. Furthermore, the fact that quotation sometimes fits awkwardly within its context, disturbing parallelism, shifting the imagery, and changing the person of address, is in keeping with the nature of quotation which, at the very least, involves the incorporation of a 'foreign body' into another context and therefore relativizes the applicability of literary-critical tools in determining what is primary and what is secondary.

Rather than attempting to resolve the diachronic issues involving Isaiah 11 and 65 or offering yet another historical reconstruction, I simply will summarize the implications of this analysis for the synchronic analysis to follow. First of all, given the fact that quotation is by nature a historical phenomenon, linking an earlier oracle which addressed another situation with a later oracle and situation, any approach which treats quotation simply as a literary device is inadequate. Secondly, the great diversity of views regarding the origin and purpose of this verbal parallel is itself an indirect acknowledgment of the complexity and multifunctionality of quotation, operating on more than one semantic level simultaneously. Thirdly, the original diachronic perspective of the author of this quotation has been blurred in the present literature, not only by its unmarked incorporation into a larger literary complex but also by the nature of that literature itself. Isaiah 11.1-9 appears to be deliberately vague, deprived of any specific historical setting, so as to encompass all of the hopes which the people place on the Davidic dynasty. Isaiah 65 is equally 'bereft of any reference which might allow one to attach to it a precise date'.[34] This suggests

33. Fishbane, *Biblical Interpretation in Ancient Israel*, p. 498, mentions both options but clearly prefers the former.
34. Hanson, *The Dawn of Apocalyptic*, p. 142.

that one should not put too much weight on any particular diachronic reconstruction. Fourthly, the diachronic dimension which is inherent *in the text*, associating ch. 11 with the Assyrian threat and ch. 65 with the plight of a devastated Jerusalem, as well as their present placement within the book of Isaiah, sets limits to historical reconstruction as a hermeneutic tool. Fohrer's interpretation, which takes Isa. 11.6-9 as a quotation from 65.25, is an impossible way to read these oracles today within their literary context. If Fohrer is correct, then the diachronic perspective of the author of ch. 11 was of little importance for those responsible for editing the present book of Isaiah. Finally, the impasse which we have observed in the diachronic analysis of this verbal parallel—and which shows little prospect of being resolved soon—makes a synchronic analysis a necessary complement if the workings of quotation are to be understood and appreciated.

Synchronic Analysis

The synchronic analysis of a verbal parallel such as Isa. 11.6-9 // 65.25 is not simply a hermeneutical move of desperation, necessitated by the impasse in the diachronic analysis and motivated by a desire to be able to say at least something about a striking quotation. Rather, it is the acknowledgment that this verbal parallel, regardless of its origin within the life of Israel, is now to be found within a canonical prophetic book which displays redactional design. The goal is to explore how such a parallel can be read in its present literary context, a reading which may be at odds with its original function but which conceivably may dovetail nicely with it.[35]

The first thing which should be observed is that this prophetic quotation is now an *internal* parallel, a repetition within one book, and functions as a type of self-quotation, a literary echo that takes its place alongside other forms of repetition, such as refrains, images and themes, which have a unifying effect on the book.[36] As such, the dynamics of the quotation's workings differ from those, for example, of a quotation of Isaiah within the book of Jeremiah.

Secondly, the context and placement of the two parallels are quite

---

35. For example, if Isa. 11.6-9 is quoted by the author of 65.17-25, then its original function may have been very close to its present function.

36. Already Owen, *Critica Sacra*, p. 8 and lists on pp. 22-23, spoke of prophets 'borrowing from themselves' or using the 'same language on different occasions'. See also Elliger, *Deuterojesaja in seinem Verhältnis zu Tritojesaja*, p. 46.

similar. Both conclude promise oracles, following a description of the improved condition of human society (11.3b-5; 65.20-24) resulting from divine intervention (spirit endowment—11.1-3a, new creation—65.17-19). Both oracles are climactic in content and are placed near the close of a major section of the book of Isaiah.[37]

In its present literary context, 11.6-9 describes two results of the messianic reign. It is characterized by safety, since even the weakest, most vulnerable human being will be able to play near and lead the wild beasts, (also established on the human level, according to v. 4); and it is characterized by harmony, the cessation of long-standing animosities between human beings and animals and between domesticated animals and predator animals which no longer are carnivorous. (These conditions also will prevail within Israel, according to the continuation of the oracle in vv. 10-16, most clearly in vv. 13-14, the יחדו [together] in v. 14 recalling its use in vv. 6-7). Isaiah 11.9 should be understood as interpreting the image of 'the peaceable kingdom' as indicating a cessation of harm and destruction in God's holy territory due to the knowledge of Yahweh permeating the land. This view, taking the imperfect verbs of v. 9 as impersonal plurals (i.e. 'one shall not harm or destroy ... '), eliminates the alleged incongruity of animals knowing God and dwelling on Mt Zion.[38] Furthermore, taking 11.1-3a, 3b-5, 6-9 as *sequential* rather than *simultaneous* reduces the potential tension within the text, tension which has been cited as a reason for labelling v. 9 as secondary.[39] The first section of the book of Isaiah ends with a promise of a righteous ruler, pervasive peace, and a restored nation; a psalm of thanksgiving (ch. 12) is the proper response.

---

37. Van Ruiten, 'The Intertextual Relationship between Isaiah 65, 25 and Isaiah 11, 6-9', p. 36, further describes the thematic connections between 11.3-5 and 65.25: the former speaks about judging the poor and the meek with righteousness and about killing the wicked; the latter describes the separation between and contrasting fates of the servants and the wicked. J.D.W. Watts, *Isaiah 34–66* (WBC, 25; Waco, TX: Word Books, 1987), p. 357, adds 35.1-2, 5-7 as a third idyllic passage which also points to 'God's original and ultimate plan for humanity in a totally nonviolent and innocent creation' and notes that each is set in a *realistic* context.

38. Duhm, *Das Buch Jesaia*, p. 108: 'the subj. of the verbs in v. 9a must be the lambs, wolves, etc., but these, of course, have no knowledge of Yahweh'. Therefore, Duhm views vv. 9-10 as redactional additions.

39. Barth, *Die Jesaja-Worte*, p. 61, 'the picture of perfect harmony in vv. 6-8 ... is in striking contrast to the situation presupposed in vv. 3f. which is by no means without tension'.

Isaiah 65.25 forms the climax of the penultimate chapter of Isaiah. Like Isaiah 11, most of the passage deals with this-worldly activities, especially vv. 21-23, and vv. 19-20 are hardly as absolute as Rev. 21.4, although the latter obviously recalls the former (compare Rev. 21.1 with Isa. 65.17). The imagery of 65.17-25 is drawn from two sources: (1) the cessation of covenant curses: vv. 21-22 reflect Deut. 28.30, 'calamity' (בהלה) in v. 23 is threatened in Lev. 26.16, as well as laboring 'in vain' (לריק) in Lev. 26.20 (one also could link v. 25 to the wild beasts in Lev. 26.22, though this appears less likely);[40] (2) the return to paradisaical circumstances, reflecting the early traditions of Genesis: creating the new heavens and new earth (v. 17—Gen. 1.1), extended life span (v. 20—Gen. 6.3), the unified emphasis on the vegetarian diet of the animals (v. 25—Gen. 1.20), and the reference to dust as the serpent's food (Gen. 3.1, 2, 4, 13, and especially v. 14). The use of נחש (serpent) in Genesis may explain its use in Isa. 65.25 instead of פתן (cobra) or צפעוני (viper) as in 11.8. If Isa. 11.8 reflects Gen. 3.15, the cessation of enmity between the serpent's seed and the woman's seed, 65.25 reflects a peculiar interpretation of Gen. 3.14. Whereas other curses are reversed, the 'curse' of Gen. 3.14 is continued, now not representing humiliation and submission (cf. Mic. 7.7, Isa. 49.23, Ps. 72.9) but rather a literal, harmless non-flesh diet.[41]

40. One also could relate v. 25 to the mention of wild beasts in Lev. 26.6, 26, though this appears less likely. Steck, ' "ein kleiner Knabe kann sie leiten", pp. 111-12, accordingly sees 11.6-8 as describing animals that endanger Israel in its land as a divine judgment, citing Lev. 26 in support; in the future age these will become, in effect, house pets (*Haustiere*). O. Kaiser, *Jesaja 1–12* (ATD, 17; Göttingen: Vandenhoeck & Ruprecht, 5th edn, 1981), p. 245, however, considers Lev. 26 to be later than Isa. 65. Regarding the covenantal blessings, see M. Rehm, *Der königliche Messias im Licht der Immanuel-Weissagungen des Buches Jesajas* (Kevelaer Rheinland: Butzon & Bercker, 1968), p. 302.

41. It is debatable whether 'eating dust', therefore, in the perspective of the author of 65.25, no longer constitutes a curse. Van Ruiten, 'The Intertextual Relationship between Isaiah 65, 25 and Isaiah 11, 6-9', pp. 39-41, notes that the 'weak' party from 11.8 is missing here, and concludes that the serpent thus is a metaphorical depiction of a 'curse for the party that was once much stronger', at the same time indicating a blessing for the unmentioned weaker party, the servants.

For a more thorough treatment of the use of Gen. 1–3 in Isa. 65, see O.H. Steck, 'Der neue Himmel und die neue Erde: Beobachtungen zur Rezeption von Gen 1-3 in Jes 65, 16B-25', in J. van Ruiten and M. Vervenne (eds.), *Studies in the Book of Isaiah: Festschrift Willem A.M. Beuken* (BETL, 132; Leuven: Leuven University Press, 1997), pp. 349-65. Vermeylen, *Du prophète Isaïe*, I, p. 275 n. 2, sees an

From a synchronic perspective, 65.25 must be viewed as a quotation of 11.6-9, a selective adaptation designed to maintain the portrait of pervasive peace yet shifting it in keeping with the imagery of the larger unit, 65.17-25. Here the animals are more clearly the subject of the verbs of v. 25b, a situation not brought about by a spread of the knowledge of Yahweh (as in 11.9b) but integral to the new heavens and new earth (v. 17) which Yahweh creates, where an intimate relationship between people and Creator prevails (v. 24). In the light of this, '*all* My holy mountain' could be broadened to embrace more than Jerusalem (similar to 11.9, so Miscall and Motyer) unlike its use in v. 11 (cf. 10.32). Certainly not all of the differences between 11.6-9 and 65.25 should be viewed as interpretive or even significant. The omissions apparently stem from a desire to abbreviate and simplify the imagery, perhaps because the future situation has already been portrayed so extensively in vv. 20-23. Here the quotation appears to be adapted to fit the context rather than the context prepared to accommodate the quotation. In any case, 65.25 is as fitting a conclusion to 65.17-24 as 11.6-9 is to 11.1-5.

The rhetoric of Isa. 65.17-25 is dominated by highly evocative repetition: the reference to 'former things' (v. 17) takes up a significant theme in Isaiah 40–55, the use of covenant curse language (vv. 20-23) recalls pentateuchal covenant texts, and the call/answer motif (v. 24) develops 58.9 (cf. also 65.1 and 66.4). These verses are followed by the quotation, the semantically richest form of repetition, from the penultimate oracle in Isaiah 1–12. These themes, in turn, are developed within the vision of the future transformation as the prophecy of 'Isaiah' moves toward its conclusion.

Regardless of the historical purposes behind this quotation, the present reader of the book of Isaiah, in reading Isaiah 65, will recall the parallel in Isaiah 11. Some of the divergences may escape notice without a studied comparison of the passages. The quotation is not made for the purpose of reinterpretation, even though it led to the reinterpretation of the snake motif, and 65.25 is not incomprehensible without a knowledge of 11.6-9. Whether or not ch. 65 *actualizes* the prophecy of ch. 11 by portraying its fulfillment as imminent,[42] depends

additional allusion to pre-Flood conditions in Isa. 11.9b—'as the waters cover the sea'.

42. Fishbane, *Biblical Interpretation in Ancient Israel*, p. 497. According to J. Oswalt, *The Book of Isaiah, Chapters 40–66* (NICOT; Grand Rapids: Eerdmans,

on how one interprets the participle בורא (creating) in vv. 17-18 and the extent to which the quoted parallel evokes the entire content of 11.1-9 or can be isolated from the rest of the oracle. In my opinion, the quotation serves merely to affirm the continuing validity of the promise.

However, the resultant recontextualization of Isa. 11.6-9, placing the promise of pervasive peace within the context of Yahweh's eschatological re-creation of the new heavens and new earth, blocks the non-messianic interpretion that sees in Isaiah 11 simply a reform movement brought about by a good contemporary king. The fulfillment of Isa. 11.6-9 is thus placed chronologically beyond the events surrounding the eighth-century Assyrian crisis and the later Babylonian conquest, the political deliverance of Cyrus, the spiritual deliverance of the servant, and the vengeance wrought by the anointed conqueror. The restored paradisical conditions, free from any covenantal curse, are the results of Yahweh's direct intervention in history and are not dependent on any human efforts. Furthermore, the placement of this parallel near the conclusion of the first and the final sections of the book of Isaiah may well serve some overall editorial purpose within the structure of the book of Isaiah, strategically recalling an earlier climactic promise near the conclusion of the prophecy, awakening new hope in a discouraged people. Such is the evocative versatility of quotation!

Isaiah 8.15 and 28.13

Most verbal parallels within the book of Isaiah are not as extensive or as striking as Isa. 11.6-9 and 65.25. Various brief images of future

1998), p. 662 n. 91, one should understand ch. 65 in the light of ch. 11; that is, see both passages as describing the same kingdom and take the blessings described in ch. 65 as those made available because of the coming of the messianic king described in ch. 11; P.D. Wegner, *An Examination of Kingship and Messianic Expectation in Isaiah 1-35* (Lewiston, NY: Edwin Mellen Press, 1992), p. 260, views 65.25 as an early messianic interpretation of 11.6-9. Interpreting the sigificance of the verbal parallel differently, Miscall, *Isaiah*, p. 146, notes that 'the attributes and work of the shoot in Isa. 11.1-5 have been transferred to the servant(s), the chosen, the one(s) called and sent, the people as prophet, priest and king'. For a discussion of the reasons for the non-mention of the messianic king in the final chapters of Isaiah, see R.L. Schultz, 'The King in the Book of Isaiah', in P.E. Satterthwaite, R.S. Hess and G.J. Wenham (eds.), *The Lord's Anointed: Interpretation of Old Testament Messianic Texts* (Grand Rapids: Baker Book House, 1995), pp. 141-65 (160-65).

promise or judgment are repeated throughout the book, such as blinded eyes, overflowing waters and wilderness highways, most of which cannot be considered quotations.[43] However, the verbal parallel found in Isa. 8.15 and 28.13 requires close examination before one can determine how it should be classified.

Text

והיה למקדש ולאבן נגף	8.14		
ולצור מכשול לשני בתי ישראל			
לפח ולמוקש ליושב ירושלם׃			
וכשלו בם רבים ונפלו	8.15	למען ילכו וכשלו אחור	28.13b
ונשברו ונוקשו ונלכדו׃		ונשברו ונוקשו ונלכדו׃	

And he will be a sanctuary; but 8.14
he will be a stone that causes
men to stumble and a rock that
makes them fall for both houses
of Israel. And for the people of
Jerusalem he will be a trap and
a snare.

Many of them will stumble; 8.15   so that they will go and   28.13b
they will fall and be broken,   stumble backward, be
they will be snared and captured.   broken and snared and
                                       captured.

Criteria
The primary question to be considered is whether the verbal parallel is extensive and notable enough to suggest dependence. Of the seven words which make up Isa. 8.15, four are found in identical form and order in 28.13. Both verses conclude with a series of three niphal verbs describing the fate of God's unbelieving people, as well as sharing the verb form וכשלו (and they will stumble). Although each verse also contains an additional verb, these do not correspond to each other, since ונפלו (and fall) in 8.15 is *subsequent* to the 'stumbling' while ילכו (go) in 28.13 *precedes* it.

That two of these verbs should be repeated is unremarkable: כשל and נפל ('stumble' and 'fall') also appear together in Isa. 3.8 and 31.3, while נוקש and נלכד ('be snared' and 'captured') are used in Prov. 6.2. However, not only do all four verbs appear both in Isa. 8.15 and 28.13,

---

43. See 'Appendix: Verbal Parallels in the Book of Isaiah', pp. 339-41.

but they relate to two different topoi, כשל and נפל to 'travelers' perils' and נוקש and נלכד to trapping animals, presumably birds,[44] and thus would not occur together naturally. Their occurrence in 8.15 is prepared for by the use of the corresponding nouns in 8.14: אבן נגף and מכשול צור (stone/rock of stumbling), פח and מוקש ('trap' and 'snare'). In 28.13, on the contrary, their use is unexpected, lacking contextual preparation. This suggests that the repetition of these four verbs in 28.13 involves dependence on their use in 8.15.

A second criterion is that of contextual awareness. As already mentioned, Isa. 8.15 completes the imagery of judgment begun in 8.14, while Isa. 28.13b, which is introduced by למען (so that), probably indicating a result clause, completes v. 13a which involves the repetition/quotation of 28.10 from the immediate context. Neither verbal parallel is marked clearly in its context, although 28.13b's use with another quotation is suggestive.

The brevity of the parallel reduces the potential for reinterpretation by reformulation. The several divergences between the two passages can be given contextual explanations. רבים (many) in 8.15 quantifies those among the 'two houses of Israel' and the 'inhabitants of Jerusalem'[45] who will be affected by the coming judgment. In 28.13, the subject of the verbs is given by להם (to them) namely 'this people' of v. 11. ב ם in 8.15, if translated correctly as 'over them' (instrumental),[46] refers to the stone and rock of v. 14 and is understandably omitted in 28.13 where they are not mentioned.

A key question in analyzing this verbal parallel is whether the mere reuse of the same verbs in 28.13 which appear in 8.15 without any mention of their related nouns (from 8.14) is sufficient to evoke a clear portrait of judgment or whether it is expected that the images will be completed by a knowledge of the context of the verbal parallel in 8.14-

44. The exact meaning of פח and מוקש in Isa. 8.14 is disputed. See the discussion by Wildberger, *Jesaja 1–39*, I, p. 339.

45. ליושב ירשלם (for the inhabitants—sing.—of Jerusalem) must be viewed as a collective noun. Several Hebrew manuscripts as well as LXX, Old Latin, Symmachus, read יושבי in agreement with the preceding בתי ישראל (houses of Israel). J.H. Hayes and S.A. Irvine, *Isaiah: The Eighth-Century Prophet* (Nashville: Abingdon Press, 1987), p. 159, translate 'ruler of Jerusalem', as in Amos 1.8 and Isa. 9.8.

46. בם can also be translated 'among them'. Kaiser, *Jesaja 1–12*, p. 187 n. 29, argues that רבב here is universal, not partitive, an incalculable number.

15.[47] One possible indicator that these verbal parallels involve a contextual linkage is the identification of further thematic and verbal parallels within the larger context.[48] Just as the 'stumbling stone' is an important image of judgment in 8.14, so the 'cornerstone' is a prominent image of salvation in 28.16.[49] Not only do both passages share the judgment imagery of stumbling and being trapped, but also the image of overflowing waters, using the verbs שָׁטַף and עָבַר (flood, pass through, 8.7-8 and 28.2, 15, 17, 18, 19).[50] Although the integrity of chs. 8 and 28 is disputed, it appears that, at least on the redactional level, these larger contexts are being associated and that the parallel in 8.15 and 28.13b involves verbal dependence.[51]

Diachronic Analysis

Once again, it is extremely difficult to determine the historical circumstances which may have led to this verbal parallel, if indeed a conscious dependence is involved, for there are few overt textual clues that offer guidance. Nevertheless, an analysis of the larger contexts reveals some striking similarities.

Isaiah 8.15 forms the conclusion of what is presented as a private prophetic oracle (vv. 11-15) which 'the LORD spoke to me with his strong hand upon me, warning me not to follow the way of this people'. Nevertheless, the use of second person plural verb forms in vv. 12-13 suggests that a wider audience is intended. This unit is at least loosely connected to the other first person sections of ch. 8—vv. 1-4, 5-10, 16-18 (19-22). Along with Isaiah 7, Isaiah 8 generally is considered to

47. One problem is that there is not a complete correspondence between the verbs used in the parallel passages. See the discussion below.

48. Fishbane, *Biblical Interpretation in Ancient Israel*, p. 285, has stated similarly that the identification of aggadic exegesis is 'proportionally increased to the extent that multiple and sustained lexical linkages between two texts can be recognized'.

49. See the further discussion of parallels under *Synchronic Analysis* below.

50. שָׁטַף is also used in Isa. 10.22 and 30.28.

51. The views of J. Oswalt, *The Book of Isaiah, Chapters 1-39* (NICOT; Grand Rapids: Eerdmans, 1986), p. 513, that 8.15 merely 'contains many of the same terms in a similar setting', and of A.J. Bjørndalen, *Untersuchungen zur allegorischen Rede der Propheten Amos und Jesaja* (BZAW, 165; Berlin: W. de Gruyter, 1986), p. 218, that 28.13b involves merely a 'corresponding combination and ordering of motifs' as 8.15 are clearly inadequate. Miscall, *Isaiah*, p. 74, however, recognizes that 28.13 'alludes to 8.15'.

consist of genuine Isaianic materials, even if originally independent of one another, stemming from the time of the Syro-Ephraimite War (c. 735–733 BCE).[52]

Accordingly, the 'conspiracy' (קֶשֶׁר) of 8.12 may refer to the people's assessment of Isaiah's efforts to dissuade Ahaz from negotiating with the Assyrians in response to the threat posed by Pekah and Rezin (7.1).[53] Instead of accepting their assessment, Isaiah is to revere Yahweh, trusting in him alone (8.17). However, those who do not heed this warning will experience Yahweh's judgment (vv. 14b-15).[54] Verse 15 describes the consequences for the people of Israel, Judah and Jerusalem in terms of v. 14's metaphors of judgment.

Isaiah 28.13b similarly forms the conclusion of a judgment oracle, consisting of vv. 7-13, or vv. 1-13 if the entire oracle is viewed as referring to Ephraim.[55] Verses 1-4 (5-6) clearly are directed to Ephraim, while vv. 14-22 are addressed to Jerusalem. Verses 7-13 are more ambiguous. The priests and prophets are criticized as drunken and incompetent, while 'this people' (הָעָם הַזֶּה) will experience God's judgment. Perhaps the passage is purposefully vague, but whether it is related to vv. 1-6 or vv. 14-22 is crucial for questions of dating.

Most scholars view Isaiah 28–33 as essentially Isaianic and stemming from the time of Hezekiah and his rebellion against Sennacherib, in c. 703 BCE. Wildberger views ch. 28 as the earliest oracle in this series. Fohrer relates it to the revolt of Ashdod (ch. 20) in 713–711 BCE.

---

52. W. Dietrich, *Jesaja und die Politik* (BEvT, 74; Munich: Chr. Kaiser Verlag, 1976), pp. 62-63. This chapter is usually considered to be a part of Isaiah's 'Memoirs' (*Denkschrift*).

53. קֶשֶׁר has been variously translated 'alliance', 'conspiracy', 'treason' and 'revolt' and, accordingly, has been interpreted as referring to the Syro-Ephraimite coalition, Ahaz's negotiations with the Assyrians, and Isaiah's efforts at dissuasion. See C.A. Evans, 'An Interpretation of Isa 8, 4-15 Unemended', *ZAW* 97 (1985), pp. 112-13.

54. Most commentators consider לְמִקְדָּשׁ (be a sanctuary) in 8.14a to be inappropriate in the context. G.R. Driver, 'Two Misunderstood Passages of the Old Testament', *JTS* NS 6 (1955), pp. 2-87 (83), emends the word to מָקְשִׁיר as well as תַּקְדִּישׁוּ (regard as holy) in v. 13 to תַּקְשִׁירוּ, translating קֶשֶׁר as 'difficulty'. Bjørndalen, *Untersuchungen zur allegorischen Rede*, p. 213, simply eliminates the word from consideration as 'unrestorable'. However, למקדשׁ lies outside out of the parallelism in v. 14b and was separated from it by an athnach by the Masoretes.

55. The latter is held by Hayes and Irvine, *Isaiah*, pp. 322-25, and Oswalt, *Isaiah 1–39*, p. 506. J.D.W. Watts, *Isaiah 1-33* (WBC, 24; Waco, TX: Word Books, 1985), pp. 352-57, translates all the verbs in vv. 1-13 as past tenses.

Watts dates the section as late as the reigns of Josiah and Jehoiakim (640–605 BCE), while Hayes and Irvine have dated the entire section, partly on the basis of the mention of Ephraim in 28.1-4, to the time of Shalmaneser (727–725 BCE).[56] Regardless of which date one chooses, the scholarly consensus is to date Isa. 28.7-13 as later (whether by a decade or a century) than 8.11-15, and most view both oracles as basically unified, possibly even Isaianic. This is confirmed by the references in the larger contexts which portray Ephraim and Aram as the primary threats in chs. 7–8, with Assyria as God's instrument of judgment, while Assyria is portrayed in chs. 28–33 both as the primary threat and as destined for God's judgment.

In the light of the historical circumstances underlying Isaiah 8 and 28, as they have been reconstructed, several explanations for the reuse of the image of judgment from 8.15 in 28.13b can be suggested: (1) Certainly, one factor could be the striking imagery of the stumbling stone and the trap, the rhetorical impact of which was appropriated to complete another oracle of judgment.[57] (2) Since the Assyrians probably are to be viewed as the instruments of divine judgment in both larger contexts (7.17, 20; 8.4, 7; 28.11; 33.18-19), one could understand 28.13 as both affirming the continuing validity of and describing more specifically how the threat of 8.15 will be fulfilled. (3) Another possibility is that the circumstances surrounding the Assyrian threat were considered to be analogous to those of the Syro-Ephraimite threat. In both crises, the Davidic monarch was tempted to trust in foreign military assistance (Assyria in chs. 7–8, Egypt in chs. 28–33) rather than in Yahweh as Isaiah instructed him. The comparative study of quotation in ancient Near Eastern literature indicates that the Egyptians were especially fond of quoting when they considered their situation to be analogous to that of an earlier historical or fictional character, whose description they then quoted.[58] Accordingly, it may be that whoever was responsible for the quotation felt that, since the sin of the people was similar, the same description of judgment was appropriate to

---

56. Wildberger, *Jesaja 1–39*, III, pp. 1056-57; and Hayes and Irvine, *Isaiah*, pp. 321-23.

57. See Bjørndalen, *Untersuchungen der allegorische Rede*, pp. 217-18, who speaks of this metaphor's 'power of expression and ability to communicate'. This may be the case even if the second and/or third suggestions are also true.

58. See Chapter 3, pp. 128-29 above.

repeat, even if the analogy is left implicit.[59]

This raises again the question of who is quoting whom. Due to the brevity and nature of the verbal parallel, some interpreters deny that any quotation or dependence is involved here.[60] However, as has been pointed out above, this is unlikely. Given the general consensus regarding the basic Isaianic origin of chs. 7–8 and 28–33, it is theoretically possible to see this parallel as a genuine example of self-quotation, where a speaker/author repeats his earlier words in another context where they are equally fitting. Self-quotation is a phenomenon which literary scholars, such as John Hollander, describe as an effective rhetorical device and biblical scholars, such as Karl Elliger, have identified within the prophetic corpus.[61]

However, most scholars deny that this is indeed the case in 8.15 // 28.13b. With regard to 8.11-15, among those who reject its Isaianic origin or literary integrity, three basic approaches may be discerned. Otto Kaiser considers the entire unit to be a retrospective judgment oracle from the early Persian period explaining the causes of decline. Dietrich reconstructs the original oracle as consisting of 8.16, 14-15 with the 'binding up of the testimony and the sealing up the law' causing Israel to fall and be snared. Duhm eliminates 'many of them will stumble' in 8.15 as a secondary addition influenced by 28.13 which disturbs the parallelism but serves to weaken the oracle by making room for exceptions to its comprehensive threat.[62]

Unlike the verbal parallel Isa. 11.6-9 and 65.25 in which the direction of quotation is much disputed, with the partial exception of Duhm who considers 8.15 and 28.13 as 'mutually enriching each other',[63] most scholars agree that it is 28.13 which is dependent on 8.15 and not vice versa but assert that v. 13 in part or in whole is a secondary addition to the oracle. Marti considers the last two or three words of 28.13 to be 'displaced' from 8.15; Duhm views them as introduced from 8.15 by a

---

59. Watts, *Isaiah 1–33*, p. 364, sees the quotation as 'reinforcing the understanding that this section points back to the events of 734-21 B.C. that are pictured in … chaps. 7-10'.

60. See n. 51 above and F. Stolz, 'Der Streit um die Wirklichkeit in der Südreichsprophetie des 8. Jahrhunderts', *Wort und Dienst* NS 12 (1973), pp. 9-30, p. 22 n. 53, cited by Dietrich, *Jesaja und die Politik*, p. 152 n. 95.

61. See Chapter 6, pp. 197-98 and n. 36 above.

62. Kaiser, *Jesaja 1–12*, p. 187; Dietrich, *Jesaja und die Politik*, pp. 73-74; Duhm, *Das Buch Jesaia*, p. 61.

63. Duhm, *Das Buch Jesaia*, pp. 60-61.

later reader. Donner and Wildberger consider the entire verse to be a prose addition, while Dietrich eliminates vv. 13b-19a as secondary, the original unit concluding with vv. 13a, 19b. Kaiser views vv. 7bβ and 13 as stemming from a proto-apocalyptic eschatological reworking of the oracle around 597–587 BCE, and Clements similarly understands v. 13 as a post-eventum reapplication of 28.10 and 8.15.[64]

In sum, nearly all commentators deny that 28.13b consists of a quotation of 8.15 by the original speaker or author of 28.7-13. In their opinion, this verbal parallel never functioned on the oral level but rather originated on the literary or, more likely, on the redactional level. On the one hand, this would tend to rule out the suggestion that this is merely a reuse of a striking image for stylistic purposes and without quotational intent. On the other hand, some reason must then be sought for inserting a secondary quotation into a previously complete literary context.

At the outset, one must wonder whether most scholars find the idea of 'self-quotation' within Isaiah inherently unacceptable, despite the reasons they give for labeling 28.13b as secondary. The stylistic argument of Donner that v. 13 is a prose addition ignores the fact that quotation may be expected, as a preformed unit, to interrupt any prosodic pattern. Furthermore, both the repeated v. 13a and v. 13b are considered to be poetic in their previous contexts.[65] Wildberger's claim that v. 13 competes with v. 11 and therefore is superfluous and secondary, is only one possible construal of the unit. If the difficult phrase צו לצו קו לקו צו לצו קו לקו קו לקו, 'Do and do ... rule or rule' in v. 13a represents the message of the 'foreign lips' of v. 11 and v. 13b represents its results (in contrast to the rejected message of v. 12, 'This is the resting place, let the weary rest' and 'This is the place of repose')—the obscure sounds imitating the Assyrian language, as van Selms has suggested—then v. 13 *resumes* and *completes* v. 11 rather than *competing with* it.[66]

---

64. K. Marti, *Das Buch Jesaja* (KHAT, 10; Tübingen: J.C.B. Mohr [Paul Siebeck], 1900), p. 207; Duhm, *Das Buch Jesaia*, p. 174; H. Donner, *Israel unter den Völkern: Die Stellung der klassischen Propheten des 8. Jahrhunderts vor Christi zur Aussenpolitik der Könige von Israel und Juda* (VTSup, 11; Leiden: E.J. Brill, 1964), p. 148; Wildberger, *Jesaja 1–39*, pp. 1054-55; Dietrich, *Jesaja und die Politik*, p. 153; O. Kaiser, *Der Prophet Jesaja, Kapitel 13-39* (ATD, 18; Göttingen: Vandenhoeck & Ruprecht, 1973), p. 197; Clements, *Isaiah 1–39*, pp. 228-29.

65. See Chapter 3, pp. 142-43. Wildberger, for example, renders both 8.15 and 28.10 as poetry, *Jesaja 1–39*, I, p. 334; III, p. 1052.

66. Wildberger, *Jesaja 1–39*, III, p. 1055. For the various views concerning the

Kaiser's identification of proto-apocalyptic features in v. 13 is rightly rejected by Wildberger.[67]

Several commentators hint at a more basic line of argumentation: v. 13 is secondary *because* it consists of quotation.[68] As has been seen already, a denigrating attitude toward quotation is rather pervasive in Old Testament scholarship, undoubtedly affecting the diachronic analysis of verbal parallels. However, this oversimplifies the matter, for quotation frequently is viewed as secondary precisely because it involves reinterpretation, which almost universally is considered to be a relatively late development within the prophetic literature. For example, Clements sees here the work of a later redactor

> who has applied the warning that God will speak to Judah through the language of foreigners in another direction. He has taken it to mean that God's word of prophecy will be treated by the people as a foreign language so that they will not need it and consequently will fall and be snared by events.[69]

In conclusion, several observations can be made regarding the diachronic analysis of Isa. 8.15 and 28.13b. First of all, it is clear that the basic problem is not simply determining in which direction the dependence lies. Although scholars are almost unanimous in agreeing that, if borrowing is involved, 8.15 is the source of 28.13 and not vice versa, no consensus has emerged regarding who is doing the quoting and for what reason. Rather, it appears that quotation remains at the

---

meaning of v. 10, see Wildberger, *Jesaja 1–39*, III, p. 1056. This is one plausible explanation for Isa. 28.9-10, See also G.R. Driver, 'Another Little Drink!—Isaiah 28:1-22', in P.R. Ackroyd and B. Lindars (eds.), *Words and Meanings: Essays Presented to David Winton Thomas* (Cambridge: Cambridge University Press, 1968), pp. 47-67; W.W. Hallo, 'Isaiah 28:9-13 and the Ugaritic Abecedaries', *JBL* 77 (1958), pp. 324-38; G. Pfeifer, 'Entwöhnung und Entwöhnungsfest im Alten Testament: Der Schlüssel zu Jesaja 28:7-13?', *ZAW* 84 (1972), pp. 341-47; G. Rice, 'Isaiah 28:1-22 and the New English Bible', *JRT* 30 (1973–74), pp. 13-17; A. van Selms, 'Isaiah 28:9-13: An Attempt to Give a New Interpretation', *ZAW* NS 85 (1973), pp. 332-39; M. Görg, 'Jesaja als "Kinderlehrer"? Beobachtungen zur Sprache und Semantik in Jes 28, 10 (13)', *BN* 29 (1985), pp. 12-16.

67. Wildberger, *Jesaja 1–39*, III, p. 1056.

68. Kaiser, *Jesaja 13–39*, p. 194, who eliminates the verse 'as a creation compiled from v. 10 and 8.15'. Similarly, Clements, *Isaiah 1–39*, p. 226.

69. Clements, *Isaiah 1–39*, pp. 228-29. Wildberger, *Jesaja 1–39*, III, p. 1061, sees in v. 13a also a reinterpretation of v. 10: שָׁם זְעֵיר (a little here) here means 'from all sides only misfortune pours down'.

mercy of the individual interpreter's analysis of the growth of the prophetic literature as a whole. Secondly, despite the brevity of the verbal parallel, several modern commentators view the quotation as interpretive in intent. This concern with purpose is in refreshing contrast to much that has been written concerning prophetic quotation. Nevertheless, little attention is given to the larger contexts of the verbal parallels as influencing or being affected by the quotation. Finally, it is remarkable how little light the diachronic analysis actually sheds on the historical aspects of quotation, focusing rather on literary-critical fine points. In order for the dynamics of this quotation to be appreciated more fully, a synchronic analysis offers an essential complement.

Synchronic Analysis
It already has been noted that the verbal, thematic and structural parallels which can be identified in Isaiah 7–8 and 28–33 may indicate that a historical analogy between the Syro-Ephraimite and Assyrian threats to Judah is being suggested literarily.[70] Accordingly, the verbal parallel would mark the climax of the analogy, indicating that the similar sin of relying on foreign alliances will call forth a similar judgment, utilizing an identical image (8.15 and 28.13). Whether or not this is the case, the verbal parallel must be examined closely in order to determine how it functions.

Isaiah 8.11 begins by setting up a contrast between the actions which Yahweh expects from Isaiah and the 'way of the people', marked (in v. 12) by contrasting attitudes toward the political policies (קשר, 'conspiracy') and the military threat (מוראו, 'its fear'). Instead, he and his followers are to declare Yahweh to be holy, thus acknowledging his awesome power.[71] As a result, Isaiah will experience a different fate: Yahweh will be a sanctuary (מקדש) for him but bring judgment upon the people as a whole.[72] Regardless of how one understands or emends

70. E.W. Conrad, 'The Royal Narratives and the Structure of the Book of Isaiah', *JSOT* 41 (1988), pp. 67-81, also suggests that Isa. 7 and 36–39 are structured in such a way as to point out the similarities between the situations of Ahaz and Hezekiah.

71. Hayes and Irvine, *Isaiah*, p. 157. Note the similar use of קדש hiphil in Num. 20.12.

72. For recent defenses of reading למקדש as 'sanctuary', see Evans, 'An Interpretation', pp. 112-13; Oswalt, *Isaiah 1–39*, pp. 233-34, and Hayes and Irvine, *Isaiah*, pp. 158-59, the latter rendering it 'for the sake of his holy domain'. It remains unclear whether 'sanctuary' refers to judgment or salvation. According to

מִקְדָּשׁ, it clearly stands apart from the remaining four elements in v. 13 which also serve as predicate complements describing Yahweh's metaphorical function. וּלְאֶבֶן נֶגֶף is paired with וּלְצוּר מִכְשׁוֹל, as is לְפַח with וּלְמוֹקֵשׁ, although it is not obvious conceptually that the first pair applies exclusively to the 'two houses of Israel', while the second pair will be experienced only by the inhabitant(s)[73] of Jerusalem. Rather, the parallelism is climactic: even Jerusalem will not escape Yahweh's trap.[74]

The paired nouns represent threats of sudden or unexpected destruction, as is made explicit by the series of verbs in v. 15. That Yahweh is the source of judgment, even though the Assyrians may be the agents (8.4, 7), is made explicit by בָּם, that is, over the stone and rock, linking v. 15 to the preceding verse. The first three verbs form a sequence—stumble, fall, be smashed—which corresponds to the stone/rock, normally an image of refuge,[75] commencing with the cognate verb of the second *nomen rectum* (וְכָשְׁלוּ/מִכְשׁוֹל). The final two verbs also represent a sequence—be snared and be captured[76]—which corresponds to the trap/snare, likewise commencing with the cognate verb of the second noun (וְנוֹקְשׁוּ/מוֹקֵשׁ). The third verb forms the transition between the two sequences, sharing the imagery of the first two and the niphal theme of the final two. Bjørndalen has noted how the verbs of v. 15, though associated with two distinct metaphorical systems, flow together to form one coherent portrayal of thorough judgment. The scope of judgment, touching 'both houses of Israel', suggests that the call to sanctify

C. von Orelli, *Der Prophet Jesaja* (Leipzig: F.C.W. Vogel, 1921), p. 40, 'but the thought, on the contrary, is that Yahweh, through judment, will make himself into a feared and unassailable sanctuary ... , in that all his scorners will come to ruin over him'. (Isa. 28.16-17 also may portray a stone that can be a refuge, v. 16b, or a place of judgment, v. 17.)

73. Hayes and Irvine, *Isaiah*, pp. 158-59, make a partial distinction, by translating לִשְׁנֵי בָתֵּי יִשְׂרָאֵל as 'to the two houses of Israel' and לְיֹשֵׁב יְרוּשָׁלַם 'for the sake of the ruler of Jerusalem', viewing the passage as a promise of protection for Zion.

74. Being trapped is a stronger image than simply stumbling over a stone. Another possibility is to see in the trap/snare an allusion to Ahaz's political entanglements with Assyria.

75. See Isa. 17.10; Deut. 32.4; Ps. 18.3; 31.3-4; 42.10; 62.8; 71.3.

76. The two verbs appear *elsewhere* in parallelism in Prov. 6.2, but in Jer. 50.24 they may indicate a sequence. See Wildberger, *Jesaja 1–39*, III, p. 1053, 'be ensnared and end up in captivity'; and Bjørndalen, *Untersuchungen zur allegorischen Rede*, pp. 214-15.

and fear Yahweh (v. 13) is not intended to be limited to Isaiah and his disciples or any specific political crisis. In effect, 8.11-15 expresses in more general, theological terms the same call to total confidence in Yahweh which is addressed to Ahaz in 7.1-13.[77]

Regardless of how one views the composition or redaction of Isa. 28.1-22[78] in its present form, it consists of three judgment oracles which are linked by several striking catchwords: drunkards (vv. 1, 3 שכורי cf. v. 7 שכר); storm images (v. 2 ברד, שטף cf. vv. 17-18); perceiving the message (v. 9 שמועה יבין cf. v. 19 הבין שמועה).[79] A central theme of the unit vv. 7-13 is the reception of the divine message. Following a threat addressed to Ephraim and preceding one addressed to Jerusalem's rulers,[80] the reference to the priests and prophets in v. 7 may be deliberately vague in order to address Israel's religious leaders as a whole. Because the mediators of divine direction are incompetent by reason of inebriation (vv. 7-8), Yahweh must address the young children, using a message suited (and comprehensible) only to them (vv. 9-10).[81]

The invective, however, is not directed here to the drunken but to 'this people'[82] (vv. 11b-12) who are *unwilling* (לא + אבה) to receive Yahweh's promise of rest. Therefore, he will use the foreign lips of

---

77. For an examination of this theme in Isa. 8, see H.-P. Müller, 'Glauben und Bleiben: Zur Denkschrift Jesajas Kapitel vi.1-viii.18', in G.W. Anderson (ed.), *Studies in Prophecy: A Collection of Twelve Papers* (VTSup, 26; Leiden: E.J. Brill, 1974), pp. 25-54.

78. For two contrasting yet complementary analyses of the chapter, see D.L. Petersen, 'Isaiah 28: A Redaction Critical Study', in P. Achtemeier (ed.), *SBL Papers 1979* (2 vols.; Missoula, MT: Scholars Press, 1979), II, pp. 101-22, and J.C. Exum, 'Isaiah 28-32: A Literary Approach', in Achtemeier (ed.), *SBL Seminar Papers: 1979*, pp. 123-51; also J.C. Exum, ' "Whom Will He Teach Knowledge?": A Literary Approach to Isaiah 28', in D.J.A. Clines, D.M. Gunn and A.J. Hauser (eds.), *Art and Meaning: Rhetoric in Biblical Literature* (JSOTSup, 19; Sheffield: JSOT Press, 1982), pp. 108-39.

79. Other repeated words include בלע (swallow) vv. 4 and 7, and רמס (trample), vv. 3 and 18.

80. משלי in v. 14 is best understood as 'rulers' rather than 'proverb-makers', despite the parallelism with לצון (scoffing), though word-play may be intended.

81. For other interpretations of צו לצו ... קו לקו (Do and do ... rule or rule) see n. 66. Exum, 'Isaiah 28-32', pp. 120-21, identifies Yahweh as the 'teacher' referred to in v. 9.

82. It is not clear that 'this people' is exclusively applied to Jerusalem. See Watts, *Isaiah 1–33*, p. 363.

invaders to render a similarly incomprehensible message (vv. 11, 13a)
which nevertheless will hit home. It is precisely at this point that the
description of judgment from 8.15 is repeated. Unlike 8.15, which
nicely completes the imagery of 8.14, in 28.13b the verbs lack any contextual motivation, other than the reference in vv. 7-8 to the stumbling
drunks. Because of the obscurity of v. 13a, a strong conjunction like
למען is needed (compare the simple waw in 8.15) to indicate that the
destruction results directly from the word of Yahweh. Perhaps it is for
this reason that the verbal parallel is modified here. The significance of
the use of ילכו (go) rather than ונפלו (fall) (as in 8.15) is unclear, but the
addition of אחור (backward) is noteworthy, since only here in the Old
Testament is כשל (stumble) followed by אחור. Possibly, since the
immediate cause is not a rock but a message, one is described not as
falling over it but rather as stumbling backward in shock upon hearing
it.[83]

The three remaining niphal verbs are repeated in identical order from
8.15. Although they represent familiar images of judgment, this
particular sequence can be explained only by their use in 8.14-15. One
could conclude that the reader of this passage is expected to supply the
unmentioned causes (the stone/rock and the trap/snare) on the basis of
his or her knowledge of this quotation's original context. This is a
common technique in quotation in modern literature, as is its placement
at the conclusion of a unit.[84] However, it could also be argued that both
immediate causes, according to the original context of the verbal parallel, have receded into the background as a result of the modification and
recontextualization of the quotation. Just as the addition of אחור following וכשלו describes a shocked response rather than an inadvertent
stumble, so the somewhat veiled reference to the *foreign* tongue in
28.11 adds an ominous note to the use of ונלכדו (be captured).
Legitimizing the reuse is the fact that the metaphorical causes of injury
and capture represent similar ultimate agents: Yahweh in Isa. 8.14-15
and the word of Yahweh in 28.13.[85] Just as those who refused to regard
God as holy and revere him alone would fall under God's judgment,

---

83. See v. 19: 'and it will be sheer terror to understand the message', picking up
the phrase from v. 9. Compare 1 Sam. 4.18 and Jn 18.6.

84. See Chapter 6, p. 197.

85. O. Procksch, *Jesaia I* (KAT, 9; Leipzig: Deichert, 1930), p. 356, notes: 'V.
13b reminds one of 8.15, so that one can understand Yahweh himself as the stumbling stone (*Ärgernis*)'.

according to Isaiah 8, so, in the case of those who rejected the divine offer of rest in a later historical crisis, that very divine word would be the source of their doom, according to Isaiah 28.

From a synchronic perspective, one must acknowledge that Isa. 28.13b is now an integral part of the book of Isaiah, not simply a redactional addition to an isolated oracle. As such, it functions, similarly to Isa. 65.25, as an *internal* parallel, a virtual self-quotation, in which an earlier message (or text) is evoked, reaffirmed, even actualized. It also alerts the reader to the possibility of a deliberate linking of two texts. A careful reading of the larger contexts, Isaiah 7–8 or 7–11 and 28–33, reveals the following parallels, in addition to those mentioned above: (1) The verb אמן (hiphil) (believe) is used both in 7.9 and 28.16, two of only four hiphil occurrences of אמן in the book of Isaiah; (2) both passages describe divinely offered refuge, if one retains מקדש (sanctuary) in 8.14a, cf. 28.12, 16; (3) a key theme in both is the people's rejection of the divine message while they resort to occult sources 8.19-20, 28.12, 15;[86] (4) in both passages Yahweh is portrayed in judgment as Israel's enemy, 8.14-15, 28.21; (5) in terms of historical setting, Assyria is the primary military threat in both; (6) Isa. 10.23 is repeated in 28.22; thus both Isa. 28.7-13 and 28.14-22 conclude with a verbal parallel from Isaiah 8–11.[87] It is evident that these two sections of the book of Isaiah have been linked, at least on the literary or redactional level, and the repetition of 8.15 in 28.13 does not constitute the *purpose* of this association but rather expresses its *implications*.

This raises again the question of the relationship between the diachronic and synchronic analysis of such verbal parallels. Can one simply dispense with one or the other? With regard to Isa. 8.15 and 28.13, the methods are clearly complementary. The work of historical reconstruction suggests a similar political crisis underlying both texts which corresponds to the analogy that is indicated literarily. The diachronic analysis of the direction of dependence coincides with the synchronic. The synchronic approach relativizes the value of Dietrich's reconstruction of the original shape of the oracles (which eliminates the quotation as a secondary addition) for understanding the present

---

86. Duhm, *Das Buch Jesaia*, p. 174, takes the reference to the 'covenant with death' in 28.1-5 literally as involving sacrifices to the gods of the underworld. The prophet, however, probably intends it sarcastically.

87. 10.23 כי־ כלה ונחרצה   אדני יהוה צבאות עשה בקרב כל־הארץ:
28.22b כי־ כלה ונחרצה שמעתי מאח אדני יהוה צבאות   על   כל־הארץ:

canonical text, while the diachronic approach reminds us of the inherently historical nature of quotation which cannot be reduced to a matter of intertextuality. In order to interpret a quotation adequately one must seek to discover both its *purpose* and its *effect*.

Isaiah 40.3, 10; 57.14; and 62.10-11

Although the individual verbal parallels just analyzed have received much scholarly attention, they have not influenced the overall assessment of Isaiah nearly as much as those between Isaiah 40–55 and 56–66, which have supplied scholars with a major reason for distinguishing between a 'Second' and 'Third' Isaiah. According to Volz, 'a compelling and decisive argument for the separation of this chapter from Deut.-Isa. is that fact that Deut.-Isa. is quoted repeatedly, sometimes even verbatim, but nevertheless with a modification/twisting (*Umbiegung*) of the meaning'.[88] Although Zimmerli's 'Zur Sprache Tritojesajas' is the best-known essay describing this 'Umbiegung', the claim goes back at least as far as Duhm. For nearly a century, the same passages within these chapters have been noted as 'internal' quotations. However, as previously observed,[89] there has been little agreement regarding the assessment and interpretation of these 'citations'.

Because of the significant role which 'Third' Isaiah's alleged use of 'Second' Isaiah has played in the overall understanding of these chapters, the issue deserves to be re-evaluated in light of this study of the dynamics of quotation. Such studies,[90] despite containing many helpful exegetical insights, display some basic flaws. For the most part, they reflect a deficient view of the purpose and function of quotation. In addition, they involve a selective analysis of individual passages and fail to investigate the effect of these verbal parallels on the overall message of these chapters.

Basic to the scholarly assessment of 'Second' and 'Third' Isaiah is the claim that all of an author's quotations fit a particular pattern (only

---

88. Volz, *Jesaja II*, p. 198.

89. See Chapter 1, pp. 42-49.

90. The primary examples of this approach are Zimmerli's 'Zur Sprache Tritojesajas', pp. 217-33, and the commentaries of Westermann and Whybray, as well as Hanson, *The Dawn of Apocalyptic*, and Michel, 'Zur Eigenart Tritojesajas', pp. 213-30, all of whom reflect or at least share, to a greater or lesser extent, Zimmerli's views regarding 'Third' Isaiah's use of 'Second' Isaiah.

exact reproduction or only with modification of the wording or meaning), so much so that this characteristic becomes a criterion for determining whether a verbal parallel is genuine or 'secondary' (*unecht*) in its present context. This can result in the elimination or overlooking of every passage that does not conform or the interpretation of all others as conforming to the pattern. To look for common features in a number of quotations is certainly valid but to declare what 'Second' or 'Third' Isaiah would never do with respect to a borrowed text is a questionable approach.[91]

Quotation is a phenomenon that is so multi-functional and semantically complex that it is difficult, if not impossible, to generalize regarding a specific author's or text's method. The analysis of Sirach and the Hodayoth indicates that the same author or text may utilize both short and long borrowings, exact reproduction and considerable adaptation, both the reuse and reapplication of convenient or appropriate language as well as instances of significant reinterpretation. Although a unified perspective or theology may underlie these quotations, this will be reflected in individual passages in a variety of ways.

Many of the German scholars analyzing 'Third' Isaiah speak of his 'Umbiegung' of 'Second' Isaiah's words, usually illustrating rather than explaining exactly what they mean by the term. What they have in mind is 'a change in meaning from the original' which basically is considered to be inappropriate or at least not intended by the original speaker or author. In their usage, 'Umbiegung' clearly has a negative connotation. However, it must be noted that every quotation will involve some change of meaning, even if the wording remains exactly the same, while some changes in wording will not necessarily affect the meaning much. On the one hand, it is not clear that the context of one passage can render its reapplication to another situation invalid, especially if it is primarily the *wording* used to describe an act of divine intervention which prompted the borrowing rather than its specific contextual *meaning*. On the other hand, a quotation always brings part of its context with it. Thus a quotation may carry with it themes, images

---

91. See Elliger, *Deuterojesaja in seinem Verhältnis zu Tritojesaja*, p. 210: 'And that is a type of writing (*Schriftstellerei*), which Trito-Isaiah never would have been guilty of'; and pp. 46-47: 'In general, it is not Deutero-Isaiah's practice to repeat himself in this manner ... Deutero-Isaiah does not repeat himself verbatim like Trito-Isaiah but in varied form.'

and associations from a first pàssage which are lacking in the second formulation and context.[92]

On the basis of these considerations, a reassessment of the verbal parallels between 'Second' and 'Third' Isaiah is in order.[93] Of all the passages in Isaiah 56–66 which contain verbal parallels to passages in Isaiah 40–55, Isa. 62.10-12 is one of the most striking and difficult to analyze, for it potentially contains a double quotation from the same context and involves one of the prominent images of the book of Isaiah: the highway through the wilderness. According to the usual analysis, Isa. 40.3 is drawn upon in 62.10 (as well as 57.14) and 40.10 is repeated in modified form in 62.11.

Texts

	40.3		62.10
קוֹל קוֹרֵא		עברו עברו בשערים	
במדבר פנו דרך יהוה		פנו דרך העם	
ישרו בערבה מסלה לאלהינו:			
	57.14		
ואמר סלו־סלו פנו־דרך		סלו סלו המסלה סקלו מאבן	
הרימו מכשול מדרך עמי:		הרימו נס על־העמים:	62.11
		הנה יהוה השמיע אל־קצה הארץ	
		אמרו לבת־ציון	
	40.10	הנה ישעך בא	
הנה אדני יהוה בחזק יבוא			
וזרעו משלה לו			
הנה שכרו אתו ופעלתו לפניו:		הנה שכרו אתו ופעלתו לפניו:	

	40.3		62.10
A voice of one calling:		Pass through, pass through the gates!	
'In the desert prepare the way for the LORD;		Prepare the way for the people	

92. See Chapter 6, pp. 196-97, 199-201. Elliger, *Deuterojesaja in seinem Verhältnis zu Tritojesaja*, pp. 284-86, denies Volz's claim of 'Umbiegung' in specific passages.

93. In this section 'Second' and 'Third' Isaiah are used to designate Isa. 40–55 and 56–66, respectively, reflecting a scholarly hypothesis, even though the origin and extent of these collections and the identity of the author(s) or group(s) behind them continue to be the object of considerable dispute. The use of this designation does not indicate the author's preference for any specific viewpoint concerning the origin of these chapters.

make straight in the wilderness a highway for our God.		
And it will be said: "Build up, build up, prepare the road",	57.14	Build up, build up the highway! Remove the stones.
Remove the obstacles out of the way of my people.'		Raise a banner for the nations.
		The LORD has made a proclamation to the ends of the earth, 62.11
		'Say to the daughter of Zion,
See, the sovereign LORD comes with power	40.10	"See, your Savior comes!
and his arm rules for him.		
See, his reward is with him, and his recompense accompanies him.		"See, his reward is with him and his recompense accompanies him." '

Criteria

Commentators usually consider Isa. 62.11 to involve a *quotation* and adaptation of 40.10 but view 62.10 as merely an *echo* or reminiscence of 40.3. Most offer little comment regarding the textual similarity between 57.14 and 62.10.[94] Interestingly, both Cannon and McKenzie see instead in 62.10 an echo of 35.8.[95] These passages illustrate the problem of trying to distinguish between quotation and topos. In quotation one is looking for the repetition of significant words and syntactical structures; with a topos one simply seeks the repetition of various terms conceptually related to a theme or topic. The topos of the highway in the wilderness is an oft-repeated theme within Isaiah (11.16; 19.23; 27.12-13; 35.8; 40.3; 42.16; 43.19; 49.11; 57.14; 58.11; 62.10) and, as a result, several of the Hebrew terms used to describe the highway, its construction and maintenance, and travel upon it necessarily will be repeated several times. This is, however, a case of reuse of imagery, not of verbal dependence or quotation. From the verse cited,

94. Whybray, *Isaiah 40–66*, p. 251, is an exception, noting that 62.10b and 57.14 are 'largely identical' but seeing dependence only in 40.3.

95. W.W. Cannon, 'Isaiah 61.1-3 an Ebed-Jahweh Poem', *ZAW* 47 (1929), pp. 284-88 (286); J.L. McKenzie, *Second Isaiah* (AB, 20; Garden City, NY: Doubleday, 1968), p. 185.

35.8, only דרך (way) and the root סלל (highway) reappear in 40.3, 57.14 and 62.10, hardly noteworthy repetitions.

However, the same question must in turn be raised with regard to the similarity between 40.3 and 57.14 // 62.10. Is this a case of quotation or merely the formulation dictated by the constraints of Hebrew to describe road construction? Of the 12 words which make up 62.10aß-b and the eight in 57.14 (excluding ואמר) only three possibly are derived from 40.3: דרך, פנו and מסלה (though it should be noted that the expression פנו דרך (prepare the way) occurs in the Old Testament only in these three verbal parallels). Which additional contextual features could strengthen the case for dependence? First, 62.10 and 40.3 share an identical syntactical construction: plural imperative—*nomen regems* (object)—*nomen rectum*, the former substituting העם (the people) for the latter's יהוה (LORD). 57.14 employs a similar syntax: פנו דרך ... מדרך עמי. Secondly, 57.14 and 62.10 both make use of the repeated imperative סלו סלו (Build up, build up) perhaps in imitation of נחמו נחמו (comfort, comfort) in 40.1, certainly a more common feature of the rhetoric in chs. 40–55 than in 56–66.[96] In the third place, it has been pointed out, probably correctly, that the puzzling ואמר (and it will be said) with which 57.14 begins is a conscious imitation of the unidentified speaker of 40.3 and especially 40.6 (where ואמר likewise is used). Whybray views this as an 'introductory formula' introducing the 'text' which the prophet then proceeds to interpret.[97] Fourthly, related to the preceding, the introduction of the imperative verbs is rather abrupt in both 57.14 and 62.10 but could be accounted for if dependent on the language and setting of 40.3.

Fifthly, Whybray and Muilenburg see 57.14-21 as a text interpreting 40.3, while Steck sees in 62.10-12 a conscious reworking of 40.1-11.[98] Reinterpretation usually involves some form of verbal dependence.[99] This would also explain 62.10's dual dependence on both 40.3 and 57.14. And finally, the strongest argument is the clear relationship

96. See J. Muilenburg, *The Book of Isaiah, Chapters 40-66: Introduction and Exegesis* (IB, 5; Nashville: Abingdon Press, 1984), p. 389.

97. Whybray, *Isaiah 40–66*, p. 209.

98. Whybray, *Isaiah 40–66*, pp. 209-10; Muilenburg, *Isaiah*, p. 671; Steck, *Bereitete Heimkehr*, p. 65.

99. Although Fishbane, *Biblical Interpretation in Ancient Israel*, pp. 497-98, gives examples of reinterpretation where verbal dependence is minimal, as in topoi, or consists of individual words rather than phrases.

between 40.10b and the identical 62.11b. If deciding solely on the basis of the extent of the verbal parallel, one might conclude that 62.10aβ-γ was dependent on 57.14 (or vice versa) rather than 40.3, since half of its words appear in 57.14, including the three which also appear in 40.3. However, given the fact that 62.11 and 40.10 clearly display dependence, it is likely that 62.10 and 40.3 are similarly related. Westermann even claims that the author of 62.10-12 has consciously drawn from the beginning and the conclusion of the 'prologue' to 'Second' Isaiah.[100] Even if one hesitates to label 62.10 a *quotation* of 40.3, the repetition of 40.10b in 62.11b is sufficient to evoke the larger context so that the choice of label is hermeneutically insignificant, since one cannot interpret 62.10-12 adequately without reference to 40.1-11.

A related question concerns the relationship between 40.10a and 62.11aß: Does הנה ישעך בא (see, your salvation comes) in 62.11 correspond to הנה אדני יהוה בחזק יבוא see, the sovereign LORD comes with power in 40.10? That two out of three words in 62.11's message also are found in 40.10 is significant, and ישעך (your salvation [MT]) could be understood as substituting for and possibly reinterpreting אדני יהוה. יהוה could be omitted because it is used at the beginning of the verse: הנה יהוה and אמרו לבת־ציון הנה ישעך בא, 'Say to the Daughter of Zion, "See your salvation comes!"', could be patterned after 40.9bß-γ: אמרי לערי יהודה הנה אלהיכם, 'Say to the towns of Judah, "Here is your God"'. Maass is correct in pointing out that what remains of 40.10 and 62.11, after excluding the latter half of each verse, cannot be designated a quotation;[101] and there are sufficient examples of quotation being limited to only one part of a verse. However, given the identity of 40.10b and 62.11b, even the limited verbal correspondence which exists between 40.10a and 62.11aß suggests some degree of influence in formulation. Hence a thorough analysis of these verses must seek to explain both the similarities and the divergences, as well as account for the omissions and additions.

In sum, the extent and degree of verbal correspondence, the existence of multiple verbal parallels, the possible use of an introductory formula, and the similarity of contexts suggest that the verbal parallels Isa. 40.10 // 62.11 involve a conscious quotation with 40.3 and 62.10 thereby

---

100. C. Westermann, *Das Buch Jesaja: Kapitel 40-66* (ATD, 19; Göttingen: Vandenhoeck & Ruprecht, 4th edn, 1966), p. 301.

101. Maass, 'Tritojesaja?', p. 160; nor, according to Maass, is any 'Umbiegung' present.

being drawn into the same rhetorical dynamics.

Diachronic Analysis

The diachronic analysis of verbal parallels within Isaiah 40–66 is hampered by a basic difficulty—the almost complete lack of textually indicated historical context. As Childs has pointed out regarding 'Second' Isaiah

> There are no date formulae used, no concrete historical situations addressed. Rarely does the prophet speak to a specific historical need with which, for example, Amos abounds ... In Third Isaiah there are a few more historical references—one hears of eunuchs and foreigners— but basically the situation is the same. The theological context completely overshadows the historical.[102]

As a result, the interpretation of these chapters since Duhm has proceeded largely on the basis of a reconstructed *Sitz im Leben*, namely late exilic Babylon for 40–55 and postexilic Jerusalem for 56–66. However, detailed textual analysis has produced an increasing number of dissenters, including those who claim a Palestinian provenance (origin), or a unified authorship for essentially all 27 chapters, as well as those who see passages by 'Second' Isaiah in 56–66 or the hand of 'Third' Isaiah in 40–55.[103]

---

102. Childs, *Introducing to the Old Testament as Scripture*, pp. 325-26. The absence of any superscription in Isa. 40, despite the efforts of many scholars to find in it the call of 'Second' Isaiah, is a fact the significance of which usually is overlooked. See C.R. Seitz, 'Isaiah 1-66: Making Sense of the Whole', in *idem* (ed.), *Reading and Preaching the Book of Isaiah* (Philadelphia: Fortress Press, 1988), pp. 105-26 (109); and *idem*, 'The Divine Council: Temporal Transition and New Prophecy in the Book of Isaiah', *JBL* 109 (1990), pp. 229-47. For an extreme example of finding historical references in 'Second' Isaiah, see S. Smith, *Isaiah: Chapters XL-LV, Literary Criticism and History* (Schweich Lectures, 1940; London: Humphrey Milford, Oxford University Press, 1944).

103. Torrey, *The Second Isaiah*; M. Haran, 'The Literary Structure and Chronological Framework of the Prophecies in Isaiah XL-XLVIII', in *Congress Volume: Bonn, 1962* (VTSup, 9; Leiden: E.J. Brill, 1963), pp. 127-55; B.O. Banwell, 'A Suggested Analysis of Isaiah XL-LXVI', *ExpTim* 76 (1964–65), p. 166; J.D. Smart, *History and Theology in Second Isaiah: A Commentary on Isaiah 35, 40-66* (Philadelphia: Westminster Press, 1965); Maass, 'Tritojesaja?', pp. 153-63; H.M. Barstad, 'Lebte Deuterojesaja in Judäa?' *Norsk Teologisk Tidsskrift* 83 (1982), pp. 77-87; *idem*, 'On the So-Called Babylonian Literary Influence', pp. 90-110; and C.R. Seitz, *Zion's Final Destiny: The Development of the Book of Isaiah: A Reassessment of Isaiah 36-39* (Minneapolis: Fortress Press, 1991), especially

The importance of this issue for the analysis of verbal parallels within Isaiah 40–66 cannot be minimized, for the interpretation of the figurative language that such parallels contain has been determined largely by its assumed historical referent. For example, Duhm, in rejecting Dillmann's explanation of Isa. 62.11, avers: 'if one considers Deut.-Isa. to be the author, one may have to explain it in this manner...'[104] In the following, the claim of 'Umbiegung' which has arisen in the course of diachronic analysis will be re-examined in order to determine whether some of the related problems can be resolved by a judicious use of synchronic analysis.

If one assumes that 40.3, 10 is the source both of 57.14 and 62.10-11, this verbal borrowing is easily explained. Given the prominence of the motif of the highway of the return in Isaiah, as a major element of the 'second exodus' theme,[105] it is understandable that the exact wording is sometimes reused to evoke the same image more clearly. This is even more expected when one views Isa. 40.1-11 as a prologue introducing the major themes of the following chapters.[106] Even if 'Second' Isaiah primarily has *the* return from the Babylonian exile in mind, given the prophetic view of the unity of all Israel, this language is equally appropriate to describe any further returns from the diaspora (of which Isa. 11.11-12 also speak). The employment of verbal parallels here would serve to underline that future returns are in continuity with past returns.

Surprisingly, despite the wide acceptance of the view that chs. 40–55 and 56–66 constitute major divisions within the book of Isaiah, no consensus has been achieved regarding the direction of the dependence in Isa. 40.3 // 57.14 // 62.10. There are two basic positions. Those who hold to the unity of chs. 56–66 consider these chapters to be later than

pp. 205-208. See also Elliger, ch. 1, in *Deuterojesaja in seinem Verhältnis zu Tritojesaja*, pp. 31-32.

104. Duhm, *Das Buch Jesaia*, p. 462.

105. For the 'second exodus' theme, see B.W. Anderson, 'Exodus Typology in Second Isaiah', in B.W. Anderson and W. Harrelson (eds.), *Israel's Prophetic Heritage: Essays in Honor of James Muilenburg* (New York: Harper & Row, 1962), pp. 177-95; and K. Kiesow, *Exodustexte im Jesajabuch: Literarkritische und motiv- geschichtliche Analysen* (OBO, 24; Göttingen: Vandenhoeck & Ruprecht, 1979).

106. R.F. Melugin, *The Formation of Isaiah 40-55* (BZAW, 141; Berlin: W. de Gruyter, 1976), p. 85, sees 40.1-8 as a 'microcosm' of chs. 41–48 and 40.9-11 as one of chs. 49–55. This is similar to Fohrer's and Clements's understanding of Isa. 1.

and dependent upon Isaiah 40, explaining these verbal parallels accordingly as modifying the original meaning (so Duhm, Zimmerli, Westermann, Whybray). Others see the verbal parallels as being so striking that they warrant the conclusion that Isa. 57.14-21 as well as 60-62 are by the same author as chs. 40–55 and accordingly see little change in meaning between 40.3, 10 and their parallels. (These include conservative commentators such as Delitzsch, Alexander, and Young but also Smart, Cannon, and Maass. Muilenburg also considers this this a possibility.)[107]

A further question concerns the integrity of Isaiah 40. Begrich sees vv. 1-8 and vv. 9-11 as representing originally independent units, the former being words of the heavenly council, forming part of the prophetic call experience, and the latter an imitation of the instructions to a messenger of victory.[108] Most modern commentators follow Begrich, although Muilenburg sees 40.1-11 as forming a unified prologue. The issue of concern is this: If the units are originally independent, then the imagery underlying 40.3 and 40.10 may differ and their reuse together in 62.10-11 probably would involve a misinterpretation. On the one hand, the combination of 40.3 and 10 in 62.10-11 does not support inherently the original unity of 40.1-11; on the other hand, it does give some indication of how the author of 62.10-11 read it. Basic to this matter is whether one conceives of 'Second' Isaiah primarily as *orally* delivered or as *written* prophecy.[109] Radically different, to be sure, is the newer literary-critical analysis of Merendino who sees 40.9-11 as stemming from the redactor who joined Isa. 49.1–52.12 to 40.12–48.22 and 40.1-8 from the redactor who added 56–66.[110] According to this theory, 40.3 could be *later* than even 60.10.

Before considering Isa. 62.10-12, diachronic issues concerning Isa. 57.14 must be discussed briefly, for, even though its exact relationship to 40.3 is unclear, its verbal parallel with 62.10 is obvious. However,

---

107. Elliger, *Deuterojesaja in seinem Verhältnis zu Tritojesaja*, p. 286, states: 'Furthermore, the judgment as to whether [a saying is] twisted (*umgebogen*) or not is largely dependent on the total interpretation of Trito-Isaiah', claiming that the quotation of 40.10b in 62.11b has the exact same sense as the original.

108. Begrich, *Studien zu Deuterojesaja*, pp. 51, 54.

109. See Y. Gitay, 'Deutero-Isaiah: Oral or Written?', *JBL* 99 (1980), pp. 185-97; *idem, Prophecy and Persuasion: A Study of Isaiah 40-48* (Forum Theologiae Linguisticae, 14; Bonn: Linguistica Biblica, 1981).

110. R.P. Merendino, *Der Erste und der Letzte: Eine Untersuchung von Jesaja 40-48* (VTSup, 31; Leiden: E.J. Brill, 1981), p. 70.

determining its historical setting is difficult. Most commentators see 57.14 as beginning a new unit which extends to v. 21. (Motyer, instead, sees vv. 13e-g, 14 as forming the bridge between two halves of the oracle: vv. 1-13d and vv. 15-21.) Westermann notes that this is the first salvation oracle in 'Third' Isaiah, a prominent genre in 'Second' Isaiah, and a parade example of the way in which 'Third' Isaiah transforms the meaning of the language he borrows from 'Second' Isaiah. Zimmerli writes:

> What is the meaning, then, of the charge to prepare the way for the people? One is thinking here of the removal of the inner obstacles of impenitence and of trusting in other powers. (This meaning is established by the harsh invective in 56.9–57.13 which precedes it.) The call to prepare the way, which in Deut.-Isa. is still understood in its proper sense, has become a component of the general pious parenesis.[111]

Bonnard and Vermeylen stress the significance of the change from a 'way for *Yahweh*' to a 'way for the people'.[112] Whybray, as already noted, sees vv. 15-21 as 'interpreting' the 'text' (v. 14) from Isaiah 40. Westermann refers to the parallel in 62.10 to confirm this 'spiritualized' understanding of the 'preparation of the way', but Smart protests that 'there is no reason to assign the 'way' any different meaning here than in 40.3-5 and elsewhere'.[113] It appears that the issue hinges not on typical diachronic issues (e.g. literary-critical tensions, *Sitz im Leben*, historical reference) but simply on the extent to which the surrounding context is determinative in interpreting figurative language, an issue which will be discussed below.

   This hermeneutical problem has led to a very different literary-critical solution. Steck has noted, along with others, that 40.3 and 62.10 speak literally of 'road preparation' while 57.14 is more spiritualized. Steck accounts for this unusual sequence by assigning 57.14 to a block of material (chs. 56–59) which was added to the growing complex of 'Isaianic' tradition before 302/301 BCE. Hence 57.14, from a historical perspective, is quoting 62.10, yet functions literarily as an anticipatory reference to the returnees of 62.10-12.[114]

111. Zimmerli, 'Zur Sprache Tritojesajas', p. 224.

112. P.-E. Bonnard, *Le second Isaïe: Son disciple et leur éditeurs: Isaïe 40-66* (Etudes Bibliques; Paris: J. Gabalda, 1972), p. 363; Vermeylen, *Du prophète Isaïe*, II, p. 462.

113. Smart, *History and Theology in Second Isaiah*, p. 244.

114. O.H. Steck, 'Beobachtungen zu Jesaja 56-59', *BZ* NS 31 (1987), pp. 228-46

Precisely how should Isa. 62.10-12 be viewed? It long has been noted that Isaiah 60–62 is more closely related to 'Second' Isaiah, both thematically and linguistically, than the rest of 'Third' Isaiah, with 62.10-12 being 'almost a catena of quotations from Second Isaiah'.[115] Although Westermann views these verses as integral to the unit 62.1-7, 10-12 (deleting vv. 8-9) and forming the conclusion of the complex 60–62, and Volz, Muilenburg, and Lack defend the original integrity of the entire chapter, others view 62.10-12 as constituting a separate unit, especially due to its summary character.[116]

A survey of the analysis of these three verses is a study in contrasts. Hanson views them as summarizing the message of 60–62, while Vermeylen denies this, seeing these verses as more closely linked to 11.11-16; 27.12-13; 35.8-10; and 56.8. While some defend the integrity of the entire chapter, Pauritsch, following Fohrer, sees 62.10 as an independent composition designed to link chs. 60 and 61 at a time when 61 was placed *before* 60; 62.11-12 was added later when 60–61 assumed their present order and 62.10 became incomprehensible.[117] Steck views 62.10-12 as added to the core of 60–62 at the end of the Persian empire, when chs. 24–27 and 35 also were integrated into the Isaianic complex.[118]

It is not the purpose of this study to resolve the impasse in diachronic analysis or to offer another reconstruction of the historical relationship between 40.3, 57.14, and 62.10-12 but rather to make some method-ological observations. First of all, it is apparent that when a verbal

---

(236-37 n. 40). See also Lau, *Schriftgelehrte Prophetie*, pp. 110-11, who similarly views 57.14 as originating in a later tradition circle than 62.10-12, understanding the 'way' in 57.14 as the 'way of the heart'.

115. Muilenburg, *Isaiah*, p. 722. See also Hanson, *The Dawn of Apocalyptic*, pp. 59-62.

116. Westermann, *Jesaja 40–66*, p. 297; Muilenburg, *Isaiah*, p. 716; R. Lack, *La symbolique du livre d'Isaïe: Essai sur l'image littéraire comme élément de struc-turation* (AnBib, 59; Rome: Biblical Institute Press, 1973), pp. 207-17. Whybray, *Isaiah 40–66*, p. 250, sees 62.10-12 as specially formulated as the conclusion of Isa. 60–62; so also E. Achtemeier, *The Community and Message of Isaiah 56–66: A Theological Commentary* (Minneapolis: Augsburg, 1982), pp. 100-101. Duhm, *Das Buch Jesaia*, p. 462, also views these verses as a separate poem. The masoretes placed a setuma following both v. 9 and v. 12.

117. Hanson, *The Dawn of Apocalyptic*, pp. 69-70; Vermeylen, *Du prophète Isaïe*, II, p. 489; Pauritsch, *Die neue Gemeinde*, p. 106.

118. Steck, *Bereitete Heimkehr*, p. 80.

parallel partakes of frequently repeated imagery, its interpretation becomes considerably more difficult. Not only the date of composition and direction of dependence but also the very meaning of 40.3; 57.14; and 62.10 are disputed. This at least raises the question of whether the claim of 'Umbiegung' arises from actual diachronic distinctions or simply from the difficulty of wrestling with figurative speech.

Secondly, it is obvious that quotation usually stimulates literary-critical efforts to explain its awkward contextual fit or defend its integral relationship to its immediate context. Nevertheless the verbal parallels themselves contribute little to this discussion, usually serving simply as minor illustrations of larger, independently developed theories of the growth and redaction of the literature. (Pauritsch's view that ch. 61 once preceded 60 was *not* developed to explain the verbal parallel in 62.10.) It is almost as if quotation, which is an inherently historical phenomenon, has been rendered diachronically mute by the nature of biblical rhetoric.

Thirdly, in the literature surveyed seldom was there any discussion of the function of quotation within oral prophecy, although the dynamics of oral quotation differ from those of literary quotation. The terminology used is clearly that of the latter—author, catena, a poet 'weaving his materials'.[119] In a sense, this is the ultimate diachronic issue: Did this verbal parallel ever function, or was it intended to function, in a context other than the growing literary complex of the book of Isaiah? Did a prophet such as 'Third' Isaiah ever cite a prophetic predecessor such as 'Second' Isaiah, evoking an image which embodied the hope of the postexilic people of God for a further regathering, an ultimate restoration of the exiled, reviving their sense of expectation that Yahweh once again would intervene, or is this simply the work of a solitary author drawing upon a favorite image of his literary model?

Finally, the newer redaction-critical work of Steck is more a complement than an alternative to synchronic analysis. In suggesting that Isaiah 56–59 was composed to fit between 1–55 and 60–62, literarily 'recalling' themes from the former and 'anticipating' the latter,[120] he is, in effect, calling for a synchronic reading, or at least one that takes seriously the intent to produce an integrated, coherent literary composition. Furthermore, many of the individual scholars' comments

---

119. Muilenburg, *Isaiah*, p. 716.

120. Steck, *Bereitete Heimkehr*, pp. 72-74; *idem*, 'Beobachtungen zu Jesaja 56-59', pp. 228-46.

regarding 62.10-12 reflect a literary sensitivity to the function of quotation regardless of their diachronic conclusions. Hence it will be useful to continue to cite examples of prior suggestions in the course of the synchronic analysis of this verbal parallel, indicating where they depart from a synchronic perspective.

Synchronic Analysis
As a point of departure, the following quotations express crucial issues for the interpretation of quotation. With regard to 62.10-12, Westermann writes: 'The relationship between God, the prophet, and the people is a different one than in Deutero-Isaiah; therefore the same words cannot say the same thing',[121] and Whybray complains: 'their meaning is, however, far from clear; and this is probably due to the fact that they are mainly constructed out of a series of quotations and near-quotations from Deutero-Isaiah used in a new sense'.[122] Is the new meaning of a quoted text determined by its assumed *Sitz im Leben* or is its *Sitz im Text* equally, or even more, determinative? If quotation results in a layering of meaning because of the convergence of multiple contexts, is this an *obscuring* or an *enriching* of meaning?

From a synchronic perspective, the three passages containing the verbal parallel must be interpreted in their present sequence within the book of Isaiah; any approach which views Isa. 40.3 or 57.14 as later and dependent upon 62.10 is an inappropriate way to read the present book of Isaiah. Furthermore, the theme of the highway which is central in the verbal parallel is not first introduced in 40.3; rather, from a synchronic perspective, it already has been encountered in 11.16; 19.23; and 35.8, whether or not these passages were added later to the present book of Isaiah.[123] And since these 'prior' contexts speak of a regathering of the 'scattered people of Judah from the four quarters of the earth' (11.12), a highway from Assyria involving the breaking of the River Euphrates (11.15-16), a highway from Egypt to Assyria (19.23), and a highway through the former desert to Zion on which neither the

121. Westermann, *Jesaja 40–66*, p. 301.

122. Whybray, *Isaiah 40–66*, p. 250. Similarly, Duhm, *Das Buch Jesaia*, p. 462: 'The extensive employment of deutero-isaianic quotations avenges itself, leading to all sorts of obscurity.'

123. Other passages related to this theme in Isa. 40–66 include 42.16; 43.19; 49.11 and 58.11. Regarding passages in Isa. 1–39, see Clements, *Isaiah 1–39*, and 'The Unity of the Book of Isaiah', pp. 117-29.

unclean person nor the dangerous beast will be found (35.5-10), these associations will not simply vanish when the theme is taken up again in 40.3. However, by virtue of the verbal parallel, 40.3, 10; 57.14; and 60.10-11 are linked more closely to each other than to any of the preceding passages or to 42.16; 43.19; 49.11; and 58.11, for that matter.

With ch. 40, a new section of the book of Isaiah commences with an emphasis on consolation and restoration. The dominant image of 40.1-11 is that of the coming of Yahweh. That this passage represents the call of 'Second' Isaiah is certainly not obvious;[124] nor is it clear who is speaking to whom. Following initial words of comfort to God's people (vv. 1-2), an unidentified voice issues the first imperatival call to 'prepare the way' for Yahweh (פנו דרך, v. 3). Just who is to do the preparation is unspecified, the emphasis being on what the preparation entails (v. 4) and the ultimate result: the revelation of Yahweh's glory to all humanity (v. 5). There is no mention here of the exiled returning from Babylon or of *human* responsibility to prepare the way.[125] The closest conceptual parallel is to the theophany of God coming through the desert to intervene on behalf of his people (Deut. 33.2, Ps. 68.7, Judg. 5.5) in which there is no thought of a literal road being prepared.

Following a brief section (vv. 6-8) contrasting the brevity of human glory with the eternality of the divine word, the image of the coming of Yahweh is taken up again (vv. 9-11) but not identically, for now the preparation is past (hence the 'way' is not mentioned here)—the advent is at hand. Again the focus is on Yahweh who comes in strength and gentleness. There is no explicit mention of anyone accompanying Yahweh, but the reference to his שכר and פעלה (reward and recompense) being with (אתו) and before him (לפניו) is suggestive. The terms used designate the wages or reward for one's labor or efforts, the possessive pronoun referring to the one who has earned them (Gen. 15.1; 30.18), though here possibly in a derived sense for the reward, the spoils for one's military efforts.[126] The juxtaposition of v. 10b with the image of the shepherd and his flock, strengthened by the use of שכר to

124. Regarding the difficulties of viewing 40.1-8 as a call narrative, see Elliger, *Deuterojesaja 40, 1–45, 7* (BKAT, 11.1; Neukirchen–Vluyn: Neukirchener Verlag, 1978), pp. 10-12; and Merendino, *Der Erste und der Letzte*, pp. 59-60.

125. Smart, *History and Theology in Second Isaiah*, pp. 45-47.

126. The claim of Begrich, *Studien zu Deuterojesaja*, p. 52, that שכר and פעלה are technical terms for spoils of battle, citing Ezek. 29.18-20, goes beyond the textual evidence.

designate sheep in Gen. 30.28, 32-33; 31.8,[127] permits one to see a veiled reference to the returnees here, although the context is deliberately vague and the focus even in v. 11 is clearly on *Yahweh*'s coming.

That such an image should be taken up twice more in similar terms in 'Third' Isaiah is not surprising. The placement, however, is striking. Delitzsch's division of Isaiah 40–66 into three enneads, each with its own theological emphasis and concluding with a description of the fate of the wicked (48.20-21; 57.20-21; and, in different form, 66.24), has found little acceptance. It is, however, intriguing to note that this call to 'prepare the way' comes precisely at the beginning of the first unit of the first ennead (40.3 in 40–48), at the beginning of the final unit of the second ennead (57.14 in 49–57), and precisely at the midway point in the final ennead (62.10 in 58–66). This at least suggests that the placement of these verbal parallels may be a part of a larger redactional strategy involving chs. 40–66.[128]

In 57.14 the primary link with 40.3 is the repetition of the imperative in פנו דרך (prepare the road). סלו סלו (Build up, build up) is related to מסלה, a favorite word in Isaiah for 'highway' (7.3; 11.16; 19.23; 33.8; 36.2; 40.3; 49.11; 59.7; 62.10), and together with הרימו מכשול מדרך עמי ('Remove the obstacles out of the way of my people'), may correspond to 40.4's description of the preparation of the 'way'. Despite the conceptual similarity between 40.3-4 and 57.14, on the basis of the latter's context, the following differences have been claimed: Whereas in 40.3 a literal highway is to be prepared for Yahweh by heavenly emissaries for a return of the exiled from Babylon, in 57.14 the people or leaders are called upon to rid themselves of sin which impedes the 'return' of salvation to them.[129]

However, one must ask whether this is a correct understanding of the use of the verbal parallel. First of all, precisely who is addressing whom is equally unclear in both 40.3 and 57.14, probably deliberately so, as indicated by the vague use of ואמר (and it will be said), so it is just as likely that the speaker and addressees are identical or similar in both chapters. The abrupt introduction of the imperatives of 'road building' strongly evokes the parallel text to complete the imagery.

127. See Elliger, *Deuterojesaja*, p. 37.
128. Isa. 62.10 is the 80th out of 160 verses in Isa. 58–66. Delitzsch, *The Prophecies of Isaiah*, II, pp. 128-29. He notes, p. 379, that the 'very same appeal ... occurs once in all three books of these prophecies'.
129. Volz, *Jesaia II*, pp. 217-28.

However, 57.14 cannot be interpreted solely on the basis of its verbal parallel in 40.3, for this incorrectly would isolate these two verses from the other occurrences of the topos of the highway within the book of Isaiah. In all of the other passages, it is Yahweh who supernaturally prepares the way and facilitates the return of the people.[130] Thus the portrait of the highway in 40.3 should be enriched by those of 42.16; 43.19; and 49.11 before one interprets its use in 57.14. This warns against assuming that the people and leaders are called upon to prepare the way in 57.14 when this is not specified.

Furthermore, in the light of these passages, it is expected that the way will be for 'the people', especially if a vague reference to the people returning with Yahweh is already contained in 40.10b-11. Chapter 40 is unique in focusing on the coming of Yahweh once again to Jerusalem but this return, according to 'Second' Isaiah, initiates the gradual restoration of God's people. Since the highway topos in Isaiah portrays multiple ways for multiple returns, it is likely that 57.14 is speaking of another such literal return (cf. 56.8), even if one concludes, on the basis of the immediate context, that the hindrances to further restoration are primarily spiritual in nature.[131] Even here it is Yahweh who takes the initiative to heal, guide and restore comfort to Israel, despite its wicked ways (vv. 18-19 with echoes of Isa. 40.1, 11), speaking peace to those

---

130. According to Merendino, *Der Erste und der Letzte*, pp. 31-34, Isa. 40.3 is unique within 'Second' Isaiah in two respects: only here are the addressees called upon to prepare the way; only here is the way prepared for God and not the people. According to Elliger, *Deuterojesaja*, p. 18, it is the spirits who prepare the way in 40.3.

131. Westermann, *Jesaja 40–66*, p. 261, argues that 'removing stones' in 57.14 must refer to preparing for the coming of salvation, because that is clearly its meaning in 62.10; but he also sees the influence here of Ezek. 7.19; 14.4, 7; 18.30; 44.12. However, Isa. 59.20, which speaks of repentance from sins, also speaks of the Redeemer (גאל) coming to Zion, very similarly to 40.3, 10; and Isa. 8.14 already uses the stumbling stone in a figurative manner. According to G. Fohrer, *Das Buch Jesaja: Kapitel 40-66* (3 vols.; Zürich: Zwingli Verlag, 1964), III, p. 19, 40.3 already refers to *inner* preparation; so also C.R. North, *The Second Isaiah* (Oxford: Clarendon Press, 1964), p. 74. Oswalt, *The Book of Isaiah, Chapters 40–66*, p. 486, correctly notes that 'there is no great difference between the use of the imagery of return here and in chs. 40-55. Both combine the physical and spiritual returns to different degrees in different places'. A return to *the land* without an accompanying return to *God* offers only a partial solution to the people's problem. See also Miscall, *Isaiah*, p. 132, who explains that Isaiah 'works on both manifest (literal) and latent (metaphorical) levels ... at the same time'.

far and near (those in Jerusalem and those still in diaspora).

Isaiah 62.10 also draws on the imagery of 40.3 but its formulation is closer to 57.14, also utilizing 49.22. Here again the highway is for the people rather than for Yahweh, however there is no contextual indication that the obstacles are spiritual in nature, unless one assumes this *on the basis of* 57.14. Instead, the metaphor may have the same signification as in ch. 40, with a different frame of reference accounting for the divergences. The addressees may be the same unspecified group as in 40.3 (the introduction of the plural imperative is equally abrupt here) or the inhabitants of Jerusalem who are called upon to go out to complete the highway described in 40.3-4, now apparently not in the desert but at the very outskirts of the city. The highway is prepared for the people (העם), the Israelites still in exile or diaspora, assisted by the nations.[132] If this interpretation is correct, then the spiritualization of the highway image which Zimmerli notes may be a shift which occurs *within* 56–66 rather than *between* 'Second' and 'Third' Isaiah.[133]

The author of 62.10-12 has selected from ch. 40 the two verses (vv. 3 and 10) which introduce and conclude the image and which express its two essential features: the highway and Yahweh's triumphal return (with the exiles). By quoting these verses he condenses and intensifies the image, and by means of a new context focuses more clearly than 40.1-11 on its impact on Jerusalem. Zimmerli describes the divergence between 40.10 and 62.11:

---

132. Compare also Isa. 49.22 from which 62.10bβ's 'raise a banner for the nations' may be derived, and see O.H. Steck, 'Heimkehr auf der Schulter oder/und auf der Hüfte: Jes 49, 22b / 60, 4b', *ZAW* 98 (1966), pp. 275-77.

133. Zimmerli, 'Zur Sprache Tritojesajas', pp. 223-25. Regarding 62.10 he writes, p. 225: 'They probably are to be understood figuratively of the inner preparation of the people'. He sees the reference to 'passing through the gates' as pilgrimage language, on the basis of Ps. 42.5 and 84.7. Contrast Duhm, *Das Buch Jesaia*, p. 462, and his openness to a literal interpretation of 'preparing the way'. See n. 107 above. One can note a similar loss in vividness of imagery or see a spiritualizing tendency in one member of each of the following verbal parallels: 49.2 // 51.16; 51.9 // 52.1; 59.16 // 63.5, each of them occurring *within* 'Second' or 'Third' Isaiah rather than *between* them. The criticism of Maass, 'Tritojesaja?', pp. 159-61; Childs, pp. 333-34; and Fishbane, *Biblical Interpretation in Ancient Israel*, p. 289 n. 23, that Zimmerli's claim of 'Umbiegung' often goes beyond the textual evidence appears to be justified. Zimmerli also bases his argument on an overly selective examination of the many verbal parallels within Isa. 40–66 (for a fuller listing, see the Appendix, p. 340).

> Here too ... the concrete discourse regarding Yahweh accompanying the procession is spiritualized into discourse regarding the coming help. The figurative language regarding the 'reward' and 'recompense' which he has brought along ... has been removed from the original complete image in 40.10 to become mere figurative expressions within the religious speech.[134]

Whybray goes a step further, virtually paraphrasing vv. 10-12, which he labels 'an inferior composition due ... to the inability of the author to handle his borrowed material', as 'live right, Jerusalem, and you will prosper'.[135]

However, an entirely different understanding of this passage is possible, if one considers the dynamics of quotation. In the first place, it already has been argued that v. 10 does not spiritualize the highway, and, if this is the case, there is no reason to see v. 11 as a spiritualization either. If 'reward and recompense' in 40.10 represent the returnees from exile portrayed as the fruits of Yahweh's labor, or the spoils of victory, as Zimmerli and Whybray suggest, there is no reason why the same cannot be designated by the words in 62.11. Only this understanding would make sense of v. 12: 'And they [the peoples] will call them [the returning Israelites], "the holy people, the redeemed of Yahweh", and you [Jerusalem] will be called "sought out, a city not forsaken"'. This would suggest that the author of 62.10-12 has made a conscious effort to retain, not drain, the image.

Secondly, the triumphant return of Yahweh is not necessarily removed from the text. If one views the author of 62.10-12 as making a quotation that would be recognized by the readers, boldly drawing twice on the inaugural vision of 'Second' Isaiah, then this vivid portrayal of Yahweh as mighty warrior would shine through from its original context and would not be lost or obscured simply by replacing אדני יהוה (sovereign LORD) with ישעך (your salvation). This substitution is intended to assure the people that Yahweh's coming represents the coming of Zion's longed-for salvation (v. 1), for Yahweh is its salvation (cf. 12.2; 33.2; 35.4) and will initiate the glorification of Jerusalem which cannot be separated from the return. Only if 'your salvation' is a metonymy for Yahweh rather than a weakened

---

134. Zimmerli, 'Zur Sprache Tritojesajas', pp. 221-22.

135. Whybray, *Isaiah 40–66*, p. 250. Summarizing v. 10, he says, p. 251, 'as in 57:14, it is the "way" of life of devotion to Yahweh which the inhabitants of Jerusalem must lead if their desire for her prosperity is to be fulfilled'.

spiritualization do the repeated pronouns of v. 11b—'*His* reward is with *Him*, and *His* recompense before *Him*'—make sense.[136]

It has been suggested that Isa. 62.10-12 summarizes chs. 60–62, but it is far more than that. Several of the key themes of these chapters find no mention here.[137] Rather, it is a key theme of Isaiah as a whole which finds it consummation here: the completion of the regathering of Israel. This theme appears at major junctures in the book (11.11-16; 27.12-13; 35.8-10, respectively concluding chs. 1–11; 24–27; 28–35), and here it concludes another coherent unit, chs. 60–62.[138] It involves far more than a double quotation of 40.3, 10: not only does it draw on the language of other 'highway' passages as well as other familiar phrases from both 'Second' and 'Third' Isaiah, but it also seems to be patterned after Isa. 40.9-11 as a whole as well as closely integrated into 62.1-12. This is not simply the 'learned vocabulary ... of a shared tradition'[139] but a purposeful building up of a major theological theme.

From 11.12 (cf. 11.11, 15-16 for the associated motifs of the regathered remnant and the highway of the return) comes the raised banner of 62.10bβ (וְנֵס נֵס לַגּוֹיִם, 'He lifts up a banner for the nations', cf. 5.26, although linguistically patterned after 49.22), as well as the idea of Israel being regathered from the 'four corners of the earth' on a divinely prepared highway (although מִקְצֵה הָאָרֶץ, cf. 62.11a, derives linguistically from 43.6 or, more likely, 48.20 עַד־קְצֵה הָאָרֶץ ... הַשְׁמִיעוּ זֹאת, 'Proclaim it ... to the ends of the earth'). From 35.4 come the promise

---

136. The LXX (and all other ancient versions) translates יִשְׁעֵךְ as 'your Savior', although this probably reflects an interpretation rather than a variant reading. The claim that the warrior aspect of Yahweh in 40.3 is toned down by 'Third' Isaiah, due to the absence of 'with might, with his arm ruling...' may be misleading, for the imagery could have been carried over through the quotation in 62.11. In addition, the verses which immediately follow—63.1-6, their initial verb בָּא (come) possibly picking up on the same verb in 62.11a—offer a fuller portrait of the 'divine warrior' than even 'Second' Isaiah (note the verbal parallel 59.16-17 // 63.5). Lau's claim, *Schriftgelehrte Prophetie*, p. 114, that, in 62.10-12 the conquering redeemer of ch. 40 is replaced by enricher of the nations thus is unwarranted.

137. For example, the riches of the nations, service of foreigners, rebuilding of Jerusalem, end of sorrow, although some of these could be read into 62.10-12.

138. Steck, *Bereitete Heimkehr*, pp. 64, 101.

139. Fishbane, *Biblical Interpretation in Ancient Israel*, p. 289. Oswalt, *The Book of Isaiah, Chapters 40–66*, pp. 588-89, sees the author here 'gathering up strands from the whole book and weaving them together into a climactic statement' regarding the various aspects of the 'return'.

of God coming, bringing salvation (הנה אלהיכם ... הוא יבוא וישעכם,
'your God will come ... he will come to save you') and the phrase גאולי
יהוה (the redeemed of the LORD) in 62.12a (35.9-10, cf. 51.10-11).[140]

According to Steck, 40.3-4, the call to prepare the way, is taken up
by 62.10aba; 40.9aßba ('Lift up your voice' הרימי) is interpreted ('Lift
up a banner..' הרימו) in 10bß; 40.10a ('See the Sovereign LORD comes
with power and his arm rules for him') corresponds to 11aα, ('See, the
LORD has made himself heard to the ends of the earth.'); 40.9bß ('Say
to the towns of Judah, "See, Here is your God!"') equals 11aß ('Say to
the daughter of Zion, "See, your help/salvation comes"'), and 40.10b is
identical to 11b.[141]

62.10-12, though a summary passage, is nevertheless integrated into
62.1-12. Lack notes the use of three perfect verbs referring to Yahweh
as marking a logical progression: v. 4—חפץ (delight), v. 8—נשבע
(swear), v. 11—השמיע (proclaim).[142] The reference to the gates in v. 10
is anticipated by the description of the watchmen on the walls of
Jerusalem in v. 6. Several key terms of vv. 10-12 are also used in vv. 1-
9: ציון (Zion) vv. 1, 11; ישע (salvation) vv. 1, 11; ל קרא (to be called)
vv. 2, 12; עזב (deserted) vv. 4, 12. Thus vv. 10-12 function on more
than one level: as a conclusion to a chapter, to a section, and, most
importantly, to a key theme within Isaiah.

Although Isa. 62.10-12 is linked by the use of the highway topos to
numerous passages, its closest relationship remains to its two verbal
parallels. Together they portray the certainty of the restoration of the

---

140. One could see in the use of נקם and גמול (vengeance and retribution) in 35.4
(and נקם and שולמים in 34.8) a basis for interpreting שכר and פעלה in 40.10 and
62.11 as 'penal recompense of vengeance on enemies' and 'reward of the righteous', respectively. E.J. Young, *The Book of Isaiah* (3 vols.; Grand Rapids:
Eardmans, 1965–72), III, p. 39, mentions but rejects this view. Note that this
'dependence' on Isa. 11 and 35 is essential to a synchronic reading of 62.10-11,
though does not necessarily correspond to diachronic reality.

141. Steck, *Bereitete Heimkehr*, pp. 65-67. For a more detailed discussion of the
intertextual relations of these verbal parallels, see Lau, *Schriftgelehrte Prophetie*,
pp. 108-20. Lau identifies the addressees in 62.10-12 as the disciples of the prophet
who are to go out and prepare for the nations's pilgrimage to Jerusalem rather than
for a new 'exodus' of God's people and, incorrectly in my opinion, views 57.14 as
an *interpretation* of 62.10-12.

142. Lack, *La symbolique*, p. 216. This involves one such verb in each of the
two words of assurance, as well as the affirmation sections (vv. 1-7, 8-9, 11-12) of
Isa. 62.

exiles by their imperatival charge to 'prepare the way' and the repetition of הנה. However, a progression is also evident. It is reflected in the
building up of the imperative verbs: 40.3 פנו...ישרו, 57.14 סלו סלו פנו;
62.10 עברו עברו...פנו...סלו סלו as well as in 57.14's dependence on
and expansion of 40.3, and 62.10's dependence on both passages
(especially 40.10). In 40.3 the building occurs in the wilderness, in
57.14 no specific place is mentioned, in 62.10 the construction presumably is complete to the very gates of the city.[143] In 40.3, the focus is on
Yahweh's coming, in 57.14 on the sinful condition and continued
judgment as hindering restoration, in 62.10 on the return of the exiled,
assisted by the nations. Perhaps the same point is underlined by the
striking yet divergent use of הרימי or הרימו (lift up) in each context: in
40.9 of lifting up the voice, in 57.14 of lifting up obstacles, in 62.10 of
lifting up a banner to the nations. Each use of the verbal parallel evokes
the imagery of the preceding, filling out detail. With the completion of
the return from the ends of the earth, Zion's salvation is realized, the
now redeemed 'holy people' of Yahweh is once again constituted. Lack
is correct in seeing here a common literary denominator, despite a
plurality of historical referents.[144] This verbal parallel offers a vivid
example of how a quotation can participate in a general theme while
developing a sub-theme through the evocative ability of the verbal
parallel and issuing its call to 'prepare the way' at structurally
significant intervals.

Isaiah 2.2-4 and Micah 4.1-3

Isaiah 2.2-4 not only is one of the 'best known texts in the Old
Testament'[145] but also represents the most extensive verbal parallel
within the prophetic corpus. The divergence between Isaiah 2.2-4 and
Micah 4.1-3 is minimal, and it is impossible to conceive of the similarities as being coincidental.[146] The two prophets associated with the

143. It is not obvious that 62.10 is referring to a pilgrimage such as that associated with the Feast of Tabernacles, partly on the basis of the mention of drinking
the new wine in the temple precincts (v. 9).

144. Lack, *La symbolique*, p. 216.

145. J.L. Mays, *Micah: A Commentary* (OTL; Philadelphia: Westminster Press,
1976), p. 93, regarding the parallel passage in Micah.

146. A.S. van der Woude, 'Micah IV 1-5: An Instance of the Pseudo-Prophets
Quoting Isaiah', in M.A. Beek *et al.* (eds.), *Symbolae Biblicae et Mesopotamicae
Francisco Mario Theodoro de Liagre Böhl Dedicatae* (Leiden: E.J. Brill, 1973), pp.

books containing this parallel are acknowledged to have been contemporaries in Judah; hence it is likely that one may have heard or been familiar with the oracles of the other. This would seem to be a classic example of one prophet borrowing from another. However, the exact nature of the dependence in this case continues to be the object of much dispute.

Text

Isaiah		Micah	
והיה באחרית הימים	2.2	והיה באחרית הימים יהיה	4.1
נכון יהיה הר בית־יהוה בראש ההרים		הר בית־יהוה נכון בראש ההרים	
ונשא מגבעות		ונשא הוא מגבעות	
ונהרו אליו כל־הגוים:		ונהרו עליו עמים:	
והלכו עמים רבים ואמרו	2.3	והלכו גוים רבים ואמרו	4.2
לכו ונעלה אל־הר־יהוה		לכו ונעלה אל־הר־יהוה	
אל־בות אלהי יעקב		ואל־בית אלהי יעקב	
וירנו מדרכיו ונלכה בארחתיו		ויורנו מדרכיו ונלכה בארחתיו	
כי מציון תצא תורה		כי מציון תצא תורה	
ודבר־יהוה מירושלם:		ודבר־יהוה מירושלם:	
ושפט בין הגוים	2.4	ושפט בין עמים רבים	4.3
והוכיח לעמים רבים		והוכיח לגוים עצמים עד־רצוק	
וכתתו חרבותם לאתים		וכתתו חרבתיהם לאתים	
וחניתותיהם למזמרות		וחניתתיהם למזמרות	
לא־ישא גוי אל־גוי חרב		לא־ישאו גוי אל־גוי חרב	
ולא־ילמדו עוד מלחמה:		ולא־ילמדון עוד מלחמה:	

Criteria

If the extent of verbal and syntactical correspondence is a valid criterion for determining dependence, then this conclusion regarding Isa. 2.2-4 and Mic. 4.1-3 is well warranted. Of the 61 words in the Isaianic parallel, 51 appear in identical form in Micah. The following divergences can be noted:

word order	Isa. 2.2	נכון יהוה הר בית־יהוה	
	Mic. 4.1	יהיה הר בית־יהוה נכון	(will be established)
	Isa. 2.2, 3, 4	כל־הגוים ... עמים רבים ... הגוים ... לעמים רבים	
	Mic. 4.1, 2, 3	עמים ... גוים רבים..עמים רבים ... לגוים עצמים	

396-402 (396); W. Rudolph, *Micha—Nahum—Habakuk—Zephanja* (KAT, 13.3; Gütersloh: Gerd Mohn, 1975), p. 77.

grammar	Isa. 2.2, 4	הגוים	Mic. 4.2, 3	גוים
	Isa. 2.3	אל	Mic. 4.2	ואל
	Isa. 2.4	לא־ישא	Mic. 4.3	לא־ישאו
word choice	Isa. 2.2	אליו	Mic. 4.1	עליו
orthography	Isa. 2.3, 4	וירנו, חרבותתם, וחניתותיהם, ילמדו		
	Mic. 4.2, 3	ויורנו, חרבתיהם, והניתתיהם, ילמדון		
unparalleled	Isa. 2.2	כל (all)		
	Mic. 4.1, 3	עצמים עד־רחוק (strong nations far and wide),		
		הוא (it)		

Ringgren claims that practically all of these variants are explained best as 'resulting from mistakes in oral transmission'.[147] Regardless of how one explains these divergences, the close correspondence clearly indicates some form of dependence.

In addition, there are several contextual features which may indicate that one author or redactor is consciously quoting the other.

Introductory formulae/explicit marking. Ackroyd has explained the superscription in Isa. 2.1 as an 'appended note stressing the Isaianic authorship of the oracle which follows', the work of an early literary critic who sought to resolve the problem of the double occurrence.[148] This would in effect function as an explicit claim that Isaiah was the originator of the oracle and that Micah was the borrower. The unparalleled use of והיה (and it will be) in Isa. 2.2 to begin the oracle also has been viewed as indicating a quotation. The anomalous waw thus lacks any antecedent context to which it is linked syntactically because it has been lifted from another text.[149] Finally, the closing formula found in

147. Ringgren, 'Oral and Written Tradition', p. 50. Similarly Mays, *Micah*, p. 95: 'It can hardly be the case that either is a copy of a literary form of the other.'

148. P.R. Ackroyd, 'A Note on Isaiah 2.1', *ZAW* 75 (1963), pp. 320-21. Seitz, *Isaiah 1-39*, pp. 23-24, however, disagrees: In Isa. 2.1 'a statement is not so much being made about the Isaianic authorship of 2:2-5, as, say against Micah authorship'.

149. Nägelsbach, *The Prophet Isaiah*, p. 55. According to E.B. Pusey, *The Minor Prophets: A Commentary* (2 vols.; Grand Rapids: Baker Book House, 1953 [1888–89), II, p. 7, Isaiah has used this syntax purposefully to mark that the prophecy is not in its original place. See GKC 154b for an analogous usage. However, if Isa. 2.1 is removed as a redactional addition, והיה would be linked to the end of ch. 1. B. Wiklander, *Prophecy as Literature: A Text-Linguistic and Rhetorical Approach*

Mic. 4.4b, כי־פי יהוה צבאות דבר (for the LORD Almighty has spoken),
possibly indicates the presence of a quotation, especially since it is used
elsewhere only in the book of Isaiah (1.20; 40.5; 58.14).[150] Of course,
none of these are certain markers of quotation but, combined with other
textual features, may prove significant.

Inversion of synonyms. Talmon, as a result of his text-critical work,
concludes that the chiastic inversion of synonymous elements (such as
גוים and עמים, nations and peoples) may be used to indicate the presence
of an inner-biblical quotation.[151]

Reinterpretation. Although most of the divergences between Isaiah and
Micah in this parallel are exegetically insignificant and inconclusive
regarding which text is prior,[152] there are several additions which are
suggestive. עד־רחוק in Mic. 4.3aß may serve to emphasize the temporal
(this refers to the distant future)[153] or, more likely, spatial scope (this
applies even to distant nations) of this prophecy. More significant is
Mic. 4.4 which is lacking in Isaiah. Talmon views it as an addition on
Micah's part which was intended to undercut the utopian perspective of
the Isaianic version and give it a more 'realistic-political' (*real-
politische*) direction.[154] Hayes views it simply as a 'rural addition' in
keeping with Micah's background.[155] However, it also refocuses the
prophecy on the benefits for the individual rather than on the nations as

to Isaiah 2-4 (ConBOT, 22; Lund: C.W.K. Gleerup, 1984), pp. 105, 113, solves the
problem by translating Isa. 2.1-2: 'This is the word which Isaiah son of Amoz saw
concerning Judah and Jerusalem; and it will come to pass at the end of days:'.

150. See p. 243 n. 9 above.

151. See Chapter 2, pp. 75-76 above and Beentjes, 'Inverted Quotations in the
Bible', pp. 506-23.

152. Isaiah and Micah both use full (plene) and defective spellings; both contain
some better readings. Though Micah is acknowledged to have the superior text,
J.M.P. Smith, *A Critical and Exegetical Commentary on the Book of Micah* (ICC;
New York: Charles Scribner's Sons, 1911), p. 85, believes these could involve *later*
improvements.

153. Rudolph, *Micha*, p. 76.

154. S. Talmon, 'Typen der Messiaserwartung um die Zeitwende', in H.W.
Wolff (ed.), *Probleme biblischer Theologie: Gerhard von Rad zum 70. Geburtstag*
(Munich: Chr. Kaiser Verlag, 1971), pp. 571-88 (579). Talmon, 'Typen der
Messiaswortung', p. 580, sees Micah's version as almost an 'inner-biblical com-
mentary' on the saying in Isaiah.

155. Hayes and Irvine, *Isaiah*, p. 82.

in v. 3.[156] Thus Mic. 4.4 could be taken as a conscious reinterpretation of the Isaiah passage.

Contextual awareness. The immediate contexts of the verbal parallel are strikingly similar. Isaiah 2.1-4 follows a portrayal of the corruption (1.21-23) and judgmental purging (1.24-25) of Jerusalem. Micah 4.1-4 also follows a presentation of Jerusalem's sinfulness (3.9-11—both Mic. 3.11 and Isa. 1.23 mention the leaders taking bribes, שֹׁחַד) and the destruction of the city (3.12). In both books, the promise oracle serves to contrast the present dismal circumstances and inevitable judgment of Jerusalem with its future exaltation.

Even more remarkable are the similar tone and function of Isa. 2.5 and Mic. 4.5.[157]

Isa. 2.5   בית יעקב לכו ונלכה באור יהוה:
Mic. 4.5   כי כל־העמים ילכו איש בשם אלהיו
ואנחנו נלך בשם־יהוה אלהינו לעולם ועד:

Although Isa. 2.5 is modeled more closely after the wording of the oracle, picking up the call of the nations in 2.3, לכו ונעלה אל־הר־יהוה, אל־בית אלהי יעקב ... ונלכה בארחתיו, 'Come, let us go up to the mountain of the LORD to the house of the God of Jacob... that we may walk in his paths' (note the assonance between בְּאׇרְחֹתָיו and בְּאוֹר), Mic. 2.5 also uses the first person plural form of address and the same key verb הלך (walk) to emphasize Judah's present calling in the light of its future position. Regardless of the origin of this further parallel, it is highly unlikely that each oracle independently received a similar application or conclusion.[158] A fair application of the criteria for determining dependence suggests that one prophetic book indeed contains a quotation from the other which has been placed in a similar context, given a similar conclusion, and adapted to conform to differing concerns.

156. Smith, *Micah*, pp. 87-88. See also Brueggemann, ' "Vine and Fig Tree" ', pp. 188-204. H. Wildberger, 'Die Völkerfahrt zum Zion. Jes. II 1-5', *VT* 7 (1957), pp. 62-81 (76), views the reuse as Isaianic in origin, omitted when a later generation took offense at its unbridled promise of peace for the nations.

157. It is amazing that Werner, *Eschatologische Texte in Jesaja 1-39*, p. 162, can speak of 'the redactional verse Isa. 2.5, which exhibits no parallel in Mic. 4.1-4', and completely ignore Mic. 4.5!

158. See the discussion of the literary-critical significance of Isa. 2.5 and Mic. 4.5 below, pp. 299-300.

Diachronic Analysis

The superscriptions to the books which contain this verbal parallel (Isa. 1.1, Mic. 1.1) indicate that the prophets associated with them were contemporaries in eighth-century Judah. Because Isaiah commenced his ministry earlier and had personal encounters with the kings of Judah, he often is considered to be older and more influential than Micah, although both assumptions may be unwarranted.[159] On the one hand, there is nothing in the content of the verbal parallel that would link it clearly to the eighth century or to the ministry of either prophet. On the other hand, in conformity with the explicit diachronicity of the texts, there are no divergences between the two passages which reflect any sense of belatedness or any indication of historical factors which may have led to a quotation.

Accordingly, many scholars, including some today, have held either Micah (so Calvin, Caspari, Nägelsbach) or Isaiah (so Duhm, Girdlestone, Sellin, Kissane, Gunneweg, Kaufmann, Scott, Junker, van der Woude, Rudolph, von Rad, Wildberger, and Motyer) to be the originator of the oracle, using criteria such as the smoothness and fullness of the text, contextual fit, consistency with the prophet's style, vocabulary, imagery, and eschatology elsewhere, and even psychological factors (according to Cheyne, Isaiah would not have quoted a younger prophet and given his oracle such a prominent position; according to Willi-Plein, Micah, the less famous, never would have dared to quote the more famous Isaiah)[160] to support their views. Girdlestone's purely historical argument displays the extent to which earlier scholars relied on contextual data:

> Now if the verse in question (Micah iii.12) is tied to the age of Hezekiah [according to Jer. XXVI.18] there is high probability that the words which immediately follow, and which are linked only by the little word 'and' or 'but' are of the same date. Can we fix the date of Isa. ii.2-4? The second, third, and fourth chapters of Isaiah seem to be one prophecy, and their position suggests that they preceded the year in which King Uzziah died (vi.1). This affords a possible answer to the question, and suggests that Isa. ii. preceded Mic. iv.[161]

159. The focus on Micah's ministry in Jer. 26 may offer a corrective to the question of influence.

160. Cheyne, *Introduction to the Book of Isaiah*, p. 10; Willi-Plein, *Vorformen der Schriftexegese*, p. 83.

161. Girdlestone, *The Building Up of the Old Testament*, p. 237.

However, this type of reasoning is no more implausible than the recent version of the historical argument: Micah never could have issued such a bold promise regarding Jerusalem's future, for then the elders of Judah in Jeremiah's day would not have remembered him instead for his prophecy of Jerusalem's destruction.[162]

Just as there always have been scholars supporting either Isaiah or Micah as the author of this text, so another explanation also has been proposed since the very inception of critical study: the oracle was incorporated into each book independently from a third, no longer extant source (so Allen, Birkeland, Budde, Cannewurf, Cheyne, Ewald, Hayes and Irvine, Lindblom, Nielsen, von Orelli, Robinson, Soggin, Sweeney, Vermeylen, Wellhausen, Werner, de Wette, Willi-Plein, R.R. Wilson, and Wolff). This view has two variations. One version suggests that an earlier, now anonymous, prophet was used by the canonical prophets. Hitzig and Ewald even posited that this prophet was Joel, probably influenced by the similarity in the imagery of Joel 4.10; Isa. 2.4; and Mic. 4.3 but likely also motivated by the desire to remove the onus of anonymity.[163] The second version argues that the eschatology of this passage is more advanced than that of the eighth-century prophets; hence it is a postexilic addition to *both* books.[164]

---

162. Van der Woude, 'Micah IV 1-5', p. 398. On the basis of the study òf quotation in the comparative materials, it is clear that it is invalid to assume that a single quotation is 'typical' of the content or of a speaker or author rather than being selected because of its contextual appropriateness. (It is ironic that the very passage which could offer the clearest example of an earlier prophet being quoted later in the Old Testament period is used instead to argue that the prophet Micah was neither quoted by nor quoting Isaiah.) Equally untenable views are that Micah would not quote Isaiah because it would not be in keeping with his powerful prophetic self-consciousness (Mic. 3.8) 'that he should adorn himself with foreign feathers', Rudolph, *Micha*, p. 78; or that the oracle cannot stem from Isaiah simply because a verbal parallel exists in Micah. Werner, *Eschatologische Texte in Jesaja 1-39*, p. 163.

163. The opinion of Hitzig and Ewald is noted by Nägelsbach, *The Prophet Isaiah*, II, p. 54, who rejects the very idea of a posited source: 'In as much as a third place, from which both may have drawn, is actually non-existent, this hypothesis is in itself superfluous and null'—a rather dubious approach. The similar wording of Joel 4.10 further complicates the matter, since the date of Joel's prophecy is also disputed. Nägelsbach, as well as Kaiser, *Jesaja 1-12*, p. 61, note the view that the oracle may have been given to both prophets by divine inspiration apart from any verbal dependence.

164. This view is defended by Cheyne, *Introduction to the Book of Isaiah*, pp. 9-

Given the difficulty of demonstrating that one prophet is dependent on another and the increasing frequency with which an 'unpreserved third source' is invoked to account for verbal parallels, one cannot help but wonder whether it is not simply the easiest option, for there is little one can say about the anonymous author of a no longer extant source. Having offered this explanation, most scholars fail to make any suggestions as to how and why this particular oracle came to be independently incorporated into two prophetic books or what implications this type of borrowing may have for an understanding of the prophetic process.[165]

The basic problem besetting the diachronic analysis of this passage is the fact that the oracle is, from a tradition-critical perspective, virtually unparalleled within the prophetic literature. Despite Vermeylen's attempt to identify the 'nations' here as scattered Israel,[166] the oracle says nothing about Israel's direct involvement in the events portrayed. Unlike 'Second' or 'Third' Isaiah, the nations do not assist in the regathering of exiled Israel or in bringing gifts to beautify Jerusalem. Any link to messianic passages such as Isa. 9.1-6 and 11.1-9 is indirect, since here it is Yahweh himself who teaches and judges. Attempts to connect the use of נהר (flow) in Isa. 2.2b to the 'river of Paradise' motif (so Fohrer) make too much out of a single word, especially when it may be preferable to translate it as 'rejoice, be radiant' rather than 'to

14, although he admits that in his earlier commentary he held that both prophets borrowed from an unknown earlier prophet. Van der Woude, 'Micah IV 1-5', p. 397, finds it difficult to believe that 'one and the same song in different redactions has been inserted in two different prophetic books by one or two interpolators'. (It is remarkable to note that scholarly thinking regarding prophetic eschatology has changed so greatly that an oracle once considered pre-Isaianic is now deemed postexilic.)

165. Soggin, *Introduction to the Old Testament*, p. 260, gives rise to this suspicion by his comment that it is 'impossible to establish which of the two versions is the earlier, unless, as seems more plausible, both are a quotation of an extract which is independent of these prophets'. It seems certain, in any case, that some type of dependence is involved. Totally unconvincing is Birkeland's view that the material simply 'wandered' from one tradition complex into another in the process of oral transmission, *Zum hebräischen Traditionswesen*, p. 19. These four basic explanations have been applied to numerous parallel passages. See Chapter 1, pp. 18, for a more complete list of possibilities. A. Motyer, *The Prophecy of Isaiah* (Leicester: Inter-Varsity Press, 1993), p. 53, may be correct in claiming that determining the nature of the dependence in this parallel is 'an insoluble problem'.

166. Vermeylen, *Du prophète Isaïe*, I, pp. 128-32. See the refutation by Werner, *Eschatologische Texte in Jesaja 1-39*, pp. 153-54.

stream'.[167] Nor is the passage directly related to the 'inviolability of Zion' or the reversal of the 'war of the nations' (*Völkerkampf*) motif,[168] for the focus here is on the cessation of war between nations in general, not on the gathering of the nations against Israel. Regarding the uniqueness of this oracle, Werner notes that only here do the nations voluntarily destroy their weapons.[169] It is even uncertain whether the initial phrase, והיה באחרית הימים (in the last days), refers to eschatological events rather than simply to the indefinite future.[170]

As a result, efforts to use vocabulary statistics or tradition-criticism to connect the oracle to the message and ministry of either Isaiah or Micah have failed to gain a consensus,[171] and these approaches are equally inadequate when attempting to assign any date to this verbal parallel. The passage simply is too unique in its timeless and universal scope. However, this observation at least offers a possible explanation as to why this oracle came to be included *in toto* in two prophetic books.

In addition to those explanations for the Micah/Isaiah parallel which already have been discussed, several other possibilities have been set out. Renaud posits a complicated interaction between the Micah and Isaiah materials. Having previously used Isa. 2.6-8 as the basis for Mic. 5.9-13, the author of Micah 4–5 (not the eighth-century prophet) then composed Mic. 4.1-4 as a positive counterpart to Mic. 3.12 and later inserted it into Isaiah as well. Still later, v. 5, in its variant formulations, was added to each passage to restrict the universalistic scope of the

167. Wiklander, *Prophecy as Literature*, pp. 70-71, who cites Isa. 60.5; Werner, *Eschatologische Texte in Jesaja 1-39*, p. 158.

168. H. Junker, 'Sancta Civitas, Jerusalem Nova: Eine formkritische und über-lieferungsgeschichtliche Studie zu Is 2', in H. Gross (ed.), *Ekklesia: Festschrift für Bischof Matthias Wehr* (TTS, 15; Trier: Paulinus Verlag, 1962), pp. 17-33 (26-27).

169. Werner, *Eschatologische Texte in Jesaja 1-39*, p. 161. Werner, p. 162, labels the entire passage as a 'special tradition' (*Sonderüberlieferung*) among the 'pilgrimage of the nations' texts.

170. Rudolph, *Micha*, p. 79.

171. E. Cannewurf, 'The Authenticity of Micah IV 1-4', *VT* 13 (1963), pp. 26-33, in particular, has criticized Wildberger's dependence on vocabulary statistics for his argumentation. The so-called Zion hymns, which are central to the argumentation of Wildberger, are equally difficult to date. Sweeney, *Isaiah 1–4*, pp. 166-68, questions Wildberger's identification of the Zion psalms with the traditions underlying Isa. 2.2-4.

oracle.[172] According to Vermeylen, Isa. 2.1-4 represents a cultic *song* which offers a rereading of 2.12-17 (e.g. the 'hills' of 2.2 are therefore 'high places', local sanctuaries) stemming from Josiah's centralization of the sanctuary which was added to Isaiah by an exilic deuteronomistic editor. Similarly, Mic. 4.1-5 is a rereading of 3.9b-10, 12.[173] Van der Woude holds that Mic. 4.1-3, though borrowed from the prophet Isaiah, is quoted *not* by Micah but by his pseudo-prophetic opponents who cite Isaiah to counter Micah's announcement of doom on Jerusalem in 3.12.[174] Finally, using a tradition-critical approach, Coggins claims that Joel, Isaiah and Micah are not dependent on a previously uttered prophetic *oracle* but are drawing independently on a common fund of *language*, an established metaphor of the Jerusalem cult.[175]

Despite the diversity of opinion regarding the origin of the verbal parallel, there is relative agreement regarding the integrity of the present oracles. Most commentators acknowledge Isaiah 2.2-4 to be the original unit, with 2.1 a later redactional addition. Micah is considered to contain several minor additions, such as עד־רחוק (at a distance). As mentioned above, Mic. 4.4 is viewed by some as reflecting Micah's own adaptation of the oracle, while Wildberger and others hold that Mic. 4.4 formed a part of the original Isaianic oracle, only later being omitted from the book of Isaiah. The nature of Isa. 2.5 // Mic. 4.5 also is debated. According to Rudolph, Mic. 4.5 flatly contradicts the preceding oracle; according to Mays, it contains the words of readers within the congregation who long for its fulfillment.[176] Isa. 2.5 is

---

172. Renaud, *Structure et attaches*, pp. 41-43. Numerous parallels between Micah and Isaiah have been noted, leading some scholars to suggest that both books were edited by the same person or group. See Wilson, *Prophecy and Society*, p. 275; Childs, *Introduction to the Old Testament as Scripture*, pp. 434-36.

173. Vermeylen, *Du prophète Isaïe*, I, p. 132; II, pp. 592-94.

174. Van der Woude, 'Micah IV 1-5', pp. 396-402; *idem, Micha* (Prediking van het Oude Testament; Nijkerk: G.F. Callenbach, 1977), pp. 131-32. With regard to van der Woude's views, see R.P. Carroll, 'Night without Vision: Micah and the Prophets', in F. García Martínez, A. Hilhurst and C.J. Labuschagne (eds.), *The Scriptures and the Scrolls: Studies in Honour of A.S. van der Woude's 65th Birthday* (Leiden: E.J. Brill, 1992), pp. 74-84.

175. Coggins, 'An Alternative Prophetic Tradition?', p. 89. However, Isa. 2.2-4 represents a structured oracle, not simply a metaphor.

176. Rudolph, *Micha*, p. 81; similarly Wildberger, *Jesaja 1–39*, I, p. 75, regarding Isa. 2.5; Mays, *Micha*, p. 99; similarly Werner, *Eschatologische Texte in Jesaja 1-39*, p. 162, regarding Isa. 2.5.

variously described as an integral conclusion to 2.2-4, a transitional link joining 2.1-4 and 2.6-21, or as belonging entirely to 2.6-21.[177] Loretz, however, basically stands alone when he concludes: 'both text forms can be conceived only as the end-product of a protracted process of growth and commentary (*Werde- und Kommentierungs-vorganges*)'.[178]

Similar disagreement prevails regarding the setting of the oracle within its respective prophetic collection. According to Renaud, Isa. 2.1-4 abruptly interrupts, without logical or material links to what precedes or follows; according to Ackroyd, it forms the original conclusion to ch. 1; according to Wiklander, it is the point of departure for Isaiah 2–4, which he views as a self-contained discourse unit.[179] With regard to Micah, J.M.P. Smith claims that 4.1-4 is incompatible with 3.9-12, and Stade suggests that 4.1-4 was added by an anonymous epigone in the post-Jeremian period to balance the one-sidedness of the doom oracles of chs. 1–3, but Willis argues that chs. 3–5 form such a coherent unit that 3.9-12 is *inseparable* from 4.1-5.[180]

Even though this overview of the diachronic analysis of Isa. 2.1-5 // Mic. 4.1-5 reveals the extent of the disagreement over basic questions and the difficulty of achieving even a minimal consensus, several observations can be made which may help guide the further study of these texts. First of all, the extent and degree of the correspondence in this verbal parallel do not simplify its analysis. Instead, further questions are raised. Because it represents a complete oracle, it cannot be dismissed as a redactional gloss, unconscious borrowing, or formulaic

177. H. Frey, *Handkommentar zum Buch Jesaja* (Bad Liebenzell: Verlag der Liebenzeller Mission, 1975), p. 74; Junker, 'Sancta Civitas', pp. 20-21; Schedl, *Rufer des Heils*, p. 53, who sees the unit as 2.5-22. In Codex Len. the masoretes placed the parasha division before Isa. 2.5 but after Mic. 4.5!

178. O. Loretz, *Der Prolog des Jesaja Buches (1, 1-2, 5): Ugaritologische und kolometrische Studien zu Jesaja-Buch* (Altenberge: CIS Verlag, 1984), pp. 74, 78, considers the words of the peoples in Isa. 2.3 to be a secondary addition.

179. Renaud, *Structure et attaches*, p. 42; Ackroyd, 'A Note on Isaiah 21', pp. 320-21; Wiklander, *Prophecy as Literature*, p. 50.

180. Smith, *Micha*, p. 84; B. Stade, 'Bemerkungen über das Buch Micha', *ZAW* 1 (1881), pp. 161-72, 170; J.T. Willis, 'The Structure of Micah 3-5 and the Function of Micah 5.9-14 in the Book', *ZAW* 81 (1969), pp. 191-214. Kaiser, *Jesaja 1–12*, p. 63, also notes that Mic. 4.1-4 fits more tightly into the surrounding context than its Isaianic parallel and therefore suggests that the prophecy was incorporated into the former earlier than into the latter.

language. Those who consider extensive quotation to be unworthy of classical prophecy cannot attribute the borrowing to either Micah or Isaiah; yet it is unsatisfying to label such a prophetic gem 'anonymous'. Because the basic correspondence is so close, the absence of a parallel to Mic. 4.4 attracts even more attention, while Isa. 2.5 // Mic. 4.5 differ sufficiently for some to claim that they are not even parallel. The fact that commentators have suggested that this oracle was incorporated *independently* into both Isaiah and Micah raises the question of whether *any* criteria for determining verbal dependence are useful.

Secondly, despite Werner's claim that Isa. 2.1-4 cannot be Isaianic *because of* the parallel in Micah 4,[181] the existence of a verbal parallel cannot be a determinative factor in dating a passage, although it may be useful in suggesting a *terminus a quo* or *ad quem*. Unless one has concluded a priori that quotation does not occur in genuine oracles and therefore is inherently suspect, contextual, linguistic and thematic factors must be the basis for assigning dates. (The verbal parallel, however, should play a crucial role in interpreting the passage.) This holds true whether one is seeking to date either of the parallel texts or trying to settle the question of priority. As a case in point, the fact that the verbal parallel appears in two books which are associated with contemporary prophets should lead one to expect that Micah would receive as many 'votes' for having priority as Isaiah. That quite the opposite has been true reveals how many considerations and presuppositions enter into the diachronic analysis.

Thirdly, despite the emphasis on diachronic analysis, such analysis often is incomplete, focusing on the reasons why the prophecy could not stem from Isaiah or Micah and why the oracle should be viewed as an earlier liturgical piece or later anonymous oracle. However, commentators often do not specify how early or late this no longer extant third source was or what its *Sitz im Leben* was. Most importantly, little is said with regard to when, why or how this liturgy or oracle came to be used in Micah or Isaiah, whether or not this anonymous oracle was, in turn, mediated from one prophetic book to the other rather than being independently incorporated into both,[182] and what significance should be given to the presence of such an extensive verbal parallel in the

181. See n. 162.
182. Kaiser, *Jesaja 1–12*, p. 63, represents an exception in stating that the oracle was incorporated first into Micah and then later, by memory, into Isaiah, although his reasons for suggesting Michan priority are unconvincing.

collections of contemporary prophets. A fruitful line of investigation, which also has significance for synchronic analysis, is the suggestion by Mowinckel, variously developed by Renaud, Wilson, and Childs,[183] that the same prophetic school, tradent or circle of editors was responsible for the transmission and reshaping of both books. Childs notes the similar theological pattern of judgment and salvation, a similar liturgical influence, and a similar style, as well as the verbal parallel, as indicative of a close relationship between the two.

Finally, it appears that whether one considers a verbal parallel to be integral or secondary to its literary context depends largely on the focus of one's attention. Those who claim that the oracle is integral to Isaiah or Micah stress repeated vocabulary, intentional contrast by literary juxtaposition, and larger redactional patterns. Those who deny this stress form-critical diversity, the abruptness of the transition, and the uniqueness of the oracle's traditions within its setting. Given the nature of quotation, with its tension between contextual assimilation and distinctiveness, both perspectives may be justified. However, the exclusive use of literary-critical, tradition-critical or redaction-critical approaches can lead one to overlook important aspects of the workings or function of quotation.

Synchronic Analysis

In analyzing this verbal parallel, a distinction must be made between these passages and those previously examined. Whereas the first three quotations involved internal parallels and their particular dynamics within the canonical book of Isaiah, Isa. 2.2-4 // Mic. 4.1-3 represents an external parallel between two canonical books and, accordingly, functions very differently.[184] Therefore, it is helpful first to consider the role of the passage within each book and then to discuss the significance of the parallel itself.

Ackroyd has analyzed correctly the function of the superscription in Isa. 2.1. From a synchronic standpoint, there can be no question about the origin of the oracle in 2.2-4. It is not derived from Micah or from an

---

183. See Chapter 2, pp. 77-82, and n. 172 above. See also J.M. Vincent, 'Michas Gerichtswort gegen Zion (3, 12) in seinem Kontext', *ZTK* 83 (1986), pp. 167-87 (183), and G. Stansell, *Micah and Isaiah: A Form and Tradition Historical Comparison* (SBLDS, 85; Atlanta: Scholars Press, 1988).

184. However, Fishbane, *Biblical Interpretation in Ancient Israel*, p. 498, has also suggested that Isa. 2.2-4 is picked up and woven into a new oracle in Isa. 60.

anonymous prophecy; it is the message that Isaiah saw (חזה) as surely as the collection (1.1) represents the larger vision (חזון) which Isaiah received (חזה) in the course of his lengthy ministry. Regardless of which traditions concerning Zion may have influenced the prophecy, it cannot be described adequately as an adaptation of a cultic song or liturgy then current in Jerusalem or as the prophet's idealized hopes for the capital city. Rather it is a prophecy of what God in the future will do for and in Zion. (Similarly, according to Mic. 4.4, it is what the LORD of Hosts has spoken.)

Because of the interruption of the superscription, 2.1-5 cannot be considered to be simply the conclusion of ch. 1; however, it cannot be isolated from ch. 1 either. Isaiah 1.1, by mentioning the kings during whose reigns Isaiah prophesied, focuses on the duration of his ministry and ch. 1 accordingly introduces the major themes of his message, perhaps even embracing the entire historical scope of the book of Isaiah,[185] ending with the judgmental purging and restoration of Jerusalem as a righteous, faithful city (1.26). Even though this summarizes Judah's and Jerusalem's future, Isaiah's vision is more universal in scope. The vision is introduced in 2.1 and presented as the point of departure for his message, anticipating, even surpassing, the portrait of Zion and the nations that will be developed in Isaiah 40–66.

However, the oracle is linked primarily to 2.5-22. There are several reasons for considering ch. 2 to be a self-contained unit.[186] In addition to the superscription in 2.1 which marks a new beginning, the masoretic parashah marker following v. 22, and the emphatic formula כי הנה האדון יהוה צבאות, 'see now the LORD Almighty', in 3.1 which parallels 2.1 in mentioning 'Judah and Jerusalem' together (possibly marking the beginning of a new unit), ch. 2 is distinct in consisting entirely of prophetic speech.[187] Both chs. 1 and 3 are marked by the use of the first person referring to the deity and related introductory formulae (1.2-3, 11-16, 18, 20, 24-26; 3.1, 15, 16). Isaiah 2 not only contains the prophet's message to the people but is unique in repeatedly offering his response to it (vv. 5, 9, 10, 22).

In this context, 2.5 presents not a liturgical response from the cultic

185. G. Fohrer, 'Jesaja 1 als Zusammenfassung der Verkündigung Jesajas', *ZAW* 74 (1962), pp. 251-68; and Seitz, 'Isaiah 1-66', pp. 113-14.

186. Junker, 'Sancta Civitas', pp. 17-33, holds a similar view but omits v. 22.

187. One might also note the verbal links: בית יעקב (house of Jacob) in 2.5 and 2.6; נשא in 2.2 and 2.12-14.

reading of the oracle but the prophet's admonition to the people and reflects his identification with their situation. It also indicates the redactional intention of the oracle's placement: in the light of the coming judgment, to challenge the people to obedience through the prospect of the coming glorification of Jerusalem.[188] The vision gives the future goal, while the remainder of the chapter portrays the present situation and what must transpire before that goal can be reached.[189] The call to obedience in v. 5 is patterned after the words of the peoples in v. 3a: Let us do now what they someday will do also, because (initial כי in v. 6) at the present God has abandoned his people. Now the land is full of idolatry ('Do not forgive them', v. 9b, a word-play with נשא, lift up), but a day of judgment is coming (initial warning: v. 10 'Go into the rocks, hide in the ground from dread of the LORD ...'). All that is lofty will be abased, idols will be abandoned (second warning: v. 22 'Stop trusting in man ...'). Only then will the temple mount alone be exalted and become the destination of a universal pilgrimage.

Given the clear statement in Isa. 2.1, a synchronic reading of the prophetic corpus must understand the oracle in Mic. 4.1-3 as a quotation from Isaiah but equally the word of the Lord of Hosts (Mic. 4.4b). This conforms with the evidence of the superscriptions, which present the prophets as contemporaries, and the fact that there are no clear signs of belatedness in Micah's appropriation of the oracle. Therefore, an interpretation also must include an examination of the effects of adaptation and recontextualization.

Scholars have noted the incongruity of offering a portrayal of Jerusalem's future exaltation immediately following an announcement of its complete destruction, and it is unlikely that a prophet ever announced both within a single breath. Yet the collection has been edited in such a way that the two descriptions clearly are connected and contrasted. Willis and Vincent have noted the numerous parallels: Zion/Jerusalem 3.10, 12; 4.2; הר (הַ)בית (the temple hill) 3.12; 4.1; agricultural imagery and terms 3.12; 4.3b, 4; the corruption of judge, priest and prophet/Yahweh as judge, teacher and spokesperson, 3.11; 4.2, 3a; the temple mount as a ruined mound (במות) / the chief peak and

---

188. Kaiser, *Jesaja 1–12*, p. 62.
189. According to Wiklander, the remainder of Isa. 2–4. See also Junker, 'Sancta Civitas', pp. 21-25. This is quite different from saying, with Vermeylen, that 2.1-4 is a reinterpretation of 2.6-21, an impossible reading from a synchronic perspective.

destination of the nations 3.12; 4.1.[190]

Micah 4 often is considered the beginning of the second section of the book, introducing promise to balance doom.[191] However, Willis has noted that each of the three major sections begins with imperatival שמעו (1.2; 3.1; 6.1) and oracles of doom (1.2–2.11; 3; 6.1–7.6) and ends with oracles of hope (2.12-13; 4-5; 7.7-20).[192] Hence Mic. 4.1-4 is structurally at the center of the book, beginning the second half of the central and longest section, and accordingly functions differently than its parallel in Isaiah, even though both serve to contrast Jerusalem's future glory with its present sinful state and coming judgment. Within the context of the book as a whole, Mic. 4.1-4 is not intended to replace, ignore, correct, repeal or replace 3.9-12. Salvation is expected only 'after of the shattering of the existing order'.[193]

Mic. 4.4 reflects an adaptation of the oracle to the concerns of the book. It individualizes the implications of universal peace, using typical Israelite descriptions of well-being. (Compare 1 Kgs 4.25, וישב יהודה וישראל לבטח איש תחת גפנו ותחת תאנתו, 'Judah and Israel... lived in safety, each man under his own vine and fig tree', and Lev. 26.6 אין מחריד, 'no one will make you afraid'—further quotations?) This conforms to the following context which emphasizes the threat of Babylonian exile (4.10) and the ultimate regathering of the exiles (4.6-7) and restoration of kingship to Zion (4.8). Unlike Isaiah, in Micah the Völkerkampf (war of the nations) theme is related to Zion's exaltation: ועתה נאספו עליך ('But now they are gathered against you', v. 11a—cf. v. 2a, also 5.1, 5-6, 9).

Scholars have noted that Mic. 4.5 is not a part of the basic oracle but rather a later response to it. This is marked clearly in the text by the divine speech formula which concludes v. 4. However, v. 5 is linked syntactically to the oracle: 'Even though (כי) all the people still walk, each in the name of their gods, we resolve to walk even now in the name of Yahweh our God and forever.'[194] This fits better with Micah's

---

190. Willis, 'The Structure of Micha 3-5', p. 196 n. 24; Vincent, 'Michas Gerichtswort', pp. 180-81.

191. For example, Mays, *Micha*, p. 96, and Smith, *Micha*, p. 82.

192. Willis, 'The Structure of Micha 3-5', p. 197. Also Allen, *The Books of Joel, Obadiah, Jonah and Micah*, p. 260. See also D.G. Hagstrom, *The Coherence of the Book of Micah: A Literary Analysis* (SBLDS, 89; Atlanta: Scholars Press, 1988).

193. Vincent, 'Michas Gerichtswort', p. 182.

194. H.W. Wolff, 'Schwerter zu Pflugscharen: Mißbrauch eines Propheten-

emphasis on the current threat of the nations. Since 4.5 expresses the *application* rather than continuing the oracle itself, it is not surprising that it does not correspond as closely to the Isaiah parallel as do the preceding verses, 4.1-3, even though it is analogous.[195]

What is the effect of this remarkable prophecy of Zion's future being placed in an equally prominent position in both prophetic books? Scholars long have noted the numerous less extensive verbal parallels between Isaiah and Micah:[196]

Micah	Isaiah	Micah	Isaiah
1.11	47.2-3	5.5	9.6
2.13	52.12	5.13	2.8
3.5	56.10-11	6.7	1.11
3.8	58.1	6.8	1.17
3.11	48.2	7.1	24.13
4.7	24.24	7.2	57.1
4.9	13.8; 21.3	7.3	1.23
4.13	41.15-16; 23.18	7.17	49.23

Although most of these involve passages which many scholars consider to be non-genuine in Isaiah, Micah, or both, their cumulative effect is the same on the reader. In keeping with the superscriptions, they suggest, first of all, that Yahweh, in a given period of Israel's history (here the eighth century) reveals to each true prophet essentially the same message. It is the *divine* message to that generation, not the prophet's own creation. Van der Woude's interpretation, that Micah is full of unmarked quotations from the pseudo-prophets which conflict with Micah's proclamation, is an unconvincing alternative explanation. Rather, the true prophet freely can quote his contemporary since both are God's spokespersons. However, in the final analysis it is not the *same* message, for the literary context, along with the distinctive emphases of each prophet, reshape and redirect even the closest paral-

wortes? Praktische Fragen und exegetische Klärungen zu Joël 4, 9-12, Jes 2, 2-5 und Mi 4, 1-5', *EvT* NS 44 (1984), pp. 280-92 (289), offers this rendering of כ.

195. A further aspect of synchronic analysis might be to examine the role of Mic. 4.1-4 within the Book of the Twelve. In the present collection, Joel 4.10 precedes its parallel in Mic. 4.3b, while Zech. 3.10 takes up the promise of Mic. 4.4 once again.

196. Raven, *Old Testament Introduction*, pp. 193, 230. These passages reflect varying degrees of verbal correspondence, but a more detailed comparison is beyond the scope of this study.

lel. Thus even the virtually identical passages Isa. 2.2-4 // Mic. 4.1-3 have differing applications.

Secondly, the parallels suggest more than chronological and theological proximity. Because of the hermeneutical dynamics of verbal parallels and the impossibility of determining priority, an intertextual relationship is established between the two books. Childs has described the result effectively:

> This common moulding has the effect that Isaiah serves as a commentary on Micah and *vice versa*. The use of a verbatim passage in such a central position consciously directs the reader to the other collection of prophecy. The two messages are not to be fused since each has been preserved with a distinct shape as a discrete entity. Yet the two are to be heard together for mutual enrichment within the larger corpus of prophecy. The canonical shaping thus emphasizes an affinity which is far closer than that established by belonging to the prophetic division of the Hebrew canon.[197]

This is pre-eminently true of Isa. 2.1-4 and Mic. 4.1-3. Regardless of the origin of the oracle, the parallel *could not* have escaped the notice of those responsible for the final form of these prophetic books and *must not* be overlooked by the modern interpreter.

Isaiah 15–16 and Jeremiah 48

Otto Procksch has called Isaiah 15–16 an 'exegetical child of sorrow' (*Schmerzenskind der Exegese*).[198] If this is true of Isaiah's oracle against Moab, whose unity at least some scholars have defended, how much more complex is the interpretation of Jeremiah's oracle against Moab which is more than twice as long. Weiser has described the latter: 'repetitions, contradictions, troublesome breaks in the continuity of thought, alternation between poetic and prose sections, striking allusions and borrowings ... infelicitously supplemented by a variety of additions ... '[199] One of the major difficulties in understanding these

---

197. Childs, *Introduction to the Old Testament as Scripture*, p. 438. Carroll, 'Night without Vision', pp. 83-84, similarly speaks of the 'intertextuality' of Micah and Isaiah.

198. Procksch, *Jesaia I*, p. 208.

199. A. Weiser, *Der Prophet Jeremia: Kapitel 25, 15-52, 34* (ATD, 21; Göttingen: Vandenhoeck & Ruprecht, 1955), p. 403.

oracles is posed by the numerous verbal parallels which these two passages share.

Criteria

Of all of the prophetic genres, the oracle against the foreign nations (hereafter OAN) is the one considered most likely to contain prophetic quotation.[200] Already Ewald noted that because the prophet was not personally well acquainted with foreign nations, having never visited them, he tended to use general, static descriptions of them and their situation, often incorporating portions of OANs which earlier prophets directed against the same nation as possessing continuing validity. The fact that these prophecies usually were written rather than orally delivered facilitated such verbal borrowing. Under these circumstances, explained Ewald, quotation should be viewed as warranted, even necessary, and not a sign of deficient creativity.[201] Since Israel and Judah continually were involved politically with their neighbors, the need continually to reissue, revise, and reapply these oracles in the light of changed circumstances is understandable.[202] Hence the identification of verbal parallels within these OANs against Moab is likely to indicate dependence on earlier oracles and not simply traditional or formulaic language. A careful comparison of Isaiah 15–16 // Jeremiah 48 reveals how extensive the interdependence is. The following parallels between these two prophetic books generally are acknowledged even though variously explained:[203]

---

200. Regarding the OANs, see D.L. Christensen, *Transformations of the War Oracle in Old Testament Prophecy: Studies in the Oracles against the Nations* (HDR, 3; Missoula, MT: Scholars Press, 1975), pp. 1-15; R.P. Carroll, *The Book of Jeremiah: A Commentary* (OTL; Philadelphia: Westminster Press, 1986), pp. 751-53; J.H. Hayes, 'The Usage of Oracles against Foreign Nations in Ancient Israel', *JBL* 87 (1968), pp. 81-92; and D.L. Petersen, 'The Oracles against the Nations: A Form-Critical Analysis', in G. MacRae (ed.), *SBL Seminar Papers: 1975* (2 vols.; Missoula, MT: SBL, 1975), I, pp. 39-61. Petersen specifically discusses the Moab oracle of Isa. 15–16 as an example (pp. 51-55).

201. Ewald, *Die Propheten des Alten Bundes*, I, pp. 67-69.

202. Clements, *Isaiah 1–39*, p. 131.

203. Wildberger, *Jesaja 1–39*, I, pp. 605-609, offers a thorough textual comparison of the verbal parallels. See also Küper, *Jeremia librorum sacrorum interpres atque vindex*, pp. 83-98.

Jer. 48.5	//	Isa. 15.5
Jer. 48.29-30	//	Isa. 16.6
Jer. 48.31	//	Isa. 16.7
Jer. 48.32	//	Isa. 16.8-9
Jer. 48.33	//	Isa. 16.10
Jer. 48.34	//	Isa. 15.4-6
Jer. 48.36	//	Isa. 16.11; 15.7
Jer. 48.37	//	Isa. 15.2
Jer. 48.38	//	Isa. 15.3

In sum, parts of 12 of Isaiah 15–16's 23 verses are paralleled in Jeremiah 48. The parallels are not only extensive but also quite close, as a comparison of Jer. 48.34-39 with its Isaianic parallels reveals:

מזעקת חשבון עד־ אלעלה עד־יהץ נתנו קולם	Jer. 48.34aα
ותזעק חשבון ואלעלה עד־יהץ נשמע קולם	Isa. 15.4a

The sound of their cry rises from Hesbon to Elealeh and Jahaz — Jer. 48.34aα
Hesbon and Elealeh cry out, their voices are heard all the way to Jahaz — Isa. 15.4a

מצער עד־חרנים עגלת שלשיה כי גם־מי נמרים למשמות יהיו:	Jer. 48.34aα-b
בריחה עד־צער עגלת שלשיה ...כי דרך חורנים זעקת־שבר יערו	Isa. 15.5aβ, bβ
כי־מי נמרים משמות יהיו	Isa. 15.6a

from Zoar as far as Horonaim and Eglath Shelishiyah, for even the — Jer. 48.34aα-b
    waters of Nimrim are dried up
her fugitives flee as far as Zoar, as far as Eglath Shelishiyah ... on — Isa. 15aβ, bβ
    the road to Horonaim they lament their destruction
the waters of Nimrim are dried up — Isa. 15.6a

Jer. 48.35 = Isa. 16.12?—both speak of Moab's במה (highplace)

על־כן לבי למואב כחללים יהמה ולבי אל־אנשי קיר ־חרש כחלילים יהמה	Jer. 48.36a
על־כן מעי למואב ככנור יהמו וקרבי לקיר חרש:	Isa. 16.11

So my heart laments for Moab like a flute; it laments like a flute for — Jer. 48.36a
    the men at Kir Hareseth
My heart laments for Moab like a harp, my inmost being for Kir — Isa. 16.11
    Hareseth

על־כן יתרת עשה אבדו:	Jer. 48.36b
על־כן יתרה עשה ופקדתם על נחל הערבים ישׂאום:	Isa. 15.7

The wealth they acquired is gone   Jer. 48.36b
so the wealth they acquired and stored up they carry away over the Isa. 15.7
    ravine of the poplars.

כי כל־ראש קרחה וכל־זקן גרעה על כל־ידים גדדת ועל־מתנים שׂק: Jer. 48.37
בכל־ראשׁיו קרחה כל־זקן גרועה: בחוצתיו חגרו שׂק Isa. 15.2bβ, 3a

Every head is shaved and every beard cut off; every hand is slashed Jer. 48.37
    and every waist is covered with sackcloth
Every head is shaved and every beard cut off. In the streets they Isa. 15.2bβ, 3a
    wear sackcloth

על כל־גגות מואב וברחבתיה כלה מספד Jer. 48.38a
על גגותיה וברחבתיה כלה יׁיליל ירד בבכי: Isa. 15.3b

On all the roofs in Moab and in the public squares there is nothing Jer. 48.38a
    but mourning
On the roofs and in the public squares they all wail, prostrate with Isa. 15.3b
    weeping

Jer. 48.38b-39 are without parallel in Isaiah 15–16

Such extensive and close correspondence is clear evidence of some
type of verbal dependence, even though some of the language may consist of formulaic expressions of mourning.

Several additional textual features also suggest the presence of verbal
dependence. Not only do the Moab oracles contain numerous parallels
between Isaiah 15–16 and Jeremiah 48, but the following additional
verbal correspondences also have been noted:

Jer. 48.40-41	//	Jer. 49.22
Jer. 48.43-44	//	Isa. 24.17
Jer. 48.45-46	//	Num. 21.28-29; 24.17

These numerous links between Jeremiah 48 and a variety of biblical
texts at least suggests that Jeremiah rather than Isaiah is the quoting
text and that the former is drawing on known (and still preserved)
sources rather than on unpreserved anonymous sources. A related feature is that of contextual awareness. With the exception of Jer. 48.40-
41—which duplicates the conclusion of Jeremiah's OAN against
Moab's near neighbor Edom and may simply be part of the shared style
of the author/redactor of the OANs in Jeremiah rather than a quotation
(note also 48.47 // 49.6, 39; 48.7 // 49.3)—all of the verbal parallels to
Jeremiah 48 come from passages which refer to Moab: Isaiah 15–16,

Num. 21.28-29 (a taunt song about a victory over Moab), Num. 24.17 (Balaam's fourth oracle, regarding Moab and Edom), Isa. 24.17 (not explicitly, but the only foreign nation mentioned in Isaiah 24–27, cf. 25.10-12).[204] This indicates that Jeremiah 48 is not drawing simply on striking imagery and formulaic expressions of judgment from OANs in general but rather on descriptive language which expressly is applied to Moab in other prophetic texts. This also explains why some very vague language from Isaiah 15–16 reappears in Jeremiah 48, even though it lacks any historical reference to or distinctive description of Moab.

Finally, there is the frequent use of divine speech formulae in Jeremiah 48 and the explicit reference to an earlier divine message in Isa. 16.13-14 which could point to quotation. It has been noted with respect to Isaiah 2 // Micah 4 that a divine speech formula may mark a quotation. Jeremiah 48 stands in stark contrast to Isaiah 15–16 by its use of 12 such formulae (vv. 1, 8, 12, 15, 25, 30, 35, 38, 40, 43, 44, 47) as well as an opening and concluding superscription (vv. 1, 47). Although it would go beyond the evidence to suggest that each use of a divine speech formula marks a distinct quotation, some striking correspondences can be observed, if one assumes that Jeremiah is dependent on Isaiah 15–16. In Jer. 48.29-30, the only first person plural saying of Isaiah (16.6) is repeated. Verse 29a follows Isaiah exactly, v. 29b reverses the order of Isa. 16.6's two synonyms for pride, a frequent feature of quotation, and then frames them with two additional synonyms. Verse 30 then inserts אני ידעתי נאם־יהוה (I know, declares the LORD) before exactly repeating the remainder of 16.6 and adding לא־כן עשו (But it is not so) which parallels ולא־כן בדיו (but her boasts are not so) in 16.6. In v. 38 the formula marks the conclusion of the final parallel to Isaiah 15–16, in v. 40 it marks the parallel to Jer. 49.22, and in v. 43 it marks the parallel in Isa. 24.17. (The parallels to Num. 21 and 24 lack a divine speech formula.)

Equally striking is Isa. 16.13-14, which begins: 'This is the word the LORD has already spoken concerning Moab. But now the LORD says … ' Verses 13-14a have been interpreted as indicating that Isaiah 15–16 is itself an earlier oracle of an unknown prophet which Isaiah reissues, adding his own update in 16.14 that all of this will be fulfilled

---

204. W.R. Millar, *Isaiah 24-27 and the Origin of Apocalyptic* (HSM, 11; Missoula, MT: Scholars Press, 1976), p. 16, notes that the only historical reference in Isa. 24–27 is to Moab in 24.10-12 and sees its verbatim repetition in Jer. 48 as reinforcing this identification with Moab.

within three years.[205] If this is the case, it is not surprising that Jeremiah also repeats various portions of the earlier oracle in addressing Moab in his day. Summing up, there is substantial evidence that verbal dependence and even extensive quotation underlie the parallel between Isaiah 15–16 and Jeremiah 48.

Diachronic Analysis

The diachronic analysis of these verbal parallels has focused on three issues: the origin and dating of the oracle, the integrity of the oracle in each of the prophetic books containing it, and the nature of the dependence. Most scholars do not consider Isaiah to be the author of the basic oracle, some considering it to be earlier and others later than the eighth-century prophet in origin. Albright contends that both Isaiah 15–16 and Jeremiah 48 have been adapted from a single ninth-century prototype, and Christensen notes that a date as early as the eleventh century has been posited. Rudolph and Hitzig support a date during the reign of Jeroboam II, Hitzig even identifying that prophet as Jonah. Van Zyl considers the oracle to be based on a bedouin mocking song from the last third of the eighth century. At the other extreme, de Jong defends a common source reflecting Josiah's conquests and reforms, Wildberger suggests the final years of the monarchy, while Fohrer and others view the oracle as postexilic, with Gray positing a fifth-century, Eissfeldt a third-century and Duhm a second-century date.[206]

---

205. The origin and significance of Isa. 16.13-14 is disputed. According to Hayes and Irvine, *Isaiah*, p. 246, v. 13 simply states that Isaiah's present oracle is in harmony with Yahweh's ancient verdict concerning Moab (i.e. not an anonymous *oracle*) such as is reflected in Deut. 23.3. According to Fishbane, *Biblical Interpretation in Ancient Israel*, p. 509, these verses acknowledge that the original oracle failed and needs to be revised. Oswalt, *Isaiah 1–39*, p. 348, suggests the possibility that the preceding words were spoken by Isaiah a few months or years prior to vv. 13-14, while noting Kaiser's view that they were added by an apocalypticist. According to Procksch, *Jesaia I*, p. 224, 16.13-14 refers solely to 16.4b-5, a messianic promise.

206. W.F. Albright, *Yahweh and the Gods of Canaan*, p. 21 n. 57, cited by S. Erlandsson, *The Burden of Babylon: A Study of Isaiah 13:2–14:23* (trans. G.J. Houser; ConBOT, 4; Lund: C.W.K. Gleerup, 1970), p. 69 n. 23; Christensen, *War Oracle*, p. 140; W. Rudolph, 'Jesaja XV-XVI', in D.W. Thomas (ed.), *Hebrew and Semitic Studies Presented to G.R. Driver* (London: Oxford University Press, 1963), pp. 130-43 (130); A.H. van Zyl, *The Moabites* (Pretoria Oriental Series, 3; Leiden: E.J. Brill, 1960), p. 37; C. de Jong, 'De volken bij Jeremia: Hun plaats in zijn prediking en het Boek Jeremiah' (2 vols.; dissertation, Theologische Academie te

Hayes and Irvine, however, have defended the Isaianic authorship of the oracle and see in it a reference to Shalmaneser V's actions against Moab, even suggesting that the order of the OANs in Isaiah 13–23 is strictly chronological.[207] Basic to most dating attempts is the identification of the attack on Moab to which the oracle refers, whether Arabian, Edomite, Assyrian or Nabatean.[208] Such an approach is understandable, given the desire to determine the underlying historical circumstances which produced the oracle. However, such an effort is fraught with difficulties, whether one is attempting to date the oracle in Isaiah, in Jeremiah, or the hypothetical oracle underlying both of them. Regarding Isaiah 15–16 Erlandsson writes: 'Because of its general character it is difficult to make a detailed exegesis of its specific historical allusions. No specific historical details are transmitted.' Clements summarizes the implications of this fact, which seems to be typical of most OANs:

> No clear or certain identification of the historical background of the prophecies can be made... There is little basis for either asserting or denying an Isaianic origin to any of the prophecies.'[209]

This suggests that, unlike Isa. 8.14 // 28.13, the quotation was not motivated by a historical *analogy* perceived between the fate of Moab in an earlier and later period but rather by a common subject matter and

Kampen, 1978), p. 123; Wildberger, *Jesaja 1–39*, I, p. 611, also citing other suggested dates noted above, I, pp. 604-605; Gray, *Isaiah*, p. 276.

207. Hayes and Irvine, *Isaiah*, pp. 221, 239-40. They view the reference to Moab in Isa. 17.2 as indicating that Isa. 15–16 preceded Isa. 17.1-3.

208. Van Zyl and König identify the invading foe as Bedouins, Marti and Nicholson as Arabs; E. Power, 'The Prophecy of Isaias against Moab (Is. 15, 1-16, 5)', *Bib* 13 (1932), pp. 435-51 (440) as Edom; Hayes and Irvine as Assyrians; Duhm and Gray as Nabateans. Christensen considers Judah to be the foe, while Rudolph suggests Israel.

209. Clements, *Isaiah 1–39*, p. 151; also Kaiser, *Jesaja 13–39*, p. 65, who even refuses to assign a definite date to the oracle; Erlandsson, *Burden of Babylon*, p. 69: 'No specific historical details are transmitted and the composition appears ... to be a synthesis.' Similarly J. Barton, *Amos's Oracles against the Nations* (Cambridge: Cambridge University Press, 1980), p. 35, argues that the historical references in Amos are so vague 'as to rule out the possibility that Amos is addressing himself to current international affairs or that the force of his words rests in their relevance to contemporary events'. According to Barton, if Amos is citing a specific historical event, then it is one *long* before his time.

possibly a prophecy-fulfillment schema.[210]

The dating of the Moab oracle in Isaiah and Jeremiah is linked inextricably to the question of the integrity of the respective chapters. What is most interesting for our purposes is the extent to which the verbal parallels influence these diachronic decisions. A common approach with regard to Isaiah 15–16 is to identify several layers in the chapter. Rudolph sees in this oracle the oldest written prophecy in the Old Testament. According to him, 16.13-14, quite possibly from Isaiah, take up an earlier prophecy. The core of the prophecy consists of an elegiac lament over the fate of Moab—15.1-4 referring to the north and 15.5-8 to the south—while 16.1 recommends a petitionary embassy to Judah, 16.3-5 containing the message and 16.6 Judah's refusal, closing with Moab's continued lament in 16.7-11. Rudolph discerns in 15.9; 16.2, 12 a secondary prophetic addition which 16.13-14 designates as 'unfulfilled'.[211] De Jong identifies the core oracle as 15.1–16.1, 3-5 which was expanded by four successive additions: 16.8-10, 6-7, 11-12 and 13-14.[212] Wildberger discerns less unity in the chapter: 15.9 and 16.12 are later additions, 16.1, 3-5 and 16.2 are interpolations, and 16.13-14 is a gloss. According to Wildberger, none of the oracle stems from Isaiah, not even 16.13-14 which several commentators attribute to him, for 'a pre-exilic prophet never quoted the word of an earlier prophet and simply reinterpreted it for his own purposes'.[213] This is a surprising statement from one who defends the Isaianic authorship of Isa. 2.2-4, for in so doing he at least must allow for the possibility that Mic. 4.1-3 is doing precisely what he denies regarding Isa. 16.13-14. Furthermore, it is not at all clear that Isa. 16.13-14 is *reinterpreting* the earlier Moab oracle.

The dating and integrity of Jeremiah 48 are equally disputed. Boadt claims that the chapter is so general that it could also be by Amos or Ezekiel, and Nicholson admits that the chapter is too complex to isolate

---

210. A. van Selms, *Jeremia en klaagliederen* (De Prediking van Het Oude Testament; Nijkerk: G.F. Callenbach, 1974), p. 37, suggests that a perceived historical *analogy* gave rise to the reuse. It would probably be more accurate to claim that a later historical *situation* concerning Moab led a prophet to recall the earlier statements regarding Moab contained in Isa. 15–16.

211. Rudolph, 'Jesaja XV-XVI', p. 142.

212. De Jong, *Jeremia*, p. 127.

213. Wildberger, *Jesaja 1–39*, II, pp. 602, 604, 606.

the genuine parts.[214] Nevertheless, most scholars still offer without hesitation a complicated historical reconstruction of the chapter's origin and growth. Christensen, following Bardtke, suggests that the basic oracle, vv. 1-28, was motivated by the events of Josiah's reign, later 'augmented by material from *ca.* 600-598, 594 (?) and/or 587-582 B. C. when earlier material was up-dated'. Van Selms traces only 14 of the chapter's verses back to Jeremiah the prophet, while Volz and Schwally deny that Jeremiah had any part in the chapter.[215]

Because of the extent of the verbal parallel between Isaiah 15–16 and Jeremiah 48, to a greater degree than with the passages already examined, questions of authorship and the integrity of the oracle largely are determined by the individual scholar's evaluation of the verbal parallels. Wildberger's denial that Isaiah would use an anonymous prophet's oracle already has been noted. With regard to Jeremiah, such statements are even more prevalent. Rudolph speaks derogatorily of 'slavish imitation of Old Testament passages' and Nicholson writes: 'It is inherently very unlikely that someone with the creative impulse and genius of Jeremiah would have felt it necessary to borrow so much from an earlier source'.[216]

Accordingly, a fascinating variety of theories has been developed to explain the relationship between Isaiah 15–16 and Jeremiah 48, more specifically, why certain sections of Jeremiah 48 consist largely of verbal parallels while others are entirely devoid of them, and why many verses in Isaiah 15–16 reappear in Jeremiah 48 while others lack any parallel. Most commentators adopt a simple yet attractive analysis of Jeremiah 48: vv. 1-28 which lack any verbal parallels (other than v. 5 // Isa. 15.5 which is considered a late interpolation) are early, possibly even Jeremianic, while vv. 29-47 which consist largely of parallels are later additions. A further distinction usually is made between vv. 29-39,

214. L. Boadt, *Jeremiah 26–52, Habakkuk, Zephaniah, Nahum* (OT Message, 10; Wilmington, DE: Michael Glazier, 1982), p. 120; E.W. Nicholson, *The Book of the Prophet Jeremiah, Chapters 26-52* (CBC; Cambridge: Cambridge University Press, 1975), p. 177.

215. Christensen, *War Oracle*, p. 244, following H. Bardtke, 'Jeremia der Fremdvölkerprophet. 2', *ZAW* 35 (1936), pp. 240-62; van Selms, *Jeremia*, pp. 35-37; P. Volz, *Der Prophet Jeremia* (KAT, 10; Leipzig: Deichert, 1922), p. 405; F. Schwally, 'Die Reden des Buches Jeremia gegen die Heiden. XXV. XLVI-LI', *ZAW* 8 (1988), pp. 177-217 (206).

216. W. Rudolph, *Jeremia* (HAT, 12; Tübingen: J.C.B. Mohr [Paul Siebeck], 1947), p. 229; Nicholson, *Jeremiah*, p. 177.

which consist of parallels from Isaiah 15–16 and vv. 40-47, which consist of parallels from a variety of Old Testament passages. The latter are considered to be later than the former and more negatively described, even though no basic differences in extent and degree of correspondence can be distinguished between these two groups of parallels.[217]

More complicated are the explanations for various parallels or the lack thereof between Isaiah's and Jeremiah's Moab oracles. According to Gray, the compiler of Jeremiah 48 and the editor of Isaiah 15–16 both drew from the same elegy over Moab, thus those verses in Isaiah without parallel in Jeremiah probably were not included in the original elegy, although he concedes (1) that some unparalleled verses in Isaiah 15–16 may have belonged to a later stage of the elegy and therefore were not included in Jeremiah 48; (2) that not all of the original elegy has been preserved (apparently assuming that *all* of the elegy was borrowed independently both by Jer. 48 and Isa. 15-16); and (3) Isa. 16.6 which is paralleled in Jer. 48.29-30 *was not* part of the elegy.[218]

Wildberger employs a similar criterion, though his results are very different, in dating the 'additions and interpolations' in Isaiah 15–16: Because 15.9 and 16.1-5, 12-14 are without parallel in Jeremiah 48 one must conclude that they had not yet been added to the Moab oracle when Jeremiah 48 was composed. However, he also suggests that 15.1-2 was present, but the author of Jeremiah 48 chose to employ his own introduction to his announcement of judgment instead, and concedes that it is unclear why Isa. 15.6b-8 is not taken up in Jeremiah 48.[219] Regardless of how extensive a verbal parallel may be, it is unwarranted to assume that a prophet is compelled to reuse all of an oracle which fits his or her message or, conversely, that the lack of borrowing can be used as a literary-critical tool. Wildberger's textual comparison is too general. Even in the example cited above, 15.6b-8, both v. 6a and v. 7a are reused in Jeremiah 48. Furthermore, many of the verses from Isaiah

217. See Christensen, *War Oracle*, p. 244; and Rudolph, *Jeremia*, pp. 239, 241, 243, who indicates which verses in the chapter *may* belong to a genuine Jeremianic core. Verses 40-47 are distinguished also because of the significant differences between the text of the MT and LXX for these verses.

218. Gray, *Isaiah*, pp. 271-72. Gray considers 15.7b-9a to have been a part of the elegy added to Isaiah after Jer. 48 drew from it; 16.6 is viewed as a reflection on the elegy which was added at an early stage of the text. He labels all 'prophetic' elements in Isa. 15–16 as secondary.

219. Wildberger, *Jesaja 1–39*, pp. 605-606.

15–16 that are considered 'borrowed' in Jeremiah 48 have only partial parallels, entire clauses being omitted. Quotation is too complex and versatile a phenomenon to formulate hard and fast rules to govern its workings.

Other criteria have been used to explain the presence or absence of parallels in Jeremiah 48 to specific verses in Isaiah 15–16. Volz suggests that the quotation of Isa. 16.8-10 in Jer. 48.32-33 led a later reader to add further quotations from Isaiah to the verses which precede and follow vv. 32-33. According to Power, Jeremiah did not utilize Isa. 15.9b–16.5 because 'it visualised a definite historical contingency which no longer existed in his time', and, according to de Jong, Jeremiah did not use Isa. 16.1-5 because future expectations regarding Zion played scarcely any role within the Jeremiah traditions. Whether Power, de Jong, or both are correct with regard to Isa. 16.1-5, their approach clearly is more satisfying than the more global theories of Gray and Wildberger.[220]

Several additional diachronic issues must be addressed before drawing some conclusions. Although it is easy to suggest why Jeremiah 48 uses some of the same descriptions of Moab as Isaiah 15–16, it is considerably more difficult to achieve any consensus regarding the nature and implications of these verbal parallels. If the possibility of an anonymous third source is excluded, nearly all scholars agree that it is Jeremiah 48 that is using Isaiah 15–16 (but not necessarily in its present canonical form) and not vice versa, noting that Isaiah 15–16 displays greater thematic unity, more appropriate contexts for the parallels, and superior textual readings, while Jeremiah 48 displays multiple borrowings and a more composite structure. Bardtke's proposal that Isaiah instead borrows from Jeremiah has found almost no support. Accordingly, commentators have tended to correct difficult readings in Jeremiah 48 to harmonize with Isaiah 15–16, a problematic procedure since Thompson concludes that the text in Isaiah is not always superior, Weiser notes that some of the quotations may be from memory, and van Selms suggests that the text in each book has been modified in the process of transmission.[221]

220. Volz, *Jeremia*, p. 403; Power, 'Prophecy of Isaias', p. 447 n. 1; de Jong, *Jeremia*, p. 126.

221. Van Selms, *Jeremia en klaagliederen*, pp. 32, 36, is an example of a scholar who posits a third source underlying both canonical oracles; thus Jer. 48 is not dependent in the least on Isa. 15–16. He also sees further borrowings in Jer. 48:

Despite the extent and closeness of the verbal parallels between
Jeremiah 48 and Isaiah 15–16, little agreement has been reached in its
diachronic assessment. Even the basic assessment of the phenomenon
is disputed. Thompson merely speaks of 'many resemblances' in Jer.
48.29-39 to Isaiah 15–16, while Fohrer describes the same verses (vv.
29-47) as 'a misdrash-like expanded judgment oracle ... a good example of inner-testamental exegesis', although one may question whether
Fohrer's definition of midrash ('in which the author has texts already
available to him with his own words') is adequate.[222]

Despite the considerable disagreement over diachronic issues, several
observations can be made on the basis of the preceding survey:

Historical background. Even though it is likely that some particular
historical circumstances gave rise to the Moab oracle in both Isaiah and
Jeremiah, either as an unintentional result of the growth of the text and
the reuse of much of the material or the conscious choice of various
prophetic forms, nearly every trace of a specific underlying historical
situation has been effaced. The multitude of scholarly reconstructions
gives ample evidence of how little *textual* evidence there is to support
these views. The subject is clearly more significant than the date:
Anything said about Moab in the past bears repeating, whether a
prophetic message or a pagan taunt![223]

v. 10 cites an old spell, v. 19 a taunt, vv. 21-24 a list of place names. Bardtke's
argumentation, 'Jeremia der Fremdvölkerprophet', pp. 247-28, is rejected expressly
by Rudolph, *Jeremia*, p. 243, and Weiser, *Jeremia*, p. 408: 'Since Isa. 15-16
possesses the better text and the more unified train of thought, whereas the text of
Jeremiah often can be reconstructed and clarified only on the basis of the former,
there can be doubt as to on which side the dependence is to be sought, and that
Jeremiah did not write these verses.' See Rudolph, *Jeremia*, pp. 238, 242, for
examples of the emendation of Jer. 48 in conformity with Isa. 15–16, but note
Thompson, *Jeremiah*, p. 709 n. 6; van Selms, *Jeremia en klaagliederen*, p. 403;
Weiser, *Jeremia*, p. 32. However, since LXX of Jer. 48 sometimes agrees with the
MT of Isa. 15–16 *against* the MT of Jeremiah, which, according to Christensen, *War
Oracle*, p. 244 and n. 100, is described as 'conflated and expanded through the
addition of standard clichés and material from proximate and parallel passages',
this practice may be justified.

222. Thompson, *Jeremiah*, pp. 710-11; G. Fohrer, 'Vollmacht über Völker und
Königreiche (Jer 46-51)', in *idem, Studien zu alttestamentlichen Texten und
Themen (1966–72)* (BZAW, 155; Berlin: W. de Gruyter, 1981), pp. 44-52 (49).

223. Carroll's remarks, *Jeremiah*, p. 781, are apt: 'The poems of 48 reflect much
of the history of Moab without being specific to the point of describing actual

Accounting for verbal parallels. No single explanation adequately accounts for the fact that some verses in Isaiah 15–16 have parallels in Jeremiah 48 while others which would seem to be equally appropriate do not. Given the nature of the OANs and the evidence offered by Isa. 16.13-14 and Jer. 48.40-47, the theory of an unpreserved third source is more attractive than in the case of Isa. 2.2-4 // Mic. 4.1-3. However, even if one posits such a source which was drawn on by both canonical prophets, this still does not explain the surprising divergence in order and wording. Furthermore, given the nature of quotation, one must exercise great caution in the text-critical use of these parallels to minimize divergence. The selection, ordering and wording of the various parallels is likely due to a combination of historical, contextual/ thematic and stylistic factors. The fact that parallels to Isaiah 15–16 are concentrated in Jer. 48.29-39 and parallels to other texts in vv. 40-47 suggests three distinct textual layers, yet the parallel Jer. 48.5 // Isa. 15.5 conflicts with such a neat division and cannot simply be ignored. One cannot help noting that this division also reflects the scholarly prejudice against quotation as a practice unworthy of the true prophet.

Evaluating verbal parallels. A clearer distinction must be made between the reuse of descriptive language from earlier OANs regarding Moab for rhetorical enrichment, the reissuing or re-actualization of earlier prophetic oracles, quotation in order to indicate that a previous prophecy is about to be fulfilled, and midrashic reinterpretation. Given the fact that Jeremiah 48 utilizes a variety of verbal parallels which display varying degrees of correspondence and are supplemented by varying amounts of unparalleled material, a verse-by-verse approach is a necessary complement to a more general assessment of the use of the verbal parallels. Even exact repetition followed by the quoting 'prophet's' own statements is not inherently evidence of 'inner-biblical exegesis'. Furthermore, whether one views the quoted source as a prophetic oracle or a bedouin taunt also is an important factor in evaluating its reuse.

events. Thus they are similar to all the poems in 46-51 which use metaphors and similes of destruction combined with allusions to Yahweh's warlike campaigns against the nations to provide a commentary on the sixth century. In the Moab collection place names take the place of specific details and give the impression of the deity roaming about the land of Moab slaughtering everything he encounters ...'

Synchronic Analysis

Rudolph has claimed that Jeremiah 48 (specifically vv. 29-39) can be understood completely only on the basis of Isaiah 15–16. Although Rudolph suggests that this is due in part to the arbitrary use of Isaiah 15–16 which obscures its meaning in Jeremiah 48, [224] his point is well taken. Precisely how the former can be used in interpreting the latter will be the focus of our synchronic analysis of the verbal parallel.

First of all, from a synchronic standpoint, this verbal parallel involves one canonical prophet quoting another. The designation OAN is not simply a scholarly label but a prophetic designation. In Isa. 13.1 a new section is marked clearly by the superscription: 'An oracle concerning Babylon that Isaiah son of Amoz saw.' This introductory formula which closely parallels Isa. 2.1 indicates that, while the subject matter is distinctive (a foreign nation), the speaker remains the eighth-century prophet. Subsequent OANs also begin with an abbreviated superscription giving the subject (15.1; 17.1; 19.1; 21.1, 11, 13; 22.1; 23.1)[225] as well as historical references linking the oracle to the time of Isaiah (14.28; 20.1-2). The implication is that these are indeed Isaiah's oracles concerning foreign nations. Even 16.13-14 need not be understood as the prophet reissuing an earlier anonymous prophecy. Rather it simply involves a prose epilogue to the poetic oracle specifying the time of fulfillment, functioning similarly to Isaiah 20 which is an epilogue to Isaiah 18–19, also referring to a three-year period.

Jeremiah similarly introduces the section of OANs in 46.1: 'This is the word of the LORD that came to Jeremiah the prophet concerning the nations.' Subsequent superscriptions also designate the subject (46.2; 47.1; 48.1; 49.1, 7, 23, 28, 34; 50.1) and link the oracle to the prophet or his times (46.13; 47.1; 49.28, 34; 50.1; 51.59-64). The Moab oracle even has an additional closing colophon (48.47b): 'Here ends the judgment on Moab', perhaps a confirmatory note due to the oracle's extraordinary length and the fact that the final verses substantially are borrowed from other Old Testament passages.[226] Especially since Jer.

---

224. Rudolph, *Jeremia*, p. 243; similarly Weiser, see n. 221 above.

225. Exceptions are the oracle against Assyria (14.24-27), which is introduced simply by a divine speech formula, and the oracle against Cush (18.1-7), which begins with a 'woe' and the mention of Cush.

226. See Weiser, *Jeremia*, p. 410: 'The final sentence represents the closing remarks of a writer who possibly felt compelled, because of various quotations from other texts, to confirm that they formed a part of the Moab poem and to estab-

48.40-47 draw from known texts, including the book of Isaiah, in a synchronic reading one is justified in assuming that Jeremiah 48 is borrowing extensively from the prophet Isaiah's Moab oracle, and thus the effort to reconstruct an unpreserved common source not only is futile but counterproductive.

Secondly, one must note the differences between the larger context of the various verbal parallels. Isaiah 15–16 presents the entire oracle as one divine message: 'This is the word the LORD has already spoken concerning Moab', while Jeremiah 48 uses a dozen divine speech formulae to indicate separate segments of the oracle. Christensen has noted Isaiah 15–16's unique status as the only pre-exilic OAN not using הוי (woe),[227] perhaps because it begins as a dirge regarding destruction which already has befallen Moab (15.1-9) which evokes the prophet's empathy (15.5aα), although it is possible to take the verbs as 'prophetic perfects'. 15.9, though obscure, suggests that relief is not near, but rather further judgment, as 16.14 confirms.[228] Therefore, the call is issued for Moab to seek refuge in Jerusalem (16.1-5). Because of Moab's excessive pride (16.6), however, there is no hope; Moab's cultic prayer is to no avail (16.12) and the prophet can only continue his lament (16.9a, 11). Isaiah 15–16 uses characteristic vocabulary: כי (for) nine times in ch. 15, the root בכה (weep) five times (in Jer. 48 only in the verbal parallels), ילל (lament) six times (in Jer. 48 three times). Even though only a few verses are specifically prophetic in content, the entire oracle now must be taken as prophetic, especially due to 16.13-14.[229]

Jeremiah 48 announces unmitigated judgment on Moab which has not yet received its due (vv. 11-12), and, hence, begins with the typical הוי (woe). Unlike Isaiah 15–16, numerous references indicate that the judgment is still future (vv. 2aβ-γ, 10, 12, 16, 41, as well as the

lish its conclusion.' Thus v. 47b could be similar in function to Isa. 2.1; see n. 148 above. According to Christensen, *War Oracle*, p. 140, Isa. 16.13 is 'calling attention to the fact that this poem was part of the received tradition and not his own composition', and thus opposite in function to Isa. 2.1.

227. Christensen, *War Oracle*, p. 140.

228. Power, 'The Prophecy of Isaias', pp. 435-39.

229. Gray, *Isaiah*, p. 271: 'An appendix, 16.13f., treats the entire oracle as a "word of Yahweh", i.e. a prophecy'. Gray, pp. 271-72, separates the 'elegy' from 15.7b–16.5; 16.12, in which the 'prophetic element is conspicuous', especially 15.9b, 16.2, 5, 12; similarly Rudolph, 'Jesaja XV-XVI', p. 138. Procksch, *Jesaia I*, p. 208, claims that the passage as a whole is a lament and not a prophecy.

repeated use of the simple imperfect). Unlike Isaiah 15–16, there is no clear movement, other than the promise of future restoration in v. 47a, but rather a series of images and descriptions of judgment and mourning. It is here that the distinctive style and emphases are most evident: The use of אֵיךְ (how, three times) שָׁבַר (break, six times, once in Isa. 15–16), נוּס, חתת, לכד (flee, shatter, capture, four times each) and בּושׁ (be ashamed, five times), the latter four verbs not appearing in Isaiah 15–16; the image of wine (vv. 11-12, 26, perhaps 38); reference to Chemosh (vv. 7, 13, 46); repeated indictments (vv. 7a, 26a, 27, 29-30, 42). Furthermore, Jeremiah 48 is structured in such a way that vv. 1-28 present the prophet's own portrait of judgment, with v. 5 (which contains the only verbal parallel) anticipating vv. 29-39, which are dominated by parallels to Isaiah 15–16. The verbal parallels in this middle section point to the harmony between Jeremiah's and Isaiah's specific descriptions of judgment on Moab, while the final section, vv. 40-47, uses further parallels to express the agreement between this portrayal and the larger testimony of the Hebrew writings, possibly implying the incipient authority (though not necessarily canonicity) of these witnesses. This suggests that the primary concern in Jeremiah 48 is compiling rather than reinterpreting earlier voices, any reinterpretation being the *byproduct* of the recontextualization.

Noting these basic differences between the structure and emphases of Isaiah 15–16 and Jeremiah 48, the latter's omissions from the former are quite understandable. Excluding for the time being the minor omissions of individual clauses, the following verses are entirely without parallel in Jeremiah: 15.1, 8-9; 16.1-5, 12, 13-14. It is not surprising that Jeremiah 48 uses its own opening and closing, especially since the parallels to Isaiah are concentrated in the middle section, utilizing its favorite verbs of destruction in v. 1 שָׁדַד (ruin, also the first verb in Isa. 15.1), בּושׁ, לכד, and חתת (be ashamed, capture, shatter); hence 15.1 and 16.13-14 are unparalleled. 16.12 is 'replaced' by 48.35 which intensifies the description of the fate of Moab's cult. 16.1-5 may be omitted because it represents a possibly historically-specific call to seek help in Zion, inapplicable in the light of Jeremiah's impending destruction of Jerusalem, and because it lacks, apart from v. 2, any language descriptive of Moab's doom and mourning which is the primary content of the verbal parallels.[230] 15.9 which contains the oracle's sole

---

230. Rudolph, 'Isaiah XV-XVI', pp. 135-36, on the basis of its form and content, considers 16.2 to be displaced from the end of ch. 15 and thus simply reverses the

announcement of *further* judgment may be omitted as unique to Isaiah's message. The omission of 15.8 remains unexplained, although its זעקה and ילל (outery and lamentation) are used elsewhere in Jeremiah 48, and it is clearly not important to the author of Jeremiah 48 to use all of the place names which appear in Isaiah 15–16. In addition, v. 34 // 15.4-6 is already very close in expression to 15.8, so that a further parallel may have been deemed unnecessary.

In order to study the reordering, rewording and reframing of the verbal parallels in Jeremiah 48, it will be helpful to concentrate on one section. The passage consisting of verses 34-39 has been selected because it marks the conclusion of the parallels to Isaiah 15–16 but is viewed as distinct from vv. 29-33 in being prose in form (although the verses in Isaiah which it closely parallels are considered poetry) and more arbitrary and careless in its use of Isaiah 15–16.[231] For ease of reference, the textual comparison already made above will be repeated here:

מזעקת חשבון עד ־אלעלה עד־יהץ נתנו קולם	Jer. 48.34aα
ותזעק חשבון ואלעלה עד־יהץ נשמע קולם	Isa. 15.4a

מצער עד־חרנים עגלת שלשיה כי גם־מי נמרים למשמות יהיו:	Jer. 48.34aαb
בריחה עד־צער עגלת שלשיה ... כי דרך חורנים זעקת־שבר יעערו	Isa. 15.5ab, bβ
כי־מי נמרים משמות יהיו	Isa. 15.6a

Jer. 48.35 = Isa. 16.12?—both speak of Moab's במה

על־כן לבי למואבכחללים יהמה ולבי אל־אנשיקיר־חרש כחלילים יהמה	Jer. 48.36a
על־כן מעי למואבככנור יהמו וקרבי לקיר חרש:	Isa. 16.11

על־כן יתרת עשה אבדו:	Jer. 48.36b
על־כן יתרה עשה ופקדתם על נחל הערבים ישׂאום:	Isa. 15.7

order: 15.1-9; 16.2; 16.1, 3-13. Hayes and Irvine, *Isaiah*, p. 243, agree but note that 16.2 once may have constituted the 'emotion laden' opening of the Moabite appeal.

231. According to Rudolph, *Jeremia*, p. 243: 'Whereas vv. 29-33 still adhere to the context of the text which serves as their model (*Vorlage*) more or less closely, ... from v. 34 on, the appropriation of the older text is quite arbitrary.' Carroll, *Jeremiah*, p. 791, labels vv. 34-39 as prose with the possible exception of v. 37. For an English translation of these parallels, see pp. 309-310.

Jer. 48.37	כי כל־ראש קרחה וכל־זקן גרעה על כל־ידים גדדת ועל־מתנים שׂק:
Isa. 15.2bβ, 3a	בכל־ראשׁיו קרחה כל־זקן גרועה: בחוצתיו חגרו שׂק
Jer. 48.38a	על כל־גגות מואב וברחבתיה כלה מספד
Isa. 15.3b	על גגותיה וברחבתיה כלה ייליל ירד בבכי:

Jer. 48.38b-39 are without parallel in Isaiah 15–16

In content, v. 34 begins a new section following the condemnation of Moab's futile pride in vv. 29-30 and first-person mourning over the ruined harvest in vv. 31-33. Verse 34a describes the geographical extent of the mourning because a major water source has dried up (v. 34b) and, by the juxtaposition of v. 35, cultic practice has been halted. The first person lament (v. 36) is followed by a description of public mourning (vv. 37-38) and a summary outcry over the extent of Moab's destruction (v. 39). The section is marked by two divine speech formulae following first person declarations of judgment: והשׁבתי למואב (And I will put an end to Moab, v. 35a) and כי־שׁברתי את־מואב (for I have broken Moab, v. 38b).

Although it is impossible to make any definitive statement due to the difficulty of identifying many of the place names mentioned in the two oracles, it appears that the author of Jeremiah 48 is abstracting a number of place names from 15.4-6 to serve a different purpose. If Schottroff is correct, v. 4a forms part of a sequence of locations north of the Arnon (vv. 2-4) while vv. 5-6 is part of a sequence south of the Arnon (vv. 5-7), perhaps originally describing the flight following two separate attacks on Moab.[232] All other material in these verses is omitted as extraneous, v. 5b having been used already in 48.5. Verse 34a now indicates that the cry over destruction is heard throughout the north and the south of Moab, for even (כי גם—in 15.6 כי is more likely an emphatic particle, as in 15.1) Nimrim's waters are dried up. Only minor grammatical changes are made to eliminate the personification of the towns and produce parallel syntax with מן ... עד (from ... as far as).

As already noted, Jer. 48.35 probably replaces Isa. 16.12. Several reasons can be given in support: (1) both use the word במה (high

232. W. Schottroff, 'Horonaim, Nimrin, Luhith und der Westrand des "Landes Ataroth": Ein Beitrag zur historischen Topographie des Landes', *ZDPV* 82 (1966), pp. 163-205 (181-84). Schottroff locates Zoar, Nimrim and the Ravine of the Poplars in the south of Moab; Power, 'Prophecy of Isaias', pp. 445, 450, locates them in the north!

place); (2) given Jeremiah 48's repeated mention of Chemosh, it is unlikely that 16.12 would be left without parallel; (3) the verse which immediately *precedes* 16.12 in Isaiah immediately *follows* v. 35 in Jeremiah.[233] However, here minor modifications do not suffice, for 16.12 is climactic (it forms an inclusio with 15.2a), claiming that Moab is completely helpless to avert further destruction, while 48.35 suggests that Moab's population will be so decimated that there no longer will be sufficient personnel to carry on the cult, although the verse also could be read as stating that Yahweh will intervene directly to cut off the pagan worship.

Verse 36a involves a minor modification of 16.11: 'flute' (חלילים) is substituted for 'harp' (כנור), perhaps considered to be a more appropriate instrument for mourning music. The wooden repetition in this verse which produces two nearly identical lines cannot be considered a poetic improvement over the source. In Isaiah 16, the first person expression of lament is motivated (על־כן) by the destruction of the harvest (v. 9b-10); in v. 36 it is more climactic, motivated by the destroyed harvest (v. 32b-33), the dried up waters of Nimrim (v. 34), and the decimated cult (v. 35). It is possible that v. 35, through its use of נאם־יהוה (declares the LORD, cf. v. 30), has changed or at least clarified the identity of the first person speaker in v. 36—it is the deity himself who mourns over the destruction of Moab and its rich vineyards. Otherwise, in light of vv. 10 and 39, it is difficult not to read the verse as sarcastic.[234] Verse 36b continues by describing the results (על־כן) for Moab: the accumulated riches are gone. Here Jeremiah 48 returns again to the sequence of verses drawn from in v. 34, taking this phrase from 15.7 where it forms

---

233. Those who consider Jer. 48.35 to correspond to Isa. 16.12 include van Selms, Rudolph, Weiser, and possibly Carroll. Volz, *Jeremia*, p. 404, connects the verse to Isa. 15.2.

234. In v. 31 it is now the speaker who wails for Moab, unlike its parallel 16.7 where it is Moab that wails for itself. According to van Selms, *Jeremia en klaagliederen*, pp. 32-33, God is the 'I' of vv. 31, 32, 36; according to Volz, *Jeremia*, p. 409, the speaker is not the poet but the disconcerted Moabites here presented as an individual; according to Rudolph, *Jeremia*, p. 243, the sincere sympathy of the poet of Isa. 15–16 has been transformed by the author of Jer. 48 into open disdain; according to Carroll, *Jeremiah*, p. 796, this first person speech is merely a convention of the mourning song, not an indication of the prophet's self-identification with Moab and its plight. According to de Jong, *Jeremia*, p. 124, the voice of Isa. 16.8-10 is that of Judah mourning over the destruction of its former rich agricultural lands which are now under Moabite control.

the conclusion of the geographical sequence in the south and immediately follows the description of the drying up of Nimrim and the vegetation it supplied with water. Thus the sequence of Isaiah 15 is maintained, even though vv. 35-36a intervene.[235] However, v. 36 changes the import of the phrase, unless אבדו (they have lost) interprets ישׂאום (they carry off) in 15.7 as referring to the enemy carrying away the spoils of the invasion.

Verses 37-38a closely follows Isa. 15.2bβ-3 which describes the activities of public mourning. In Isaiah 15–16 it directly follows the initial general description of destruction; here it immediately precedes the conclusion of the second section of the oracle as the final verbal parallel drawn from Isaiah's Moab oracle. In the latter context it suggests that the first person lament of v. 36 is in harmony with (כי) the mood of the people of Moab as a whole, as expressed by the final words of v. 38a: 'there is nothing but mourning' (כלה מספד; the parallel in Isaiah 15 uses its author's favorite expressions for mourning, ילל and בכי). Jeremiah 48.37-38a involves only minor changes, producing a more parallel syntax by adding כל (all) twice, eliminating pronominal suffixes, and adding a fourth gesture ('every hand is cut').

The section in Jeremiah 48 concludes with two unparalleled statements in vv. 38b and 39. This procedure also is followed in vv. 40-47: Each sequence of verbal parallels from an earlier passage is followed by the author's own words (cf. v. 42 which picks up phrases from vv. 2 and 26; vv. 44b-45a; v. 47). Verse 38b states emphatically that the destruction of Moab is Yahweh's doing, smashing it (שׁבר, a favorite word in the oracle for destruction) like an unwanted jar. Verse 39 is a summary expression of shock (אי) over the extent of Moab's devastation, echoing vv. 17 and 26bβ-27aα and using the favorite words חתת and בושׁ ('shatter' and be 'ashamed').

Summing up, Jer. 48.34, 36-38a is composed almost entirely of verbal parallels drawn from Isaiah 15–16, which are incorporated with a minimum of syntactical modification, word substitution and supplementation. Because of the distinct emphases and structure of Jeremiah's Moab oracle, the content of the initial section (vv. 1-28), and the historical decontextualization of Isaiah 15–16 as a result of its reuse, only selected portions are used in a reordered sequence. It is even necessary to substitute v. 35 for the *thematically* parallel 16.12. However, there is

235. Christensen, *War Oracle*, p. 239, considers v. 34b to be dislocated from the end of v. 36 due to the position of the same colon in a different context in 15.6.

little evidence of significant reinterpretation (although it may offer some clarification), much less of arbitrary misconstrual, of the source. Rather, it appears that the author of the section simply is drawing on an earlier portrayal of Moab's destruction in order to supplement and enrich his own description.

What, then, is the significance of this reuse of earlier material? With regard to Jer. 48.34-39 at least, Rudolph's claim that these verses cannot be completely understood without reference to Isaiah 15–16 is unfounded, although the latter may help to clarify the selection and ordering of the content. On the one hand, the text of vv. 34-39 is hardly obscure; on the other hand, even a knowledge of 16.12 does not fully explain the form and placement of v. 35. Given the complex process of selection, ordering and modification of these parallels, it is highly unlikely that the author of this section expected the readers, much less any listeners, to be competent to catch all of the nuances of the recontextualization to enrich their reading of the oracle. In the preceding analysis of these verses, an effort has been made to explain this process of recontextualization, but this is not inherently hermeneutically necessary or even useful for future interpreters of these verses. Furthermore, contra Fohrer, this surely is *not* proto-midrash or inner-biblical exegesis, even though it may contain some evidence of reinterpretation. Nor is there any clear indication of a prophecy/fulfillment pattern.

Rather, it appears that, in this parallel, language is being reused merely for rhetorical effect, with the expectation that the audience or reader will have at least a general awareness that the same language also is applied in Isaiah 15–16 to the same nation. The verbal parallels in vv. 29-39 certainly are not essential to the oracle; they add very little that is not already contained in some form in vv. 1-28 other than the first person lament. This does not necessarily imply that they are secondary, for they serve as a confirmatory compilation of descriptions of the coming judgment on Moab. It is significant to note that, except for those of vv. 40-41 and possibly 43-44, all of the verbal parallels are drawn from material concerned with Moab, even though many equally striking and fitting images of destruction could have been quarried elsewhere. It appears that Ewald's description of the use of verbal borrowing in the OANs is quite apt with respect to Isaiah 15–16 // Jeremiah 48. (Note also the parallels between Obadiah and Jeremiah's OAN against Edom in 49.7-22.)

That this is not the only possible use of verbal parallels in an OAN is made clear by a contrasting example. Habakkuk 2.6-20 contains five 'woes' which are described as the 'taunt' (מָשָׁל) of the nations against the Chaldean, most likely forming part of the OAN tradition. The third of the woes consists entirely of three verbal parallels: Hab. 2.12 // Mic. 3.10 where it is applied to Jerusalem; 2.13 // Jer. 51.58b where it is applied to Babylon, possibly dependent on Habakkuk; and 2.14 // Isa. 11.9b where it concludes a messianic prophecy.[236] Three contrasts between this set of verbal parallels and those of the Moab oracle are apparent. (1) Micah 3.10 and Isa. 11.9 have nothing to do with the Chaldeans. (2) Micah 3.10 and Isa. 11.9 are part of an invective-threat and promise oracle, respectively, not an OAN. (3) Isaiah 11.9b ('for the earth will be full of the knowledge of the LORD as the waters cover the sea') is given a radically different application in Hab. 2.14. The addition of 'glory' in the latter is quite significant, and the verse in its new setting is both theologically enriching and contextually crucial, contrasting with v. 16 (the Chaldean's fading glory) and anticipating v. 20 ('But the LORD is in his holy temple; let all the earth be silent before him'). This brief example at least warns against a generalizing characterization of the use of verbal parallels in OANs.

In a synchronic reading of Isaiah 15–16 // Jeremiah 48, the latter will be viewed as the borrower, which also coincides with the scholarly diachronic consensus. The use of other verbal parallels in 48.40-47 argues against positing a third source. In any case, it is likely that whoever was responsible for the final form of the OANs of Jeremiah was aware of the verbal parallel in Isaiah 15–16. Together, the two prophets bear witness to the continuity in the divine pronouncement regarding Moab.[237] The synchronic reading relativizes the significance

---

236. Regarding the verbal parallels of Hab. 2.12-14, see W.W. Ward, *A Critical and Exegetical Commentary on Habakkuk* (ICC; Edinburgh: T. & T. Clark, 1912), pp. 16-17: 'Here is a remarkable succession of quotations, definitely designated as such and depending on a previous collection of sacred books.' Also Thompson, *Jeremiah*, p. 769; Pusey, *The Minor Prophets*, II, p. 200; Kaiser, *Jesaja 1–12*, pp. 246-47; Rudolph, *Micha*, p. 223; E. Sellin, *Das Zwölfprophetenbuch*. I. *Hälfte Hosea—Micha* (KAT, 12; Leipzig: Deichert, 1929), p. 354.

237. According to Boadt, *Jeremiah 26-52*, p. 131, 'the purpose of repeating so many well-worn phrases and old poems is to bring their power and effectiveness to bear once again ... There can be no better way of saying how awful Moab's fate will be than by repeating these favorite gems'. Van Selms, *Jeremia en klaaglie deren*, p. 37, sees in the reuse an 'actualization' of the prophecy. According to

of a diachronic reconstruction of the original circumstances which gave rise to these oracles, but the diachronic analysis of the complex structure of the oracles warns against a simplistic synchronic understanding of Jer. 48.29-47 as a mere anthology of analogous statements regarding Moab. The verbal parallel Isaiah 15–16 // Jeremiah 48 is significant not only because of the extent of the correspondence but also because it warns against the excessive interpretation of verbal borrowing which attributes great significance to every divergence. It offers a striking illustration of the variety and versatility of prophetic quotation.

Rudolph, *Jeremia*, p. 243, the borrowed material offered a harsher characterization of the Moabites for the purpose of his woe oracle.

Chapter 9

CONCLUSION: PROPHETIC QUOTATION—
PROBLEMS, PERSPECTIVES, PROSPECTS

The phenomenon of verbal dependence is one of the most versatile and complex aspects of prophetic speech. The analysis of five verbal parallels in the preceding chapter reflects the diversity and difficulty of prophetic quotation. Whether involving brief or extensive correspondence, central oracles or simple imagery, these verbal parallels present an intriguing hermeneutical challenge.

This study has examined quotation within the prophetic writings as well as in other literatures in order to understand its workings more fully and assess its significance more accurately. Through the analysis of more than a century of, for the most part, not previously surveyed scholarly literature discussing the phenomenon, many helpful, often long-forgotten, methodological insights and suggestions were 're-discovered'. In the process, it also became evident that much of the employment of alleged prophetic quotations in Old Testament research is defended inadequately or supported insufficiently by the textual data. In the future, greater caution should be taken in the use of verbal parallels in constructing critical theories.

In this study, prophetic quotation has been placed within its larger context, highlighting its functional kinship with quotation in ancient Near Eastern, early Jewish, and world literature in general. As a result, the hermeneutical complexity, rhetorical diversity and semantic richness of prophetic quotation has emerged, making evident the necessity of distinguishing between external and internal parallels and of combining diachronic with synchronic analysis in interpreting them.

In concluding this study, it is useful to summarize the problems that remain, the new perspectives that have been culled from the comparative study, and the prospects for further investigation and application.

Problems

Each of the aspects of the model for analyzing verbal parallels suggested in Chapter 7 is still beset with problems. The use of multiple criteria for identifying quotation adds a degree of objectivity which is lacking in much of the relevant scholarly literature. However, the question remains as to why verbal parallels are not marked more clearly, such as is the case in many New Testament examples. Yet the comparative material suggests that minimal marking generally is the practice in literature contemporary to the Old Testament and even later Jewish literature. Even those features which could be considered clear markers, such as the divine speech formulae as noted in Micah 4 and Jeremiah 48, also are used in numerous examples where verbal dependence probably is *not* involved. One is forced to draw one of two conclusions: either the readers or listeners are not expected to identify the verbal parallel or they are considered competent to recognize it despite only minimal marking. Perhaps further detailed study of the comparative material will indicate how such marking functions.

The analysis of specific verbal parallels in the preceding chapter as well as the survey of the scholarly literature in the first section of this study indicates the total lack of consensus in the diachronic analysis of prophetic quotation. The only matter on which there is substantial agreement is that quotation usually is considered to be secondary, contemporary interpreters concluding this as readily as those at the turn of the century. However, this conclusion not only is based on an unnecessarily narrow understanding of the nature and purpose of verbal dependence but also is in conflict with the evidence from ancient extrabiblical literature.

On the basis of our extensive examination of secondary literature, it must be admitted that diachronic analysis is *unable* to determine conclusively the direction of dependence or even the redactional level in which the verbal parallel was incorporated into the literature. This has two primary implications. First, it warns against moving too quickly from a list of verbal parallels to the construction of any critical theory, such as discussed in Chapter 2, *on the basis of* these passages, especially since this usually assumes that these passages have a uniform origin and function. Indeed, much that has been written regarding diachronic aspects of prophetic quotation needs to be rethought.

Secondly, given the limitations of diachronic analysis, synchronic analysis must be viewed as a necessary supplement to the diachronic and as a possible means of moving beyond the impasse in historical analysis. The inadequacy of the diachronic approach is especially evident in the case of internal parallels, in which the *effect* of the verbal parallels is at least as important to discuss as their *origin*. However, the synchronic method cannot stand alone, since quotation is an inherently historical phenomenon whose oral origins, which the scholarly literature seldom treats, and literary expression demand diachronic analysis.

Unfortunately, the synchronic analysis of verbal parallels is equally fraught with problems, three of which will be noted here. First of all, there is the danger of countering the under-interpretation of verbal parallels in diachronic analysis by over-interpreting them, attributing significance to every divergence, even though some are as likely to result from other factors, such as quotation by memory, as from intentional change, and it is difficult, if not impossible, to tell the difference. It often requires great hermeneutical sensitivity to discern the limitations to interpretation which the text in its present form imposes. To try to delve beyond these limits is to ask questions about quotation's dynamics which the text cannot answer.

Secondly, there is the related difficulty of trying to determine intentionality. Although the comparative evidence indicates that verbal dependence is more a conscious than an unconscious practice, one is never far from speculative psychologizing when suggesting what an author or redactor 'intended' with a given parallel. This problem is particularly acute when one seeks to identify examples of the reinterpretive use of verbal parallels: Is this evidence of inner-biblical exegesis or merely a by-product of recontextualization? On the basis of the definitions proposed earlier in this study, one must use caution in labelling a given verbal parallel a 'quotation'.

Thirdly, there is the unclarified relationship between diachronic and synchronic analysis. It is far too easy to advocate an exclusively diachronic or synchronic approach or to pay mere lip-service to one of the two without seriously considering how the one supplements, limits, corrects or gives guidance to the other. It must be admitted that, with respect to this issue, the analysis of the verbal parallels in the preceding chapter is not completely satisfying. Yet even the consideration of the question provided a helpful check on the interpretive process.

New Perspectives

The examination of the comparative material has proven helpful in gaining a better understanding of the nature and workings of quotation and suggesting some methodological possibilities for moving beyond the impasse in the analysis of prophetic quotation. It is not necessary to note here the numerous insights from the comparative material which were summarized in Chapter 7, most of which have not been applied previously in any systematic manner to the biblical phenomenon. It is hoped that the proposed model for 'quotation criticism' will not merely offer a corrective to some of the methods presently used in assessing verbal parallels in the prophetic corpus but also make a positive hermeneutical contribution. However, a more thorough analysis of quotation in each of the literatures surveyed in this study is also needed. Verbal parallels in a variety of texts have been examined, but there have been few systematic assessments of the phenomenon. Where this has been undertaken, as in Brunner's most recent treatment of quotation in Egyptian literature in the *Lexikon der Ägyptologie*, significant progress can be noted over earlier studies.

Equally helpful is the renewed interest in inner-biblical interpretation. Fishbane's comprehensive work, *Biblical Interpretation in Ancient Israel*, is exemplary in its analysis of numerous passages as well as its synthetic approach to the topic. Even though his impressive contribution to the subject is both broader in scope, dealing with all types of biblical literature, and narrower in focus, emphasizing only the reinterpretive reuse of earlier traditions, than this study, it already has stimulated further work on verbal parallels within the prophets. Despite the lack of terminological clarity in much that has been written regarding 'proto-midrashic' elements in the Old Testament, the increased attention given to this aspect of prophetic literature is refreshing. However, it must be noted that verbal dependence in the prophets does not necessarily involve 'biblical interpretation', and the analysis of non-interpretive borrowing is not less significant for a proper understanding of the literature.

It is evident that one's approach to verbal parallels is incomplete if one simply seeks to identify and list them, even if one proceeds to explain the direction of dependence and suggest a date at which a specific parallel was incorporated into its present literary context. It is necessary also to evaluate the meaning and significance of the verbal parallel.

It is crucial to approach each set of passages without any preconceived ideas of how quotation *must* be understood in any individual case. The analysis of five representative passages in the preceding chapter indicates the flexibility and diversity of the phenomenon. In the parallel Isa. 11.6-9 // Isa. 65.25 a lengthier passage apparently has been summarized and refocused, while in Isaiah 15–16 // Jeremiah 48 material simply has been extracted and reused to supplement by means of 'borrowed' imagery the description of judgment already given. In the parallel Isa. 2.2-4 // Mic. 4.1-3 an entire oracle has been reused and placed in an equally prominent position within the prophetic collection whereas in Isa. 8.15 // Isa. 28.13 the correspondence consists merely of a few words. In Isa. 28.13 the knowledge of the parallel in Isa. 8.15 was deemed essential for a proper understanding of the imagery whereas in Jeremiah 48 a similar knowledge of Isaiah 15–16 was judged to be an interesting but not crucial aid in the hermeneutical process. In Isa. 40.3, 10 // Isa. 57.14 // Isa. 62.10-11 the verbal parallel contributes along with various other passages to the development of a major theme within the book, while the repeated material in Jeremiah 48 serves simply to supplement an individual oracle. Far from presenting any clear patterns of reuse, each verbal parallel presents its own hermeneutical challenge and textual dynamics.

Prospects

Given the vast number of verbal parallels that have been identified within and between the various prophetic books, few of which have been subjected to a thorough analysis, there remains much work to be done. On the basis of the criteria discussed throughout this study a reduced list of *external* verbal parallels could be produced, similar to the list of *internal* parallels within the book of Isaiah offered in the Appendix, as well as a list of *internal* parallels within other prophetic books. Then it would be possible to characterize and compare more fully the types of materials that found reuse within the prophetic corpus. Similarly, the analysis of additional passages might reveal some distinctive patterns of reuse not apparent from the study of just five verbal parallels.

There are four larger topics of scholarly investigation to which this present work contributes and, accordingly, should be the subject of further study.

The Development of Biblical Interpretation

Fishbane's work in this regard already has been mentioned. Many scholars see within the Old Testament the beginnings of exegesis. The reuse of prophetic oracles or segments thereof represents one type of reinterpretation. If one compares the reuse of specific prophetic traditions within the prophetic corpus (involving both early and later prophets) with the reuse of the same traditions within early Judaism (Qumran and the Apocrypha), is any trajectory of development identifiable? Can the use of the Old Testament in the New Testament shed further light on its reuse *within* the Old Testament? Can this study shed further light on the complex issue of the New Testament quotations of the Old?

Parallel Passages within the Old Testament

Girdlestone in his intriguing book *Deuterographs* lists and briefly discusses numerous repeated passages within the Old Testament. Most notable are the extensive parallels between Samuel–Kings and Chronicles, but there are also many additional parallels between other historical books (such as Josh. // Judg. 1), duplicate psalmic material and proverbial sayings, and repeated legal material, most of which cannot be interpreted as proto-midrashic. Given the limited amount of literature included in Israel's canonical writings, within which many other sources are mentioned explicitly, why are so many traditions included more than once? Is this an indication of the haphazard process of redaction or of a growing canonical consciousness? Do repeated prophetic words share any common features or functions with these other parallels?

The Nature of Prophecy

It has been claimed repeatedly above that verbal parallels are neither a sign of deficient creativity nor especially characteristic of the postexilic waning of the prophetic movement. On the one hand, verbal parallels are numerous enough within the prophetic corpus to represent a significant feature of prophetic rhetoric. The reuse of earlier prophetic traditions is clearly as prominent as the reuse of historical traditions, even though they are more difficult to identify and evaluate. On the other hand, no prophetic book or section thereof is so filled with verbal parallels (not even Joel, Zechariah or 'Third' Isaiah), as to be dominated by them, despite the exaggerated claims of some scholars. Thus, prophetic quotation must be viewed as one element within the prophet's rhetorical repertoire which is employed sparingly, selectively and purposefully. Just what does this obvious verbal dependence indicate regarding continuity among the prophets, the inherent authority of earlier oracles and the (resultant?) need to revise and correct, to actualize and reissue them? What does this suggest about the knowledge of earlier oracles which the prophet or author assumes on the part of his or her audience or readers? Just how much competence is required in order to comprehend these prophetic quotations?

The Unity of the Book of Isaiah. A major emphasis in Isaianic studies during recent decades has been on the unity of the present canonical book.[1] Few scholars still suggest that the present canonical book

---

1. Recent discussions of the nature of Isaiah's 'unity' include Ackroyd, 'Isaiah I-XII'; J. Becker, *Isaias: Der Prophet und sein Buch* (SBS, 30; Stuttgart: Verlag Katholisches Bibelwerk, 1968); W. Brueggemann, 'Unity and Dynamic in the Isaiah Tradition', *JSOT* 29 (1984), pp. 89-107; D. Carr, 'Reaching for Unity in Isaiah', *JSOT* 57 (1993), pp. 61-80; Childs, *Introduction to the Old Testament as Scripture*; R.E. Clements, 'Beyond Tradition-Criticism: Deutero-Isaianic Development of First Isaiah's Themes', *JSOT* 31 (1985), pp. 95-113; *idem*, 'The Unity of the Book of Isaiah'; R.J. Clifford, 'The Unity of the Book of Isaiah and Its Cosmogonic Language', *CBQ* 55 (1993), pp. 1-17; T. Collins, *The Mantle of Elijah: The Redaction Criticism of the Prophetical Books* (Sheffield: JSOT Press, 1993), Ch. 2; E.W. Conrad, *Reading Isaiah* (Philadelphia: Fortress Press, 1991); W.J. Dumbrell, 'The Purpose of the Book of Isaiah', *TynBul* 36 (1985), pp. 111-28; J.H. Eaton, *Festal Drama in Deutero-Isaiah* (London: SPCK, 1979); *idem*, 'The Isaiah Tradition', in Coggins, Phillips and Knibb (eds.), *Israel's Prophetic Tradition*, pp. 58-76; S. Erlandsson, 'The Unity of Isaiah—A New Solution?', in K.E. Marquart *et al.* (eds.), *A Lively Legacy: Essays in Honor of Robert Preus* (Fort Wayne, IN: Concordia Theological Seminary, 1985), pp. 33-39; C.A. Evans, 'The Unity and Parallel Structure of Isaiah', *VT* 38 (1988), pp. 129-47; F.G. Meade, *Pseudonymity and Canon: An Investigation into the Relationship of Authorship and Authority in Jewish and Earliest Christian Tradition* (Grand Rapids: Eerdmans, 1987); Miscall, *Isaiah*; *idem*, 'Isaiah: The Labyrinth of Images', *Semeia 54* (1991), pp. 103-21; A. Motyer, 'Three in One or One in Three: A Dipstick into the Isaianic Literature', *Churchman* 108 (1994), pp. 22-36; R. Rendtorff, 'The Book of Isaiah: A Complex Unity. Synchronic and Diachronic Reading', in R.F. Melugin and M.A. Sweeney (eds.), *New Visions of Isaiah* (JSOTSup, 214; Sheffield: Sheffield Academic Press, 1996), pp. 32-49; *idem*, 'Zur Komposition des Buches Jesaja'; Seitz, 'Isaiah 1-66',

resulted from the haphazard inclusion of additional material in order to 'fill out the scroll'. However, little agreement has emerged regarding the *nature* of that unity. Is it liturgical (Eaton), sociological (Brueggemann), redactional (Clements, Rendtorff, Williamson), canonical (Childs, Seitz), structural (Evans), exegetical (Becker), tradition-critical (Ackroyd) or theological (Roberts)? Interestingly, until recently verbal parallels have received surprisingly little attention in these studies, with the exception of the work of Steck and Williamson, which focus on the significance of verbal parallels in the redactional structuring of the book. Whether or not their historical reconstructions of this process are correct, their redaction-critical conclusions suggest that verbal parallels too often have been neglected in the discussions of the nature of Isaiah's unity.

This comparative study has led to a re-evaluation of the phenomenon of prophetic quotation and to a renewed appreciation for verbal parallels within the prophetic corpus. If various critical abuses of verbal parallels are corrected and their exegetical import receives due attention, then an enriched meaning will be given to the prophetic claim, when repeating the words of a prophetic predecessor: 'Thus says the LORD'. Emerson wrote:

> We are as much informed of a writer's genius by what he selects as by what he originates. We read the quotation with his eyes, and find a new a fervent sense; as a passage from one of the poets, well recited, borrows new interest from the rendering.[2]

idem, 'On the Question of Divisions Internal to the Book of Isaiah', in E.H. Lovering, Jr (ed.), *SBL 1993 Seminar Papers* (Atlanta: Scholars Press, 1993), pp. 260-66; *idem*, *Zion's Final Destiny*; G.T. Sheppard, 'The Book of Isaiah: Competing Structures According to a Late Modern Description of its Shape and Scope', in E.H. Lovering, Jr (ed.), *SBL 1992 Seminar Papers* (Atlanta: Scholars Press, 1992), pp. 549-82; Sweeney, *Isaiah 1–4*; *idem*, 'Textual Citations in Isaiah 24–27'; A.J. Tomasino, 'Isaiah 1.1–2.4 and 63–66, and the Composition of the Isaianic Corpus', *JSOT* 57 (1993), pp. 81-98; B.G. Webb, 'Zion in Transformation: A Literary Approach to Isaiah', in D.J.A. Clines, S.E. Fowl and S.E. Porter (eds.), *The Bible in Three Dimensions* (Sheffield: JSOT Press, 1990), pp. 65-84. See also the overviews by J.J. Schmitt, *Isaiah and his Interpreters* (Mahwah, NJ: Paulist Press, 1986), pp. 117-27; Vermeylen, 'L'unité du livre d'Isaïe', in *idem* (ed.), *Le livre d'Isaïe*, pp. 11-53; Sweeney, 'Reevaluating Isaiah 1-39 in Recent Critical Research', *Currents in Research: Biblical Studies* 4 (1996) pp. 79-113; and Williamson, *The Book Called Isaiah*.

2. Emerson, *Letters and Social Aims*, VIII, p. 194.

Too long marginalized by scholars or maligned as a sign of deficient creativity and an institution in decline, prophetic quotation is a powerful and effective rhetorical device for actualizing past words and enriching present words regarding God's work in the world. It is time for interpreters of the Hebrew prophets to take up a refocused 'search for quotation'!

In the course of our analysis of verbal parallels *within* the book of Isaiah, a number of problems were encountered. In the scholarly literature regarding Isaiah literally hundreds of similarities were noted. Many of these, however, consist primarily of a similarity in theme or subject matter, sharing at most one or two Hebrew nouns or verbs in common. Since our goal was to identify the most extensive or distinctive verbal parallels rather than to compile a comprehensive list of all possible parallels, further criteria were needed to eliminate the correspondences that are merely coincidental while retaining those in which the opposite forces of preservation and adaptation combine to effectively disguise the correspondence.

Nearly half of the verbal parallels cited fit into one of the following two categories: (1) The verbal correspondence consists almost entirely of repeated near-synonyms, or so-called 'word pairs', such as רום/נשא (lofty—2.13; 6.1; 52.13; 57.14), שמיר/שית (briars—5.6; 7.23-25; 10.17; 27.4), עברה/חרון אף (wrath—13.9, 13), האזין/שמע קולי (listen—28.23; 32.9), שקט/נטה (quiet—30.15; 32.17), שאון/עלז (revelers—5.14; 24.28), ירש/שכן (dwell—34.11; 65.9), שוש/גיל (rejoice—35.2; 61.10; 65.18; 66.14), ששון/שמחה (joy—35.10; 22.13; 51.3), נקם/גמול (vengeance—35.4; 59.17-18), and שד/שבר (ruin—51.19; 60.18).

(2) Similar imagery which involves, almost of necessity, some verbal correspondence, such as agricultural/vegetative: the vineyard (5.1-6; 27.2-5; 32.12-14); harvest (17.6; 24.13), righteousness described as a plant springing up (45.8; 61.11); a fading leaf (1.30; 34.4; 64.5); physical infirmities—blindness, deafness, dumbness, lameness (6.9; 29.9-10, 18; 30.10-11; 32.3-4; 33.23; 35.5-6; 42.7, 18-20; 43.8; 44.18; 59.10); the highway (11.16; 19.23; 35.8; 40.3; 42.16; 43.19; 49.11; 57.14; 58.11; 62.10); the banner (5.26; 11.10-12; 13.2; 18.3; 36.17; 49.11; 57.14; 58.11; 62.10); birth and child care (26.18; 49.20-23; 60.16; 66.7-9, 11); pottery making (29.16; 45.9; 64.8); idol building (40.19-20; 41.6-7; 44.9-14; 45.20; 46.6-7); and the revivification of the desert (35.6-7; 41.18; 43.19-20; 48.21; 49.10).[1]

---

1. Several of of these images have been studied in greater detail. See, for example, R.E. Clements, 'Patterns in the Prophetic Canon: Healing the Blind and the Lame', in G.M. Tucker, D.L. Petersen and R.R. Wilson (eds.), *Canon, Theology, and Old Testament Interpretation* (Philadelphia: Fortress Press, 1988), pp. 189-200, and J.L. McLaughlin, 'Their Hearts *Were* Hardened: The Use of Isaiah 6, 9-10 in the Book of Isaiah', *Bib* 75 (1994), pp. i-25; also Kiesow, *Exodustexte im Jesajabuch*; and H.M. Barstad, *A Way in the Wilderness: The 'Second Exodus' in the Message of Second Isaiah* (JSSM, 12, Manchester: The Victoria University of Manchester, 1989). Other

Also deemed less significant were verbal parallels involving physical gestures, such as hiding one's face (54.8; 59.2), in which similarities in grammatical structure are more dominant than verbal correspondence, such as 2.3. כי מציון תצא תורה ודבר־יהוה מירושלם, 'The law will go out from Zion, the word of the LORD from Jerusalem' // 37.32. כי מירושלם תצא שארית ופליטה מהר ציון, 'For out of Jerusalem will come a remnant, and out of Mt Zion a band of survivors', compare 51.4 תורה מאתי תצא, 'the law will go out from me'; in which the correspondence consists solely of a two-member construct chain, such as כבוד הלבנון, 'the glory of Lebanon' (35.2; 60.13); and expressions which, although strikingly similar in wording and rarely found in the Old Testament, were not necessarily uncommon in contemporary Hebrew usage and are found in rather unrelated contexts, such as, אחת מהנה לא נעדרה 'none of these will be missing' (34.16)// איש לא נעדר (40.26).

Finally, all but the following 50 passages were eliminated:[2]

1.	2.9, 11, 17	//	5.15	23.	45.23	//	55.11
2.	2.20	//	31.7	24.	46.13	//	51.5
3.	4.6	//	25.4	25	48.22	//	57.21
4.	5.30	//	8.22	26.	49.2	//	51.16
5.	8.15	//	28.13	27.	49.18, 22-23	//	60.4
6.	10.23	//	28.22	28.	49.26	//	60.16
7.	11.6-9	//	65.25	29.	50.2	//	59.1
8.	11.12	//	56.8	30.	51.5	//	60.9
9.	13.21-22	//	34.13-14	31.	51.9	//	52.1
10.	14.27	//	43.13	32.	51.16	//	59.21
11.	24.4	//	33.9	33.	52.12	//	58.8
12.	25.12	//	26.5	34.	53.6	//	56.11
13.	29.17	//	32.15	35.	55.3	//	61.8
14.	35.10	//	51.11	36.	55.5	//	60.9
15.	40.10	//	62.11	37.	55.13	//	56.5
16.	40.21	//	48.8	38.	57.14	//	62.10 (40.3)
17.	40.25	//	46.5	39.	58.12	//	61.4
18.	41.8-10	//	44.1-2	40.	59.16	//	63.5
19.	41.19	//	60.13	41.	60.21	//	61.3
20.	42.6-7	//	49.8-9	42.	61.9	//	65.23
21.	43.18-19	//	65.17	43.	65.12	//	66.4
22.	44.23	//	49.13//52.9	44.	5.25; //9.11, 16, 20; //10.4		

---

repeated images include the boats of Tarshish: 2.16; 23.1; the beautiful crown: 28.5; 62.3; the messenger on the mountain: 40.9; 52.7; and moaning like a dove: 38.14; 59.11.

    2.   It is being asserted here that these verbal parallels are the least likely to be coincidental and the most easily recognized by the reader. However, it is not being claimed that these are the only identifiable verbal parallels within Isaiah. All parallels are based on the Hebrew text alone. For an example of a verbal parallel within an English translation which does not have a correspondence in Hebrew, compare 40.31 with 57.10 and the words 'renew strength' and 'faint'. This problem already was noted by F.W. Farrar, *History of Interpretation* (Brampton Lectures, 1885; London: Macmillan, 1886), pp. 469-70 n. 5.

45.	18.2	//	18.7	48.	8.11; //18.4; //21.16; //31.4
46.	45.5, 6, 14, 18, 21, 22; //46.9			49.	9.6	//	37.32
47.	1.20; //40.5; //58.14			50.	21.20	//	28.22

Of these, 44-46 represent refrains, while 47-50 probably are formulae.

In studying the content, form and distribution of these verbal parallels, several interesting observations can be made. Of the 50 passages, 18 are promissory in content, while only 10 convey judgment. This may be due to the fact that many of the verbal parallels are drawn from chs. 40–66. Fourteen passages express assurance or authority, describing the unique actions or attributes of God or his relationship to his servant. Four passages basically are accusatory (Isa. 56.11 is part of an indictment, while 53.6, its parallel, is part of a corporate confession), two form an appeal or call to action, and one contains liturgical praise.[3] Very few of the verbal parallels are primarily descriptive in content, though one must note the description of the foreign nation in 45, as well as the positive and negative portrayal of animal behavior in 7 and 9, respectively. For the most part, then, these verbal parallels do not involve simply attractive formulations which are repeated to enhance style; they are promises, threats and assurances which are repeated for emphasis or reapplied either to situations or to individuals or groups deemed analogous.

In these verbal parallels, various types of revision are evident. In some of the parallels, one formulation is considerably more developed and the other succinct (3 7), one seems to combine several expressions from another (1), or one reflects, in its context, a very different mood from the other (28, 31, 34), in addition to numerous modifications in word order, grammar, and vocabulary. In some passages the poetic parallelism is retained (15, 40), while in others the order is reversed (38), the key phrases of two lines are combined in one line (3), or only one line of the couplet is shared (35).

A final interesting observation concerns the distribution of verbal parallels within the book of Isaiah. Of the 50 passages selected, 15 are contained within Isaiah 1–39, 30 within 40–66, and only five involve both 1–39 and 40–66. Nearly half (14) of the parallels in 40–66 'link' 'Second' and 'Third' Isaiah. Five of the parallels are found in adjoining chapters. Forty-seven chapters of Isaiah contain a verse which is paralleled elsewhere within the book.

3.	Promise:	3, 7, 8, 13-15, 19, 21, 24, 27, 30, 33, 35-37, 39, 41-42
	Judgment:	1-2, 4-6, 9, 11-12, 25, 44
	Assurance, Authority:	10, 18, 20, 23, 26, 28-29, 32, 40, 46-50
	Accusation:	16-17, 34, 43
	Appeal:	31, 38
	Praise:	22
	Description:	45

BIBLIOGRAPHY

Achtemeier, E., *The Community and Message of Isaiah 56–66: A Theological Commentary* (Minneapolis: Augsburg, 1982).

Ackroyd, P.R., *Continuity: A Contribution to the Study of the Old Testament Religious Tradition* (Oxford: Basil Blackwell, 1962).

—'Continuity and Discontinuity: Rehabilitation—Authentication', in D.A. Knight (ed.), *Tradition and Theology in the Old Testament* (Philadelphia: Fortress Press, 1977), pp. 215-34.

—'Criteria for the Maccabaean Dating of Old Testament Literature', *VT* 3 (1953), pp. 113-32.

—'Hosea and Jacob', *VT* 13 (1963), pp. 245-59.

—'An Interpretation of the Babylonian Exile: A Study of 2 Kings 20, Isaiah 38-39', *SJT* 27 (1974), pp. 329-52.

—'Isaiah I–XII: Presentation of a Prophet', in W. Zimmerli *et al.* (eds.), *Congress Volume: Göttingen 1977* (VTSup, 29; Leiden: E.J. Brill, 1978), pp. 16-48.

—'Isaiah 36–39: Structure and Function', in W.C. Delsman *et al.* (eds.), *Von Kanaan bis Kerala: Festschrift für Prof. Mag. Dr. Dr. J.P.M. van der Ploeg O.P. Zur Vollendung des siebzigsten Lebensjahres am 4. Juli 1979* (AOAT, 211; Neukirchen–Vluyn: Neukirchener Verlag, 1982), pp. 3-21.

—'A Note on Isaiah 2.1', *ZAW* 75 (1963), pp. 320-21.

—'The Vitality of the Word of God in the Old Testament: A Contribution to the Study of the Transmission of Old Testament Material', *ASTI* 1 (1962), pp. 7-23.

Ahlström, G.W., *Joel and the Temple Cult of Jerusalem* (VTSup, 21; Leiden: E.J. Brill, 1971).

Albani, M. *et al.* (eds.), *Studies in the Book of Jubilees* (TSAJ, 65; Tübingen: Mohr Siebeck, 1997).

Albertz, R., 'Das Deuterojesaja-Buch als Fortschreibung der Jesaja-Prophetie', in E. Blum *et al.* (eds.), *Die hebräische Bibel und ihre zweifache Nachgeschichte* (Festschrift Rolf Rendtorff; Neukirchen–Vluyn: Neukirchener Verlag, 1990), pp. 241-56.

Alexander, J.A., *Commentary on the Prophecies of Isaiah* (Grand Rapids: Zondervan, 1953, reprint of 1875 revised edition).

Allen, L.C., *The Books of Joel, Obadiah, Jonah and Micah* (NICOT; Grand Rapids: Eerdmans, 1976).

—'Isaiah liii.11 and its Echoes', *Vox Evangelica* 1 (1962), pp. 24-28.

Alster, B., *The Instructions of Suruppak: A Sumerian Proverb Collection* (Copenhagen: Akademisk Forlag, 1974–75).

Alt, A., 'Jesaja 8, 23–9, 6: Befreiungsnacht und Krönungstag', in *idem, Kleine Schriften zur Geschichte des Volkes Israel* (3 vols.; Munich: C.H. Beck, 1953), II, pp. 206-25.

—'Zwei Vermutungen zur Geschichte des Sinuhe', *ZÄS* 58 (1923), pp. 48-50.

Altick, R.D., and J.J. Fenstermaker, *The Art of Literary Research* (New York: W.W. Norton, 4th edn, 1993).

Anderson, B.W., 'Exodus Typology in Second Isaiah', in B.W. Anderson and W. Harrelson (eds.), *Israel's Prophetic Heritage: Essays in Honor of James Muilenburg* (New York: Harper & Row, 1962), pp. 177-95.

Anderson, G.W., 'Isaiah XXIV–XXVII reconsidered', in *Congress Volume: Bonn 1962* (VTSup, 9; Leiden: E.J. Brill, 1963), pp. 118-26.

Anstensen, A., *The Proverb in Ibsen: Proverbial Sayings and Citations as Elements in his Style* (New York: Columbia University Press, 1936).

Archer, G., *A Survey of Old Testament Introduction* (Chicago: Moody Press, 1975).

Auerbach, E., 'Die grosse Überarbeitung der biblischen Bücher', in G.W. Anderson *et al.* (eds.), *Congress Volume: Copenhagen 1953* (VTSup, 1; Leiden: E.J. Brill, 1953), pp. 1-10.

Auld, A.G., 'Poetry, Prophecy, Permeneutic: Recent Studies in Isaiah', *SJT* 33 (1980), pp. 567-81.

Axelson, B., 'Lygdamus und Ovid: Zur Methodik der literarischen Prioritätsbestimmung', *Eranos* 58 (1960), pp. 92-111.

Bakhtin, M.M., *The Dialogic Imagination: Four Essays by M.M. Bakhtin* (ed. M. Holquist; trans. C. Emerson and M. Holquist; Austin: University of Texas Press, 1981).

Baltzer, D., *Ezechiel und Deuterojesaja: Berührungen in der Heilserwartung der beiden grossen Exilspropheten* (BZAW, 121; Berlin: W. de Gruyter, 1971).

Banwell, B.O., 'A Suggested Analysis of Isaiah XL–LXVI', *ExpTim* 76 (1964–65), p. 166.

Barns, J.W.B., *Five Ramesseum Papyri* (Oxford: Oxford University Press, 1956).

Bardtke, H., 'Jeremia der Fremdvölkerprophet. 2.', *ZAW* 35 (1936), pp. 240-62.

Barstad, H.M., 'Lebte Deuterojesaja in Judäa?', *Norsk Teologisk Tidssgrift* 83 (1982), pp. 77-87.

—'On the So-Called Babylonian Influence in Second Isaiah', *Scandinavian Journal of Theology* 2 (1987), pp. 90-110.

—*A Way in the Wilderness: The 'Second Exodus' in the Message of Second Isaiah* (JSS, 12; Manchester: The Victoria University of Manchester, 1989).

Barta, W., 'Das Schulbuch Kemit', *ZÄS* 105 (1978), pp. 6-14.

Barth, H., *Die Jesaja-Worte in der Josiazeit* (WMANT, 48; Neukirchen–Vluyn: Neukirchener Verlag, 1977).

Barthes, R., 'The Death of the Author', in *idem, Image, Music, Text* (trans. S. Heath; New York: Hill & Wang, 1977), pp. 142-48.

Bartlett, J.R., 'The Moabites and Edomites', in D.J. Wiseman (ed.), *Peoples of Old Testament Times* (Oxford: Clarendon Press, 1973), pp. 229-58.

Barton, J., *Amos's Oracles against the Nations* (Cambridge: Cambridge University Press, 1980).

Bate, W.J., *The Burden of the Past of the English Poet* (Cambridge, MA: Belknap Press, 1970).

Baumgarten, J., and M. Mansoor, 'Studies in the New *Hodayot* (Thanksgiving Hymns)', *JBL* 74 (1955), pp. 115-24, 188-95; 75 (1956), pp. 107-13.

Baumgartner, W., 'Die literarischen Gattungen in der Weisheit des Jesus Sirach', *ZAW* 34 (1914), pp. 161-98.

Beal, T.K., 'Glossary' and 'Ideology and Intertexuality: Surplus of Meaning and Controlling the Means of Production', in Fewell (ed.), *Reading between Texts*, pp. 21-24, 27-39.

Beaugrande, R. de, *Critical Discourse: A Survey of Literary Theorists* (Norwood, NJ: Ablex, 1988).

Beentjes, P.C., 'Inverted Quotations in the Bible: A Neglected Stylistic Pattern', *Bib* 63 (1982), pp. 506-23.

Begrich, J., *Studien zu Deuterojesaja* (TBü, 20; Munich: Chr. Kaiser Verlag, 1963).

Behr, J.W., *The Writings of Deutero-Isaiah and the Neo-Babylonian Royal Inscriptions: A Comparison of the Language and Style* (Pretoria: University of Pretoria, 1937).

Behrens, E., *Assyrisch-Babylonische Briefe kultischen Inhalts aus der Sargonidenzeit* (LSS, 2/1; Leipzig: J.C. Hinrichs, 1906).

Bendavid, A., *Parallels in the Bible* (Jerusalem: Carta, 1972).

Ben-Porat, Z., 'The Poetics of Allusion—a Text Linking Device—in Different Media of Communication (Literature versus Advertising and Journalism)', in S. Chatman, U. Eco and J.-M. Klinkenberg (eds.), *A Semiotic Landscape: Proceedings of the First Congress of the International Association for Semiotic Studies: Milan, June 1974* (Approaches to Semiotics, 29; The Hague: Mouton, 1979), pp. 588-93.

—'The Poetics of Literary Allusion', *PTL: A Journal for Descriptive Poetics and Theory of Literature* 1 (1976), pp. 105-28.

Bentzen, A., *Introduction to the Old Testament* (2 vols.; Copenhagen: G.E.C. Gad, 4th edn, 1958).

Berg, H.K., *Ein Wort wie Feuer: Wege lebendiger Bibelauslegung* (Munich: Kösel; Stuttgart: Calwer Verlag, 1991).

Bergler, S., *Joel als Schriftinterpret* (Beiträge zur Erforschung des Alten Testaments und des antiken Judentums, 16; Main: Peter Lang, 1988).

Berridge, J.M., 'Jeremia und die Prophetie des Amos', *TZ* 35 (1979), pp. 321-41.

Betz, O., *Offenbarung und Schriftforschung in der Qumrantexte* (WUNT, 6; Tübingen: J.C.B. Mohr [Paul Siebeck], 1960).

Beuken, W.A.M., 'Does Trito-Isaiah Reject the Temple? An Intertextual Inquiry into Isa. 66.1-6', in S. Draisma (ed.), *Intertextuality in Biblical Writings: Essays in Honor of Bas van Iersel* (Kampen: Kok, 1989), pp. 53-66.

—'Isaiah lxv–lxvi: Trito-Isaiah and the Closure of the Book of Isaiah', in J.A. Emerton (ed.), *Congress Volume: Leuven 1989* (VTSup, 43; Leiden: E.J. Brill, 1991), pp. 204-21.

—'Isa. 56.9–57.13: An Example of the Isaianic Legacy of Trito-Isaiah', in J.W. Henten *et al.* (eds.), *Tradition and Re-Interpretation in Jewish and Early Christian Literature. Essays in Honour of Jürgen C.H. Lebram* (Leiden: E.J. Brill, 1986), pp. 48-64.

—*Jesaja* (De Prediking van het Oude Testament; Vols. 3A, 3B; Nijkerk: G.F. Callenbach, 1989).

—'Jesaja 33 als Spiegeltext im Jesajabuch', *ETL* 67 (1991), pp. 5-35.

Beyerlin, W., *Die Kulttradition in der Verkündigung des Propheten Micha* (FRLANT, 72; Göttingen: Vandenhoeck & Ruprecht, 1959).

Bič, M., *Das Buch Joel* (Berlin: Evangelische Verlagsanstalt, 1960).

Birkeland, H., *Zum hebräischen Traditionswesen: Die Komposition der prophetischen Bücher des alten Testaments* (Oslo: Jacob Dybwad, 1938).

Bjørndalen, A.J., *Untersuchungen zur allegorischen Rede der Propheten Amos und Jesaja* (BZAW, 165; Berlin: W. de Gruyter, 1986).

Blank, S.H., 'Irony by Way of Attribution', *Semitics* 1 (1970), pp. 1-6.

—*Prophetic Faith in Isaiah* (New York: Harper & Brothers, 1958).

Blenkinsopp, J., *Prophecy and Canon: A Contribution to the Study of Jewish Origins* (Notre Dame: University of Notre Dame Press, 1977).

Bloch, R., 'Ecriture et tradition dans le judaïsme: Aperçus sur l'origine du midrash', *Cahiers Sioniens* 8 (1954), pp. 9-34.

—'Ezéchiel XVI: Exemple parfait du procédé midrashique dans la Bible', *Cahiers Sioniens* 9 (1955), pp. 193-223.

—'Midrash', *DBSup*, V, cols. 1263-81.

—'Note methodologique pour l'étude de la littérature rabbinique', *RSR* 43 (1955), pp. 194-227.

Bloom, H., *The Anxiety of Influence: A Theory of Poetry* (New York: Oxford University Press, 1973).

—*Figures of Capable Imagination* (New York: Seabury, 1976).

—*A Map of Misreading* (New York: Oxford University Press, 1975).

Blumenthal, E., 'Ägyptologie und Textkritik', *OLZ* 78 (1983), pp. 229-39.

Boadt, L., *Jeremiah 26–52, Habakkuk, Zephaniah, Nahum* (OT Message, 10; Wilmington, DE: Michael Glazier, 1982).

Boelter, F., 'From the Old Testament: An Isaiah Apocalypse?', *Explor* 4 (1978), pp. 75-78.

Bogaert, P.-M., 'Le personnage de Baruch et l'histoire du livre de Jérémie', in E.A. Livingstone (ed.), *Studia Evangelica. VII. Papers Presented to the Fifth International Congress on Biblical Studies Held at Oxford, 1973* (TUGAL, 126; Berlin: Akademie Verlag, 1982), pp. 73-81.

Boller, P.F., Jr, *Quotemanship: The Use and Abuse of Quotations for Polemical and Other Purposes* (Dallas: Southern Methodist University Press, 1967).

Bonnard, P.-E., *Le second Isaïe: Son disciple et leurs éditeurs: Isaïe 40-66* (Etudes Bibliques; Paris: J. Gabalda, 1972).

Bonsirven, J., *Exégèse rabbinique et exégèse paulinienne* (Bibliothèque de Théologie historique; Paris: Beauchesne, 1938).

Borger, R., 'Marduk-zākir-šumi I und der Kodex Ḫammurapi', *Or* NS 34 (1965), pp. 168-69.

Bosshard, E., 'Beobachtungen zum Zwölfprophetenbuch', *BN* 40 (1987), pp. 30-62.

Boyd, J.O., 'Ezekiel and the Modern Dating of the Pentateuch', *PTR* 6 (1908), pp. 29-51.

Bradley, D.G., 'The Topos as a Form in the Pauline Paraenesis', *JBL* 72 (1953), pp. 238-46.

Brewer, D.A., *Techniques and Assumptions in Jewish Exegesis before 70 CE* (TSAJ, 30; Tübingen: Mohr Siebeck, 1992).

Bright, J., *A History of Israel* (Philadelphia: Westminster Press, 2nd edn, 1976).

Brin, G., 'Concerning Some of the Uses of the Bible in the Temple Scroll', *RevQ* 12 (1987), pp. 519-28.

Brodie, L.T., 'Jacob's Travail (Jer 30:1-13) and Jacob's Struggle (Gen 32:22-32): A Test Case for Measuring the Influence of the Book of Jeremiah on the Present Text of Genesis', *JSOT* 15 (1981), pp. 31-60.

Brooke, J.G., *Exegesis at Qumran: 4Q Florilegium in its Jewish Context* (JSOTSup, 29; Sheffield: JSOT Press, 1985).

—*Exegesis at Qumran: 4QFlorilegium in its Jewish Context* (JSOTSup, 29; JSOT Press, 1985).

Brower, R., *Alexander Pope: The Poetry of Allusion* (Oxford: Clarendon Press, 1959).

—*Mirror on Mirror: Translation. Imitation. Parody* (Cambridge, MA: Harvard University Press, 1974).

Brownlee, W.H., *The Meaning of the Qumrân Scrolls for the Bible* (New York: Oxford University Press, 1964).

Bruce, F.F., *Biblical Exegesis in the Qumran Texts* (Grand Rapids: Eerdmans, 1954).

—'The Earliest Old Testament Interpretation', *OTS* 17 (1972), pp. 37-52.

Brueggemann, W., *A Commentary on Jeremiah: Exile and Homecoming* (Grand Rapids: Eerdmans, 1998).

—'Unity and Dynamics in the Isaiah Tradition', *JSOT* 29 (1984), pp. 89-107.

—' "Vine and Fig Tree": A Case Study in Imagination and Criticism', *CBQ* 43 (1981), pp. 188-204.

Brunner, H., 'Eine neue Entlehnung aus der Lehre des Djedefhor', *MDAIK* 14 (1956), pp. 17-19.

—'Ein weiteres Djedefhor-Zitat', *MDAIK* 19 (1963), p. 53.

—'Zitate', in W. Helck and W. Westendorf (eds.), *Lexikon der Ägyptologie* (7 vols.; Wiesbaden: Otto Harrassowitz, 1986), VI, cols. 1415-20.

—'Zitate aus Lebenslehren', in E. Hornung and O. Keel (eds.), *Studien zu altägyptischen Lebenslehren* (Göttingen: Vandenhoeck & Ruprecht, 1979), pp. 105-71.

Buber, M., 'Falsche Propheten', *Die Wandlung* 2 (1947), pp. 277-81.

Buchanan, G.W., *Introduction to Intertextuality* (Mellen Biblical Press Series, 26; Lewiston, NY: Edwin Mellen Press, 1994)

Büchmann, G., *Geflügte Worte: Der Citatenschatz des deutschen Volkes* (Berlin: Hande & Spenersche [Max Pasche], 1925).

Burkard, G., *Textkritische Untersuchungen zu ägyptischen Weisheitslehren des Alten und Mittleren Reiches* (Ägyptologische Abhandlungen, 34; Wiesbaden: Otto Harrassowitz, 1977).

Burrows, M., *The Literary Relations of Ezekiel* (Philadelphia: Jewish Publication Society of America, 1925).

Caird, G.B., 'Ben Sira and the Dating of the Septuagint', in E.A. Livingstone (ed.), *Studia Evangelica, Volume VII: Papers Presented to the Fifth International Congress on Biblical Studies Held at Oxford, 1973* (TUGAL, 126; Berlin: Akademie Verlag, 1982), pp. 95-100.

Cannewurf, E., 'The Authenticity of Micah IV 1-4', *VT* 13 (1963), pp. 26-33.

Cannon, W.W., 'The Integrity of Habakkuk 1-2', *ZAW* 43 (1925), pp. 62-90.

—'Isaiah 61.1-3 an Ebed-Jahweh Poem', *ZAW* 47 (1929), pp. 284-88.

—'Isaiah c. 57.14-21. cc. 60-62', *ZAW* 52 (1934), pp. 75-77.

Carmignac, J., 'Les citations de l'Ancien Testament dans "La Guerre des Fils de Lumière contre les Fils de Ténèbres" ', *RB* 63 (1956), pp. 234-60, 375-90.

—'Les citations de l'Ancien Testament, et spécialement des Poèmes du Serviteur, dans les Hymnes de Qumrân', *RevQ* 2 (1959–60), pp. 357-94.

—'Les rapports entre l'Ecclésiastique et Qumrân', *RevQ* 3 (1961–62), pp. 209-18.

—'Six passages d'Isaïe éclairés par Qumran', in S. Wagner (ed.), *Bibel und Qumran: Beiträge zur Erforschung der Beziehungen zwischen Bibel- und Qumranwissenschaft. Hans Bardtke zum 22.6.1966* (Berlin: Evangelische Haupt-Bibelgesellschaft zu Berlin, 1968), pp. 37-46.

Carmignac, J., and P. Guilbert (eds.), *Les textes de Qumran: Traduits et annotés* (Paris: Letouzey et Ané, 1961).

Carr, D., 'Reaching for Unity in Isaiah', *JSOT* 57 (1993), pp. 61-80.

Carroll, R.P., *The Book of Jeremiah: A Commentary* (OTL; Philadelphia: Westminster Press, 1986).

—'Night without Vision: Micah and the Prophets', in F. García Martínez, A. Hilhurst and C.J. Labuschagne (eds.), *The Scriptures and the Scrolls: Studies in Honour of A.S. van der Woude's 65th Birthday* (Leiden: E.J. Brill, 1992), pp. 74-84.

—'Prophecy and Dissonance: A Theoretical Approach to the Prophetic Tradition', *ZAW* NS 92 (1980), pp. 108-19.

—'Prophecy, Dissonance and Jeremiah XXVI', *Glasgow University Oriental Society Transactions* 25 (1973–74), pp. 12-23.

—*When Prophecy Failed: Cognitive Dissonance in the Prophetic Traditions of the Old Testament* (New York: Seabury, 1979).

Carson, D.A., and H.G.M. Williamson (eds.), *It Is Written: Scripture Citing Scripture. Essays in Honour of Barnabas Lindars* (Cambridge: Cambridge University Press, 1988).

Caspari, C.P., *Beiträge zur Einleitung in das Buch Jesaia und zur Geschichte der jesaianischen Zeit* (Berlin: L. Oehmigke's Verlag, 1848).

—'Jesajanische Studien. I. Jeremia ein Zeuge für die Aechtheit von Jes. c. 34 und mithin auch für die Aechtheit von Jes. c. 33, c. 40–66, c. 13–14, 23 und c. 21, 1-10', *Zeitschrift für die Gesamte Lutherische Theologie und Kirche* 4 (1843), pp. 1-73.

—'Jesajanische Studien. III. Über die Eingangsworte der ersten jesajanischen Weissagung und des ganzen Buches Jesaja', *Zeitschrift für die Gesamte Lutherische Theologie und Kirche* 6 (1845), pp. 76-106.

—*Über Micha den Morasthiten und seine prophetische Schrift: Ein monographischer Beitrag zur Geschichte des alttestamentlichen Schriftthums und zur Auslegung des Buches Micha* (Christiania: P.T. Malling, 1852).

Caspari, W., 'Jesaja 34 und 35', *ZAW* NS 8 (1931), pp. 67-86.

Cassuto, U., 'On the Formal and Stylistic Relationship between Deutero-Isaiah and Other Biblical Writers', in *idem, Biblical and Oriental Studies. I. Bible* (trans. I. Abrahams; repr.; Jerusalem: Magnes Press, 1973), pp. 141-77, originally published in *Rivista Israelitica* 8–10 (1911–13).

—'The Sequence and Arrangement of the Biblical Sections', *Biblical and Oriental Studies. I. Bible* (trans. I. Abrahams; repr.; Jerusalem: Magnes Press, 1973), pp. 1-6.

Cazelles, H., 'Qui aurait visé, à l'origine, Isaïe II 2-5?', *VT* 30 (1980), pp. 409-20.

Cheon, S., *Exodus in the Wisdom of Solomon: A Study in Biblical Interpretation* (JSPSSup, 23; Sheffield: Sheffield Academic Press, 1997).

Chester, A., 'Citing the Old Testament', in D.A. Carson and H.G.M. Williamson (eds.), *It Is Written: Scripture Citing Scripture. Essays in Honour of Barnabas Lindars* (Cambridge: Cambridge University Press, 1988), pp. 141-69.

Cheyne, T.K., *Introduction to the Book of Isaiah* (London: A. & C. Black, 1895).

—*The Prophecies of Isaiah: A New Translation with Commentary and Appendices* (2 vols.; New York: Thomas Whittaker, 5th edn, 1890).

Childs, B.S., 'The Canonical Shape of the Prophetic Literature', *Int* 32 (1978), pp. 46-55.

—'The Enemy from the North and the Chaos Tradition', *JBL* 78 (1959), pp. 187-98.

—'The Exegetical Significance of Canon for the Study of the Old Testament', in W. Zimmerli (ed.), *Congress Volume: Göttingen 1977* (VTSup, 29; Leiden: E.J. Brill, 1977), pp. 66-80.

—*Introduction to the Old Testament as Scripture* (Philadelphia: Fortress Press, 1979).

—*Isaiah and the Assyrian Crisis* (SBT, 2/3; Naperville, IL: Allenson, 1967).

—'Midrash and the Old Testament', in J. Reumann (ed.), *Understanding the Sacred Text: Essays in Honor of Morton S. Enslin* (Valley Forge, PA: Judson Press, 1972), pp. 47-59.

—*Myth and Reality in Ancient Israel* (London: SCM Press, 1960).

—'Psalm Titles and Midrashic Exegesis', *JSS* 16 (1971), pp. 137-50.

Christensen, D.L., *Transformations of the War Oracle in Old Testament Prophecy: Studies in the Oracles against the Nations* (HDR, 3; Missoula, MT: Scholars Press, 1975).

Clark, D.J., *A Translator's Handbook on the Books of Obadiah and Micah* (New York: United Bible Societies, 1982).

Clements, R.E., 'Beyond Tradition-Criticism: Deutero-Isaianic Development of First Isaiah's Themes', *JSOT* 31 (1985), pp. 95-113.

—*Isaiah 1–39* (NCB; Grand Rapids: Eerdmans, 1980).

—'Patterns in the Prophetic Canon', in G.W. Coats and B.O. Long (eds.), *Canon and Authority: Essays in Old Testament Religion and Theology* (Philadelphia: Fortress Press, 1977), pp. 42-55.

—*Prophecy and Tradition* (Atlanta: John Knox Press, 1978).

—'The Ezekiel Tradition: Prophecy in a Time of Crisis', in R. Coggins, A. Phillips, and M. Knibb (eds.), *Israel's Prophetic Tradition: Essays in Honour of Peter R. Ackroyd* (Cambridge: Cambridge University Press, 1982), pp. 119-36.

—'The Unity of the Book of Isaiah', *Int* 36 (1982), pp. 117-29.

Clifford, R.J., 'The Unity of the Book of Isaiah and its Cosmogonic Language', *CBQ* 55 (1993), pp. 1-17.

Cobb, W.H., 'The Integrity of the Book of Isaiah', *BSac* 39 (1882), pp. 519-54.

—'The Language of Isaiah XL–LXVI', *BSac* 38 (1881), pp. 658-86; 39 (1882), pp. 104-32.

—'Two Isaiahs, or one?', *BSac* 38 (1881), pp. 230-53.

Coggins, R., 'An Alternative Prophetic Tradition?', in R. Coggins, A. Phillips and M. Knibb (eds.), *Israel's Prophetic Tradition: Essays in Honour of Peter R. Ackroyd* (Cambridge: Cambridge University Press, 1982), pp. 77-94.

Collins, T., *The Mantle of Elijah: The Redaction Criticism of the Prophetical Books* (Sheffield: JSOT Press, 1993).

Compagnon, A., *La seconde main: Ou le travail de la citation* (Paris: Editions du Seuil, 1979).

Conrad, E.W., *Reading Isaiah* (Philadelphia: Fortress Press, 1991).

—'The Royal Narratives and the Structure of the Book of Isaiah', *JSOT* 41 (1988), pp. 67-81.

Cooper, J., 'Symmetry and Repetition in Akkadian Narrative', *JAOS* 97 (1977), pp. 508-12.

Craghan, J.F., 'Mari and its Prophets: The Contributions of Mari to the Understanding of Biblical Prophets', *BTB* 5 (1975), pp. 32-55.

Craig, H., 'Shakespeare and Wilson's *Art of Rhetorique*: An Inquiry into the Criteria for Determining Sources', in S.P. Zitner (ed.), *The Practice of Modern Literary Scholarship* (repr.; Glenview, IL: Scott, Foresman & Co., 1966), pp. 103-12.

Crenshaw, J.L., *Prophetic Conflict: Its Effect upon Israelite Religion* (BZAW, 124; Berlin: W. de Gruyter, 1971).

Crook, M.B., 'Did Amos and Micah Know Isaiah 9.2-7 and 11.1-9?', *JBL* 73 (1954), pp. 144-51.

—'A Suggested Occasion for Isaiah 9, 2-7 and 11, 1-9', *JBL* 68 (1949), pp. 213-24.

Culler, J., *Structuralist Poetics* (Ithaca, NY: Cornell University Press, 1975).

Culpepper, R.A., *Anatomy of the Fourth Gospel: A Study in Literary Design* (Philadelphia: Fortress Press, 1983).

Dahl, N.A., 'Widersprüche in der Bibel: Ein altes hermeneutisches Problem', *ST* 25 (1971), pp. 1-19.

Damrosch, D.N., 'Scripture and Fiction: Egypt, the Midrash, and Finnegan's Wake' (PhD dissertation, Yale University, 1980).

Davies, E.W., *Prophecy and Ethics: Isaiah and the Ethical Traditions of Israel* (JSOTSup, 16; Sheffield: JSOT Press, 1981).

Davies, W.D., 'Reflections about the Use of the Old Testament in the New in its Historical Context', *JQR* 74 (1983), pp. 105-36.

Day, J., 'A Case of Inner Scriptural Interpretation: The Dependence of Isaiah XXVI.13–XXVII.11 on Hosea XIII.4–XIV.10 (Eng. 9) and its Relevance to Some Theories of the Redaction of the "Isaiah Apocalypse" ', *JTS* NS 31 (1980), pp. 309-19.

—'Da'at "Humiliation" in Isaiah LIII 11 in the Light of Is 53 3 and Dan. 12 4 and the Oldest Known Interpretation of the Suffering Servant', *VT* 30 (1980), pp. 97-101.

—'Prophecy', in D.A. Carson and H.G.M. Williamson (eds.), *It Is Written: Scripture Citing Scripture. Essays in Honour of Barnabas Lindars* (Cambridge: Cambridge University Press, 1988), pp. 39-55.

Deist, F.E., 'Notes on the Structure of Isa. 2:2-22', *Theologia Evangelica* 10 (1977), pp. 1-6.

Delcor, M., 'Les sources du Deutéro-Zacharia et ses procédés d'emprunt', *RB* 59 (1952), pp. 385-411.

Delitzsch, F., *The Prophecies of Isaiah* (trans. J. Martin; 2 vols.; repr.; Grand Rapids: Eerdmans, 3rd edn, 1976 [1877]).

Derchain, P., 'Allusion, citation, intertextualité', in M. Minas and J. Zeidler (eds.), *Aspekte spätägyptischer Kultur: Festschrift für Erich Winter zum 65. Geburtstag* (Mainz: Philipp von Zabern, 1994), pp. 69-76.

Dhorme, E., Review of *Problèmes du livre d'Habacuc* (Neuchâtel: Secrétariat de l'Université, 1944), by P. Humbert, in *RHR* 131 (1946), pp. 176-82.

Diedrich, F., *Die Anspielungen auf die Jakob-Tradition in Hosea 12, 1-13: Ein literaturwissenschaftlicher Beitrag zur Exegese früher Prophetentexte* (FzB, 27; Würzburg: Echter Verlag, 1977).

Dietrich, W., *Jesaja und die Politik* (BEvT, 74; Munich: Chr. Kaiser Verlag, 1976).

Dodd, C.H., *According to the Scriptures* (London: Lowe & Brydone, 1952).

Donner, H., *Israel unter den Völkern: Die Stellung der klassischen Propheten des 8. Jahrhunderts vor Christi zur Aussenpolitik der Könige von Israel und Juda* (VTSup, 11; Leiden: E.J. Brill, 1964).

Dozeman, T.B., 'Inner-Biblical Interpretation of Yahweh's Gracious and Compassionate Character', *JBL* 108 (1989), pp. 207-23.

Draisma, S. (ed.), *Intertextuality in Biblical Writings: Essays in Honor of Bas van Iersel* (Kampen: Kok, 1989).

Driver, G.R., 'Another Little Drink!—Isaiah 28:1-22', in P.R. Ackroyd and B. Lindars (eds.), *Words and Meanings: Essays Presented to David Winton Thomas* (Cambridge: Cambridge University Press, 1968), pp. 47-67.

—'Two Misunderstood Passages of the Old Testament', *JTS* NS 6 (1955), pp. 2-87.

Driver, S.R., *The Book of the Prophet Jeremiah* (New York: Charles Scribner's Sons, 1906).

—*The Books of Joel and Amos* (Cambridge: Cambridge University Press, 1915).

—*An Introduction to the Literature of the Old Testament* (New York: Charles Scribner's Sons, 6th edn, 1897).

Duhm, B., *Das Buch Jesaia: Übersetzt und erklärt* (HKAT, 3.1; Göttingen: Vandenhoeck & Ruprecht, 4th edn, 1922 [1892]).

Dumbrell, W.J., 'The Purpose of the Book of Isaiah', *TynBul* 36 (1985), pp. 111-28.

Dupont-Sommer, A., *Le livre des hymnes découvert près de la mer Morte (1QH)* (Semitica, 7; Paris: Librairie d'Amérique et d'Orient Adrien Maisonneuve, 1957).

Eakins, J.K., 'Ezekiel's Influence on the Exilic Isaiah' (ThD thesis, Southern Baptist Theological Seminary, 1971).

Eaton, J.H., *Festal Drama in Deutero-Isaiah* (London: SPCK, 1979).

—'The Isaiah Tradition', in R. Coggins, A. Phillips and M. Knibb (eds.), *Israel's Prophetic Tradition: Essays in Honour of Peter R. Ackroyd* (Cambridge: Cambridge University Press, 1982), pp. 58-76.

—'The Origin of the Book of Isaiah', *VT* 9 (1959), pp. 138-57.

Ebeling, E., 'Ein philosophisches Zwiegespräch in akkadischer Sprache', *Mitteilungen der vorderasiatischen Gesellschaft* 23.1 (1918), pp. 50-70.

—'Quellen zur Kenntnis der babylonischen Religion II', *Mitteilungen der vorderasiatischen Gesellschaft* 23.2 (1919), pp. 1-82.

Eberharter, A., *Der Kanon des Alten Testaments zur Zeit des Ben Sira: Auf Grund der Beziehungen des Sirachbuches zu den Schriften des Alten Testaments dargestellt* (Münster: Aschendorff, 1911).

Edgar, S.L., 'Respect for Context in Quotations from the Old Testament', *NTS* 9 (1963), pp. 55-62.

Eichhorn, J.G., *Einleitung in das Alte Testament* (5 vols.; Göttingen: Carl Eduard Rosenbusch, 4th edn, 1823–25).

—*Introduction to the Study of the Old Testament: A Fragment Translated by George Tilly Gollop* (London: Spottiswoode, 1888, from 3rd edn, 1803).

Eldridge, V.J., 'The Influence of Jeremiah on Isaiah 40–55' (ThD dissertation, Southern Baptist Theological Seminary, 1978).

Eliot, T.S., *The Complete Poems and Plays* (New York: Harcourt, Brace & Company, 1934).

Elliger, K., *Deuterojesaja in seinem Verhältnis zu Tritojesaja* (BWANT, 63; Stuttgart: W. Kohlhammer, 1933).

—*Die Einheit Tritojesajas* (BWANT, 45; Stuttgart: W. Kohlhammer, 1928).

—*Deuterojesaja 40, 1–45, 7* (BKAT, 11.1; Neukirchen–Vluyn: Neukirchener Verlag, 1978).

—*Studien zum Habakuk-Kommentar vom Toten Meer* (BHT, 15; Tübingen: J.C.B. Mohr [Paul Siebeck], 1953).

Ellis, E.E., *The Old Testament in Early Christianity: Canon and Interpretation in the Light of Modern Research* (WUNT, 54; Tübingen: J.C.B. Mohr [Paul Siebeck], 1991).

Emerson, R.W., *The Complete Works of Ralph Waldo Emerson. VIII. Letters and Social Aims* (12 vols.; New York: W.H. Wise & Company, 1920 [1875]).

Empson, W., *Seven Types of Ambiguity* (Edinburgh: T. & A. Constable Ltd., 1930).

Endres, C., and B.K. Gold, 'Joannes Secundus and his Roman Models: Shapes of Imitation in Renaissance Poetry', *Renaissance Quarterly* 35 (1982), pp. 577-89.

Engnell, I., 'Profetia och tradition: Några synpunkter på ett gammaltestamentligt central-problem', *SEÅ* 12 (1947), pp. 94-123.

—*A Rigid Scrutiny: Critical Essays on the Old Testament by Ivan Engnell* (trans. and ed. J.T. Willis; Nashville: Vanderbilt University Press, 1969).

Epstein, I. (ed.), *The Hebrew–English Edition of the Babylonian Talmud* (trans. M. Simon and I. Slotki; Hindhead, Surrey: Soncino, 1948).

Erlandsson, S., *The Burden of Babylon: A Study of Isaiah 13:2–14:23* (trans. G.J. Houser; ConBOT, 4; Lund: C.W.K. Gleerup, 1970).

Erman, A., *The Ancient Egyptians: A Sourcebook of their Writings* (trans. A.M. Blackman; New York: Harper & Row, 1966).

Eslinger, L.M., 'Hosea 12:5a and Genesis 32:29: A Study in Inner Biblical Exegesis', *JSOT* 18 (1980), pp. 91-99.

—'Inner-biblical Exegesis and Inner-biblical Allusion: The Question of Category', *VT* 42 (1992), pp. 47-58.

Evans, C.A., 'An Interpretation of Isa 8, 4-15 Unemended', *ZAW* 97 (1985), pp. 112-13.

—'On Isaiah's Use of Israel's Sacred Tradition', *BZ* 30 (1986), pp. 92-99.

—'The Unity and Parallel Structure of Isaiah', *VT* 38 (1988), pp. 129-47.

Evans, C.A., and J.A. Sanders (eds.), *The Function of Scripture in Early Jewish and Christian Tradition* (JSNTSup, 154; Sheffield: Sheffield Academic Press, 1998).

Ewald, H., *Die Propheten des Alten Bundes* (3 vols.; Göttingen: Vandenhoeck & Ruprecht, 1867–68; originally published as 2 vols. in 1840–41).

Exum, J.C., 'Isaiah 28-32: A Literary Approach', in P. Achtemeier (ed.), *SBL Seminar Papers: 1979* (2 vols.; Missoula, MT: Scholars Press, 1979), II, pp. 123-151.

—' "Whom Will He Teach Knowledge?": A Literary Approach to Isaiah 28', in D.J.A. Clines, D.M. Gunn and A.J. Hauser (eds.), *Art and Meaning: Rhetoric in Biblical Literature* (JSOTSup, 19; Sheffield: JSOT Press, 1982), pp. 108-39.

Eybers, I.H., 'Micah, the Morasthite: The Man and his Message', in A.H. van Zyl (ed.), *Old Testament Studies: Papers Read at the Eleventh Meeting Held at the University of Pretoria, January 1968* (OTWSA; Potchefstroom: Pro Rege, n.d.), pp. 9-24.

Eyre, C.J., 'The Semna Stelae: Quotation, Genre, and Functions of Literature', in S. Israelit-Groll (ed.), *Studies in Egyptology Presented to Miriam Lichtheim*, I (Jerusalem: Magnes Press, 1990), pp. 134-65.

Falkenstein, A., *Die Haupttypen der sumerischen Beschwörung literarisch untersucht* (LSS, NS 1; Leipzig: J.C. Hinrichs, 1931).

Farley, W.J., *The Progress of Old Testament Prophecy in the Light of Modern Scholarship* (New York: Fleming H. Revell, 1925).

Farrar, F.W., *History of Interpretation* (Bampton Lectures, 1885; London: Macmillan, 1886).

Faulkner, R.O., 'The Installation of the Vizier', *JEA* 41 (1955), pp. 18-29.

—*A Concise Dictionary of Middle Egyptian* (Oxford: Oxford University Press, 1962).

Fecht, G., 'Ägyptische Zweifel am Sinn des Opfers: Admonitions 5, 7-9', *ZÄS* 100 (1973), pp. 6-16.

—*Der Habgierige und die Maat in der Lehre des Ptahhotep (5. und 19. Maxime)* (ADAIK, 1; Glückstadt: Verlag J.J. Augustin, 1958).

Feldmann, F., *Das Buch Isaias übersetzt und erklärt* (HAT, 14; 2 vols.; Münster: Aschendorff, 1925–26).

Fewell, D.N. (ed.), *Reading between Texts: Intertextuality and the Hebrew Bible* (Louisville, KY: Westminster/John Knox Press, 1992).

Fey, R., *Amos und Jesaja: Abhängigkeit und Eigenständigkeit des Jesaja* (WMANT, 12; Neukirchen–Vluyn: Neukirchener Verlag, 1963).

Fishbane, M.A., *Biblical Interpretation in Ancient Israel* (Oxford: Clarendon Press, 1985).

—*The Garments of Torah: Essays in Biblical Hermeneutics* (Bloomington: Indiana University Press, 1989).

—'Revelation and Tradition: Aspects of Inner-Biblical Exegesis', *JBL* 99 (1980), pp. 343-61.

—'Torah and Tradition', in D.A. Knight (ed.), *Tradition and Theology in the Old Testament* (Philadelphia: Fortress Press, 1977), pp. 275-300.

Fitzmyer, J.A., 'The Use of Explicit Old Testament Quotations in Qumran Literature and in the New Testament', *NTS* 7 (1961), pp. 297-333.

Fohrer, G., *Das Buch Jesaja: Kapitel 1-23* (3 vols.; Zürcher Bibelkommentar, 1; Zürich: Zwingli-Verlag, 1960).

—*Das Buch Jesaja: Kapitel 40-66* (Zürcher Bibelkommentar, 3; Zürich: Zwingli-Verlag, 1964).

—*Die Hauptprobleme des Buches Ezechiel* (BZAW, 72; Berlin: Alfred Töpelmann, 1952).

—*Introduction to the Old Testament* (trans. D.E. Green; Nashville: Abingdon Press, 1968).

—'Jesaja 1 als Zusammenfassung der Verkündigung Jesajas', *ZAW* 74 (1962), pp. 251-68.

—*Studien zur alttestamentlichen Prophetie (1949-1965)* (BZAW, 99; Berlin: Alfred Töpelmann, 1967).

—'Vollmacht über Völker und Königreiche (Jer 46-51)', in *idem*, *Studien zu alttestamentlichen Texten und Themen (1966-72)* (BZAW, 155; Berlin: W. de Gruyter, 1981), pp. 44-52.

Fohrer, G., and E. Sellin, *Introduction to the Old Testament* (trans. D.E. Green; Nashville: Abingdon Press, 1968).

Fontaine, C.R., *Traditional Sayings in the Old Testament: A Contextual Study* (Bible & Literature, 5; Sheffield: Almond Press, 1982).

Foster, B.R., *Before the Muses: An Anthology of Akkadian Literature* (2 vols.; Bethesda, MD: CDL Press, 2nd edn, 1996).

Fowler, R.M., 'Who Is "the Reader" in Reader Response Criticism?', *Semeia* 31 (1985), pp. 5-23.

—'Who is "the Reader" of Mark's Gospel?', in K.H. Richards (ed.), *SBL Seminar Papers: 1983* (Chico, CA: Scholars Press, 1983), pp. 31-53.

Fox, M.V., 'The Identification of Quotations in Biblical Literature', *ZAW* 92 (1980), pp. 416-31.

—'A Study of Antef', *Or* 46 (1977), pp. 393-423.

—'Two Decades of Research in Egyptian Wisdom Literature', *ZÄS* 107 (1980), pp. 120-35.

France, R.T., and D. Wenham (eds.), *Studies in Midrash and Historiography* (Gospel Prespectives, 3; Sheffield: JSOT Press, 1983).

Freedman, D.N., 'The Law and the Prophets', in *Congress Volume: Bonn 1962* (VTSup, 9; Leiden: E.J. Brill, 1963), pp. 250-65.

Frey, H., *Handkommentar zum Buch Jesaja* (Bad Liebenzell: Verlag der Liebenzeller Mission, 1975).

Fuerst, W.J., 'Micah among the Prophets: A Study of Prophetic Disagreement', *The Bible Today* 20 (1982), pp. 20-25.

Fullerton, K., 'The Stone of the Foundation' *AJSL* 37 (1920), pp. 1-50.

Fyfe, W.H. (trans.), 'Longinus: On the Sublime', in G.P. Goold (ed.), *Aristotle: The Poetics, XXIII* (LCL, 199; Cambridge, MA: Harvard University Press, 1973).

Gallard, C., 'The Problem of Quotation of One Text in Another Text', in A.M. Johnson, Jr (ed. and trans.), *Structuralism and Biblical Hermeneutics: A Collection of Essays* (Pittsburgh: Pickwick Press, 1979), pp. 207-208.

Gammie, J.G., 'On the Intention and Sources of Daniel 1-6', *VT* 31 (1981), pp. 282-92.

Gardiner, A.H., 'The Earliest Manuscripts of the Instruction of Amenemmes I', in *Mélanges Maspero*. I. *Orient Ancien* (3 vols.; Cairo: Imprimerie de l'institut français d'archéologie orientale, 1935–38), pp. 478-96.

—'The Eloquent Peasant', *JEA* 9 (1923), pp. 5-25.

—*Notes on the Story of Sinuhe* (Paris: Librairie Honoré Champion, 1916).

—'The Tomb of Amenemhet, High Priest of Amon', *ZÄS* 47 (1910), pp. 87-99.

Gaster, T.H., *The Dead Sea Scriptures in English Translation* (Garden City, NY: Doubleday, 1964).

Gayley, C.M., and F.N. Scott, *An Introduction to the Methods and Materials of Literary Criticism: The Bases in Aesthetics and Poetics* (Boston: Ginn & Co, 1899).

Gelin, A., 'La question des "relectures" bibliques a l'intérieur d'une tradition vivante', in J. Coppens, A. Descamps and E. Massaux (eds.), *Sacra Pagina* (2 vols.; Gembloux: Duculot, 1959), I, pp. 303-15.

Genctte, G., *Palimpsestes: La littérature au second degré* (Paris: Editions du Seuil, 1982).

Germann, H., 'Jesus ben Siras Dankgebet und die Hodajoth', *TZ* 19 (1963), pp. 81-87.

Gerstenberger, E., 'The Woe-Oracles of the Prophets', *JBL* 81 (1962), pp. 249-63.

Gertner, M., 'The Masorah and the Levites: An Essay in the History of a Concept', *VT* 10 (1960), pp. 241-84.

—'Midrashim in the New Testament', *JSS* 7 (1962), pp. 267-92.

—'Terms of Scriptural Interpretation: A Study in Hebrew Semantics', *London School of Oriental and African Studies* 25 (1962), pp. 1-27.

Gesenius, W., *Der Prophet Jesaia* (Leipzig: F.C.W. Vogel, 1921).

Geyer, J.B., 'Mythology and Culture in the Oracles against the Nations', *VT* 36 (1986), pp. 129-45.

Gibson, J.C.L. (ed.), *Canaanite Myths and Legends* (Edinburgh: T. & T. Clark, 2nd edn, 1978).

Gilula, M., '*Hirtengeschichte* 17-22 = *CT* VII 36 m-r', *GM* 29 (1978), pp. 21-22.

Girdlestone, R.B., *The Building Up of the Old Testament* (New York: Fleming H. Revell, 1912).

—*Deuterographs: Duplicate Passages in the Old Testament. Their Bearing on the Text and Compilation of the Hebrew Scriptures* (Oxford: Clarendon Press, 1894).

—*The Foundations of the Bible: Studies in Old Testament Criticism* (London: Eyre & Spottiswoode, 2nd edn, 1891).

—*The Grammar of Prophecy: A Systematic Guide to Biblical Prophecy* (Grand Rapids: Kregel Publications, 1955).

Gitay, Y., 'Deutero-Isaiah: Oral or Written?', *JBL* 99 (1980), pp. 185-97.

—*Isaiah and his Audience: The Structure and Meaning of Isaiah 1-12* (Studia Semitica Neerlandica, 30; Assen: Van Gorcum, 1991).

—*Prophecy and Persuasion: A Study of Isaiah 40-48* (Forum Theologiae Linguisticae, 14; Bonn: Linguistica Biblica, 1981).

Glatzer, N.N., 'A Study of the Talmudic-Midrashic Interpretation of Prophecy', in *idem* (ed.), *Essays in Jewish Thought* (Birmingham, AL: University of Alabama Press, 1978), pp. 16-35.

Görg, M., 'Jesaja als "Kinderlehrer"? Beobachtungen zur Sprache und Semantik in Jes 28, 10 (13)', *BN* 29 (1985), pp. 12-16.

Goldin, J., 'From Text to Interpretation and from Experience to the Interpreted Text', *Prooftexts* 3 (1983), pp. 157-68.

Goldingay, J., *Approaches to Old Testament Interpretation* (Downers Grove, IL: InterVarsity Press, 1981).

Good, E.M., 'Hosea and the Jacob Tradition', *VT* 16 (1966), pp. 137-51.

Gordis, R., *The Book of God and Man: A Study of Job* (Chicago: University of Chicago Press, 1965).

—*The Book of Job: Commentary, New Translation, and Special Studies* (New York: Jewish Theological Seminary of America, 1978).

—*Koheleth: The Man and his World. A Study of Ecclesiastes* (New York: Schocken Books, 3rd edn, 1973 [1951]).

—'Midrash in the Prophets', *JBL* 49 (1930), pp. 417-22.

—'Quotations in Biblical, Oriental, and Rabbinic Literature', *HUCA* 22 (1949), pp. 157-219; reprinted in *Poets, Prophets, and Sages: Essays in Biblical Interpretation* (Bloomington: Indiana University Press, 1971), pp. 104-59.

—'Quotations in Wisdom Literature', *JQR* NS 30 (1939–40), pp. 123-47.

—'Virtual Quotations in Job, Sumer, and Qumran', *VT* 31 (1981), pp. 410-27.

Graetz, H., 'Isaiah XXXIV and XXXV', *JQR* 4 (1892), pp. 1-8.

Gray, G.B., *A Critical and Exegetical Commentary on the Book of Isaiah I-XXVII* (ICC; New York: Charles Scribner's Sons, 1912).

—'The Parallel Passages in "Joel" in their Bearing on the Question of Date', *The Expositor* 4.8 (1893), pp. 208-25.

Grayson, A.K., *Babylonian Historical-Literary Texts* (Toronto Semitic Texts and Studies, 3; Toronto: University of Toronto Press, 1975).

Grech, P., 'Interprophetic Re-interpretation and Old Testament Eschatology', *Augustinianum* 9 (1969), pp. 235-65.

Greene, T.M., *The Light in Troy: Imitation and Discovery in Renaissance Poetry* (New Haven: Yale University Press, 1982).

—'Petrarch and the Humanist Hermeneutic', in G. Rimanelli and K.J. Atchity (eds.), *Italian Literature: Roots and Branches. Essays in Honor of Thomas Goddard Bergin* (New Haven: Yale University Press, 1976), pp. 201-24.

Gressmann, H., 'Die literarische Analyse Deuterojesajas', *ZAW* 34 (1914), pp. 254-97.

Griffith, F.L., 'The Milligen Papyrus (Teaching of Amenemhat)', *ZÄS* 34 (1890), pp. 345-51.

—'The Teaching of Amenophis the Son of Kanakht: Papyrus B.M. 10474', *JEA* 12 (1926), pp. 191-231.

Grimal, N.-C., *La stèle triomphale de Pi('ankh)y au musée du Caire: JE 48862 et 47086–47089* (Cairo: Institut français d'archéologie orientale, 1981).

Grimm, A., 'Ein Zitat aus den Pyramidentexten in einem ptolemäischen Ritualtext des Horus-Tempels von Edfu: Edfou III, 130.14-15 = Pyr. 376b (Spr. 269). Zur Tradition altägyptischer Texte: Voruntersuchungen zu einer Theorie der Gattungen', *GM* 31 (1979), pp. 35-46.

Gross, K., *Die literarische Verwandschaft Jeremias mit Hosea* (Leipzig: Universitätsverlag von Robert Noske, 1930).

Gruber, M.I., *Aspects of Nonverbal Communication in the Ancient Near East* (Studia Pohl, 12; 2 vols.; Rome: Biblical Institute Press, 1980).

Guglielmi, W., 'Eine "Lehre" für einen reiselustigen Sohn', *WO* 14 (1983), pp. 147-68.

—'Zur Adaption und Funktion von Zitaten', in H. Altenmüller and D. Wildung (eds.), *Festschrift für Wolfgang Helck zu seinem 70. Geburtstag* (SAK, 11; Hamburg: Helmut Buske Verlag, 1984), pp. 347-64.

Gunn, B., 'Some Middle-Egyptian Proverbs', *JEA* 12 (1926), pp. 282-84.

Gunn, D.M., 'Deutero-Isaiah and the Flood', *JBL* 94 (1975), pp. 493-508.

Gunneweg, A.H.J., *Mündliche und schriftliche Tradition der vorexilischen Prophetenbücher als Problem der neueren Prophetenforschung* (FRLANT, 73; Göttingen: Vandenhoeck & Ruprecht, 1959).

Gurney, O.R., 'The Sultantepe Tablets VII: The Myth of Nergal and Ereshkigal', *AnSt* 10 (1960), pp. 105-31.

Habel, N.C., 'Appeal to Ancient Tradition as a Literary Form', *ZAW* 88 (1976), pp. 253-72.

Hagstrom, D.G., *The Coherence of the Book of Micah: A Literary Analysis* (SBLDS, 89; Atlanta: Scholars Press, 1988).

Hallo, W.W., 'Akkadian Apocalypses', *IEJ* 16 (1966), pp. 231-42.

—'Isaiah 28:9-13 and the Ugaritic Abecedaries', *JBL* 77 (1958), pp. 324-38.

—'New Viewpoints on Cuneiform Literature', *IEJ* 12 (1962), pp. 13-26.

—'Notes from the Babylonian Collection. I. Nungal in the Egal: An Introduction to Colloquial Sumerian?', *JCS* 31 (1979), pp. 161-65.

—'Notes from the Babylonian Collection. II. Old Babylonian HAR-ra', *JCS* 34 (1982), pp. 81-92.

—'Problems in Sumerian Hermeneutics', in B.L. Sherwin (ed.), *Perspectives in Jewish Learning*, V (Chicago: Spertus College of Judaica Press, 1973), pp. 1-12.

—review of *The Instructions of Suruppak: A Sumerian Proverb C Collection* by B. Alster, *JNES* 37 (1978), pp. 269-73.

Hallo, W.W., and J.J.A. van Dijk, *The Exaltation of Inanna* (New Haven: Yale University Press, 1968).

Hambourg, G.R., 'Reasons for Judgment in the Oracles against the Nations in the Prophet Isaiah', *VT* 31 (1981), pp. 145-59.

Hammill, L.R., 'Biblical Interpretation in the Apocrypha and Pseudepigrapha' (PhD dissertation, University of Chicago, 1950).

Hanson, P.D., *The Dawn of Apocalyptic* (Philadelphia: Fortress Press, 1979).

—'Old Testament Apocalyptic Reexamined', *Int* 25 (1971), pp. 454-79.

Haran, M., 'From Early to Classical Prophecy: Continuity and Change', *VT* 27 (1977), pp. 385-97.

—'The Literary Structure and Chronological Framework of the Prophecies in Isaiah XL-XLVIII', in *Congress Volume: Bonn, 1962* (VTSup, 9; Leiden: E.J. Brill, 1963), pp. 127-55.

Hardmeier, C., 'Gesichtspunkte pragmatischer Erzähltextanalyse. "Glaubt ihr nicht, so bleibt ihr nicht": Ein Glaubensappell an schwankende Anhänger Jesajas', *Wort und Dienst* 15 (1979), pp. 33-54.

—'Jesajaforschung im Umbruch', *VF* 31 (1986), pp. 3-31.

—*Texttheorie und biblische Exegese: Zur rhetorischen Funktion der Trauermetaphorik in der Prophetie* (BEvT, 79; Munich: Chr. Kaiser Verlag, 1978).

Harris, B.F., 'Biblical Echoes and Reminiscences in Christian Papyri', in *Proceedings of the XIV International Congress of Papyrologists, Oxford, 24–31 July 1974* (Oxford: Oxford University Press, 1975), pp. 155-60.

Hart, J.H.A., *Ecclesiasticus: The Greek Text of Codex 248* (Cambridge: Cambridge University Press, 1901).

Hartman, G.H., *Criticism in the Wilderness: The Study of Literature Today* (New Haven: Yale University Press, 1980).

Hartman, L., *Prophecy Interpreted: The Formation of Some Jewish Apocalyptic Texts and of the Eschatological Discourse of Mark* (Lund: C.W.K. Gleerup, 1966).

Haspecker, J., *Gottesfurcht bei Jesus Sirach: Ihre religiöse Struktur und ihre literarische und doktrinäre Bedeutung* (AnBib, 30; Rome: Pontifical Biblical Institute, 1967).

Hayes, J.H., 'The History of the Form-Critical Study of Prophecy', in G. MacRae (ed.), *SBL Seminar Papers: 1973* (2 vols.; Cambridge, MA: SBL, 1973), I, pp. 60-99.

—'The Usage of Oracles against Foreign Nations in Ancient Israel', *JBL* 87 (1968), pp. 81-92.

Hayes, J.H., and S.A. Irvine, *Isaiah: The Eighth-Century Prophet* (Nashville: Abingdon Press, 1987).

Hays, R.B., *Echoes of Scripture in the Letters of Paul* (New Haven: Yale University Press, 1989).

Helberg, J.L., 'Nahum—Jonah—Lamentations—Isaiah 51-53 (A Possibility for Establishing a Connection)', in A.H. van Zyl (ed.), *Biblical Essays: Proceedings of the 12th Meeting of Die Ou-Testamentiese Werkgemeenskap in Suid-Afrika* (Potchefstroom: Pro Rege, 1969), pp. 46-55.

Helck, W., 'Eine kleine Textverbesserung', in *Jaarbericht van het vooraziatisch-egyptisch genootschap Ex oriente lux* (*Annuaire de la Société orientale 'Ex oriente lux'* 19 [1965–66]), pp. 464-67.

Helweg, F., 'Einige Bemerkungen zu Micha Cap. III-V', *Zeitschrift für die Gesamte Lutherische Theologie und Kirche* 2 (1841), pp. 1-35.

Hengel, M., and H. Löhr (eds.), *Schriftauslegung im antiken Judentum und im Urchristentum* (WUNT, 73; Tübingen: Mohr Siebeck, 1994).

Hengstenberg, E.W., *Christology of the Old Testament and a Commentary on the Messianic Predictions* (trans. T. Meyer and J. Martin; 4 vols.; Grand Rapids: Kregel, 1956).

Henshaw, T., *The Latter Prophets* (London: George Allen & Unwin, 1958).

Hermann, A., *Altägyptische Liebesdichtung* (Wiesbaden: Otto Harrassowitz, 1959).

Hermann, S., 'Prophetie in Israel und Ägypten: Recht und Grenze eines Vergleichs', in *Congress Volume: Bonn 1962* (VTSup, 9; Leiden: E.J. Brill, 1963), pp. 47-65.

Hermisson, H.-J., 'Deuterojesaja-Probleme: Ein kritischer Literaturbericht', *VF* 31 (1986), pp. 53-84.

—'Einheit und Komplexität Deuterojesajas: Probleme der Redaktionsgeschichte von Jes 40–55', in J. Vermeylen (ed.), *The Book of Isaiah. Le livre d'Isaïe. Les oracles et leurs relectures unité et complexité de l'ouvrage* (BETL, 81; Leuven: Leuven University Press, 1989), pp. 287-312.

Herntrich, V., *Der Prophet Jesaja, Kapitel 1-12 übersetzt und erklärt* (ATD, 17; Göttingen: Vandenhoeck & Ruprecht, 2nd edn, 1954).

Hertzberg, H.W., 'Die Nachgeschichte alttestamentlicher Texte innerhalb des Alten Testaments', in P. Volz, F. Stummer and J. Hempel (eds.), *Wesen und Werden des Alten Testaments* (BZAW, 66; Berlin: Alfred Töpelmann, 1936), pp. 110-21.

Hill, A.E., *Malachi* (AB, 25D; New York: Doubleday, 1998).

Hillers, D.R., *A Commentary on the Book of the Prophet Micah* (Hermeneia; Philadelphia: Fortress Press, 1984).

—'A Convention in Hebrew Literature: The Reaction to Bad News', *ZAW* 77 (1965), pp. 86-90.

—*Treaty Curses and the Old Testament Prophets* (BibOr, 16; Rome: Pontifical Biblical Institute, 1964).

Hirsch, E.D., *Validity in Interpretation* (New Haven: Yale University Press, 1967).

Hoffman, Y., 'The Technique of Quotation and Citation as an Interpretive Device', in B. Uffenheimer and H.G. Reventlow (eds.), *Christian and Jewish Hermeneutics through the Centuries* (JSOTSup, 59; Sheffield: JSOT Press, 1988), pp. 71-79.

Holladay, W.L., *Isaiah: Scroll of a Prophetic Heritage* (Grand Rapids: Eerdmans, 1978).

—*Jeremiah: Spokesman Out of Time* (Philadelphia: United Church Press, 1974).

—'On Every High Hill and Under Every Green Tree', *VT* 11 (1961), pp. 170-76.

Hollander, J., *The Figure of Echo: A Mode of Allusion in Milton and After* (Berkeley: University of California Press, 1981).

Holm-Nielsen, S., *Hodayot: Psalms from Qumran* (Acta Theologica Danica, 2; Aarhus, Denmark: Universitetsforlaget, 1960).

—'The Importance of Late Jewish Psalmody in the Understanding of Old Testament Psalmodic Tradition', *ST* 14 (1960), pp. 1-53.

Horton, F.L., Jr, 'Formulas of Introduction in the Qumran Literature', *RevQ* 7 (1969–71), pp. 505-14.

Hossfeld, F.L., and I. Meyer, *Prophet gegen Prophet: Eine Analyse der alttestamentlichen Texte zum Thema. Wahre und falsche Propheten* (BibB, 9; Fribourg: Schweizerisches Katholisches Bibelwerk, 1973).

Hoy, D., *The Critical Circle: Literature, History, and Philosophical Hermeneutics* (Berkeley: University of California Press, 1978).

Hubmann, F.D., 'Der "Weg" zum Zion: Jesaja 35:8-10', in J.B. Bauer and J. Marböck (eds.), *Memoria Jerusalem: Freundesgabe Franz Sauer zum 70. Geburtstag* (Graz: Akademische Druck- und Verlagsanstalt, 1977), pp. 29-41.

Hughes, G.R., 'The Cruel Father', in G.E. Kadish (ed.), *Studies in Honor of John A. Wilson. September 12, 1969* (Studies in Ancient Oriental Civilization, 35; Chicago: University of Chicago Press, 1969), pp. 43-54.

Humbert, P., *Problèmes du livre d'Habacuc* (Neuchâtel: Secrétariat de l'Université, 1944).

Hurvitz, A., *A Linguistic Study of the Relationship between the Priestly Source and the Book of Ezekiel: A New Approach to an Old Problem* (Cahiers de la Revue Biblique, 20; Paris: J. Gabalda, 1982).

Ihroni, 'Die Häufung der Verben des Jubelns in Zephanja iii.14f, 16-18: rnn, rw', śmḥ, 'lz, śwś, und gîl', *VT* 33 (1983), pp. 106-10.

Jacob, E., 'Quelques remarques sur les faux prophètes', *TZ* 13 (1957), pp. 478-86.

Jahn, J., *Einleitung in die göttlichen Bücher des Alten Bundes. II. Abschnitt* (Wien: C.F.. Wappler & Beck, 2nd edn, 1803).

Janzen, J.G., 'Double Readings in the Text of Jeremiah', *HTR* 60 (1967), pp. 433-47.

—*Studies in the Text of Jeremiah* (Cambridge, MA: Harvard University Press, 1973).

Jenny, L., 'The Strategy of Form', in T. Todorov (ed.), *French Literary Theory Today: A Reader* (trans. R. Carter; Cambridge: Cambridge University Press, 1982), pp. 34-63.

Jeremias, J., *Kultprophetie und Gerichtsverkündigung in der späten Königszeit Israels* (WMANT, 35; Neukirchen–Vluyn: Neukirchener Verlag, 1970).

Johnson, A.L., 'Allusion in Poetry', *PTL: A Journal of Descriptive Poetics and Theory of Literature* 1 (1976), pp. 579-87.

Johnson, A.M., Jr (ed.), *The New Testament and Structuralism* (Pittsburgh: Pickwick Press, 1976).

Johnson, F., *The Quotations of the New Testament from the Old Considered in the Light of General Literature* (Philadelphia: American Baptist Publication Society, 1846).

Jong, C. de, 'De volken bij Jeremia: Hun plaats in zijn prediking en in het Boek Jeremia' (2 vols.; dissertation, Theologische Academie te Kampen, 1978).

Jongeling, B., *A Classified Bibliography of the Finds in the Desert of Judah 1958–1969* (STDJ, 7; Leiden: E.J. Brill, 1971).

Junker, H., 'Sancta Civitas, Jerusalem Nova: Eine formkritische und überlieferungsgeschichtliche Studie zu Is 2', in H. Gross (ed.), *Ekklesia: Festschrift für Bischof Matthias Wehr* (TTS, 15; Trier: Paulinus Verlag, 1962), pp. 17-33.

Kadish, G.E., 'British Museum Writing Board 5645: The Complaint of Kha-Kheper-Re-Senebu' *JEA* 59 (1973), pp. 77-90.

Kaiser, G.R., *Proust—Musil—Joyce. Zum Verhältnis von Literatur und Gesellschaft am Paradigma des Zitats* (Frankfurt: Athenäum Verlag, 1972).

Kaiser, O., *Introduction to the Old Testament: A Presentation of its Results and Problems* (trans. J. Sturdy; Minneapolis: Augsburg, 1975).

—'Jesaja/Jesajabuch', *TRE*, XVI, pp. 636-58.

—*Jesaja 1–12* (ATD, 17; Göttingen: Vandenhoeck & Ruprecht, 5th edn, 1981); ET *Isaiah 1-12* (trans. J. Bowden; OTL; Philadelphia: Westminster Press, 1983).

—*Der Prophet Jesaja, Kapitel 13-39* (ATD, 18; Göttingen: Vandenhoeck & Ruprecht, 1973); ET *Isaiah 13-39* (trans. R.A. Wilson; OTL; Philadelphia: Westminster Press, 1974).

Kapelrud, A.S., 'Eschatology in the Book of Micah', *VT* 11 (1961), pp. 392-405.

Kaplony, P., 'Eine neue Weisheitslehre aus dem alten Reich (Die Lehre des Mttj) in der altägyptischen Weisheitsliteratur', *Or* NS 37 (1968), pp. 1-62.

Kaufman, S.A., 'Prediction, Prophecy, and Apocalypse in the Light of New Akkadian Texts', in A. Shinen (ed.), *Proceedings of the Sixth World Congress of Jewish Studies* (3 vols.; Jerusalem: Jerusalem Academic Press, 1977), I, pp. 221-28.

Kaufmann, Y., *The Religion of Israel* (trans. and ed. M. Greenberg; New York: Schocken Books, 1972).

Kees, H., 'Die Lebensgrundsätze eines Amonpriesters der 22. Dynastie', *ZÄS* 74 (1947), pp. 73-87.

Keil, K.F., *Manual of Historico-Critical Introduction to the Canonical Scriptures of the Old Testament* (trans. G.C.M. Douglas; 2 vols.; Edinburgh: T. & T. Clark, 1869–70).

—*The Prophecies of Jeremiah*, II (trans. J. Kennedy; Edinburgh: T. & T. Clark, 1874).

Kellett, E.E., *Literary Quotation and Allusion* (Cambridge: W. Heffer & Sons, 1933).

Kenner, H., 'Notes to "The Waste Land"', in J. Martin (ed.), *A Collection of Critical Essays on 'The Waste Land'* (Englewood Cliffs, NJ: Prentice–Hall, 1968), pp. 36-38.

Keown, G.L., P.J. Scalise and T.G. Smothers, *Jeremiah 26-52* (WBC, 27; Dallas: Word Books, 1995).

Kiesow, K., *Exodustexte im Jesajabuch: Literarkritische und motiv- geschichtliche Analysen* (OBO, 24; Göttingen: Vandenhoeck & Ruprecht, 1979).

Kilian, R., *Jesaja 1–39* (Erträge der Forschung, 200; Darmstadt: Wissenschaftliche Buchgesellschaft, 1983).

Kimura, H., 'Is 6:1-9:6: A Theatrical Section of the Book of Isaiah' (ThD dissertation; Uppsala University, 1981).

King, L.W., *Enuma Elish: The Seven Tablets of Creation* (2 vols.; London: Luzac & Co., 1902).

Kissane, E.J., *The Book of Isaiah* (2 vols.; Dublin: Browne & Nolan, 1941–43).

Kitchen, K.A., 'Proverbs and Wisdom Books of the Ancient Near East', *TynBul* 28 (1977), pp. 69-114.

Kittel, B.P., *The Hymns of Qumran: Translation and Commentary* (SBLDS, 50; Chico, CA: Scholars Press, 1981).

Klostermann, A., 'Jesaja Cap. 40-66', *Zeitschrift für die Gesamte Lutherische Theologie und Kirche* 37 (1976), pp. 1-60.

Knight, D.A., *Rediscovering the Traditions of Israel: The Development of the Traditio-Historical Research of the Old Testament, with Special Consideration of Scandinavian Contributions* (SBLDS, 9; Missoula, MT: SBL, 1973).

Knight, G.A., *Isaiah 56-66: The New Israel* (ITC; Grand Rapids: Eerdmans, 1985).

Koch, K., *The Prophets*. I. *The Assyrian Period* (trans. M. Kohl; Philadelphia: Fortress Press, 1983).

König, F.E., *Das Buch Jesaja eingeleitet, übersetzt und erklärt* (Gütersloh: C. Bertelsmann, 1926).

—*De criticae sacrae argumento e linguae legibus repetito: Ratione ducta maxime Geneseos capp. 1–11 eius historiam, naturam, vim examinavit* (Leipzig: J.C. Hinrichs, 1879).

—*Einleitung in das Alte Testament mit Einschluss der Apokryphen und der Pseudepigraphen Alten Testaments* (Bonn: Eduard Weber's Verlag, 1893).

—'Gibt es "Zitate" im Alten Testament?', *NKZ* 15 (1904), pp. 734-46.

—'Die letzte Pentateuchschicht und Hesekiel', *ZAW* 28 (1908), pp. 174-79.

—'Der Sprachbeweis in der Litteraturkritik, insbesondere des Alten Testaments', *TSK* 66 (1893), pp. 445-79.

—*Stilistik, Rhetorik, Poetik in Bezug auf die biblische Literatur komparativisch dargestellt* (Leipzig: Dieterich, 1900).

Koenig, J., *L'herméneutique analogique du judaïsme antique d'après les témoins textuels d'Isaïe* (VTSup, 33; Leiden: E.J. Brill, 1982).

Koole, J.L., 'Die Bibel des Ben-Sira', *OTS* 14 (1965), pp. 374-96.

Kramer, S.N., 'Gilgamesh and the Land of the Living', *JCS* 1 (1944), pp. 1-46.

Kraus, H.-J., *Prophetie in der Krisis: Studien zu Texten aus dem Buch Jeremia* (Biblische Studien, 43; Neukirchen–Vluyn: Neukirchener Verlag, 1964).

Kristeva, J., *Desire in Language: A Semiotic Approach to Literature and Art* (trans. T. Gora, A. Jardine and L.S. Roudiez; ed. L.S. Roudiez; New York: Columbia University Press, 1980 [1969]).

—*The Kristeva Reader* (ed. T. Moi; New York: Columbia University Press, 1986).

Kronfeld, C., 'Allusion: An Israeli Perspective', *Prooftexts* 5 (1985), pp. 137-63.

Küper, A., *Jeremias librorum sacrorum interpres atque vindex* (Berlin: Georg Reimer, 1837).

—*Das Prophetenthum des Alten Bundes* (Leipzig: Dörffling & Franke, 1870).

Kugel, J.L., 'The Bible's Earliest Interpreters', *Prooftexts* 7 (1987), pp. 269-83.

—' "James Kugel Responds." Response to "On the Bible as Literature", by A. Berlin', *Prooftexts* 2 (1982), pp. 328-32.

—'On the Bible and Literary Criticism', *Prooftexts* 1 (1981), pp. 217-36.

—'Two Introductions to Midrash', *Prooftexts* 3 (1983), pp. 131-55.

Kuhl, C., review of *The Literary Relations of Ezekiel* (Philadelphia: Jewish Publication Society of America, 1952), by M. Burrows, in *TLZ* 53 (1928), pp. 121-22.

Kuhlmann, K.P., 'Eine Beschreibung der Grabdekoration mit der Aufforderung zu kopieren und zum Hinterlassen von Besucherinschriften aus saitischer Zeit', *MDAIK* 29 (1973), pp. 205-13.

Lack, R., *La symbolique du livre d'Isaïe: Essai sur l'image littéraire comme élément de structuration* (AnBib, 59; Rome: Biblical Institute Press, 1973).

Lambert, W.G., 'Ancestors, Authors, and Canonicity', *JCS* 11 (1957), pp. 1-14.

—*Babylonian Wisdom Literature* (Oxford: Clarendon Press, 1960).

—'Dingir . šà.dib.ba Incantations', *JNES* 33 (1974), pp. 267-322.

Lambert, W.G., and A.R. Millard, *Atra-hasis: The Babylonian Story of the Flood* (Oxford: Clarendon Press, 1969).

Lande, I., *Formelhafte Wendungen der Umgangssprache im Alten Testament* (Leiden: E.J. Brill, 1949).

Landsberger, B., 'Jahreszeiten in Sumerisch-Akkadischen', *JNES* 8 (1949), pp. 248-97.

—'Zur vierten und siebenten Tafel des Gilgamesch-Epos', *RA* 62 (1968), pp. 97-135.

Lau, W., *Schriftgelehrte Prophetie in Jes 56–66: Eine Untersuchung zu den literarischen Bezügen in den letzten elf Kapiteln des Jesajabuches* (BZAW, 225; Berlin: W. de Gruyter, 1994).

LeDéaut, R., 'A propos d'une définition du midrash', *Bib* 50 (1969), pp. 395-413.

Lee, A.G., *Allusion, Parody and Imitation: The St John's College Cambridge Lecture 1970–71 Delivered at the University of Hull 11th March, 1971* (Hull: University of Hull, 1971).

Lehmann, M.R., 'Ben Sira and the Qumran Literature', *RevQ* 3 (1961–62), pp. 103-16.

Leiman, S.Z., *The Canonization of Hebrew Scripture: The Talmudic and Midrashic Evidence* (Hamden, CT: Archon Books, 1976).

Lévi, I., *The Hebrew Text of the Book of Ecclesiasticus* (Leiden: E.J. Brill, 1904).

Lichtheim, M., *Ancient Egyptian Literature: A Book of Readings* (3 vols.; Berkeley: University of California Press, 1973–78).

—'The Songs of the Harper', *JNES* 4 (1945), pp. 178-212.

Lim, T.H., *Holy Scripture in Qumran Commentaries and Pauline Letters* (Oxford: Oxford University Press, 1997).

Lindars, B., 'Good Tidings to Zion: Interpreting Deutero-Isaiah Today', *BJRL* 68 (1985–86), pp. 473-97.

Lindblom, J., *Prophecy in Ancient Israel* (Philadelphia: Fortress Press, 1962).

Lipiński, E., 'באחרית ימים dans les textes préexiliques', *VT* 20 (1970), pp. 445-50.

Löfstedt, E., 'Reminiscence and Imitation: Some Problems in Latin Literature', *Eranos* 47 (1949), pp. 148-64.

Loewenstamm, S.E., *Comparative Studies in Biblical and Ancient Oriental Literatures* (AOAT, 204; Neukirchen–Vluyn: Neukirchener Verlag, 1980).

Lohfink, N., 'Isaias 8, 12-14', *BZ* NS 7 (1963), pp. 98-104.

Lohse, E., *Die Texte aus Qumran: Hebräisch und deutsch* (Munich: Kösel, 1986).

Long, B.O., 'Prophetic Authority as Social Reality', in G.W. Coats and B.O. Long (eds.), *Canon and Authority: Essays in Old Testament Religion and Theology* (Philadelphia: Fortress Press, 1977), pp. 3-20.

Longman, T., III, *Literary Approaches to Biblical Interpretation* (Foundations of Contemporary Interpretation, 3; Grand Rapids: Zondervan, 1987).

Loretz, O., *Der Prolog des Jesaja Buches (1, 1-2, 5): Ugaritologische und kolometrische Studien zu Jesaja-Buch* (Altenberge: CIS Verlag, 1984).

Lorton, D., 'The Expression *'Iri Hrw Nfr'*, *JARCE* 21 (1975), pp. 23-31.

—'The Expression *Šmš-ib'*, *JARCE* 7 (1968), pp. 41-54.

Lutz, H.F., *Selected Sumerian and Babylonian Texts* (PBS, 1.2; Philadelphia: The University Museum, 1919).

McFadden, W.R., 'Micah and the Problem of Continuities and Discontinuities in Prophecy', in W.W. Hallo, J.C. Moyer and L.G. Perdue (eds.), *Scripture in Context. II. More Essays on the Comparative Method* (Winona Lake, IN: Eisenbrauns, 1983), pp. 127-46.

McIvor, J.G., *The Literary Study of the Prophets from Isaiah to Malachi* (New York: George H. Doran Co., n.d.).

McKenzie, J.L., *Second Isaiah* (AB, 20; Garden City, NY: Doubleday, 1968).

McKeon, R., 'Literary Criticism and the Concept of Imitation in Antiquity', *Modern Philology* 34 (1936), pp. 1-35.

McKnight, E.V., *Meaning in Texts: The Historical Shaping of a Narrative Hermeneutics* (Philadelphia: Fortress Press, 1978).

McLaughlin, J.L., '"Their Hearts *Were* Hardened: The Use of Isaiah 6, 9-10 in the Book of Isaiah', *Bib* 75 (1994), pp. 1-25.

Maass, F., 'Tritojesaja?', in *idem* (ed.), *Das ferne und nahe Wort: Festschrift Leonhard Rost* (BZAW, 105; Berlin: Alfred Töpelmann, 1967), pp. 153-63.

Macholz, G.C., 'Jeremia in der Kontinuität der Prophetie', in H.W. Wolff (ed.), *Probleme biblischer Theologie: Gerhard von Rad zum 70. Geburtstag* (Munich: Chr. Kaiser Verlag, 1971), pp. 306-34.

Malinowski, B., 'The Problem of Meaning in Primitive Languages', in C.K. Ogden and I.A. Richards (eds.), *The Meaning of Meaning* (New York: Harcourt, Brace & Company, 1945), pp. 296-336.

Manahan, R.E., 'An Interpretive Survey: Audience Reaction Quotations in Jeremiah', *GTJ* 1 (1980), pp. 163-83.

—'A Theology of Pseudoprophets: A Study in Jeremiah', *GTJ* 1 (1980), pp. 77-96.

Mansoor, M., 'The Massoretic Text in the Light of Qumran', in *Congress Volume: Bonn 1962* (VTSup, 9; Leiden: E.J. Brill, 1963), pp. 305-21.

—*The Thanksgiving Hymns* (STDJ, 3; Leiden: E.J. Brill, 1961).

—'The Thanksgiving Hymns and the Massoretic Text', *RevQ* 3 (1961–62), pp. 387-94.

Marböck, J., 'Das Gebet um die Rettung Zions Sir 36, 1-22 (G: 33, 1-13a; 36, 16b-22) im Zusammenhang der Geschichtsschau Ben Siras', in J.B. Bauer and J. Marböck (eds.), *Memoria Jerusalem: Freundesgabe Franz Sauer zum 70. Geburtstag* (Graz: Akademische Druck- und Verlagsanstalt, 1977), pp. 93-115.

Marciniak, M., 'Une formule empruntée à la sagesse de Ptahhotep', *BIFAO* 73 (1973), pp. 109-12.

Margalioth, R., *The Indivisible Isaiah: Evidence for the Single Authorship of the Prophetic Book* (New York: Sura Institute for Research; Jerusalem; Yeshiva University, New York, 1964).

Marshall, I.H., 'An Assessment of Recent Developments', in D.A. Carson and H.G.M. Williamson (eds.), *It Is Written: Scripture Citing Scripture. Essays in Honour of Barnabas Lindars* (Cambridge: Cambridge University Press, 1988), pp. 1-21.

Marti, K., *Das Buch Jesaja* (KHAT, 10; Tübingen: J.C.B. Mohr [Paul Siebeck], 1900).

Martínez, F.G., *The Dead Sea Scrolls Translated: The Qumran Texts in English* (Leiden: E.J. Brill, 1994).

Marx, A., 'A propos des doublets du livre de Jérémie: Réflexions sur la formation d'un livre prophétique', in J.A. Emerton (ed.), *Prophecy: Essays Presented to Georg Fohrer on his Sixty-Fifth Birthday, 6 September 1980* (BZAW, 150; Berlin: W. de Gruyter, 1980), pp. 106-20.

Mason, R.A., 'The Relation of Zech 9-14 to Proto-Zechariah', *ZAW* 88 (1976), pp. 227-39.

—'Some Examples of Inner Biblical Exegesis in Zech IX-XIV', in E.A. Livingstone (ed.), *Studia Evangelica. VII. Papers Presented to the Fifth International Congress on Biblical Studies Held at Oxford, 1973* (TUGAL, 126; Berlin: Akademie Verlag, 1982), pp. 343-54.

Maunowicz, L., 'Citations bibliques dans l'épigraphie greque', in E.A. Livingstone (ed.), *Studia Evangelica. VII. Papers Presented to the Fifth International Congress on Biblical Studies Held at Oxford, 1973* (TUGAL, 126; Berlin: Akademie Verlag, 1982), pp. 333-37.

Mayenowa, M.R., 'Expressions Guillemetées: Contribution à l'étude de la sémantique du texte poétique', *Janua Linguaram* 1 (1970), pp. 645-57.

Mays, J.L., *Amos: A Commentary* (OTL; Philadelphia: Westminster Press, 1969).

—*Micah: A Commentary* (OTL; Philadelphia: Westminster Press, 1976).

Mead, R.T., 'A Dissenting Opinion about Respect for Context in Old Testament Quotations', *NTS* 10 (1964), pp. 279-89.

Meade, F.G., *Pseudonymity and Canon: An Investigation into the Relationship of Authorship and Authority in Jewish and Earliest Christian Tradition* (Grand Rapids: Eerdmans, 1987).

Meier, G., review of *A Dictionary of Assyrian Chemistry and Geology* (Oxford: Oxford University Press, 1936) by R. Campbell Thompson, in *AfO* 13 (1939–41), pp. 71-74.

Melugin, R.F., 'Deutero-Isaiah and Form Criticism', *VT* 21 (1971), pp. 326-37.

—*The Formation of Isaiah 40-55* (BZAW, 141; Berlin: W. de Gruyter, 1976).

—' "Form" versus "Formation" of Prophetic Books', in K.H. Richards (ed.), *SBL Seminar Papers: 1983* (Chico, CA: Scholars Press, 1983), pp. 13-29.

Merendino, R.P., *Der Erste und der Letzte: Eine Untersuchung von Jesaja 40-48* (VTSup, 31; Leiden: E.J. Brill, 1981).

Merwe, B.J. van der, 'Echoes from the teaching of Hosea in Isaiah 40-55', in A.H. van Zyl (ed.), *Studies on the Books of Hosea and Amos: Papers Read at the 7th and 8th meetings of Die Ou-Testamentiese Werkgemeenskap in Suid-Afrika, 1964–1965* (Potchefstroom: Pro Rege, 1965), pp. 90-99.

Metzger, B.M., 'The Formulas Introducing Quotations of Scripture in the New Testament and the Mishnah', *JBL* 70 (1951), pp. 297-307.

Meyer, H., *Das Zitat in der Erzählkunst: Zur Geschichte und Poetik des europäischen Romans* (Stuttgart: J.B. Metzlersche Verlagsbuchhandlung, 1961).

Meyer, I., *Jeremia und die falschen Propheten* (OBO, 13; Göttingen: Vandenhoeck & Ruprecht, 1977).

Meyer, R.M., 'Kriterien der Aneignung', *Neue Jahrbücher für das klassische Altertum, Geschichte und deutsche Literatur und für Pädagogik* 17 (1906), pp. 349-89.

Michaelis, D., 'Das Buch Jesus Sirach als typischer Ausdruck für das Gottesverhältnis des nachalttestamentlichen Menschen', *TLZ* 83 (1958), pp. 602-608.

Michel, D., 'Deuterojesaja', *TRE*, VII, pp. 510-30.

—'Zur Eigenart Tritojesajas', *Theologia Viatorum* 10 (1965–66), pp. 213-30.

Middendorp, T., *Die Stellung Jesu Ben Siras zwischen Judentum und Hellenismus* (Leiden: E.J. Brill, 1973).

Millar, W.R., *Isaiah 24-27 and the Origin of Apocalyptic* (HSM, 11; Missoula, MT: Scholars Press, 1976).

Millard, A.R., 'The Old Testament in its Ancient World: Aspects of Prophetic Writings', *The Scottish Bulletin of Evangelical Theology* 7 (1989), pp. 88-99.

—'La prophète et l'écriture Israël, Aram, Assyrie', *RHR* 202 (1985), pp. 125-45.

Miller, J.H., 'The Critic as Host', in H. Bloom *et al.* (eds.), *Deconstruction and Criticism* (New York: Seabury, 1979), pp. 217-53.

Miller, J.W., *Das Verhältnis Jeremias und Hesekiels sprachlich und theologisch untersucht mit besonderer Berücksichtigung der Prosareden Jeremias* (Assen: Van Gorcum, 1955).

Miller, M.P., 'Targum, Midrash, and the Use of the Old Testament in the New Testament', *JSJ* 2 (1971), pp. 29-82.

Miner, E., 'Allusion', in A. Preminger (ed.), *Princeton Encyclopedia of Poetry and Poetics* (Princeton, NJ: Princeton University Press, enlarged edn, 1974), p. 18.

Miscall, P.D., *Isaiah* (Readings; Sheffield: JSOT Press, 1993).

—'Isaiah: New Heavens, New Earth, New Book', in Fewell (ed.), *Reading between Texts*, pp. 41-56.

—'Isaiah: The Labyrinth of Images', *Semeia* 54 (1991), pp. 103-21.

Moo, D.J., *The Old Testament in the Gospel Passion Narratives* (Sheffield: Almond Press, 1983).

Morawski, S., 'The Basic Function of Quotation', in C.H. van Schooneveld (ed.), *Janua Linguaram: Studia Memoriae Nicolai van Wijk Dedicata. Sign, Language, Culture* (Series Maior, 1; The Hague: Mouton, 1970), pp. 690-705.

Motyer, A., *The Prophecy of Isaiah* (Leicester: Inter-Varsity Press, 1993).

—'Three in One or One in Three: A Dipstick into the Isaianic Literature', *Churchman* 108 (1994), pp. 22-36.

Moule, C.F.D., 'Fulfillment-Words in the New Testament: Use and Abuse', *NTS* 14 (1967–68), pp. 293-320.

Mowinckel, S., *Jesaja-Disiplene: Profetien fra Jesaja til Jeremia* (Oslo: H. Aschehoug & Co., 1926).

—*Prophecy and Tradition: The Prophetic Books in the Light of the Study of the Growth and History of the Tradition* (Oslo: Jacob Dybwad, 1946).

—*Zur Komposition des Buches Jeremia* (Oslo: Jacob Dybwad, 1914).

Müller, D.H., 'Ezechiel entlehnt eine Stelle aus Zephanja und glossiert sie', in *Biblische Studien. III. Komposition und Strophenbau* (Vienna: Alfred Hölder, 1907), pp. 30-36.

Müller, H.-P., 'Glauben und Bleiben: Zur Denkschrift Jesajas Kapitel vi.1-viii.18', in G.W. Anderson (ed.), *Studies in Prophecy: A Collection of Twelve Papers* (VTSup, 26; Leiden: E.J. Brill, 1974), pp. 25-54.

Münderlein, G., *Kriterien wahrer und falscher Prophetie: Entstehung und Bedeutung im Alten Testament* (Europäische Hochschulschriften, 23, Theologie, 33; Bern: Peter Lang, 2nd edn, 1979).

Muilenburg, J., *The Book of Isaiah, Chapters 40-66: Introduction and Exegesis* (IB, 5; Nashville: Abingdon Press, 1984).

Mullins, T.Y., 'Topos as a New Testament Form', *JBL* 99 (1980), pp. 541-47.

Myers, J.M., *Hosea—Jonah* (Layman's Bible Commentary, 14; Richmond, VA: John Knox Press, 1959).

—'Some Considerations Bearing on the Date of Joel', *ZAW* NS 33 (1962), pp. 177-95.

Nägelsbach, C.W.E., *The Prophet Isaiah* (trans. S.T. Lowrie and D. Moore; A Commentary on the Holy Scriptures by J.P. Lange, 11; New York: Charles Scribner's Sons, 1878).

Nelson, L., Jr, 'Baudelaire and Virgil: A Reading of "Le Cygne"', *CompLit* 13 (1961), pp. 332-45.

Neumann, P.H.A. (ed.), *Das Prophetenverständnis in der deutschsprachigen Forschung seit Heinrich Ewald* (Wege der Forschung, 307; Darmstadt: Wissenschaftliche Buchgesellschaft, 1979).

Nicholson, E.W., *The Book of the Prophet Jeremiah, Chapters 26-52* (CBC; Cambridge: Cambridge University Press, 1975).

Nickelsburg, G.W.E., *Jewish Literature between the Bible and the Mishnah: A Historical and Literary Introduction* (Philadelphia: Fortress Press, 1981).

Nielsen, E., *Oral Tradition: A Modern Problem in Old Testament Introduction* (SBT, 11; Naperville, IL: Allenson, 1955).

Nielsen, K., *There is Hope for a Tree: The Tree as Metaphor in Isaiah* (JSOTSup, 65; Sheffield: JSOT Press, 1989).

Nitchie, E., *The Criticism of Literature* (New York: Macmillan, 1928).

Nitzan, B., *Qumran Prayer and Religious Poetry* (STDJ, 12; Leiden: E.J. Brill, 1994).

Nogalski, J., *Literary Precursors to the Book of the Twelve* (BZAW, 217; Berlin: W. de Gruyter, 1993).

—*Redactional Processes in the Book of the Twelve* (BZAW, 218; Berlin: W. de Gruyter, 1993).

North, C.R., 'The "Former Things" and the "New Things" in Deutero-Isaiah', in H.H. Rowley (ed.), *Studies in Old Testament Prophecy* (New York: Charles Scribner's Sons, 1950), pp. 111-26.

—*The Second Isaiah* (Oxford: Clarendon Press, 1964).

Ockinga, B.G., 'The Burden of Kha kheperre sonbu', *JEA* 69 (1983), pp. 88-95.

O'Connell, R.H., *Concentricity and Continuity: The Literary Structure of Isaiah* (JSOTSup, 188; Sheffield: Sheffield Academic Press, 1994).

O'Day, G.R., 'Jeremiah 9:22-23 and 1 Corinthians 1:26-31: A Study in Intertextuality', *JBL* 109 (1990), pp. 259-67.

Odeberg, H., *Trito-Isaiah (Isaiah 56–66): A Literary and Linguistic Analysis* (Uppsala: Lundeqvist, 1931).

Oesterley, W.O.E., *The Wisdom of Jesus the Son of Sirach or Ecclesiasticus* (Cambridge: Cambridge University Press, 1912).

Ogdon, J.R., 'CT VII, 36 i-r = Spell 836', *GM* 58 (1982), pp. 59-64.

Olley, J.W., ' "Hear the Word of YHWH": The Structure of the Book of Isaiah in 1QIsaᵃ', *VT* 43 (1993), pp. 19-49.

Olmstead, A.T., 'Critical Notes: II Isaiah and Isaiah, Chapter 35', *AJSL* 53 (1936–37), pp. 251-53.

Oppenheim, A.L., 'A New Prayer to the "Gods of the Night"', in *Studia biblica et orientalia. III. Oriens antiquus* (AnBib, 12; Rome: Pontifical Biblical Institute, 1959), pp. 282-301.

Orelli, C. von, *Der Prophet Jesaja* (Leipzig: F.C.W. Vogel, 1921), pp. 226-72.

Osswald, E., *Falsche Prophetie im Alten Testament* (Sammlung gemeinverständlicher Vorträge und Schriften aus dem Gebiet der Theologie und Religionsgeschichte, 237; Tübingen: J.C.B. Mohr [Paul Siebeck], 1962).

—'Zum Problem der Vaticinia ex Eventu', *ZAW* 75 (1963), pp. 27-44.

Oswalt, J., *The Book of Isaiah, Chapters 1–39* (NICOT; Grand Rapids: Eerdmans, 1986).

—*The Book of Isaiah, Chapters 40-66* (NICOT; Grand Rapids: Eerdmans, 1998).

Otto, E., *Die biographischen Inschriften der ägyptischen Spätzeit: Ihre geistes-geschichtliche und literarische Bedeutung* (Probleme der Ägyptologie, 2; Leiden: E.J. Brill, 1954).

Otzen, B., 'Traditions and Structures of Isaiah XXIV-XXVII', *VT* 24 (1974), pp. 196-206.

Overholt, T.W., 'Jeremiah 2 and the Problem of "Audience Reaction" ', *CBQ* 41 (1979), pp. 262-73.

Owen, H., *Critica Sacra; or, a Short Introduction to Hebrew Criticism* (London: W. Bowyer & J. Nichols, 1774).

Panzer, F., 'Vom mittelalterlichen Zitieren', in *Sitzungsberichte der Heidelberger Akademie der Wissenschaften* 35/2 (Heidelberg: Carl Winter, 1950), pp. 1-44.

Parpola, S., *Letters from Assyrian Scholars*, II (Neukirchen–Vluyn: Neukirchener Verlag, 1983).

Partee, B.H., 'The Syntax and Semantics of Quotation', in S.R. Anderson and P. Kiparsky (eds.), *A Festschrift for Morris Halle* (New York: Holt, Rinehart & Winston, 1973), pp. 410-18.

Pasco, A.H., *Allusion: A Literary Graft* (Toronto: University of Toronto Press, 1994).

Patte, D., *Early Jewish Hermeneutic in Palestine* (SBLDS, 22; Missoula, MT: Scholars Press, 1975).

Paul, S.M., 'Deutero-Isaiah and Cuneiform Royal Inscriptions', *JAOS* 88 (1968), pp. 180-86.

—'Literary and Ideological Echoes of Jeremiah in Deutero-Isaiah', in P. Peli (ed.), *Proceedings of the Fifth World Congress of Jewish Studies (1969)* (5 vols.; Jerusalem: World Union of Jewish Studies, 1972), I, pp. 102-20.

Paulien, J., 'Elusive Allusions: The Problematic Use of the Old Testament in Revelation', *BR* 33 (1988), pp. 37-53.

Pauritsch, K., *Die neue Gemeinde: Gott sammelt Ausgestossene und Arme (Jesaia 56-66): Die Botschaft des Tritojesaia-Buches literar-, form-, gattungskritisch und redaktions-geschichtlich untersucht* (AnBib, 47; Rome: Biblical Institute Press, 1971).

Peake, A.S., 'Isaiah', in *idem* (ed.), *Commentary on the Bible* (London: T.C. & E.C. Jack, 1920).

—*Jeremiah* (NCB; New York: Henry Frowde, 1911).

Perri, C., 'On Alluding', *Poetics* 7 (1978), pp. 289-307.

Perri, C., *et al.* (eds.), 'Allusion Studies: An International Annotated Bibliography, 1921-1977', *Style* 13 (1979), pp. 178-225.

Peters, N., *Das Buch Jesus Sirach oder Ecclesiasticus* (EHAT; Münster: Aschendorff, 1913).

Petersen, D.L., 'Isaiah 28: A Redaction Critical Study', in P. Achtemeier (ed.), *SBL Seminar Papers: 1979* (2 vols.; Missoula, MT: Scholars Press, 1979), II, pp. 101-22.

—'Israelite Prophecy and Prophetic Traditions in the Exilic and Post-Exilic Periods' (PhD dissertation, Yale University, 1972).

—*Late Israelite Prophecy: Studies in Deutero-Prophetic Literature and in Chronicles* (SBLMS, 23; Missoula, MT: Scholars Press, 1977).

—'The Oracles against the Nations: A Form-Critical Analysis', in G. MacRae (ed.), *SBL Seminar Papers: 1975* (2 vols.; Missoula, MT: SBL, 1975), I, pp. 39-61.

Peterson, S.L., 'Babylonian Literary Influence in Deutero-Isaiah: A Bibliographic and Critical Study' (PhD dissertation, Vanderbilt University, 1975).

Pfeifer, G., 'Entwöhnung und Entwöhnungsfest im Alten Testament: Der Schlüssel zu Jesaja 28:7-13?', *ZAW* 84 (1972), pp. 341-47.

Pieper, M., *Die Grosse Inschrift des Königs Neferhotep in Abydos* (MVG, 32.2; Leiden: J.C. Hinrichs, 1927).

Pigman, G.W., III, 'Versions of Imitation in the Renaissance', *Renaissance Quarterly* 33 (1980), pp. 1-32.

Ploeg, J.P.M. van der, 'Zur Literatur- und Stilforschung im Alten Testament', *TLZ* 100 (1975), pp. 801-14.

Pohl, A., and R. Follet, *Codex Hammurabi* (Rome: Pontifical Biblical Institute, 1950).

Polan, G.J., *In the Ways of Justice toward Salvation: A Rhetorical Analysis of Isaiah 56-59* (AUSS, 7/13; New York: Peter Lang, 1986).

Polaski, D., 'Reflections on a Mosaic Covenant: The Eternal Covenant (Isaiah 24.5) and Intertextuality', *JSOT* 77 (1998), pp. 55-73.

Polk, T., *The Prophetic Persona: Jeremiah and the Language of the Self* (JSOTSup, 32; Sheffield: JSOT Press, 1984).

Polzin, R.M., *Biblical Structuralism: Method and Subjectivity in the Study of Ancient Texts* (Semeia Supplements; Missoula, MT: Scholars Press, 1977).

Pope, M.H., 'Isaiah 34 in Relation to Isaiah 35, 40-66', *JBL* 71 (1952), pp. 235-43.

—'Mid Rock and Scrub, a Ugaritic Parallel to Exodus 7:19', in G.A. Tuttle (ed.), *Biblical and Near Eastern Studies: Essays in Honor of William Sanford LaSor* (Grand Rapids: Eerdmans, 1978), pp. 146-50.

Popper, W., 'A Literary Problem in the Book of Isaiah', *University of California Chronicle* 32 (1930), pp. 284-317.

Porten, G.G., 'Defining Midrash', in J. Neusner (ed.), *The Study of Ancient Judaism. I. Mishnah, Midrash, Siddur* (New York: Ktav, 1981), pp. 55-92.

Porteous, N.W., 'Actualization and the Prophetic Criticism of the Cult', in E. Würthwein and O. Kaiser (eds.), *Tradition und Situation: Studien zur alttestamentlichen Prophetie. Artur Weiser zum 70. Geburtstag* (Göttingen: Vandenhoeck & Ruprecht, 1963), pp. 93-105.

—'Prophets and the Problem of Continuity', in B.W. Anderson and W. Harrelson (eds.), *Israel's Prophetic Heritage: Essays in Honor of James Muilenburg* (New York: Harper & Row, 1962), pp. 1-25.

Posener, G., 'Le début de l'enseignement de Hardjedef', *REg* 9 (1952), pp. 109-17.

Power, E., 'The Prophecy of Isaias against Moab (Is. 15, 1-16, 5', *Bib* 13 (1932), pp. 435-51.

Price, I.M., *The Great Cylinder Inscription A & B of Gudea* (Leipzig: J.C. Hinrichs, 1927).

Procksch, O., *Jesaia I* (KAT, 9; Leipzig: Deichert, 1930).

Pusey, E.B., *The Minor Prophets: A Commentary* (2 vols.; Grand Rapids: Baker Book House, 1953 [1888–89]).

Rabinowitz, P.J., ' "What's Hecuba to Us?" The Audience's Experience of Literary Borrowing', in S.R. Suleiman and I. Crosman (eds.), *The Reader in the Text: Essays on Audience and Interpretation* (Princeton, NJ: Princeton University Press, 1980), pp. 241-63.

Rad, G. von, 'The City on the Hill', in *The Problem of the Hexateuch and Other Essays* (trans. E.W.T. Dicken; New York: McGraw-Hill, 1966) reprinted from *EvT* 8 (1948–49), pp. 232-42.

—'The Levitical Sermon in I and II Chronicles', in *The Problem of the Hexateuch and Other Essays* (trans. E.W.T. Dicken. New York: McGraw–Hill, 1966), pp. 267-80.

Raven, J.H., *Old Testament Introduction: General and Special* (New York: Fleming H. Revell, 1906).

Redditt, P.L., 'The Book of Joel and Peripheral Prophecy', *CBQ* 48 (1986), pp. 225-40.

Rehm, M., *Der königliche Messias im Licht der Immanuel-Weissagungen des Buches Jesajas* (Kevelaer Rheinland: Butzon & Bercker, 1968).

Reiner, E., 'The Babylonian Fürstenspiegel in Practice', in J.N. Postgate (ed.), *Societies and Languages of the Ancient Near East: Studies in Honour of I.M. Diakonoff* (Warminster: Aris & Phillips, 1982), pp. 320-23.

Renaud, B., *Structure et attaches littéraires de Michée IV–V* (Cahiers de la Revue Biblique, 2; Paris: J. Gabalda, 1964).

Rendtorff, R., *Das Alte Testament: Eine Einführung* (Neukirchen–Vluyn: Neukirchener Verlag, 1983).

—'The Book of Isaiah: A Complex Unity. Synchronic and Diachronic Reading', in R.F. Melugin and M.A. Sweeney (eds.), *New Visions of Isaiah* (JSOTSup, 214; Sheffield: Sheffield Academic Press, 1996), pp. 32-49

'Erwägungen zur Frühgeschichte des Prophetentums', *ZTK* 59 (1962), pp. 145-67.

—*Kanon und Theologie: Vorarbeiten zu einer Theologie des ATs* (Neukirchen–Vluyn: Neukirchener Verlag, 1991).

—'Zur Komposition des Buches Jesaja', *VT* 34 (1984), pp. 295-320.

Resseguire, J.L., 'Reader-Response Criticism and the Synoptic Gospels', *JAAR* 52 (1984), pp. 307-24.

Reuss, E., *Die Geschichte der Heiligen Schriften: Alten Testaments* (Braunschweig: C.A. Schwetschke & Son, 1881).

Rey, P.-L., review of *La second main: Ou le travail de la citation* (Paris: Editions du Seuil, 1979), by A. Compagnon, in *La Nouvelle Revue Française* 318 (1979), pp. 116-18.

Rice, G., 'Isaiah 28:1-22 and the New English Bible', *JRT* 30 (1973–74), pp. 13-17.

Richards, I.A., *Principles of Literary Criticism* (New York: Harcourt, Brace & Company, 4th edn, 1930).

Rickman, J., 'On Quotations', *The International Journal of Psycho-Analysis* 10 (1929), pp. 242-48.

Rimmon-Kenan, S., 'The Paradoxical Status of Repetition', *Poetics Today* 1 (1980), pp. 151-59.

Ringgren, H., 'Oral and Written Transmission in the Old Testament: Some Observations', *ST* 3 (1949), pp. 34-59.

Robert, A., 'Les attaches littéraires bibliques de Prov. i-ix', *RB* 43 (1934), pp. 42-68, 172-204, 374-84; 44 (1935), pp. 344-65, 502-25.

—*Initiations bibliques: Introduction à l'etude des saintes écritures* (ed. A. Robert and A. Tricot; Paris: Desclée de Brouwer, 1948).

—'Littéraires (Genres)', *DBSup*, V, pp. 405-21.

Roberts, A., and J. Donaldson (eds.), *The Ante-Nicene Fathers*. II. *Fathers of the Second Century* (10 vols.; trans. M. Dods; Grand Rapids: Eerdmans, 1979).

Robinson, H.W., *Inspiration and Revelation in the Old Testament* (Oxford: Clarendon Press, 1946).

Robinson, T.H., *Die zwölf kleinen Propheten* (trans. O. Eissfeldt and F. Horst; HAT, 14; Tübingen: J.C.B. Mohr [Paul Siebeck], 1938).

Rosenthal, F., 'Die Parallelstellen in den Texten von Ugarit', *Or* NS 8 (1939), pp. 213-37.

Rost, L., *Judaism outside the Hebrew Canon: An Introduction to the Documents* (trans. D.E. Green; Nashville: Abingdon Press, 1976).

Roth, W., 'Interpretation as Scriptural Matrix: A Panel on Fishbane's Thesis', *BR* 35 (1990), pp. 36-57 (with contributions by L.J. Hoppe, R.D. Haak and P.A. Viviano).

Rudolph, W., *Jeremia* (HAT, 12; Tübingen: J.C.B. Mohr [Paul Siebeck], 1947).

—'Jesaja XV-XVI', in D.W. Thomas (ed.), *Hebrew and Semitic Studies Presented to G.R. Driver* (London: Oxford University Press, 1963), pp. 130-43.

—*Micha—Nahum—Habakuk—Zephanja* (KAT, 13.3; Gütersloh: Gerd Mohn, 1975).

—'Wann wirkte Joel?', in Maass (ed.), *Das ferne und nahe Wort*, pp. 193-98.

Rüger, H.P., *Text und Textform im hebräischen Sirach* (BZAW, 112; Berlin: W. de Gruyter, 1970).

Ruiten, J.T.A.G.M. van, 'The Intertextual Relationship between Isaiah 65, 25 and Isaiah 11, 6-9', in F. García Martínez, A. Hilhurst and C.J. Labuschagne (eds.), *The Scriptures and the Scrolls: Studies in Honour of A.S. van der Woude's 65th Birthday* (Leiden: E.J. Brill, 1992), pp. 31-42.

Rummel, S. (ed.), *Ras Shamra Parallels: The Text from Ugarit and the Hebrew Bible* (Rome: Pontifical Biblical Institute, 1981).

Ruppert, L., 'Herkunft und Bedeutung der Jakob-Tradition bei Hosea', *Bib* 52 (1971), pp. 488-504.

Saebø, M., *Sacharja 9-14: Untersuchungen von Text und Form* (WMANT, 34; Neukirchen–Vluyn: Neukirchener Verlag, 1969).

Sanders, J.A., 'Adaptable for Life: The Nature and Function of Canon', in F.M. Cross, W.E. Lemke and P.D. Miller, Jr (eds.), *Magnalia Dei: The Mighty Acts of God. Essays on the Bible and Archaeology in Memory of G. Ernest Wright* (Garden City, NY: Doubleday, 1976), pp. 531-60.

—*Canon and Community: A Guide to Canonical Criticism* (Philadelphia: Fortress Press, 1984).

—*From Sacred Story to Sacred Text: Canon as Paradigm* (Philadelphia: Fortress Press, 1987).

—'Hermeneutics in True and False Prophecy', in G.W. Coats and B.O. Long (eds.), *Canon and Authority: Essays in Old Testament Religion and Theology* (Philadelphia: Fortress Press, 1977), pp. 21-41.

—'Text and Canon: Concepts and Method', *JBL* 98 (1979), pp. 5-29.

—*Torah and Canon* (Philadelphia: Fortress Press, 1972).

Sandmel, S., 'The Haggada within Scripture', *JBL* 80 (1961), pp. 105-22.

—'Parallelomania', *JBL* 81 (1962), pp. 1-13.

Sarna, N.M., 'Psalm 89: A Study in Inner Biblical Exegesis', in A. Altmann (ed.), *Biblical and Other Studies* (Cambridge, MA: Harvard University Press, 1963), pp. 29-46.

Saussure, F. de, *Course in General Linguistics* (New York: McGraw-Hill, 1966).

Saviv, S., 'The Antiquity of Song of Songs: The Song of Songs' Influence on Isaiah and Jeremiah', *Beth Mikra* 29 (1983–84), pp. 295-304.

Savran, G.W., *Telling and Retelling: Quotation in Biblical Narrative* (Indiana Studies in Biblical Literature; Bloomington: Indiana University Press, 1988).

Schaefer, K.R., 'Zechariah 14: A Study in Allusion', *CBQ* 57 (1995), pp. 66-91.

Schakel, P.J., *The Poetry of Jonathan Swift: Allusion and the Development of a Poetic Style* (Madison: University of Wisconsin Press, 1978).

Scharbert, J., 'Die prophetische Literatur: Der Stand der Forschung', in H. Cazelles (ed.), *De Mari à Qumrân. L'Ancien Testament. Son milieu. Ses écrits. Ses relectures juives. Hommage à Mgr J. Coppens* (Gembloux: Duculot, 1969), pp. 58-118.

Schechter, S., and C. Taylor, *The Wisdom of Ben Sira* (Cambridge: Cambridge University Press, 1899).

Schedl, C., *Rufer des Heils in heilloser Zeit: Der Prophet Jesajah Kapitel I-XII logotechnisch und bibeltheologisch erklärt* (Paderborn: Ferdinand Schöningh, 1973).

Schlack, B.A., *Continuing Presences: Virginia Woolf's Use of Literary Allusion* (University Park, PA: Pennsylvania State University Press, 1979).

Schmitt, A., *Prophetischer Gottesbescheid in Mari und Israel: Eine Strukturuntersuchung* (BWANT, 114; Stuttgart: W. Kohlhammer, 1982).

Schmitt, J.J., *Isaiah and his Interpreters* (Mahwah, NJ: Paulist Press, 1986).

Schneider, D.A., 'The Unity of the Book of the Twelve' (PhD dissertation, Yale University, 1979).

Schneider, U., *Die Funktion der Zitate im 'Ulysses' von James Joyce* (Studien zur englischen Literatur, 3; Bonn: Bouvier, 1970).

Scholes, R., *Semiotics and Interpretation* (New Haven: Yale University Press, 1982).

—*Structuralism in Literature: An Introduction* (New Haven: Yale University Press, 1974).

Schoors, A., *I am God your Saviour: A Form-Critical Study of the Main Genres in Is. XL-LV* (VTSup, 24; Leiden: E.J. Brill, 1973).

—*Jesaja* (De Boeken van het Oude Testament, 9A; Roermond: J.J. Romen & Sons, 1972).

—'Literary Phrases', in L.R. Fisher (ed.), *Ras Shamra Parallels* (3 vols.; Rome: Pontifical Biblical Institute, 1972), I, pp. 3-70.

Schottroff, W., 'Horonaim, Nimrin, Luhith und der Westrand des "Landes Ataroth": Ein Beitrag zur historischen Topographie des Landes', *ZDPV* 82 (1966), pp. 163-208.

Schreiner, J., 'Das Buch jesajanischer Schule', in J. Schreiner (ed.), *Wort und Botschaft* (Würzburg: Echter Verlag, 1967), pp. 143-62.

—'Interpretation innerhalb der schriftlichen Überlieferung', in J. Maier and J. Schreiner (eds.), *Literatur und Religion des Frühjudentums: Eine Einführung* (Würzburg: Echter Verlag, 1973), pp. 19-30.

Schultz, R.L., 'The King in the Book of Isaiah', in P.E. Satterthwaite, R.S. Hess and G.J. Wenham (eds.), *The Lord's Anointed: Interpretation of Old Testament Messianic Texts* (Grand Rapids: Baker Book House, 1995), pp. 141-65.

Schwally, F., 'Die Reden des Buches Jeremia gegen die Heiden. XXV. XLVI-LI', *ZAW* 8 (1988), pp. 177-217.

Scott, R.B.Y., 'The Relation of Isaiah, Chapter 35, to Deutero-Isaiah', *AJSL* 52 (1935-36), pp. 178-91.

Seeligmann, I.L., 'Voraussetzungen der Midraschexegese', in G.W. Anderson *et al.* (eds.), *Congress Volume: Copenhagen 1953* (VTSup, 1; Leiden: E.J. Brill, 1953), pp. 150-81.

Segal, M.S., *Sefer Ben Sira ha-Shalem* (Jerusalem: Bialik Institute, 1958).

Sehmsdorf, E., *Die Prophetenauslegung bei J.G. Eichhorn* (Göttingen: Vandenhoeck & Ruprecht, 1971).

—'Studien zur Redaktionsgeschichte von Jesaja 56-66', *ZAW* 84 (1972), pp. 517-62.

Seibert, P., *Die Charakteristik: Untersuchungen zu einer altägyptischen Sprechsitte und ihren Ausprägungen in Folklore und Literatur. I. Philologische Bearbeitung der Bezeugungen* (Ägyptologische Abhandlungen, 17; Berlin: Otto Harrassowitz, 1967).

Seidel, M., חקרי מקרא (Jerusalem: Mossad Harav Kook, 1978).

Seitz, C.R., 'The Divine Council: Temporal Transition and New Prophecy in the Book of Isaiah', *JBL* 109 (1990), pp. 229-47.

—*Isaiah 1–39* (Interpretation; Louisville, KY: Westminster/John Knox Press, 1993).

—'Isaiah 1-66: Making Sense of the Whole', in *idem* (ed.), *Reading and Preaching the Book of Isaiah* (Philadelphia: Fortress Press, 1988), pp. 105-26.

—'On the Question of Divisions Internal to the Book of Isaiah', in E.H. Lovering, Jr (ed.), *SBL 1993 Seminar Papers* (Atlanta: Scholars Press, 1993), pp. 260-66.

—'Third Isaiah', *ABD*, III, pp. 501-507.

—*Zion's Final Destiny: The Development of the Book of Isaiah: A Reassessment of Isaiah 36-39* (Minneapolis: Fortress Press, 1991).

Sellin, E., *Das Zwölfprophetenbuch*. I. *Hälfte Hosea—Micha* (KAT, 12; Leipzig: Deichert, 1929).

Selms, A. van, 'Isaiah 28:9-13: An Attempt to Give a New Interpretation', *ZAW* NS 85 (1973), pp. 332-39.

—*Jeremia en klaagliederen* (De Prediking van Het Oude Testament; Nijkerk: G.F. Callenbach, 1974).

Seux, M.-J., *Hymnes et prières aux dieux de Babylonie et d'Assyrie* (Paris: Cerf, 1976).

Sheppard, G.T., 'The Book of Isaiah: Competing Structures According to a Late Modern Description of its Shape and Scope', in E.H. Lovering, Jr (ed.), *SBL 1992 Seminar Papers* (Atlanta: Scholars Press, 1992), pp. 549-82.

—'Canonization: Hearing the Voice of the Same God through Historically Dissimilar Traditions', *Int* 36 (1982), pp. 21-33.

Shinan, A., and Y. Zakovitch, 'Midrash on Scripture and Midrash within Scripture', *Scripta Hierosolymitana* 31 (1986), pp. 257-77.

Silva, M., *Biblical Words and their Meaning: An Introduction to Lexical Semantics* (Grand Rapids: Zondervan, 1983).

—'The Pauline Style as Lexical Choice: Γινωσκειν and Related Terms', in D.A. Hagner and M.J. Harris (eds.), *Pauline Studies: Essays Presented to Professor F.F. Bruce* (Grand Rapids: Eerdmans, 1980), pp. 184-207.

Silverman, D.P., 'Coffin Text Spell 902 and its Later Usages in the New Kingdom', in J. Leclant (ed.), *L'égyptologie en 1979: Axes prioritaires de recherches* (2 vols.; Colloques internationaux du Centre National de la Recherche Scientifique, 595; Paris: Centre National de la Recherche Scientifique, 1982), I, pp. 67-70.

Simpson, W.K., 'Allusions to "The Shipwrecked Sailor" and "The Eloquent Peasant" in a Ramesside Text', *JAOS* 78 (1958), pp. 50-51.

Simpson, W.K. (ed.), *The Literature of Ancient Egypt: An Anthology of Stories, Instructions, and Poetry* (trans. R.O. Faulkner, E.F. Wente, Jr and W.K. Simpson; New Haven: Yale University Press, 1972).

Sjöberg, A., *Der Mondgott Nanna-Suen in der sumerischen Überlieferung* (Stockholm: Almqvist & Wiksell, 1960).

Skehan, P.W., 'Isaiah and the Teaching of the Book of Wisdom', *CBQ* 2 (1940), pp. 289-99.

Skehan, P.W., and A.A. DiLella, *The Wisdom of Ben Sira* (AB, 39; New York: Doubleday, 1987).

Slomovic, E., 'Toward an Understanding of the Formation of Historical Titles in the Book of Psalms', *ZAW* NS 91 (1979), pp. 350-80.

Smart, J.D., *History and Theology in Second Isaiah: A Commentary on Isaiah 35, 40-66* (Philadelphia: Westminster Press, 1965).

Smend, R., *Der Prophet Ezechiel* (KeHAT; Leipzig: S. Hirzel, 2nd edn, 1880).

—*Die Weisheit des Jesus Sirach* (Berlin: Georg Reimer, 1906).

Smith, A.J., 'Theory and Practice in Renaissance Poetry: Two Kinds of Imitation', *BJRL* 47 (1964–65), pp. 212-43.

Smith, D.M., Jr, 'The Use of the Old Testament in the New', in J.M. Efird (ed.), *The Use of the Old Testament in the New and Other Essays: Studies in Honor of W.F. Stinespring* (Durham, NC: Duke University Press, 1972), pp. 3-65.

Smith, G.V., 'The Use of Quotations in Jeremiah XV 11-14', *VT* 29 (1979), pp. 229-31.

Smith, J.M.P., *A Critical and Exegetical Commentary on the Book of Micah* (ICC; New York: Charles Scribner's Sons, 1911).

Smith, R.L., *Micah—Malachi* (WBC, 32; Waco, TX: Word Books, 1984).

Smith, S., *Isaiah: Chapters XL-LV, Literary Criticism and History* (Schweich Lectures, 1940; London: Humphrey Milford, Oxford University Press, 1944).

Snaith, J.G., 'Biblical Quotations in the Hebrew of Ecclesiasticus', *JTS* NS 18 (1967), pp. 1-12.

—*Ecclesiasticus, or the Wisdom of Jesus Son of Sirach* (Cambridge: Cambridge University Press, 1914).

Soggin, J.A., *Introduction to the Old Testament from its Origins to the Closing of the Alexandrian Canon* (trans. J. Bowden; OTL; Philadelphia: Westminster Press, 1976).

Sommer, B.D., 'Allusions and Illusions: The Unity of the Book of Isaiah in Light of Deutero-Isaiah's Use of Prophetic Tradition', in R.F. Melugin and M.A. Sweeney (eds.), *New Visions of Isaiah* (JSOTSup, 214; Sheffield: Sheffield Academic Press, 1996), pp. 156-86.

—'*Leshon Limmudim*: The Poetics of Allusion in Isaiah 40–66' (PhD thesis, University of Chicago, 1994).

—*A Prophet Reads Scripture: Allusion in Isaiah 40–66* (The Contraversions Series; Stanford: Stanford University Press, 1998).

Speiser, E.A., 'The Case of the Obliging Servant', *JCS* 8 (1954), pp. 98-105.

—'Sultantepe Tablet 38.73 and Enuma Eliš III 69', *JCS* 11 (1957), pp. 43-44.

Sperber, A., 'Hebrew Based upon Biblical Passages in Parallel Transmission', *HUCA* 14 (1939), pp. 153-239.

Spiegel, S., 'Ezekiel or Pseudo-Ezekiel?', *HTR* 24 (1931), pp. 245-321.

Stade, B., 'Bemerkungen über das Buch Micha', *ZAW* 1 (1881), pp. 161-72.

—'Deuterosacharja: Eine kritische Studie', *ZAW* 1 (1881), pp. 1-96; 2 (1882), pp. 151-72.

Stadelmann, H., *Ben Sira als Schriftgelehrter: Eine Untersuchung zum Berufsbild des vor-makkabäischen Sofer unter Berücksichtigung seines Verhältnisses zu Priester-, Propheten- und Wesheitslehrertum* (WUNT, 2.6; Tübingen: J.C.B. Mohr [Paul Siebeck], 1980).

Stanley, C.D., *Paul and the Language of Scripture: Citation Technique in the Pauline Epistles and Contemporary Literature* (Cambridge: Cambridge University Press, 1992).

Stansell, G., *Micah and Isaiah: A Form and Tradition Historical Comparison* (SBLDS, 85; Atlanta: Scholars Press, 1988).

Steck, O.H., 'Beobachtungen zu Jesaja 56-59', *BZ* NS 31 (1987), pp. 228-46.

—'Beobachtungen zur Anlage von Jes 65-66', *BN* 38/39 (1987), pp. 103-16.

—*Bereitete Heimkehr: Jesaja 35 als redaktionelle Brücke zwischen dem ersten und dem zweiten Jesaja* (SBS, 121; Stuttgart: Katholisches Bibelwerk, 1985).

—' "ein kleiner Knabe kann sie leiten": Beobachtungen zum Tierfrieden in Jesaja 11, 6-8
und 65, 25', in J. Hausmann and H.-J. Zobel (eds.), *Alttestamentlicher Glaube und
biblische Theologie* (Stuttgart: W. Kohlhammer, 1992), pp. 104-13.

—'Heimkehr auf der Schulter oder/und auf der Hüfte: Jes 49, 22b/60, 4b', *ZAW* 98 (1966),
pp. 275-77.

—'Der neue Himmel und die neue Erde: Beobachtungen zur Rezeption von Gen 1-3 in Jes
65, 16B-25', in J. van Ruiten and M. Vervenne (eds.), *Studies in the Book of Isaiah:
Festschrift Willem A.M. Beuken* (BETL, 132; Leuven: Leuven University Press,
1997), pp. 349-65.

—*Old Testament Exegesis: A Guide to the Methodology* (trans. J.D. Nogalski; SBL
Resources for Biblical Study, 33; Atlanta: Scholars Press, 1995).

—*Studien zu Tritojesaja* (BZAW, 203; Berlin: W. de Gruyter, 1991).

Sternberg, M., *The Poetics of Biblical Narrative: Ideological Literature and the Drama of
Reading* (Bloomington: Indiana University Press, 1985).

—'Proteus in Quotation-Land: Mimesis and the Forms of Reported Discourse', *Poetics
Today* 3 (1982), pp. 107-56.

Stolz, F., 'Der Streit um die Wirklichkeit in der Südreichsprophetie des 8. Jahrhunderts',
Wort und Dienst NS 12 (1973), pp. 9-30.

Strack, H.L., *Introduction to the Talmud and Midrash* (Philadelphia: Jewish Publication
Society of America, 1931).

—review of *De criticae sacrae argumento e linguae legibus repetito* by E. König, *TLZ* 4
(1879), pp. 441-42.

Suggs, M.J., 'Wisdom of Solomon 2:10-15: A Homily Based on the Fourth Servant Song',
JBL 76 (1957), pp. 26-33.

Sundberg, A.C., Jr, 'On Testimonies', *NevT* 3 (1959), pp. 208-81.

Sweeney, M.A., *Isaiah 1–4 and the Post-Exilic Understanding of the Isaianic Tradition*
(BZAW, 171; Berlin: W. de Gruyter, 1988).

—'New Gleanings from an Old Vineyard: Isaiah 27 Reconsidered', in C.A. Evans and
W.F. Stinespring (eds.), *Early Jewish and Christian Exegesis: Studies in Memory of
William Hugh Brownlee* (Atlanta: Scholars Press, 1987), pp. 51-66.

—'Reevaluating Isaiah 1-39 in Recent Critical Research', *Currents in Research: Biblical
Studies* 4 (1996), pp. 79-113.

—'Textual Citations in Isaiah 24–27: Toward an Understanding of the Redactional
Function of Chapters 24–27 in the Book of Isaiah', *JBL* 107 (1988), pp. 39-52.

Talmon, S., 'Aspects of the Textual Transmission of the Bible in the Light of the Qumran
Manuscripts', *Textus* 4 (1964), pp. 95-132.

—'Double Readings in the Massoretic Text', *Textus* 1 (1960), pp. 144-84.

—'Synonymous Readings in the Textual Traditions of the Old Testament', *Scripta
Hierosolymitana* 8 (1961), pp. 335-83.

—'The Textual Study of the Bible: A New Outlook', in F.M. Cross and S. Talmon (eds.),
Qumran and the History of the Biblical Text (Cambridge, MA: Harvard University
Press, 1975), pp. 321-400.

—'Typen der Messiaserwartung um die Zeitwende', in H.W. Wolff (ed.), *Probleme
biblischer Theologie: Gerhard von Rad zum 70. Geburtstag* (Munich: Chr. Kaiser
Verlag, 1971), pp. 571-88.

Talmon, S., and M. Fishbane, 'The Structuring of Biblical Books: Ezekiel', *ASTI* 10
(1975–76), pp. 129-53.

Tannert, W., 'Jeremia und Deuterojesaja: Eine Untersuchung zur Frage ihres literarischen und theologischen Zusammenhanges' (Phd dissertation, University of Leipzig, 1956); summarized in *TLZ* 83 (1958), pp. 725-26.

Taylor, A., *The Proverb* (Cambridge, MA: Harvard University Press, 1931).

Thompson, J.A., *The Book of Jeremiah* (NICOT; Grand Rapids: Eerdmans, 1980).

—*The Book of Joel* (IBC, 6; Nashville: Abingdon Press, 1956).

—'The Date of Joel', in H.N. Bream, R.D. Heim and C.A. Moore (eds.), *A Light unto my Path: Old Testament Studies in Honor of J.M. Myers* (Philadelphia: Temple University Press, 1974), pp. 453-64.

Thun, H., *Probleme der Phraseologie* (Beihefte zur Zeitschrift für Romanische Philologie, 168; Tübingen: Max Niemeyer, 1978).

Tigay, J.H., *The Evolution of the Gilgamesh Epic* (Philadelphia: University of Pennsylvania Press, 1982).

—'On Evaluating Claims of Literary Borrowing', in M.E. Cohen, D.L. Snell and D.B. Weisberg (eds.), *The Tablet and the Scrolls: Near Eastern Studies in Honor of W.W. Hallo* (Bethesda, MD: CDL Press, 1993), pp. 250-55.

Tomasino, A.J., 'Isaiah 1.1–2.4 and 63–66, and the Composition of the Isaianic Corpus', *JSOT* 57 (1993), pp. 81-98.

Torrey, C.C., *Pseudo-Ezekiel and the Original Prophecy* (YOS, 18; New Haven: Yale University Press, 1930).

—*The Second Isaiah: A New Interpretation* (New York: Charles Scribner's Sons, 1928).

—'Some Important Editorial Operations in the Book of Isaiah', *JBL* 57 (1938), pp. 109-39.

Touzard, J., 'L'Ame juive au temps des perses', *RB* 35 (1926), pp. 174-205.

Treves, M., 'The Date of Joel', *VT* 7 (1957), pp. 149-56.

Tromp, N.J., *Primitive Conceptions of Death and the Nether World in the Old Testament* (Rome: Biblical Institute Press, 1969).

Tucker, G.M., 'Prophetic Speech', *Int* 32 (1978), pp. 31-45.

Tushingham, A.D., 'Ben Sira's Attitude toward Scripture' (BD dissertation; University of Chicago, Divinity School, 1941).

Uchelen, N.A. van, 'Isaiah I 9: Text and Context', *OTS* 21 (1981), pp. 155-63.

Ugnad, A., 'Zur akkadischen Weisheitsliteratur', *OLZ* 23 (1920), pp. 249-50.

Unger, L., *Eliot's Compound Ghost: Influence and Confluence* (University Park, PA: Pennsylvania State University Press, 1981).

Untermann, J., *From Repentance to Redemption: Jeremiah's Thought in Transition* (JSOTSup, 54; Sheffield: JSOT Press, 1987).

Vermes, G., 'Bible and Midrash: Early Old Testament Exegesis', in P.R. Ackroyd and C.F. Evans (eds.), *The Cambridge History of the Bible*. I. *From the Beginnings to Jerome* (Cambridge: Cambridge University Press, 1970), pp. 199-231.

—*Scripture and Tradition in Judaism: Haggadic Studies* (SPB, 4; Leiden: E.J. Brill, 1961).

Vermeylen, J., *Du prophète Isaïe à l'apocalyptique: Isaïe, I-XXXV, miroir d'un demi-millénaire d'expérience religieuse en Israël* (Etudes Bibliques; 2 vols.; Paris: J. Gabalda, 1977–78).

—'L'unité du livre d'Isaïe', in *idem* (ed.), *The Book of Isaiah. Le livre d'Isaïe. Les oracles et leurs relectures unité et complexité de l'ouvrage* (BETL, 81; Leuven: Leuven University Press, 1989), pp. 11-53.

Vernus, P., 'La formula "Le souffle de la bouche" au moyen empire', *REg* 28 (1976), pp. 139-45.

Vincent, J.M., 'Michas Gerichtswort gegen Zion (3, 12) in seinem Kontext', *ZTK* 83 (1986), pp. 167-87.

Vollmer, J., 'Jesajanische Begrifflichkeit?', *ZAW* 83 (1971), pp. 389-91.

Volz, P., *Jesaia II* (KAT, 9; Leipzig: Deichert, 1932).

—*Der Prophet Jeremia* (KAT, 10; Leipzig: Deichert, 1922).

Vorster, W.S., 'Intertextuality and Redaktionsgeschichte', in S. Draisma (ed.), *Intertextuality in Biblical Writings: Essays in Honor of Bas van Iersel* (Kampen: Kok, 1989), pp. 15-26.

Vriezen, T.C., 'La tradition de Jacob dans Osee 12', *OTS* 1 (1942), pp. 64-78.

Waard, J. de, *A Comparative Study of the Old Testament Text in the Dead Sea Scrolls and in the New Testament* (STDJ, 4; Leiden: E.J. Brill, 1965).

Waldman, N.M., 'A Biblical Echo of Mesopotamian Royal Rhetoric', in A.I. Katsh and L. Nemoy (eds.), *Essays on the Occasion of the Seventieth Anniversary of the Dropsie University* (Philadelphia: Dropsie University, 1979), pp. 449-55.

Walker, H.H., and N.W. Lund, 'The Literary Structure of the Book of Habakkuk', *JBL* 53 (1934), pp. 355-70.

Walle, B. van de, *La transmission des textes littéraires égyptiens* (Brussels: Fondation Egyptologique Reine Elisabeth, 1948).

Walton, J.H., 'New Observations on the Date of Isaiah', *JETS* 28 (1985), pp. 129-32.

Ward, W.W., *A Critical and Exegetical Commentary on Habakkuk* (ICC; Edinburgh: T. & T. Clark, 1912).

Watanabe, K., 'Rekonstruktion von Vte 438 auf Grund von *Erra* III a 17', *Assur* 3 (1983), pp. 164-66.

Watson, W.G.E., 'Ugaritic and Mesopotamian Literary Texts', *UF* 9 (1977), pp. 273-84.

Watters, W.R., *Formula Criticism and the Poetry of the Old Testament* (BZAW, 138; Berlin: W. de Gruyter, 1976).

Watts, J.D.W., *Isaiah 1–33* (WBC, 24; Waco, TX: Word Books, 1985).

—*Isaiah 34–66* (WBC, 25; Waco, TX: Word Books, 1987).

Webb, B.G., 'Zion in Transformation: A Literary Approach to Isaiah', in D.J.A. Clines, S.E. Fowl and S.E. Porter (eds.), *The Bible in Three Dimensions* (Sheffield: JSOT Press, 1990), pp. 65-84.

Wegner, P.D., *An Examination of Kingship and Messianic Expectation in Isaiah 1-35* (Lewiston, NY: Edwin Mellen Press, 1992).

Weinfeld, M., 'Ancient Near Eastern Patterns in Prophetic Literature', *VT* 27 (1977), pp. 178-95.

Weingreen, J., *From Bible to Mishna: The Continuity of Tradition* (Manchester: Manchester University Press, 1976).

Weiser, A., *Der Prophet Jeremia: Kapitel 25, 15-52, 34* (ATD, 21; Göttingen: Vandenhoeck & Ruprecht, 1955).

Weisgerber, J., 'The Use of Quotations in Recent Literature', *CompLit* 22 (1970), pp. 36-45.

Wellhausen, J., *Prolegomena to the History of Ancient Israel* (trans. J.S. Black and A. Menzies; New York: Meridian Books, 1957).

Wendel, U., *Jesaja und Jeremia: Worte, Motive und Einsichten in der Verkündigung Jeremias* (Biblisch-theologische Studien, 25; Neukirchen–Vluyn: Neukirchener Verlag, 1955).

Werblowsky, R.J.Z., 'Stealing the Word', *VT* 6 (1956), pp. 105-106.

Wernberg-Moller, P., 'The Contribution of the Hodayot to Biblical Textual Criticism', *Textus* 4 (1964), pp. 133-75.

Werner, W., *Eschatologische Texte in Jesaja 1-39: Messias, Heiliger Rest, Völker* (FzB, 46; Würzburg: Echter Verlag, 1982).

Westermann, C., *Das Buch Jesaja: Kapitel 40-66* (ATD, 19; Göttingen: Vandenhoeck & Ruprecht, 4th edn, 1966).

—*Isaiah 40-66* (trans. D.M.G. Stalker; OTL; Philadelphia: Westminster Press, 1969).

Wette, W.M.L. de, *A Critical and Historical Introduction to the Canonical Scriptures of the Old Testament* (trans. T. Parker; 2 vols.; Boston: Little, Brown & Company, 2nd edn, 1858 [1817]).

Whallon, W., *Formula, Character, and Context: Studies in Homeric, Old English, and Old Testament Poetry* (Cambridge, MA: Harvard University Press, 1969).

Wheeler, M., *The Art of Allusion in Victorian Fiction* (London: Macmillan, 1979).

Whitaker, R.E., 'A Formulaic Analysis of Ugaritic Poetry' (PhD dissertation, Harvard University, 1970).

—'Ugaritic Formulae', in S. Rummel (ed.), *Ras Shamra Parallels: The Texts from Ugarit and the Hebrew Bible* (3 vols.; Rome: Pontifical Biblical Institute, 1981), III, pp. 209-19.

Whitt, W.D., 'The Jacob Traditions in Hosea and their Relation to Genesis', *ZAW* 103 (1991), pp. 18-43.

Whybray, R.N., 'The Identification and Use of Quotations in Ecclesiastes', in J.A. Emerton (ed.), *Congress Volume: Vienna 1980* (VTSup, 32; Leiden: E.J. Brill, 1981), pp. 435-51.

—*Isaiah 40-66* (NCB; London: Marshall, Morgan & Scott, 1975).

Widengren, G., *Literary and Psychological Aspects of the Hebrew Prophets* (Uppsala: Lundeqvist, 1948).

Wierzbicka, A., 'Descriptions or Quotations?', in *Janua Linguaram. Studia Memoriae Nicola van Wijk Dedicata. Sign. Language. Culture* (Series Maior, 1; The Hague: Mouton, 1970), pp. 627-44.

Wiklander, B., *Prophecy as Literature: A Text-Linguistic and Rhetorical Approach to Isaiah 2-4* (ConBOT, 22; Lund: C.W.K. Gleerup, 1984).

Wilcke, C., *Das Lugalbandaepos* (Wiesbaden: Otto Harrassowitz, 1969).

Wildberger, H., *Jesaja 1-39* (BKAT, 10; 3 vols.; Neukirchen–Vluyn: Neukirchener Verlag, 1965-82).

—'Die Völkerfahrt zum Zion: Jes. II 1-5', *VT* 7 (1957), pp. 62-81.

Willey, P.T., *Remember the Former Things: The Recollection of Previous Texts in Second Isaiah* (SBLDS, 161; Atlanta: Scholars Press, 1997).

Willi, T., *Die Chronik als Auslegung: Untersuchungen zur literarischen Gestaltung der historischen Überlieferung Israels* (FRLANT, 106; Göttingen: Vandenhoeck & Ruprecht, 1972).

Willi-Plein, I., 'Das Geheimnis der Apokalyptik', *VT* 27 (1977), pp. 62-81.

—*Vorformen der Schriftexegese innerhalb des Alten Testaments* (BZAW, 123; Berlin: W. de Gruyter, 1971).

Williamson, G., *A Reader's Guide to T.S. Eliot: A Poem-by-Poem Analysis* (New York: Noonday Press, 1955).

Williamson, H.G.M., *The Book Called Isaiah: Deutero-Isaiah's Role in Composition and Redaction* (Oxford: Clarendon Press, 1994).

Willis, J.T., 'The First Pericope in the Book of Isaiah', *VT* 34 (1984), pp. 63-77.

—*Isaiah* (Austin, TX: Sweet, 1980).

—'The Structure of Micah 3-5 and the Function of Micah 5.9-14 in the Book', *ZAW* 81 (1969), pp. 191-214.

Wilson, R.R., 'Form Critical Investigation of the Prophetic Literature: The Present Situation', in G. MacRae (ed.), *SBL Seminar Papers: 1973* (2 vols.; Cambridge, MA: SBL, 1973), I, pp. 100-27.

—*Prophecy and Society in Ancient Israel* (Philadelphia: Fortress Press, 1980).

Wimsatt, W.K., and M.C. Beardsley, 'The Intentional Fallacy', in W.K. Wimsatt (ed.), *The Verbal Icon* (Lexington: University Press of Kentucky, 1954), pp. 3-18.

Wiseman, D.J., 'A Lipšur Litany from Nimrud', *Iraq* 31 (1969), pp. 175-83.

Wolde, E. van, 'Trendy Intertextuality?', in Draisma (ed.), *Intertextuality in Biblical Writings*, pp. 43-49.

Wolfe, R.E., 'The Editing of the Book of the Twelve', *ZAW* 53 (1935), pp. 90-129.

Wolff, H.W., *A Commentary on the Book of the Prophet Hosea* (trans. G. Stansell; Hermeneia, 28; Philadelphia: Fortress Press, 1974).

—*A Commentary on the Books of the Prophets Joel and Amos* (trans. W. Janzen, S.D. McBride, Jr, and C.A. Muenchow; Hermeneia, 29–30; Philadelphia: Fortress Press, 1977).

—*Dodekapropheten 4, Micha* (BKAT, 14.4; Neukirchen–Vluyn: Neukirchener Verlag, 1980–82).

—'Die eigentliche Botschaft der klassischen Propheten', in H. Donner, R. Hanhart and R. Smend (eds.), *Beiträge zur alttestamentlichen Theologie: Festschrift für Walther Zimmerli zum 70. Geburtstag* (Göttingen: Vandenhoeck & Ruprecht, 1977), pp. 547-57.

—'Prophecy from the Eighth through the Fifth Century', *Int* 32 (1978), pp. 17-30.

—'Schwerter zu Pflugscharen: Mißbrauch eines Prophetenwortes? Praktische Fragen und exegetische Klärungen zu Joël 4, 9-12, Jes 2, 2-5 und Mi 4, 1-5', *EvT* NS 44 (1984), pp. 280-92.

—'Das Zitat im Prophetenspruch: Eine Studie zur prophetischen Verkündigungsweise', in *idem, Gesammelte Studien zum Alten Testament* (TBü, 22; Munich: Chr. Kaiser Verlag, 1964 [1937]), pp. 36-129.

Woude, A.S. van der, 'Micah IV 1-5: An Instance of the Pseudo-Prophets Quoting Isaiah', in M.A. Beek *et al.* (eds.), *Symbolae Biblicae et Mesopotamicae Francisco Mario Theodoro de Liagre Böhl Dedicatae* (Leiden: E.J. Brill, 1973), pp. 396-402.

—*Micha* (Prediking van het Oude Testament; Nijkerk: G.F. Callenbach, 1977).

—'Seid nicht wie eure Väter! Bemerkungen zu Sacharja 1.5 und seinem Kontext', in J.A. Emerton (ed.), *Prophecy: Essays Presented to Georg Fohrer on his Sixty-Fifth Birthday. 6 September 1980* (BZAW, 150; Berlin: W. de Gruyter, 1980), pp. 163-73.

—'Three Classical Prophets', in R. Coggins, A. Phillips and M. Knibb (eds.), *Israel's Prophetic Tradition: Essays in Honour of Peter R. Ackroyd* (Cambridge: Cambridge University Press, 1982), pp. 32-57.

Wright, A.G., 'The Literary Genre Midrash', *CBQ* 28 (1966), pp. 105-38, 417-57.

Young, E.J., *The Book of Isaiah* (3 vols.; Grand Rapids: Eerdmans, 1965–72).

—'Isaiah 34 and its Position in the Prophecy', *WTJ* 27 (1964–65), pp. 93-114.

—*An Introduction to the Old Testament* (Grand Rapids: Eerdmans, 1960).

Žabkar, L.W., 'Adaptation of Ancient Egyptian Texts to the Temple Ritual at Philae', *JEA* 66 (1980), pp. 127-36.

Zeitlin, S., 'Midrash: A Historical Study', *JQR* NS 44 (1953–54), pp. 21-36.

Zimmerli, W., 'Das Phänomen der "Fortschreibung" im Buch Ezechiel', in J.A. Emerton (ed.), *Prophecy: Essays Presented to Georg Fohrer on his Sixty-Fifth Birthday. 6 September 1980* (BZAW, 150; Berlin: W. de Gruyter, 1980), pp. 174-91.

—*A Commentary on the Book of the Prophet Ezekiel Chapters 1–24* (trans. R.E. Clements; Hermeneia, 26; Philadelphia: Fortress Press, 1979).

—'Prophetic Proclamation and Reinterpretation', in D.A. Knight (ed.), *Tradition and Theology in the Old Testament* (Philadelphia: Fortress Press, 1977), pp. 69-100.

—'Vom Prophetenwort zum Prophetenbuch', *TLZ* 104 (1979), pp. 481-96.

—'Zur Sprache Tritojesajas', in *Gottes Offenbarung: Gesammelte Aufsätze zum Alten Testament* (TBü, 19; Munich: Chr. Kaiser Verlag, 1963), pp. 217-33.

—'Erkenntnis Gottes nach dem Buch Ezechiel', in *Gottes Offenbarung: Gesammelte Aufsätze zum Alten Testament* (TBü, 19; Munich: Chr. Kaiser Verlag, 1963), pp. 41-119.

Zink, J.K., 'The Use of the Old Testament in the Apocrypha' (PhD dissertation, Duke University, 1963).

Zyl, A.H. van, *The Moabites* (Pretoria Oriental Series, 3; Leiden: E.J. Brill, 1960).

INDEXES

INDEX OF REFERENCES

BIBLE

INDEX OF AUTHORS

JOURNAL FOR THE STUDY OF THE OLD TESTAMENT
SUPPLEMENT SERIES